The Epistemic Role of Consciousness

PHILOSOPHY OF MIND SERIES
SERIES EDITOR: David J. Chalmers, *Australian National University*

The Epistemic Role of Consciousness

DECLAN SMITHIES

OXFORD
UNIVERSITY PRESS

Oxford University Press is a department of the University of Oxford. It furthers
the University's objective of excellence in research, scholarship, and education
by publishing worldwide. Oxford is a registered trade mark of Oxford University
Press in the UK and certain other countries.

Published in the United States of America by Oxford University Press
198 Madison Avenue, New York, NY 10016, United States of America.

© Oxford University Press 2019

First issued as an Oxford University Press paperback, 2023

CIP data is on file at the Library of Congress
ISBN 978–0–19–991766–2 (Hbk.)
ISBN 978–0–19–768000–1 (Pbk.)

1 3 5 7 9 8 6 4 2

Paperback printed by Integrated Books International, United States of America

This book is dedicated to all the philosophers on the job market.

Contents

Acknowledgments

This book has been a long time coming. While it's hard to identify the exact moment of conception, it's fair to say that I've been working on the central ideas of this book for my whole adult life. As I approach midlife, the appearance of this book gives me an opportunity to reflect on this time and to express my gratitude to the many people who have shaped my academic path until now.

My first debt is to my parents for encouraging me to pursue my passion for philosophy. My father, who originally inspired my interest in the subject, died while I was writing this book. It saddens me that I didn't finish while he was still alive, but I am grateful to share the moment with my mother, who has always supported me.

I first started thinking about the relationship between consciousness and rationality while I was an undergraduate at the University of Oxford from 1997 to 2000. My philosophy of mind tutorials with David Mackie covered two major challenges for physicalism: the problem of explaining consciousness and the problem of explaining rationality. I was sure these two problems must be connected somehow, but the philosophers on my reading list seemed to treat them quite separately. After finals, while reading John McDowell's fascinating book *Mind and World*, I began to see how the two problems might be connected in the philosophy of perception.

When I started the PhD program at New York University in 2000, I studied perception with Christopher Peacocke, consciousness with Ned Block, self-knowledge with Crispin Wright, and epistemic internalism with Paul Boghossian. These courses gave me the background I needed to begin working out a more unified account of the relationship between consciousness and epistemic rationality. By the summer of 2001, the basic ideas of the dissertation were already beginning to take shape. In 2006, I defended my PhD dissertation, *Rationality and the Subject's Point of View*, which was my first attempt to defend the thesis that the epistemic role of consciousness is to justify belief in a way that is accessible to the subject through reflection alone.

It was exhilarating to live in New York in my early twenties and to work with some of the world's best philosophers. Peacocke chaired my committee until he left for Columbia, when Boghossian took over as chair, with Block and Wright also serving on the committee. At the same time, I learned much from conversations with Jerry Fodor, who was visiting from Rutgers, and with James Pryor, who joined the department in my final year. I am forever grateful to these philosophers for their formative influence on my own thinking and for their own inspirational work. Of course, I also learned—and I continue to learn—a huge amount from other NYU graduate students, especially David Barnett, Sinan Dogramaci, Geoff Lee, Anna-Sara Malmgren, Adam Pautz, Karl Schafer, Joshua Schechter, Jon Simon, and Sebastian Watzl.

I spent the year in 2004–2005 as a visiting student at the University of Warwick, where Bill Brewer was my advisor. His work on the epistemic role of consciousness made a strong impression on me, and he was generous in helping me to develop an account that diverged from his own. I also had wonderful conversations during that year with Steven Butterfill, Naomi Eilan, Christoph Hoerl, Susan Hurley, Johannes Roessler, and especially Rory Madden.

In 2006, I started a tenure-track position at the Ohio State University. In ret-rospect, this was a huge stroke of fortune, since I had no publications at the time; indeed, I had nothing accepted for publication until 2009. The job market then was not what it is now, where many candidates are unable to find tenure-track positions despite publishing more than enough work to secure tenure. I am grateful to my colleagues who took a gamble in hiring me. Ohio State has been my home now for more than a decade. I am especially grateful to a se-ries of department chairs—George Pappas, Don Hubin, William Taschek, and Justin D'Arms—for everything they've done to support my research during this time.

I was thrilled to spend three years at the Australian National University as a postdoctoral fellow between 2007 and 2010. Daniel Stoljar was my advisor: working with him was an education in how to do philosophy. I also learned a huge amount from conversations with David Chalmers, Alan Hajek, and Frank Jackson, as well as the many terrific postdocs who overlapped with me, including John Bengson, Berit Brogaard, Patrick Greenough, Carrie Jenkins, Fiona MacPherson, Joe Salerno, Susanna Schellenberg, Nico Silins, Nicholas Southwood, Daniel Star, and Michael Titelbaum. Many of the central ideas in this book were presented at seminars and conferences during this time.

In 2013–2014, I spent the year as a visiting associate professor at MIT. The academic highlight was a graduate seminar on the topic of this book. Alex Byrne came to every session with incisive comments and witty observations. There were seminar visits from Selim Berker, Geoff Lee, Susanna Siegel, and Roger White, and an impressive group of graduate students in attendance, in-cluding Sophie Horowitz, Bernhard Salow, and Ginger Schultheis.

Over the last few years, I've enjoyed a series of visiting positions back home in the United Kingdom. I was a member of New Directions in Religious Epistemology at the University of Oxford in Trinity 2013, the Northern Institute of Philosophy at the University of Aberdeen in summer 2013, the London Institute of Philosophy in summer 2015, and New Directions in the Study of

Mind at the University of Cambridge in Lent 2017. I'm extremely grateful to Tim Crane, John Hawthorne, Barry Smith, and Crispin Wright for making these visits possible and for giving me opportunities to share work in progress with their research groups.

The first complete draft of the book manuscript was written during a year of research leave in 2016–2017. This research leave was funded by a Faculty Professional Leave from the Ohio State University and by a grant from the John Templeton Foundation administered by Tim Crane at the University of Cambridge. Needless to say, the ideas expressed in this book are my own, and should not be taken to reflect the views of the John Templeton Foundation.

I spent three months in summer 2017 as a visiting fellow at the Australian National University. The Philosophy of Mind Reading Group did me a huge favor by working through the first half of the book manuscript, which gave me the stimulus I needed to finish. I'm grateful to everyone who came, especially Melissa Ebbers, Frank Jackson, Matthew Kopec, Erick Llamas, Don Nordblom, Blake Roeber, Luke Roelofs, Alex Sandgren, and Daniel Stoljar.

At Ohio State, I've taught two graduate seminars on the book: one back in fall 2009 when the project was first conceived and another in fall 2017 when the manuscript was finally complete. I've been helped by conversations with many graduate students, especially Ethan Brauer, Jamie Fritz, John Hurst, Brian McLean, Erin Mercurio, Brentyn Ramm, Lindsay Rettler, and Jeremy Weiss. I'm also grateful to Maria Lasonen-Aarnio and Nico Silins for enjoyable visits to my seminar in 2017.

The book draws heavily on themes in my previous work, although the content has been substantially revised, expanded, and reorganized to yield a more unified and systematic account of the epistemic role of consciousness. Where I am relying on previously published work, I have indicated this in the footnotes. I am grateful to the editors concerned for the opportunity to reuse this work in substantially revised form.

In 2018, I received three sets of extremely helpful comments from referees for Oxford University Press: they were Ram Neta, Adam Pautz, and Susanna Siegel. I'm also grateful to the series editor, David Chalmers, and the acquisitions editor, Peter Ohlin, for advice and guidance throughout the process.

I am indebted to many others for illuminating comments and conversations about my work, including Robert Audi, David Bourget, Jessica Brown, John Campbell, David Christensen, Elijah Chudnoff, Jeremy Fantl, Kati Farkas, Richard Feldman, Brie Gertler, Daniel Greco, Benj Hellie, Terry Horgan, Ole Koksvik, Hilary Kornblith, Uriah Kriegel, Clayton Littlejohn, Brent Madison, Matthew McGrath, Angela Mendelovici, Andrew Moon, David Pitt, Eric Schwitzgebel, Charles Siewert, Joshua Smart, David Sosa, Chris Tucker, Ralph Wedgwood, Timothy Williamson, and Wayne Wu. It's hard to remember everyone, since I've discussed the topics of this book with almost everyone in philosophy I know over the years. If I've forgotten you, please forgive me. As a penance, I promise to write one referee report for each person I've unjustly neglected.

My final debt is to my wife, Janet Beard, whom I met when I was on the job market back in 2005. Since then, she has been with me through all of this, from New York where we met, to Columbus where we decided to move together, to Australia where we got engaged, to England where we got married, to Boston where our daughter was born, and back again to Columbus where we now live. Jenny, thank you for everything we've experienced together.

PART I
PHILOSOPHY OF MIND

1

Consciousness

Consciousness is a puzzling phenomenon. In fact, it is puzzling in at least two different ways. First, there are puzzles about the nature of consciousness. And second, there are puzzles about the significance of consciousness. Puzzles of the first kind are about what consciousness *is*, while puzzles of the second kind are about what consciousness *does*.

We can illustrate both of these puzzles by considering what philosophers like to call *zombies*.[1] Philosophical zombies are not the same as Hollywood zombies. They look and act just like you or me. The key difference is that you and I are conscious, whereas zombies are not. By definition, a zombie is an unconscious creature—that is, a creature that has no conscious states at all. As we might say, there is "nothing it is like" to be a zombie.

Zombies generate a puzzle about the *nature* of consciousness. It seems possible that a perfect physical duplicate of mine could be a zombie—that is, a creature entirely lacking in consciousness. But if so, then how can consciousness be a physical phenomenon? Physicalism says that every phenomenon is a physical phenomenon. And yet the apparent possibility of zombies suggests that consciousness is a counterexample. Hence, we seem forced to deny that consciousness is a physical phenomenon after all.

Zombies also generate a puzzle about the *significance* of consciousness. It seems possible that a perfect physical duplicate of mine could do everything that I can do, but without the assistance of consciousness. But if so, then what is the point of being conscious? What can conscious creatures do that cannot be done without consciousness? If zombies can do everything we can do, then the answer seems to be: nothing at all. Hence, we seem forced to accept that consciousness plays no indispensable role in our lives.

Much recent work in philosophy has been preoccupied with the first puzzle, whereas this book is exclusively concerned with the second. To highlight this distinction, let me contrast the following pair of questions:

(1) *A metaphysical question*: What is the nature of consciousness and how is it physically realized in the brain?

---

[1] See Chalmers (1996) and Crick and Koch (2001) for two prominent examples of how zombies have figured in recent discussions in the philosophy and science of consciousness.

(2) *An epistemological question*: What is the role of consciousness in giving us knowledge and justified belief about the external world?

This book is about the epistemological question, rather than the metaphysical question: it is about what consciousness does, rather than what consciousness is. It makes no attempt to engage with metaphysical issues about the nature of consciousness or its physical realization in the brain. Instead, it is primarily concerned with epistemological issues about the role of consciousness as a source of knowledge and justified belief. The conclusions of this book are metaphysically neutral in the sense that you can accept them whatever your views about the nature of consciousness and its physical realization in the brain. Even so, I will need to begin by explaining what I mean by the word 'consciousness' so that you know what this book is about.

1.1. What Is Consciousness?

If you're reading this book, then it's probably safe to assume that you're conscious. What I mean is not just that you're awake and alert, although I hope that's true, but also that you're the subject of various conscious mental states, including thoughts, feelings, and sensory experiences. These mental states are conscious in the sense that there is "something it's like" for you to have them. As Thomas Nagel puts the point, "an organism has conscious mental states if and only if there is something it is like to *be* that organism—something it is like *for* that organism" (1974: 436).

This is what Ned Block calls the *phenomenal concept* of consciousness. As he defines it, "Phenomenal consciousness is experience; what makes a state phenomenally conscious is that there is something 'it is like' to be in that state" (1995: 228). One problem with this definition, as Block acknowledges, is that if you don't already know what he means by the word 'consciousness', then using synonymous expressions like 'experience' or 'what it's like' is unlikely to prove helpful. Moreover, this problem seems unavoidable, since the phenomenal concept of consciousness cannot be defined in more basic terms. Like many other concepts, it is primitive and indefinable. Our only option is to define the concept ostensively—that is, by giving examples that illustrate when it applies and when it doesn't.

Here are some paradigmatic examples of phenomenal consciousness: consider the experience of feeling pain, visualizing red, or thinking about mathematics. All of these experiences have *phenomenal character*: that is, there is something it's like for you to have them. Moreover, they all differ in their phenomenal character, since what it's like to feel pain is different from what it's like to visualize red or to think about mathematics. In contrast, there is typically nothing it's like for you to digest food, to secrete hormones, or to be in a coma. These states are not examples of phenomenal consciousness, since they have no phenomenal character at all.

Block warns against confusing the phenomenal concept of consciousness with any functional concept of consciousness defined in terms of its causal role in cognition or action. This is the main point of his influential distinction between *phenomenal consciousness* and *access consciousness*. To a first approximation, a mental state is access conscious just when it is poised for use in the direct control of action, reasoning, or verbal report. The guiding idea is that access consciousness is an "information-processing correlate" of phenomenal consciousness (1997: 384). In other words, a mental state is access conscious when it does what phenomenally conscious mental states normally do. As Block argues, however, it is at least conceivable that phenomenal consciousness and access consciousness can come apart.

Zombies provide the simplest illustration of access consciousness without phenomenal consciousness. By definition, a zombie is not conscious in the phenomenal sense: there is nothing it is like to be a zombie. But it is at least conceivable that a zombie can do everything that you can do: for every phenomenal state in you, there is some corresponding nonphenomenal state in your zombie twin that plays the same kind of causal role in the control of action, reasoning, and verbal report. If so, then your zombie twin is conscious in the functional sense but not the phenomenal sense. Zombies can have access consciousness, but not phenomenal consciousness.

Personally, I doubt that there is any good sense in which zombies are conscious. Block maintains that our ordinary concept of consciousness is a "mongrel concept" that conflates two distinct kinds of consciousness—namely, phenomenal consciousness and access consciousness. On this view, there is one sense in which zombies are conscious and another sense in which they are not. As others have complained, however, this is really quite implausible: there is no ordinary sense in which zombies are conscious.[2] If zombies satisfy Block's definition of access conscious, then we shouldn't conclude that there are two kinds of consciousness. Instead, we should conclude that access consciousness is merely an ersatz functional substitute for phenomenal consciousness. In my view, the phenomenal concept is our most basic concept of consciousness and all other concepts of consciousness are defined explicitly or implicitly in terms of this one.[3] In any case, this book is about the phenomenal concept of

---

[2] For example, Searle (1992: 84) and Burge (1997: 428) raise this objection.
[3] Burge (1997) and Smithies (2011a) propose accounts of rational-access consciousness that presuppose some connection with phenomenal consciousness.

consciousness. Whenever I speak about consciousness without qualification, it is phenomenal consciousness that I have in mind.

What can we learn from Block's distinction? He may be wrong to claim that there are two kinds of consciousness, but he is quite right to warn us against confusing consciousness—the real thing—with mere ersatz functional substitutes that occupy the same causal role. We shouldn't confuse consciousness with its function, since it's conceivable that everything consciousness does can be done equally well without it. This is what zombies teach us. Block's contribution is to highlight this distinction between what consciousness is and what it does. As I will now explain, we can use this distinction to raise a challenging question about the significance of consciousness and its role in our mental lives.

1.2. The Significance of Consciousness

What is the significance of consciousness? Does consciousness play any significant role in our lives that cannot equally be played without consciousness? If so, then we can say that consciousness has *unique significance*.

To make this question vivid, imagine that we all suddenly become zombies. Are we thereby guaranteed to lose anything of significance in our lives? How much of our lives could remain intact? As we've seen, it's at least conceivable that zombies can do everything we can do. For example, it's conceivable that we might wake up tomorrow without consciousness and yet still be able to do everything we could do before. If so, then there is nothing we conscious creatures can do that cannot equally be done without consciousness. This makes it hard to resist the conclusion that consciousness has no unique significance in our lives. For future reference, let's call this *the zombie challenge*.

The main aim of this book is to answer the zombie challenge by arguing that consciousness has unique epistemic significance. First, however, I want to clarify the nature of the challenge by addressing two replies: the "scientific" reply and the "metaphysical" reply. This will clarify my project and disentangle it from scientific debates about the function of consciousness and philosophical debates about the metaphysical basis of consciousness. While these debates are interesting and important in their own right, they are largely orthogonal to my central concerns in this book.

The *scientific reply* to the zombie challenge is that the science of consciousness will tell us what we can and cannot do without consciousness. This is Fred Dretske's view:

The function of experience, the reason animals are conscious of objects and their properties, is to enable them to do all those things that those who do not have it cannot do. This is a great deal indeed. If . . . there are many things people with experience can do that people without experience cannot do, then *that* is a perfectly good answer to questions about what the function of experience is. (1997: 14)

Dretske's main goal is to argue that questions about the function of consciousness are empirical questions that can be answered experimentally by studying the differences between conscious and unconscious vision. His own hypothesis is that the function of conscious vision is to enable visual identification and recognition of objects. As he puts the point, "Remove visual sensations of X and S might still be able to tell *where* X is, but S will not be able to tell *what* X is" (1997: 13).

Dretske's specific hypothesis can be questioned on empirical grounds, but let's just assume it's correct for the sake of argument, since the exact details won't matter.[4] Suppose we're built in such a way that we cannot visually identify and recognize objects without consciousness. Even so, the question remains: couldn't we have been built differently? It seems possible, at least in principle, that a zombie could identify and recognize objects in the absence of conscious vision. Perhaps there are no such zombies. Still, we can ask, is this just an accident of evolutionary history or is there some principled reason why only conscious vision can play this functional role?

Dretske doesn't argue that consciousness has unique significance in the sense that nothing else can play the same functional role. Instead, he argues that even if something else can play the same functional role, it doesn't follow that consciousness is an epiphenomenon that has no function at all. After all, functional roles can be multiply realized. He writes:

Maybe something else besides experience would enable us to do the same things, but this would not show that experience didn't have a function. All it would show is that there was more than one way to skin a cat—more than one way to get the job done. (1997: 14)

This point is well taken, but whether it constitutes an adequate response to the zombie challenge depends on how exactly the challenge is understood. Dretske is primarily concerned with a scientific question about the function of consciousness: is it merely an epiphenomenon or does it play some causal role in our lives? In contrast, I am primarily concerned with a more distinctively

---

[4] Milner and Goodale (2006: 221–228) give examples of unconscious perception in the ventral stream, which are hard to square with Dretske's proposal. They propose instead that the function of consciousness is to serve as an input to working memory.

philosophical question about whether consciousness has any unique function: does it play any role in our lives that cannot in principle be played by anything else? The scientific facts about our constitution simply don't address this
question, since they leave open the possibility that we could in principle have
been built differently. For this reason, we can now set aside the scientific reply
to the zombie challenge.

The *metaphysical reply* to the zombie challenge is that it has no force because
zombies are impossible. If so, then it's trivial that zombies cannot do everything
we can do, since they cannot exist at all. The objection is that we cannot use
zombies to raise a challenge for the significance of consciousness without assuming that zombies are possible and thereby taking a controversial stance on
the metaphysics of consciousness.

I'll make two points in response. The first point is that whether zombies are
possible depends on what kind of zombies we're talking about. If zombies are
defined as unconscious creatures, then not only can they exist, but in fact they
do. Examples include coma patients, human embryos, paramecia, oak trees,
and laptop computers. What's more controversial is whether a zombie can be
just like a conscious creature in all other respects.

David Chalmers (1996) argues that there could be a *physical zombie* who
resembles a conscious creature in all physical respects. This is highly controversial, of course, since it implies that physicalism is false. A weaker assumption
is that there could be a *functional zombie* who resembles a conscious creature
in abstract functional respects; for instance, a silicon robot that duplicates the
functional organization of our brain without being conscious.[5] This assumption is much less controversial, but it is still not completely innocuous: it is
consistent with physicalism, but inconsistent with functionalist versions of
physicalism.

This brings me to my second point. We can remain neutral on these metaphysical issues about the status of physicalism and functionalism by framing
the zombie challenge in terms of conceivability rather than possibility.[6] Our
question is whether consciousness plays any significant role in our mental lives
that cannot conceivably be played without it. If zombies are so much as conceivable, then we seem forced to conclude that there is no significant role in
our lives that cannot conceivably be played without consciousness. After all, it's

---

[5] Compare Block's (1978) homunculi-headed robots.

[6] In other words, we should understand the zombie challenge in terms of epistemic possibility, rather than metaphysical possibility. Chalmers (2002a) defines an epistemic possibility as a
hypothesis about the actual world that is ideally conceivable in the sense that it cannot be ruled out
conclusively by any ideal process of a priori reasoning.

conceivable that zombies can do everything we can do. This makes it hard to resist the conclusion that consciousness has no unique significance.

It's relatively uncontroversial that zombies are conceivable in the sense that they cannot be ruled out on a priori grounds alone. What is much more controversial is whether there is a valid argument from the premise that zombies are conceivable to the conclusion that zombies are possible. Many proponents of physicalism and functionalism accept the premise about conceivability, while rejecting the inference from conceivability to possibility. The relationship between conceivability and possibility is exactly the kind of disputed metaphysical issue that I want to set aside in this book. That is one reason why I prefer to understand the zombie challenge in terms of conceivability rather than possibility.[7]

Another reason is that this book is primarily concerned with conceptual questions, rather than metaphysical questions, about the significance of consciousness. My question is whether there is any conceptual, analytic, or a priori connection between the phenomenal concept of consciousness and our other psychological and epistemic concepts, including concepts of mental representation, belief, and knowledge. That is why I'm asking how much of our mental lives could be preserved in zombies. Is it conceivable—in the sense that it's not ruled out on a priori grounds—that a zombie could have the capacity for mental representation, belief, or knowledge?

Our initial reflections on the zombie challenge suggest that much of our mental life can be preserved in zombies in the absence of consciousness. After all, zombies can do everything we can do. If our psychological and epistemic capacities are functionally defined in terms of their causal roles, then it is inconceivable that zombies lack the same capacities as conscious creatures. I'll argue, however, that our psychological and epistemic capacities cannot be functionally defined in terms of their causal roles. Instead, they are defined in terms of their connections with phenomenal consciousness. On this view, it is inconceivable that zombies share our mental lives.

In the next section, I'll situate this proposal in the context of contemporary debates about how to solve the "hard problem" of explaining phenomenal consciousness. As I'll explain, metaphysical puzzlement about the nature of phenomenal consciousness leads many philosophers to marginalize its role in theories of mental representation, cognition, and knowledge. In this way, metaphysical perplexity tends to result in epistemological distortion. Although this

---

[7] I'm assuming what Block (2002: 392) and Chalmers (2003: 221) call *phenomenal realism*, the thesis that the phenomenal concept of consciousness cannot be defined a priori in purely physical or functional terms. This is compatible with a posteriori (but not a priori) versions of physicalism and functionalism about phenomenal consciousness.

book takes no stand on contemporary debates about the metaphysics of consciousness, it is important to recognize how they have shaped the intellectual background for contemporary debates in epistemology.

1.3. The Hard Problem of Consciousness

For much of the twentieth century, phenomenal consciousness occupied a curious status within the philosophy of mind: it was absolutely central in some ways, and yet largely peripheral in others. On the one hand, much of the preoccupation with the mind-body problem was fueled by metaphysical puzzles about the nature of phenomenal consciousness and its place in the physical world. On the other hand, these metaphysical puzzles provided much of the impetus for a research program of understanding the mind as far as possible without making reference to phenomenal consciousness. One defining characteristic of this research program was the idea that the "hard problem" of explaining phenomenal consciousness could be divorced from the comparatively "easy problems" of explaining mental representation, cognition, and knowledge of the external world.

In a classic discussion, David Chalmers (1996) explains the distinction between the hard and easy problems in terms of a distinction between two concepts of mind. On the one hand, we have the *phenomenal* concept of mind: this is the concept of mind as conscious experience. A state is mental in the phenomenal sense just in case there is "something it is like" for the subject of that mental state to have it. On the other hand, we have the *psychological* concept of mind: this is the concept of mind as the causal or explanatory basis of behavior. A state is mental in the psychological sense just in case it plays the right kind of role in the causal explanation of behavior. Chalmers sums up the distinction as follows:

> On the phenomenal concept, mind is characterized by the way it *feels*; on the psychological concept, mind is characterized by what it *does*. There should be no question of competition between these aspects of mind. Neither of them is *the* correct analysis of mind. They cover different phenomena, both of which are quite real. (1996: 11)

Consider, for example, the concept of pain. We have a phenomenal concept of pain as a mental state that feels a certain way—it feels painful. But we also have a psychological concept of pain as a mental state that is caused by bodily damage and causes aversive behavior. We use the word 'pain' to express both of these concepts. And while these concepts are normally coextensive, they are nevertheless distinct. It is at least conceivable that a zombie might engage in pain behavior without feeling pain or, conversely, that a "madman" (Lewis 1980b) might feel pain without engaging in pain behavior.

According to Chalmers, we can give a functional analysis of our psychological concepts, but not our phenomenal concepts. Psychological states can be functionally defined in terms of their causal roles, which can be abstractly described in nonpsychological terms.[8] In contrast, phenomenal states cannot be defined in terms of their causal role, since it's conceivable that zombies can have nonphenomenal states that play the same causal role as our phenomenal states. The mere conceivability of functional zombies is enough to undermine the functional analysis of phenomenal concepts: no further inference from conceivability to possibility is required.

With this conceptual distinction in hand, Chalmers divides the mind-body problem into a hard problem and an easy problem. Explaining the phenomenal aspects of mind is a hard problem because there is an "explanatory gap" (Levine 1983) between physical facts and phenomenal facts: it is conceivable that the same physical facts could give rise to different phenomenal facts or to none at all. In contrast, explaining the psychological aspects of mind is an easy problem because there is no such explanatory gap between physical facts and psychological facts. We just need to specify a physical mechanism that plays the causal role in terms of which the psychological facts are defined. In the case of phenomenal facts, however, we cannot do this because they are not defined in terms of their causal role. Chalmers sums up the situation like this:

> There is no great mystery about how a state might play some causal role, although there are certainly technical problems there for science. What is mysterious is why that state should *feel* like something; why it should have a phenomenal quality. (1996: 15)

In sum, the problem of explaining psychological aspects of mind is an easy problem because the psychological concept of mind can be functionally defined, whereas the problem of explaining phenomenal consciousness is a hard problem because the phenomenal concept of mind cannot be functionally defined.

---

[8] As David Lewis (1972) explains, we start by using our mental terms to state the causal connections between mental states, environmental inputs, and behavioral outputs. Next, we generate the "Ramsey sentence" for the theory by systematically replacing each mental term with a variable bound by an existential quantifier. The result of this technique is a reductive analysis of our mental terms in the form of a complex definite description that specifies the causal role of our mental states in nonmental terms.

Which aspects of mind generate hard problems and which generate easy problems? That depends on which concepts of mind can be functionally defined. As I use the terms, it's not true by definition that our psychological concepts can be functionally defined. It's a substantive question—not one that can be settled by terminological stipulation—whether our ordinary psychological concepts (including our concepts of mental representation, belief, and knowledge) can be functionally defined. In the rest of this section, I'll contrast three distinct theoretical perspectives on this question and explain how they bear on our initial question about the significance of consciousness.[9]

The first view is *bifurcationism*: it says that there is no conceptual connection between our phenomenal concepts and our psychological concepts. Although we cannot give any functional definition of our phenomenal concepts, our ordinary psychological concepts can be functionally defined without mentioning phenomenal consciousness at all. On this view, it's conceivable that there could be a functional zombie with no phenomenal states. However, it's inconceivable that a functional zombie has no psychological states, since its nonphenomenal states play all the causal roles in which psychological states are defined. As Jaegwon Kim puts the point, "It would be incoherent to withhold states like belief, desire, knowledge, action, and intention from these creatures" (2005: 165).

Bifurcationism has important consequences for the metaphysical project of solving the mind-body problem. If bifurcationism is true, then the hard problem of explaining phenomenal consciousness can be divorced from the easy problems of explaining mental representation, cognition, and knowledge. We don't need to explain phenomenal consciousness in order to make progress in explaining these other aspects of mind. Instead, we can explain mental representation, cognition, and knowledge in purely causal terms without mentioning phenomenal consciousness at all. Ned Block gives expression to this viewpoint when he writes, "We cannot now conceive how psychology could explain qualia, though we *can* conceive how psychology could explain believing, desiring, hoping, etc." (1978: 307).

Bifurcationism also bears on our initial question about the significance of consciousness. If bifurcationism is true, then phenomenal consciousness has no uniquely significant role to play in our psychological lives. It's conceivable that we can remove phenomenal consciousness entirely while leaving our psychological lives perfectly intact. This is because the psychological roles played by our phenomenal states can conceivably be played by the nonphenomenal

---

[9] Chalmers (1996) is officially agnostic on this question. Although some of his remarks are friendly toward bifurcationism, he argues that some aspects of cognition are conceptually tied to phenomenal consciousness, including the contents of perceptual and phenomenal belief. This is a central theme in his later work, including Chalmers (2003) and (2004).

states of our functional zombie twins. Hence, bifurcationism implies that there is no role in our psychological lives that cannot conceivably be played without phenomenal consciousness. In other words, phenomenal consciousness has no unique significance in our psychological lives.

If bifurcationism is false, however, then the significance of consciousness begins to look rather different. Bifurcationism contrasts with *unificationism*, which says that there is some conceptual, analytic, or a priori connection between our phenomenal and psychological concepts of mind. The nature of this connection is disputed: some argue that we should analyze phenomenal consciousness in terms of its psychological role, while others argue that we should analyze our psychological states and processes in terms of their connections with phenomenal consciousness. As I'll explain, these opposing views have very different consequences for questions about the nature and significance of consciousness.

One version of unificationism says that *psychological functions come first*. On this view, phenomenal consciousness can be defined in terms of its causal role in the psychological processes that produce action, cognition, or metacognition. Moreover, the psychological concepts used in the definition of phenomenal consciousness can be functionally defined in purely causal terms. Putting these two claims together, the result is that both phenomenal and psychological concepts can be functionally defined in purely causal terms.[10]

On this view, we cannot divorce the hard problem of explaining phenomenal consciousness from the easy problem of explaining its associated psychological functions. On the contrary, these problems are intimately connected; moreover, they are connected in ways that make the hard problem easier to solve. To explain phenomenal consciousness, we just need to explain the psychological functions in terms of which it is defined. Since explaining these psychological functions is an easy problem, explaining phenomenal consciousness is an easy problem too.

Another consequence of this view is that phenomenal consciousness has a uniquely significant role to play in our psychological lives. On this view, phenomenal consciousness is functionally defined in terms of its causal role in our psychology. Therefore, it's inconceivable that there can be a functional zombie who does everything we conscious creatures can do. Any functional duplicate of a conscious creature is thereby a psychological duplicate of that creature, and any psychological duplicate of a conscious creature is thereby a phenomenal

---

[10] Psychological theories of consciousness are proposed by Armstrong (1968), Dretske (1995), Tye (1995), Lycan (1996), Rosenthal (1997), and Carruthers (2000), although many of these theories are advanced as empirical conjectures, rather than conceptual analyses.

duplicate of that creature. Hence, the causal role that phenomenal consciousness plays in our psychological lives cannot conceivably be played in zombies.

This is also the main problem with this view: it rules out the conceivability of functional zombies. This is sufficiently implausible that many proponents of functionalism about phenomenal consciousness prefer to recast it as an empirical or metaphysical hypothesis, rather than a conceptual analysis. We needn't conclude, however, that there is no analytic connection at all between phenomenal and psychological concepts. Instead, we can simply reverse the direction of analysis. Rather than analyzing phenomenal consciousness in terms of its role in our psychology, we can analyze our psychological states and processes in terms of phenomenal consciousness.

This alternative version of unificationism says that *phenomenal consciousness comes first*. On this view, the phenomenal concept of consciousness is our basic concept of mind. Our concepts of psychological states, including mental representation, belief, and knowledge, are analyzed in terms of their connections with phenomenal consciousness. As John Searle writes, "All of the processes that we think of as especially mental—whether perception, learning, inference, decision making, problem solving, the emotions, etc.—are in one way or another crucially related to consciousness" (1992: 227).

On this view, neither our phenomenal concepts nor our psychological concepts of mind are amenable to functional analysis. If our psychological concepts are analyzed in terms of their relations to phenomenal consciousness, and phenomenal consciousness resists functional definition, then our psychological concepts resist functional definition too. It's conceivable that there could be a functional zombie, but it's inconceivable that a functional zombie could have the same psychology as a conscious creature. This is because neither phenomenal states nor psychological states can be functionally defined in terms of their abstract causal structure.

Again, this means that we cannot we cannot divorce the hard problem of explaining phenomenal consciousness from the easy problem of explaining its associated psychological functions. These problems are intimately connected. Rather than making the hard problem easier to solve, however, this makes the easy problems much harder to solve. If our psychological states are analyzed in terms of their connections with phenomenal consciousness, then we cannot explain our psychological lives without explaining phenomenal consciousness too.

This view also has the consequence that phenomenal consciousness has a uniquely significant role to play in our psychological lives. This is not because functional zombies are inconceivable, but rather because they cannot conceivably share our psychology. They don't have the same psychological states and processes as we do, since our psychological states and processes are defined in terms of their connections with phenomenal consciousness. It's conceivable that functional zombies can do everything we can do, but it's inconceivable that their psychological lives are just like ours. This is the kind of response to the zombie challenge that I will develop in this book. In the next section, I'll distinguish several different versions of this response.

1.4. Putting Consciousness First

This section explores the program of putting phenomenal consciousness first. There are many different versions of this program. One version says that zombies cannot *represent* the world because phenomenal consciousness is the basis of all mental representation. Another version says that zombies cannot *think* about the world because phenomenal consciousness is the basis of all conceptual thought. My own version says that zombies cannot *know* anything about the world, since they have no epistemic justification to form beliefs: on this view, phenomenal consciousness is the basis of all epistemic justification. This section explains what's distinctive about my response to the zombie challenge by distinguishing it from others in the same vicinity.

1.4.1. Mental Representation

Proponents of bifurcationism tend to regard the problem of explaining mental representation as an easy problem, which can be divorced from the hard problem of explaining phenomenal consciousness. Consider the research program of "naturalizing" mental representation: the aim is to analyze mental representation in nonrepresentational terms that can be stated without mentioning consciousness. Naturalistic theories of mental representation typically appeal to internal causal relations between physical states of the brain or external causal relations between physical states of the brain and the external world. According to a simple causal theory, for example, a mental state represents that p just in case it is caused by the fact that p under optimal conditions in which the representational system fulfills its biological function.[11]

If mental representation can be analyzed without mentioning consciousness, then perhaps consciousness can be analyzed in terms of mental representation. This is the goal of *representational theories* of consciousness, which come in at least three kinds. First-order representational theories say that a mental state

---

[11] Those who defend causal theories of mental representation include Dretske (1981), Millikan (1984), Stalnaker (1984), and Fodor (1987). See Stich and Warfield (1994) for a volume of essays on the topic and Loewer (1997) for a critical survey.

is conscious just in case it represents the external world in a way that plays the right kind of functional role in the control of action, reasoning, and verbal report. Higher-order representational theories say that a mental state is conscious just in case it is the target of some higher-order mental representation, such as a higher-order thought or perception. Finally, self-representational theories say that a mental state is conscious just in case it represents itself in the right way.[12]

Combining these two ideas yields an influential strategy for solving the hard problem of consciousness. According to *the representational solution*, we can close the explanatory gap between physical and phenomenal concepts by combining a causal theory of mental representation with a representational theory of phenomenal consciousness. For example, David Armstrong (1968) combines a higher-order representational theory of phenomenal consciousness with a causal-informational theory of mental representation. The first step is that consciousness results from a process of "self-scanning" that carries information about your own informational states. The second step is that physical states carry information about other physical states when there is a systematic causal dependence of the former on the latter. The result is a version of unificationism that puts psychological functions first: it defines phenomenal consciousness in terms of its causal role in the psychological process of self-scanning.

Unfortunately, there are problems with both steps in the representational solution. The main problem with causal theories of mental representation is that they tend to face an underdetermination problem. This is the problem of explaining what makes it the case that a mental representation has the content that it does, rather than some deviant alternative. For example, Quine (1960: ch. 2) asks what makes it the case that our word 'rabbit' refers to rabbits, rather than undetached rabbit parts. Similarly, Kripke (1982) asks what makes it the case that our word 'plus' refers to the plus function, rather than the deviant quus function. These problems were originally raised for theories of linguistic meaning, but the same problems arise for theories of mental representation. The problem is that causal relations between me and my environment underdetermine whether I refer to rabbits or undetached rabbit parts, plus or quus, and so on. So, if mental representation is grounded in causal relations to the environment, then its content is radically indeterminate.

Even if this problem can be solved, the conceivability of zombies presents a problem for the representational analysis of consciousness. After all, it's conceivable that a zombie could have representational states that play the same kind

---

[12] For first-order representational theories, see Harman (1990), Tye (1995), Dretske (1995), and Jackson (2003). For higher-order representational theories, see Armstrong (1968), Rosenthal (1997), and Carruthers (2000). For self-representational theories, see Kriegel (2009) and the essays in Kriegel and Williford (2006).

of abstract causal role as our own conscious states. In the case of Armstrong's self-scanning theory, for example, it's conceivable that zombies could have higher-order states that carry information about their own first-order informational states. Some proponents of representational theories deny that zombies are conceivable, but this is rather hard to swallow. A more popular response is to block the inference from conceivability to possibility—say, by endorsing some version of the phenomenal concept strategy. But this is to abandon the representational strategy for solving the hard problem of consciousness. On this view, we cannot close the explanatory gap by giving a representational analysis of our phenomenal concepts.[13]

We can summarize these problems in the form of a dilemma. Is it conceivable that zombies can have mental representations or not? If so, then the representational analysis of consciousness is false, since zombies can satisfy all the relevant representational conditions without being conscious. If not, then the causal analysis of mental representation is false, since zombies can satisfy all the relevant causal conditions without having mental representations. Either way, the representational solution to the hard problem fails: we cannot close the explanatory gap by combining a representational analysis of consciousness with a causal analysis of mental representation.

Why does the representational solution to the hard problem fail? One diagnosis is that phenomenal consciousness comes first: mental representation should be analyzed in terms of phenomenal consciousness, rather than vice versa. The argument for this view is that only phenomenal consciousness provides a sufficiently determinate ground of mental representation. Zombies cannot have mental representations because only phenomenal consciousness can ground mental representation in a way that avoids radical indeterminacy. John Searle puts the point in terms of the claim that all intentional states have "aspectual shape"—that is, they present their intentional objects under some aspects, rather than others. He argues, "For a zombie, unlike a conscious agent, there simply is no fact of the matter as to exactly which aspectual shapes its alleged intentional states have" (1990: 595).

On this view, consciousness is the unique source of all mental representation: in other words, all mental representation is either conscious or otherwise grounded in consciousness. As Terry Horgan and George Graham (2012) put the point, consciousness is the "anchor point" for all mental representation.

---

[13] Michael Tye (1995) combines a causal theory of mental representation with a representational theory of phenomenal consciousness, but he endorses a version of the phenomenal concept strategy to block the inference from the premise that zombies are conceivable to the conclusion that zombies are possible. This is, in effect, to abandon the project of solving the hard problem by closing the explanatory gap.

This view provides a striking answer to our question about the significance of consciousness. If we become zombies, then we cannot represent the external world at all.[14]

In chapter 2, I'll argue against the proposal that consciousness is the unique source of all mental representation. More specifically, I'll argue that it cannot account for the indispensable explanatory role of unconscious mental representation in cognitive science. Following Tyler Burge (2010), I'll recommend that we solve the indeterminacy problems by treating mental representation as an autonomous scientific kind. Even if we cannot give a naturalistic reduction of unconscious mental representation in nonrepresentational terms, we are committed to its existence insofar as it plays an indispensable explanatory role in our best scientific theories. On this view, zombies can have mental representations so long as they play an indispensable role in explaining their behavior.

Our question about the significance of consciousness therefore remains. Is there any significant distinction to be drawn between the kind of mental representation that has its source in consciousness and the kind that has its source elsewhere? One answer is that consciousness is the ultimate source of our capacity to think about the empirical world. Bertrand Russell (1912) argues that our capacity to think about objects and properties in the external world depends ultimately on conscious acquaintance with our own experience. A contemporary version of this Russellian program says that all our empirical thought depends on demonstrative thought about objects and properties in the external world, and all such demonstrative thought depends upon conscious acquaintance with those objects and properties. On this view, zombies can have nonconceptual representations of the external world, but they have no conceptual capacity to think about the external world.[15]

In chapter 2, I'll argue that the epistemic role of consciousness is more fundamental in the order of explanation than the role of consciousness in thought. We can explain the role of consciousness in conceptual thought as a consequence of the epistemic role of consciousness together with epistemic constraints on conceptual thought. This yields a more fundamental answer to the zombie question. My claim is that mental representation provides epistemic justification for belief only if it has its source in consciousness. On this view, zombies can represent the world, but they cannot know anything about the world, since they have no epistemic justification to form beliefs about the world.

---

[14] McGinn (1989: 235) calls this the "converse Brentano thesis," but he doesn't go so far as to endorse it. Proponents include Searle (1990), Strawson (2008), Kriegel (2011), Horgan and Graham (2012), and Mendelovici (2018).
[15] Those who defend some essential connection between consciousness and thought include McDowell (1994), Davies (1995), Brewer (1999), Campbell (2002), Chalmers (2003), Pautz (2013), and Dickie (2015).

1.4.2. Epistemic Justification

To put this proposal into perspective, let's consider how phenomenal consciousness has figured—or otherwise failed to figure—in contemporary epistemology. What role does phenomenal consciousness play in contemporary theories of knowledge and epistemic justification? According to bifurcationism, the problem of explaining knowledge and epistemic justification is regarded as an easy problem that can be divorced from the hard problem of explaining phenomenal consciousness. Here are two prominent examples.

Jerry Fodor (1975) argues that we can explain epistemic rationality in terms of a computational theory of mind. The key idea is that the mind contains mechanisms that are sensitive to the formal properties of symbols. Moreover, there is an isomorphism between the formal properties of symbols and their semantic properties: there is a one-to-one mapping from one set of properties to the other that preserves relations between them. As a result, computational mechanisms that are directly sensitive to the formal properties of symbols are thereby indirectly sensitive also to their semantic properties. So long as we can explain the semantic properties of symbols without mentioning consciousness—say, in terms of a causal theory of mental representation—there is no need to mention consciousness in giving a mechanistic explanation of rational cognition.[16]

Similarly, Alvin Goldman (1979) and other proponents of reliabilism in epistemology explain knowledge and epistemic justification in terms of reliable connections between the mind and the external world that can be specified without mentioning consciousness. On a simple form of process reliabilism, for example, a belief is epistemically justified just in case it is held on the basis of a process that reliably yields true beliefs. Given this kind of reliabilism, the problem of explaining knowledge and justified belief can be regarded as an easy problem that can be tackled independently of the hard problem of explaining consciousness.[17]

If epistemic justification can be explained without appealing to phenomenal consciousness, then perhaps phenomenal consciousness can be explained in terms of epistemic justification. This is the goal of epistemic theories of consciousness. Epistemic theories are less popular than representational theories in the recent literature, but they have much the same structure. Higher-order epistemic theories say that a mental state is conscious just in case it serves as a

---

[16] Fodor (1983) is much less optimistic about the prospects of using the computational theory of mind to explain the rationality of inductive reasoning than deductive reasoning.
[17] Reliabilism was originally proposed as theory of knowledge by Armstrong (1973), Goldman (1976), Dretske (1981), and Nozick (1981). Goldman (1979) was the first to extend reliabilism from knowledge to epistemic justification.

basis for higher-order knowledge or epistemically justified belief that you're in that mental state. First-order epistemic theories, in contrast, say that a mental state is conscious just in case it serves as a basis for first-order knowledge or epistemically justified belief about the external world. According to Fred Dretske's epistemic criterion for consciousness, you are conscious of an object just in case information about the object is available to you as a justifying reason for belief or action. He writes, "S is aware of x if and only if information about x is available to S as a reason. It is the availability of information for rationalizing and motivating intentional action . . . that makes it conscious" (2006: 174).

Combining these two ideas yields a new strategy for solving the hard problem. According to *the epistemic solution*, we can close the explanatory gap by combining an epistemic analysis of phenomenal consciousness with a reliabilist analysis of epistemic justification. Unfortunately, the epistemic solution fails for much the same reason as the representational solution. Again, the problem can be posed in the form of a dilemma. Is it conceivable that zombies have epistemically justified beliefs or not? If so, then the epistemic analysis of consciousness is false, since zombies can satisfy all the relevant epistemic conditions without being conscious. If not, then the reliabilist analysis of epistemic justification is false, since zombies can satisfy all the relevant reliability conditions without having epistemically justified beliefs. Either way, the epistemic solution to the hard problem fails: we cannot close the explanatory gap by combining a reliabilist analysis of epistemic justification with an epistemic analysis of consciousness.

Why does the epistemic solution to the hard problem fail? My own diagnosis is that phenomenal consciousness comes first: we should analyze epistemic justification in terms of phenomenal consciousness, rather than vice versa. It is extremely plausible that there is some analytic connection between consciousness and knowledge: indeed, this connection seems to be encoded in the etymology of the word 'consciousness', which derives from the Latin words, *con* (together), and *scire* (to know). We can preserve this connection by giving a phenomenal analysis of epistemic justification, rather than an epistemic analysis of phenomenal consciousness. That is exactly what I will do in this book.

The main aim of this book is to argue that consciousness has unique epistemic significance. On this view, all epistemic justification has its source in consciousness. More precisely, all mental representations that provide epistemic justification for belief are either conscious or otherwise grounded in consciousness. This generates an answer to the zombie challenge. Zombies can represent the world, but they cannot know anything about the world, since they have no epistemic justification to form beliefs about the world. Only conscious creatures can know anything about the world.

Although this book is about the epistemic role of consciousness, I've argued elsewhere that the normative significance of consciousness extends in a unified way across epistemic and practical domains.[18] Just as consciousness is a unique source of epistemic justification for belief, so it is a unique source of practical justification for action. Conscious experience gives us justifying reasons for belief and action and thereby enables us to believe and act rationally on the basis of those reasons. Moreover, conscious experience is a unique source of epistemic and practical reasons. If we become zombies, then we have no justifying reasons for belief and action, and so we cannot believe or act rationally on the basis of reasons. Let me illustrate the point with a mundane example.

Consider the experience you have when you see a tempting piece of cake and you feel the desire to eat it. Your visual experience seems to present you with cake and thereby gives you an epistemic reason to believe that there is cake before you. Similarly, your affective experience of desire presents the prospect of eating the cake in a positive light and thereby gives you a practical reason to intend to eat the cake. These reasons are defeasible, of course, but the phenomenal character of your experience counts to some degree in favor of eating the cake. In the absence of defeating reasons, these reasons are strong enough to act upon. If you are rational, then you will eat the cake, and you will do so for good reasons.

Now contrast your zombie twin who is in exactly the same external predicament. Your zombie twin has an internal state that represents the presence of cake and an internal state that motivates eating the cake. Even so, there is nothing it is like for the zombie to have these representational and motivational states. The zombie has no visual experience that seems to present it with cake and no experience of desire that seems to present the cake in a positive light. In consequence, the zombie has no epistemic reason to believe there is cake to be eaten and it has no practical reason to intend to eat cake. Of course, we can explain why your zombie twin behaves as it does by citing its unconscious representational and motivational states. We can also explain why acting that way is good for the zombie—for instance, it may need food in order to survive. What we cannot do is to explain the zombie's behavior in a way that shows it to be rational in light of the zombie's own reasons for belief or action. This is because the zombie has no conscious experience.

That, in any case, is what I will argue in this book. Your zombie twin doesn't have the same reasons as you, since consciousness is a unique source of reasons for belief and action. Moreover, it follows—or so I will argue—that your zombie

---

[18] Smithies and Weiss (2019) argue that affective experience plays an essential role in explaining how desires provide practical reasons for action.

twin doesn't have the same mental states that you do. By stipulation, your zombie twin has no conscious mental states. Still, we can ask, does it have all the same beliefs, desires, and intentions?

Resolving this question depends on how these mental states are defined. Are they defined by their *causal role* in motivating belief and action or by their *normative role* in providing reasons for belief and action? If mental states are defined by their causal role, then your zombie twin has the same mental states as you, since their states play the same causal role as yours. If mental states are defined by their normative role, however, then your zombie twin doesn't have the same mental states as you, since their states don't play the same normative role as yours. I'll now suggest that beliefs, desires, and intentions are defined by their normative roles in providing reasons for belief and action, rather than their causal roles in motivating belief and action.

There is often a mismatch between the causal roles of our mental states and their normative roles: we don't always believe and act on the basis of our reasons. After all, we're not ideally rational agents. Nevertheless, ideally rational agents can have beliefs, desires, and intentions, just as we can. Their mental states don't play the same causal role as our mental states in motivating belief and action, since they are much more rational than we are, but their mental states play the same abstract normative role in providing reasons for belief and action. For example, their beliefs and intentions provide reasons for action and are supported by reasons provided by perception and desire. This suggests that these mental states are defined by their normative roles in providing us with reasons for belief and action, rather than their causal roles in motivating us to believe and act for those reasons. In this sense, the mental is normative.

When I say that the mental is normative, I mean that there are normative roles that are both necessary and sufficient for having certain mental states, such as beliefs, desires, and intentions. I'm not making the stronger claim that the most fundamental characterization of these mental states is given by their normative roles. Presumably, there must be some more fundamental explanation that explains why beliefs, desires, and intentions play different kinds of normative roles. In my view, the most fundamental characterization of these standing attitudes concerns their phenomenal dispositions. Beliefs, desires, and intentions are disposed to cause different kinds of phenomenal experience. These phenomenal dispositions explain why beliefs, desires, and intentions play the normative roles that they do. On this view, phenomenal consciousness comes first in explaining the normativity of the mental.[19]

---

[19] Zangwill (2005) defines "normative functionalism" as the thesis that beliefs and desires have normative essences, but he distinguishes the strong thesis that their whole essence is normative from the weaker thesis that their normative essence is a consequence of some more basic essence. My

If the mental is normative, and consciousness is a unique source of normativity, then it follows that consciousness plays a unique role in our mental lives. On this view, zombies cannot have exactly the same mental states as conscious creatures, since their unconscious states cannot play the same normative role in giving and receiving support from reasons. In this way, we can use the normative significance of consciousness as a premise in arguing that consciousness plays an essential role in our mental lives.

Zombies pose a challenge to the significance of consciousness because they can do everything we conscious creatures can do: the unconscious states of a zombie play the same abstract causal role as our conscious states. My response to this challenge is to explain the significance of consciousness in terms of its normative role, rather than its causal role. Consciousness has no unique causal significance, but it has unique normative significance: it is inconceivable that the normative role of consciousness can be duplicated by any merely ersatz functional substitute for consciousness. This is because the unique normative significance of consciousness depends on its phenomenal character, rather than its causal role. This means that our epistemic and psychological concepts cannot be functionally defined in terms of their abstract causal role. We cannot understand the mind by putting psychological functions first. Instead, we need to put phenomenal consciousness first.[20]

1.5. An Overview of This Book

This book is about the connection between phenomenal consciousness and epistemic justification. But what is epistemic justification? Like the concept of phenomenal consciousness, the concept of epistemic justification cannot be defined in more basic terms, but only by giving examples. Justified beliefs include those based on perceptual experience, or inferred from other justified beliefs by good deductive and inductive reasoning. Unjustified beliefs include those based on wishful thinking, hasty generalization, fallacious reasoning, or ungrounded hunches. We all have some intuitive understanding of what it means to say that a belief is justified, which we can use as a starting point in building a theory of epistemic justification. At the same time, we can use more abstract

---

view is consistent with a weak form of normative functionalism on which the normative essence of belief and desire is consequential upon a more basic essence that is defined in terms of phenomenal dispositions.

[20] Lee (2013, 2019) argues that if reductive physicalism is true, then consciousness has no unique normative significance. In my view, however, his argument relies on a dubious premise about how evaluatively significant distinctions must be grounded in fundamental physical reality. I hope to discuss this argument in future work.

theoretical considerations to sharpen and refine our intuitive grasp on the nature of epistemic justification.

It is sometimes said that 'justified belief' is a philosopher's idiom, but a quick search of the internet reveals multiple uses in the news, including the sports pages. Here is a representative example from the soccer fan website *Pain in the Arsenal*:

> Alexis Sanchez is clearly unhappy with life at the Emirates and could well be edging towards a summer exit. Repeated strops and tantrums . . . have led many to conclude that Sanchez is nearing the end of his Arsenal tenure. And that is a justified belief.[21]

Admittedly, beliefs are more commonly described as 'reasonable' or 'rational' than 'justified', but these are all perfectly good uses of English language, and they are all standardly used with the same meaning. To say that a belief is justified is to say that it is rational or reasonable—in other words, it is based on good reasons. Some epistemologists insist on drawing distinctions between justification, rationality, and reasonableness. I am not opposed to drawing such distinctions; indeed, I'll draw a distinction between ideal and nonideal senses of these epistemic terms. My claim here is just that these are theoretical distinctions, which are not obviously reflected in our ordinary use of the terms.

'Epistemic justification' is a philosopher's idiom, but this technical terminology is designed to mark an intuitive distinction. An epistemically justified belief is a belief that is justified by evidence—that is, by epistemic reasons, rather than practical reasons. If you believe that God exists because you want to avoid the threat of eternal damnation, then you believe for practical reasons, rather than epistemic reasons. You have no epistemic reason to believe that God exists because your desire gives you no evidence that God exists. Arguably, beliefs cannot be justified by practical reasons at all, since these are the "wrong kinds of reasons" to justify belief. In any case, it seems clear that you cannot know anything on the basis of practical reasons. Epistemic justification is the kind of justification that is necessary for knowledge. All knowledge is justified by evidence.

We can say that all knowledge is justified by evidence without prejudging questions about the nature of evidence. Given the framework of evidentialism, we can define your evidence in terms of its epistemic role in determining which propositions you have epistemic justification to believe. Different theories of evidence disagree about which facts play this epistemic role. This book argues

---

[21] https://paininthearsenal.com/2017/03/28/arsenal-50-million-alexis-sanchez-good-deal/.

for a *phenomenal conception* of evidence, according to which your evidence is exhausted by the facts about your current phenomenally individuated mental states. Given that epistemic justification is determined by evidence, this yields the central organizing thesis of the book:

Phenomenal Mentalism: Necessarily, which propositions you have epistemic justification to believe at any given time is determined solely by your phenomenally individuated mental states at that time.

These "phenomenally individuated" mental states include not only your experiences, which are individuated by their phenomenal character, but also your standing beliefs, desires, and intentions, which are individuated by their dispositions to cause certain kinds of phenomenal experiences under phenomenal conditions. At the same time, this criterion excludes your "subdoxastic" mental states, which are individuated by their role in unconscious computational processes, and all your mental states that are externally individuated by their relations to the external world.

The book as a whole provides an extended argument for phenomenal mentalism. The book is divided into two parts, which converge on phenomenal mentalism from opposite directions. Part I argues "from below" by using intuitions about cases to build a more general argument for phenomenal mentalism. Part II, in contrast, argues "from above" by using general epistemic principles (such as the JJ principle) to argue for phenomenal mentalism. These two argumentative strategies are mutually reinforcing. The judgments about cases provide intuitive support for the general principles, while the general principles provide theoretical support for the judgments about cases. The result is a theory of epistemic justification that achieves stable reflective equilibrium between intuitions about cases and general principles.

Here, in summary form, are some intuitive considerations that are adduced in support of phenomenal mentalism in the first part of the book:

- It explains why perceptual experience provides epistemic justification for beliefs about the external world.
- It explains why unconscious perceptual information in blindsight doesn't provide epistemic justification for beliefs about the external world.
- It explains why you and your phenomenal duplicates in skeptical scenarios have epistemic justification to believe the same propositions to the same degree.
- It explains why your beliefs, as well as your perceptual experiences, can affect which propositions you have epistemic justification to believe.

- It explains why your "subdoxastic" mental representations, unlike your beliefs, cannot affect which propositions you have epistemic justification to believe.

Much of the first part of the book is devoted to motivating these claims, defending them against objections, and explaining how they support phenomenal mentalism.

The second part of the book is designed to address an explanatory challenge for phenomenal mentalism. Why are only phenomenally individuated mental states capable of determining epistemic justification? Phenomenal mentalism is intuitively compelling, but the challenge is to provide some kind of theoretical understanding of why it should be true. The second part of the book develops a form of *accessibilism* about epistemic justification that is designed to explain why phenomenal mentalism is true. *Phenomenal accessibilism* is the view that results from combining phenomenal mentalism with accessibilism in the manner that I'll explain.

My answer to the explanatory challenge appeals to a threefold connection between epistemic justification, phenomenal consciousness, and introspection. What's special about phenomenally individuated mental states is that they are "luminous" in the sense that you're always in a position to know by introspection whether or not you're in those mental states. Moreover, accessibilism makes it plausible that only luminous mental states provide epistemic justification for belief. This explains why only phenomenally individuated mental states provide epistemic justification for belief. Here is the argument in outline:

(1) Only introspectively luminous mental states can provide epistemic justification for belief.
(2) Only phenomenally individuated mental states are introspectively luminous.
(3) Therefore, only phenomenally individuated mental states can provide epistemic justification for belief.

I'll now briefly comment on each of these premises.

The second premise articulates an epistemic connection between introspection and phenomenal consciousness. Although I'll motivate this premise and defend it against objections in chapter 5, I won't attempt to derive it from more fundamental assumptions, since I very much doubt that this can be done. Some philosophers argue that we can explain the epistemic connection between introspection and phenomenal consciousness in terms of metaphysical claims about the nature of phenomenal consciousness. For example, one influential view says that phenomenal consciousness is introspectively luminous because it (and it alone) is "self-presenting" in the sense that it constitutes a primitive form of awareness of itself. In my view, however, there is no good motivation for this claim about the nature of phenomenal consciousness. Indeed, I suspect that the epistemic connection between introspection and phenomenal consciousness says much more about the nature of introspection than it does about the nature of phenomenal consciousness. My strategy is to use this epistemic connection as my starting point in explaining a more general connection between epistemic justification and phenomenal consciousness. Of course, this still leaves me with the burden of motivating the first premise.

The first premise says that only introspectively luminous mental states can provide epistemic justification for belief. I motivate this premise by arguing for a form of accessibilism about epistemic justification:

Accessibilism: Epistemic justification is luminously accessible in the sense that, necessarily, you're always in a position to know which propositions you have epistemic justification to believe at any given time.

If accessibilism is true, then it stands in need of explanation. What explains how you're always in a position to know which propositions you have epistemic justification to believe? The best explanation, or so I will argue, is that epistemic justification is determined by introspectively luminous facts about your phenomenally individuated mental states. Whenever you're in some phenomenally individuated mental state M that gives you epistemic justification to believe that *p*, you're thereby in a position to know the following:

(1) I'm in M [by introspection].
(2) If I'm in M, then I have justification to believe that *p* [by a priori reasoning].
(3) Therefore, I have justification to believe that *p* [by deduction from (1) and (2)].

The upshot is that phenomenal mentalism is an essential part of the best explanation of accessibilism. If accessibilism can be motivated and defended on independent grounds, then phenomenal mentalism is supported by inference to the best explanation.

In the second part of the book, I give three distinct arguments for accessibilism. First, it explains and vindicates the intuitions about cases that I use to motivate phenomenal mentalism in the first part of the book. Second, it is needed for explaining the irrationality of epistemic akrasia—that is, roughly, believing things you believe you shouldn't believe. And third, it follows from the plausible thesis that epistemic justification is what gives a belief the potential to survive an ideally rational process of critical reflection.

I also defend accessibilism against a series of influential objections. These include Timothy Williamson's anti-luminosity argument, Ernest Sosa's version of the problem of the speckled hen, David Christensen's arguments from misleading higher-order evidence, Hilary Kornblith's arguments against the connection between epistemic justification and reflection, and Eric Schwitzgebel's arguments for the unreliability of introspection. A central theme in my responses to all these objections is that we need to respect a distinction between ideal and nonideal standards of epistemic rationality. I argue that this is not just an ad hoc move designed to avoid objections, but is independently well motivated: in effect, everyone needs some version of this distinction. What is distinctive about my account is not the appeal to ideal rationality itself, but rather my specific account of what ideal rationality consists in.

Any version of evidentialism says that ideal rationality is a matter of proportioning your beliefs to the evidence. But different versions of evidentialism disagree about which propositions are supported by your evidence. According to accessibilism, you're always in a position to know what your evidence is and what it supports. Otherwise, your evidence can make it rational to be epistemically akratic—that is, to believe things that you believe you shouldn't believe. Plausibly, however, epistemic akrasia is never permitted by ideal standards of rationality. The best explanation of accessibilism is that your evidence is exhausted by introspectively luminous facts about your mental states. But only phenomenally individuated facts about your mental states are introspectively luminous in the requisite way. Hence, phenomenal mentalism emerges as an inevitable consequence of an independently motivated account of the nature of ideal rationality.

1.6. Chapter Summaries

This book is divided into two parts. The first part is more closely engaged with issues in the philosophy of mind, including debates about the role of phenomenal consciousness in theories of mental representation, perception, cognition, and introspection. The second part is more exclusively concerned with issues in epistemology, including the debates between internalism and externalism about the nature of epistemic justification. This division is somewhat artificial, however, since one of the main aims of the book is to highlight interconnections between epistemology and philosophy of mind. Throughout this book, epistemology informs and is informed by philosophy of mind.

I hope you will read this book from beginning to end. If you're looking to read more selectively, however, here is some advice about how to proceed. While the book as a whole builds a cumulative argument for the epistemic role of consciousness, each individual chapter is relatively self-standing, and each of the two parts can be read on its own. If you're primarily interested in issues in the philosophy of mind, including debates about the nature and epistemic role of phenomenal consciousness, then it makes sense to start with chapters 1–7. If you're primarily interested in issues in epistemology, including the debate between internalism and externalism about epistemic justification, then you could just as well start with chapters 6–12. Either way, chapters 6 and 7 are essential to understanding the overall contours of the view. And if you want to know how it all fits together, then you should probably read the whole thing.

Chapter 2: Representation

Chapter 2 explores the relationship between consciousness and mental representation. Section 2.1 argues for a version of representationalism, the thesis that consciousness is a kind of mental representation. Section 2.2 argues against the representational grounding thesis, which says that all unconscious mental representation is grounded in consciousness. Section 2.3 argues that the representational grounding thesis is not supported by failure of the program of naturalizing mental representation. Section 2.4 examines the conceptual grounding thesis, which says that all conceptual representation is grounded in consciousness. The role of consciousness in thought is best explained as a consequence of the epistemic role of consciousness together with epistemic constraints on conceptual thought. Section 2.5 presents the epistemic grounding thesis, which says that all mental representation that provides epistemic justification for belief is grounded in consciousness. This thesis sets the agenda for the rest of the book.

Chapter 3: Perception

Chapter 3 explores the epistemic role of consciousness in perception. Section 3.1 argues that unconscious perceptual representation in blindsight cannot justify beliefs about the external world. Section 3.2 argues that this is because phenomenal consciousness, rather than access consciousness or metacognitive consciousness, is necessary for perceptual representation to justify belief. Section 3.3 argues that perceptual experience has a distinctive kind of phenomenal character—namely, presentational force—that is not only necessary but also sufficient for perception to justify belief. Section 3.4 uses a version of the new evil demon problem to argue that the justifying role of perceptual experience supervenes on its phenomenal character alone. Section 3.5 defends this supervenience thesis against the objection that phenomenal duplicates who perceive distinct objects thereby have justification to believe different de re propositions.

Chapter 4: Cognition

Chapter 4 explores the epistemic role of consciousness in cognition. Section 4.1 argues that all beliefs provide epistemic justification for other beliefs. Section 4.2 contrasts beliefs with subdoxastic states, which provide no epistemic justification for belief. Section 4.3 argues that this epistemic distinction between beliefs and subdoxastic states cannot be explained in terms of the functional criterion of inferential integration. Section 4.4 argues that this epistemic distinction must be explained in terms of the phenomenal criterion of conscious accessibility: the contents of beliefs are accessible to consciousness as the contents of conscious judgments. Section 4.5 argues that conscious judgments have phenomenal contents that supervene on their phenomenal character. Section 4.6 concludes with some proleptic remarks to explain why beliefs can provide epistemic justification for other beliefs only if their contents are accessible to consciousness.

Chapter 5: Introspection

Chapter 5 explores the epistemic role of consciousness in introspection. Section 5.1 presents a simple theory of introspection, which says that some mental states provide introspective justification that puts you in a position to know with certainty that you're in those mental states. Section 5.2 defends the simple theory against Eric Schwitzgebel's arguments for the unreliability of introspection. Section 5.3 motivates the simple theory on the grounds that it explains a plausible connection between epistemic rationality and introspective self-knowledge. Section 5.4 argues that all and only phenomenally individuated mental states fall within the scope of the simple theory of introspection. Section 5.5 explores the role of consciousness in explaining our introspective knowledge of what we believe. Section 5.6 concludes with some pessimism about the prospects for explaining the connection between consciousness and introspection in more basic terms.

Chapter 6: Mentalism

Chapter 6 develops a theory of epistemic justification designed to capture the epistemic role of phenomenal consciousness: namely, phenomenal mentalism. Section 6.1 defines epistemic justification within the framework of evidentialism. Section 6.2 defines mentalism about epistemic justification and explores its connection with evidentialism. Section 6.3 argues for phenomenal mentalism, the thesis that epistemic justification is determined solely by your phenomenally individuated mental states, by appealing to intuitions about clairvoyance, super-blindsight and the new evil demon problem. Section 6.4 argues for a phenomenal conception of evidence, which says that your evidence is exhausted by facts about your current phenomenally individuated mental states, and defends it against Timothy Williamson's arguments for the E = K thesis. Finally, section 6.5 outlines an explanatory challenge for phenomenal mentalism, which sets the agenda for the second part of the book.

Chapter 7: Accessibilism

Chapter 7 answers the explanatory challenge by combining phenomenal mentalism with accessibilism to yield phenomenal accessibilism. Section 7.1 defines accessibilism as the thesis that epistemic justification is luminous in the sense that you're always in a position to know which propositions you have epistemic justification to believe. Section 7.2 argues that phenomenal mentalism is part of the best explanation of accessibilism: if accessibilism can be motivated on independent grounds, then phenomenal mentalism is supported by inference to the best explanation. Sections 7.3 and 7.4 use accessibilism to motivate the intuitions about cases that support phenomenal mentalism—namely, clairvoyance, super-blindsight, and the new evil demon problem. Finally, section 7.5 answers the explanatory challenge for phenomenal mentalism: epistemic justification is determined by your current phenomenally individuated mental states because they are luminous by introspection.

Chapter 8: Reflection

Chapter 8 motivates accessibilism by appealing to William Alston's hypothesis that the value of epistemic justification is tied to reflection, an activity that is the distinctive mark of persons who can be held responsible for their beliefs and actions. Section 8.1 argues that epistemic justification is what makes our beliefs stable under an idealized process of reflection. Section 8.2 uses this proposal in arguing for the JJ principle, which says that you have justification to believe a proposition if and only if you have justification to believe that you have justification to believe it. Sections 8.3–8.6 defend this proposal against a series of objections raised by Hilary Kornblith: the overintellectualization problem, the regress problem, the empirical problem, and the value problem. Section 8.7 concludes with some reflections on the debate between internalism and externalism about epistemic justification.

Chapter 9: Epistemic Akrasia

Chapter 9 argues that accessibilism is needed to explain the epistemic irrationality of epistemic akrasia—roughly, believing things you believe you shouldn't believe. Section 9.1 defines epistemic akrasia and separates questions about its possibility and its rational permissibility. Section 9.2 argues from the premise that epistemic akrasia is never rationally permissible to the conclusion that the JJ principle is true. The remaining sections motivate the premise that epistemic akrasia is never rationally permissible: section 9.3 appeals to an epistemic version of Moore's paradox, section 9.4 to the slogan that knowledge is the aim of belief, and section 9.5 to the connection between epistemic justification and reflection.

Chapter 10: Higher-Order Evidence

Chapter 10 explores a puzzle about epistemic akrasia: if you can have misleading higher-order evidence about what your evidence supports, then your total evidence can make it rationally permissible to be epistemically akratic. Section 10.1 presents the puzzle and three options for solving it: Level Splitting, Downward Push, and Upward Push. Section 10.2 argues that we should opt for Upward Push: you cannot have misleading higher-order evidence about what your evidence is or what it supports. Sections 10.3 and 10.4 defend Upward Push against David Christensen's objection that it licenses irrational forms of dogmatism in ideal and nonideal agents alike. Section 10.5 responds to his argument that misleading higher-order evidence generates rational dilemmas in which you're guaranteed to violate one of the ideals of epistemic rationality. Section 10.6 concludes with some general reflections on the nature of epistemic rationality and the role of epistemic idealization.

Chapter 11: Luminosity

Chapter 11 defends the thesis that some phenomenal and epistemic conditions are luminous in the sense that you're always in a position to know whether or not they obtain. Section 11.1 draws a distinction between epistemic and doxastic senses of luminosity and argues that some conditions are epistemically luminous even if none are doxastically luminous. Section 11.2 uses this distinction in solving Ernest Sosa's version of the problem of the speckled hen. The same distinction is applied to Timothy Williamson's anti-luminosity argument in section 11.3, his argument against epistemic iteration principles in section 11.4, and his argument for improbable knowing in section 11.5. Section 11.6 concludes by explaining why this defense of luminosity is not merely a pointless compromise.

Chapter 12: Seemings

Chapter 12 concludes the book by contrasting phenomenal accessibilism with Michael Huemer's phenomenal conservatism. Section 12.1 defines phenomenal conservatism as the global principle that you have epistemic justification to believe a proposition just when it seems strongly enough on balance to be true. Section 12.2 explains the concept of a seeming and outlines an argument that there are no nonperceptual seemings. Section 12.3 argues that phenomenal conservatism imposes implausible restrictions on evidence: all seemings are evidence, but not all evidence is seemings. Section 12.4 argues that phenomenal conservatism gives an overly simplistic account of the evidential support relation: it cannot explain why epistemic rationality requires not only perceptual coherence, but also introspective coherence, logical coherence, and metacoherence. Section 12.5 argues that phenomenal accessibilism is needed to explain these essential characteristics of epistemically rational thinkers. Section 12.6 concludes by summarizing why phenomenal accessibilism is superior to phenomenal conservatism.

2

Representation

The first chapter of this book posed a question about the significance of consciousness and its role in our mental lives. How much of our mental life depends upon consciousness? To put the question more vividly: if we all become zombies, then how much of our mental life are we thereby guaranteed to lose? One prominent answer is that consciousness is the ultimate source of all mental representation (the scholastic term is "intentionality"). On this view, it is only because we are conscious creatures that we are capable of representing the world around us. If we become zombies, then we cannot represent the external world at all.

The main goal of this chapter is to explore the relationship between consciousness and mental representation. This will allow me to distinguish my account of the epistemic significance of consciousness from nearby alternatives, while also laying out some of the background assumptions in the philosophy of mind that I'll be assuming throughout the book. I'll argue that zombies can represent the world, although they cannot know anything about the world, since their mental representations cannot provide them with epistemic justification to form beliefs about the world. On this view, consciousness is the ultimate basis of epistemic justification.

In section 2.1, I'll begin by presenting and motivating an influential thesis about the nature of consciousness known as "representationalism" (or "intentionalism"):

Representationalism: All consciousness is a kind of mental representation.

I'll argue for this thesis on broadly phenomenological grounds: representationalism provides the best explanation of the way conscious experience seems to us through introspection. As we saw in section 1.4, some philosophers are interested in representationalism for metaphysical reasons: they regard it as the key to solving the hard problem of consciousness. In contrast, I am interested in representationalism primarily for epistemological reasons: it will figure centrally in my account of the epistemic role of consciousness in chapters 3 and 4.

Representationalism says that all consciousness is a kind of mental representation, but it doesn't imply that all mental representation is conscious. Some philosophers combine representationalism with the further thesis that all unconscious mental representation is grounded in consciousness. This is to endorse the following representational grounding thesis:

The Representational Grounding Thesis: All mental representation is either conscious or grounded in consciousness.

On this view, consciousness is the unique source of all mental representation. If we become zombies, then we thereby lose our capacity for representing the external world.

In sections 2.2 and 2.3, I'll argue that the representational grounding thesis is both false and unmotivated. We should believe in the existence of unconscious mental representation because it plays an indispensable explanatory role both in folk psychology and in cognitive science. Moreover, not all unconscious mental representation that plays an indispensable role in psychological explanation is grounded in consciousness. Since unconscious mental representation is indispensable for explaining zombie behavior, we should conclude that zombies have mental representations after all. Our question about the significance of consciousness therefore remains. What is the significance of the distinction between conscious and unconscious mental representation?

In section 2.4, I'll consider the answer that consciousness is the ultimate source of all conceptual thought. On this view, the distinction between conceptual and nonconceptual representation is ultimately explained in terms of consciousness. According to the conceptual grounding thesis, all conceptual representation has its source in consciousness in the following sense:

The Conceptual Grounding Thesis: All conceptual mental representation is either conscious or grounded in consciousness.

This means that zombies can represent the world, but only conscious creatures can think about the world. I'll argue that the role of consciousness in thought is best explained as a consequence of the epistemic role of consciousness together with epistemic constraints on conceptual thought. If so, then the epistemic role of consciousness is more fundamental than the role of consciousness in thought.

This brings me finally to my own account of the significance of consciousness, which I'll introduce in section 2.5 and develop in the rest of this book.

On this view, consciousness is the unique source of epistemic justification. All epistemic justification has its source in consciousness in the sense here defined:

The Epistemic Grounding Thesis: All mental representation that plays an epistemic role in the justification of belief is either conscious or grounded in consciousness.

On this view, a mental representation cannot provide justifying reasons for belief, and so cannot play a role in the rational explanation of belief, unless it is either conscious or grounded in consciousness. Zombies can have mental representations that causally explain their behavior, but they cannot have mental representations that rationally explain their beliefs or their behavior. Hence, they cannot know anything about the world.

Here is the plan for this chapter. I'll begin by arguing that representationalism is true (section 2.1). Next, I'll argue that the representational grounding thesis is false (section 2.2) and unmotivated (section 2.3). Finally, I'll examine the conceptual grounding thesis (section 2.4), and I'll argue that it is best explained as a consequence of the epistemic grounding thesis (section 2.5), which I'll argue for in the rest of the book.

2.1. Representationalism

Take a moment to inspect the front cover of this book and reflect on your visual experience. You'll notice that your experience has two aspects. On the one hand, your experience is phenomenally conscious in the sense that there is something it's like for you to have the experience. On the other hand, your experience represents the external world: for example, it represents that the book has a certain shape and color. Now, it is surely not just a coincidence that your experience has these two aspects. On the contrary, there is an intimate connection between what it's subjectively like for you to have the experience and the way your experience represents the external world. Colin McGinn was among the first to make this point in the following passage:

Perceptual experiences are Janus-faced: they point outward to the external world but they also present a subjective face to their subject: they are of something other than the subject and they are like something for the subject. But these two faces do not wear different expressions: for what the experience is like is a function of what it is of, and what it is of is a function of what it is like. (1989: 231)

This is an evocative metaphor, but we need a more precise statement of the idea it is designed to evoke. What exactly is the nature of the connection between what it's subjectively like to have the experience and what your experience is about? The simplest answer, and I think the best, is that the connection is one of identity. According to representationalism, the phenomenal character of experience *just is* a way of representing the external world.[1]

In order to give a more precise statement of representationalism, we need to introduce some terminology. Let's start with phenomenal consciousness. A mental state is *phenomenally conscious* just when there is something it's like for the subject to be in that mental state. The *phenomenal character* of a mental state is what it's like for the subject to be in it. And the *phenomenal properties* of a mental state are simply aspects of its phenomenal character: they are more or less determinate ways of being phenomenally conscious.

Now let's consider mental representation. A *representational state* is a mental state that represents the world. The *representational content* of a mental state is the way it represents the world to be: if the world is that way, then its content is true; otherwise, its content is false. The *representational force* of a mental state is the way in which it represents its content: for example, belief and desire can represent the same contents in different ways: belief represents its content as true, whereas desire represents its content as to be made true. The *representational properties* of a mental state are simply aspects of its representational force or content: they are more or less determinate ways of representing the world.[2]

With these definitions in hand, we can now define representationalism more precisely as the following identity thesis:

Representationalism: Necessarily, every phenomenal property is identical with some representational property.

Since identity is a symmetric relation, representationalism implies that some representational properties are identical with phenomenal properties, but it doesn't imply that all of them are. Representationalism is therefore consistent with the existence of unconscious mental representation (see section 2.2).

In this book, I'll assume that perceptual experience has representational content. This assumption is motivated by a combination of phenomenological and epistemological considerations. For example, the content of your perceptual experience determines accuracy conditions that can be satisfied or unsatisfied

---

[1] This view is also called "intentionalism." Aside from McGinn (1989), proponents include Harman (1990), Dretske (1995), Tye (1995), Lycan (1996), Siewert (1998), Byrne (2001), Horgan and Tienson (2002), Crane (2003), Jackson (2003), Chalmers (2004), Speaks (2009), Pautz (2010), Brogaard (2018), and Mendelovici (2018).

[2] The distinction between force and content derives from Frege (1956). Force is a relation to content: it is what Searle (1983) and Crane (2003) call "intentional mode" and Chalmers (2004) calls "manner of representation." The contents of representational states are usually regarded as propositions, but I take no stand on the nature of propositions, or the question of whether there can be nonpropositional contents.

depending on whether you perceive the world as it is or merely suffer a perceptual illusion or hallucination. Moreover, the content of your perceptual experience determines which contents you thereby have epistemic justification to believe. In chapter 3, I'll put these assumptions to work in developing an account of the epistemic role of consciousness in perception. Unfortunately, I won't have space to explore how much of the epistemic role of consciousness can be preserved if you reject these foundational assumptions in the philosophy of mind.[3]

It's one thing to claim that perceptual experience has representational content, but it's another thing to claim that the phenomenal character of perceptual experience can be identified with its representational properties. Proponents of "the qualia theory" often accept the first claim while rejecting the second. On this view, experience has some phenomenal properties that are distinct from any representational property: these nonrepresentational, phenomenal properties are known as "qualia." A strong version of the theory says that all phenomenal properties are qualia, whereas a weak version says that only some are qualia. All else being equal, however, we should avoid the weak version of the qualia theory, since it gives a disjunctive theory of phenomenal consciousness that identifies some phenomenal properties with representational properties and others with qualia. As Daniel Stoljar remarks, "It would be an odd sort of position indeed which postulates qualia but then adds that qualia are only instantiated in cases in which you face the sun with closed eyes, or else are in states of sexual climax" (2004: 368).

Why should we prefer representationalism to the qualia theory? In chapters 3 and 4, I'll motivate representationalism on epistemological grounds by putting it to work in explaining how perceptual and cognitive experience provides epistemic justification for belief. In this section, however, I'll argue that representationalism is more plausible than the qualia theory on broadly phenomenological grounds. This will allow me to clarify some background assumptions about the nature of phenomenal consciousness that I'll assume in my account of its epistemic role. It will also provide context for asking whether all mental representation is grounded in phenomenal consciousness.

In my view, the best argument for representationalism is abductive: it best explains a complex set of phenomenological and epistemological data. Since abductive arguments are holistic by nature, I can only sketch a small part of the abductive case for representationalism here. My strategy will be to motivate and defend the following phenomenological claims:

---

[3] See Byrne (2009), Pautz (2010), Siegel (2010), and Schellenberg (2011) for arguments in defense of the claim that perception has content, and see Travis (2004) and Brewer (2006) for arguments against this claim.

(1) All phenomenal states are representational states.
(2) All phenomenal duplicates share representational properties.
(3) All phenomenal differences are representational differences.

I'll argue that representationalism provides the best explanation of why these phenomenological claims are true. First, all phenomenal states are representational states because having a phenomenal property just is having a representational property. Second, all phenomenal duplicates share representational properties because sharing phenomenal properties just is sharing representational properties. And third, all phenomenal differences are representational differences because a difference in phenomenal properties just is a difference in representational properties.

In contrast, the qualia theory cannot explain these claims. Given Hume's dictum that there are no necessary connections between distinct existences, the qualia theory implies that there is only a contingent connection between phenomenal properties and representational properties. As a result, it cannot rule out the following possibilities:

(1) Some phenomenal states have no representational properties.
(2) Some phenomenal duplicates share no representational properties.
(3) Some phenomenal states share all the same representational properties, but differ in their phenomenal properties.

Plausibly, however, these scenarios are impossible. Much of the motivation for representationalism derives from its ability to explain why they are impossible.

I'll set aside a view that we might call *quasi-representationalism*, which says that phenomenal properties are distinct from representational properties and yet necessarily connected with them.[4] This view combines the letter of qualia theory with the spirit of representationalism. Representationalism is superior for at least two reasons. First, it explains the modal connections between phenomenal properties and representational properties. Modal connections of supervenience are not brute necessities: they need to be explained in more fundamental terms, and identity provides an explanatory stopping point. Second, representationalism is more faithful to the intimate connection between phenomenal and representational properties. If phenomenal properties are distinct from representational properties, then in principle their nature can be characterized in nonrepresentational terms. Intuitively, however, there is simply no way to characterize the phenomenal character of experience

---

[4] See Farkas (2013) for an explicit defense of this view.

except in terms of the way in which it represents the world. The identity thesis explains why this is true.

2.1.1. All Phenomenal States Are Representational States

The first argument is that representationalism best explains the datum that all phenomenal states are representational states. Qualia theorists sometimes accept this claim, but they cannot explain why it is true. Since phenomenal properties are distinct from representational properties, there is no necessary connection between them. If phenomenal states have representational properties at all, then this is a contingent matter that depends, for example, on their causal relations to the external world. On this view, phenomenal states can have qualia without having any representational properties at all. In contrast, representationalism explains why all phenomenal states are representational states. This is because all phenomenal properties are identical with representational properties.

Is it really a datum that all phenomenal states are representational states? I don't want to suggest that this should be immediately obvious or that it is immune to reasonable objections. Nevertheless, I think the claim can be made plausible by reflection on experience and can be defended against purported counterexamples. That's what I'll try to make plausible by summarizing some key points from the large literature on this issue.

Let's start with visual experience. When you look at this book, your experience represents that the book has a certain shape and color. Your experience is accurate only if the book has that shape and color; otherwise, it is inaccurate. As Charles Siewert (1998) puts the point, your experience has "accuracy conditions" that must be satisfied if the experience is to be an accurate representation of the world. Moreover, as Siewert notes, your experience has accuracy conditions just in virtue of its phenomenal properties, since the phenomenal character of your experience guarantees that it is accurate only if there is a book in front of you with a certain shape and color. But the properties of your experience in virtue of which it can be assessed for accuracy are representational properties. Therefore, it follows that the phenomenal properties of your experience are representational properties.[5]

---

[5] This argument from accuracy conditions is developed in different ways by Siewert (1998: ch. 7), Horgan and Tienson (2002), Chalmers (2004), and Siegel (2010: ch. 2).

The same argument extends to all visual experience. Some philosophers claim that visual experiences of phosphenes and afterimages have no representational content.[6] But these visual experiences also have accuracy conditions in virtue of their phenomenal character: they represent that there are colors and shapes at various locations around you. If there are no colors or shapes at those locations, then your visual experience is inaccurate. Indeed, the same argument extends to experiences in other sensory modalities besides vision. Auditory and olfactory experiences don't represent colors or shapes, of course, but they do represent other properties—including sounds and smells—at various locations in the external world around the perceiver.

Again, some philosophers claim bodily sensations, like pain and orgasm, have no representational content. And yet bodily sensations have a felt location: they represent parts of the body as being a certain way. For example, when I feel a pain in my foot, my experience represents that my foot hurts, and when I feel an itch in my foot, my experience represents that it itches. These experiences have different contents. Moreover, these experiences are accurate only if my foot really is the way it feels. If my foot has been amputated, and I am experiencing phantom limb pain, then my experience misrepresents that my foot hurts, when in fact the pain is all in my mind.

Some bodily sensations also have an affective or emotional component: for instance, bodily pain feels bad, whereas bodily pleasure feels good. Indeed, one and the same bodily condition can feel good for a while, but then start to feel bad, such as a massage that goes on for too long. Some versions of representationalism explain this as a difference in the representational content of experience, while others explain it as a difference in representational force. On the content view, there is a difference in evaluative content—that is, whether the bodily condition is represented as being good or bad. On the attitude view, in contrast, there is a difference in evaluative force—that is, whether the bodily condition is represented in a positive or negative way, which need not affect which contents are represented.[7]

Emotional experiences always have some representational content, which may concern aspects of the body, or aspects of the external world, or both at the same time. John Searle claims that there are objectless emotions and moods that have no representational content at all, such as "undirected anxiety, depression, and elation" (1983: 1). But these emotional states are best construed as having very general representational contents: for instance, a general feeling

---

[6] See Boghossian and Velleman (1989: 93–94) and Block (1996: 31–35) for this objection.
[7] See Smithies and Weiss (2019) for the distinction between the content view and the attitude view as it applies to affective experience.

of depression tends to make everything seem much worse than usual. These emotional states are about nothing in particular, but it doesn't follow that they are about nothing at all. They are positive or negative feelings, or dispositions to have such feelings, that are directed toward everything, rather than anything in particular.[8]

All phenomenal experience falls within the scope of representationalism. Some proponents of representationalism claim that all phenomenal experience is reducible to sensory perception, broadly construed to include perceptual imagery and inner speech. Others claim that there is nonsensory experience in cognition, attention, or emotion. If there is any nonsensory experience, then it falls within the scope of representationalism too. I'll revisit this point in connection with the cognitive experience of judgment in section 4.5.

2.1.2. All Phenomenal Duplicates Share Representational Properties

The second argument is that representationalism explains the datum that all phenomenal duplicates share representational properties. The qualia theory leaves open the possibility that a pair of phenomenal duplicates can have all the same qualia without having any of the same representational properties. However, this seems impossible: all phenomenal duplicates must share at least some of their representational properties. Moreover, representationalism explains why. All phenomenal duplicates share representational properties because sharing phenomenal properties *just is* sharing representational properties.

Terry Horgan and John Tienson (2002) argue that all of your phenomenal duplicates share representational properties in virtue of their shared phenomenal character. Recall Siewert's claim that your experience determines accuracy conditions in virtue of its phenomenal character alone. All of your phenomenal duplicates have experiences with the same phenomenal character, so their experiences thereby share accuracy conditions. Therefore, all of your phenomenal duplicates share representational properties. Horgan and Tienson illustrate this point with an example:

Suppose that you have the experience of seeing a picture hanging crooked. Each of your phenomenal duplicates has a phenomenally identical

---

[8] See Tye (1995: ch. 4) and Crane (2003) for more detailed discussion of the intentionality of bodily sensations, emotions, and moods.

experience. Some of these experiences will be accurate and some will be inaccurate. Whether or not a given duplicate's picture-hanging-crooked experience is accurate—that is, whether or not things are as the experience presents things as being—will depend upon the duplicate's actual environment. Thus, the sensory-phenomenal experience, by itself, determines conditions of accuracy: i.e. a class of ways the environment must be in order for the experience to be accurate. (2002: 524)

This example makes it plausible that all of your phenomenal duplicates can be assessed for accuracy in the same general way: their visual experience is accurate only if there is a picture hanging crooked in front of them. Their visual experiences share accuracy conditions precisely because they have the same phenomenal character.

Horgan and Tienson acknowledge that phenomenal duplicates can share some of their representational properties without sharing all of them. If you and your phenomenal duplicate are looking at different pictures, then your experiences have different accuracy conditions in virtue of your different relations to the environment. Your experience is accurate only if the picture you see is crooked, whereas the experience of your phenomenal duplicate is accurate only if the picture they see is crooked. Even so, the point remains that your experiences share accuracy conditions because of their shared phenomenal character: each experience is accurate only if there is a picture hanging crooked in front of the perceiver. Your experience has two kinds of representational content: (i) *phenomenal content*, which depends solely on its phenomenal character, and (ii) *externalist content*, which depends in part on its relations to the external world.[9]

Representationalism implies that perceptual experience has phenomenal content, since it says that the phenomenal character of perceptual experience is identical with a way of representing contents about the external world. And yet it doesn't imply that the representational content of perceptual experience is exhausted by its phenomenal content. Representationalism is compatible with the plausible thesis that perceptual experience also has externalist content, which depends on extrinsic relations to the external world that fail to supervene on its intrinsic phenomenal character. I'll revisit this point in section 3.5.

---

[9] Chalmers (2002, 2004) uses the framework of two-dimensional semantics to model these two dimensions of content: phenomenal content is a "primary intension," i.e. a function from centered epistemically possibilities to extensions, while externalist content is a "secondary intension," i.e. a function from metaphysical possibilities to extensions.

2.1.3. All Phenomenal Differences Are
Representational Differences

The third argument is that representationalism explains the datum that all phenomenal differences are representational differences. The qualia theory leaves open the possibility that experiences with exactly the same representational properties can nevertheless differ in qualia. If so, then we can radically change the phenomenal properties of your experience without thereby changing any of its representational properties. Plausibly, however, this is impossible. We cannot change the phenomenal character of your experience without thereby changing either what is represented by your experience or how it is represented. Moreover, representationalism explains this. All phenomenal differences are representational differences because a difference in phenomenal properties *just is* a difference in representational properties.

In evaluating this argument, it is important to contrast *pure* and *impure* versions of representationalism. All versions of representationalism agree that every phenomenal property is identical with some representational property. The difference is that the pure version identifies every phenomenal property with the pure representational property of representing some content, whereas the impure version identifies every phenomenal property with the impure representational property of representing some content with a certain kind of force. In my view, impure representationalism is much more plausible than pure representationalism because it allows that differences in representational force, as well as differences in representational content, can make a phenomenal difference.

Some philosophers argue for pure representationalism by appealing to the so-called "transparency" of experience.[10] As Jeff Speaks puts the point, experience is transparent in the sense that "nothing is available to introspection other than the objects represented as in one's environment, and the properties they are represented as having" (2009: 542). Speaks appeals to the transparency thesis in constructing the following argument for pure representationalism:

(1) If two experiences differ in phenomenal character, there is an introspectible difference between them.

(2) If there is an introspectible difference between two experiences, then there is a difference in the objects and properties those two experiences represent as in one's environment (the transparency/difference principle).

---

[10] The argument from transparency is developed in different ways by Gilbert Harman (1990), Michael Tye (1995), Alex Byrne (2001), and Jeff Speaks (2009).

(3) If there is a difference in the objects and properties two experiences represent as in one's environment, there is a difference in the content of the two experiences.

(4) Therefore, if two experiences differ in phenomenal character, they differ in content. (2009: 543)

On a pure version of representationalism, there can be no phenomenal difference between experiences without some difference in representational content. Moreover, the best explanation of this supervenience thesis is that the phenomenal character of experience is identical with its representational content.

Arguably, however, pure representationalism is false: two experiences can have the very same representational content while nevertheless differing in their overall phenomenal character. Indeed, a conscious experience can have the same content as an unconscious mental representation that has no phenomenal character at all. We can divide potential counterexamples to pure representationalism into several categories:

(1) *Conscious versus unconscious mental states*: The contents of visual experience can be represented unconsciously in blindsight or stored unconsciously in the belief system.

(2) *Perceptual versus nonperceptual experiences*: The contents of visual experience can be represented in conscious thought, emotion, or imagination.

(3) *Perceptual experiences in different modalities*: The contents of visual experience can be represented in tactile experience (e.g. there's a cubical object in my hand) or in auditory experience (e.g. there's something moving to my left).

(4) *Perceptual experiences in the same modality*: The contents of visual experiences can remain the same while differing in blurriness or in the focus of visual attention.

Together, these examples make a compelling case that differences in representational force—that is, differences in the way that content is represented—can make a phenomenal difference. If so, then pure representationalism is false, but an impure version is true: namely, there can be no difference in the phenomenal character of experience without some difference in its representational content or representational force. This is because every phenomenal property is identical with some impure representational property of representing some content with a certain kind of force.[11]

---

[11] Lycan (1996), Crane (2003), Chalmers (2004), and Speaks (2010) argue for impure versions of representationalism based on the kinds of examples listed here.

Where does the argument from transparency go wrong? Arguably, the thesis that experience is transparent captures the phenomenal contribution of representational content, while ignoring representational force. For example, the second premise in Speaks's argument is the transparency/difference principle, which says that any introspectible difference in the phenomenal character of experience is a difference in its representational content. The examples just mentioned make it plausible that some introspectible differences in the phenomenal character of experience are differences in representational force, rather than representational content. We can know by introspection not only which contents are represented in our experience, but also the way in which those contents are represented.[12]

Impure representationalism might be regarded with suspicion on the grounds that representational force is nothing more than qualia under a different name. On this view, representing that p with a certain phenomenal force is nothing more than representing that p in a way that is associated with certain qualia. This objection is, however, misconceived. Qualia are nonrepresentational properties: they are distinct from representational properties and merely contingently related with them. In contrast, representational force is essentially a way of representing content. Therefore, experience cannot have a certain phenomenal force without thereby representing some content or other. Mental representation is essentially a matter of representing some content with a certain kind of representational force.

2.2. Unconscious Mental Representation

Representationalism implies that all consciousness is mental representation, but it doesn't imply that all mental representation is conscious. If representationalism is true, then there is a kind of mental representation that zombies cannot have—namely, the conscious kind—but it doesn't follow that they cannot have any kind of mental representation at all. If there can be unconscious mental representation, then our question about the significance of consciousness remains. What is the significance of the distinction between conscious and unconscious mental representation?

One answer is that consciousness is the source of all mental representation. On this view, consciousness is the original source of mental representation,

---

[12] It's no accident that proponents of the transparency of experience have a hard time explaining how we can know by introspection what attitudinal relations we stand in toward the contents of our experience. Indeed, Dretske (2003) uses this point as the basis of an argument for introspective skepticism.

and all unconscious mental representation derives ultimately from consciousness. Given the further thesis that mental representation is the source of all nonmental representation, including linguistic and pictorial forms of conventional representation, it follows that all representation has its source in consciousness. This thesis is the cornerstone of what Uriah Kriegel calls *the phenomenal intentionality research program*. As he puts the point, "intentionality is injected into the world with the appearance of . . . phenomenal character" (2013: 3).

On this view, consciousness is a kind of mental representation, and all unconscious mental representation is grounded in consciousness, so all mental representation is either conscious or grounded in consciousness. Here is a more precise statement of the view:

> *The Representational Grounding Thesis*: Necessarily, every representational property is either identical with or grounded in some phenomenal property.[13]

If all unconscious mental representation is grounded in conscious states of the same creature, then it follows that only conscious creatures can have representational states. Therefore, zombies cannot represent the world at all.

I'll argue against the representational grounding thesis on broadly empirical grounds. We should believe in unconscious mental representation insofar as it plays an indispensable role in psychological explanation. Not all unconscious mental representations that play an indispensable explanatory role are grounded in consciousness. Therefore, the representational grounding thesis is false. How might proponents of the representational grounding thesis account for the existence of unconscious mental representation? In this section, I'll consider four different options: eliminativism, dispositionalism, functional holism, and interpretivism. I'll argue that all four options are inadequate.

2.2.1. Eliminativism

The first option is *eliminativism*: the thesis that there is no unconscious mental representation at all. On this view, all mental representation is conscious.

---

[13] McGinn calls this the "converse Brentano thesis" (1997: 300), but he doesn't go as far as to endorse it. Proponents include Searle (1990), Strawson (2008), Kriegel (2011), Horgan and Graham (2012), and Mendelovici (2018).

According to Galen Strawson, for example, "all true or real intentionality essentially involves consciousness" (2008: 281).

Why suppose there is any unconscious mental representation at all? The best argument is an *indispensability argument*. We should believe there is unconscious mental representation because it plays an indispensable role in psychological explanation both in common sense and in cognitive science. This follows from the more general methodological principle that we should believe in the entities posited by a theory when they play an indispensable role in theoretical explanation. The indispensability argument can be summarized as follows:

(1) Unconscious mental representation plays an indispensable explanatory role in common-sense psychology and scientific psychology.
(2) We should believe in the existence of the entities posited by a theory when they play an indispensable role in theoretical explanation.
(3) Therefore, we should believe in the existence of unconscious mental representations.

How might proponents of eliminativism resist this argument for the existence of unconscious mental representation?

One strategy is to reject premise (1) on the grounds that psychological theories that appeal to unconscious mental representation are explanatorily redundant. So, for example, Paul Churchland (1981) and Stephen Stich (1983) argue that our common-sense belief-desire psychology is false and can be replaced without loss of explanatory power by neurophysiological or syntactic theories of the mind. In response, however, Jerry Fodor (1987: ch. 1) makes a persuasive case in defense of the predictive success, theoretical depth, and explanatory indispensability of common-sense psychology. Similarly, Tyler Burge (1986), Christopher Peacocke (1994), and Michael Rescorla (2017) have argued that content-involving computational explanations in cognitive science cannot be replaced without loss of explanatory power by neurophysiological or syntactic explanations. Since these issues have been extensively discussed elsewhere, I'll simply assume that premise (1) is true. There is, at the very least, a substantial burden on proponents of eliminativism to show that premise (1) is false. As far as I can see, they are swimming against the tide.[14]

Another strategy is to reject premise (2) in favor of *instrumentalism* about unconscious mental representation. On this view, there are no unconscious mental representations, although it is sometimes useful to talk *as if* there were.

---

[14] See Egan (1995) and Orlandi (2014) for skepticism about the explanatory power of unconscious mental representation in cognitive science, but see Peacocke (1999) and Rescorla (2015) for critical discussion.

So, for example, Daniel Dennett's intentional stance theory "does not say that Intentional systems *really* have beliefs and desires, but that one can explain and predict their behavior by *ascribing* beliefs and desires to them" (1971: 91). The problem with instrumentalism is that the predictive and explanatory value of supposing that there is unconscious mental representation is a good reason to think it's true. As Jerry Fodor remarks, "there is surely a presumptive inference from the predictive successes of a theory to its truth" (1985: 79). Proponents of instrumentalism therefore need to make the case that unconscious mental representation is not explanatorily indispensable after all. As a result, the second strategy collapses into the first.

If sound, the indispensability argument establishes *realism* about unconscious mental representation: the thesis that some unconscious mental states have representational properties that play an indispensable role in causal explanation. Moreover, it establishes realism about the kinds of unconscious mental representations that figure in common-sense psychology and scientific psychology alike. So, we are committed not only to the beliefs and desires that figure in common-sense explanations of behavior, but also to the "subdoxastic" mental representations that figure in psychological explanations in cognitive science. We should endorse realism about doxastic and subdoxastic states alike.[15]

2.2.2. Dispositionalism

John Searle (1990) argues that all unconscious mental representation must be in principle accessible to consciousness. According to his Connection Principle:

> The ascription of an unconscious intentional phenomenon to a system implies that the phenomenon is in principle accessible to consciousness. (1990: 586)

But what exactly does it mean to say that an unconscious mental state is accessible to consciousness? Searle seems to move between two different interpretations of the Connection Principle, which I'll call *potentialism* and *dispositionalism*.

---

[15] Compare Fodor's (1987: 10) realism about the propositional attitudes. Realism does not entail the representational theory of mind, according to which believing that *p* is standing in the belief relation to a mental representation that means that *p*. On this view, mental representations are internal symbols, such as sentences in the language of thought. This is a much more loaded use of the term 'mental representation' than mine.

Potentialism is the thesis that every unconscious mental representation is accessible to consciousness in the sense that it has the potential to be conscious; in other words, it is possible for that very mental state to be conscious. Thus, Searle writes, "The notion of an unconscious intentional state is the notion of a state that is a possible conscious thought or experience" (1990: 588).

The main problem with potentialism is that it cannot account for beliefs and desires. While the contents of beliefs and desires are potentially conscious, the states themselves are not. We do sometimes draw a distinction between conscious and unconscious beliefs, but this is best understood as a distinction between beliefs whose contents are easily accessible to consciousness and beliefs whose contents are not so easily accessible, perhaps owing to repression or some other blocking mechanism. Beliefs and desires are standing states that can persist through changes in the stream of consciousness, and periods of total absence of consciousness, including dreamless sleep. Although they are disposed to cause thoughts, judgments, and other episodes in the stream of consciousness, they cannot be identified with the conscious episodes they are disposed to cause. That would be to confuse a disposition with its occurrent manifestations. Beliefs and desires have the potential to cause conscious episodes, but they don't have the potential to become conscious themselves. Therefore, potentialism collapses into eliminativism about beliefs and desires.[16]

Some philosophers distinguish between dispositional and occurrent senses of belief, but this terminology is misleading. It makes no more sense to describe the manifestation of a dispositional belief as an occurrence of belief than to describe the manifestation of fragility as an occurrence of fragility. Just as the fragility of a glass causes it to break when dropped, so my beliefs cause me to make judgments when I consider whether their contents are true. The fragility of the glass cannot be identified with its breaking, since it causes the breaking to occur. Similarly, my belief cannot be identified with its occurrent manifestation in judgment, since it causes the judgment to occur. A judgment is an occurrent event in the stream of consciousness, whereas a belief is a standing state that persists through changes in the stream of consciousness. Beliefs are disposed to cause episodes of conscious judgment, but they are distinct from the conscious judgments they are disposed to cause.

Dispositionalism, in contrast with potentialism, can be initially defined as the thesis that every unconscious mental representation is accessible to consciousness in the sense that it is disposed to cause some conscious experience. Thus, Searle writes, "Unconscious beliefs are indeed dispositional states of the brain, but they are dispositions to produce conscious thoughts" (1990: 588).

---

[16] See Crane (2013) for a congenial discussion of much the same point.

The main problem with dispositionalism, as defined here, is that it's too weak to capture any significant constraint on unconscious mental representation. Unconscious states don't need representational content in order to cause conscious experiences. Just consider the neurological states that are disposed to cause headaches: they are disposed to cause conscious mental representations, but they are not mental representations themselves. What makes beliefs and desires any different? Without a satisfying answer to this question, dispositionalism collapses into eliminativism. According to Galen Strawson, for example, "no dispositional states can be intentional" (2008: 282).

On Strawson's view, beliefs and desires are disposed to cause experiences that have representational content, but beliefs and desires have no representational content themselves. The problem with this view is that it cannot account for the fact that beliefs and desires can play a role in the causal and rational explanation of action without manifesting the disposition to cause conscious experience. When I open the fridge to make my morning coffee, I'm so preoccupied with my plans for the day that I don't consciously think about what I'm doing. Even so, my action is explained by the fact that I want milk in my coffee and I believe that there is milk in the fridge. We cannot explain why I'm acting this way, and why my action is rational, except by appealing to the contents of beliefs and desires that currently make no impact on my stream of consciousness.

In chapter 4, I'll propose a new and improved version of dispositionalism, which says that beliefs are individuated wholly by their dispositions to cause conscious judgments. On this view, the representational content of belief is grounded in the representational content of the judgments it is disposed to cause. In other words, beliefs have their contents in virtue of their dispositions to cause judgments with those very same contents. Therefore, the contents of beliefs are accessible to consciousness as the contents of judgments.

This dispositional theory of unconscious mental representation cannot be extended from beliefs to subdoxastic states. This is because the representational properties of subdoxastic states are not grounded just in their dispositions to cause conscious experience. On the contrary, they have their representational properties in virtue of their dispositions to figure in computational processes that occur below the level of consciousness. Martin Davies describes a hypothetical scenario in which "low-level representational states—*prima facie* examples of subdoxastic states—surfaced in conscious awareness, as distinctive itches or tickles" (1989: 138). As Davies notes, we wouldn't classify these states as beliefs, despite their disposition to cause conscious experiences. After all, they have their representational properties not in virtue of their disposition to cause itches and tickles, but in virtue of their role in unconscious computational processes.

Consider Quine's (1970) challenge to Chomsky's (1965) claim that we implicitly know the syntactic rules of our language. Quine's challenge is to explain what constitutes implicit or tacit knowledge of a syntactic rule: it should be less demanding than explicit knowledge of the rule, but also more demanding than merely exhibiting linguistic behavior that conforms to the rule. The standard response is that implicit knowledge of a rule is constituted by causal structure of the right kind in the psychological processes that underpin one's linguistic behavior. According to Davies (1987), for instance, one has implicit knowledge of a rule just in case the causal structure of one's psychological processes mirrors the logical structure of a syntactic theory that includes the rule in question. In principle, two subjects could be disposed to exhibit the very same linguistic behavior, although this results from distinct psychological processes that embody implicit knowledge of different syntactic theories. Therefore, implicit knowledge of syntax is constituted not by dispositions to exhibit linguistic behavior, but rather by dispositions to figure in unconscious psychological processes that causally explain linguistic behavior.

We can make exactly the same point in the case of the theory of vision. According to David Marr (1982), the aim of the theory of vision is to explain how our visual system solves the "inverse problem" of computing the function from a pair of two-dimensional retinal images to a three-dimensional representation of the external world. A theory of vision specifies which rules and representations are used by the visual system in computing this function and explains how these computations are implemented in the brain. But if the same function can be computed in different ways, then what makes it the case that we are computing it one way rather than another? Once again, this depends on the causal structure of the unconscious psychological processes that underpin conscious visual experience. In principle, two subjects could have exactly the same visual experiences in actual and counterfactual circumstances, although their visual systems use very different rules and representations. Therefore, the representational properties of these unconscious visual states are not grounded solely in their disposition to cause conscious visual experiences, but also in their disposition to figure in unconscious psychological processes.

Searle's dispositionalism is therefore committed to a restricted form of eliminativism about unconscious mental representation: he can account for beliefs and desires, but not for the subdoxastic mental representations that figure in computational explanations in cognitive science. Searle recognizes this commitment, but his response is to bite the bullet:

> If we are looking for phenomena which are intrinsically intentional but inaccessible in principle to consciousness there is nothing there: no rule following, no mental information processing, no unconscious

inferences, no mental models, no primal sketches, no 2½D images, no three-dimensional descriptions, no language of thought and no universal grammar. (1990: 589)

Searle's proposal is therefore extremely revisionary about psychological explanation in cognitive science. This is also the main reason to reject his proposal: it cannot do justice to the explanatory power of our best psychological theories in cognitive science, which make indispensable reference to mental representations.

To illustrate the point, consider Marr's (1982) proposal that the visual system solves the inverse problem by performing computational processes defined over a series of unconscious mental representations that are physically realized in the brain. According to Searle, this can be nothing more than a metaphorical description of neurophysiological processes in the brain. The problem is that removing the language of representation deprives the theory of much of its explanatory power. Even if we knew exactly which parts of the brain were involved in solving the inverse problem, we wouldn't thereby know how they were solving it. As Marr says, "Trying to understand perception by studying only neurons is like trying to understand bird flight by studying only feathers. It just cannot be done" (1982: 27).

Does Searle's dispositionalism improve on Strawson's eliminativism? Yes, insofar as it accounts for beliefs and desires; but no, insofar as it fails to account for subdoxastic mental representations. Since the indispensability argument supports realism about beliefs and subdoxastic states alike, Searle's proposal is an unstable compromise.

2.2.3. Functional Holism

Terry Horgan and George Graham (2012) propose that consciousness is an "anchor point" for mental representation. On this view, all unconscious mental representation must be functionally integrated within a holistic network that also includes conscious mental representation. Unlike Searle, they do not claim that all unconscious mental representation is accessible to consciousness. Instead, they claim that all unconscious mental representation is functionally integrated with consciousness.

This proposal is hard to motivate. Horgan and Graham cannot claim that unconscious mental states have their representational properties solely in virtue of their functional connections with conscious experience. Otherwise, their proposal fares no better than Searle's. But if they concede that unconscious mental states can have representational properties in virtue of their functional connections with each other, then it's not clear why functional connections with conscious experience should also be needed.[17] In the next section, I'll argue that their stated motivation for this proposal is inadequate. Meanwhile, in this section, I'll argue that there are strong empirical grounds to reject the proposal that all unconscious mental representation is functionally connected with consciousness.

Consider the distinction between two visual systems advanced by David Milner and Melvyn Goodale (1995). They argue that the anatomical distinction between ventral and dorsal pathways in the primate brain corresponds to a functional distinction between "vision for perception" and "vision for action." In the ventral stream, visual information is processed for the purpose of identifying and recognizing objects, whereas the dorsal stream serves the purpose of guiding action. Moreover, visual information in the ventral stream is sometimes but not always conscious, whereas visual information in the dorsal stream is never conscious. According to Milner and Goodale, "Visual phenomenology . . . can arise only from processing in the ventral stream" (1995: 200).

Milner and Goodale present multiple sources of evidence for this proposal, but here are just two. First, patient studies reveal double dissociations between conscious vision and action. For instance, patients with visual form agnosia, resulting from damage in the ventral stream, can post a card in a slot without being able to report its orientation. In contrast, patients with optic ataxia, resulting from damage in the dorsal stream, can report the orientation of a slot without being able to orient their hand correctly when trying to post a card in the slot. Second, studies with normal subjects reveal discrepancies between conscious vision and action in cases of visual illusion. In the Ebbinghaus illusion, for example, subjects can accurately proportion their grip to the size of the disc when reaching to grasp it, although their visual experience misrepresents its size.

These studies demonstrate that the spatial parameters of visually guided action are sometimes explained by visual representations in the dorsal stream that are neither conscious nor accessible to consciousness. We cannot explain the accuracy of someone's grip size, for example, without appealing to unconscious visual representations in the dorsal stream that accurately represent the size of the object. According to Milner and Goodale, the dorsal stream processes information in a way that is relatively independent from the ventral stream. If so, then these unconscious visual representations in the dorsal stream are functionally isolated to a significant extent from conscious experience.

---

[17] Bourget (2010) argues that all unconscious mental representation is derived from holistic networks of relations with other conscious or unconscious mental representations. This view incurs no commitment to the representational grounding thesis.

Of course, there are both functional and anatomical connections between ventral and dorsal streams, although these are not yet well understood. Milner and Goodale (1995: 201–204) argue that visual experience can influence action in at least two ways: first, in selecting which objects to act upon; and second, in selecting which actions to perform based on identification of those objects. How you reach for and grasp an object is often guided by your visual recognition of what kind of object it is; for instance, you tend to pick up a knife by the handle and not the blade. Milner and Goodale (2006: 231–234) suggest that these functional interactions between the ventral and dorsal streams may be subserved by feedback and feedforward projections into the primary visual cortex.

Even in humans, however, the functional interactions between ventral and dorsal streams are highly circumscribed. In more primitive nonhuman animals, the connections between conscious vision and unconscious visual control of action are likely to be even more circumscribed or entirely absent. If vision originally evolved in response to motor demands, as Milner and Goodale claim, then we should expect to find unconscious visual control of action in more primitive creatures that have no conscious experience at all. Indeed, this is just what we find in the case of many arthropods, including bees and jumping spiders. As Tyler Burge reports:

> Bees and certain spiders visually perceive color, shape, motion, spatial location, and so on. They exhibit associated perceptual constancies. Whether bees and spiders are phenomenally conscious is unknown. These cases are not *known* to illustrate individual perception without consciousness. But the epistemic situation supports not taking consciousness to be constitutive of individual perception. (2010: 375)

Burge emphasizes that we can't be certain that bees and spiders are unconscious creatures, although it seems very likely that they are. And yet we can know they have mental representations, since this hypothesis is confirmed by our best scientific theories. But if we can know that some creatures have mental representations without knowing whether they're conscious, then it is at least conceivable that unconscious creatures can have mental representations.

Consider zombies: it is conceivable that there can be functional or physical duplicates of conscious creatures that lack consciousness entirely. We cannot explain the behavior of such creatures without attributing unconscious mental states that represent their environment and play some causal role in guiding their behavior. Therefore, it is at least conceivable that zombies can have mental representations. Moreover, it is not only conceivable, but also empirically well confirmed, that we have "zombie systems" (Crick and Koch 2001) in the dorsal stream that figure in the unconscious visuomotor control of action.

Does Horgan and Graham's functional holism fare any better than Searle's dispositionalism? Yes: insofar as it accounts for subdoxastic mental representations that are functionally connected with consciousness, such as the visual representations that figure in computational explanations of vision. But no: insofar as it fails to account for subdoxastic mental representations that are functionally isolated from consciousness, such as the visual representations that figure in the unconscious visual control of action. Since the indispensability argument supports realism about subdoxastic mental representations whether or not they are functionally integrated with consciousness, Horgan and Graham's proposal is an unstable compromise.

2.2.4. Interpretivism

Uriah Kriegel (2011) rejects all these proposals—eliminativism, dispositionalism, and functional holism—on the grounds that there are unconscious mental representations that are neither accessible to consciousness nor functionally integrated with consciousness. He even accepts that there could be a representational zombie. But he argues that this can be reconciled with the representational grounding thesis by opting for *interpretivism* about unconscious mental representation.

What makes it the case that an unconscious mental state has the representational properties it does? According to Kriegel's interpretivism, the answer is that "an ideal interpreter would, under ideal conditions, experientially interpret that item to have that content" (2011: 202). The representational states of an unconscious creature are grounded in conscious acts of interpretation performed by an ideal interpreter, who is fully rational and fully informed of all the nonrepresentational facts about the unconscious creature in question.

Kriegel contrasts his restricted form of interpretivism with the global form endorsed in Daniel Dennett's early work.[18] According to Dennett, an intentional system has intentional states in virtue of the fact that it can be interpreted from the *intentional stance*: in other words, its behavior can be usefully interpreted using intentional concepts. As Dennett writes, "A particular thing is an intentional system only in relation to the strategies of someone who is trying to explain and predict its behavior" (1971: 87).

---

[18] In his later work, Dennett (1991) proposes a version of the intentional stance that may be compatible with realism about intentionality.

One major problem with Dennett's theory is that it doesn't explain what makes an interpreter an intentional system. If an interpreter is an intentional system only in relation to the strategies of some other interpreter who is trying to explain and predict its behavior, then we face an infinite regress. The regress is vicious because it fails to explain the original source of intentionality. Kriegel's interpretivism blocks the regress because it applies only to unconscious mental representation. The regress comes to an end in acts of interpretation that have their representational content in virtue of their phenomenal character. Therefore, consciousness is the ultimate source of all mental representation.

I'll argue that Kriegel's interpretivism falls victim to the indispensability argument, since it is inconsistent with the kind of realism about unconscious mental representation that the argument supports. Kriegel claims that his view is realist in the minimal sense that there are unconscious mental states that have representational properties. At the same time, he acknowledges that it is antirealist in the more demanding sense that the representational properties of unconscious mental states are *response-dependent* properties. As he explains, "it is not so much because certain intentional facts hold that certain interpretations are justified, as that because those interpretations are justified that the intentional facts hold" (2011: 201).

Does Kriegel's antirealism imply that unconscious creatures cannot have mental representations in a world without consciousness? If so, then it is ruled out by the indispensability argument, since unconscious mental representation can play an indispensable explanatory role even if there are no conscious creatures around to recognize this fact. In fact, the problem is even worse, since Kriegel's theory of unconscious mental representation appeals to an *ideal interpreter* defined as a conscious creature who is fully rational and fully informed. Since there are no ideal interpreters, it seems to follow that there is no unconscious mental representation at all. Thus, Kriegel's interpretivism threatens to collapse into eliminativism.

In fact, Kriegel allows that unconscious creatures can have mental representations in a world without conscious creatures, so long as they have states that are *disposed* to cause the right kinds of responses in the right kinds of conscious creatures. The idea is that if there were ideal creatures with full rationality and full information about the nonrepresentational facts, they would consciously interpret unconscious creatures as having mental representations. The problem comes when we try to explain what makes this counterfactual true. The best explanation is that ideal creatures would interpret unconscious creatures as having mental representations because they succeed in tracking response-independent facts about the indispensable role of unconscious mental representation in causal explanation. But if that's right, then Kriegel's interpretivism is false. So Kriegel must deny that the counterfactual is grounded in response-independent facts about unconscious creatures. But then he cannot accommodate the realist claim that unconscious mental representation plays an indispensable role in causal explanation. Why think unconscious mental representation plays an indispensable role if there are no response-independent facts about unconscious creatures that require invoking it? And if it is not indispensable, why think ideal agents would interpret unconscious creatures as having it? The dilemma is to explain how interpretivism avoids the collapse into realism on the one hand or eliminativism on the other.

I don't see how this dilemma can be avoided, but even if it can, there is a further challenge that remains. The challenge is to motivate interpretivism about unconscious mental representation without capitulating to a more general form of antirealism in the philosophy of science. Presumably, ionic bonding, biological fitness, and neural activation are not response-dependent properties. Why suppose interpretivism is true of the properties that figure in explanations in psychology, but not neuroscience, biology, or chemistry?

Ultimately, Kriegel's interpretivism seems to be motivated primarily by its role in securing the representational grounding thesis. But why should we accept this thesis in the first place? In the next section, I'll examine an influential argument for the representational grounding thesis, which can be found in various different forms in the work of Searle (1990), Strawson (2008), and Horgan and Graham (2012).

2.3. Grounding Representation in Consciousness

Why would anyone accept the representational grounding thesis? It is often put forward as a diagnosis of the indeterminacy problems that arise for naturalistic theories of mental representation. On this view, only consciousness can ground mental representation in a way that avoids the problems of radical indeterminacy. Zombies cannot have mental representations because there is nothing besides consciousness that can give them determinate contents. As Searle writes, "For a zombie, unlike a conscious agent, there simply is no fact of the matter as to exactly which aspectual shapes its alleged intentional states have" (1990: 595).

The main aim of this section is to present and criticize this argument for the representational grounding thesis. The argument aims to show that if unconscious mental representation is not grounded in consciousness, then it cannot play an indispensable role in psychological explanation. Here is the argument in outline:

(1) All unconscious mental representation plays an indispensable role in psychological explanation.

(2) If unconscious mental representation is not grounded in consciousness, then it must be grounded in tracking relations.

(3) If unconscious mental representation is grounded in tracking relations, then it is representational only in a deflationary sense that plays no indispensable role in psychological explanation.

(4) Therefore, all unconscious mental representation is grounded in consciousness.

I'll begin by explaining the motivation for each of the premises and then I'll explain why the argument is unsound.

Premise (1) is a consequence of the indispensability argument. The argument for realism about unconscious mental representation is that it plays an indispensable role in psychological explanation. If unconscious mental representation is explanatorily superfluous, then we have no good reason to believe that it exists in the first place. In that case, there is no good objection to eliminativism about unconscious mental representation.

Premise (2) is motivated by the consideration that unconscious mental representation is not a fundamental aspect of reality and hence must be grounded in something more fundamental. As Jerry Fodor writes:

> It's hard to see . . . how one can be a Realist about intentionality without also being . . . a Reductionist. If the semantic and the intentional are real properties of things, it must be in virtue of . . . properties that are themselves *neither* intentional *nor* semantic. If aboutness is real, it must be really something else. (1987: 97)

According to dualism, consciousness is a fundamental aspect of reality. If dualism is combined with representationalism, then some mental representation is fundamental—namely, the kind that is identical with consciousness. But even dualists can allow that unconscious mental representation must be grounded in something more fundamental. If it is not grounded in consciousness, then what else could it be grounded in aside from the kinds of tracking relations that figure in reductive theories of mental representation?

Reductive theories of mental representation aim to identify some relation specified in nonrepresentational terms that obtains when and only when an internal state of the brain represents an external state of the world. In other words, the aim is to give a reductive definition or analysis of mental representation in nonrepresentational terms. Different reductive theories appeal to different sorts of relations between the mind and the external world, but we can use the phrase 'tracking relations' as an umbrella term for the causal, teleological, or functional relations that figure in such theories.[19]

Premise (3) is motivated by the apparent intractability of various problems that arise for reductive theories of mental representation. We can set aside problems that arise in the explanation of conscious mental representation, since we're concerned here only with unconscious mental representation. I'll mention two problems, which I'll call the *underdetermination problem* and the *overgeneration problem*.[20]

The underdetermination problem is the problem of explaining what makes it the case that a mental representation has the representational content that it does, rather than some deviant alternative. For example, Quine (1960: ch. 2) asks what makes it the case that your word 'rabbit' refers to rabbits, rather than undetached rabbit parts. Similarly, Kripke (1982) asks what makes it the case that your word 'plus' refers to the plus function, rather than the quus function. These problems were originally raised for theories of linguistic meaning, but similar problems arise for theories of mental representation. The problem is that tracking relations underdetermine whether I refer to rabbits or undetached rabbit parts, plus or quus, and so on. If mental representation is grounded in tracking relations, then it's radically indeterminate, and so explanatorily useless. In this way, the underdetermination problem threatens to undercut the explanatory power of mental representation.

One version of the underdetermination problem is the problem of *misrepresentation*.[21] The problem is to explain how we can draw a distinction between accurate representation and misrepresentation in purely causal terms. Consider Grice's (1957) natural signs, which represent whatever they are caused by or correlated with. So, for example, smoke represents fire, and tree rings represent the age of the tree. The basic problem is that mental representations can be caused by and correlated with things they misrepresent. For instance, my mental representation HORSE can be caused not only by horses, but also by cows on a dark night. But then what makes it the case that it represents the property of being a horse, rather than the disjunctive property of being either a horse or a cow on a dark night?

One answer is that mental states represent whatever they are caused by in *optimal conditions*. But what are optimal conditions? If they are simply defined as

---

[19] The major reductive theories are causal or informational theories (Dretske 1981, Stalnaker 1984, Fodor 1987), teleological theories (Millikan 1984), and long-arm functional role theories (Block 1986, Harman 1987).

[20] Searle (1990) and Horgan and Graham (2012) raise the underdetermination problem, while Strawson (2008) raises the overgeneration problem, which he calls "the stopping problem."

[21] This is an instance of Fodor's (1987: 102) disjunction problem.

conditions in which mental states represent accurately, then the theory is trivial and so cannot provide a reductive definition of mental representation. But if optimal conditions are defined reductively, say as conditions in which representational systems fulfill their biological functions, then the theory is vulnerable to counterexamples. After all, there's no guarantee that mental representations are veridical when they are fulfilling their biological function. So it's not clear that optimal conditions can be defined in a way that avoids counterexamples without triviality.[22]

The overgeneration problem is the problem of explaining how there can be principled grounds for attributing representational properties to unconscious mental states without thereby attributing them to everything, including paramecia, plants, and thermostats. The problem is that if representation is ubiquitous, then it is explanatorily useless. After all, mental representation plays no indispensable role in explaining the behavior of paramecia, plants, and thermostats. Again, the problem arises most clearly for Grice's natural signs, which carry information about whatever they are caused by or correlated with. As Strawson says, "Every effect can be said to carry information about its cause, and in that sense to be about its cause, and in that sense to represent its cause" (2008: 286).

Once again, we might try to solve the problem by saying that mental states represent whatever they are caused by when they are in optimal conditions in which they fulfill their function. However, this is not enough to avoid the overgeneration problem. Even plants, paramecia, and perhaps even thermostats have the function of carrying information about their causes. Nevertheless, there is no explanatory purpose served by ascribing representational properties to them, since the behavior of these organisms and mechanisms can be adequately explained in terms of simple associations between stimulus and response. Mental representation should be distinguished from merely having the function of carrying information insofar as it plays an indispensable role in psychological explanation.[23]

Following Tyler Burge (2010: 292–308), I am skeptical that the concept of mental representation can be reductively defined in nonrepresentational terms using statistical, causal, or biological concepts. While the prospects for reduction cannot be ruled out definitively, the failures of existing proposals provide strong inductive grounds for pessimism. In any case, for current dialectical

---

[22] See Fodor (1987: 104–106), Boghossian (1989b: 537–540), and Loewer (1997: 115–117) for versions of this objection.
[23] See Burge (2010: chs. 8 and 9) for the distinction between representation and mere sensory registration of information: he argues that the most primitive form of genuine representation is perception, which is distinguished from mere sensation by perceptual objectification.

purposes, we can assume for the sake of argument that no such reductive definition can be given. If so, then what conclusions are we entitled to draw?

One diagnosis is that reductive theories of mental representation fail because that they ignore the role of consciousness in grounding mental representation. If all mental representation is grounded in consciousness, then the overgeneration problem can be solved quite easily. Paramecia, plants, and thermostats don't have mental representations because they are not conscious creatures. The underdetermination problem can also be solved because it is introspectively manifest that conscious experience has determinate representational content; for instance, I can know by introspection whether I'm thinking about rabbits or undetached rabbit parts, plus or quus, and so on. Therefore, unconscious mental representation can inherit determinate representational content from its connections with conscious experience. If unconscious mental representation is not anchored in consciousness, however, then it must be radically indeterminate. As Searle writes, "For a zombie, unlike a conscious agent, there is simply no fact of the matter as to exactly which aspectual shapes its alleged intentional states have" (1990: 595).

In fact, however, we already have good reasons to reject this diagnosis. As we've seen in section 2.2, the representational grounding thesis raises its own undergeneration problem: it cannot account for all unconscious mental representation that plays an indispensable role in psychological explanation. And yet unconscious mental representation cannot play an indispensable explanatory role if it is utterly ubiquitous, or radically indeterminate in content. So we have good reasons to think that there must be some other way in which unconscious mental representation is grounded in fundamental reality that does not involve consciousness. At the same time, we're assuming that unconscious mental representation can't be reductively defined in nonrepresentational terms. We should therefore regard unconscious mental representation as an autonomous or irreducible scientific kind. As Tyler Burge writes, "Perception and representation . . . do not need reduction to be scientifically acceptable. For all that is now known, they are *irreducible explanatory* notions" (2010: 308).

This is a familiar predicament in science. Sometimes we can reduce higher-level scientific kinds to lower-level scientific kinds without loss of explanatory power, such as the reduction of heat to molecular motion. More often, however, there are scientific kinds that play an indispensable explanatory role in some higher-level science, although we cannot reduce them to the kinds that figure in lower-level sciences. As Stephen Stich writes:

> There is no naturalistic account of *grooming behavior* in primate ethology. Nor is there a naturalistic account of *attack behavior* in stickleback ethology. But surely it would be simply perverse to deny the existence of

grooming behavior, simply because we can't define it in the language of physics and biology . . . The situation for *mental representation* looks entirely parallel. (1992: 258)

The general conclusion to draw is that higher-level kinds don't need to be reductively defined in order to be scientifically respectable. The mark of a scientific kind is that it plays an indispensable role in scientific explanation.

This does not mean that we should regard unconscious mental representation as a fundamental aspect of reality on par with the properties that figure in fundamental physics, such as mass, spin, and charge. Compare Timothy Williamson's (2000) view that knowledge is a mental state that cannot be reductively defined in more basic terms—say, as a justified true belief that meets further conditions designed to rule out Gettier cases. There is no commitment here to the view that knowledge is metaphysically fundamental. Presumably, knowledge is grounded in more fundamental features of reality, but in a way that eludes reductive definition.

Similarly, unconscious mental representation is grounded in more fundamental aspects of reality, but it doesn't follow that it can be reductively defined in terms of necessary and sufficient conditions stated in fundamental terms. It may be instead that there is an infinite set of sufficient conditions that has no systematic unity at the level of fundamental reality. As Barry Loewer writes in the conclusion of his survey of reductive theories of mental representation, "It may be that the naturalistic conditions that are sufficient for semantic properties are too complicated or too unsystematic" (1997: 122). In principle, a Laplacian demon could list an infinite set of physical conditions that are sufficient for mental representation, but there is no guarantee that these conditions have anything much in common aside from the fact that they are sufficient conditions for mental representation. They may have no unity at the level of fundamental reality.

All this suggests an alternative diagnosis of the failure of reductive theories of mental representation. These theories fail not because they neglect consciousness, but because reductive definition is not required for grounding. The failure to produce a reductive definition of unconscious mental representation is no good reason to deny the possibility of unconscious mental representation that is not grounded in consciousness.

2.4. Grounding Thought in Consciousness

Here's what I've argued in this chapter so far. All consciousness is mental representation, but not all mental representation has its source in consciousness.

Hence, there are at least two different kinds of mental representation: one that has its source in consciousness and another that has its source elsewhere. Our question about the significance of consciousness therefore remains wide open. What is the significance of the distinction between these two kinds of mental representation?

The answer I want to consider in this section is that consciousness is the ultimate source of all conceptual thought. On this view, all conceptual representation is either conscious or grounded in consciousness. Here is a more precise statement of the thesis:

> *The Conceptual Grounding Thesis*: Necessarily, every conceptual representational property is either identical with or grounded in some phenomenal property.

This view draws a distinction between conceptual and nonconceptual representation. The crux of the distinction is that conceptual representation requires some capacity for thought, whereas nonconceptual representation requires no such capacity for thought. For example, the computational modules involved in early visual processing can represent the world, but they have no conceptual capacity to think about the world. If the conceptual grounding thesis is true, then the same is true of zombies: they are capable of mental representation, but not conceptual thought.

Martin Davies (1995) rejects the representational grounding thesis, but he accepts the conceptual grounding thesis. He criticizes Searle's Connection Principle because it implies that subdoxastic states have no representational properties. At the same time, he concedes that the representational properties of our subdoxastic states are importantly different from those of our beliefs, desires, and other propositional attitudes. On this view, there are at least two different kinds of mental representation, which he calls "attitude aboutness" and "subdoxastic aboutness." Attitude aboutness is conceptual in the sense that it requires having a capacity to think about things. For example, you can't believe that dogs bark unless you have the conceptual capacity to think about dogs and barking. According to Davies, these conceptual capacities are fine-grained in the sense that they are capacities to think about things under certain modes of presentation; moreover, they are systematic in the sense that they conform to what Gareth Evans (1982: 104) calls "the generality constraint."[24]

---

[24] See section 4.3 for a statement and discussion of Evans's generality constraint.

With this distinction between conceptual and nonconceptual representation in hand, Davies proceeds to sketch an argument for the conceptual grounding thesis:

Attitude aboutness involves conceptualization, and conceptualization involves senses or modes of presentation. Among modes of presentation, those demonstrative modes of presentation that are afforded by perceptual experience constitute particularly clear examples. Suppose, even, that we could argue that in order to be able to think about objects at all, a subject needs to be able to think about objects under perceptual demonstrative modes of presentation. Then there would be a deep connection between intentionality and consciousness, just as Searle says, although not one that holds intentional state by intentional state. (1995: 381)

Here is the argument in outline: (i) in order to think about any objects at all, you must be able to think about some objects under perceptual-demonstrative modes of presentation; but (ii) you need conscious perception of an object in order to think about that object under a perceptual-demonstrative mode of presentation; so (iii) all thought about objects is grounded ultimately in conscious perception. Before examining these premises, let's explain what it means to think a perceptual-demonstrative thought about an object; that is, to think about an object under a perceptual-demonstrative mode of presentation.[25]

What is demonstrative thought? We might begin by saying it's the kind of thought that is characteristically expressed by a demonstrative utterance of the form, 'That F is G'. On reflection, however, this is inadequate. Suppose I am surrounded by white mugs and blindfolded. In that case, I could point to one of the mugs at random and say, "That mug is white," but I would not thereby express a demonstrative thought about the mug in question. Rather, I would be thinking of it by description, as the mug to which I am pointing. But if I were to remove the blindfold and take a look at the mug, then I would be able to think demonstrative thoughts about the mug. As Evans puts the point, "Thinking about an object demonstratively is thinking about an object in a way which depends crucially upon the subject's currently *perceiving* that object" (1982: 72).

Evans highlights the role of perception in making it possible for you to think demonstrative thoughts. Your perception of an object enables you to think demonstrative thoughts about the object by giving you information (or misinformation) that is causally derived from the object. Your demonstrative thought

---

[25] The rest of this section draws on my discussion of the role of consciousness in demonstrative thought in Smithies (2011b).

is about that object only because you're disposed to use information from the object in forming beliefs about the object without mediation by inference. So when you think a demonstrative thought about an object, you thereby exploit an information link with the object. In that sense, demonstrative thoughts are *information-based* thoughts.

Not all information-based thoughts are demonstrative thoughts, since they include thoughts involving proper names as well as demonstratives. Moreover, not all demonstrative thoughts are based on perception, since they can be based on memory and testimony as well as perception. Arguably, however, these other ways of thinking information-based thoughts ultimately depend upon perception. If so, then our most fundamental kind of information-based thought is demonstrative thought that is based upon perception.

With these clarifications in mind, let's revisit Davies's argument for the conceptual grounding thesis, which can be summarized like this:

(1) All conceptual thought is grounded in perceptual-demonstrative thought.

(2) All perceptual-demonstrative thought is grounded in conscious perception.

(3) Therefore, all conceptual thought is grounded in conscious perception.

I'll briefly consider both premises in turn. On the first premise: why should we suppose that all conceptual thought is grounded in demonstrative thought?

Peter Strawson's (1959: 20–23) massive reduplication argument is suggestive here. Massive reduplication occurs when there is a distant region of the universe that is qualitatively identical to our own region of the universe. Intuitively, you can refer to the objects in your own region of the universe even in the event that massive reduplication occurs. If all of your thoughts are purely descriptive thoughts, however, then this cannot be so. None of your thoughts refer to anything at all in the massive reduplication scenario, since their descriptive contents are not uniquely satisfied. There is nothing to secure reference to your own region of the universe, rather than the qualitatively identical region elsewhere. Hence, your thoughts are not all purely descriptive thoughts.

Strawson argues that your capacity to think about objects located in space depends upon your capacity to think about them demonstratively on the basis of perception. There is a slight gap in the argument here, since the distinction between descriptive thoughts and demonstrative thoughts based on perception is not an exhaustive one. Nevertheless, there is some prospect of closing this gap by arguing that all our nondescriptive modes of thought about the external world are ultimately grounded in demonstrative thoughts based on perception. Another complication is that this argument may not deliver an unrestricted conclusion about conceptual thought, but only a more restricted conclusion about our capacity to think about objects located in space. Even so, this conclusion would certainly be substantial enough to answer our initial question about the significance of consciousness.

Turning now to the second premise: why think only conscious perception grounds demonstrative thought about objects? According to Evans, perception enables us to think demonstrative thoughts about objects by giving us information about those objects. But why think our perceptual information must be conscious in order to play this role? Not all perceptual information is conscious: as Evans (1982: 158) notes, there must be unconscious perceptual information that explains how blindsighted subjects are able to make accurate reports about objects in their blind field that they cannot consciously perceive. But then why can't these blindsighted subjects use unconscious perceptual information in thinking demonstrative thoughts about objects in their blind field?

Intuitively, this is impossible. Blindsighted subjects cannot think demonstrative thoughts about objects in the blind field precisely because they are not perceptually conscious of them. They can think about them by description: say, as the objects in their blind field that they cannot see. But they cannot think demonstrative thoughts about those objects on the basis of unconscious perceptual information. Moreover, this is not just a medical limitation that can be explained in terms of empirical facts about their neural wiring. It seems inconceivable that anyone could think demonstrative thoughts on the basis of unconscious perceptual information. John Campbell pumps this intuition using his example of "the sea of faces":

> You and I are sitting at a dinner table with a large number of people around and you make a remark to me about "that woman." There are a lot of people around: I can't yet visually single out which one you mean. So on anyone's account, I do not yet know which woman you are talking about. Suppose now that we add to the example. My visual experience remains as before: a sea of faces. I cannot consciously single out the person you mean. All I get consciously is the sea of faces. But now we add some of what the blindseer has. . . . So I can make reliable guesses about what the person is eating, wearing, and so on, as well as reaching and pointing appropriately. But so long as my conscious experience remains a sea of faces, there is an ordinary sense in which I do not know who you mean. (2002: 8–9)

The suggestion is that it doesn't matter how much unconscious perceptual information you receive from the object or how you're able to use it in the control of action and speech. If you're not conscious of the object, and you cannot single out the object in consciousness, then you cannot think demonstratively about the object because you don't know which object is in question.[26]

If this intuition is correct, then it needs an explanation. Why must perceptual information be conscious to serve as a basis for demonstrative thought? If there is a necessary connection between consciousness and demonstrative thought, then it must derive either from the nature of consciousness or from the nature of demonstrative thought. Evans and Campbell give contrasting accounts of this connection: Evans explains consciousness in terms of its functional role in demonstrative thought, whereas Campbell explains the nature of demonstrative thought in terms of consciousness.

In the following passage, Evans sketches a broadly functionalist analysis of consciousness in terms of conceptual thought:

> We arrive at conscious perceptual experience when sensory input . . . serves as input to a *thinking, concept-applying, and reasoning system*; so that the subject's thoughts, plans, and deliberations are also systematically dependent on the informational properties of the input. When there is such a further link, we can say that the person, rather than just some part of his brain, receives and possesses the information. (1982: 158)

The suggestion is that what makes perceptual information conscious is that it serves as input to a conceptual system—most fundamentally, through the formation of perceptually based demonstrative thoughts. On this view, it is sufficient for perceptual information to be conscious that it serves as a basis for demonstrative thought. Equivalently, it is necessary for perceptual information to serve as a basis for demonstrative thought that it is conscious. Hence, Evans's functionalist analysis of consciousness rules out the possibility that blindsighted subjects could think demonstrative thoughts on the basis of unconscious perceptual information.[27]

One problem with this functionalist analysis of consciousness is that it seems conceivable that a primitive creature could have conscious perception without having any conceptual system at all. Another problem is that it seems conceivable that a zombie could have unconscious perceptual information that serves as input to a central system with the same abstract causal structure as our conceptual system. Perhaps zombies cannot have a genuine conceptual system, but only an ersatz functional substitute. But if so, then we need to reverse the

---

[26] For current purposes, I'll ignore issues about the role of conscious attention in demonstrative thought, but see Smithies (2011a) and (2011b: 26–32) for discussion.

[27] Compare Tye's (1995) PANIC theory, which says that phenomenal consciousness is abstract nonconceptual intentional content that is poised to make an impact on the conceptual system.

direction of analysis: that is, we need to analyze conceptual thought in terms of consciousness, rather than analyzing consciousness in terms of its role in conceptual thought. Campbell's (2002) account of demonstrative thought puts consciousness first: on this view, perception explains demonstrative thought because it is conscious; it's not conscious because it explains demonstrative thought.

Campbell argues that conscious perception is necessary for knowing which object is the reference of a demonstrative concept. On a classical view, grasping a demonstrative concept is a matter of knowing its reference—that is, knowing to which object it refers. Moreover, your knowledge of the reference of a demonstrative concept is what causes and justifies your use of the demonstrative concept in thought and action. Campbell argues that conscious perception of an object is what plays this causal and justifying role by setting in motion and defining the targets for the unconscious information processing that underpins your use of the demonstrative concept in thought and action.[28] Therefore, he concludes, conscious perception is what provides you with your knowledge of the reference of demonstrative concepts. On this view, blindsighted subjects cannot think demonstrative thoughts about objects in their blind field because they violate the requirements for knowing the reference of a demonstrative concept.

My main objection to Campbell's account is that it remains unclear why consciousness is needed to set in motion and define the targets for unconscious information processing that is directed toward a particular object. Even if we assume the empirical hypothesis that consciousness actually plays this role, it seems conceivable that something remote from consciousness could play the same functional role in a zombie. Indeed, given that subjects with blindsight and visual form agnosia are capable of reporting and acting upon objects that they cannot consciously perceive, there must be something remote from consciousness that actually plays this role. Otherwise, we simply cannot explain the reliability of their verbal reports and actions.

The problem with Campbell's account is that it's located at the wrong level of psychological explanation. I agree that consciousness explains our grasp of demonstrative concepts by causing and justifying our use of those concepts in thought, but I disagree with his account of what this role consists in. Campbell argues that consciousness plays an essential computational role: it sets in motion and defines the targets for the unconscious information processing that underpins our use of demonstrative concepts in thought. In contrast, I argue

---

[28] Compare Milner and Goodale's (1995) proposal that conscious visual processing in the ventral stream sets the targets for unconscious visual processing in the dorsal stream.

that consciousness plays an essential epistemic role: it enables subjects to use demonstrative concepts in forming noninferentially justified beliefs about objects in the world around them. Campbell's account concerns the role of consciousness in the computational explanation of subpersonal-level processes of information processing, whereas mine concerns the role of consciousness in the rationalizing explanation of personal-level processes of belief formation.

I argue that the role of consciousness in demonstrative thought can be explained as a consequence of the epistemic role of consciousness together with epistemic constraints on demonstrative thought. Here is the argument in outline:

(1) You can think perceptual demonstrative thoughts about an object only if you have perceptual information that gives you defeasible, noninferential justification to form beliefs about the object.

(2) You have perceptual information that gives you defeasible, noninferential justification to form beliefs about an object only if you are perceptually conscious of the object.

(3) Therefore, you can think perceptual demonstrative thoughts about an object only if you are perceptually conscious of the object.

On this view, perception explains our capacity to think demonstrative thoughts about an object by giving us defeasible, noninferential justification to form beliefs about the object. However, only conscious perception can play this epistemic role. Hence, perception must be conscious in order to explain our capacity for demonstrative thought.

The first premise is an instance of a more general thesis that there are epistemic constraints on concept possession. What distinguishes a conceptual capacity from any other representational capacity? A plausible answer is that there are epistemic constraints on the possession and exercise of conceptual capacities. To have a concept, you must be disposed to use the concept in a way that is subject to norms of epistemic rationality. The early visual system does not have conceptual capacities because its representations are not epistemically constrained in this way: they are not subject to norms of epistemic rationality.

What are the epistemic constraints on demonstrative concepts? According to Evans, you can think demonstrative thoughts about an object only if you have perceptual information from the object, which you can use in forming beliefs about the object without inferential mediation by background beliefs. These beliefs are epistemically rational only if your perceptual information gives you defeasible, noninferential justification to form beliefs about the object. Otherwise, it would be irrational to form beliefs about objects on the basis of this perceptual information without inferential mediation. Hence, you can think demonstrative thoughts about an object only if you have perceptual information that gives you defeasible, noninferential justification to form beliefs about the object. This secures our first premise.

The second premise is an instance of a more general thesis about the epistemic role of consciousness. I've argued that your perception of an object must play an epistemic role in order to enable you to think demonstrative thoughts about the object, but what must your perception be like in order to play this epistemic role? In chapter 3, I'll argue that the phenomenal character of perceptual experience plays an indispensable epistemic role. It is only because perceptual experience has the phenomenal character of seeming to present me with objects and properties in the external world that it noninferentially justifies me in forming beliefs about those objects and properties. What's missing in blindsight is any such experience of apparently being presented with objects and properties in the blind field. Therefore, subjects with blindsight are not justified in forming beliefs about the blind field on the basis of unconscious perceptual information without mediation by inference.

This explains why blindsighted subjects cannot think demonstrative thoughts, but only descriptive thoughts, about objects in their blind field. They cannot satisfy the epistemic constraints on demonstrative thought. More specifically, unconscious perceptual information in blindsight cannot provide them with defeasible, noninferential justification to form beliefs about objects in the blind field. Hence, the role of consciousness in demonstrative thought can be explained in terms of the epistemic role of consciousness together with epistemic constraints on demonstrative thought.

In *The Problems of Philosophy*, Bertrand Russell writes, "All our knowledge, both knowledge of things and knowledge of truths, rests upon acquaintance as its foundation" (1912: 48). Acquaintance, for Russell, is a conscious state of direct and unmediated awareness of things. Meanwhile, his distinction between knowledge of things and knowledge of truths corresponds roughly to the distinction between our conceptual ability to think about things and our epistemic ability to know truths about those things. So Russell's thesis is that consciousness plays a dual role in explaining our conceptual ability to think about things and our epistemic ability to know truths about those things.

What is the relationship between these two aspects of the role of consciousness? Russell does not answer this question, but the arguments of this section suggest a more general account of the relationship between the epistemic role of consciousness and its role in grounding conceptual thought. I've argued, in effect, that the role of consciousness in thought can be explained as a consequence of the epistemic role of consciousness together with epistemic constraints on conceptual thought. If that is right, then the epistemic role of consciousness is more fundamental than the role of consciousness in thought.

2.5. Grounding Epistemic Justification in Consciousness

This brings me, finally, to my own account of the significance of consciousness. The central thesis of this book is that consciousness has unique epistemic significance: all epistemic justification has its source in consciousness. On this view, it is not true that all unconscious mental representation is grounded in consciousness, but only the kind that provides epistemic justification of belief. All mental representation that provides epistemic justification for belief is either conscious or grounded in consciousness. Here is a more precise statement of this epistemic grounding thesis:

The Epistemic Grounding Thesis: Necessarily, every representational property that plays a role in the epistemic justification of belief is either identical with or grounded in some phenomenal property of the same subject.

On this view, zombies can have mental representations, but their mental representations cannot provide epistemic justification for beliefs about the world. As a result, zombies cannot have knowledge or epistemically justified beliefs about the external world.

The epistemic grounding thesis is consistent with the representational grounding thesis, but it is a much weaker claim, and a more plausible one. We can defend the epistemic significance of consciousness without making the further claim that all mental representation has its source in consciousness. One might argue for the epistemic grounding thesis by deriving it from the representational grounding thesis, but that is not my strategy. I'll be arguing for the epistemic grounding thesis on independent grounds.

On my view, mental representation is a genus that has at least two different species. All mental representation figures in psychological explanation, but some mental representation figures in a distinctively rationalizing kind of psychological explanation. This kind of psychological explanation makes belief and action intelligible by explaining it in terms of the subject's reasons for belief or action. The reasons for which we believe and act are not always justifying reasons. Accordingly, our beliefs and actions are not always justified by reasons. Even so, the reasons for which we believe and act are the kinds of things that can in principle serve as justifying reasons for belief or action. According to the epistemic grounding thesis, all justifying reasons for belief are provided by mental representations that are either conscious or otherwise grounded in consciousness. Hence, these are the only kinds of mental representations that can figure in distinctively rationalizing explanations of belief.

The epistemic grounding thesis also provides a plausible explanation of the conceptual grounding thesis. What is the basis of the distinction between conceptual and nonconceptual species of mental representation? My answer is that there are epistemic constraints on conceptual representation: that is, all conceptual representation provides epistemic justification for belief. It follows that all conceptual representation is either conscious or grounded in consciousness, since this is necessary for mental representation to provide epistemic justification for belief. In this way, we can explain the role of consciousness in thought as a consequence of its epistemic role.

I'll argue for the epistemic grounding thesis in the remaining chapters of Part I. In chapter 3, I'll argue that perception must be conscious in order to provide epistemic justification for beliefs about the external world. In chapter 4, I'll argue that beliefs must be accessible to consciousness in order to provide epistemic justification for other beliefs. In chapter 5, I'll argue that your mental states must be either conscious or accessible to consciousness in order to give you epistemic justification for introspectively believing that you're in those very mental states. In chapter 6, I'll argue that epistemic justification is determined solely by mental states that are either conscious or accessible to consciousness. Finally, in Part II, I'll situate this account of the epistemic role of consciousness within a broader epistemological framework.

3

Perception

How does perception justify beliefs about the external world? I'll begin from the assumption that skepticism is false and hence that some of our beliefs about the external world are justified by perception. My main goal in this chapter is to examine what perception must be like in order to play this justifying role. More specifically, I want to examine the role of phenomenal consciousness in explaining how perception justifies beliefs about the external world. Does perception justify belief solely in virtue of its phenomenal character?

A note on terminology: I'll use the terms 'justified' and 'rational' more or less interchangeably. Justification is always relative to a standard: here, I'm talking about justification by standards of epistemic rationality, rather than morality or prudence. Although this assumption is dispensable, I'll tend to assume a version of evidentialism, which says that all epistemic justification for belief has its source in evidence—that is, epistemic reasons, rather than practical reasons, for belief. Evidentialism is neutral between various rival conceptions of evidence: we can say that evidence is what epistemically justifies belief without thereby prejudging the nature of evidence. The main aim of this chapter is to argue that all perceptual evidence has its source in phenomenal consciousness.

Following Roderick Firth (1978), we can draw a distinction between *propositional* and *doxastic* senses of epistemic justification. All doxastically justified beliefs are propositionally justified, but not vice versa. A belief is propositionally justified when you have justification to hold the belief, whether or not you hold the belief, whereas a belief is doxastically justified when you hold the belief in a justified way. In an evidentialist framework, a belief is propositionally justified when you have strong enough evidence that its content is true, whereas a belief is doxastically justified when you hold the belief in a way that is properly based on such evidence. In a slogan, doxastic justification is propositional justification plus proper basing.

Perception justifies beliefs about the external world in both senses, but I will focus on propositional justification, rather than doxastic justification. I'll make the following assumptions about the kind of propositional justification that is provided by perception. First, perceptual justification is *defeasible* in the sense that it can be defeated by a posteriori justification to believe other propositions—for instance, that your perception is unreliable. Second, perceptual justification is *immediate* or *noninferential* in the weak sense that it doesn't depend on a posteriori justification to believe any other propositions—for instance, that perception is reliable. After all, a posteriori justification to believe that perception is reliable depends upon perception. If we deny that perceptual justification is immediate in the weak sense just defined, then we generate a vicious epistemic circle.

These assumptions are neutral in the debate between dogmatism and its rivals. James Pryor (2000) defines *dogmatism* as the thesis that perceptual justification is immediate in the stronger sense that it doesn't depend on either a priori or a posteriori justification to believe anything else. Some opponents of dogmatism, including Crispin Wright (2004), Roger White (2006), and Stewart Cohen (2010) argue that dogmatism generates bootstrapping problems. To avoid these problems, they argue that perceptual justification depends on a priori justification to believe that perception is reliable. Nicholas Silins (2008) and Ralph Wedgwood (2013) combine dogmatism with the claim that perceptual justification entails a priori justification to believe that your perception is reliable, although the former doesn't depend on the latter. This version of dogmatism avoids the usual objections. In any case, the weak immediacy thesis is common ground in the debate between dogmatism and its opponents.

This chapter is about the epistemic role of perception, so we can postpone questions about the epistemic role of cognition until the next chapter. Background beliefs can defeat the immediate justification provided by perception, and they can combine with perception to yield inferentially mediated justification. For current purposes, however, the justifying role of perception can be understood in a way that brackets the justifying role of background beliefs. When I refer to the justifying role of perception, I mean its role in providing us with a source of propositional justification for beliefs about the external world that is defeasible and immediate in the weak sense just defined.

Here is the plan. In section 3.1, I begin by arguing that unconscious visual information in blindsight cannot justify beliefs about objects in the blind field. In section 3.2, I argue that this is because perception must have phenomenal character in order to justify beliefs about the external world: the epistemic role of phenomenal consciousness cannot be supplanted by access consciousness or metacognitive consciousness instead. In section 3.3, I explain how representationalism makes it plausible that perceptual experience justifies some beliefs about the external world in virtue of its phenomenal character alone. In sections 3.4 and 3.5, I argue that the justifying role of perceptual experience supervenes on its phenomenal character, and I apply this supervenience thesis to skeptical scenarios and duplication scenarios. Finally, I conclude in section 3.6.

3.1. Blindsight

Normal human perception has *phenomenal character*: in other words, there is something it is like for us to perceive the external world. According to representationalism, the phenomenal character of perception is identical with some way of representing the external world. It doesn't follow, however, that perception must have phenomenal character in order to represent the external world at all. Indeed, there is substantial empirical evidence that our perceptual systems can represent the external world without any associated phenomenal character at all. In this chapter, I'll focus on the example of *blindsight*.[1]

Blindsight is caused by neural damage in the primary visual cortex. It results in large blind spots (or "scotoma") in the visual field. Patients with blindsight claim that they cannot see anything in these blind areas, but when forced to choose between a range of alternatives, they can make accurate reports about stimuli presented in the blind field with a high degree of reliability. The stimuli detected in blindsight include position, movement, orientation, simple shapes, colors, and emotions. What explains the reliable accuracy of these reports is that information about stimuli in the blind field is represented and processed in the visual system, although it doesn't surface in conscious experience.

Blindsight can influence action as well as verbal report. When prompted, patients with blindsight can orient their eyes or point their finger toward a spot of light in the blind field. Some can catch a ball, grasp a stick, or post a card in a slot. There is even one documented patient with bilateral blindsight who can navigate his way through a narrow corridor crowded with obstacles. We cannot explain these remarkable abilities except by appealing to the representation and processing of visual information about the blind field that has no associated phenomenal character.

It is perhaps worth mentioning that some blindsighted subjects do sometimes report experiences in response to certain kinds of stimuli. For example, Weiskrantz's patient, DB, reports "'seeing' some peculiar waves" (1997: 19) when he is presented with rapidly moving stimuli of high luminance contrast. These experiences do not accurately represent the stimuli in question, though, and they tend to impair his performance in detection tasks. Moreover, in other cases, DB reports that he can see nothing at all in his blind field. I'll focus on what Weiskrantz calls "type 1" rather than "type 2" cases of blindsight in which patients report having no experience at all. Moreover, I'll assume that these

---

[1] See Weiskrantz (1997: ch. 1) for a review of empirical work on blindsight. Prinz (2015) reviews other empirical evidence for unconscious perceptual representation, including visual agnosia, unilateral neglect, achromatopsia, masking, binocular rivalry, interocular suppression, and transcranial magnetic stimulation.

subjective reports are accurate and that subjects with blindsight are not mistaken about their own lack of experience.[2]

Do patients with blindsight *see* the objects and properties in their blind field? Some philosophers say yes: blindsight is an example of unconscious perception. Others say no: there can be no genuine perception without consciousness.[3] Is there anything at stake in this debate aside from the purely verbal question of whether we define "seeing" or "perception" in terms of consciousness? I think so. What is at stake is whether consciousness is necessary for perception to play its distinctive functional role. If so, then defining perception in terms of consciousness is not merely a terminological maneuver, since it marks out an important theoretical kind.

What is the distinctive functional role of perception? One key role is to give us knowledge and epistemically justified beliefs about the external world. Perceiving an object is a matter of receiving perceptual information from the object that gives you immediate, defeasible justification to form beliefs about the object. Now, we need to ask whether unconscious visual information in blindsight plays the right kind of epistemic role in justifying beliefs about the blind field. If not, then it doesn't satisfy the epistemic constraints on perception.

In this section, I'll argue that blindsight cannot justify beliefs about the blind field. In the next section, I'll argue that this is because it has no phenomenal character. In contrast, normal human perception justifies belief only because it has some phenomenal character. So, I'll argue, the presence or absence of phenomenal character is what explains the justificational difference between blindsight and conscious sight. This is the basis of my argument for the following thesis:

> *The Phenomenal Condition*: Necessarily, perception justifies belief about the external world if and only if it has some phenomenal character.

Anyone who rejects the Phenomenal Condition must either deny that there is a justificational difference between blindsight and conscious sight or else explain it in some other way. I'll argue that neither of these options is viable.

Here is a thought experiment to warm you up. Suppose you wake up in the hospital feeling normal. The doctor holds her hand in front of your face and asks you to count how many fingers she is holding up. You answer correctly and she gives you some candy as a reward. Now she holds her hand just outside your conscious field of vision and asks you to count how many fingers she is

---

[2] For the rival view that blindsight is degraded conscious vision, see Campion et al. (1983), Lau and Passingham (2006), and Overgaard et al. (2008).
[3] See, for example, the recent debate between Block (2016) and Phillips (2016).

holding up. You tell her you can't see her hand, but she asks you to guess anyway. You say, "What the hell" and hazard a guess. To your surprise, she says you got the right answer and gives you some more candy. Again she holds up her hand and asks you to guess the number of fingers, and again you give the right answer. The experiment continues until you've eaten so much candy you begin to feel sick.

How are you getting the answers right? You have absolutely no idea. In fact, while you were sleeping in the hospital, a neurosurgeon implanted a mechanism in your brain that accurately detects conditions outside your visual field. It's like an internal video camera, except that you can't see what's on the screen. When you're asked to guess, your answers are sensitive to whatever the camera detects. Of course, you have no way of knowing that there's a camera inside your head, nor that it exerts any influence on what you say.

Do you have any justification to form beliefs about how many fingers the doctor is holding up? You surely do when you can see the doctor's hand, but not when the doctor's hand falls outside your conscious field of vision. It makes no difference that the camera inside your head can "see" the doctor's hand and enables you to guess the right answer. After all, you have no way of knowing about the existence of this mechanism at all. Since you have no relevant background evidence about how many fingers the doctor is holding up, the only reasonable option is to withhold belief altogether.

The same applies in the case of blindsight. A blindsighted subject has justification to form beliefs about objects when they're presented in the conscious field of vision, but not when they're presented in the blind field. It makes no difference that some visual system in his brain can "see" the stimulus and thereby help him to guess the right answer. Again, he has no way of knowing about the existence of this mechanism. Since he has no relevant background evidence about the blind field, the only reasonable option is to withhold belief.

Of course, there are various differences between my hypothetical case of the internal video camera and actual cases of blindsight. For example, the internal video camera is implanted, rather than innate, and it is designed by an agent, rather than by natural selection. Perhaps we could tamper with these details of the example, but it is not clear why this should make any difference. What matters is that the subject has no way of knowing about the existence and functioning of the relevant internal mechanism whatever the specific details of its causal etiology. I'll now reply to a series of objections.

Objection 1: Given a long enough track record, subjects with blindsight can learn that they are reliable about the blind field and hence that their guesses are likely to be true. In that case, a blindsighted subject might have justification to believe (i) I'm inclined to guess that there's an X in my blind field, and (ii) my guesses are reliably accurate, so (iii) it's probably true that there's an X in my blind field.

In reply, this is true but irrelevant. In this scenario, your inferential justification for beliefs about the blind field has its source not in unconscious visual information, but rather in background beliefs about the reliability of your guesses. Our question is whether unconscious visual information in blindsight is a source of *noninferential* justification for beliefs about the blind field. To address this question, we need to focus on cases in which you have no background empirical evidence that you are reliable about the blind field. In such cases, the only reasonable option is to withhold belief.

Objection 2: The absence of conscious visual experience in blindsight gives you evidence that you're unreliable. After all, you have inductive evidence that you're not typically reliable when you make noninferential reports about the immediate environment except when they are based on perceptual experience. Hence, the absence of conscious visual experience in blindsight gives you an undercutting defeater.[4]

Again, this is irrelevant. Our question is whether unconscious visual information in blindsight provides even *defeasible* justification for beliefs about the blind field, whether or not it is defeated. To address this question, we need to focus on cases in which you have no defeaters in the form of background empirical evidence that you are unreliable. In such cases, withholding belief is still the only reasonable option.

Objection 3: We cannot make sense of the stipulation that you have no evidence for or against the thesis that you have a reliable faculty of blindsight. Alvin Goldman (1986) makes a similar point in response to Laurence BonJour's (1985) stipulation that Norman the clairvoyant has no evidence for or against the thesis that he has a reliable clairvoyant power. He says that Norman can reason as follows: "If I had a clairvoyant power, I would surely find *some* evidence for this. . . . Since I lack any such signs, I apparently do not possess reliable clairvoyant processes" (1986: 112).

In reply, you cannot settle a priori whether or not you have a reliable faculty of blindsight or clairvoyance. This is an a posteriori question that needs to be settled on the basis of empirical evidence. Moreover, we can stipulate that your total body of empirical evidence is silent on this question. Perhaps you just came into existence and have no track record to draw upon. There is no incoherence in supposing that you have no evidence either for or against the thesis that you have a reliable faculty of blindsight.

---

[4] Goldman (1986: 109–112), Lyons (2009: 176–177) and Nagel (2016) appeal to undercutting defeaters in responding to BonJour's (1985) case of the clairvoyant, Norman.

Objection 4: If we stipulate that you have no evidence about your own reliability, then there is no epistemic disparity between blindsight and conscious perception. On this view, conscious perception justifies belief about the external world only when you have background empirical evidence that it is reliable. In the absence of such evidence, even conscious perception is justificationally inert.

In reply, this contradicts our initial assumption that conscious perception provides immediate justification for beliefs about the external world in the absence of empirical evidence that perception is reliable. The motivation for this assumption is that there is no way to acquire empirical evidence for the reliability of perception except by relying on perception itself. In light of this circularity problem, it is extremely plausible that conscious perception provides a source of immediate justification that doesn't depend on background empirical evidence. It is not equally plausible—in fact, it is extremely implausible—that unconscious perceptual information in blindsight can play the same kind of justifying role.

Our question is whether blindsight can play the same kind of epistemic role as conscious perception in providing immediate, defeasible justification for beliefs about the external world. So far, I've been pumping the intuition that it doesn't, but in case you're not yet convinced, here is a further argument designed to persuade you.

The first premise of the argument is the empirical observation that patients with blindsight do not typically *believe* the reports they make about objects in the blind field under forced choice conditions. Instead, they say they are just guessing and are surprised to learn of their own reliability. Here is Larry Weiskrantz reporting on his patient, DB:

> In many cases he said he was just guessing, and thought he was not performing better than chance. When he was shown his results . . . he expressed open astonishment in the early days. (1997: 18)

The second premise is that this reaction—namely, withholding belief about objects in the blind field—seems entirely rational. There's nothing rationally deficient about patients who suffer from blindsight: after all, it's a perceptual deficit, rather than a cognitive one. The third premise is that if you have evidence that justifies holding some belief, and yet you withhold belief instead, then you're less than fully rational. After all, epistemic rationality is a matter of conforming your beliefs to the evidence in your possession. Put all this together and we can draw the conclusion that unconscious perception in blindsight doesn't provide evidence that justifies forming beliefs about the blind field.

Here is the argument in outline:

(1) Blindsighted subjects are not disposed to form beliefs noninferentially on the basis of unconscious visual information, but rather to withhold belief instead.

(2) Blindsighted subjects are not thereby any less than fully rational.

(3) If unconscious visual information in blindsight provides a source of noninferential justification for belief, then blindsighted subjects are less than fully rational insofar as they are not disposed to form beliefs noninferentially on the basis of unconscious visual information, but rather to withhold belief instead.

(4) Therefore, unconscious visual information in blindsight does not provide a source of noninferential justification for belief.

Suppose, for the sake of argument, that unconscious perceptual information in blindsight provides evidence that justifies forming beliefs about the blind field. On this view, blindsighted subjects are less than fully rational insofar as they ignore this evidence in withholding belief about the blind field. But this view seems wrong. Blindsight is not a cognitive deficit in which subjects ignore perceptual evidence that justifies forming beliefs about the blind field. Rather, it is a perceptual deficit in which subjects lack the perceptual evidence that is needed to justify beliefs about the blind field in the first place.

One objection to this argument is that it ignores the role of background evidence about reliability. After all, blindsighted subjects are disposed to form beliefs about the blind field when they have positive evidence that they're reliable and to refrain when they have negative evidence that they're unreliable. So perhaps blindsighted subjects refrain from forming beliefs about the blind field only because they have undercutting defeaters in the form of negative evidence about their own reliability. As I've explained, however, our question is whether unconscious perceptual information in blindsight provides immediate, defeasible justification for beliefs about the external world. To answer this question, we need to focus on cases in which subjects have no background empirical evidence about their own reliability. With this background stipulation in place, the objection can be set aside.

The crucial point for our purposes is that blindsighted subjects are not disposed to form beliefs noninferentially on the basis of unconscious visual information in the absence of either positive or negative evidence about their own reliability. The empirical evidence shows that their beliefs are not directly responsive to what's represented in the blind field, but only when indirectly mediated by inferences about what they're inclined to guess. And yet they are not rationally deficient because they are disposed to refrain from forming beliefs noninferentially on the basis of unconscious visual information in the absence of any background empirical evidence about their own reliability. Therefore, we may conclude that unconscious perceptual information in blindsight doesn't provide a source of immediate, defeasible justification for beliefs about the external world.

3.2. Concepts of Consciousness

So far, I've argued that conscious perception justifies belief about the external world, whereas unconscious perceptual information in blindsight does not. What explains this epistemic asymmetry between conscious perception and blindsight? Here is my proposed explanation:

> *The Phenomenal Condition*: Necessarily, perception justifies belief about the external world if and only if it has some phenomenal character.

In this section, I'll argue that blindsight cannot justify beliefs about the blind field because it has no phenomenal character. In contrast, normal human perception justifies belief about the external world only because it has some phenomenal character. In other words, the presence or absence of phenomenal character is what explains the justificational difference between blindsight and conscious sight.

My goal in this section is to argue that this explanation is better than the alternatives. Opponents will insist—quite correctly—that there are functional differences, as well as phenomenal differences, between blindsight and conscious sight. If so, then perhaps we can explain the justificational difference between blindsight and conscious sight in terms of the difference in their functional role, rather than their phenomenal character. Ned Block (1995) argues that our ordinary concept of consciousness is a "mongrel concept" that conflates phenomenal and functional concepts of consciousness. So can we explain the justificational difference between blindsight and conscious sight in terms of access consciousness or metacognitive consciousness, rather than phenomenal consciousness? I think not: even a functional zombie has no justification to form beliefs about the external world on the basis of visual information with no phenomenal character. Since this case is so remote from the actual world, however, we shouldn't try to eyeball it directly. Instead, we'll get there by means of a series of small steps from actual cases of blindsight.

Block defines access consciousness in terms of its functional role in the control of cognition and action:

> A state is A-conscious if it is poised for direct control of thought and action. To add more detail, a representation is A-conscious if it is poised

for free use in reasoning and for direct "rational" control of action and speech. (1997: 382)

The guiding idea here is that access consciousness is an "information-processing correlate" of phenomenal consciousness (1997: 384). In other words, a mental state is access conscious when it plays the same role in cognition and action that our mental states normally do when they're phenomenally conscious. As Block notes, however, these are distinct concepts, since there are conceptually possible cases in which they come apart. For example, a functional zombie has access consciousness, but lacks phenomenal consciousness.

In section 1.1, I complained that there is no ordinary sense in which a zombie is conscious. If so, then access consciousness is not another kind of consciousness, but merely an ersatz functional substitute for phenomenal consciousness. For current purposes, however, we can ignore this point. What matters is Block's claim that we sometimes confuse phenomenal consciousness with its functional role in making information accessible for use in cognition and action. If these can come apart, as in the case of a functional zombie, then we can ask whether the justifying role of perception should be explained in terms of its phenomenal consciousness or its functional role in making information accessible.

Can we explain the justificational difference between blindsight and conscious sight in terms of access consciousness, rather than phenomenal consciousness? As Block notes, blindsight is conscious in neither sense. Phenomenal consciousness is missing because there is nothing it's like for a blindsighted subject to visually represent objects and properties in their blind field. Access consciousness is missing because these visual representations are not poised for direct control of thought and action. Blindsighted subjects do not spontaneously use unconscious perceptual information in acting upon objects in the blind field, or making reports about them, but only when they are prompted to do so. Hence, visual information in blindsight is neither phenomenally conscious nor access conscious.

Can we explain why blindsight fails to justify beliefs about the blind field in terms of the absence of access consciousness, rather than phenomenal consciousness? If so, then we can replace the Phenomenal Condition with the following Accessibility Condition:

The Accessibility Condition: Necessarily, perception justifies belief about the external world if and only if it is access conscious.

In order to decide the issue, we need to ask whether perception justifies belief when phenomenal consciousness and access consciousness come apart. If there are no such cases, then we don't have a rival proposal. We can therefore proceed on the assumption that access consciousness and phenomenal consciousness can be dissociated. I'll rely on this assumption in arguing that access consciousness is neither necessary nor sufficient for perception to justify beliefs about the external world.

Block gives examples of inattentive perception to illustrate the conceptual possibility of phenomenal consciousness without access consciousness:

> Suppose you are engaged in intense conversation when suddenly at noon you realize that right outside your window, there is—and has been for some time—a pneumatic drill digging up the street. You were aware of the noise all along, one might say, but only at noon are you *consciously aware* of it. That is, you were P-conscious of the noise all along, but at noon you are both P-conscious *and* A-conscious of it. (1995: 234)

Before noon, you were peripherally aware of the drilling sound. At noon, when the sound captured your attention, your awareness of the sound became poised for direct control of thought and action. You didn't notice the sound until it captured your attention, but it doesn't follow that you weren't aware of it beforehand. Sometimes we're aware of things that we fail to notice because we're not paying attention. Attention normally makes perceptual information access conscious as well as phenomenally conscious.[5]

Can perception justify beliefs in the absence of access consciousness? You might say no because access consciousness is needed to form justified beliefs on the basis of perception. At noon, when the drilling sound captures your attention, you can form a justified belief that it's noisy outside. But if you form the same belief before noon, when the sound of the drill has not yet captured your attention, then your belief is unjustified. A belief formed in this way seems no better than mere guesswork, since you could easily have formed the same belief in the same way without any peripheral awareness of the sound. After all, your peripheral awareness of the sound is not accessible for use in forming beliefs.

This argument supports the conclusion that access consciousness is necessary for forming doxastically justified beliefs on the basis of perception. Still, it doesn't follow that access consciousness is necessary for having propositional justification to form those beliefs in the first place. We're assuming that perceptual experience can represent contents that are phenomenally conscious but not access conscious. So, in Block's example, your experience represents that

---

[5] Block (2007) makes an empirical case for the thesis that phenomenal consciousness "overflows" access consciousness. For current purposes, though, we can abstract away from the empirical details, since we just need to assume that such cases are conceptually possible.

it's noisy outside before this content becomes poised for use in the direct control of thought and action. But if your perceptual experience represents that p, then you thereby have immediate, defeasible justification to believe that p (see section 3.3). Therefore, access consciousness is not necessary for perceptual experience to give you propositional justification for forming beliefs about an object.[6]

I conclude that access consciousness is not necessary for perception to justify beliefs about the external world, but is it sufficient? To answer this question, we need to consider cases of access consciousness without phenomenal consciousness in perception. Block uses the example of *super-blindsight*:

> A real blindsight patient can only guess when given a choice from a small set of alternatives (X/O; horizontal/vertical, etc.). But suppose—interestingly, apparently contrary to fact—that a blindsight patient could be trained to prompt himself at will, guessing what is in the blind field without being told to guess. The super-blindsighter spontaneously says, "Now I know that there is a horizontal line in my blind field even though I don't actually see it." (1995: 233)

Block says that visual information in super-blindsight is access conscious but not phenomenally conscious. As Michael Tye (1995: 143) notes, however, there is a problem here. If the super-blindsighter needs to prompt himself to guess, and then believes whatever he guesses, then his visual representations are not poised for *direct* control of thought and action, since their impact on cognition is mediated by an act of self-prompting. As such, they don't satisfy Block's conditions for access consciousness.

To avoid this problem, let's stipulate that the super-blindsighter forms beliefs about the blind field spontaneously and without prompting himself to guess. These beliefs are formed directly and noninferentially on the basis of unconscious visual information about the blind field. There is no inferential mediation of the form (i) I'm disposed to guess that p, and (ii) I'm reliable, so (iii) it's probably true that p. The idea is that super-blindsight has the same causal influence in belief-formation as conscious sight, but with no phenomenal character. We can also suppose that super-blindsight has the same degree of reliability and richness of content as conscious sight. This is a better example of access consciousness without phenomenal consciousness in perception.[7]

---

[6] In Smithies (2011a) and (2011b), I argue that attention is necessary for doxastic justification but not propositional justification.

[7] Tye (1995: 142–143) denies that super-blindsight is possible, but all we really need for current purposes is that it's conceivable, whether or not it's possible.

Is perceptual information in super-blindsight available for direct *rational* control of belief and action? If not, then we still don't have an example of access consciousness without phenomenal consciousness. As Block explains, however, he uses the term 'rational' as a mere placeholder to exclude the kind of control that obtains in blindsight. In this deflationary sense, the kind of control that obtains in super-blindsight counts as rational. As Block puts the point, "I mean the 'rationally' to exclude the 'guessing' kind of guidance of action that blind-sight patients *are* capable of in the case of stimuli presented to the blind field" (1995: 228).

Still, this leaves our target question wide open. Does unconscious percep-tual information in super-blindsight provide epistemic justification for beliefs about the blind field? There is considerable pressure to say no. After all, there is no relevant difference between super-blindsight and ordinary blindsight that could plausibly explain why justification is present in the first case, but absent in the second case. The only difference is that the super-blindsighter is dis-posed to spontaneously form beliefs about the blind field, whereas the ordinary blindsighter is disposed only to make tentative guesses under forced choice conditions. But the mere fact that you are disposed to form beliefs under cer-tain conditions is not enough to make your disposition justified. So either the disposition is justified in both cases or neither. Since the disposition is not justi-fied in ordinary cases of blindsight, we should conclude that it is not justified in cases of super-blindsight either.

Of course, there is a phenomenal difference between these cases, since the super-blindsighter has feelings of confidence that are absent in ordinary blind-sight. Could this make a justificational difference between these cases? I think not. First, the mere feeling of confidence is not sufficient to justify you in forming beliefs—justification is not so easy to come by. Second, even if cognitive experi-ence plays some epistemic role, it cannot play the same foundational epistemic role as perceptual experience in justifying belief without standing in need of justifica-tion (see section 3.3). And third, our question is whether unconscious perception in super-blindsight can justify beliefs about the blind field. If the justifying work is done by conscious cognition, such as feelings of confidence, then it is not done by unconscious perception. Either way, unconscious perception in super-blindsight cannot justify beliefs about the external world.

Block's example of super-blindsight thereby serves as an intuitive counterexample to a simple form of reliabilism about justified belief. Reliabilism is the thesis that a belief is doxastically justified if and only if it is formed on the basis of a sufficiently reliable process. The super-blindsighter satisfies this condition, since he forms beliefs about the blind field on the basis of reliable visual information. As I've just argued, however, these beliefs are not doxastically justified. Therefore, reliability is not sufficient for doxastically justified belief.[8]

I conclude that access consciousness is not sufficient for perception to justify beliefs about the external world. One reaction is to impose more demanding functional conditions for perception to justify beliefs about the external world. As Block notes, there are some important functional differences between super-blindsight and conscious sight:

> The super-blindsighter himself contrasts what it is like to know visually about an X in his blind field and an X in his sighted field. There is something it is like to experience the latter, but not the former, he says. It is the difference between *just knowing* and knowing via a visual experience. (1995: 233)

When normal human adults acquire perceptual knowledge, we know by reflection how we know what we know. And even when our perceptual beliefs fail to be knowledge, as in cases of perceptual illusion, we know by reflection why we believe what we believe. We know that perceptual experience gives us justifying reasons for our beliefs. In contrast, the super-blindsighter cannot know by reflection why he believes what he does about the blind field. So perhaps what's missing in super-blindsight is higher-order knowledge or metacognition about the visual states on which your beliefs are based.[9]

We can put this proposal in terms of Ned Block's concept of *metacognitive consciousness*. According to Block, "A conscious state in this sense is a state accompanied by a thought to the effect that one is in that state . . . arrived at nonobservationally and noninferentially" (1995: 235). Normal human perception is metacognitively conscious in the sense that we can know without inference how our perceptual experience represents the world around us. In contrast, neither blindsight nor super-blindsight is metacognitively conscious in the sense that we can know without inference what information is perceptually represented about objects in the blind field.

Can the absence of metacognitive consciousness explain why super-blindsight fails to justify beliefs about the blind field? If so, then we can replace the Phenomenal Condition with the following Metacognitive Condition:

---

[8] This example has the same structure as more standard counterexamples to reliabilism, including BonJour's (1985) case of Norman the clairvoyant, Lehrer's (1990: 163–164) Truetemp case, and Plantinga's (1993: 199) case of the epistemically serendipitous brain lesion.

[9] Ayers (1991) suggests that super-blindsight involves knowing without knowing how you know: in his terms, it's a case of secondary knowledge without primary knowledge.

The Metacognitive Condition: Necessarily, perception justifies belief about the external world if and only if it is metacognitively conscious.

To decide the issue, we need to ask whether perception justifies belief when phenomenal consciousness and metacognitive consciousness come apart. As before, if there are no such cases, then we don't have a rival proposal. So we can assume that phenomenal consciousness comes apart from metacognitive consciousness. I'll now use this assumption in arguing that metacognitive consciousness is neither necessary nor sufficient for perception to justify beliefs about the external world.

I'll begin by arguing that metacognitive consciousness is not necessary for perception to justify beliefs about the external world. Human infants and non-human animals can acquire knowledge about the external world on the basis of perceptual experience without knowing how they know. For example, Alison Gopnik (1993) reports that three-year-old children can reliably say what's inside a drawer, although they cannot reliably say whether they know this by perception, inference, or testimony. She argues that this reflects more general difficulties that three-year-olds have in understanding concepts of mental states. And yet surely these children can form justified beliefs on the basis of perceptual experience without forming higher-order beliefs about the perceptual experiences on which their beliefs are based. If so, then metacognitive consciousness is not necessary for perception to justify beliefs about the external world.

A similar point holds for human adults too, since we often know things without knowing how we know them. As David Lewis says, "We know the name that goes with the face, or the sex of the chicken, by relying on subtle visual clues, without knowing what those clues may be" (1996: 551). In these cases, we form beliefs on the basis of visual experience, although we don't have metacognitive awareness of the aspects of visual experience on which our first-order beliefs are based. Again, this shows that metacognitive consciousness is not necessary for perception to justify beliefs about the external world.[10]

I'll now argue that metacognitive consciousness is not sufficient for perception to justify beliefs about the external world. To illustrate the conceptual possibility of metacognitive consciousness without phenomenal consciousness, Block gives the example of *super-duper-blindsight*:

---

[10] These cases are compatible with the luminosity of epistemic justification, since we're always in a position to know the justifying reasons for our beliefs even if we're not always capable of taking advantage of our epistemic position.

A super-duper-blindsighter whose blindsight is every bit as good, functionally speaking, as his sight. In the case of the super-duper-blindsighter, the only difference between vision in the blind and sighted fields, functionally speaking, is that the quasi-zombie himself regards them differently. (1995: 246 n. 16)

In super-blindsight, the subject is disposed to form beliefs about the blind field on the basis of nonphenomenal information without mediation by inference. In super-duper-blindsight, in contrast, the subject is also disposed to form higher-order beliefs about the nonphenomenal information on which these first-order beliefs are based. So, for example, when the subject believes that there's an 'X' in the blind field on the basis of vision, he also believes that his visual system represents that there's an 'X' in the blind field. These visual states are not only access conscious, but also metacognitively conscious in the sense that they serve as the basis for higher-order beliefs formed without inferential mediation.

Does super-duper-blindsight justify beliefs about the blind field? Again, surely not, since there is no relevant difference between super-blindsight and super-duper-blindsight. The only difference is that the super-duper-blindsighter is reliable not only about the objects in his blind field, but also about his visual representations of those objects. As we've seen, however, the presence of a reliable doxastic disposition is not sufficient for justification. If a reliable first-order doxastic disposition is not sufficient to justify first-order beliefs about the external world, then why should adding a reliable second-order doxastic disposition be sufficient to justify higher-order beliefs about the internal world? Intuitively, the super-duper-blindsighter is no more justified in forming higher-order beliefs about subcortical vision than the super-blindsighter is justified in forming beliefs about the blind field on the basis of subcortical vision. And we cannot turn unjustified beliefs into justified beliefs just by adding more unjustified beliefs!

As Block notes, the super-duper-blindsighter is not a functional zombie. Even a super-duper-blindsighter knows the difference between phenomenal and nonphenomenal vision. There is a functional difference between these two kinds of vision because the super-duper-blindsighter regards them differently. If we take one step further, and imagine that these two kinds of vision play exactly the same functional role in metacognition, then we are imagining a *partial functional zombie*. This is a creature that falsely believes that his visual representations are phenomenally conscious even when they are not.

Does unconscious perceptual information justify beliefs about the blind field in the partial functional zombie? Again, the answer is no, since there is no relevant difference between the partial functional zombie and super-duper-blindsighter. The only difference is that the super-duper-blindsighter is disposed to believe *truly* that his beliefs about the blind field are based on phenomenally unconscious vision, whereas the partial functional zombie is disposed to believe *falsely* that his beliefs about the blind field are based on phenomenally conscious vision. But this makes no justificatory difference to the status of his beliefs about the blind field. We cannot turn unjustified beliefs into justified beliefs by adding more unjustified false beliefs, rather than more unjustified true beliefs!

Now for the final step in the argument. There is no relevant difference between the partial functional zombie and the total functional zombie. The only difference is that the partial functional zombie has some preserved phenomenal vision, whereas the total functional zombie has none. But if nonphenomenal vision cannot justify beliefs when restricted to one region of the visual field, then it cannot do so when it encompasses the whole visual field. After all, it's hard to see how the presence or absence of phenomenal vision elsewhere makes any justificational difference. If you doubt this, we can repeat the whole argument using cases of bilateral blindsight that leave no phenomenal vision intact.

I conclude that the epistemic role of phenomenal consciousness cannot be replaced by any functional criterion defined in causal terms. A functional zombie has unconscious perceptual states that exactly duplicate the causal role of our conscious perceptual experiences, but they do not thereby provide any justification to form beliefs about the world. The causal role of perceptual experience can be mirrored in a functional zombie, but its epistemic role cannot be mirrored in the same way. Phenomenal consciousness is necessary for perception to justify beliefs about the external world.

3.3. Presentational Force

The Phenomenal Condition says that phenomenal character is both necessary and sufficient for perception to justify beliefs about the external world. We need both directions of the biconditional to explain why justification is present in conscious sight and yet absent in blindsight. So far, I've been primarily concerned to argue that phenomenal character is necessary for perception to justify beliefs about the external world. In this section, I'll argue that phenomenal character is sufficient for perception to justify beliefs about the external world. More precisely, I'll argue for *the phenomenal sufficiency thesis*, which says that every perceptual experience provides immediate, defeasible justification for believing propositions about the external world in virtue of its phenomenal character alone.

My argument for the phenomenal sufficiency thesis assumes *representationalism*, the thesis that the phenomenal character of experience is a kind of mental representation (see section 2.1). On the qualia theory, the phenomenal sufficiency thesis is much harder to sustain. If perceptual experience is just a matter of instantiating qualia, then it cannot plausibly justify beliefs about the external world in virtue of its phenomenal character alone. To explain how perceptual experience justifies beliefs about the external world, we would need to invoke the causal relations to the external world that determine its representational content. Otherwise, there would be no nonarbitrary answer to the question why perceptual experience justifies believing some contents about the external world, rather than others.

If representationalism is true, however, there is a nonarbitrary connection between the phenomenal character of perceptual experience and the beliefs it justifies about the external world. This is because the phenomenal character of perceptual experience *just is* a way of representing the external world. Moreover, it is in virtue of representing that the external world is a certain way that perceptual experience justifies believing that it is that way. Hence, perceptual experience can plausibly justify belief about the external world in virtue of its phenomenal character alone.

Now, representationalism cannot explain the distinctive epistemic role of perceptual experience all by itself. After all, representationalism is a global thesis: it implies that all experiences have representational contents. And yet not all experiences justify believing their representational contents. Hence, an explanatory task remains. What explains why perceptual experience plays its distinctive epistemic role in justifying beliefs about the external world without standing in need of justification? My answer is that perceptual experience has a distinctive kind of phenomenal character that sets it apart from other experiences with the same content. More specifically, the phenomenal character of perceptual experience is a way of representing its content with *presentational force*. Moreover, it is because perceptual experience represents its content with presentational force that it plays its distinctive epistemic role in justifying beliefs without standing in need of justification.[11]

Here is the outline of my argument for the phenomenal sufficiency thesis:

(1) *Representationalism about Perceptual Experience*: Every perceptual experience has phenomenal character that is identical with the property of representing some content with presentational force.

---

[11] On the presentational force of perceptual experience, see Heck (2000: 508–511), Huemer (2001: 77–79), Pryor (2004: 357), Chudnoff (2013: 32–40), Bengson (2015: 10–19) and Siegel and Silins (2015: 790–793). I'm inclined to agree with Morrison (2016) and Munton (2016) that presentational force comes in degrees, which determine the degree of justification provided by perceptual experience.

(2) *The Content Principle*: Every experience that represents that *p* with presentational force thereby provides immediate, defeasible justification to believe that *p*.[12] Therefore,

(3) *The Phenomenal Sufficiency Thesis*: Every perceptual experience provides immediate, defeasible justification to believe some content in virtue of its phenomenal character alone.

The first premise captures the distinctive phenomenal character of perceptual experience. What sets the phenomenal character of perceptual experience apart from other experiences with the same content is that it represents its content with presentational force. Meanwhile, the second premise explains why perceptual experience plays its distinctive epistemic role in justifying beliefs without standing in need of justification. Perceptual experience plays its distinctive epistemic role because it represents its contents with presentational force.

I'll motivate the first premise by rebutting an objection to representationalism. The objection is that it seems possible that two experiences can have exactly the same representational content while nevertheless differing in their overall phenomenal character. Consider, for example, the phenomenal contrast between seeing that *p* and merely visualizing that *p*. There is a phenomenal difference between seeing and visualizing even if their representational contents are exactly the same.

One response is that there is always some difference in the representational contents of seeing and visualizing. For example, the contents of visual perception are usually much richer and more determinate than the contents of visual imagination. In David Hume's terminology, they have more "force and vivacity." The problem is that this is just a contingent truth about human psychology. We can therefore consider possible scenarios in which the contents of visual experience are impoverished or in which our powers of visual imagination are enriched. In such cases, we can visually imagine scenes with as much richness and determinacy as we can visually perceive them. Nevertheless, the phenomenal contrast between perceptual experience and imaginative experience remains.

My own response appeals to the distinction between *pure* and *impure* forms of representationalism. Pure representationalism says that every difference in the phenomenal character of experience is a difference in representational content. The phenomenal contrast between seeing and visualizing therefore presents an apparent counterexample to pure representationalism. Impure

---

[12] The content principle resembles Pryor's (2000) version of phenomenal dogmatism and Huemer's (2001) principle of phenomenal conservatism. See chapter 12 for a comparison between my view and phenomenal conservatism.

representationalism, in contrast, allows that the phenomenal difference between seeing and visualizing can be explained as a difference in representational force, rather than representational content. On this view, perceptual experience is set apart from perceptual imagination by its distinctive phenomenal force.

What is the distinctive phenomenal force of perceptual experience? One answer is that perceptual experience has *assertive force*: it represents its contents as being true. When you have a perceptual experience with the content that *p*, it thereby seems true that *p*. In contrast, when you have an imaginative experience with the content that *p*, it doesn't thereby seem true that *p*, but merely seems possible that *p*. Moreover, this phenomenal difference between perceptual experience and perceptual imagination goes some way toward explaining their different epistemic roles. Perceptual experience justifies believing its contents only because it represents its contents as true. In contrast, imaginative experience doesn't justify believing its contents precisely because it doesn't represent its contents as true.[13]

The appeal to assertive force doesn't go quite far enough, since it fails to distinguish perceptual experience from cognitive experience. After all, judgments represent their contents with assertive force: if you judge that *p*, it thereby seems true to you that *p*. Even so, there is a phenomenal difference between seeing that *p* and merely judging that *p*. Typically, the contents of visual experience are much richer than the contents of judgment, but this is just another contingent truth about human psychology. As before, we can consider possible scenarios in which the contents of visual experience are impoverished or in which our cognitive powers are enriched. In such cases, we can make judgments that are just as rich and fine-grained as our perceptual experiences. Nevertheless, the phenomenal contrast between perceptual experience and cognitive experience remains.[14]

I suggest that what sets perceptual experience apart from the cognitive experience of judgment is that it represents its contents with *presentational force*. To a first approximation, we can say that presentational force is the kind of phenomenal character you have when it seems to you that you're presented with the very things that make your experience true. James Pryor articulates a very similar idea in the following passage:

---

[13] Phenomenal and etiological classifications of experience can crosscut each other: for example, an experience produced by imagination could have exactly the same phenomenal character as a veridical perception. The content principle implies that the epistemic role of experience is determined by its phenomenal character, rather than its etiology. In Descartes's dreaming scenario, for instance, it's plausible that our justifying evidence is the same whether we are perceiving or merely dreaming so long as the phenomenal character of experience is exactly the same.

[14] Huemer (2001), Chudnoff (2013), Bengson (2015), and Koksvik (2017) argue that some cognitive experiences—namely, intuitions—have the same kind of presentational force and epistemic role as perceptual experience. I argue against this view in chapter 12.

> I think there's a distinctive phenomenology: the feeling of seeming to as-
> certain that a given proposition is true. This is present when the way a
> mental episode represents its content makes it feel as though, by enjoying
> that episode, you can thereby just tell that content obtains. . . . When you
> have a perceptual experience of your hands, that experience makes it feel
> as though you can just see that hands are present. It feels as though hands
> are being shown or revealed to you. (2004: 357)

Pryor says that when you have a perceptual experience that represents that you
have hands, it seems to you not only that you have hands, but also that you are
presented with the things that *make* it true that you have hands. As he puts the
point, it seems as if you just see that hands are present. Moreover, this is how
it seems to you whether you're genuinely seeing that you have hands or merely
suffering a visual illusion or hallucination.

Although Pryor is gesturing toward an important phenomenon here, I think
there is a serious problem with the way he articulates it. We cannot explain the
distinctive phenomenal character of perceptual experience in terms of a 'that'-
clause that articulates the content of how things seem to you when you have the
experience. This is because you might judge such contents to be true without
currently having any visual experience at all. If you're in the grip of Anton's syndrome, for example, you might sincerely judge that you can see your hands even
if you're completely blind. In that case, it seems to you that you can just see that
hands are present, since that's what you sincerely judge to be true, but you're
not thereby enjoying the distinctive phenomenal character of visual experience.

Impure representationalism allows that some phenomenal differences are
differences in representational force, rather than differences in representational
content. These differences cannot always be defined by stating a 'that'-clause
that specifies how things seem when you have the experience. Instead, they are
best defined ostensively by giving examples. Presentational force is a kind of
phenomenal character that we know ostensively by introspecting perceptual experience and contrasting it with other experiences. It is the kind of phenomenal
character that your experience has when you perceive things, and when you
hallucinate them, but not when you merely visualize or make judgments about
things. To rephrase what Pryor says, it is the kind of phenomenal character that
your experience has *when* you can just see that hands are present. What impure
representationalism says is that this phenomenal character is a distinctive way
of representing contents about the external world. That is the first premise in
my argument for the phenomenal sufficiency thesis.

The motivation for the second premise is that the distinctive phenomenal character of perceptual experience explains its distinctive epistemic role.
Perceptual experience justifies beliefs about the external world without standing

in need of any further justification: in that sense, it is a justificational "regress-stopper." In contrast, imaginative experience doesn't justify believing its content because it doesn't represent its content with assertive force. Meanwhile, the cognitive experience of judgment represents its content with assertive force, but it cannot play the same epistemic role as perceptual experience. Judgments cannot justify other beliefs and judgments without standing in need of justification themselves. We can always ask what justifies you in making a judgment. Moreover, your judgments cannot justify other beliefs and judgments unless they are justified themselves. In the case of perceptual experience, however, the question of justification simply doesn't arise. This is because perceptual experience, unlike cognitive experience, represents its contents with presentational force. Presentational force explains why perception has a distinctive epistemic role that sets it apart from imaginative and cognitive experience.

This view also provides the resources for answering what has become known as the "Sellarsian dilemma." Laurence BonJour argues, following Wilfrid Sellars, that nothing can justify belief without standing in need of justification. He writes:

> It is one and the same feature of a cognitive state, namely, its assertive or at least representational content, which both enables it to confer justification on other states and also creates the need for it to be itself justified—thus making it impossible in principle to separate these two aspects. (1985: 78)

The argument takes the form of a dilemma. Either perceptual experience has representational content or it doesn't. The first horn: if it has no representational content, then it cannot justify beliefs about the external world, since there is no nonarbitrary connection between the perceptual experience itself and the beliefs it is supposed to justify. The second horn: if perceptual experience does have representational content, then it can justify belief, but only insofar as it is justified by other beliefs or experiences. Either way, perceptual experience cannot justify belief without standing in need of justification.

The first horn of the dilemma is implicit in Davidson's (1986: 310) argument that nothing can justify a belief except another belief. His argument is that only beliefs can justify other beliefs by assertively representing contents that stand in appropriate logical or probabilistic relations to the contents of the beliefs they justify. If perceptual experience is just a matter of having sensations with no representational content at all, then it cannot justify beliefs about the external world in virtue of its phenomenal character alone. Instead, your justification depends on background evidence that your sensations are reliably caused by facts in the external world. On this view, however, your beliefs about the external world are justified by evidence about the reliability of your own perceptual experience, and not by the phenomenal character of your perceptual experience alone.

The problem with Davidson's argument is that perceptual experience is not just a matter of having sensations. According to representationalism, the phenomenal character of perceptual experience is a way of representing contents about the external world. Moreover, perceptual experience represents its content with assertive force. It can therefore justify beliefs by assertively representing contents that stand in appropriate logical or probabilistic relations to the contents of the beliefs it justifies. On this view, there is a nonarbitrary connection between the phenomenal character of perceptual experience and the beliefs it justifies about the external world. Hence, perceptual experience can justify beliefs about the external world in virtue of its phenomenal character alone.

This brings us to the second horn of the dilemma. If perceptual experience is like belief in representing its contents with assertive force, then how can it be unlike belief in its capacity to justify beliefs without standing in need of any further justification? The challenge here is to explain what makes perceptual experience different from belief in virtue of which it plays its distinctive epistemic role. My answer is that perceptual experience is like belief in representing its contents with assertive force, but it is unlike belief in representing its contents with presentational force. Moreover, it is in virtue of representing its contents with presentational force that perceptual experience has the capacity to justify believing those contents without standing in need of any further justification.

In summary, the presentational force of perceptual experience explains both its distinctive phenomenal character and its distinctive epistemic role. The presentational force of perceptual experience explains why it is phenomenally different from imaginative and cognitive experiences with the same content. It also explains why perceptual experience plays a different epistemic role from imaginative and cognitive experiences with the same content. This is because perceptual experience plays its epistemic role in justifying belief in virtue of its phenomenal character alone.

This argument for the phenomenal sufficiency thesis is plausible, but it is not conclusive. Some philosophers will resist the argument by challenging the content principle. On some views, presentational force is necessary but not sufficient for perceptual experience to play its distinctive epistemic role. Perhaps the absence of presentational force explains why cognitive and imaginative experiences cannot play the same epistemic role as perceptual experience. Even so, presentational force may not be sufficient to explain why perceptual experience plays its epistemic role unless it also satisfies further conditions, which fail to supervene on its phenomenal character. According to radical externalism, the content principle is false: perceptual experience justifies believing its content only if it is reliable, or has the right kind of etiology, or serves as a basis for perceptual knowledge.

I haven't argued directly for the content principle in this section. In the next section, however, I'll argue that radical externalism makes implausible predictions about skeptical scenarios precisely because it rejects the content principle. Moreover, I'll bolster this argument in chapter 7 by drawing out more implausible consequences of radical externalism. These arguments provide indirect support for the content principle and thereby shore up my argument for the phenomenal sufficiency thesis in this section.[15]

3.4. Skeptical Scenarios

One dimension of the debate between internalism and externalism in the epistemology of perception concerns the justifying role of phenomenal character. I'll have much more to say in due course about how to understand this debate. For current purposes, though, we can define *phenomenal internalism* as the view that perceptual experience justifies belief solely in virtue of its phenomenal character, while *phenomenal externalism* is the view that perceptual experience justifies belief at least partly in virtue of externalist facts, which don't supervene on its phenomenal character. So defined, the debate between phenomenal internalism and externalism concerns whether the justifying role of perceptual experience supervenes on its phenomenal character in the following sense:

Phenomenal Internalism: Necessarily, there can be no difference in which propositions you have defeasible, noninferential justification to believe on the basis of perceptual experience without some difference in its phenomenal character.

We can further distinguish between *radical* and *moderate* versions of phenomenal externalism. Moderate externalism says that externalist facts about perceptual experience can make a justificational difference only by affecting its representational content, whereas radical externalism allows that externalist facts can make a justificational difference between perceptual experiences with exactly the same representational content. Therefore, moderate and radical

---

[15] Also, I haven't addressed the "tainted sources" objection to the content principle proposed by Markie (2005), Siegel (2012), McGrath (2013), and Teng (2018). For the record, I agree with the responses given by Tucker (2010: 538–540), Huemer (2013: 747–748), and Pautz (forthcoming).

externalism disagree about whether the content principle is true. I'll argue against radical externalism in this section, and I'll revisit moderate externalism in the next section.

Radical externalism says the content principle is false: a perceptual experience with the content that p justifies believing that p only if it satisfies further externalist conditions, which fail to supervene on its phenomenal character. This view comes in many different forms, including the following broad categories:

Reliabilism: Necessarily, a perceptual experience with the content that p justifies believing that p only if it reliably indicates that p.[16]

Factivism: Necessarily, a perceptual experience with the content that p justifies believing that p only if you veridically perceive that p.[17]

Etiologism: Necessarily, a perceptual experience with the content that p justifies believing that p only if it has the right kind of etiology.[18]

Different forms of radical externalism impose different external conditions on the so-called "good case" in which a perceptual experience with the representational content that p justifies believing that p. What all forms of radical externalism have in common is that there is some justificatory difference between the good case and the bad case, despite the fact that they are phenomenally identical. This is because the justifying role of perceptual experience depends on the satisfaction of certain externalist conditions, which obtain only in the good case.

On the simplest versions of radical externalism, you have justification for belief only in the good case. On more complex versions, you have justification for belief in both cases, but you have more justification in the good case than the bad case, which means that you have justification to believe with more confidence in the good case than the bad case. Either way, there are doxastic attitudes that you have justification to hold in the good case but not in the bad case. To simplify the discussion, I'll ignore this complication in what follows.

---

[16] Proponents of reliabilism include Goldman (1979), Sosa (1991), Burge (2003), Bergmann (2006), and Lyons (2009), although they disagree among themselves about the kind of reliability that is necessary for perceptual justification.

[17] Proponents of factivism include McDowell (1995), Williamson (2000), Roessler (2009), Littlejohn (2009), Pritchard (2012), and Schellenberg (2013). Some of these authors allow that you have some degree of justification in the bad case, but more in the good case.

[18] Proponents of etiologism include Siegel (2012), McGrath (2013), and Teng (2018). They impose etiological conditions on perceptual justification designed to rule out cases of cognitive penetration of experience by unjustified beliefs, desires, and so on. See Siegel (2017) for the most recent development of this view.

Here is a general form of argument against radical externalism:

(1) Subjects in the bad case form the same beliefs as subjects in the good case.
(2) If perceptual experience doesn't provide equal justification for belief in the good case and the bad case, then subjects in the bad case are less rational than subjects in the good case insofar as they form the same beliefs as subjects in the good case.
(3) Subjects in the bad case are no less rational than subjects in the good case. Therefore,
(4) Perceptual experience provides equal justification for belief in the good case and the bad case.

This argument makes explicit the reasoning that lies behind Stewart Cohen's (1984) new evil demon problem for reliabilism. Consider your phenomenal duplicate who is systematically deceived by an evil demon. Your phenomenal duplicate holds many of the same beliefs and seems no less rationally justified than you are. The upshot is that your perceptual experience provides equal justification for beliefs about the external world whether or not it represents the external world in a reliable way. Hence, reliability is not necessary for justification.

Cases of perceptual illusion and hallucination raise similar problems for factivism. Suppose that Macbeth undergoes a "seamless transition" from the good case of seeing that there is a dagger before him to the bad case of merely hallucinating that there is a dagger before him. The transition is seamless in the sense that Macbeth cannot know by introspection when it is occurring and it makes no relevant impact on his doxastic attitudes—in particular, he continues to believe that there is dagger before him with the same high level of confidence throughout. Factivism makes the implausible prediction that Macbeth's belief is justified at the start of this transition but unjustified by the end, since he has more justification for his belief in the good case than the bad case. What is hard to swallow is the idea that rationality requires Macbeth to abandon his belief or to reduce his confidence in the course of this transition. Indeed, this seems rationally prohibited: anyone who reduces her confidence in this way would be grossly irrational.[19]

We can raise exactly the same problem for etiologism by considering seamless transitions between good and bad etiologies. To adapt a case from Susanna Siegel (2012), suppose Jill undergoes a seamless transition from the good case

[19] We can make the transition extremely gradual to block the objection that Macbeth's belief is not safe from error at the start of the transition. Alternatively, we can shift from intrasubjective to intersubjective comparisons: the seamless transitions are useful only because they make the judgment of equal rationality so compelling.

of seeing that Jack is angry to the bad case in which her experience is not causally responsive to the external facts, but rather to her own antecedent beliefs. The transition is seamless in the sense that Jill cannot know by introspection when the transition is occurring and it makes no relevant impact on her beliefs. Etiologism makes the implausible prediction that Jill's belief that Jack is angry is justified at the start of the transition, but unjustified by the end. Again, what seems hard to swallow is the idea that rationality requires Jill either to abandon her belief or to reduce her confidence in the course of the transition. As before, this seems grossly irrational.[20]

Proponents of radical externalism cannot block this argument by rejecting the first premise. It is true that subjects in the bad case cannot form de re beliefs about objects when they are merely hallucinating. I'll address this point in section 3.5. All we need for current purposes is that there is significant overlap between the contents of the beliefs formed in the good case and the bad case. At a minimum, subjects in the good case and the bad case are guaranteed to share the phenomenal contents of their beliefs and experiences, which supervene on phenomenal character alone. Radical externalism says that subjects in the good case have more justification for some of these beliefs than subjects in the bad case. This is because externalist facts about perceptual experience can impact on its justifying role without impacting on its representational content at all.

The second premise should also be common ground in the debate between phenomenal internalism and externalism. We encountered the same idea in section 3.1. Epistemic rationality is a matter of proportioning your beliefs to the evidence in your possession. If your justifying evidence for a proposition is stronger in the good case than the bad case, then you should be more confident in the good case than the bad case. Otherwise, you violate the rational requirement to proportion your beliefs to the evidence.

Proponents of radical externalism often reject the third premise by appealing to a distinction between justification and blamelessness. The suggestion is that although your beliefs are unjustified in the bad case, you nevertheless have an excuse for holding them. Since you have an excuse, you cannot be blamed for holding these beliefs without adequate justification. In the bad case, you are blameless, but irrational or unjustified.[21]

I agree that blamelessness is not sufficient for justification by standards of rationality. After all, victims of brainwashing, drugs, or mental illness sometimes form unjustified beliefs through no fault of their own. Consider, for example, patients with Capgras delusion who believe that their spouse has been

---

[20] See Pautz (forthcoming) for this objection to Siegel's etiologism.

[21] Williamson (2007), Littlejohn (2009), and Pritchard (2012) give various different versions of this response.

replaced by an imposter. Although such beliefs are clearly unjustified, we do not blame these patients because they are delusional. Intuitively, however, there is a rational difference between perceptual illusions on the one hand and cognitive delusions on the other. Our evaluations of rationality are sensitive to the distinction between perceptual malfunction and cognitive malfunction. Both kinds of malfunction are blameless, but the former is consistent with rationality, whereas the latter is not. We obscure this distinction insofar as we maintain that both are examples of blameless irrationality.

Following James Pryor (2001: 117), we can illustrate the point by contrasting two different versions of the bad case. In "the good-bad case," subjects form beliefs that conform to the contents of their experiences, although their experiences are systematically illusory. In "the bad-bad case," in contrast, subjects form beliefs in conflict with the contents of their illusory experiences owing to the influence of some cognitive delusion. Subjects in both cases are blameless, but those in the good-bad case seem justified, whereas those in the bad-bad case seem unjustified. The challenge for radical externalism is to explain the epistemic difference between subjects in the bad case without conceding that some of them hold justified beliefs. Let's call this "the reverse new evil demon problem."

As far as I can see, the only way to solve the problem in full generality is to accept that there is some epistemic status that supervenes on phenomenal character alone. To deny that this epistemic status is called 'justification' would be a purely terminological maneuver. So this option seems tantamount to accepting phenomenal internalism. The alternative is to deny that there is any epistemic status that supervenes on phenomenal character alone. But this kind of view cannot adequately solve the reverse new evil demon problem. I'll illustrate this point in connection with two recently proposed solutions.

Timothy Williamson (forthcoming) proposes to solve the new evil demon problem by drawing a distinction between *complying* with a norm and merely being *disposed* to comply with a norm. The claim is that while subjects in the bad case don't comply with norms of rationality, they are generally disposed to comply with such norms, and they do what subjects with those general dispositions would do when they are in the bad case. As a result, they have a much better excuse than delusional subjects who lack any general disposition to comply with rational norms at all. The basic idea is that your beliefs in the bad case are excusable when they result from the exercise of general dispositions that would yield justified beliefs in the good case. As Williamson writes, "the general dispositions of the brain in the vat remain truth-tracking and knowledge-producing ones, we may suppose, although the unfavorable circumstances block those manifestations."

For illustration, Williamson asks us to imagine Connie, a generally competent mathematician who believes contradictions in the presence of a brain-scrambling machine. The effect of this machine is not to destroy her mathematical reasoning abilities, but rather to serve as a distorting influence that temporarily impairs her exercise of those abilities. Connie is generally disposed to form justified beliefs about mathematics, and she believes what a person with those general dispositions would believe in the presence of a brain-scrambling machine. Even so, Connie is not justified in believing contradictions, but she is blameless because the influence of the brain-scrambling machine gives her an excuse.

Williamson's proposal faces the reverse evil demon problem. Compare two versions of the bad case: the subject in the good-bad case forms beliefs in conformity with her experiences, while the subject in the bad-bad case forms beliefs in contradiction with her experiences owing to the temporary operation of a brain-scrambling machine. Both are excusable by Williamson's lights because both are generally disposed to form justified beliefs and both believe what someone with those general dispositions would believe in their current circumstances. And yet neither is justified, by Williamson's lights, since both are victims of deception. The problem is that this fails to explain the obvious rational difference between these subjects—namely, that only one of them forms beliefs in conformity with her experience.

Maria Lasonen-Aarnio (forthcoming b) proposes to solve the new evil demon problem by drawing a distinction between *rationality* and *reasonableness*. Rationality or justification is a matter of achieving a certain kind of *success*: namely, proportioning your beliefs to the evidence. Reasonableness, in contrast, is a matter of exercising a certain kind of *competence*: namely, a general disposition to proportion your beliefs to the evidence. Lasonen-Aarnio endorses a knowledge-first conception of evidence, according to which your evidence supports believing that p only if you know that p. On this view, all rational beliefs are knowledge, but false beliefs can be reasonable when they are formed by exercising a competence to acquire knowledge in bad circumstances.

According to Lasonen-Aarnio, the new evil demon problem is an example of epistemic competence without success. The demon doesn't destroy your competence to acquire knowledge altogether, but merely puts you in circumstances that prevent you from exercising your competence successfully. If you're deceived by an evil demon, then your beliefs are reasonable, but they are not rational, or justified, or supported by your evidence.

Lasonen-Aarnio's proposal does better than Williamson's in dealing with the reverse new evil demon problem. The subject in the good-bad case who forms beliefs in conformity with her illusory experiences is reasonable because she exercises a competence to acquire knowledge, though in bad circumstances. In contrast, the subject in the bad-bad case who forms beliefs in conflict with her illusory experiences is unreasonable because she fails to exercise any competence to acquire knowledge. Hence, the epistemic difference between the good-bad case and the bad-bad case can be explained in terms of reasonable-ness, rather than rationality, justification, or evidence.

Even so, the reverse new evil demon problem arises here too. This is because the competence to acquire knowledge is an *extrinsic* disposition: it requires being anchored to a normal environment. Not all subjects in the bad case are anchored to a normal environment. For example, we can imagine victims of the evil demon who are deceived permanently, rather than temporarily, and who are not even members of species that evolved in normal environments. A more extreme ex-ample is the Bolztmann brain, which arises by random fluctuations from a state of thermodynamic equilibrium. Lasonen-Aarnio is forced to deny that these subjects have reasonable beliefs, since they exercise no competence to acquire knowledge. Instead, she explains our tendency to think otherwise as an error that arises from confusing these subjects with those anchored to normal environments.

I think we should resist this error theory. Boltzmann brains can be per-fect intrinsic duplicates of your brain. Assuming that phenomenal character supervenes on intrinsic properties of the brain, it follows that any intrinsic duplicate is a phenomenal duplicate. Given that representationalism is true, it follows that your phenomenal duplicates have experiences with the same phe-nomenal contents as your own. Given the content principle, it follows that your phenomenal duplicates have defeasible, noninferential justification to believe the same phenomenal contents as you do on the basis of experience. So we can argue against the error theory using assumptions motivated in the first two chapters of this book.

3.5. Duplication Scenarios

In the previous section, I argued that the new evil demon problem cannot be solved without endorsing phenomenal internalism. In this section, I'll de-fend phenomenal internalism against an objection that appeals to duplication scenarios. The objection is that externalist facts about your perceptual relations to the external world can affect which propositions you have justification to believe without making any phenomenal difference. This generates apparent counterexamples in which phenomenal duplicates have justification to believe different propositions because they stand in different perceptual relations to the external world. I'll focus on de re propositions about objects, although the gen-eral form of argument applies to externalist contents more generally.[22]

---

[22] Williamson (2007) argues against phenomenal internalism by adapting the Twin Earth ex-ample from Putnam (1975) and Burge (1982). The following example from Davies (1997) has exactly the same structure: in effect, it is a Twin Earth example for de re belief.

A *de re proposition* is a proposition about an object that is true or false of that object in every possible world in which the object exists. Believing de re propositions about an object requires not only that the object exists, but also that it stands in some appropriate relation—such as a perceptual relation—to the believing subject. This relation is what guarantees that her belief is about that object, rather than another object, or none at all. De re beliefs can be based not only on perception, but also memory, testimony, and perhaps other ways besides. In this section, however, I'll focus exclusively on de re beliefs based on perception.

Perception enables me to believe de re propositions about the objects that I currently perceive. It doesn't enable me to believe de re propositions about numerically distinct but qualitatively identical objects that I'm not currently perceiving. Here is an example from Martin Davies to illustrate the point:

> If I look at an apple, Fido, and think, "That apple is rotten," and you look at a numerically distinct but qualitatively indistinguishable apple, Fifi, and think, "That apple is rotten," then—be we ever so similar internally—our beliefs have different contents in virtue of our being related to different apples. My belief, concerning Fido, to the effect that it is rotten, is a belief whose correctness depends upon how things are with Fido: whether Fido is indeed a rotten apple. Your belief, in contrast, is one whose correctness is indifferent to how things are with Fido, but depends instead upon how things are with Fifi. In that sense, the contents of our beliefs are object-involving. (1997: 313–314)

In this example, you and I are intrinsic duplicates perceiving numerically distinct but qualitatively identical apples—namely, Fido and Fifi. Since we're intrinsic duplicates, it seems plausible that we're phenomenal duplicates too. It visually seems to each of us that there is a rotten apple ahead. Moreover, each of us believes this general proposition. In addition, however, each of us believes a de re proposition about the apple we're perceiving to the effect that it is rotten. I believe a de re proposition about Fido, whereas you believe a de re proposition about Fifi, and not vice versa. Since we're both fully rational, each of us believes everything that we have justification to believe. It follows that we don't have justification to believe the same propositions on the basis of perceptual experience, despite the fact that we are phenomenal duplicates. This is a counterexample to phenomenal internalism.

Here is a summary of the duplication argument against phenomenal internalism:

(1) You and I are phenomenal duplicates who see distinct objects.

(2) I believe the de re proposition that Fido is rotten, whereas you believe the de re proposition that Fifi is rotten, and not vice versa.

(3) You and I are fully rational, so each of us believes every proposition that we have justification to believe on the basis of perceptual experience.

(4) Therefore, phenomenal internalism is false: you and I are phenomenal duplicates, but we have justification to believe different propositions on the basis of perceptual experience.

In Smithies (2016b), I explored the consequences of accepting this conclusion. I argued that moderate externalism is a stable compromise between phenomenal internalism and the more radical forms of externalism discussed in section 3.4.

Moderate externalism says that externalist facts can affect the justifying role of perceptual experience, but only insofar as they impact on its representational content. They make no independent epistemic contribution of the kind that radical externalism claims. Hence, moderate externalism is consistent with the content principle, which says that if your experience represents that p with presentational force, then you thereby have justification to believe that p. On this view, perceptual experience provides justification to believe its phenomenal contents in virtue of its phenomenal character alone, while also providing justification to believe its externalist contents in virtue of its relations to the external world. Therefore, moderate externalism preserves a fundamental role for the phenomenal character of perceptual experience, while also extending a derivative role to externalist facts.

While this fallback position is worth exploring, and while it is broadly congenial to the main conclusions of this book, I'm now inclined to think that phenomenal internalism can be defended against the duplication argument. In the rest of this section, I'll consider three different strategies for defending phenomenal internalism. My own strategy is to accept the first two premises of the argument and to reject the third premise instead.

One strategy is to reject the first premise in the duplication argument by denying that all intrinsic duplicates are phenomenal duplicates. According to *the relational view* of experience, the phenomenal character of experience in cases of veridical perception consists in the perceptual relation that holds between the subject and the external world.[23] On this view, the phenomenal character of experience depends not just on intrinsic properties of the subject but on their extrinsic relations to the external world. Intrinsic duplicates can differ

---

[23] This view is sometimes called "naive realism." Aside from Campbell (2002), other proponents include Martin (2004) and Brewer (2006).

in phenomenal character if they are perceptually related to distinct objects (or none at all). Moreover, these phenomenal differences explain the corresponding epistemic differences in which de re propositions subjects have justification to believe.

One problem for the relational view of experience is to explain how the transition from perceiving one object to perceiving another, or from perceiving to hallucinating, can be "seamless" in the sense that it cannot be detected through introspection. The standard explanation is that the phenomenal character of experience remains constant throughout the transition. But proponents of the relational view insist that the phenomenal character of experience can change in ways that you're unable to detect. Thus, John Campbell writes:

> It may seem to you that you have kept track of just one thing when in fact you have not. Perhaps one object was substituted for another in the twinkling of an eye. . . . But that does not show that you are in the same conscious state whether or not it is the same object; rather, it shows it may be impossible to tell, simply by having the experience, which sort of experience it is. (2002: 130)

On this view, perceptions of qualitatively identical but numerically distinct objects are indiscriminable by reflection alone, although they differ in their phenomenal character.

This is reminiscent of Michael Martin's (2004) epistemic conception of hallucination, according to which there is no shared phenomenal character in virtue of which hallucinations are indiscriminable from matching veridical perceptions. As Susanna Siegel (2004) argues, however, experiences that differ radically in their phenomenal character may be indiscriminable from the same veridical perceptions because the subject is inattentive, unreflective, or delusional. So the epistemic conception fails to capture the match between perfect hallucinations and veridical perceptions.

Martin replies that perfect hallucinations match veridical perceptions in the sense that they're indiscriminable from those veridical perceptions in an "impersonal" sense that abstracts away from the subject's limited cognitive capacities. Impersonal indiscriminability is most naturally understood in counterfactual terms: if the subject's cognitive capacities were idealized in relevant ways, the subject would be unable to discriminate a perfect hallucination from a corresponding veridical perception by introspection. The problem is that we cannot evaluate the truth of this counterfactual without holding fixed the phenomenal character of the subject's experience. The epistemic conception of hallucination must therefore take epistemic facts about impersonal indiscriminability as primitive, rather than explaining them in counterfactual terms. In contrast, the standard conception of hallucination can explain epistemic facts about impersonal indiscriminability, rather than taking them as primitive. Perfect hallucinations are impersonally indiscriminable from matching veridical perceptions because they have the same phenomenal character. This should be preferable to anyone who wants to ground epistemic justification in phenomenal consciousness.

The second strategy for defending phenomenal internalism is to reject the second premise by denying that phenomenal duplicates who perceive distinct objects thereby believe distinct de re propositions about those objects. In Davies's example, each of us believes the general proposition that there is a rotten apple ahead of us. Our beliefs refer to different apples, so they have different truth-conditions, but they have exactly the same propositional content. What this view denies is that each of us believes a de re proposition about the apple in our own environment. More generally, our beliefs and experiences have phenomenal contents that depend on phenomenal character, but no externalist contents that depend on our relations to the external world. This means that all phenomenal duplicates believe exactly the same propositions. Katalin Farkas (2008a) calls this view "phenomenal intentionality without compromise."[24]

Is there any compelling argument that our beliefs have externalist contents? Many are persuaded by duplication scenarios in which phenomenal duplicates in different environments think thoughts with different truth-conditions. The problem is that Farkas denies that a difference in truth-conditions requires a difference in content, since she holds that content determines truth-conditions only relative to a context. Instead of relying solely on intuitions about duplication scenarios, I suggest it is more productive to consider whether externalist content plays an indispensable explanatory role.

Some philosophers argue that externalist content plays an indispensable role in explaining relational facts about behavior.[25] The general idea is that we need to explain relational facts about my behavior in terms of relational facts about my mental states. For instance, my de re belief that Fido is rotten explains why I throw it in the trash. Opponents must claim that my behavior is explained by the general belief that there is a rotten apple in my environment together with the environmental fact that Fido is in fact the rotten apple in my environment. Arguably, however, we cannot preserve the explanatory power of relational facts about my mental states simply by conjoining intrinsic facts about my mental states with relational facts about my environment. As Timothy Williamson

---

[24] Other proponents of this view include Jackson (2003) and Pitt (2013).
[25] See Burge (1986), Peacocke (1993), and Williamson (2000: ch. 3).

(2000: ch. 3) argues, our behavior is best explained by "prime" conditions that cannot be conjunctively analyzed into internal and external components. Those who reject the second premise in the duplication argument take on the burden of addressing this explanatory argument.

I propose to defend phenomenal internalism by accepting the first two premises of the duplication argument and rejecting the third premise instead. On this view, phenomenal duplicates have justification to believe exactly the same propositions. Nevertheless, they believe different propositions in virtue of their different perceptual relations to the external world. In short, phenomenal duplicates can differ in doxastic justification, but not propositional justification.[26]

Applying this to our duplication example, you and I have justification to believe exactly the same set of propositions, including the de re proposition that Fido is a rotten apple and the de re proposition that Fifi is a rotten apple. Nevertheless, we believe different propositions in this set because of our different perceptual relations to the external world. My experience represents the de re proposition that Fido is rotten, while yours represents the de re proposition that Fifi is rotten, and not vice versa. Unlike you, I cannot believe de re propositions about Fifi because I'm not in perceptual contact with Fifi. Nevertheless, I have justification to believe de re propositions about Fifi, which I cannot use in forming justified beliefs. This is not because of any rational deficiency of mine, but simply because I am not perceptually related to Fifi in the right way.

I'll now defend this proposal against three objections.[27] First, Williamson (2007) argues that it has the implausible consequence that our perceptual experience is always misleading. After all, it implies that my perceptual experience justifies believing many false propositions, including the de re proposition that Fifi is within reach. Intuitively, however, there is nothing misleading about my perceptual experience when I am not suffering from illusions or hallucinations. In reply, my perceptual experience is misleading only when it misrepresents the external world. In such cases, I am in danger of believing the false propositions represented by my perceptual experience. My perceptual experience is not misleading whenever it justifies believing false de re propositions that are not represented in my perceptual experience. After all, I am in no danger of believing these false propositions.

A second objection is that my perceptual experience gives me immediate justification to believe that p only if it represents that p. This is the reverse of the

---

[26] Compare Audi (2001: 32). This is the strategy I endorsed in Smithies (2014: 112) but abandoned in Smithies (2016b) for reasons that I'll explain in what follows.

[27] I'm indebted here to conversations with Alex Byrne, Adam Pautz, and Nico Silins.

content principle, which says that if my perceptual experience represents that p, then it gives me immediate justification to believe that p (see section 3.3). But even if we accept the content principle, why should we accept the reverse? It seems initially plausible because it gives us a principled account of the connection between perceptual experience and the propositions it justifies believing without inference. In reply, however, we can give a principled account of this connection without accepting the reverse content principle. My perceptual experience gives me immediate justification to believe that p only if there is some epistemically possible state of the world in which my perceptual experience represents that p.

A third objection is that this view implies that my experience can justify believing inconsistent propositions, which conflicts with logical and probabilistic constraints on epistemic rationality. For example, I have justification to believe not only that Fido is the only apple within reach, but also that Fifi is the only apple within reach. In reply, however, this result is plausible on independent grounds. Consider Saul Kripke's (1979) puzzle about belief: Pierre believes that London is pretty and also that London is not pretty. The puzzle is to explain why Pierre is rational, despite the fact that he believes inconsistent propositions. David Chalmers (2002b) argues that Pierre is rational because the phenomenal contents of his beliefs are consistent, although their externalist contents are inconsistent. The more general conclusion is that logical and probabilistic constraints on epistemic rationality are best understood as constraints on the phenomenal contents of belief, rather than its externalist contents. My evidence can justify believing inconsistent externalist contents, but it cannot justify believing inconsistent phenomenal contents.

In Smithies (2016b), I argued that this proposal conflicts with a plausible principle linking propositional and doxastic senses of justification:

> *The Linking Principle*: Necessarily, if you are fully rational, and you have sufficient propositional justification to believe that p, then you have a doxastically justified belief that p.

The linking principle is motivated by the consideration that epistemic rationality requires that you proportion your beliefs to your evidence. If your total evidence justifies believing that p, but you don't believe that p on the basis of your evidence, then you're violating this requirement of epistemic rationality. The same consideration figured in my discussion of blindsight (section 3.1) and the new evil demon problem (section 3.4).

The current proposal generates absurd consequences when it is combined with the linking principle. Suppose my total evidence justifies believing de re propositions about Fifi, although I cannot believe these propositions because

I'm not in perceptual contact with Fifi. The linking principle entails that this makes me less than fully rational, which is absurd. My rationality is in no way impugned by the fact that I'm not in perceptual contact with Fifi. After all, rationality doesn't require that I should be omnipresent! If we accept the linking principle, then we must deny that I have justification to believe de re propositions about Fifi.

I now think we can answer this objection by modifying the linking principle in a way that makes it much more plausible:

> *The Modified Linking Principle*: Necessarily, if you are fully rational, you have sufficient propositional justification to believe that *p*, and you adopt some doxastic attitude toward the proposition that *p*, then you have a doxastically justified belief that *p*.

Epistemic rationality requires that you proportion your beliefs to your evidence, but it doesn't require that you are fully opinionated in the sense that you adopt some doxastic attitude toward every single proposition. The requirements of epistemic rationality are conditional in form: if you hold some doxastic attitude toward the proposition that *p*, then your doxastic attitude must be justified by your evidence. These conditional requirements prohibit holding doxastic attitudes that are not justified by your evidence, but they also permit holding no doxastic attitudes at all. I'll now give three examples to motivate this modified version of the linking principle.

Example 1: Clutter Avoidance. When your evidence justifies believing that *p*, it thereby justifies believing that *p* or *q*, that *p* or *q* or *r*, and so on ad infinitum. As Gilbert Harman (1986: 12) notes, however, epistemic rationality doesn't require cluttering up your mind with pragmatically irrelevant disjunctions. Epistemic rationality requires you to believe these disjunctions if you adopt some doxastic attitude toward them. But there is no failure of epistemic rationality involved in failing to hold any doxastic attitude at all. The question whether you should clutter up your mind by adopting some doxastic attitude falls within the province of practical rationality, rather than epistemic rationality.

Example 2: A Priori Justification. It is a priori that nothing is red and green all over. Your justification to believe this proposition doesn't have its source in color experience, but you need color experience in order to believe it at all. As it is often said, your color experience is an *enabling* condition, rather than a *justifying* condition. How can we make sense of this distinction? I suggest that it is best understood as a distinction between psychological conditions for believing propositions and epistemic conditions for having justification to believe propositions. On this view, everyone has justification to believe that nothing is red and green all over, no matter what experiences you have, but you need color experience in order to believe this proposition. If so, then epistemic rationality cannot plausibly require that you believe everything you have justification to believe, since you may not satisfy the relevant psychological conditions. Epistemic rationality doesn't require color experience!

Example 3: Duplication Cases. The distinction between enabling conditions and justifying conditions can be usefully extended to the a posteriori domain. Consider the Fido and Fifi example: you cannot form de re beliefs about Fido because you are not in perceptual contact with Fido. However, it doesn't follow that you lack justification to form beliefs about Fido. Perceiving Fido is an *enabling* condition, rather than a *justifying* condition: it is a psychological condition on believing de re propositions about Fido, rather than an epistemic condition on having justification to believe them. Hence, you can have justification to believe de re propositions about Fido even if you're unable to believe them.

If we modify the linking principle as I'm recommending, then we can defend phenomenal internalism by rejecting the third premise in the duplication argument. You and I can be fully rational without believing every proposition that we have justification to believe. In particular, we are no less than fully rational because we fail to satisfy the enabling conditions for believing de re propositions about objects that we cannot perceive. I conclude that the duplication argument against phenomenal internalism fails.

3.6. Conclusions

In this chapter, I argued that the phenomenal character of perceptual experience is both necessary and sufficient for justifying beliefs about the external world. More specifically, perceptual experience justifies beliefs about the external world because its phenomenal character is a way of representing content with presentational force. Moreover, I argued that there can be no difference in which propositions you have justification to believe on the basis of perceptual experience without some difference in its phenomenal character. This is what I called *phenomenal internalism*.

My arguments for these conclusions relied on judgments about cases, including blindsight cases and skeptical scenarios. These are not just brute intuitions, since I have motivated them with arguments, and defended them against objections. Even so, these arguments depend primarily on consideration of particular cases, rather than general theoretical principles.

In the second part of this book, I will supplement the argument from cases with an argument from general epistemic principles. For example, in chapter 7, I'll argue that the judgments that I've relied on in this chapter can be explained and vindicated by appealing to the independently motivated thesis of accessibilism. These arguments will provide additional support for the conclusions of this chapter.

4

Cognition

What is the relationship between consciousness and cognition? This chapter explores the question whether there could be a *cognitive zombie*—that is, an unconscious creature with the capacity for cognition. By definition, zombies cannot be conscious, but it's a further question whether they can have cognitive states and processes. Can zombies have beliefs and can they engage in reasoning and other forms of rational belief revision?

John Searle (1990) argues that zombies cannot have beliefs because they cannot have any representational states at all. According to Searle's Connection Principle, all unconscious representational states are accessible to consciousness. In chapter 2, I argued that this view fails to accommodate the explanatory role of unconscious mental representation in cognitive science. Zombies, like the zombie systems within us, have unconscious representational states that are inaccessible to consciousness, but which nevertheless play an indispensable role in explaining their behavior.

This chapter argues for an Epistemic Connection Principle, which says that all unconscious representational states that provide epistemic justification for belief are accessible to consciousness. On this view, zombies can have unconscious mental representations, but their representational states cannot play any epistemic role in justifying belief because they are inaccessible to consciousness. These representational states are not beliefs because they are not subject to epistemic norms: they don't play the epistemic role of belief in justifying and being justified by other beliefs. Hence, zombies cannot have beliefs, but only "z-liefs."

A note on terminology: as I use the term, 'cognition' refers to representational states and processes that are subject to epistemic norms, and hence can be assessed for epistemic justification, rationality, or reasonableness. Some writers use the term 'cognition' in a much broader sense to include all representational states and processes that figure in psychological explanation. For instance, Noam Chomsky coins the term 'cognizing' for the way in which we represent the syntactic rules and principles of our native language. He writes, "Cognizing has the structure and character of knowledge, but may be, and in the interesting cases is, inaccessible to consciousness" (1980: 9).

I have no quarrel with Chomsky's claim that we mentally represent a grammar for our language. These mental representations are not examples of cognition in my sense of the term, however, since they are inaccessible to consciousness and so not subject to norms of epistemic rationality. They are not beliefs, but "subdoxastic" mental representations. Although Chomsky and I use the term 'cognition' in different ways, our disagreement is not merely terminological, since this reflects an underlying disagreement about the theoretical significance of consciousness. I claim that conscious accessibility marks an important theoretical distinction between beliefs and subdoxastic states, whereas Chomsky denies that conscious accessibility has any theoretical significance. Thus, he writes, "It may be expected that conscious beliefs will form a scattered and probably uninteresting subpart of the full cognitive structure" (1976: 163).

Here is an overview of the chapter. In section 4.1, I'll begin by arguing that all beliefs provide epistemic justification for other beliefs. In section 4.2, I'll distinguish beliefs from subdoxastic states, which play no such epistemic role in justifying other beliefs. In section 4.3, I'll argue that we cannot explain this epistemic distinction between beliefs and subdoxastic states in terms of the functional criterion of inferential integration. In section 4.4, I'll argue that we must explain it by appealing instead to the phenomenal criterion of conscious accessibility: the contents of beliefs are accessible to consciousness as the contents of conscious judgments. In section 4.5, I'll argue that conscious judgments have representational force and content that is identical with their phenomenal character. Finally, in section 4.6, I'll conclude with some proleptic remarks about why beliefs must be consciously accessible in order to play their epistemic role in justifying other beliefs.

4.1. The Epistemic Role of Belief

In this section, I'll argue for a view that is intermediate between two extremes. At one extreme, Donald Davidson (1986) claims that only beliefs can justify other beliefs. In chapter 3, however, I argued that beliefs can be justified by perceptual experiences, which are distinct from the beliefs they justify. At the other extreme, Richard Feldman (2004: ch. 9) claims that only experiences can justify beliefs. I'll argue instead for the *intermediate view* that both experiences and beliefs can justify beliefs. Moreover, I'll argue for an *inclusive version* of this intermediate view, according to which all of your beliefs play an epistemic role in justifying other beliefs. On this view, which propositions you have justification to believe at any given time depends not only on your total experiential state at that time, but also on your total doxastic state at that time.

Richard Feldman and Earl Conee (2008) hold the extreme view that only experiences can justify beliefs. They endorse a version of *evidentialism*, which says that your ultimate evidence at any given time determines which beliefs you have epistemic justification to hold at that time. Moreover, they hold that your ultimate evidence at any given time is exhausted by your experience at that time:

> All ultimate evidence is experiential. Believing a proposition, all by itself, is not evidence for its truth. Something at the interface of your mind and the world—your experiences—serves to justify belief in a proposition, if anything does. (2008: 88)

On this view, your beliefs don't affect which beliefs you have epistemic justification to hold unless they currently impinge on the contents of your experience. On this view, the epistemic role of belief is mediated by its impact on what you're currently thinking about. As Feldman states the view, "S has p available as evidence at t iff S is currently thinking of p" (2004: 232).

Feldman (2004) defends this view against a series of objections: (i) the problem of stored defeaters, (ii) the problem of stored beliefs, (iii) the problem of forgotten evidence, and (iv) the problem of background beliefs. In this section, I'll argue that Feldman's responses to these objections are unsuccessful, and hence that we should reject his extreme view in favor of the intermediate view.

Objection 1: The problem of stored defeaters. Sometimes your beliefs are unjustified, despite being supported by your current thoughts and experiences, because you have defeating evidence stored in memory that you fail to recall when it is relevant. In Feldman's example, your friend tells you that you can complete the hike to Precarious Peak, and you believe him, forgetting the past occasions on which he overestimated your abilities. Intuitively, your belief is unjustified, since you have defeating evidence stored in memory.

In reply, Feldman compares this with a case in which you have information about the difficulty of the hike stored in a notebook. In each case, there is evidence available to you that would defeat your justification if you came to possess it. Until you access this information, however, your justification remains undefeated because you don't yet possess the defeating evidence. Perhaps you were negligent in failing to access the information in your memory or your notebook. If so, then we can say that the evidence you possess now results from using bad methods for gathering evidence. Nevertheless, your belief is justified in the sense that it is supported by the evidence that you currently possess. As Feldman (2004: 233) puts the point, your belief is rational or justified in the *current-state* sense, but not the *methodological* sense.[1]

---

[1] For a more compelling illustration of this distinction, see Feldman and Conee's (2004: 89–90) discussion of Kornblith's (1983) example of the headstrong physicist.

The problem with Feldman's reply is that information stored in memory is not relevantly similar to information stored in a notebook. There is always some failure of epistemic rationality associated with failing to access relevant information stored in memory. You're not always blameworthy, since recalling the information may be difficult, and you may be doing all that can be reasonably expected under the circumstances. Even so, you are blamelessly violating standards of epistemic rationality. Epistemic rationality requires using all relevant evidence in your possession. In contrast, there need be no violation of epistemic rationality associated with failing to access the information stored in your notebook—for instance, when your eyesight fails or it is too dark to read. Your evidence includes information stored in memory, but not information stored in your notebook.[2]

Objection 2: The problem of stored beliefs. Beliefs stored in memory can be justified, and they can constitute knowledge, even when they are not justified by anything you are currently thinking about. For example, you can retain your knowledge that Washington is the capital of the United States even while you're listening to a philosophy lecture and thinking only about philosophy.

In reply, Feldman draws a distinction between occurrent and dispositional senses of epistemic terms:

> A person knows a thing dispositionally provided the person would know it occurrently if he thought of it. Since the thought that Washington is the capital would, presumably, be accompanied by an awareness of justifying evidence, this fact can be known dispositionally by most of us. Hence, the intuition that we know simple facts even when we are not thinking of them can be accommodated by the minimalist view of evidence possessed: they are known dispositionally but not occurrently. (2004: 236)

The claim is that my dispositional beliefs constitute dispositional knowledge because their occurrent manifestations as conscious judgments would constitute occurrent knowledge. For example, I have dispositional knowledge that Washington is the capital because I would have occurrent knowledge if only I were to think consciously about the matter.

This response commits a version of the conditional fallacy. Consider the proposition that you're now thinking about rhubarb: you don't know this proposition when it's false, but you would know it whenever you make it true by thinking about rhubarb. Feldman recognizes this problem, and tries to

[2] In Smithies (2018a), I develop this point in arguing against Clark and Chalmers's (1998) extended mind thesis. There is no epistemic parity between Inga's memory and Otto's notebook, since only the former is subject to norms of epistemic rationality.

circumvent it by endorsing a form of skepticism about dispositional knowledge. He writes, "In the most fundamental sense, one does not know things such as that Washington is the capital when one is not thinking of them" (2004: 237). On this view, we don't know anything we're not currently thinking about, although we're disposed to have such knowledge when we need it. One consequence of skepticism about dispositional knowledge is that we cannot use it to explain occurrent knowledge. As we'll see, this makes trouble for Feldman's responses to other objections.

Objection 3: The problem of forgotten evidence. You can retain your knowledge that Washington is the capital of the United States without retaining your knowledge of how you originally formed the belief. So, for example, you may have forgotten whether you learned this by watching TV, reading a book, or listening to a teacher in class. In that case, there may be no justifying evidence stored in memory that would occur to you now when you consciously think about the matter. Nevertheless, you still know, and have justification to believe, that Washington is the capital.

In reply, Feldman argues that his justification to believe that Washington is the capital has its source in his "current conviction or feeling of certainty" (2004: 238). But what justifies this feeling of conviction? Presumably, it needs to be justified, since we sometimes feel too strongly convinced that something is true, and yet feelings of conviction cannot justify belief unless they are justified themselves. In this case, however, there is no other experience that could plausibly justify the feeling of conviction that Washington is the capital. To explain why the feeling of conviction is justified, we need to appeal to its coherence with your system of dispositional beliefs, including your belief that your memory is generally reliable. This threatens to undermine Feldman's proposal because he cannot explain our occurrent knowledge in terms of dispositional knowledge.

One potential rejoinder is that feelings of conviction can defeasibly justify themselves without standing in need of any further justification. But if feelings of conviction can defeasibly justify themselves, then why not standing dispositions to feel conviction? Consider the following principle of doxastic conservatism:

Doxastic Conservatism: Necessarily, if you believe that p, then you thereby have defeasible justification to believe that p.

Is there any principled motivation for restricting the principle of doxastic conservatism to occurrent doxastic feelings, rather than standing doxastic states? Feldman claims that believing a proposition is not evidence for its truth and hence that justifying evidence for beliefs must be supplied by experiences that are distinct from those beliefs. But this claim is self-undermining: if believing a proposition is not evidence for its truth, then neither is the feeling of conviction that it is true. In order to solve the problem of forgotten evidence, we should accept the principle of doxastic conservatism, and allow that believing a proposition is defeasible evidence for its truth.[3]

Objection 4: The problem of background beliefs. Your background beliefs can affect what you know, and what you have justification to believe, on the basis of perceptual experience. Suppose an expert and a novice birdwatcher see a scarlet tanager and it looks exactly the same way to each of them. The expert believes it's a scarlet tanager because she knows what these birds look like, whereas the novice leaps to the conclusion that it's a scarlet tanager without knowing or having justification to believe that this is what they look like. The expert and the novice have exactly the same experiences, but only the expert has justification to believe that the bird is a scarlet tanager.

In reply, Feldman concedes that the expert can know that the bird is a scarlet tanager without bringing her background knowledge into consciousness. There is no need to make the inference consciously once it has become automatic. Instead, Feldman appeals to the expert's feelings of certainty that the bird is a scarlet tanager. The problem is that the novice may have exactly the same feelings of certainty, although his feelings of certainty are unjustified. Hence, we cannot explain the justificational difference between the expert and the novice without appealing to the justifying role of background beliefs.

A similar point applies in the case of abductive inference. Suppose you observe that the streets are wet and you infer that it has been raining. Your justification to draw this conclusion depends on vast amounts of background information that is represented unconsciously in the belief system, including information about the conditional probabilities of various hypotheses given that the streets are wet. You cannot bring all of this information into consciousness in the process of drawing the inference. After all, attention imposes limits on the capacity of conscious thought: we cannot think about too many things at once. Nevertheless, vast amounts of background information are crucially implicated in your justification to draw the inference.

I conclude that your justifying evidence includes not only facts about your experience, but also facts about what you believe. On this *intermediate* view, both your experiences and your beliefs play an epistemic role in justifying other beliefs. This raises a further question. Are there any restrictions on which of your beliefs are included in your justifying evidence? I'll argue for an *inclusive* version of the intermediate view, which says that all of your beliefs are part of

---

[3] Harman (1986: ch. 4) argues that doxastic conservatism solves the problem of forgotten evidence, while McGrath (2007) criticizes alternative solutions and defends doxastic conservatism against objections.

your evidence. I'll begin by defending this inclusive view against the objection that there are psychological or epistemic constraints on which beliefs are included in your evidence.

The first objection is that there are psychological constraints on which beliefs are included in your evidence. Feldman argues that your evidence excludes beliefs that are deeply buried in memory, and so not easily accessible, but which can be triggered by certain kinds of prompting or therapy. He gives an example in which his parents tell him that his childhood house was white, although he also has a deeply buried memory that it was yellow. Feldman claims that this memory cannot be accessed easily enough to undermine his justification to believe his parents. He writes, "In this situation it would be most unfair to claim that I am epistemically irresponsible or blameworthy for failing to make proper use of my evidence" (2004: 228).

In reply, it's not always reasonable to blame you when you violate the requirements of epistemic rationality. In this case, it would be unreasonable to blame you for believing what your parents tell you, since it's hard to recall your childhood memories, and you're doing all that can be reasonably expected under the circumstances. Even so, you are blamelessly violating the requirements of epistemic rationality. After all, you believe that your house was white, and you also believe that your house was yellow. Epistemic rationality requires that you avoid having inconsistent beliefs. In this case, you violate the requirements of epistemic rationality, although you cannot be blamed for doing so.[4]

We can turn this reply into a positive argument for the inclusive view. The first premise is that epistemic rationality requires all of your beliefs to be consistent: for example, it's rationally prohibited to believe that p while also having the belief that not-p stored in memory. The second premise is that epistemic rationality requires your representational states to be consistent with each other only if they are included within your total body of evidence. If not, there is no rational pressure to make them consistent. These two premises entail that all beliefs stored in memory are included within your total body of evidence.

The second objection is that there are epistemic constraints on which beliefs are included in your evidence. Feldman argues that unjustified beliefs cannot be included in your evidence, since otherwise we face a bootstrapping problem. If I believe that p without good evidence, I don't thereby have good enough

---

[4] See section 8.4 for further discussion of the connection between epistemic rationality and blameworthiness. I argue that blameworthiness is constrained by your capacities, whereas the requirements of epistemic rationality are not so constrained. I therefore reject the epistemic 'ought' implies 'can' principle on one natural reading.

evidence to justify believing that p. And yet the inclusive view seems to imply otherwise.

In reply, we can avoid this bootstrapping problem without endorsing epistemic constraints on which beliefs are included in your evidence. The key point is that the evidence provided by an unjustified belief is always defeated by whatever makes the belief unjustified. All of your beliefs are included in your evidence and provide some degree of justification for believing their contents. However, the justification provided by a belief is defeated when that belief is not justified by your total evidence—say, because it fails to cohere with the rest of your belief system. Doxastic conservatism says that if you believe that p, then you thereby have some defeasible evidence that p, but this defeasible evidence is defeated when your belief is not supported by your total evidence. Hence, the bootstrapping problem can be avoided.[5]

Again, we can turn this reply into a positive argument for the inclusive view. The first premise is that whether a belief is justified depends on how well it coheres with the rest of your belief system. The second premise is that coherence is a global property: how well a belief coheres with the rest of your belief system depends on its relations to all of your beliefs and not just the justified ones. The third premise is that your total body of evidence is what determines whether your beliefs are justified. Since all of your beliefs are relevant in determining the justification of any other belief, it follows that all of your beliefs are included in your total body of evidence.

4.2. Beliefs and Subdoxastic States

In the previous section, I defended the inclusive view that all of your beliefs are included in your justifying evidence. In this section, I'll argue against the *all-too-inclusive* view that all of your representational states are included in your justifying evidence. I'll distinguish between two kinds of representational states—beliefs and subdoxastic states—and I'll argue that subdoxastic states are excluded from your justifying evidence.

Stephen Stich defines subdoxastic states as "psychological states that play a role in the proximate causal history of beliefs, though they are not beliefs themselves" (1978: 499). This definition isn't quite right. On the one hand, it's too permissive, since it includes perceptual experiences, which are distinct from the beliefs they cause and justify. On the other hand, it's too restrictive, since it

---

[5] Compare Schroeder's (2011) argument against what he calls "the high bar" on evidence, which says that a belief provides evidence only if it is justified.

excludes unconscious representational states involved in guiding action, rather than forming belief. A better definition is that subdoxastic states are unconscious representational states that are distinct from belief, but which nevertheless play a causal role in representational processes. As usual, however, it's probably best to define subdoxastic states ostensively through example and contrast. We can argue about the classification of hard cases in due course. Meanwhile, here are some paradigm examples from the recent history of cognitive science.

Noam Chomsky (1965) argues that we can understand language only because we have tacit knowledge of a grammar for our language. A grammar is a syntactic theory comprised of rules and principles that generate a syntactic description of every sentence in the language. Chomsky claims that we know the grammar for our language: this knowledge is tacit in the sense that it is inaccessible to consciousness, but its content is drawn upon by computational processes that enable us to produce and understand sentences. On this view, understanding the syntactic structure of a sentence is the output of an unconscious computational process that draws upon the content of a tacitly known grammar.[6]

Similarly, David Marr (1982) explains our visual experience of the environment as the output of an unconscious computational process that manipulates a series of representational states according to certain algorithms or rules. This computational process takes as input the representation of light intensity in a pair of two-dimensional retinal images and yields as output a three-dimensional representation of shapes and their spatial organization in an object-centered frame of reference. The task for a computational theory of vision is to identify the representations and rules that are used in computing this function and to explain how this computational process is implemented in the brain.

Beliefs and subdoxastic states are in many ways alike. They are both species of unconscious mental representation: they represent their contents with assertive force, but they have no phenomenal character. Moreover, they figure in representational processes in which causal transitions between representational states are sensitive to the representational properties of those states.[7] Even so there is a normative difference between these representational states: beliefs,

---

[6] Evans (1981) and Davies (1987) argue for the "mirror constraint," which says that the causal structure of the computational process should mirror the logical structure of a derivation of the syntactic form of the sentence in the tacitly known grammar.

[7] Fodor (1980) argues that computation is directly sensitive only to syntax, but indirectly sensitive to semantics in virtue of an isomorphism between syntax and semantics. In contrast, Peacocke (1994) argues that some computation is directly sensitive to semantics. See Rescorla (2012, 2017) for a helpful overview and analysis of the debate.

unlike subdoxastic states, figure in representational processes that are subject to norms of epistemic rationality. As I'll put the point, beliefs figure in *cognitive* processes, whereas subdoxastic states figure in merely *computational* processes. The sine qua non for cognition, as I use the term, is being subject to epistemic norms.

Cognitive processes include not only inferential processes, such as deductive and inductive reasoning, but also noninferential processes, such as forming beliefs on the basis of perception, memory, and testimony. The inputs to a cognitive process can vary depending on whether it is an inferential or noninferential process, but the output is always some revision to one's system of beliefs—for instance, forming new beliefs, abandoning old beliefs, adjusting one's credences, and so on.

Not all processes resulting in belief revision are cognitive processes. Your beliefs can change as a direct result of brain injury without thereby resulting from any cognitive process. What sets cognitive processes apart from these noncognitive processes is that they result in believing something *for a reason*. Needless to say, the reasons for which we believe things are not always good reasons. After all, our reasoning is often irrational. Nevertheless, a cognitive process is always subject to norms of epistemic rationality, and so it can be assessed as rational or irrational, depending on whether the reasons for which we believe something are good or bad reasons. In short, the mark of cognition is being subject to norms of epistemic rationality.

Since Helmholtz, and before, perception has been described as an *inferential process* in which our perceptual systems make "unconscious inferences" from sensory data to conclusions about the external world.[8] This description seems appropriate because our perceptions result from computational processes that operate on mental representations according to certain algorithms or rules. These computational processes are *inference-like* insofar as they manipulate mental representations in ways that are sensitive to their representational properties.

Unlike genuine inferences, however, these computational processes are not subject to norms of rationality, since they are not responsive to reasons. It makes no sense to assess the language module as rational or irrational when it computes the syntactic description of a sentence. Likewise, it makes no sense to assess the visual system as rational or irrational when it computes a representation of the distal environment from a pair of retinal images. These

---

[8] Hatfield (2002) reviews the history. In psychology and philosophy, the inferential conception of perception figures prominently in the work of Marr (1982) and Fodor (1983) among many others.

computational processes are not subject to rational assessment because they are not performed for reasons: they are neither rational nor irrational but *arational*. This is not to deny that computational processes are subject to normative assessment at all. We can assess them in terms of reliability, proper functioning, contribution to biological fitness, and so on. The claim is merely that they are not subject to distinctively epistemic norms of rationality. The normative standards that apply to computational processes are distinct from those that apply to cognitive processes.[9]

Here is an example to illustrate the point. Suppose your parents tell you that pronouns are bound in their governing category and you believe them. At the same time, you subdoxastically represent the contradictory proposition that pronouns are free in their governing category. You are no less than fully rational on this account. Epistemic rationality requires your beliefs to be consistent with each other, but it doesn't require your beliefs to be consistent with your subdoxastic states. This is because your evidence includes your beliefs, while excluding your subdoxastic mental representations.

This suggests the following argument against the all-too-inclusive view. The first premise is that epistemic rationality permits believing that p while also subdoxastically representing that not-p. The second premise is that epistemic rationality requires your unconscious representational states to be logically consistent with each other if they are included within your total evidence. Given that your beliefs are included within your total evidence, it follows that your subdoxastic states are not included within your total evidence. Otherwise, epistemic rationality would require your beliefs to be consistent with your subdoxastic states.

In summary, there is a normative difference between beliefs and subdoxastic states: beliefs are subject to norms of epistemic rationality, whereas subdoxastic states are not. This much I take to be relatively uncontroversial. The controversial question is what explains this normative difference between beliefs and subdoxastic states. Presumably, it is not just a brute fact. There must be some nonnormative difference between beliefs and subdoxastic states that explains this normative difference between them. What grounds this distinction? This is the question to which I now turn.

[9] Why not think the very same norms, such as avoiding inconsistency, apply to these different kinds of representational processes? In the second part of this book, I'll argue that the epistemic norms governing belief are constrained by structural principles, such as the JJ principle, which have no analogue in the subdoxastic domain.

4.3. Inferential Integration

Can we explain the normative difference between beliefs and subdoxastic states without appealing to consciousness? The challenge is to identify some functional difference between beliefs and subdoxastic states that explains the normative difference between them. In this section, I'll focus on Stich's (1978) criterion of inferential integration, but I'll also connect this with Evans's (1981) generality constraint, Fodor's (1983) account of nonmodular cognition, and Block's (1995) definition of access consciousness. I'll argue that the normative difference between beliefs and subdoxastic states cannot be explained in terms of inferential integration, but must be explained in terms of conscious accessibility instead.[10]

Stephen Stich (1978) argues that there are two important differences between beliefs and subdoxastic states:

(1) Beliefs are *consciously accessible* in the sense that their contents can be accessed in conscious judgment: if I believe that p, then I'm thereby disposed to judge that p when I entertain the question whether p. In contrast, the contents of subdoxastic states are *consciously inaccessible*: if I subdoxastically represent that p, then I'm not thereby disposed to judge that p when I entertain the question whether p.

(2) Beliefs are *inferentially integrated* with other beliefs in the sense that they combine to generate further beliefs in their deductive and inductive consequences, and they are mutually adjusted to avoid logical inconsistency and probabilistic incoherence. In contrast, subdoxastic states are *inferentially isolated* from beliefs and from subdoxastic states in other subsystems.

These two properties—conscious accessibility and inferential integration—are conceptually distinct. So, we can ask, which of them accounts for the normative distinction between beliefs and subdoxastic states? My main goal in this section is to argue that the normative distinction between beliefs and subdoxastic states cannot be explained in terms of inferential integration, but must be explained in terms of conscious accessibility instead.

---

[10] This section and the next one build on my defense of the phenomenal individuation of belief in Smithies (2012d).

Here is a statement of the rival explanation that I will be arguing against:

(1) *The Inferential Integration Principle*: Unconscious mental representations can justify belief if and only if they are inferentially integrated with other beliefs.
(2) *The Functional Distinction*: Beliefs are inferentially integrated with other beliefs, whereas subdoxastic states are inferentially isolated from beliefs and from subdoxastic states in other subsystems. Therefore,
(3) *The Normative Distinction*: Beliefs can justify other beliefs, whereas subdoxastic states cannot justify beliefs.

This is what Michael Dummett calls *an explanatory argument*: the conclusion states the datum that needs to be explained, and the premises are supported insofar as they are needed to explain the datum. As he writes, "An explanation often takes the form of constructing a deductive argument, the conclusion of which is a statement of the fact needing explanation: but, unlike what happens in a suasive argument, in an explanatory argument the epistemic direction may run counter to the direction of logical consequence" (1978: 296).

Stich claims that our beliefs are inferentially integrated in the sense that they combine with each other to generate further beliefs in their deductive and inductive consequences, and they are mutually adjusted to avoid logical inconsistency and probabilistic incoherence. Of course, we are not perfectly rational agents. Even so, the point remains that our beliefs form a system of mutually supporting inferential relations. As Stich writes, "A person's body of beliefs forms an elaborate and interconnected network with a vast number of potential inference patterns leading from every belief to almost any other" (1978: 507).

In contrast, our subdoxastic states are inferentially isolated not only from our beliefs, but also from subdoxastic states in other subsystems. Stich puts the point like this:

If we think in terms of a cognitive simulation model, the view I am urging is that beliefs form a consciously accessible, inferentially integrated cognitive subsystem. Subdoxastic states occur in a variety of separate, special purpose subsystems. And even when the subdoxastic states within a specialized subsystem generate one another via a process of inference, their inferential interactions with the integrated body of accessible beliefs are severely limited. Similarly, in all likelihood, the potential inferential connections among subdoxastic states in different specialized subsystems are extremely limited or non-existent. (1978: 507–508)

Stich is not making the definitional point that only beliefs stand in inferential connections with other beliefs. He uses the term 'inference' more liberally to include representational transitions between subdoxastic states as well as beliefs. His point is rather that the inferential connections between subdoxastic states are relatively impoverished in comparison with the inferential connections between beliefs. In fact, there are three distinct points to be made here: (i) subdoxastic states don't combine with beliefs to generate further beliefs; (ii) they don't combine with beliefs to generate further subdoxastic states; and (iii) they don't combine with subdoxastic states in other subsystems to generate further subdoxastic states.

Gareth Evans (1981) extends Stich's point by noting that our beliefs are integrated not only with other beliefs, but also with our desires. Beliefs combine with desires to produce action and, given the right set of background beliefs, almost any belief can combine with any desire in the production of action. As he writes, "It is of the essence of a belief state that it be at the service of many distinct projects, and that its influence on any project be mediated by other beliefs" (1981: 132). Subdoxastic states, in contrast, are not poised to combine with the subject's beliefs and desires in the production of action. Their inferential interactions are largely restricted to other subdoxastic states within the same representational subsystem.

Evans explains this point in terms of a distinction between conceptual and nonconceptual species of mental representation. He argues that beliefs are conceptually structured in the following sense: you cannot believe that a is F unless you have a general conception of what it is for an arbitrary object to be F, and hence you are capable of entertaining the thought that b is F for any object b of which you have a conception. In other words, beliefs must conform to what he calls "the generality constraint":

> We shall not be prepared to attribute to a subject the belief that a is F . . . unless we can suppose the subject to be capable of entertaining the supposition (having the thought) that b is F, for every object b of which he has a conception. (1981: 133)

In contrast, subdoxastic states need not conform to the generality constraint: you can subdoxastically represent that a is F without having any general conception of what it is for an arbitrary object to be F. As Evans says, "When we attribute to the brain computations whereby it localizes the sounds we hear, we ipso facto ascribe to it representations of the speed of sound and of the distance between the ears, without any commitment to the idea that it should be able to represent the speed of light or the distance of anything else" (1982: 104 n. 22).

Evans's generality constraint is a consequence of Stich's requirement that beliefs are inferentially integrated with each other. Suppose my beliefs are inferentially integrated in the sense that when I believe that *a is F*, and I believe that *a = b*, I'm also disposed to infer that *b is F*. This requires that I can recombine the contents of my belief that *a is F*, and my belief that *a = b*, in order to entertain the content that *b is F*. If my beliefs are to be inferentially integrated in this way, then they must also conform to the generality constraint. As Evans writes, "Behind the idea of a system of beliefs lies that of a system of concepts, the structure of which determines the inferential properties which thoughts . . . are treated as possessing" (1981: 133).

Stich's criterion of inferential integration also figures in Fodor's (1983) account of central cognition. Fodor develops Stich's cognitive simulation model by drawing an architectural distinction between perception and cognition. On this view, perceptual systems are *modules*: they are "domain-specific" in the sense that they are restricted in the kinds of information they can take as input and "informationally encapsulated" in the sense that they are restricted in the kinds of information they can use in processing their inputs. These modules tend to exhibit a cluster of related symptoms, including conscious inaccessibility, fast and mandatory operation, fixed neural architecture, and characteristic patterns of breakdown and development. According to Fodor, however, informational encapsulation is "the essence of . . . modularity" (1983: 71).

Fodor argues that the cognitive system, in contrast, must be *nonmodular* in order to play its distinctive functional role in the fixation of belief. He argues in two steps. First, the inductive processes involved in belief fixation are holistic in the sense that they are sensitive to global properties of the belief system, such as simplicity and explanatory power. Second, modular processes cannot exhibit these holistic properties because they are domain specific and informationally encapsulated. Hence, our beliefs must be integrated within a nonmodular system in order to play their distinctive functional role in inductive inference. This argument partially vindicates Stich's claim that our beliefs are inferentially integrated with each other, whereas our subdoxastic states are inferentially isolated from each other.[11]

Finally, Stich's criterion of inferential integration also figures in Ned Block's (1995) original definition of access consciousness. Stich says that our beliefs are "inferentially promiscuous" in the sense that "almost any belief can play a role in the inference to any other" (1978: 506). Block includes inferential promiscuity as one of three sufficient conditions for access consciousness:

A state is access-conscious . . . if, in virtue of one's having the state, a representation of its content is (1) inferentially promiscuous (Stich 1978), that

---

[11] Fodor (1983: 83–86) agrees with Stich that our beliefs are inferentially integrated with each other, but he denies that all of our subdoxastic states are inferentially isolated, since he thinks our capacity for deductive inference is underwritten by subdoxastic representations of the validity of argument forms, such as modus ponens.

is, poised for use as a premise in reasoning, (2) poised for rational control of action, and (3) poised for rational control of speech. (1995: 231)

It's worth noting that the requirements for access consciousness are different for perception and cognition: the contents of cognition are directly poised for use in reasoning, whereas the contents of perception are indirectly poised for use in reasoning only by way of their impact on cognition. In section 3.2, I argued that access consciousness is neither necessary nor sufficient for perception to provide reasons for belief. This section extends the argument from perception to cognition.

What is the relationship between conscious accessibility and inferential integration? Stich claims that these two properties tend to "run in tandem" (1978: 517), and he conjectures that this is no accident, although he doesn't attempt to explain the correlation. There may well be some explanatory connection between conscious accessibility and inferential integration. When I can access the contents of my beliefs in judgment, this tends to promote their inferential connections with other beliefs. Otherwise, their inferential connections tend to be much more attenuated. As Block suggests, "Perhaps there is something about consciousness that greases the wheels of accessibility" (1997: 402).

Conscious accessibility may tend to promote inferential integration, but there is no conceptually necessary connection between these properties. On the one hand, conscious accessibility is not *necessary* for inferential integration. Zombies can have unconscious mental representations that are access conscious in the sense that their contents are inferentially promiscuous. And yet the contents of these mental representations are not accessible to consciousness as the contents of conscious judgments. On the other hand, conscious accessibility is not *sufficient* for inferential integration. When patients with Capgras delusion believe their spouse has been replaced by an imposter, the contents of these beliefs are accessible to consciousness as the contents of judgments. At the same time, these "monothematic delusions" tend to be inferentially isolated from other beliefs—for example, patients often neglect to call the police in order to report the imposter. Conscious accessibility may tend to promote inferential integration, but these properties are conceptually distinct.

If conscious accessibility is distinct from inferential integration, then we can ask which of these properties explains the normative distinction between beliefs and subdoxastic states. Since these properties are normally coinstantiated, we'll need to examine conceptually possible cases in which they come apart. I'll argue that a representational state is subject to epistemic norms of rationality when it is consciously accessible and yet inferentially isolated, but not when it is inferentially integrated and yet consciously inaccessible. I'll therefore conclude that the normative distinction between beliefs and subdoxastic states is explained by conscious accessibility, rather than inferential integration.

Stich gives the following example to illustrate the difference in inferential integration between beliefs and subdoxastic states:

> Suppose that, for some putative rule r, you have come to believe that if r then Chomsky is seriously mistaken. Suppose further that, as it happens, r is in fact among the rules stored by your language processing mechanism. That belief along with the subdoxastic state will not lead to the belief that Chomsky is seriously mistaken. By contrast, if you believe (perhaps even mistakenly) that r, then the belief that Chomsky is seriously mistaken is likely to be inferred. (1978: 508–509)

In this passage, Stich is making a descriptive claim about the inferential dispositions correlated with believing a proposition. There is also a normative counterpart to this descriptive claim, which concerns the inferential dispositions that one is rationally required to have when one believes a proposition. The descriptive claim is that one's beliefs tend to be inferentially integrated with each other, whereas the normative claim is that they ought to be. My argument relies on this normative claim.

To adapt Stich's example, if you believe (i) that if r is true, then Chomsky is mistaken, and you also believe (ii) that r is true, then you are rationally committed to believing (iii) that Chomsky is mistaken. In other words, it is irrational to believe that (i) and (ii) while withholding belief that (iii). It is a violation of the norms of epistemic rationality to believe the premises of a deductively valid argument while also withholding belief in its conclusion. Epistemic rationality requires that your beliefs are logically consistent and closed under logical consequence.[12] In contrast, if you believe (i) and you merely subdoxastically represent (ii), then you are not thereby rationally committed to believing (iii). Epistemic rationality requires your beliefs to be inferentially integrated with each other, but it doesn't require your beliefs to be inferentially integrated with your subdoxastic states. What explains this normative difference between beliefs and subdoxastic states? To answer this question, I'll consider two hypothetical variations on Stich's example in which conscious accessibility and inferential integration come apart.

Case 1: Your mental representation of rule r is accessible to consciousness, but it is inferentially isolated from your other beliefs, including the conditional

---

[12] Christensen (2004) argues that the norms of rationality require probabilistic coherence, rather than logical consistency and closure. But we can easily reformulate the argument in terms of probabilistic constraints on epistemic rationality.

belief that if r is true, then Chomsky is mistaken. In this case, you are disposed to judge that r is true, but you are not disposed to infer that Chomsky is mistaken. This seems irrational, or anyway less than fully rational. If you believe a conditional, and you are disposed to judge its antecedent, then you are rationally committed to believe its consequent: it is irrational to withhold belief in the consequent while also being disposed to judge the antecedent. But if an unconscious mental representation grounds a rational commitment to use its content as a premise in deductive inference, then it is a belief, rather than a subdoxastic state. Therefore, a disposition to judge r is sufficient for believing r even if this belief is not inferentially integrated with your other beliefs.

Case 2: Your mental representation of rule r is inaccessible to consciousness, but it is inferentially integrated with your other beliefs, including the conditional belief that if r is true, then Chomsky is mistaken. In this case, you are not disposed to judge that r is true, but you are nevertheless disposed to infer that Chomsky is mistaken. Again, this seems irrational, or anyway less than fully rational: if you believe a conditional, but you're not disposed to judge that the antecedent is true, then you have no rational commitment to believe the consequent. Indeed, you have a rational commitment to refrain from believing the consequent unless you have other grounds for making the inference: it's irrational to believe a conclusion by inference from some premises unless you are disposed to judge that the premises are true. But if an unconscious mental representation does not ground a rational commitment to use its content as a premise in deductive inference, then it is not a belief, but a subdoxastic state. Therefore, it's not sufficient for believing r that you have a mental representation of r that is inferentially integrated with your other beliefs. On the contrary, a disposition to judge that r is necessary for believing r.

I conclude that the normative distinction between beliefs and subdoxastic states is explained in terms of conscious accessibility, rather than inferential integration. Moreover, we cannot explain the distinction by imposing more demanding functional constraints on belief, since the same arguments apply. No matter how much a mental representation mirrors the functional role of belief, it is not subject to epistemic norms unless its content is accessible to consciousness as the content of a conscious judgment.

4.4. Conscious Accessibility

In the previous section, I argued that the normative difference between beliefs and subdoxastic states is best explained by a nonnormative difference in conscious accessibility: beliefs are accessible to consciousness, whereas subdoxastic states are inaccessible to consciousness. The explanation appeals to an epistemic analogue of Searle's Connection Principle, which says that unconscious representational states can justify belief if and only if they are accessible to consciousness. Here is the explanatory argument in outline:

(1) *The Epistemic Connection Principle*: Unconscious representational states can justify belief if and only if they are accessible to consciousness.
(2) *The Phenomenal Distinction*: Beliefs are accessible to consciousness, whereas subdoxastic states are inaccessible to consciousness.
(3) *The Normative Distinction*: Therefore, beliefs can justify other beliefs, whereas subdoxastic states cannot justify beliefs.

My main goal in this section is to explain why the contents of beliefs are accessible to consciousness and to defend this claim against objections.

What does it mean to say that a mental state is accessible to consciousness? According to John Searle's (1990) Connection Principle, all unconscious representational states are accessible to consciousness. As we saw in section 2.2.2, Searle gives two distinct criteria for conscious accessibility: one of them is too strong to include beliefs, while the other is too weak to exclude subdoxastic states. I'll propose an intermediate criterion that gets the extension right: it includes beliefs, while also excluding subdoxastic states.

The *strong criterion* says that a mental state is accessible to consciousness just in case it is disposed to become conscious. This criterion excludes beliefs, since beliefs are disposed to cause conscious judgments, but they cannot be identified with the conscious judgments they are disposed to cause. A judgment is an occurrent event in the stream of consciousness, whereas a belief is a standing state that persists through changes in the stream of consciousness. We can sometimes explain why someone judges a proposition by citing the fact that they believe it, but the truth of this causal explanation requires that the belief is distinct from the judgment it is disposed to cause.

The *weak criterion* says that a mental state is accessible to consciousness just in case it is disposed to cause conscious experiences. This criterion includes subdoxastic states, since some of them are disposed to cause conscious experiences. Martin Davies (1989) gives a hypothetical example in which subdoxastic states of tacit knowledge are disposed to cause distinctive itches or tickles. But we can also give more realistic examples, including the subdoxastic visual representations that figure in computational explanations of conscious visual experience.

My *intermediate criterion* says that an unconscious representational state is accessible to consciousness just in case it is individuated by its dispositions to cause conscious experiences. Beliefs satisfy this criterion because they are individuated by their dispositions to cause conscious judgments. In contrast, subdoxastic states fail to satisfy this criterion because they are individuated by their role in unconscious computational processes. So the intermediate criterion is weak enough to include beliefs, but also strong enough to exclude subdoxastic states.

As Stich (1978) notes, the contents of belief are accessible to consciousness as the contents of conscious judgments. If you believe a proposition, then you're thereby disposed to judge that it's true when you entertain it consciously in thought. Moreover, when you exercise this disposition, your judgment can be said to express what you believe. If you merely subdoxastically represent a proposition, in contrast, you're not thereby disposed to judge that it's true. For example, you subdoxastically represent various syntactic principles without thereby having any disposition to judge that they are true. Of course, you might be disposed to judge what you also subdoxastically represent, but if so, that is just a coincidence. It is not guaranteed by the individuation of your subdoxastic representations. In contrast, the individuation of your beliefs guarantees that you're disposed to judge their contents when you entertain them consciously in thought.

How does the individuation of belief guarantee that its contents are accessible to consciousness in conscious judgment? My answer is that belief is a disposition toward judgment: to believe that p is to be disposed to consciously judge that p when you consciously entertain whether p. Your belief derives its representational content and its assertive force from the conscious judgments it disposes you to make. This is why the judgments you're disposed to make express what you believe and do not merely coincide with what you believe. After all, your belief is individuated wholly by its disposition to cause these very conscious judgments.

In contrast, subdoxastic states are individuated by their disposition to figure in unconscious computational processes. Even if they are disposed to cause conscious experiences, they are not individuated by those dispositions. For example, subdoxastic states that embody tacit knowledge of syntax are individuated by their role in syntactic processing, rather than their role in causing conscious itches and tickles. Likewise, subdoxastic visual states are individuated by their role in unconscious visual processes, rather than their dispositions to cause conscious visual experience. This explains why the contents of subdoxastic states, unlike the contents of beliefs, are inaccessible to consciousness as the contents of conscious judgments. If you are disposed to judge what you also subdoxastically represent, then this is just a coincidence, since it is not guaranteed by the individuation of your subdoxastic states. In that case, your judgments do not express your subdoxastic representations, but merely coincide with them.

In summary, the contents of beliefs are accessible to consciousness as the contents of conscious judgments, whereas the contents of subdoxastic states are inaccessible to consciousness. This is because beliefs are individuated by their disposition to cause conscious judgments, whereas subdoxastic states are individuated by their role in unconscious computational processes. In the rest of this section, I'll defend this account of belief against a series of objections.

Objection 1: The disposition to judge that *p* is not necessary for believing that *p*. Recall Feldman's (2004: 228) example in which your belief that your childhood house was yellow is deeply buried in memory. The content of this belief is not easily accessible to consciousness, since it is triggered only by certain kinds of prompting or therapy. When you consider the question, you're disposed to judge that your childhood house was white, rather than yellow, since that's what your parents tell you. Isn't this a counterexample in which you believe a proposition without being disposed to judge that it is true?

In reply, this is a case in which you have inconsistent beliefs, since you're disposed to make conflicting judgments in different circumstances. You're normally disposed to judge that your house was white, but you also have some disposition to judge that it was yellow given the right kind of prompting or therapy. This disposition is normally blocked from manifesting itself because the belief is so deeply buried in memory. Nevertheless, the disposition remains, despite the fact it is not easily triggered. We can extend this account to the unconscious beliefs that figure in psychoanalytic theory. These are dispositions toward judgment that are normally blocked from manifesting themselves. One of the goals of psychoanalytic therapy is to remove these blockages so as to give you conscious access to what you believe. Moreover, one of the goals of psychoanalytic theory is to give an account of the nature of these blocking mechanisms, such as repression and denial.

Objection 2: The disposition to judge that *p* is not sufficient for believing that *p*. Consider Alvin Goldman's (1999: 278–279) example of the train passenger who is just waking up from a nap. He is disposed to make various judgments about the neighboring landscape, but he doesn't acquire any beliefs about the landscape until he opens his eyes and looks out the window. Isn't this a counterexample in which you're disposed to judge that *p* without believing that *p*?

In reply, the sleepy passenger doesn't acquire the disposition to make judgments about the landscape until he opens his eyes. Until then, he has only a second-order disposition to acquire this first-order disposition when he opens his eyes. Any adequate theory of dispositions needs to respect this distinction between having a disposition and merely having a disposition to acquire it under certain circumstances. Following Robert Audi (1994), we can say that the sleepy passenger has a *disposition to believe* that the landscape is hilly, but no *dispositional belief*. We can accept this distinction without endorsing Audi's claim that all dispositional beliefs must have been entertained in the past. You can dispositionally believe a proposition that you've never previously entertained so long as you're disposed to judge that it's true without acquiring new evidence or engaging in new enquiry. For example, perhaps you dispositionally believe that elephants don't wear underpants in the wild, since you're disposed to judge this without a moment's thought. Other cases may be harder to classify, but it goes without saying that the boundaries of this distinction are somewhat vague.

Objection 3: Beliefs are not dispositions, since beliefs cause behavior, but dispositions cannot be causes. Ned Block (1990) argues that the causal role of a disposition is preempted by its physical realizer: for instance, what causes me to fall asleep when I take a sleeping pill is its specific chemical properties, rather than its general disposition to induce sleep.

In reply, however, I deny that dispositions cannot be causes. Arguably, the general disposition of a sleeping pill to induce sleep is more proportional to its effects than its specific physical realizer. After all, the sleeping pill would have the same effect if its dormative virtue were realized by another chemical instead. Stephen Yablo (1992) argues that causes are proportional to their effects. If so, then we should conclude that dispositions can be causes after all.

Objection 4: Beliefs are *multitrack* dispositions: they are dispositions to cause bodily actions as well as mental acts of judgment. Believing a proposition requires being disposed to act as if it is true. Without the right kind of dispositions toward action, a mere disposition toward judgment is not sufficient for belief.

In reply, let me first clarify that I'm not denying that beliefs are normally disposed to cause bodily actions. What I'm denying is that beliefs are *individuated* by those dispositions. After all, it is conceivable that believers might lack any dispositions to engage in bodily action at all. Consider Galen Strawson's example of the weather watchers:

> The weather watchers are a race of sentient, intelligent creatures. They are distributed across the surface of their planet, rooted to the ground, profoundly interested in the local weather. They have sensations, thoughts, emotions, beliefs, desires. They possess a conception of an objective, spatial world. But they are constitutionally incapable of any sort of behavior, as this is ordinarily understood. They lack the necessary physiology. Their mental lives have no other-observable effects. They are not even disposed to behave in any way. (1994: 251)

These creatures have beliefs about the weather because they are disposed to make conscious judgments about the weather, although they are not disposed to act upon these judgments. It is merely a contingent fact about normal humans that our beliefs tend to combine with our desires to cause actions that are more or less rational. We could have been wired up quite differently, like David Lewis's (1980b) madman, to do exactly the opposite of what is rationalized by our beliefs and desires. Or we could have wired up, like Strawson's weather watchers, to do nothing at all. These scenarios are conceivable because beliefs and desires are not individuated by their dispositions to cause bodily actions. Rather, they are individuated by their dispositions to cause conscious experiences.[13]

Objection 5: When our dispositions toward judgment come apart from our dispositions toward action, our beliefs are not reflected in what we judge to be true, but rather in what we do. Christopher Peacocke gives the following example to make this point:

> Someone may judge that undergraduate degrees from countries other than her own are of an equal standard to her own, and excellent reasons may be operative in her assertions to that effect. All the same, it may be quite clear, in decisions she makes on hiring, or in making recommendations, that she does not really have this belief at all. (1998: 90)

Peacocke's academic—I'll call her Alice—is disposed to act in ways that conflict with her judgments. We can assume that there is no conflict in her dispositions toward judgment; otherwise, she has inconsistent beliefs that are manifested in different circumstances. For the sake of argument, let's assume that she is disposed to judge that foreign degrees are equal to domestic degrees, and she is not disposed to judge the opposite. Nevertheless, she is disposed to act as if they are inferior. What does Alice believe? Peacocke's answer is that she doesn't really believe what she judges to be true—namely, that foreign degrees are equal. Instead, what she really believes, as revealed in her actions, is that foreign degrees are inferior. Hence, a disposition to judge that *p* is neither necessary nor sufficient for believing that *p*.[14]

In reply, I dispute Peacocke's description of the example. I claim that Alice believes that foreign degrees are as good as domestic degrees, although she is not disposed to act as if she believes this. Moreover, I deny that Alice believes that foreign degrees are inferior to domestic degrees, although she is disposed to act as if she believes it. What motivates this description of the example? My

---

[13] See Smithies and Weiss (2019) for further elaboration of this point.

[14] Schwitzgebel (2010) gives examples with much the same structure. He regards these as examples of "in-between belief," since he holds that beliefs require dispositions toward action as well as dispositions toward judgment.

answer is that it best preserves an important theoretical distinction between two kinds of irrationality—namely, epistemic and practical irrationality.[15]

To see this, compare Alice with her colleague, Bob. Both have evidence that foreign degrees are equal to domestic degrees, but they respond to this evidence in different ways:

(A)   Alice is disposed to make judgments that accord with the evidence, but she is disposed to act in conflict with those judgments.

(B)   Bob is disposed to make judgments that conflict with the evidence, and he is disposed to act in accord with those judgments.

Both Alice and Bob are subject to rational criticism insofar as they are disposed to act in conflict with the evidence. However, the nature of this rational criticism is rather different in each case. Bob is epistemically irrational, since he is disposed to make judgments that conflict with his evidence. In contrast, Alice is epistemically rational insofar as she is disposed to make judgments that respect her evidence. Nevertheless, she is practically irrational, since she is disposed to act in conflict with her own judgments.

To capture this difference between Alice and Bob, we should recognize that there is something that Alice believes and Bob disbelieves—namely, that foreign degrees are equal to domestic degrees. After all, people are epistemically irrational in virtue of what they believe, whereas they are practically irrational in virtue of how they act. Bob is epistemically irrational because he believes in conflict with the evidence. In contrast, Alice is epistemically rational, but practically irrational: she believes in accordance with the evidence, but her rational beliefs fail to constrain her actions. We obscure the normative difference between Alice and Bob if we say that both of them, or neither of them, believe that foreign degrees are inferior to domestic degrees. In order to capture the difference in epistemic rationality, we should say that Alice believes in accordance with the evidence, whereas Bob believes in conflict with the evidence.

Eric Schwitzgebel (forthcoming) complains that this reply gives Alice more credit than she is due by classifying her belief as a rational one. More generally, it risks downgrading our responsibility for our actions. In reply, however, we are responsible not only for forming beliefs rationally in accordance with the evidence, but also for acting rationally in accordance with the evidence. Alice fulfills her responsibilities in the epistemic domain, but she violates her responsibilities in the practical domain. We can recognize that her epistemic

---

[15] Compare Zimmerman's claim that "cognitive evaluations . . . can be pried apart from those properly aimed at absentmindedness, phobia and prejudice" (2007: 79).

conduct is better than Bob's without excusing her practical conduct. Perhaps we should focus more attention on practical conduct than epistemic conduct, but this is no basis for obscuring the distinction altogether.

Another objection appeals to the role of belief in the explanation of action. If Alice does not believe that foreign degrees are inferior to domestic degrees, then how can we explain her disposition to act as if she does? Suppose that we cannot explain her behavior without ascribing some belief-like representational state with the content that foreign degrees are inferior to domestic degrees. Even so, Alice cannot access the content of this state in making conscious judgments. Because its content is inaccessible to consciousness, this representational state cannot provide epistemic justification for belief. As such, it is properly classified as a subdoxastic state, rather than a belief.[16]

On this view, not all representational and motivational states that play a role in the explanation of action are beliefs and desires. Beliefs and desires are the kinds of representational and motivational states that can figure in the *rational* explanation of action because they provide justifying reasons for belief and action. My claim is that unconscious representational states provide justifying reasons only if they are individuated in such a way that their contents are accessible to consciousness.

Tamar Gendler (2008a, 2008b) draws a similar distinction between beliefs and other belief-like representational states that she calls *aliefs*. What is my attitude when I'm standing on a glass viewing platform and I know that I'm safe, but I act and react as if I'm in danger? According to Gendler, I *believe* that I'm safe, but I *alieve* that I'm in danger. I agree with Gendler that we need to distinguish beliefs from other belief-like representational states that play a role in the causal explanation of action. At the same time, I disagree with her about the basis of this distinction. This is worth highlighting because her account of the distinction is vulnerable to compelling objections that don't apply to mine.

First, Gendler claims that beliefs are distinguished from aliefs by their sensitivity to evidence. She writes, "Beliefs change in response to changes in evidence; aliefs change in response to changes in habit" (2008b: 566). In response, Eric Schwitzgebel (2010: 539–541) argues that there is no threshold for sensitivity to evidence that is low enough to include our beliefs, but also high enough to exclude our habits. On the one hand, our beliefs and judgments are not perfectly sensitive to evidence. On the other hand, our habits and emotional

---

[16] Since I draw the distinction between beliefs and subdoxastic states in terms of conscious accessibility, I'm not committed to the claim that all subdoxastic states are alike in other respects, such as modularity or inferential isolation.

reactions are imperfectly sensitive to evidence, since they can change given repeated exposure to evidence. This is Schwitzgebel's dilemma.

Second, Gendler claims that beliefs are distinguished from aliefs by their
role in inferential processes. Aliefs, in contrast, figure solely in associative
processes. Thus, she writes, "Alief is associative, automatic, and arational"
(2008a: 641). In response, Eric Mandelbaum (2013) argues that if aliefs are
merely associational states, then they cannot do the explanatory work required of them. In the phenomenon of celebrity contagion, for instance,
people are willing to pay much more money for a sweater when a celebrity
has worn it, but not so much when it has been washed. Mandelbaum argues
that this is because subjects engage in the unconscious inference that washing
the sweater erases valuable traces left by physical contact with the celebrity.
We cannot explain this unconscious inference by appealing to states that
figure only in associative processes. But if we say that aliefs can figure in unconscious inferences too, then we collapse the distinction between aliefs and
beliefs. This is Mandelbaum's dilemma.

My proposal avoids these objections. I don't claim that beliefs are distinguished from subdoxastic representational states either by their sensitivity to
evidence or by their capacity to figure in inference-like transitions. Instead,
I claim that beliefs are distinguished from subdoxastic states because their
contents are accessible to consciousness. Conscious accessibility, rather than
evidential sensitivity or inferential potential, is what grounds the normative
distinction between beliefs and subdoxastic states. Aliefs are not properly classified as beliefs because their contents are not accessible to consciousness as the
contents of conscious judgments. As a result, they are not subject to norms of
epistemic rationality at all.

4.5. Cognitive Experience

In the last section, I argued that beliefs are individuated wholly by their
dispositions to cause conscious judgments. On this view, beliefs derive their
representational force and content from the conscious judgments they are disposed to cause. You *believe* that p just when and because you're disposed to
consciously *judge* that p. But what accounts for the representational force and
content of these conscious judgments themselves? In this section, I'll argue that
conscious judgments have representational force and content that is identical
with their phenomenal character. In other words, they have *phenomenal force
and content*.

In chapter 2, I argued for *representationalism*, the thesis that the phenomenal character of experience is identical with a certain kind of representational

force and content. Since representationalism is a global thesis, it implies that all experience has phenomenal force and content. In chapter 3, I explored the epistemological consequences of applying representationalism to perceptual experience. According to *perceptual representationalism*, all perceptual experience has phenomenal force and content. In this section, I'll extend representationalism from perceptual experience to cognitive experience. According to *cognitive representationalism*, all cognitive experience has phenomenal force and content. Although I'm primarily concerned with the cognitive experience of judgment, much of my discussion extends to other kinds of cognitive experience, including conscious thinking, reasoning, and understanding, as well as feelings of confidence, certainty, and doubt.[17]

Some philosophers accept perceptual representationalism, while denying cognitive representationalism. This is because they endorse a kind of *reductionism*, which says that all experience is reducible to perceptual experience, broadly construed to include inner speech and other forms of perceptual and motor imagery.[18] On this view, all cognitive experience can be explained in terms of the occurrence of perceptual experience that is associated with episodes of cognition. Perceptual experience underdetermines the representational properties of cognition: the contents of your thoughts and judgments cannot be explained solely in terms of associated perceptual experience. Hence, there is a tension between reductionism and cognitive representationalism. The argument can be summarized as follows:

(1) Reductionism is true.
(2) If reductionism is true, then cognitive representationalism is false.
(3) Therefore, cognitive representationalism is false.

In section 4.5.1, I'll explore two different strategies for blocking this argument: one option is to reject reductionism, while the other option is to reconcile reductionism with cognitive representationalism.

The main goal of this section is to argue for cognitive representationalism about the cognitive experience of judgment. On this view, judgment has representational force and content that is identical with its phenomenal character. I give two arguments for this conclusion: a phenomenological argument and an epistemological argument. In section 4.5.1, I argue that cognitive representationalism provides the best explanation of the phenomenal contrast between

---

[17] This section draws from my survey of the literature on cognitive experience in Smithies (2013b) and (2013c).

[18] Proponents of representationalism who also endorse reductionism include Dretske (1995), Tye (1995), and Carruthers (2000).

the presence and absence of judgment. In section 4.5.2, I argue that it provides the best explanation of our introspective knowledge of which judgments we're making at any given time.

4.5.1. The Argument from Phenomenal Contrast

A *judgment*, as I use the term, is an episode in the stream of consciousness: it is an episode of conscious thought. Not all conscious thought is judgment: for instance, you can entertain a proposition, wonder whether it is true, or assume it for the sake of argument, without thereby judging that it's true. Judgment is different from these other forms of conscious thought insofar as it is a mental event of affirming a proposition to be true. Judgment is the phenomenal counterpart of assertion.

All conscious thought has some phenomenal character, but judgment has a distinctive phenomenal character that sets it apart from all other kinds of conscious thought. What it's like to judge that you've just woken up, for example, is different from what it's like to entertain the same proposition, to wonder whether it's true, or to assume it for the sake of argument. More generally, what it's like to judge a proposition is different from what it's like to adopt any other attitude toward the same proposition. This is because judgment has a distinctive *phenomenal force* that distinguishes it from all other kinds of conscious thought. More specifically, it has an *assertive* kind of phenomenal force.

While all judgments have the same kind of assertive phenomenal force, they can differ in their overall phenomenal character. What it's like to judge that you just woke up, for example, is different from what it's like to judge that you've been awake for hours. More generally, what it's like to judge a proposition is different from what it's like to adopt the same attitude toward a different proposition in the same external conditions. This is because judgment has a distinctive kind of *phenomenal content* that distinguishes it from all other conscious judgments made in the same external conditions. Of course, judgments can also have externalist contents, which vary between phenomenal duplicates depending on external conditions. Representationalism implies that all experience has phenomenal content, but it doesn't imply that all the representational contents of experience are phenomenal contents.

This argument is an application of what Susanna Siegel (2010: 87–96) calls "the method of phenomenal contrast." It starts with the datum that there is a phenomenal contrast between two scenarios and then seeks to confirm a hypothesis by inference to the best explanation. The datum to be explained is that if we vary which judgments you're making, while holding fixed your external conditions, we thereby change the phenomenal character of your experience.

The best explanation of this datum, I'll argue, is that judgment has phenomenal force and content. Suppose, for example, that two subjects entertain the same proposition, but one of them judges this proposition to be true, while the other suspends judgment. This makes a phenomenal difference because judgment has phenomenal force. Alternatively, suppose that two subjects entertain the same proposition, but one of them judges that it's true, while the other judges that it's false, or that if it's true, then either it's true or it's false. This makes a phenomenal difference because judgment has phenomenal content.

How will opponents respond to this argument? One option is to deny that making a judgment ever makes a phenomenal difference, but this is hard to take seriously. Surely making a judgment sometimes makes a difference causally, if not constitutively, to the phenomenal character of your experience. A better option is to argue that this datum can be explained without accepting that judgment has phenomenal force and content. On this view, judgment makes a phenomenal difference only insofar as it is causally associated with sensory experiences, including sensory imagery and inner speech.[19]

I'll raise two objections to this proposal. The first objection is that not all conscious thought is expressed in inner speech or sensory imagery. Some cognitive experience is entirely nonsensory. Charles Siewert (1998) calls this "noniconic thought." He writes:

> I think you will, if you try, be able to recognize examples from your own daily life . . . of unverbalized noniconic thought. These are sometimes fairly primitive or simple, and sometimes remarkably complicated, so that to say what one was thinking would require a lengthy syntactically complex utterance—but in either event thought occurs, wordlessly, without imagery, condensed, and evanescent. (1998: 277–278)

Siewert's examples include suddenly realizing that he's locked himself out of his apartment, or finding himself lost in thought about the topic of the book he is writing. These examples resonate strongly with my own experience. Although I sometimes talk to myself, or imagine what I'm thinking about, much of my conscious thought is devoid of any form of sensory expression. That, in any case, is how it seems to me upon introspection.[20]

Some philosophers disagree, however, and this introspective disagreement is problematic because it calls into question the reliability of our introspective

---

[19] For the reductionist view that all cognitive experience can be explained in sensory terms, see Tye (1995), Lormand (1996), Wilson (2003), Robinson (2005), and Prinz (2007).
[20] For another example, see Strawson's (1994: 18–21) virtuosic description of a stream of "four seconds of thought" that unfolds "too fast for subvocalized words."

reports about nonsensory thought. Perhaps the disagreement can be explained away as the result of interpersonal variation in the extent to which people think in imagery or inner speech. A more unsettling possibility, though, is that these introspective disagreements may be driven by background theoretical commitments about the nature of consciousness. If so, then perhaps introspective reports of nonsensory thinking cannot be trusted, especially when they are made by philosophers (like me) who are concerned to advance a specific theoretical agenda.[21]

This qualm can be alleviated to some extent by Russell Hurlburt's (1990) empirical studies using the method of "descriptive experience sampling." In these studies, subjects are instructed to record their experiences when a paging device beeps at random intervals throughout the day. Subjects frequently report the experience of *unsymbolized thinking*, which is defined as "the experience of an explicit, differentiated thought that does not include the experience of words, images, or any other symbols" (Hurlburt and Akhter 2008: 1364). This is one of the five categories of experience that are most frequently reported by subjects, together with sensory awareness, sensory imagery, inner speech, and emotional feelings. According to Heavey and Hurlburt (2008), there is some interpersonal variation in the frequency of these experiences, but each occurs in about a quarter of all samples. It is reasonable to conclude that unsymbolized thinking is not just a philosopher's invention. On the contrary, it is a widespread and frequently occurring human experience.

The second objection I'll raise is more concessive. Suppose we grant for the sake of argument that all conscious thought and judgment is expressed in some sensory medium. We still cannot explain its phenomenal character without appealing to its phenomenal force and content. This is because the same sensory medium can express different thoughts or judgments in a way that makes an overall phenomenal difference. I'll divide this objection into two parts.

First, sensory experience cannot explain the distinctive *force* associated with the experience of judgment. This is because the same sensory experience can be associated with different kinds of phenomenal force. As Christopher Peacocke (2007: 365–366) points out, the words "Meeting tomorrow!" can occur in the context of judgment, decision, memory, or imagination. In each case, the overall experience is very different. Jesse Prinz (2007: 349–350) replies that judgment and decision are associated with different "epistemic emotions," which he identifies with perceptions of bodily changes. The problem is that it seems quite implausible that there is always some experience of bodily

---

[21] Of course, many opponents of nonsensory thinking have a theoretical agenda too. One traditional motivation for denying cognitive representationalism is the desire to insulate the easy problem of explaining cognition from the hard problem of explaining consciousness.

perception associated with the experience of judging or deciding that there will be a meeting tomorrow. A much more plausible explanation is that judgments and decisions have different kinds of phenomenal force.[22]

Second, sensory experience cannot explain the distinctive *content* associated with the experience of judgment. This is because interpretation makes a phenomenal difference to the experience of imagery and inner speech. For instance, Galen Strawson (1994: 5–9) notes that there is a distinctive kind of experience associated with understanding speech. He illustrates this point by contrasting the experience of two monoglots, an Englishman called 'Jack' and a Frenchman called 'Jacques', as they listen to the same news broadcast on French television. A similar point applies when the speech is not heard, but subvocalized in inner speech.[23]

One problem with Strawson's example is that understanding language affects one's experience of various nonsemantic properties, including syntactic, phonological, and orthographic properties. So perhaps we can explain the phenomenal difference between Jack and Jacques without appealing to the content of their auditory experience or inner speech. Understanding speech involves segmenting it into words and phrases, while foreign speech in contrast sounds like a continuous, unstructured stream of noise. Moreover, understanding a language affects one's experience of phonemes, the language-specific types of sounds that are treated as equivalent by any given language. For example, the words 'raw' and 'law' sound the same to Japanese speakers, but different to English speakers, while the 't' in 'stun' and 'ton' sound the same to English speakers, but different to Chinese speakers.[24]

Plausibly, however, understanding speech involves experience of semantic as well as nonsemantic properties. Consider the phenomenal contrast involved in switching between different interpretations of a lexically ambiguous utterance, such as "I hope the food's not too hot for you" (Siewert 1998: 278). In this case, there is no change in your experience of its sound or structure. Rather, your understanding of its semantic content makes a phenomenal difference. This content need not be reflected in your imaginative or emotional experience. You simply experience the utterance as meaning one thing or another. Again, the same point applies when the utterance is not heard, but subvocalized in inner speech. More generally, the experience of understanding, thought, and judgment varies depending on its semantic content. This is because all cognitive experience has phenomenal content.

---

[22] Peacocke (2007) argues that these are two different species of *action awareness*, the experience of mental action. Arguably, however, not all judgments are actions: consider the experience of suddenly realizing that you've left your keys at home.
[23] Similar points are made by Peacocke (1992: 89–90), Siewert (1998: 275–276), Horgan and Tienson (2002: 522–523), Pitt (2004: 26–29), and Siegel (2010: 99–100).
[24] See O'Callaghan (2010) for an informative discussion of phoneme perception.

Understanding speech is a kind of high-level perception.[25] Consider phoneme perception: it requires high-level processing of sensory inputs, since the boundaries between phonemes do not correspond directly to acoustic properties of speech. At the same time, this perceptual processing is largely encapsulated from cognition. This is illustrated by the McGurk effect, an illusion of phoneme perception that is resistant to influence by your beliefs and desires. In much the same way, perception of syntactic and semantic properties requires high-level processing of sensory inputs, although this perceptual processing is largely encapsulated from your beliefs and desires. As Jerry Fodor remarks, "You can't hear speech as noise *even if you would prefer to*" (1983: 53).

If understanding speech involves high-level perception, then it's plausible that inner speech involves high-level perceptual imagery. Unlike the experience of hearing voices, it may involve motor imagery, rather than pure auditory phenomenology. In any case, the experience of inner speech depends on interpretation just as much as the experience of external speech. The experience of subvocalizing an ambiguous sentence varies depending on how its content is understood. Similarly, the experience varies depending on whether the subvocalized sentence is used in making a judgment or forming a decision.

This suggests an alternative strategy for resolving the conflict between reductionism and cognitive representationalism. One strategy is to argue that reductionism is false because there is some nonsensory cognitive experience, such as the experience of unsymbolized thinking. An alternative response is that reductionism is compatible with cognitive representationalism because all cognitive experience has phenomenal force and content even when couched in a sensory medium: for example, there are high-level perceptual experiences in which sensory imagery is given a semantic interpretation. Arguably, this kind of high-level perceptual experience is rich enough to determine the representational contents of cognition. This means that we can defend cognitive representationalism without taking issue with the reductionist thesis that all cognitive experience is reducible to perceptual experience. In my view, the truth of reductionism is hard to evaluate because its proponents have not clearly defined the distinction between perceptual experience and cognitive experience. Since this issue remains obscure, proponents of cognitive representationalism can remain neutral on whether or not reductionism is true.[26]

---

[25] For further discussion of high-level perception, see Siewert (1998: 361–362), Bayne (2009), and Siegel (2010). See also Fodor (1983: 96–97) on the outputs of perceptual modules.

[26] Compare Levine (2011) for a similar point about the independence of reductionism and cognitive representationalism.

4.5.2. The Argument
from Introspective Knowledge

I'll now give an epistemological argument for the thesis that judgment has phenomenal force and content. This argument is another inference to the best explanation. The epistemological datum to be explained is that we can sometimes know by introspection alone which judgments we're currently making. The best explanation of this datum, or so I will argue, is that judgment has phenomenal force and content.[27]

This is an instance of a more general strategy for arguing that experience has phenomenal force and content. We all have some introspective knowledge about the contents of our own sensory experience. For instance, I can know by introspection whether I'm visualizing red or green. How can I know this on the basis of introspection alone? The answer is that there is a phenomenal difference between visualizing red and green. The difference in content between these experiences is constituted by the phenomenal difference between them. Moreover, this phenomenal difference explains how I can know by introspection whether I am visualizing the one content or the other.

This line of reasoning can be extended from perception to cognition. We all have some introspective knowledge about the contents of our own cognitive experience. I can know by introspection, for example, whether I am consciously thinking about politics or religion. How can I know what I'm thinking on the basis of introspection alone? As before, the answer is that there is a phenomenal difference between thinking about politics and religion. The difference in content between these thoughts is constituted by the phenomenal difference between them. This phenomenal difference explains how I can know by introspection whether I'm thinking about one thing or the other.

The argument has exactly the same structure in each case. The datum to be explained is that we have some introspective knowledge of the representational properties of experience. Moreover, the best explanation of the datum is that experience has phenomenal force and content: it has representational properties that are identical with its phenomenal properties. Since we have some introspective knowledge of the phenomenal properties of experience, we thereby have some introspective knowledge of its representational properties, since every phenomenal property of experience is identical with some

---

[27] Goldman (1993) and Pitt (2004) give epistemological arguments that conscious thought has representational force and content in virtue of its phenomenal character, but their arguments rely on broadly perceptual models of introspection. I'll formulate the argument here in a way that is relatively neutral between different theories of introspection, but I'll defend what I call a "simple theory" of introspection in chapter 5.

representational property. Although this argument applies more generally, I'll focus on its application to the cognitive experience of judgment:

(1) I can sometimes know by introspection which judgments I'm currently making.
(2) I can sometimes know by introspection which judgments I'm currently making only because judgment has phenomenal force and content.
(3) Therefore, judgment has phenomenal force and content.

Blocking this argument requires either denying that we can have introspective knowledge of judgment or explaining our introspective knowledge of judgment without appealing to its phenomenal force and content. I'll consider each of these options in turn.

A radical version of the first option would be to deny that we can have any introspective knowledge of experience at all. Gilbert Ryle (1949) is sometimes credited with the thesis that we can only know our own minds in the same way that we know the minds of others—that is, by inference from observed behavior. The problem with this thesis, whether or not Ryle endorsed it, is that it cannot explain how we know our own experience when it has no causal influence on our behavior. To borrow Paul Boghossian's example, you might know by introspection that you're currently thinking that even lousy composers sometimes write great arias. He writes, "Your knowledge of that occurrent thought could not have been inferred from any premises about your behavior because that thought could not yet have come to have any traction on your behavior" (1989a: 8).

A slightly less radical version of the first option would be to claim, as Peter Carruthers (2011) does, that we have introspective knowledge of perceptual states, but not cognitive states. On this view, what we take to be introspective knowledge of conscious thought is in fact the result of an unconscious inference from premises about our sensory experiences, behavior, or external circumstances. This proposal, like Ryle's, faces a version of Boghossian's problem. It cannot explain how we know what we're thinking when we have no relevant sensory, behavioral, or circumstantial evidence to draw upon—say, when we're lying motionless in bed. The problem is clearest in cases of unsymbolized thought. But the problem remains even if our thoughts are couched in inner speech, since the low-level sensory aspects of experience cannot fix a unique interpretation for our thoughts.[28]

---

[28] Ultimately, Carruthers adopts an error theory: we don't know as much as we think we do about our own thoughts and judgments. To motivate this, he appeals to empirical evidence that people sometimes engage in confabulation. Even so, it's not clear that self-ascription of cognition is always based on inference. Nichols and Stich (2003: ch. 4) and Goldman (2006: ch. 9) defend dual-process

The second option is to concede that we have introspective knowledge of our own thoughts and judgments, but to explain this without appealing to the thesis that cognitive experience has phenomenal force and content. The usual strategy is to endorse a version of reliabilism that explains our introspective knowledge in terms of the operation of a reliable introspective mechanism. So, for example, Shaun Nichols and Stephen Stich explain our introspective knowledge of what we believe in terms of the operation of what they call a "Monitoring Mechanism":

> To have beliefs about one's own beliefs, all that is required is that there be a Monitoring Mechanism (MM) that, when activated, takes the representation p in the Belief Box as input and produces the representation *I believe that p* as output. This mechanism would be trivial to implement. To produce representations of one's own beliefs, the Monitoring Mechanism merely has to copy representations from the Belief Box, embed the copies in a representation schema of the form: *I believe that* —, and then place the new representations back in the Belief Box. (2003: 160–161)

Joseph Levine (2011: 106–107) explains our introspective knowledge of thought in much the same way. We just need a mechanism that takes as input a mental representation that p, embeds it in a representation schema of the form *I think that p*, and then deposits it in the Belief Box without mediation by inference. Levine claims that this kind of mechanism can yield introspective knowledge so long as it is sufficiently reliable. There is no further requirement that the mental representations it takes as input must have phenomenal force and content.

This reliabilist account of introspective knowledge is implausible, since reliability is not sufficient for a belief to be justified (see section 3.2). Recall Ned Block's (1995) example of the *super-blindsighter* who has a reliable disposition to form true beliefs about the blind field on the basis of unconscious visual information. These first-order beliefs are reliable, but they are unjustified. The same applies to the *super-duper-blindsighter* who has a reliable disposition to form true beliefs about his unconscious visual states without mediation by inference. Again, these higher-order beliefs are reliable, but unjustified. The same kinds of counterexamples apply in perception and introspection alike. Moreover, the absence of phenomenal consciousness explains why these reliable beliefs are unjustified in each case. Hence, we should conclude that

---

theories, according to which which we can use inferential and noninferential processes in self-ascribing cognitive states.

phenomenal consciousness plays an essential role in explaining our introspective knowledge of our own thoughts and judgments.

Nichols and Stich (2003: 197–198) argue that phenomenal consciousness plays no essential role in explaining our introspective knowledge of cognition. After all, we can know by introspection what we believe, but phenomenal consciousness plays no role in explaining this introspective knowledge, since beliefs have no phenomenal character at all. In my view, this objection is much too quick. In this chapter, I've argued that the contents of belief are accessible to phenomenal consciousness as the contents of judgment. Moreover, in the next chapter, I'll argue that this point is crucial for explaining our introspective knowledge of what we believe. We can know what we believe by means of introspection only because the contents of belief are accessible to consciousness as the contents of conscious judgment. On this view, we cannot explain our introspective knowledge of what we believe without appealing to phenomenal consciousness.

4.6. Conclusions

Can zombies have beliefs? Searle argues that zombies cannot have beliefs because they cannot have representational states at all. According to Searle's Connection Principle, all unconscious representational states are accessible to consciousness. On my view, in contrast, zombies can have mental representations, but they cannot have beliefs, since their mental representations cannot provide epistemic justification for belief. According to my Epistemic Connection Principle, all unconscious representational states that provide epistemic justification for belief are accessible to consciousness.

In this chapter, I argued for the Epistemic Connection Principle on the grounds that it provides the best explanation of the normative distinction between beliefs and subdoxastic states. I motivated this claim by appealing to intuitions about cases in which conscious accessibility comes apart from other functional criteria, such as inferential integration. Although these intuitions about cases make it plausible that the Epistemic Connection Principle is true, they don't provide much reflective understanding of why it is true. An explanatory challenge therefore remains. Why must unconscious representational states be accessible to consciousness in order to play an epistemic role in the justification of belief?

In the second part of this book, I'll answer this explanatory challenge by appealing to a form of *accessibilism*, which says that epistemic justification is luminous in the sense that you're always in a position to know which beliefs you have epistemic justification to hold. I'll argue that epistemic justification is luminous only because it is determined by mental states that are luminous through introspection. Moreover, I'll argue in the next chapter that mental states are luminous through introspection only if they are conscious or accessible to consciousness. It follows that only conscious and consciously accessible mental states play a role in determining which propositions you have epistemic justification to believe. This gives us a more principled theoretical argument for the Epistemic Connection Principle:

(1) All mental states that provide epistemic justification for belief are introspectively luminous.
(2) All introspectively luminous mental states are either conscious or accessible to consciousness.
(3) Therefore, all mental states that provide epistemic justification for belief are either conscious or accessible to consciousness.

Accessibilism therefore plays an important role in explaining why beliefs must be accessible to consciousness in order to provide epistemic justification for other beliefs.

Let me close by contrasting my account of the role of consciousness in cognition with a nearby alternative proposed by Adam Pautz (2013). The contrast is worth exploring because Pautz and I agree that a zombie cannot have beliefs, although we disagree about why not. On my account, the contents of beliefs are derived from the contents of the judgments they are disposed to cause. On Pautz's account, in contrast, the contents of beliefs are derived from the contents of the perceptual experiences that make them rational. So the disagreement between us concerns whether the contents of belief are grounded in the contents of cognitive experience or perceptual experience.

Pautz argues for a view he calls "phenomenal functionalism," which combines David Lewis's (1974) functionalism about belief and desire with a broadly phenomenal conception of perceptual evidence. According to Lewis, the contents of your beliefs and desires are fixed by the "best interpretation" of your behavior—that is, the one that maximizes the rationality of your behavior given your perceptual evidence. Pautz combines Lewis's functionalism about belief and desire with a phenomenal conception of perceptual evidence, according to which perceptual evidence is constituted by perceptual experience. On this view, the contents of your most basic beliefs are fixed by the contents of the perceptual experiences that make them rational, while the contents of your perceptual experiences are fixed by their phenomenal character. In this way, the contents of cognition are ultimately grounded in phenomenal consciousness.

Lewis's functionalism implies that the mental is normative in a much stronger sense than I'm willing to countenance. On his view, the mental is normative in the sense that beliefs and desires are essentially the kinds of states that conform—if not perfectly, then well enough—with norms of epistemic and practical rationality. This version of functionalism seems much too demanding to explain the kind of systematic irrationality that is not only conceptually possible, but also scientifically confirmed.[29] On my own view, in contrast, the mental is normative in a much weaker sense: beliefs and desires are always subject to norms of epistemic and practical rationality, although they do not always comply with those norms. On this view, beliefs and desires are subject to rational norms in virtue of their phenomenal dispositions. We can explain why beliefs and desires are governed by different norms by appealing to their different phenomenal dispositions. This view gives us much more latitude in explaining the presence of beliefs and desires in delusional patients and other extremely irrational agents who systematically violate the norms of epistemic and practical rationality.

Setting this problem aside, I want to close by suggesting that phenomenal functionalism is unstable because Lewis's functionalism undermines the best motivation for the phenomenal conception of perceptual evidence. Why suppose that only perceptual experience provides evidence or epistemic reasons that justify beliefs about the external world? If unconscious perception in zombies has determinate content, and if it justifies beliefs about the external world, then why can't it play the same role as perceptual experience in fixing determinate contents for zombie beliefs? Here are two contrasting strategies for answering this challenge.

The first strategy appeals to the role of phenomenal consciousness in fixing determinate contents for our mental representations. On this view, only phenomenal consciousness can supply a determinate ground of mental representation, since the alternative is to ground consciousness in tracking relations that leave the contents of mental representation radically indeterminate. For example, Pautz (2013: 222–224) motivates a nonreductive version of representationalism about perceptual experience in part by appealing to indeterminacy problems for causal theories of perceptual content. The idea is that only the phenomenal character of perceptual experience suffices to fix its determinate content. This means that if there is unconscious perception in zombies, then its content is radically indeterminate. This is why unconscious perception in zombies cannot play the same role as perceptual experience in fixing determinate belief content.

---

[29] Bortolotti (2010) argues against rationality constraints on belief by defending a doxastic conception of delusion. Smithies and Weiss (2019) argue that Lewis's (1980b) case of "mad pain" also has analogues for belief and desire.

I criticized this style of argument in chapter 2. Even if we cannot give a reductive definition of mental representation in terms of tracking relations, we should nevertheless regard it as a legitimate scientific kind insofar as it plays an indispensable role in psychological explanation. Moreover, we have good reason to believe that zombies, like the zombie systems in our brains, have unconscious representations that play an indispensable role in psychological explanation. Since the first strategy is committed to denying that zombies have mental representations with reasonably determinate contents, it should be rejected on empirical grounds.

The second strategy appeals to the epistemic role of phenomenal consciousness in providing epistemic justification for beliefs about the external world. On this view, perception provides evidence or epistemic reasons that justify beliefs about the external world only if it is phenomenally conscious. This view allows that zombies can have unconscious perceptions with determinate contents, although these unconscious perceptions cannot provide epistemic justification for beliefs about the external world. That is why unconscious perception in zombies cannot play the same role as perceptual experience in fixing determinate belief content.

The problem is that the best theoretical motivation for this claim about the epistemic role of phenomenal consciousness is in tension with Lewis's functionalism about belief and desire. As I've just indicated, the best argument for the epistemic role of phenomenal consciousness appeals to accessibilism, the thesis that epistemic justification is luminous. On this view, perceptual evidence must be phenomenally conscious in order to provide epistemic justification for belief in a way that is luminous through introspection. For the same reason, doxastic evidence must be accessible to phenomenal consciousness in order to provide epistemic justification for belief in a way that is luminous through introspection. Phenomenal functionalism is self-undermining because functionalism about belief undermines this motivation for the phenomenal conception of evidence. If your beliefs are individuated by their behavioral dispositions, rather than their phenomenal dispositions, then they are not luminous through introspection.

Phenomenal functionalism faces a choice between three unattractive options. The first option is to reject accessibilism about epistemic justification, which undermines the best motivation for endorsing the phenomenal conception of evidence in the first place. The second option is to deny that beliefs provide epistemic justification for other beliefs, which results in an implausible version of the phenomenal conception of evidence. The third option is to insist that beliefs are introspectively luminous even if they are functionally individuated by their behavioral dispositions, which is hard to sustain. Lewis (1972: 258) takes the third option: he argues that we can build introspective self-knowledge into the functional role of belief: on this view, it is true by definition that you always know by introspection whatever you believe. The problem is that this strategy builds luminosity into the psychological conditions for belief, rather than the normative conditions for epistemic rationality. This exacerbates the more general problem with functionalism that I've already mentioned—namely, that it results in an implausibly demanding version of the thesis that the mental is normative.

This is ultimately why the contents of belief must be grounded in cognitive experience, rather than perceptual experience. Why privilege cognitive-phenomenal dispositions over sensory-behavioral dispositions in the individuation of belief and desire? The answer is that our beliefs and desires are introspectively luminous only if they are individuated by their cognitive-phenomenal dispositions, rather than their sensory-behavioral dispositions. As I'll explain in chapter 5, our beliefs are introspectively luminous only because they are phenomenally individuated by their dispositions to cause phenomenally conscious judgments. And as I'll explain in the rest of the book, our beliefs provide epistemic justification only because they are introspectively luminous.

5

Introspection

What is introspection? According to William James, "The word 'introspection' need hardly be defined—it means, of course, the looking into our own minds and reporting of what we there discover" ([1890] 1981: 85). We shouldn't assume, however, that introspection is a form of inner perception. Instead, we can use the term 'introspection' as a label for the distinctive way—whatever it is—in which we know our own minds. This is to make the reasonable assumption that we have some distinctive way of knowing about our own minds, but without prejudging its nature. The task for a theory of introspection is to account for our knowledge of our own minds in a way that explains what makes it distinctive.

Introspection has a distinctive subject matter: to a first approximation, it is a way of knowing about one's own current mental states, as contrasted with one's past mental states, the mental states of others, or the physical states of the external world. We cannot define introspection solely in terms of its subject matter, however, since this would collapse the distinction between knowing about one's own mental states by introspection and knowing about them in some third-personal way—say, by inference from premises about behavior. This distinction between first-person and third-person perspectives on our own minds is exactly what a theory of introspection needs to explain.

Following Alex Byrne (2005), we can distinguish two dimensions of the epistemic asymmetry between first-person and third-person perspectives on the mind—that is, between the way in which we know about our own minds and the way in which we know about the minds of others. First, introspection is "peculiar" in the sense that it is epistemically different from other ways of knowing about the world; and second, it is "privileged" in the sense that it is epistemically more secure than other ways of knowing about the world. Any theory of introspection should explain the sense in which it gives us peculiar and privileged epistemic access to our own mental states.

This chapter argues for what I call "the simple theory" of introspection, which says that some mental states are introspectively luminous in the sense that you're always in an epistemic position to know whether or not you're in those mental states.[1] The simple theory is compatible with various different answers to "the scope question": that is, which mental states are introspectively luminous in this sense? I'll argue that all introspectively luminous mental states are individuated by their phenomenal character or by their phenomenal dispositions. Hence, phenomenal consciousness plays an indispensable role in explaining our introspective knowledge of our own minds.

Here is the plan for the chapter. I'll begin by presenting the simple theory (section 5.1), defending it against objections (section 5.2) and explaining the motivations for the theory (section 5.3). Next, I'll give my answer to the scope question (section 5.4) and explore the role of phenomenal consciousness in explaining our introspective knowledge of what we believe (section 5.5). Finally, I'll consider whether the connection between phenomenal consciousness and introspection can be further explained (section 5.6).

5.1. The Simple Theory of Introspection

It is sometimes said that our knowledge of our own minds, like our knowledge of the minds of others, must be based on either perception, inference, or nothing at all. For example, Paul Boghossian (1989a) argues for skepticism about introspective knowledge by showing that none of these options can be made to work. One response to this skeptical challenge is to reject the initial assumption that our knowledge of our own minds must be based on perception, inference, or else nothing at all. This is the option taken by Christopher Peacocke, who regards this assumption as a "spurious trilemma" (1998: 83).

Peacocke argues that you can know that you're in some conscious state by making what he calls a "consciously-based self-ascription"—that is, by forming a belief immediately or noninferentially on the basis of that conscious state. For example, you can know that you feel pain by forming the belief that you feel pain immediately and noninferentially on the basis of the feeling of pain. This knowledge is based on neither perception nor inference, but it is not based on nothing at all. The feeling of pain gives you an introspective reason to believe that you feel pain. Moreover, you can believe that you feel pain on the basis of this reason without relying on either perception or inference. As Peacocke says, "An experience of pain can be a thinker's reason for judging that he is in pain" (1998: 72).

The simple theory of introspection extends this proposal. It says that when you have an introspective reason to believe that you're in a certain kind of

---

[1] I first presented the simple theory of introspection in Smithies (2012a), but similar proposals are defended by Ayer (1963), Chisholm (1989), Peacocke (1998), Pryor (2005), Zimmerman (2004), Shoemaker (2009), and Neta (2011). These are all versions of what Alston (1989: ch. 10) calls the "truth-sufficiency" account of privileged access.

mental state, you have that reason just by virtue of being in that mental state. There is no further requirement that you have some inner perception that you're in that mental state, or that you have reason to believe the premises of a noncircular argument for the conclusion that you're in that mental state. The mere fact that you're in that mental state is sufficient to give you an introspective reason to believe that you're in that mental state. This is what sets the simple theory apart from perceptual and inferential theories of introspection.[2]

According to the simple theory, some mental states are *self-intimating* in the sense that they provide introspective reasons for beliefs about themselves:

> *The Self-Intimation Thesis*: For some mental states M, necessarily, if you're in M, then you thereby have an introspective reason to believe that you're in M.

An *introspective reason* is a reason for believing that you're in some mental state, which you have just by virtue of the fact that you're in that mental state. As always, these reasons for belief are sensitive to modes of presentation. Suppose pain is identical with C-fiber firing. If you feel pain, then you have an introspective reason to believe that you feel pain, but you don't have an introspective reason to believe that your C-fibers are firing. In other words, you have an introspective reason to believe this phenomenal fact under a phenomenal mode of presentation, rather than a neurophysiological mode of presentation. I'll take this point for granted in the discussion to follow.

Because you have introspective reasons in virtue of facts about your mental states, they have various distinctive epistemological properties. In particular, they are immediate, infallible, indubitable, indefeasible, and immune from error in epistemically close cases:

(1) *Immediacy*: Necessarily, if you have an introspective reason to believe that you're in M, then you have that reason just because you're in M, and not because you have reason to believe anything else.

(2) *Infallibility*: Necessarily, if you have an introspective reason to believe that you're in M, then you're in M, since you have the reason just because you're in M.

(3) *Indubitability*: Necessarily, if you have an introspective reason to believe that you're in M, then it is certain that you're in M, since having the reason entails that you're in M.

---

[2] Perceptual theories of introspection are defended by Armstrong (1968), Lycan (1995), and Goldman (2006), while inferential theories are defended by Ryle (1949), Byrne (2005), Carruthers (2011), and Cassam (2014).

(4) *Indefeasibility*: Necessarily, if you have an introspective reason to believe that you're in M, then it is not defeated by reasons to believe anything else, since it is certain that you're in M.

(5) *Epistemic safety*: Necessarily, if you have an introspective reason to believe that you're in M, then you're immune from error in all epistemically close cases in which you have the same reasons for belief, since you have those reasons only if you're in M.

Because introspective reasons have all these distinctive epistemic features, we can endorse what we might call *the bridging thesis*, which says that having an introspective reason to believe that you're in a mental state puts you in a position to know by introspection that you're in that mental state:

The Bridging Thesis: For all mental states M, necessarily, if you have an introspective reason to believe that you're in M, then you're in a position to know by introspection that you're in M.

If we combine the self-intimation thesis with the bridging thesis, we can derive the further conclusion that some mental states are *luminous* in the following sense:

The Luminosity Thesis: For some mental states M, necessarily, if you're in M, then you're in a position to know by means of introspection that you're in M.

Timothy Williamson (2000: ch. 4) argues that nothing is luminous in the sense that you're always in a position to know that it obtains when it does. However, I'll defend the luminosity thesis against Williamson's argument in chapter 11.

Introspection provides you with knowledge of negative facts as well as positive facts about your mental states.[3] Just as you can know by introspection when you're in pain, so you can know by introspection when you're *not* in pain. But when you know by introspection that you're not in pain, what is your reason for believing that you're not in pain? We cannot say that the negative fact that you're not in pain is your reason for believing that you're not in pain. After all, an inanimate object like my laptop is not in pain, but it doesn't thereby have a reason to believe that it's not in pain. Given that you're not an inanimate object,

---

[3] Sosa (2003: 135–137) raises this point as an objection to Peacocke's (1998) theory of introspective self-knowledge. Stoljar (2012a: 395–398) argues that the response proposed here violates a safety condition for knowledge. This objection raises many of the same issues discussed in connection with the problem of the speckled hen in section 11.2.

however, your reason for believing that you're in pain is the fact that you're in some total mental state that *includes* being in pain, whereas your reason to believe that you're not in pain is the fact that you're in some total mental state that *excludes* being in pain.

In other words, the simple theory says that some mental states are *strongly luminous* in the sense that you're always in a position to know whether or not you're in them:

> *The Strong Luminosity Thesis*: For some mental states M, necessarily, you're always in a position to know by means of introspection whether or not you're in M.

You're always in a position to know, for example, whether or not you're in pain: if your total conscious state includes being in pain, then you're in a position to know that you're in pain, and if it excludes being in pain, then you're in a position to know that you're not in pain.

The simple theory explains the sense in which introspection gives us peculiar access to our own mental states. Introspection is peculiar because our introspective reasons for beliefs about mental states have their source in those very mental states. When I feel cold, this gives me an introspective reason to believe that I feel cold, and I'm thereby in a position to know that I feel cold by forming a belief on the basis of this reason. Other people are sometimes in a position to know that I feel cold on the basis of reasons provided by perception, testimony, or inference, but they're never in a position to know that I feel cold on the basis of reasons provided by the fact that I feel cold. This way of knowing about our own mental states is different from our ways of knowing about the mental states of other people.

The simple theory also explains the sense in which introspection gives us privileged access to our own mental states. Introspection is privileged because I am always in a position to know whether or not I feel cold. When I feel cold, I thereby have a reason to believe that I feel cold, which puts me in a position to know that I feel cold by forming a belief on the basis of that reason. Similarly, mutatis mutandis, if I don't feel cold. Other people are sometimes in a position to know whether I feel cold when they have good reasons provided by perception, testimony, or inference. And yet no one else is always guaranteed to have good reasons of this kind. We're always in a position to know whether we ourselves feel cold, but we're not always in a position to know whether other people feel cold. In that sense, introspection is epistemically superior to other ways of knowing about the world.

The simple theory is a version of *constitutivism*—the thesis that there is a constitutive, essential, or necessary connection between being in a certain mental state and standing in some doxastic or epistemic relation to that mental state. We can distinguish further between doxastic and epistemic forms of constitutivism:

> *Doxastic constitutivism*: For some M, necessarily, if you're in M, then you *know*, and hence *believe*, that you're in M.

> *Epistemic constitutivism*: For some M, necessarily, if you're in M, then you're in a *position to know*, and hence you have *justification to believe*, that you're in M.

The simple theory is a form of epistemic constitutivism, rather than doxastic constitutivism. Epistemic constitutivism doesn't imply doxastic constitutivism because we don't always convert our epistemic position into knowledge. In some cases, we have introspective reasons that justify believing that we're in some mental state, but we don't succeed in forming a justified belief on the basis of those reasons. An ideally rational agent always converts her epistemic position into knowledge when she forms an opinion on some question. Sadly, we humans are not ideally rational agents.

Doxastic constitutivism is implausible because of these human limitations. Even if we restrict the thesis to phenomenal states, such as feeling pain, we can find cases in which subjects are in phenomenal states without believing that they are in them. Here are some of the most obvious counterexamples:

(1) *Conceptual poverty*: A newborn infant feels pain, but she lacks the conceptual abilities required to form the belief that she feels pain.

(2) *Inattention*: An athlete incurs a painful injury while playing football, but her attention is distracted, so she doesn't notice that she feels pain until the game is over.

(3) *Miscategorization*: A student in a fraternity initiation trick is threatened with a red-hot poker, and then an ice cube is pressed on the back of his neck, which dupes him into believing that he feels an intensely painful sensation of heat, when in fact he feels a mildly unpleasant sensation of cold.

(4) *Delusion*: A patient with Anton's syndrome believes he can see, and believes he has visual experiences, although in fact he is completely blind.

These cases pose no serious problems for epistemic constitutivism. In each case, the subject has an introspective reason that justifies believing some fact about her experience, but she cannot form an introspectively justified belief on the basis of this reason. These are cases in which the subject cannot convert propositional justification into doxastic justification because of some fact about her psychological limitations: she is conceptually impoverished, or inattentive, or undiscriminating, or delusional. As a result, the subject is unable to convert her epistemic position into knowledge.

The luminosity thesis doesn't entail that you're always capable of converting your epistemic position into knowledge. If you have an introspective reason to believe that you're in a mental state, and you form that belief in a way that is properly based on your reason, then you thereby know by introspection that you're in that mental state. However, there is no guarantee that you always have the capacity to form beliefs that are properly based on your introspective reasons. We can do this sometimes, but not always. In the next section, I'll use this point in defending the simple theory against some objections.

5.2. The Reliability Challenge

My goal in this section is to defend the simple theory against the objection that it makes implausible psychological commitments concerning the reliability of introspection. Let us begin by distinguishing the following pair of questions about introspection:

(1) *An epistemological question*: What is the source of our introspective reasons to form beliefs about our own mental states?

(2) *A psychological question*: What are the psychological processes or mechanisms that we use in forming introspective beliefs about our own mental states?

The simple theory is an account of the source of our introspective reasons, rather than the psychological processes we use in forming introspective beliefs on the basis of these reasons. It says an introspective reason to believe that you're in a certain mental state has its source in the fact that you're in that mental state. It's another question which psychological processes are involved when you form beliefs about your mental states. For reasons that I'll explain, however, the simple theory cannot remain entirely silent on this question. So it remains to be seen whether the psychological commitments incurred by the simple theory are defensible. The main goal of this section is to argue that these psychological commitments are weak enough to be plausible.

It is a Moorean fact that we have some introspective knowledge about our own mental states: this is more certain than the premises of skeptical arguments to the contrary. We may not have quite as much introspective knowledge as we often suppose, but it is beyond the pale to suppose that we have none at all.

Any plausible theory of introspection should explain how introspective knowledge is possible for creatures like us. But can the simple theory of introspection satisfy this Moorean constraint? In order to answer this question, we need an account of what our psychological processes must be like in order to yield introspective knowledge. Therefore, the simple theory of introspection cannot remain entirely silent about the answer to the psychological question.

We cannot acquire introspective knowledge unless our introspective processes are sufficiently reliable. Only beliefs held on the basis of reliable processes can be knowledge. Sometimes, our beliefs are justified even when they are not reliable enough to be knowledge. In the case of introspection, however, this possibility is ruled out by the proper basing condition for doxastic justification. Your beliefs are properly based on your reasons only if they are held in a way that is reliably responsive to your possession of those reasons. The simple theory says that your introspective reasons have their source in facts about your mental states. Hence, your beliefs are properly based on your introspective reasons only if they are held in a way that is reliably responsive to the mental facts in virtue of which you possess those reasons. This means that your beliefs are introspectively justified only when they are formed in a sufficiently reliable way. Reliability is therefore necessary for beliefs to be doxastically justified on the basis of introspection.[4]

The simple theory is not a version of reliabilism, however, since reliability is neither necessary nor sufficient for beliefs to be propositionally justified by introspective reasons. According to the simple theory, introspective reasons have their source not in the reliability of your introspective processes for forming beliefs about your mental states, but rather in your mental states themselves. Reliability is not *necessary* for propositional justification because you can have introspective reasons for beliefs about your mental states without having any reliable means of forming justified beliefs on the basis of those reasons. Reliability is not *sufficient* for propositional justification because false beliefs are not supported by introspective reasons even when they result from a generally reliable introspective process. On the simple theory, reliability is implicated in doxastic justification, rather than propositional justification.

With these clarifications in place, I'll now defend the simple theory of introspection against the objection that it is incompatible with Eric Schwitzgebel's (2011) *unreliability thesis*.[5] This is the thesis that introspection is unreliable

---

[4] Reliability is also sufficient for beliefs to be doxastically justified by introspection: there cannot be an introspective clairvoyant who forms beliefs about his own experience in a reliable way, but whose beliefs are not introspectively justified.

[5] This section draws on the exchange between Smithies (2013a) and Schwitzgebel (2013).

in the sense that we are highly prone to uncertainty and error in making introspective judgments about our own current conscious experience. Schwitzgebel motivates the unreliability thesis by examining a series of hard cases—including dreams, depth perception, echolocation, imagery, inattention, emotion, conscious thought, and phosphenes—in which we encounter introspective uncertainty or disagreement about the nature of conscious experience. These cases serve as the basis for extrapolating to the more general conclusion that our introspective judgments about the most general features of conscious experience are unreliable in the sense that they are prone to uncertainty and error.

I won't attempt to summarize Schwitzgebel's rich and intriguing discussion of these various case studies, since that would be an impossible task. Instead, let me simply concede his unreliability thesis, at least for the sake of argument, in order to examine its implications for the simple theory. I'll consider three objections to the simple theory, which concern its implications for (i) introspective skepticism, (ii) the nature of privileged access, and (iii) the possibility of reasonable disagreement and uncertainty in hard cases.

The first objection is that if the unreliability thesis is true, then introspective skepticism follows. According to the simple theory, we cannot have introspective knowledge unless our beliefs are formed in a sufficiently reliable way. If the unreliability thesis is true, however, then this necessary condition for introspective knowledge seems to be violated. The simple theory therefore fails to satisfy the Moorean constraint of explaining how introspective knowledge is possible for creatures like us.

In reply, Schwitzgebel's unreliability thesis does not license introspective skepticism. What he shows is that there are many hard cases in which introspection is powerless to resolve disagreement or uncertainty about the nature of conscious experience. But the existence of hard cases in which we cannot acquire introspective knowledge does not preclude the existence of easier cases in which we can. Schwitzgebel's achievement is to show that there are more hard cases, and fewer easier cases, than we might otherwise have recognized. But he doesn't show—or even claim to show—that introspective knowledge can never be had at all. Indeed, he explicitly says, "I am not an utter skeptic" (2011: 139).

Schwitzgebel's unreliability thesis motivates a moderate position that falls between two extremes. One extreme is *infallibilism*: the thesis that introspection is always reliable enough to yield knowledge. The other extreme is *skepticism*: the thesis that introspection is never reliable enough to yield knowledge. In between lies the *moderate position* that introspection is sometimes, but not always, reliable enough to yield knowledge. The challenge that remains for the moderate position is to "quarantine" the threat of skepticism by identifying the conditions under which introspection is reliable enough to yield knowledge.[6]

The second objection is that if the unreliability thesis is true, then much of the motivation for the simple theory of introspection is undermined. In particular, there is no basis for the claim that introspection gives us privileged epistemic access to our own mental states. If the unreliability thesis is true, then introspection is no more reliable than other ways of knowing about the world, including sensory perception; indeed, if anything, it is less reliable. As Schwitzgebel puts the point, "Descartes, I think, had it quite backward when he said the mind—including especially current conscious experience—was better known than the outside world" (2011: 136).

In reply, the simple theory doesn't imply that introspection is more reliable than other ways of knowing about the world. The psychological processes that we use in forming introspective beliefs about our own mental states are no less prone to uncertainty and error than our other ways of forming beliefs about the world. The claim is not that introspection is immune from uncertainty and error, but rather that all introspective uncertainty and error reflects some departure from ideal rationality. In this respect, introspection is epistemically privileged in comparison with other ways of knowing about the world, including perception. After all, perceptual illusion, hallucination, and distortion result in uncertainty and error that reflects no rational failing on the part of the believer. Following Tyler Burge, let's call this *brute* uncertainty and error: "Brute errors do not result from any sort of carelessness . . . or irrationality on our part" (1988: 657). Introspection is epistemically privileged in the sense that it is immune from brute uncertainty and error.

There is no commitment here to the claim that introspection is more reliable than other ways of knowing about the world. If we were fully rational, then introspection would be perfectly reliable, since it's immune from brute uncertainty and error. As a matter of fact, however, we are not fully rational and so there is no reason to suppose that introspection is perfectly reliable. Indeed, we may even be more prone to failures of rationality in the case of introspection than perception. The simple theory is therefore consistent with Schwitzgebel's claim that perception is more reliable than introspection.

What grounds the epistemic difference between introspection and perception if not some difference in their comparative reliability? Presumably, there must be some psychological difference between these processes that explains the epistemic difference between them. In my view, this is not a difference in reliability, however, but a difference in the psychological role of mental

---

[6] This challenge is addressed in various different ways by Bayne and Spener (2010), Watzl and Wu (2012), Spener (2015), and Ramm (2016).

representation. In perception, you form beliefs about the external world on the basis of perceptual experience, which represents the external world. In introspection, by contrast, you form beliefs about your own experience directly on the basis of experience without mediation by any intermediate representation of your own experience. This psychological difference between perception and introspection is what grounds the epistemic difference between them.

The content principle says that if your perceptual experience represents that p with presentational force, then you thereby have defeasible, noninferential justification to believe that p (see section 3.3). Brute error results when your perceptual experience misrepresents that p and thereby justifies believing falsely that p. In contrast, introspective justification has its source in facts about your mental states, rather than intermediate representations that are capable of misrepresenting those facts. As a result, brute errors cannot arise in the case of introspection. This is why introspection is epistemically privileged in comparison with perception. Perceptual justification has its source in representations of the facts, whereas introspective justification has its source in the facts themselves.

The third objection is that the simple theory cannot explain the possibility of reasonable disagreement and uncertainty in hard cases. Suppose you and I disagree about the nature of conscious experience on purely introspective grounds—for example, perhaps we disagree about whether there is unsymbolized thinking (see section 4.5). If you're right and I'm wrong, then the simple theory seems to imply that you're justified by introspection, whereas I'm unjustified. Intuitively, however, there is disparity in the truth of our respective opinions, but no such disparity in our degree of justification. Can the simple theory explain how reasonable disagreement and agnosticism are possible in hard cases like this? It seems to imply that rational agents always know the phenomenal facts whatever they are.

I'll make two points in reply to this objection. The first point appeals to the distinction between *propositional* and *doxastic* senses of justification. Whenever you're in some phenomenal state M, you thereby have propositional justification to believe that you're in M, but it doesn't follow that you can form a doxastically justified belief that you're in M. If you believe you're in M on the basis of an unreliable introspective process, then your belief is not doxastically justified because it's not sufficiently responsive to your introspective reasons to satisfy the proper basing condition. In hard cases, we may have introspective reasons that decide disagreement in one way or another, but we may still be unable to rationally resolve the disagreement because our beliefs are insufficiently responsive to those reasons. This is exactly what the simple theory of introspection predicts in combination with Schwitzgebel's unreliability thesis.

Although this explains why introspective belief is not always justified in hard cases, it doesn't explain why introspective agnosticism is sometimes justified. In fact, the simple theory seems to imply that introspective agnosticism is never justified. Given bivalence, either you're in M or you're not in M. Assuming strong luminosity, it follows that either you have justification to believe that you're in M or you have justification to believe that you're not in M. Given uniqueness, it follows that you never have justification for agnosticism about whether you're in M. And yet this seems implausible, since agnosticism is often the most reasonable attitude for limited creatures like us to adopt in hard cases.[7]

This brings me to my second point, which is that we need a further distinction between *ideal* and *nonideal* standards of justification, rationality, or reasonableness. Ideal rationality always requires respecting your evidence, whether or not you're capable of doing so, whereas nonideal rationality just requires doing the best you can. Since you're not always capable of respecting your evidence, the requirements of ideal and nonideal rationality sometimes diverge. This point is often made in connection with the thesis that rationality requires logical omniscience: if it's a logical truth that p, then ideal rationality requires being certain that p, but if you can't reliably tell whether it's a logical truth, then nonideal rationality requires being uncertain that p.[8] Exactly the same point applies if it's a phenomenal truth that p, but you cannot reliably tell whether it's a phenomenal truth that p. These are Schwitzgebel's hard cases of introspective uncertainty and disagreement.

In chapter 10, I'll propose a more general account of the epistemic significance of disagreement and other forms of higher-order evidence about the reliability of your own cognitive processes. To anticipate, higher-order evidence about the unreliability of introspection in hard cases doesn't defeat your introspective reasons for belief about your own experience. Rather, your unreliability in hard cases prevents you from responding to those reasons in the way that ideal rationality requires. Moreover, evidence about the unreliability of introspection in hard cases makes it nonideally rational for you to "bracket" those reasons and hence to be agnostic about your own experience. We cannot explain intuitions about nonideal rationality in terms of the defeasibility of introspective reasons without thereby obscuring the epistemic asymmetry between introspection and perception. As I'll explain in the next

---

[7] In conversation, Adam Pautz has pressed a related objection concerning *degrees* of justification: the simple theory says that you always have maximal justification for beliefs about your experience, so it cannot explain why you have more justification for belief about your phenomenal states in easy cases than hard cases. In reply, intuitions about grades of introspective justification can be explained in terms of the same distinction: ideal rationality always requires certainty, whereas nonideal rational permits varying degrees of uncertainty.

[8] In Smithies (2015a), I defend the thesis that rationality requires logical omniscience by appealing to the distinction between ideal and nonideal rationality.

section, this epistemic asymmetry is part of what motivates the simple theory in the first place.

5.3. Rationality and Self-Knowledge

Why accept the simple theory of introspection? In this section, I'll argue that the simple theory is supported by (i) reflection on examples, (ii) our ordinary talk about reasons for belief about experience, and (iii) an important epistemic asymmetry between perception and introspection. The third argument is by far the most important because it connects with one of the central motivations for the version of accessibilism about epistemic justification developed in the second half of this book.

First, the simple theory is supported by reflection on examples. Intuitively, your reason for believing that you feel pain has its source in the fact that you feel pain. It doesn't have its source in some higher-order representation of the fact that you feel pain, or in some reason to believe the premises of a noncircular argument for the conclusion that you're in pain. The mere fact that you feel pain is enough to give you a reason to believe that you feel pain. Moreover, if you are sufficiently responsive to your reasons, you can know that you feel pain by believing that you feel pain on the basis of this reason. The same point applies, mutatis mutandis, to other experiences: feeling cold, seeming to see red, thinking about rhubarb, and so on. Other things being equal, we should extend the simple theory to all cases, rather than complicating the theory to deal with hard cases.

Second, the simple theory explains some otherwise puzzling features of our ordinary talk about our reasons for belief about our own experience. Suppose you know that you feel cold, and someone asks you, "What is your reason for believing that you feel cold?" It would be strange to answer by giving an argument for the conclusion that you feel cold or by alluding to some inner perception that represents that you feel cold. A much more natural response would be, "What do you mean? I just feel cold!"

Admittedly, we don't usually ask other people to give reasons for beliefs about how they feel. You might be taken aback, or even lost for words, if someone asks you to give reasons in defense of your belief that you feel cold. But why is this? The problem is not that you don't know whether or not you feel cold. It's a Moorean fact that you sometimes know how you feel. Moreover, the problem is not that your knowledge of how you feel is not based on reasons. All knowledge is based on reasons. The problem is that you can't articulate your reasons for believing that you feel cold without simply reiterating that you feel cold, which seems more like begging the question than answering it. Fred Dretske (2003) uses this point to argue for introspective skepticism, but his argument can be resisted. Just because we can't give dialectically satisfying reasons for our beliefs about our own experiences, it doesn't follow that we can't have reasons for those beliefs at all.[9]

When someone asks you to give reasons in support of your belief that p, giving a dialectically satisfying answer requires citing some further premise q that entails or makes it probable that p. In this case, however, there need be no further premise that you can cite in support of your belief that you feel cold. After all, you haven't inferred that you feel cold from other premises, and you don't believe it on the basis of an inner perception that represents that you feel cold. Rather, your reason for believing that you feel cold is just that you feel cold. The simple theory explains why there is no dialectically satisfying response to the challenge: you can't give reasons for your belief that you feel cold except by just reiterating the fact that you feel cold. That is why the game of giving and asking for reasons breaks down in the case of introspection.

Third, and most important, the simple theory explains an important epistemic asymmetry between introspection and perception: epistemic rationality requires introspective knowledge of your own mind, but it doesn't require perceptual knowledge of the external world. The connection between epistemic rationality and introspective self-knowledge is a central theme in the work of Sydney Shoemaker (1996), Tyler Burge (1996), and Richard Moran (2001), but I will argue for this connection in my own way.

Epistemic rationality doesn't require perceptual knowledge of the external world. In the First Meditation, Descartes observed that an evil demon could deceive us about the external world by causing our perceptual experiences to be systematically unreliable. Intuitively, however, this kind of demonic deception undermines knowledge but not epistemic rationality. The victim of an evil demon can form rationally justified beliefs on the basis of perceptual experience, although this is an unreliable way to form beliefs in the circumstances. Indeed, this point is the basis of Stewart Cohen's (1984) "new evil demon problem" for reliabilism. Reliabilism says that our beliefs are justified only if they are held in a reliable way, but reliabilism seems false because it's plausible that an evil demon can make your beliefs unreliable without thereby making them unjustified.

This point about perceptual knowledge has no analogue for introspective knowledge. An evil demon cannot deceive you about your own conscious experience without thereby compromising your rationality. In the Second Meditation, Descartes insists that a fully rational subject can know

---

[9] See Stoljar (2012b) for a more detailed critical discussion of Dretske's argument for skepticism about introspection.

not just *that* she is thinking and experiencing, but also *what* she is thinking and experiencing, even if she cannot know whether or not her thoughts and experiences correspond with reality. He writes: "Because I may be dreaming, I can't say for sure that I now see the flames, hear the wood crackling, and feel the heat of the fire; but I certainly *seem* to see, to hear, and to be warmed."

We can certainly imagine an evil demon with the power to deceive us about our own conscious experience. As Eric Schwitzgebel writes:

> If you admit the possibility that you are dreaming, I think you should admit the possibility that your judgment that you are having red phenomenology is a piece of delirium not accompanied by any reddish phenomenology. (2011: 124)

Introspective delirium of this kind is possible; indeed, an actual case is found in patients with Anton's syndrome, who are blind but believe they can see. In the First Meditation, Descartes entertains the skeptical hypothesis that we are like "brain-damaged madmen" who hold outlandish beliefs that they are pumpkins or made of glass. Of course, madmen can believe outlandish things about their own experience as well as about the external world. But this madness hypothesis is crucially different from other Cartesian skeptical hypotheses. If I am dreaming or deceived by an evil demon, then my beliefs are not only false, but also justified by the evidence of my senses. These Cartesian skeptical scenarios involve a kind of deception that leaves my epistemic rationality intact. But this is not what happens when an evil demon induces delirium by making me think that I'm a pumpkin, when I seem to be a man, or by making me think I seem to see red when I seem to see nothing at all. These beliefs are false, but they are not justified by the evidence of my senses. Hence, this kind of delirium compromises my epistemic rationality, rather than leaving my epistemic rationality intact.

We can illustrate the point by considering a standard objection to *pure coherentism*, the thesis that epistemic rationality is just a matter of having coherent beliefs. The objection is that an evil demon can induce a kind of delirium or madness in which your beliefs cohere with each other without also cohering with your experiences. Ernest Sosa writes:

> Suppose the victim has much sensory experience, but that all of this experience is wildly at odds with his beliefs. Thus he believes he has a splitting headache, but he has no headache at all; he believes he has a cubical piece of coal before him, while his visual experience is as if he had a white and round snowball before him. And so on. (1991: 136)

This is a compelling counterexample to pure coherentism because internal coherence within your belief system is not sufficient for epistemic rationality. Epistemic rationality also requires a kind of internal coherence between your beliefs and your experiences, which excludes deception about your own experience. If you're an epistemically rational agent, and it visually seems to you that p, then you believe not only that p, but also that it visually seems to you that p. Your beliefs about the external world may be false, since things aren't always how they seem, but your beliefs about your own experience are nevertheless true.

To develop this point, let's assume for *reductio* that it can be epistemically rational to form false beliefs about your own experience—for example, to believe that it seems that there is a black cube before you, when in fact it seems that there is a white sphere before you. If so, then it's rational to believe that there is a white sphere before you, since that is just how things seem. At the same time, it's rational for you to believe that it's *irrational* for you to believe that there is a white sphere before you, since it's rational for you to believe that this is *not* how things seem. In other words, it's rational for you to be *epistemically akratic*—that is, to believe that there is a white sphere before you, while also believing that it's irrational to believe this. Intuitively, however, it is never rational to be epistemically akratic in this way. After all, it seems irrational to believe the conjuncts of the following Moorean conjunction: "There is a white sphere before me, although it's irrational to believe this." Therefore, it is never rational to form false beliefs about your own experience.[10]

Some philosophers may challenge this argument by invoking defeaters. The response is that it's rational to believe that things are the way they seem only in the absence of defeaters. But when it's rational to form false beliefs about how things seem, this defeats the rationality of believing that things are how they seem. So, for example, if it seems that there is a white sphere before you, but it's rational to believe that things seem otherwise, then this defeats the rationality of believing that there is a white sphere before you. Moreover, if it's rational for you to believe that it seems that there is a black sphere before you, then it may be rational to believe that there is a black cube before you, rather than a white sphere. This response avoids the implication that epistemic akrasia can be rational, but as I'll explain, it conflicts with the intuitions about epistemic rationality that motivate the objection to pure coherentism in the first place.

---

[10] Epistemic akrasia is a central theme of the second part of this book. In chapter 7, I motivate intuitions about super-blindsight and the new evil demon by appealing to the irrationality of epistemic akrasia. In chapters 9 and 10, I argue for the irrationality of epistemic akrasia and explain this by appealing to phenomenal accessibilism. In chapter 12, I appeal to the irrationality of epistemic akrasia in arguing against phenomenal conservatism.

The objection to pure coherentism relies on the intuition that epistemic rationality requires a kind of internal coherence between your beliefs and your experiences. The victim of the evil demon in Sosa's example is epistemically irrational because his beliefs are systematically divorced from his own experience. However, the reply we are now considering implies that Sosa's victim may be perfectly rational after all. So long as he is rationally permitted to form false beliefs about his own experience, he is rationally permitted to refrain from forming beliefs about the world that cohere with his own experience, and he may be rationally permitted to form beliefs about the world that conflict with his own experience. Intuitively, however, this kind of disconnection between your experiences and your beliefs is beyond the pale as far as epistemic rationality is concerned. An essential feature of epistemically rational agents is that they form beliefs about the external world that cohere with the perceptual appearances. To preserve this platitude, we need to combine it with the claim that epistemically rational agents form beliefs about the perceptual appearances that cohere with those perceptual appearances. In other words, epistemically rational agents do not form false beliefs about their own perceptual appearances.[11]

To sum up, there is an important epistemic asymmetry between introspection and perception. Epistemic rationality is compatible with deception about the external world, but it is not compatible with deception about our own experience. Epistemic rationality requires introspective knowledge of your own experience, but it doesn't require perceptual knowledge of the external world. Moreover, the simple theory of introspection best explains this epistemic asymmetry between perception and introspection. Your perceptual justification for beliefs about the external world is fallible and defeasible because it has its source in perceptual representations of the external world that are capable of misrepresentation. In contrast, your introspective justification for beliefs about your experience is infallible and indefeasible because it has its source in facts about your experience themselves, rather than introspective representations of those facts that are capable of misrepresentation. When you have an experience, you're in a position to know by introspection that you have the experience. If you're epistemically rational, and you consider the question, then you know that you have the experience by forming a belief on the basis of your introspective reason. In that sense, epistemic rationality requires introspective knowledge of your own experience.

---

[11] In section 12.4.1, I use much the same argument against phenomenal conservatism as a global theory of epistemic justification that subsumes introspection under the same model as perception.

5.4. The Scope Question

In this section, I'll address a question about the scope of introspection: namely, which mental states can be known by introspection? Given a simple theory of introspection, this question takes on a distinctive form: which mental states are introspectively luminous in the sense that you're always in a position to know by introspection whether or not you're in them? The simple theory is compatible with various different answers to the scope question: it says that some mental states are introspectively luminous, but it doesn't say which ones. In this section, I'll argue that mental states are introspectively luminous if and only if they are *phenomenally individuated* in the sense that they are individuated by their phenomenal character or by their phenomenal dispositions.

Some philosophers, including Brie Gertler (2007) and Katalin Farkas (2008b), claim that introspection is the mark of the mental. On this view, what sets mental states apart from nonmental states is precisely that they can be known by means of introspection. This yields an extremely simple answer to the scope question: all mental states, and only mental states, can be known by introspection. Although I reject this claim, I accept that introspection marks out an important class of mental states: namely, those that provide epistemic justification for belief. Not all mental states fall within the scope of introspection, since not all mental states provide epistemic justification for belief. Nevertheless, the scope of introspection includes all mental states that provide epistemic justification for belief. This will serve as an important constraint on my answer to the scope question.

Consider the subdoxastic mental representations that figure in computational explanations in cognitive science, such as Chomsky's (1965) tacit knowledge of syntactic rules and Marr's (1982) primal and 2.5D sketch. These representational states are mental by any neutral criterion, but our knowledge of them is based on scientific theory, rather than introspection. Similarly, we cannot know just by introspection what implicit biases we harbor toward minority groups. To uncover these biases, we need to observe our own behavior—for instance, by taking implicit association tests. Therefore, we need some further restriction on which of our mental states can be known by means of introspection.

It is tempting to exclude subdoxastic mental representations by appealing to some *phenomenal criterion* for introspective knowledge. So, for example, we might say that a mental state is introspectively luminous just in case it has some phenomenal character. This version of the phenomenal criterion is too weak to exclude factive mental states, such as seeing that p. This state is phenomenally conscious in the sense that there is something it's like to see that p. At the same time, it's a factive mental state, which means that you cannot see that p in the bad case in which it merely seems to you that p. And yet part of what's bad about the bad case is that you're not in a position to know by introspection when you're in it. Therefore, seeing that *p* is not introspectively luminous in the strong sense that you're always in a position to know by introspection whether or not you see that *p*. Hence, this version of the phenomenal criterion is too weak as stated.

A revised version of the phenomenal criterion says that a mental state is introspectively luminous just in case it is *individuated* by its phenomenal character in the following sense: there is some phenomenal character that is both necessary and sufficient for instantiating that mental state. Factive mental states, such as seeing that *p*, violate this criterion because you can have the same phenomenal character in the bad case without seeing that *p*. Hence, the revised version of the phenomenal criterion is strong enough to rule out factive mental states.

Unfortunately, both versions of the phenomenal criterion are too strong, since they exclude not only subdoxastic states, but also beliefs. Beliefs are disposed to cause phenomenally conscious episodes of judgment, but they're not phenomenally conscious states themselves. Rather, beliefs are standing, dispositional states that are distinct from their manifestations in phenomenal consciousness. Nevertheless, I'll argue that we can know what we believe in just the same way that we can know what we are currently thinking or judging. In other words, we can extend the simple theory of introspection from experience to belief:

The Extended Simple Theory: Necessarily, if you believe that *p*, then you thereby have an introspective reason that puts you in a position to know by introspection that you believe that *p*.

Just as thinking that *p* gives you an introspective reason to believe that you're thinking that *p*, so believing that *p* gives you an introspective reason to believe that you believe that *p*. In each case, we can acquire introspective knowledge by forming beliefs noninferentially on the basis of introspective reasons provided by our mental states themselves.[12]

Why should we extend the simple theory from experience to belief? In the previous section, I argued that the simple theory of introspection explains a plausible connection between epistemic rationality and introspective self-knowledge. I'll now argue that this connection between epistemic rationality

---

[12] The literature on self-knowledge includes many rival theories of our introspective knowledge of what we believe, including those proposed by Evans (1982), Shoemaker (1996), Moran (2001), Nichols and Stich (2003), Byrne (2005), Zimmerman (2004), Silins (2012), and Fernandez (2013). I critically discuss some of these theories in Smithies (2016a).

and introspective self-knowledge extends from experience to belief. Here is my argument in outline:

(1) Both experience and belief provide epistemic justification for belief.
(2) All mental states that provide epistemic justification for belief are intro-spectively luminous.
(3) Therefore, both experience and belief are introspectively luminous.

In chapters 3 and 4, I argued for the intermediate view that both experience and belief play a role in providing epistemic justification for belief. Moreover, in this chapter, I'm arguing that all mental states that provide epistemic justifica-tion for belief must be introspectively luminous. Otherwise, there will be cases in which your mental states give you epistemic justification to be epistemically akratic. Intuitively, however, this cannot happen, since epistemic akrasia is al-ways epistemically irrational and unjustified. Hence, both experience and belief must be included within the scope of introspection.

We've already seen how this argument works in the case of experience, but now let's extend it to the case of belief. If your beliefs are excluded from the scope of introspection, then you can believe that p without thereby being in a position to know by introspection that you believe that p. On this view, since your beliefs don't provide conclusive evidence about themselves, your total ev-idence can make it rational to hold false beliefs about what you believe. So, for example, it may be that you believe that p, although your evidence makes it rational to believe that you *don't* believe that p. But since your beliefs provide epistemic reasons for holding other beliefs, then this has the consequence that your evidence can make it rational to be epistemically akratic, which seems absurd.

Consider a case in which the rationality of believing that q depends on whether or not I believe that p. And suppose I know this; that is, I know that it's rational to believe that q if and only if I believe that p. Now let's assume for *reductio* that I believe that p, although it's rational to believe that I don't believe that p. Since I believe that p, it's rational to believe that q. But since it's rational to believe that I *don't* believe that p, it's rational to believe that it's *irrational* to believe that q. In other words, it's rational to be epistemically akratic—that is, to believe that q, while also believing that it's irrational to believe that q. Intuitively, however, epistemic akrasia is always irrational. After all, it seems irrational to believe the conjunctions of the following Moorean conjunction: "q, although it's irrational to believe that q." Therefore, it can never be rational to form false beliefs about what you believe in the first place.

Moreover, the simple theory explains why it cannot be rational to form false beliefs about what you believe. Consider the classic version of Moore's paradox, which is the problem of explaining why there's always some irrationality involved in believing Moorean conjunctions of the following omissive form:

The omissive form: p and I don't believe that *p*.

The problem arises because believing a Moorean conjunction seems irrational in much the same way as believing a contradiction, and yet Moorean conjunctions, unlike contradictions, can be true. Since I am neither omniscient nor infallible, it can be true that *p* when I don't believe that *p*. But although Moorean conjunctions can be true, they cannot be believed without some irrationality. Moore's paradox is the problem of explaining why not.[13]

The simple theory provides an elegant solution to Moore's paradox, since it implies that you cannot rationally believe Moorean conjunctions of the omissive form. According to the simple theory, you're always in a position to know what you believe by introspection. Whenever you believe the first conjunct of an omissive Moorean conjunction, you're thereby in a position to know by introspection that the second conjunct is false. As a result, you're in a position to know that the whole conjunction is false whenever you believe it. But you cannot rationally believe a conjunction when you're in a position to know that it's false. Therefore, you cannot rationally believe an omissive Moorean conjunction.

To see why the simple theory is indispensable, let's suppose for the sake of argument that you're *not* always in a position to know what you believe. In that case, you can rationally believe an omissive Moorean conjunction when you're not in a position to know that you believe it. You can never *know* an omissive Moorean conjunction because if you believe the first conjunct, then the second conjunct is false. That doesn't mean you can never *rationally believe* an omissive Moorean conjunction, since rational beliefs can be false.[14] If you rationally believe the first conjunct, but you're not in a position to know that you believe it, then the second conjunct might be true for all you're in a position to know. Indeed, you might have very strong evidence that the second conjunct is true. In that case, there's no reason why you cannot rationally believe the whole conjunction. Intuitively, however, believing an omissive Moorean conjunction is always irrational. We cannot plausibly explain this without extending the simple theory of introspection from experience to belief.

---

[13] See Smithies (2016a) for a more extended discussion of Moore's paradox and its implications for an account of our introspective knowledge of what we believe.
[14] Here I'm setting aside Williamson's (2013) view that a belief is fully rational or justified only if it is knowledge. See section 9.4 for some brief discussion.

One neglected aspect of Moore's paradox is that you can have evidence that makes it rational to believe an omissive Moorean conjunction. For example, you might have evidence that it will rain tomorrow, while also having evidence that you are epistemically irrational, and hence that you fail to believe what the evidence supports. In that case, your total evidence makes it rational to believe the omissive Moorean conjunction, "It will rain, but I don't believe it will rain." Even so, believing the Moorean conjunction seems irrational. This is all rather puzzling. If your evidence makes it rational to believe a Moorean conjunction, then why can't you rationally believe it?

The simple theory solves this puzzle. It implies that evidence for an omissive Moorean conjunction is always *finkish* in the sense that it is destroyed in the attempt to use it in forming a doxastically rational belief. After all, believing that *p* has the effect of destroying the evidence that makes it rational to believe that you don't believe that *p*. On the simple theory, your evidence about what you believe is constituted by the psychological facts about what you believe. You can have meteorological evidence that it will rain, while also having psychological evidence that you don't believe it will rain, so long as you don't believe it will rain. But if you come to believe it will rain on the basis of the meteorological evidence, then your psychological evidence changes: you lose your earlier evidence that you don't believe it will rain and you acquire new evidence for the opposite conclusion. Therefore, your evidence for an omissive Moorean conjunction is always finkish.[15]

Moore's paradox provides additional support for the claim that the connection between rationality and introspective self-knowledge extends from experience to belief.[16] Rationality requires knowing what you believe, since otherwise you're liable to fall into an irrational Moorean predicament. The simple theory of introspection explains why rationality requires knowing what you believe, just as it requires knowing what experiences you have. This is because facts about your beliefs, just like facts about your experiences, are introspectively luminous.

Not everyone agrees that we can know what we believe by means of introspection. For instance, Brie Gertler (2011: 77–80) argues that we cannot have introspective knowledge of our beliefs, but only the phenomenally conscious episodes they are disposed to cause. Her argument can be summarized as follows:

---

[15] The allusion here is to what Martin (1994) calls "finkish dispositions," which are destroyed whenever their manifestation conditions obtain. I introduced the notion of finkish evidence in Smithies (2012c: 288) and I explore it further in Smithies (2016a: 404–406).

[16] Sobel (1987) and Milne (1991) also give Dutch book arguments for the thesis that rationality requires knowing your own credences.

(1) Beliefs are dispositional states.

(2) We cannot have introspective knowledge of our dispositional states.

(3) Therefore, we cannot have introspective knowledge of our beliefs.

The support for this argument derives from a more general account of the epistemology of dispositions. We typically know the dispositions of an object by making inferences from premises about its manifestations. So, for example, we can infer that an object is fragile by observing that it shatters when it is dropped. Similarly, it may be said, we can know what we believe only by making inferences from premises about the way in which our beliefs manifest themselves in our conscious experiences and in our actions.

Gertler (2011) endorses a view of just this kind.[17] She claims that we know what we believe by making explanatory inferences from premises about what we consciously think or judge to be true. This explains why we often know what we ourselves believe without knowing what others believe. After all, these explanatory inferences rely on premises about our own experience that we know by introspection. On this view, however, we don't know the conclusions of these inferences in the same way as we know the premises. We know the premises by introspection alone, whereas we know the conclusions by explanatory inference from these premises.

The main problem with Gertler's account is that it cannot guarantee a connection between epistemic rationality and knowledge of what you believe. On this view, epistemically rational thinkers can have misleading evidence about what they believe. Given that beliefs provide epistemic justification for other beliefs, however, this has the implausible consequence that your total evidence can make epistemic akrasia rational. This problem is not unique to Gertler's account, of course, since it arises for any account that denies that our beliefs are introspectively luminous. But the problem is serious enough to motivate turning her argument on its head. Since beliefs are dispositional states, and since we can have introspective knowledge of what we believe, it follows that we can have introspective knowledge of at least some of our dispositional states after all. Of course, we cannot have introspective knowledge of all of our dispositional states. An answer to the scope question should therefore articulate what it is about belief that sets it apart from other dispositional states that cannot be known by means of introspection.

In chapter 4, I argued that our beliefs are individuated by their dispositions to cause phenomenally conscious judgments: to believe that p is to be disposed

---

[17] This kind of inferential account of our knowledge of what we believe was originally proposed by Ryle (1949), and more recently by Carruthers (2011) and Cassam (2014).

to judge that p when you consciously entertain whether p. In other words, our beliefs are individuated in such a way that their contents are accessible to consciousness as the contents of judgments. If so, then we're always in a position to know what we believe by accessing the contents of our beliefs in making conscious judgments. If you believe that p, then you're thereby disposed to judge that p when you consider whether p. Moreover, if you express your belief that p in exercising the disposition to judge that p, then you're thereby in a position to know that you believe that p. In contrast, the contents of our subdoxastic states are inaccessible to consciousness as the contents of judgments. This is why we cannot know by introspection which contents are represented subdoxastically, but only which contents we believe. It is precisely because the contents of our beliefs are accessible to consciousness, whereas the contents of our subdoxastic states are inaccessible to consciousness.

Can we explain our introspective knowledge of what we believe without appealing to the fact that their contents are accessible to phenomenal consciousness? Aaron Zimmerman (2004) explains our introspective knowledge of what we believe in terms of *access consciousness*, rather than *conscious accessibility*. As we've seen in section 4.3, these are distinct properties. A zombie's mental states are access conscious when they are inferentially promiscuous and poised for direct control of speech and action. But a zombie cannot have mental representations whose contents are accessible to phenomenal consciousness. Which of these properties explains our introspective knowledge of what we believe? Zimmerman writes:

> It is at least *difficult* to imagine a subject who believes that p in a fully A-conscious manner—where this belief is poised to guide her inferences and behavior in all the customary ways—and who is also caused to believe that she believes that p by the fact that she believes that p, but who is nevertheless unjustified in believing that she has this belief. And this lends considerable *prima facie* support to the claim that A-consciousness is sufficient for direct [introspective] accessibility. (2004: 357)

In reply, however, Block's (1995: 233) example of super-blindsight suggests that access consciousness is not sufficient for mental representations to fall within the scope of introspective knowledge. In super-blindsight, visual information about the blind field is not phenomenally conscious, but it is access conscious because it is poised for use in the direct control of action, speech, and reasoning. Nevertheless, a super-blindsighter cannot know by introspection what information about the blind field is represented in her visual system. She can only make abductive inferences from observational data about her own speech and action. In this respect, she is no better off than the ordinary blindsighter. The same point applies if we stipulate that this visual information is inferentially integrated in the sense that it combines with beliefs to yield new beliefs. The super-blindsighter may be disposed to use this visual information in making new inferences, but she won't be able to know by introspection which premises she is using in making these inferences.

What is more, we cannot explain introspective knowledge in terms of met-acognitive consciousness either. A mental representation M is *metacognitively conscious* when you form the higher-order thought that you have M without in-ferential mediation. Block's (1995: 246 n. 16) example of super-duper-blindsight suggests that metacognitive consciousness is not sufficient for a mental repre-sentation to fall within the scope of introspective knowledge. This case is just like super-blindsight, except that the subject has a reliable disposition to form higher-order thoughts about visual representations of the blind field without inferential mediation. Intuitively, the hyper-blindsighter cannot know by in-trospection what information about the blind field is represented in her visual system any more than the super-blindsighter can. She has a reliable disposition to form true beliefs about her visual representations of the blind field, just as the super-blindsighter has a reliable disposition to form true beliefs about the blind field, but this is not enough to make them justified. As I argued in section 3.2, these beliefs are reliable, but unjustified.

In summary, what explains our introspective knowledge of what we believe is accessibility to phenomenal consciousness, rather than access consciousness or metacognitive consciousness. We're in a position to know what we believe be-cause the contents of our beliefs are accessible to consciousness as the contents of judgments. Moreover, this is a consequence of the fact that our beliefs have their contents in virtue of their dispositions to make us judge those contents to be true. To believe that p is to be disposed to judge that p when you consider the question. On this view, our beliefs inherit their representational force and content from the judgments they are disposed to cause. In other words, they are individuated by their dispositions to cause the conscious experience of judgment.

We can extend this account to explain our introspective knowledge of other standing attitudes, including desire, emotion, and intention. All of these standing attitudes inherit their representational force and content from the experiences they are disposed to cause. To a first approximation: desiring that p is being disposed to feel desire when you consider the prospect that p, being sad that p is being disposed to feel sad when you consider the fact that p, intending to do A is being disposed to feel resolve when you consider whether to do A, and so on. The details may need refinement, but the basic idea is that all of these standing attitudes are individuated by their dispositions to cause experiences.

That is why we can know by introspection not only what we believe, but also what we desire, feel, and intend.[18]

We need an answer to the scope question that is weak enough to include our beliefs and other standing attitudes, as well as our experiences, while also being strong enough to exclude our subdoxastic mental representations. I propose the following answer:

> *The Phenomenal Individuation Constraint*: Necessarily, a mental state is introspectively luminous if and only if it is phenomenally individuated by its phenomenal character or by its phenomenal dispositions.[19]

To be in a phenomenally individuated mental state is to have a certain phenomenal character or a certain phenomenal disposition. If a mental state is phenomenally individuated, then there is some phenomenal character or some phenomenal disposition that is both necessary and sufficient for being in that mental state. This criterion is weak enough to include not only your experiences, which are individuated by their phenomenal character, but also your beliefs and desires, which are individuated by their phenomenal dispositions. At the same time, it is strong enough to exclude your subdoxastic mental representations, which are individuated by their role in unconscious computational processes. They are not phenomenally individuated in either sense.

Let me close this section by defending the phenomenal individuation constraint against three objections. The first objection is that it's too weak to exclude phenomenal dispositions that clearly fall outside the scope of introspection. Consider the disposition to feel nauseated when you think about mathematics. You cannot know by introspection alone whether or not you have this disposition. The mere presence of the disposition doesn't give you an introspective reason to believe that you have it. Rather, you need to infer the presence of the disposition in the usual way: by thinking about mathematics and then seeing whether you feel nauseated. If so, then you may conclude that you have the disposition on the basis of inference to the best explanation.

In reply, the phenomenal individuation constraint excludes these phenomenal dispositions, since it includes only mental states within its scope. It applies to mental states that are phenomenally individuated in the sense that they inherit their representational properties from the phenomenal states

---

[18] Smithies and Weiss (2019) explore the extension from belief to desire.

[19] We can also state the phenomenal individuation constraint in terms of facts, rather than mental states: necessarily, you're in a position to know that *p* by introspection if and only if it's a phenomenally individuated fact that *p*, where a phenomenally individuated fact is one that is wholly about your phenomenally individuated mental states.

they are disposed to cause in phenomenal conditions. There is no representational mental state corresponding to the disposition to feel nauseated when
you think about mathematics. Not every set of dispositions—even phenomenal
dispositions—individuates a mental state by its representational properties.

The second objection is that the phenomenal individuation constraint fails
to explain much of the knowledge that is available to us in a distinctively first-
personal way. Consider my knowledge that I am raising my arm, that my legs
are crossed, or that I see my hands. None of this knowledge concerns phenomenally individuated mental states, since not all of my phenomenal duplicates
have arms, legs, or hands; indeed, some of them are disembodied brains in vats.
In reply, not all knowledge that is available in a distinctively first-personal way
is explained by introspection alone. Much of this knowledge can be explained
in terms of inference from premises known by introspection. For example,
I know by introspection that I seem to be raising my arms, crossing my legs, or
seeing my hands, and I infer that things are the way they seem. I don't always
make the inference consciously, but my knowledge has an inferential structure
all the same. It is not based solely on introspection.

The third objection is that the phenomenal individuation constraint fails to
explain our knowledge of the externally individuated contents of our beliefs
and experiences. Presumably, I can know by introspection that I'm thinking
about Fido. This thought is not phenomenally individuated, however, since not
all my phenomenal duplicates are able to think about Fido. According to the
phenomenal individuation constraint, only phenomenally individuated mental
states give me introspective reasons that put me in a position to acquire introspective knowledge. Hence, the phenomenal individuation constraint cannot
explain my introspective knowledge that I'm thinking about Fido.

In reply, the conclusion doesn't follow from the premises. When I'm in
the right kind of environment, I can acquire introspective knowledge that
I'm thinking an externally individuated thought on the basis of an introspec-
tive reason provided by a phenomenally individuated thought. Whenever
I think an externally individuated thought that q, I also think a phenomenally
individuated thought that p, which I share with all my phenomenal duplicates.
Unlike my phenomenal duplicates, I succeed in thinking that q only because
I'm thinking that p in the right kind of environment. If I think that p, and I do
this in the right kind of environment, then I thereby think that q. Similarly, if
I believe that I think that p, and I do this in the right kind of environment, then
I thereby believe that I think that q.

The phenomenal individuation constraint implies that I have an introspective reason to believe that I'm thinking that p, since this thought is individuated
by its phenomenal character. Moreover, I can acquire introspective knowledge
that I'm thinking that p by forming a belief on the basis of this introspective

reason. Suppose I do this in an environment where I succeed in thinking that q by thinking that p. If so, then I can know that I'm thinking that q by knowing that I'm thinking that p. After all, my belief that I'm thinking that q is both justified and nonaccidentally true. In the right kind of environment, I acquire introspective knowledge that I'm thinking the externally individuated thought that q on the basis of an introspective reason that is provided by my phenomenally individuated thought that p. That is to say, we can have introspective knowledge of the externalist contents of our beliefs and experiences after all.[20]

5.5. The Role of Conscious Judgment

What is the role of conscious judgment in explaining your introspective knowledge of what you believe? On my account, judging that p is neither necessary nor sufficient for having introspective justification to believe that you believe that p. It's not necessary because you can have standing introspective knowledge of your beliefs when you're not making any judgment at all. Moreover, it's not sufficient because even when you judge that p, the source of your introspective justification to believe that you believe that p is not the judgment itself, but rather the standing belief expressed by the judgment.

At the same time, I've argued that we can know what we believe by means of introspection only because the contents of our beliefs are accessible to consciousness as the contents of conscious judgments. Hence, consciousness plays an important role in explaining our introspective knowledge of what we believe. The disposition to judge that p is both necessary and sufficient for having introspective justification to believe that you believe that p, although the act of judgment itself is neither necessary nor sufficient.

I want to defend this proposal against two challenges. The first challenge concerns cases in which you believe that p without judging that p because your disposition to judge that p is *masked*—for instance, by repression. The simple theory implies that you have introspective justification to believe that you believe that p in such cases, but is this plausible? The second challenge concerns cases in which you judge that p without believing that p because the disposition to judge that p is *mimicked*—for instance, by the interventions of an evil demon. The simple theory implies that you lack introspective justification to believe

---

[20] Smithies (2016b) explores a version of moderate externalism that allows the externalist contents of experience and belief to play a role in grounding propositional justification. Moderate externalism can be combined with a weaker version of the phenomenal individuation constraint that includes the "phenomenally mediated contents" of experience and belief within the scope of introspection. This view is similar in spirit to the more uncompromising version of phenomenal internalism defended in this book.

that you believe that *p* in such cases, but again, is this plausible? The main goal of this section is to defend these consequences of extending the simple theory to explain our introspective knowledge of what we believe.[21]

5.5.1. Belief without Judgment

First, let's consider a case in which your disposition toward judgment is *masked*. Suppose you believe that you're ill, but your belief is repressed, so your disposition to access its content in making judgments is blocked from its normal manifestations. If the blockage were removed in the course of psychotherapy, then you would judge that you are ill when the question arises. As things are, however, you tend to judge that you're in good health. Isn't it implausible then to suppose, as the simple theory implies, that you have any introspective justification to believe that you believe that you are ill?

Here is one way to press the objection. If you form the second-order belief that you believe you are ill, when the first-order belief is repressed, and you have no other relevant evidence, then your second-order belief is unjustified. And, the objection continues, this is because your repressed first-order belief gives you no introspective justification to form a second-order belief that you have it. On this view, you have no introspective justification to believe that you believe that *p* when your disposition to judge that *p* is blocked from manifesting itself in the normal way.

In reply, I accept the datum, but not the proposed explanation. Your second-order belief is unjustified not because you lack introspective justification to form it, but rather because you're unable to form the belief in a way that is properly based on your introspective justification. On this view, the epistemic role of conscious judgment is not to provide introspective justification for second-order beliefs about what you believe. Rather, its epistemic role is to enable you to form second-order beliefs that are properly based on the introspective justification provided by the corresponding first-order beliefs. In a slogan, judgment plays an *enabling* role, rather than a *justifying* role, in explaining your introspective knowledge of what you believe.

This is an instance of the more general point that you can have propositional justification to believe that *p* without being able to form a doxastically justified belief that *p*. A belief is doxastically justified only if it is properly based on the reasons that give you propositional justification to hold the belief. But you can have reasons that justify forming a belief without being able to form a justified

---

[21] See Johnston (1992) for the distinction between masking and mimicking a disposition.

belief on the basis of those reasons. I already made this point in sections 5.1 and 5.2, but the goal of this section is to argue that repressed belief is another instance of the same general phenomenon.[22]

What is proper basing? To a first approximation, a belief is properly based on a reason only if it is reliably responsive to your possession of that reason. Your introspective reasons to form second-order beliefs have their source in corresponding first-order beliefs. Hence, your second-order beliefs are properly based on these introspective reasons only if they are reliably responsive to your first-order beliefs. This proper basing condition is not normally satisfied when your first-order beliefs are repressed. If you form the second-order belief, and you have no other relevant evidence, then it is no more justified than a belief formed on the basis of blind guesswork. After all, you just got lucky: you could easily have formed the second-order belief in much the same way without having any corresponding first-order belief. You simply cannot form second-order beliefs in a reliable way when your first-order beliefs are blocked from manifesting themselves in judgment.

Under normal conditions, our second-order beliefs can satisfy the proper basing requirement. I'll mention three different ways this can happen. One way is by forming second-order beliefs on the basis of conscious judgments that express our first-order beliefs. In other words, we can follow what Nicholas Silins calls the Transparency Method:

> *The Transparency Method*: If you judge that *p*, believe you believe that *p*! (2012: 302)

Following a method, we can assume, is a matter of complying with the consequent because the antecedent obtains. In particular, following the Transparency Method is a matter of believing that you believe that *p* because you judge that *p*. When your beliefs are not repressed, you can express those beliefs in making judgments. In those conditions, following the Transparency Method is a way of forming second-order beliefs in a way that is reliably responsive to your corresponding first-order beliefs.[23]

This is not the only way we can have introspective knowledge of what we believe. Even when I'm not currently judging that *p*, I can have standing introspective knowledge that I believe that *p*, so long as there is an appropriate connection between my first-order disposition to judge that *p* and my second-order disposition to judge that I believe that *p*. When I have standing

---

[22] Other examples with the same structure include the cases of perception without attention discussed in section 3.2 and the problem of the speckled hen discussed in section 11.2.

[23] In section 5.5.2, I'll discuss cases in which your judgments don't express what you believe.

introspective knowledge of what I believe, these two dispositions are not merely accidentally connected. Rather, my second-order disposition depends upon my first-order disposition: that is, I'm disposed to judge that I believe that p only because I'm disposed to judge that p. Moreover, this dependence is constitutive and not merely causal. If I'm disposed to follow the Transparency Method, then I'm disposed to judge that I believe that p by exercising my disposition to judge that p. In that sense, my disposition to judge that I believe that p is partially constituted by my disposition to judge that p.[24]

As Christopher Peacocke (1998) observes, we can express our standing introspective knowledge of what we believe by making second-order judgments without mediation by any corresponding first-order judgments. These are what he calls "NICS" self-ascriptions of belief because they are based on no intermediate conscious states. He writes:

> Most of us, when it becomes conversationally appropriate to say "I know my name is NN," or "I know my address is such-and-such," have no need to wait upon its surfacing in consciousness what our names and addresses are. We make these utterances intentionally and knowledgeably, but not because it has just occurred to us that our names and addresses are such-and-such. (1998: 91)

As we've seen, my self-ascription of the belief that p is justified only if it is reliably responsive to my first-order disposition to judge that p. If that first-order disposition is blocked by repression, however, then this condition isn't satisfied. This is why Peacocke endorses the requirement of "first-order ratifiability":

> *The Requirement of First-Order Ratifiability*: An NICS self-ascription of (say) a belief that p is knowledge only if it is made in circumstances in which the thinker is also willing to make the first-order judgment that p. (1998: 93)

This requirement gives an explanatory role for conscious judgment even in NICS cases where self-ascriptions of belief are not based on any intermediate conscious act of judgment.

I've just mentioned three different ways in which we can have justified second-order beliefs about what we believe. In each case, the second-order belief that you believe that p is justified only if it is reliably responsive to your

---

[24] Compare Shoemaker's (1996) claim that our second-order beliefs are partially constituted by first-order beliefs in the following sense: insofar as we're rational, the dispositions that realize our second-order beliefs include the dispositions that realize our first-order beliefs.

first-order disposition to judge that p. My central claim is that this condition is not typically satisfied when the first-order disposition toward judgment is blocked by repression. That is why you cannot form a justified second-order belief that you believe that p when your first-order belief that p is repressed.

Any theory of introspection needs to explain the sense in which repression constitutes a failure of epistemic rationality. Ideally rational agents do not have repressed beliefs. When your beliefs are repressed, they are not poised for use in conscious judgment and reasoning. Moreover, they are not poised for use as a basis for forming second-order beliefs about what you believe. What I'm suggesting is that there's an important connection between these two points. When your beliefs are poised for use in making first-order judgments about the world, they are also poised for use in making second-order judgments about what you believe. Rationality requires that your beliefs are always poised for use in making judgments of both kinds. That is why ideally rational agents always know what they believe.

5.5.2. Judgment without Belief

Now let's consider a case in which your disposition toward judgment is *mimicked*. Suppose you're taking a quiz under time pressure and you're primed with distracting stimuli designed to induce mistakes. So, for example, you're shown an image of the Sydney Opera House when you're asked, "What is the capital of Australia?" You make the judgment that Sydney is the capital, but then you catch yourself a moment later and wonder what you were thinking. You know full well that Canberra is the capital city, and you don't have contradictory beliefs, you just made a temporary slip in judgment. In that case, your judgment fails to express what you believe.[25]

As I use the terms, judgment is a conscious mental episode that is individuated by its phenomenal character, whereas belief is a standing state that is individuated by its disposition to cause judgment. Judging that p is not sufficient for believing that p because it doesn't guarantee that you have a stable disposition to judge that p across a wide enough range of circumstances. Slips of judgment do not express what you believe because they fail to manifest any stable disposition toward judgment. Indeed, you might even be caused to make judgments without thereby manifesting any disposition at all. Suppose an evil demon causes you to make judgments that conflict with what you believe. In

[25] Zimmerman (2004: 362–368) claims that judging that p entails believing that p, but he also defines a *seeming judgment* as an episode that has the same phenomenal character as judgment, but which doesn't entail belief. This is exactly what I mean by the term 'judgment'.

this case, your dispositions toward judgment are masked, and the contrary dispositions are mimicked, by the interventions of the evil demon. This case presents two distinct problems for the simple theory of introspection.[26]

The old evil demon problem is the problem of explaining how we can know we're not in the evil demon scenario. Brie Gertler states the problem like this:

> Descartes' meditator can introspect his occurrent beliefs [i.e. judgments] that "I doubt that I am sitting before the fire" or "2 + 3 = 5," but cannot introspect the causal sources of those beliefs, including standing beliefs or past cognitive processes. This is why he cannot rule out, through introspection alone, the possibility that these beliefs are caused by an evil genius, rather than by a standing belief. (2007: 206 n. 8)

If I can know by introspection that I believe that p, then I can know by deduction that I'm not in an evil demon scenario in which I merely judge that p without believing that p. But that seems too easy. Can I really know that I'm not in the evil demon scenario just by a combination of introspection and deduction?

I'm not going to try to solve this problem here, since it's a general problem that everyone faces—namely, the problem of skepticism. As Descartes observed, an evil demon can deceive me about the external world by inducing perceptual experiences that are systematically false. So we face the problem of explaining how we can know that we're not in the evil demon scenario. If I can know by perception that I have hands, then I can know by deduction that I'm not deceived by an evil demon in such a way that it merely seems to me that I have hands. Again, that seems too easy. Can I really know that I'm not in the evil demon scenario just by a combination of perception and deduction?

There is an ongoing debate about how best to solve this problem. On the one hand, Mooreans maintain that we really can know that we're not in the evil demon scenario by deduction from premises we know on the basis of perception. On the other hand, rationalists maintain that we cannot know anything on the basis of perception unless we already know on a priori grounds that we're not in the evil demon scenario. For current purposes, I'll remain neutral between these options. Given the epistemic asymmetries between perception and introspection, however, it's not clear that we are forced accept the same solution in both cases.[27]

---

[26] I borrow the labels from Nicholas Silins. See Silins (2013) for the old evil demon problem and Silins (forthcoming) for the new evil demon problem.

[27] Moorean responses to the problem of skepticism about the external world are defended by Pryor (2004) and Pritchard (2012), while Rationalist responses are defended by Wright (2004), White (2006), Silins (2008), and Cohen (2010).

The new evil demon problem, in contrast, is the problem of explaining how we can form justified second-order beliefs about what we believe in the demon scenario when those beliefs are reliably false. Nicholas Silins puts the challenge like this:

> Suppose that whenever René judges at a time that p, an evil demon typically but indiscernibly ensures that René at that time fails to believe that p. . . . Here René's use of the Transparency Method is not reliable, without René having any inclination of the disruption. . . . René still seems to form a justified belief that he believes that p when he does so on the basis of his judgment that p. (forthcoming: 12)

The problem, according to Silins, is that René can form introspectively justified beliefs about what he believes by following the Transparency Method, although this way of forming beliefs is unreliable in the circumstances.

If we extend the simple theory to our introspective knowledge of what we believe, then we face a version of the new evil demon problem. We cannot say that René forms introspectively justified beliefs about what he believes by following the Transparency Method. After all, the simple theory implies the following pair of claims:

(1) *The negative claim*: If René judges that p without believing that p, then he *lacks* introspective justification to believe that he *believes* that p.

(2) *The positive claim*: If René judges that p without believing that p, then he *has* introspective justification to believe that he *doesn't believe* that p.

The simple theory implies the negative claim because it says that introspective justification is *infallible*: you cannot have introspective justification to believe that you believe that p unless you believe that p. It implies the positive claim because it says that belief is positively and negatively *self-intimating*: if you believe that p, then you have introspective justification to believe that you believe that p, and if you don't believe that p, then you have introspective justification to believe that you don't believe that p. Can these claims be defended?

My response is to deny that following the Transparency Method always yields introspectively justified beliefs about what you believe. We can distinguish the *good case* in which your first-order judgments reflect what you believe from the *bad case* in which they do not. Second-order beliefs formed by following the Transparency Method are justified in the good case, but not in the bad case. This is because your introspective justification for believing that you believe that p has its source not in the judgment that p, but rather in the belief that p, which your judgment serves to express. Your judgment expresses belief in the good case, but not in the bad case. Hence, it is only in the good case that you have introspective justification to believe that you believe that p.

Some epistemologists will insist that you're equally justified whether you're in the good case or the bad case.[28] But why should we accept this? It's true that the phenomenal character of your experience is the same in each case, but we cannot assume that justification supervenes on the phenomenal character of experience. In section 4.1, I rejected this supervenience thesis on the grounds that it cannot accommodate the justifying role of standing belief. Justification depends not just on your current experiential state, but on your current doxastic state. Differences in what you believe can suffice for corresponding differences in what you have justification to believe, including differences in what you have introspective justification to believe about what you believe.

My response faces a version of the *reverse new evil demon problem* (section 3.4). Even in the evil demon scenario, following the Transparency Method seems much more reasonable than following some blatantly silly method, such as divining entrails. But if following the Transparency Method doesn't yield justified beliefs in the evil demon scenario, then what makes it any more reasonable than divining entrails? The challenge for the simple theory is to explain the intuitive epistemic difference between these methods.

Here I'm inclined to borrow Maria Lasonen-Aarnio's (2010) distinction between *justification* or *rationality* on the one hand and *reasonableness* on the other. A justified belief is one that is properly based on the evidence, whereas a reasonable belief is one that is based on dispositions that would yield justified belief in normal circumstances. Lasonen-Aarnio uses this distinction to address the reverse new evil demon as it arises in the case of perception (see section 3.4). She argues that the victim of the evil demon cannot form justified beliefs, since all justified beliefs are knowledge. Nevertheless, she argues, the victim of an evil demon can form reasonable beliefs, since her beliefs are formed by exercising dispositions that would yield justified beliefs under normal circumstances.[29]

I propose a parallel solution to the reverse new evil problem as it arises in the case of introspection. Although René has no justification to believe that he believes that p in the bad case, it is reasonable for him to believe this all the same. This is because following the Transparency Method yields justified beliefs

---

[28] Moon (2012) argues that the new evil demon problem arises for anyone who denies that justification supervenes on phenomenal character alone, since an evil demon can change your dispositional beliefs without changing what you have epistemic justification to believe. I respond briefly to Moon's argument in section 6.3.

[29] I draw a similar distinction between ideal and nonideal senses of rationality in chapter 10, and elsewhere, but here I'm using Lasonen-Aarnio's distinction to highlight the similarities and differences between her response to the new evil demon problem and mine.

in normal circumstances in which our judgments express what we believe. Even if René doesn't employ the Transparency Method on some occasion, it is nevertheless reasonable for him to do so. Hence, the negative claim can be defended against the charge of intuitive implausibility. Moreover, the positive claim can be defended in much the same way. Although René has justification to believe that he doesn't believe that p, it is nonetheless unreasonable for him to believe this. After all, believing this would require following the Anti-Transparency Method, "If you judge that p, believe that you *don't* believe that p!" But following this method yields unjustified beliefs about what you believe in normal circumstances in which your judgments express what you believe.

Given that I criticized Lasonen-Aarnio's response to the reverse new evil demon problem in the case of perception, what entitles me to give the same response in the case of introspection? This may seem cheeky, perhaps, but it is not without motivation. We can accept Lasonen-Aarnio's distinction between justification and reasonableness without accepting the applications she makes with it. This is because applying the distinction presupposes an account of the nature of evidence to which your justified beliefs must be responsive. I allow that perceptual evidence can be misleading, but I deny that introspective evidence can be misleading. We needn't assume that evidence is misleading in both cases or neither. Indeed, this would obscure the epistemic asymmetry between perception and introspection.

One final challenge is to explain why René cannot rationally judge an omissive Moorean conjunction of the form, p *but I don't believe that* p. As Silins notes, the simple theory allows that René's evidence in the bad case can support this Moorean conjunction. But then what explains why he can't judge the Moorean conjunction in a rationally justified way? My response is that even if René's evidence supports the Moorean conjunction, he cannot make the judgment in a way that is properly based on the evidence. This is because he cannot follow the Anti-Transparency Method in a nonaccidental way. If he succeeds in conforming to the method on a particular occasion by judging that p and hence judging that he doesn't believe that p, then he just gets lucky. His second-order judgment is not formed in a way that is reliably responsive to the absence of the first-order belief. So his second-order judgment is supported by the evidence, but it is not properly based on the evidence.[30]

---

[30] We cannot solve the problem by appealing to the fact that evidence for an omissive Moorean conjunction is "finkish" in the sense that it is destroyed whenever you believe it. After all, René doesn't believe the Moorean conjunction, since he judges the first conjunct without believing it. Hence, finkishness doesn't rule out the possibility of rationally judging the Moorean conjunction without believing it.

In section 5.5.1, I argued that judgment plays an *enabling* role, rather than a *justifying* role, in explaining our introspective knowledge of what you believe. The role of judgment is not to provide introspective justification for second-order beliefs, but rather to enable us to form second-order beliefs in a way that is introspectively justified. When you believe that *p* without judging that *p* because your disposition to judge that *p* is masked, you have introspective justification to believe that you believe that *p*, but you cannot form the second-order belief in a way that is introspectively justified. Similarly, I'm now suggesting, when you judge that *p* without believing that *p* because the disposition to judge that *p* is mimicked, you have introspective justification to believe that you don't believe that *p*, but you cannot form the second-order belief in a way that is introspectively justified. The explanation is the same in each case. Masking or mimicking the dispositions that constitute your first-order beliefs prevents you from forming second-order beliefs that are reliably responsive to the presence or absence of those first-order beliefs.

5.6. Conclusions

This chapter argues for a connection between introspection and phenomenal consciousness. According to the phenomenal individuation constraint, a mental state is introspectively luminous just in case it is individuated either by its phenomenal character or by its phenomenal dispositions. Can we further explain this connection between introspection and phenomenal consciousness?

Some philosophers seek to explain this epistemological claim about the role of phenomenal consciousness in terms of metaphysical claims about its nature. Terry Horgan and Uriah Kriegel (2007) claim that consciousness is *self-presenting* in the sense that it's in the nature of consciousness to consciously present itself. Your visual experience of this book, for example, not only makes you aware of the book, but it also makes you aware of your awareness of the book. The claim is not merely that having an experience puts you in a position to know by introspection that you're having that experience. Rather, it is because an experience makes you aware of itself that it puts you in a position to know by introspection that you're having that experience. On this view, every conscious experience constitutes a form of awareness of itself that is more primitive than introspective knowledge, and which explains how introspective knowledge is possible.[31]

---

[31] Compare Russell's (1912) claim that *acquaintance* is a form of direct conscious awareness of things that explains our knowledge of things, and our knowledge of facts about those things. Some contemporary theories of introspection appeal to the claim that we have acquaintance with our experiences, including Fumerton (1995), Gertler (2001), BonJour (2003), Chalmers (2003), Pitt (2004), and Feldman (2004).

This proposal, which I'll call *self-presentationism*, faces at least three problems. The first problem is that it gives the wrong answer to the scope question. Which of our mental states can we know by means of introspection? According to self-presentationism, only consciousness can be known by introspection, since only consciousness is self-presenting. In this chapter, however, I've argued that we can also know what we believe by means of introspection, despite the fact that beliefs are not conscious states. Self-presentationism must therefore deny that we can know what we believe by introspection. But this is hard to square with the claim that beliefs provide epistemic justification for other beliefs, since all mental states that provide epistemic justification are introspectively luminous. Therefore, self-presentationism cannot account for the epistemic role of belief in providing epistemic justification for other beliefs.

The second problem is that self-presentationism is not well motivated on epistemological grounds. Why must an experience be self-presenting in order to justify believing that you have the experience? One answer is to invoke what James Pryor calls the Premise Principle:

The Premise Principle: The only things that can justify a belief that *p* are other states that assertively represent propositions, and those propositions have to be ones that *could be used as premises* in an argument for *p*. (2005: 189)

Applied to the case of introspection, the Premise Principle says that what justifies believing that you have an experience is that you're in some state that assertively represents that you have that experience. This makes it hard to explain introspective knowledge without supposing that every experience presents itself, and thereby assertively represents that you have the experience in question. But why accept the Premise Principle, rather than simply regarding introspection as a counterexample? The main attraction is theoretical unity: it gives us a way of subsuming introspection under a more general epistemological principle that includes perception and inference too. Arguably, however, this kind of theoretical unification results in distortion, since introspection is epistemologically different from other ways of knowing about the world. We needn't assume that we know our own minds by perception, inference, or nothing at all. As Peacocke insists, this is a "spurious trilemma."

The third problem is that self-presentationism is not well motivated on phenomenological grounds. By definition, there is something it is like for a subject to have an experience. But what kind of relation must hold between a subject S and an experience E when there is something it's like for S to have E? Horgan and Kriegel (2007) claim that E must be *presented* to S in such a way that S is *aware* of having E. But this is far from obvious. Why isn't it enough that S *has* E?

After all, you cannot have an experience, or instantiate a phenomenal property, unless there's something it's like for you to have that property. It's not clear that we need to explain this by appealing to some special relation that subjects stand in toward phenomenal properties, rather than something special about phenomenal properties themselves. That extra step is a piece of speculative metaphysics that goes beyond anything justified by the phenomenal character of experience.[32]

We cannot explain the epistemological connection between introspection and consciousness in terms of more fundamental claims about the nature of consciousness. Instead, we should take the epistemological connection between introspection and consciousness as our starting point and put it to work in explaining other things. I will use it as a basis for explaining the more general connection between consciousness and epistemic justification, and for explaining why epistemic justification is luminous upon reflection. That is my overarching goal in the rest of this book.

---

[32] Stoljar (2018) argues that there are also good reasons to reject self-presentationism because it generates a vicious kind of infinite regress. Compare section 12.4.1

6

Mentalism

What is the epistemic role of phenomenal consciousness? In the last three chapters, I argued that phenomenal consciousness is a unique source of epistemic justification to form beliefs on the basis of perception, cognition, and introspection. In this chapter, I'll integrate these claims about the epistemic role of phenomenal consciousness into a more general theory of epistemic justification. The main goal of this chapter is to explain the sense in which phenomenal consciousness is the basis of epistemic justification.

Any theory of epistemic justification should explain what makes it the case that we have epistemic justification to believe some propositions, rather than others. Sometimes, you have justification to believe propositions that I have no justification to believe, and vice versa. What explains these epistemic differences between us? Presumably, these are not just brute facts. All epistemic facts depend upon nonepistemic facts, so there must be some nonepistemic difference between us that explains why these epistemic differences obtain. A theory of the basis of epistemic justification needs to explain *how* facts about epistemic justification depend on nonepistemic facts; moreover, it needs to explain *which* nonepistemic facts they depend on. That is the agenda for this chapter.

One influential theory of the basis of epistemic justification is *reliabilism*: it says that the reliability of your belief-forming processes determines which propositions you have epistemic justification to believe. As we saw in chapter 3, and as I'll explain here, reliabilism is vulnerable to some intuitive counterexamples. These counterexamples are often supposed not only to undermine reliabilism, but also to support *mentalism*, which says that epistemic justification depends solely on your mental states, rather than the reliability of their connections to the external world. One problem with mentalism is that some of our mental states play no epistemic role in determining which beliefs we have epistemic justification to hold. Without imposing any further restriction on which of our mental states play such an epistemic role, mentalism is vulnerable to exactly the same counterexamples as reliabilism.

In this chapter, I argue for *phenomenal mentalism*, which says that epistemic justification is determined solely by your phenomenally individuated mental states. These include not only your conscious experiences, which are individuated by their phenomenal character, but also your consciously accessible beliefs, which are individuated by their phenomenal dispositions. At the same time, these exclude your externally individuated mental states, which are individuated by their relations to the environment, and your subdoxastic mental representations, which are individuated by their role in unconscious computational processes. Phenomenal mentalism avoids the intuitive counterexamples to reliabilism; moreover, it explains why the intuitive judgments about these examples are correct: it is therefore strongly supported on intuitive grounds.

Notwithstanding the intuitive support for phenomenal mentalism, an explanatory challenge remains. Why is it that only phenomenally individuated facts about our mental states can make a justificational difference? This claim might seem plausible on intuitive grounds, but without any deeper explanation, it can seem arbitrary and theoretically unmotivated. The main goal of the second part of this book is to answer this explanatory challenge by arguing that phenomenal mentalism is the best explanation of accessibilism, which can be motivated and defended on independent grounds.

Here is the plan for this chapter. In section 6.1, I explain the concept of epistemic justification by locating it within the theoretical framework of evidentialism. In section 6.2, I defend mentalism about epistemic justification against the objection that evidential support facts are not mental facts. In section 6.3, I argue that phenomenal mentalism avoids the intuitive counterexamples to reliabilism and explains why our intuitive judgments are correct. In section 6.4, I propose a phenomenal conception of evidence and defend it against Williamson's (2000: ch. 9) arguments for the E = K thesis. Finally, in section 6.5, I outline the explanatory challenge for phenomenal mentalism.

6.1. Evidentialism

What is epistemic justification? As I said in section 1.5, the concept of epistemic justification cannot be defined in more basic terms, but only by giving examples of when it applies and when it doesn't. Although we cannot give any reductive definition of epistemic justification, we can provide some elucidation of this concept by locating it within the theoretical framework of evidentialism.

Epistemic justification is justification by epistemic reasons, rather than moral or practical reasons. We can illustrate this distinction by giving examples, such as Pascal's Wager: if you believe that God exists only because you want to avoid the risk of eternal damnation, then you believe for practical reasons, rather than epistemic reasons. You don't have an epistemic reason for believing that God exists because your desire gives you no evidence that God exists. More generally, you have an epistemic reason for believing that p only if you have evidence that supports the proposition that p. If all epistemic justification for belief is justification by epistemic reasons, and all epistemic reasons for belief are evidence, then all epistemic justification for belief is justification by evidence. Evidentialism explains epistemic justification in terms of evidence.

Epistemologists sometimes explain the concept of epistemic justification by appealing to its connection with truth. Unfortunately, the nature of this "truth-connection" is a matter of controversy. Reliabilism says that epistemically justified beliefs are objectively likely to be true in the sense that they are held on the basis of belief-forming processes that reliably track the truth. As I'll explain in section 6.3, however, reliabilism is vulnerable to convincing counterexamples. Can we give a more neutral account of the truth-connection that doesn't require taking on such controversial theoretical commitments?

Evidentialism provides a more neutral explanation of the truth-connection: it says that epistemically justified beliefs are evidentially likely to be true in the sense that they are probable given your evidence. Not everyone accepts evidentialism, of course, but it has the advantage of theoretical flexibility insofar it can be combined with many different conceptions of evidence, including phenomenal, reliabilist, and knowledge-first conceptions of evidence. At the same time, evidentialism is not completely vacuous, since any reasonable conception of evidence must be sensitive to the intuitive distinction between epistemic and pragmatic reasons.

Earl Conee and Richard Feldman (2004) define evidentialism in terms of the following pair of commitments:

EJ: Doxastic attitude D toward proposition p is epistemically justified for S at t if and only if having D toward p fits the evidence S has at t. (2004: 83)

ES: The justification of anyone's doxastic attitude toward any proposition at any time strongly supervenes on the evidence that the person has at the time. (2004: 101)

ES says that epistemic justification supervenes on evidence in the following sense: there can be no difference in which doxastic attitudes you have epistemic justification to hold at any given time without some difference in your evidence at that time. This tells us nothing about which doxastic attitudes are justified by which evidence. EJ is designed to fill in this lacuna: it says you have epistemic justification to adopt a doxastic attitude just in case it fits with your current evidence. Moreover, EJ explains why ES is true: the only way to change which doxastic attitudes you have epistemic justification to hold is by changing your evidence and thereby changing which doxastic attitudes fit with your evidence.

What does it mean to say that a doxastic attitude "fits" with your evidence? The basic idea is that which doxastic attitude you have epistemic justification to hold toward a proposition is a function of the degree to which that proposition is supported by your evidence. Here is a simple way of applying evidentialism to coarse-grained doxastic attitudes of belief, disbelief, and withholding:

(1) If your evidence supports p to a high enough degree, then you have justification to believe that p.

(2) If your evidence supports not-p to a high enough degree, then you have justification to believe that not-p.

(3) If your evidence supports neither p nor not-p to a high enough degree, then you have justification to withhold belief that p.

We can also apply evidentialism to more fine-grained degrees of confidence. A simple and plausible version of evidentialism says that your degree of confidence in a proposition should be proportioned to its degree of evidential support. So, for example, if your evidence supports the proposition that p to degree n, then you have justification to be confident that p to degree n. On the threshold view, you believe that p just when you have a high enough degree of confidence that p. Hence, you have justification to believe that p just when your evidence justifies a high enough degree of confidence that p.

Evidentialism makes good sense of the distinction between propositional and doxastic senses of epistemic justification. This is an instance of a more general distinction between prospective and retrospective senses of justification that applies equally in epistemic and practical domains. You can have justification to perform an action, for example, without performing the action in a justified way. After all, you might fail to perform the action at all, or you might perform the action for the wrong reasons. Given that this distinction between prospective and retrospective senses of justification applies to actions as well as beliefs, why are epistemologists tempted to explain the distinction by appealing to relations to propositions? As I'll explain, this makes perfect sense within an evidentialist framework that explains epistemic justification in terms of evidence.

Evidentialism explains your prospective justification to adopt beliefs and other doxastic attitudes in terms of the evidential support relation that holds between your evidence and a proposition. Evidentialism says that you have prospective justification to hold a certain doxastic attitude toward the proposition that p just when your evidence supports the proposition that p to a fitting degree. In contrast, your doxastic attitude toward p is retrospectively justified just in case it is properly based on evidence that supports p to a fitting degree. Retrospective justification depends on whether your doxastic attitudes are properly based on your evidence, whereas propositional justification depends solely on which propositions are supported by your evidence. That is why it is apt to use the terminology of "propositional" and "doxastic" justification.

Evidentialism explains epistemic justification in terms of what your evidence supports, so we need to understand two concepts: (i) *evidence* and (ii) *evidential support*. Let's take these in reverse order. Evidential support is the relation between your evidence and a proposition that determines which doxastic attitude you have epistemic justification to hold toward the proposition in question. It is a relation that comes in degrees: the more your evidence supports a proposition, the more epistemic justification you have to believe it. On a probabilistic conception of evidential support, the degree to which a proposition is supported by your evidence is given by its evidential probability—that is, by its probability conditional upon your evidence.

Evidential probability cannot be defined in terms of chance or credence—that is, objective probability or subjective probability.[1] Instead, evidential probability is a sui generis kind of probability. What it means to say that evidential support is a kind of probability is that it is constrained by the axioms of the probability calculus. On this view, evidential support is modeled as a probability function that maps each proposition onto a real number in the interval between 1 and 0. If your evidence entails that p, then the probability that p is 1. If your evidence is inconsistent with p, then the probability that p is 0. Degrees of evidential support are degrees of probability between 1 and 0. It is unrealistic to suppose that degrees of evidential support have the same degree of precision as real numbers, but this is a harmless idealization of the kind that is ubiquitous in science.[2]

What about evidence? In an evidentialist framework, your evidence can be defined by its epistemic role: it is what gives you epistemic justification to hold certain beliefs and other doxastic attitudes by supporting their contents to a fitting degree. As I'll explain in section 6.4, however, the justifying role of evidence can be understood in two different ways. James Pryor (2005) puts the point in terms of a distinction between "justification-makers" and "justification-showers." Your evidence in the *justification-making* sense is constituted by facts that make it the case that you have epistemic justification to hold some doxastic attitudes, rather than others. Meanwhile, your evidence in the *justification-showing* sense is constituted by propositions you have epistemic justification to believe, which you are rationally permitted to use as premises in reasoning. Both conceptions of evidence are perfectly legitimate, but we need to keep them apart in order to avoid confusion. Unless I explicitly say otherwise, I will use the term 'evidence' in the justification-making sense, rather than the justification-showing sense.

---

[1] Williamson (2000: 209–213) argues that epistemic probability cannot be reduced to objective probability or subjective probability.

[2] See Christensen (2004: 143–150) for a helpful discussion of this point.

Your evidence in the justification-making sense is defined by its epistemic role in determining which doxastic attitude you have epistemic justification to hold toward any given proposition. It plays this epistemic role by supporting the proposition in question to a fitting degree. All proponents of evidentialism can agree that your evidence is what plays this epistemic role, but they can disagree about which facts play this epistemic role. Evidentialism is therefore compatible with various rival conceptions of evidence, including the following:

Reliabilism: Your evidence consists of facts about you that are reliable indicators of facts about the external world.

Knowledge-First: Your evidence consists of facts about your knowledge.

The Phenomenal Conception: Your evidence consists of facts about your phenomenally individuated mental states.

This chapter assumes evidentialism with the aim of arguing for a phenomenal conception of evidence, according to which your evidence is identified with the totality of phenomenally individuated facts about your current mental states.

Although evidentialism provides a convenient and plausible framework, it is not an indispensable component of the theory of epistemic justification that I defend in this chapter. My core proposal— phenomenal mentalism—can be defended without any commitment to evidentialism. I'll mention this point from time to time, but otherwise I'll tend to operate on the default assumption that evidentialism is true.

6.2. Mentalism

Let's define 'the justificational facts' about a person at a time as the total set of facts about which doxastic attitudes that person has epistemic justification to hold at that time. To a first approximation, *mentalism* is the thesis that the justificational facts about a person at a time depend solely on mental facts about that person at that time. This preliminary definition of mentalism raises two questions:

(1) *The Dependence Question*: How do the justificational facts *depend* on mental facts?

(2) *The Scope Question*: Which are the *mental facts* on which the justificational facts depend?

In this section, I'll address the dependence question. I'll postpone discussion of the scope question until the next section.

Here are three distinct answers to the dependence question, which are listed in order of logical strength from weakest to strongest:

The Mentalist Supervenience Thesis: Justification *supervenes* on the mental in the sense that every justificational difference necessitates some mental difference.

The Mentalist Determination Thesis: Justification is *determined* by the mental in the sense that every justificational difference holds in virtue of some mental difference.

The Mentalist Grounding Thesis: Justification is *grounded* in the mental in the sense that every justification fact holds in virtue of some mental fact.

I'll argue that the supervenience thesis is too weak, whereas the grounding thesis is too strong, to capture the sense in which justificational facts depend on mental facts. Mentalism should instead be defined as the determination thesis.[3]

Mentalism is often defined as a supervenience thesis. For example, when Conee and Feldman originally coined the term 'mentalism', they defined it like this:

The justificatory status of a person's doxastic attitudes strongly supervenes on the person's occurrent and dispositional mental states, events, and conditions. If any two possible individuals are exactly alike mentally, then they are alike justificationally, e.g., the same beliefs are justified for them to the same extent. (2004: 56)

This definition is too weak to capture the sense in which justification depends on the mental. Dependence is an *asymmetric* relation: if the A-facts depend on the B-facts, then it follows that the B-facts don't depend on the A-facts. In contrast, supervenience is a *nonsymmetric* relation: it is neither symmetric nor asymmetric. If the A-facts supervene on the B-facts, then it doesn't follow that the B-facts don't also supervene on the A-facts. In some cases, the supervenience relation holds in both directions.

Here is a case in point. In chapter 3, I argued that the justifying role of perceptual experience supervenes upon its phenomenal character. Moreover, it is not implausible that the phenomenal character of perceptual experience also supervenes on its justifying role. Given representationalism, there can be no

---

[3] See Kim (1984) and Bennett and McLaughlin (2005) on the definition of supervenience. On the definition of grounding, see Fine (2001), Schaffer (2009), and Rosen (2010).

difference in the phenomenal character of perceptual experience without some difference in its representational properties. Arguably, however, any difference in the representational properties of perceptual experience affects which doxastic attitudes you have epistemic justification to hold. If so, then supervenience holds in both directions. In contrast: dependence holds only in one direction: the justifying role of perceptual experience depends on its phenomenal character, and not vice versa. Supervenience is too weak to capture this asymmetric dependence.

A similar point holds much more generally. If justification supervenes on the mental, then some of the mental facts constitute a *minimal* supervenience base. There can be no difference in the mental facts that figure in this minimal supervenience base without some corresponding difference in the justificational facts. Hence, supervenience holds in both directions between justificational facts and the mental facts on which they minimally supervene. In contrast, dependence holds only in one direction: the justificational facts depend on the mental facts in the minimal supervenience base, but not vice versa. Again, supervenience is too weak to capture this asymmetric dependence.

To capture this asymmetric dependence, mentalism is sometimes defined as the thesis that justification is *grounded* in the mental in the sense that every justification fact holds in virtue of some mental fact. So, for example, Juan Comesaña defines mentalism as follows:

All the factors that contribute to the epistemic justification of a doxastic attitude towards a proposition by a subject S are mental states of S. (2005b: 59)

Having defined mentalism in this way, Comesaña proceeds to reject it on the grounds that epistemic justification is partially grounded in facts about the evidential support relation, which are nonmental facts. Evidentialism says you have epistemic justification to believe that p just when and because your evidence supports p to a sufficiently high degree. But whether your evidence supports a proposition depends not only on facts about what evidence you have, but also on facts about the evidential support relation. On a logical or probabilistic conception of evidential support, for example, your evidence supports the proposition that p when it logically entails that p or makes it sufficiently probable that p. If so, then epistemic justification is partially grounded in nonmental facts about logical entailment or evidential probability.[4]

---

[4] Compare Goldman's (1999: 282) objection that mentalism cannot accommodate the role of logical and probabilistic relations in a theory of epistemic justification.

Comesaña's point is well taken, but this is no reason for rejecting mentalism. Instead, we should reformulate mentalism in a way that is more sensitive to the division of epistemic labor between evidence and evidential support. The key point for my purposes is that it's a contingent matter what evidence you have, whereas the evidential support relation holds necessarily for all subjects, times, and possible worlds. You and I can differ in what evidence we have, but we cannot differ in how the evidential support relation applies to us: it is the same for everyone no matter what evidence we happen to have. If we have the same evidence, then there can be no difference in which propositions we have epistemic justification to believe, since our evidence supports the same propositions to the same degree. Contraposing, if we have epistemic justification to believe different propositions, then there must be some difference in our evidence that explains why this is so.

What I'm suggesting is that evidentialism is best understood as a determination thesis, rather than a grounding thesis or a supervenience thesis:

The Evidentialist Supervenience Thesis: Justification *supervenes* on evidence in the sense that every justificational difference necessitates some difference in evidence.

The Evidentialist Determination Thesis: Justification is *determined* by evidence in the sense that every justificational difference holds in virtue of some difference in evidence.

The Evidentialist Grounding Thesis: Justification is *grounded* in evidence in the sense that every justification fact holds in virtue of some facts about evidence.

The supervenience thesis is too weak to capture the asymmetric dependence of epistemic justification on evidence. Meanwhile, the grounding thesis is too strong to respect Comesaña's point that epistemic justification is grounded partly in facts about the nature of the evidential support relation. The determination thesis is strong enough to capture the asymmetric dependence of epistemic justification on evidence, but also weak enough to allow evidential support facts to play a role in grounding epistemic justification. Since these evidential support facts hold necessarily, they cannot make a justificational difference. Only a difference in evidence can make a justificational difference.

If we define evidentialism as a determination thesis, then we can define mentalism as a thesis about the nature of your evidence. *Mentalism about evidence* says that your evidence is exhausted by mental facts: these are the only contingent facts about you that can make a justificational difference. Moreover, mentalism can be defined without commitment to evidentialism. *Mentalism about justification* says that justification is determined by the mental in the sense that every justificational difference holds in virtue of some difference in mental facts. It is a further question whether these mental facts are evidence. According to *nonevidentialist* versions of mentalism, they might include facts about your epistemic standards, practical interests, and goals.

Determination is a relation of "difference-making": the A-facts are determined by the B-facts just in case every difference in A-facts is grounded in some difference in B-facts. Mentalism is a thesis about the nature of justificational difference-makers: it says that all justificational difference-makers are mental facts. When mentalism is defined in this way, the scope question becomes salient. Which mental facts are justificational difference-makers? All of them, or only some of them? And, if only some of them, then which ones? This is the question to which I'll now turn.

6.3. Phenomenal Mentalism

To answer the scope question for mentalism, we need to begin by considering what makes mentalism an attractive option in the first place. In this section, I'll outline an explanatory argument for mentalism that appeals to intuitions about cases. The argument is that mentalism provides the best explanation of some well-known intuitive counterexamples to reliabilism, including clairvoyance and the new evil demon problem. I'll argue that without some further restriction on which mental facts can make a justificational difference, mentalism is vulnerable to the very same counterexamples as reliabilism. Moreover, I'll argue that avoiding these counterexamples requires a commitment to *phenomenal mentalism*, which says that justificational facts are determined solely by the phenomenally individuated facts about your current mental states.[5]

Reliabilism comes in many different forms, but the central idea is that the reliability of your belief-forming processes determines which beliefs you have epistemic justification to hold. On a simple version of reliabilism, you have justification to believe a proposition just in case you're disposed to believe it on the basis of a reliable belief-forming process. To a first approximation, your belief-forming processes are reliable just in case they yield a sufficiently high proportion of true beliefs to false beliefs in counterfactual conditions that are sufficiently similar to your actual conditions.[6]

---

[5] This section builds on my argument for phenomenal mentalism in Smithies (2014b).

[6] Goldman (1979) was the first to propose a reliabilist theory of justification, but compare Goldman (1986), Sosa (1991), Burge (2003), Bergmann (2006), and Lyons (2009) for various different ways of explaining the relationship between justification and reliability. For simplicity, I will ignore these complications here.

There are well-known counterexamples to reliabilism. On the one hand, there are counterexamples to the thesis that reliability is *necessary* for justification. Suppose you're a disembodied soul being deceived by an evil demon; or, to use the updated version, suppose you're a disembodied brain in a vat being deceived by an evil neuroscientist. In these skeptical scenarios, your visual experience has exactly the same phenomenal character as it does in the real-world scenario, although it represents the external world in a way that is systematically unreliable. Intuitively, you have justification to form beliefs on the basis of visual experience in the skeptical scenario, despite the fact that forming beliefs in this way is unreliable in those circumstances. For example, your belief that you have hands is justified, although it is formed in an unreliable way. Hence, reliability is not necessary for justification. This is Stewart Cohen's (1984) new evil demon problem for reliabilism.

On the other hand, there are counterexamples to the thesis that reliability is *sufficient* for justification. Consider BonJour's example of the clairvoyant, Norman:

Norman, under certain conditions which usually obtain, is a completely reliable clairvoyant with respect to certain kinds of subject matter. He possesses no evidence or reasons of any kind for or against the general possibility of such a cognitive power or for or against the thesis that he possesses it. One day Norman comes to believe that the President is in New York City, though he has no evidence either for or against this belief. In fact the belief is true and results from his clairvoyant power under circumstances in which it is completely reliable. (1985: 41)

Let's stipulate that Norman has no experience that represents that the president is in New York City. In fact, his experiences are no different from yours or mine. Even so, Norman believes that the president is in New York City on the basis of a wholly unconscious process that results from the operation of his reliable clairvoyant power. Nevertheless, he has no evidence that he has such a reliable clairvoyant power. Intuitively, Norman has no justification to form beliefs on the basis of clairvoyance, despite the fact that this is a reliable way of forming beliefs in the circumstances. For example, his belief about the location of the president is unjustified, although it is formed in a reliable way. Hence, reliability is not sufficient for justification.

So understood, BonJour's clairvoyance case has the same structure as Block's case of super-blindsight (see section 3.2). Suppose you have a form of super-blindsight that disposes you to form beliefs about objects that fall outside your conscious visual field on the basis of reliable but unconscious visual information. In this scenario, your visual experience has exactly the same phenomenal character as it does in the actual world, but in addition you have unconscious visual information that represents objects in "the blind field" with a high degree of reliability. At the same time, you have no evidence that you have this reliable source of unconscious visual information. Intuitively, you lack justification to form beliefs on the basis of super-blindsight, despite the fact that forming beliefs in this way is reliable in the circumstances. If you believe that there is an X in your blind field, for example, then your belief is unjustified, despite the fact that it is formed in a reliable way. This is another counterexample to the thesis that reliability is sufficient for justification.

These counterexamples to reliabilism are often thought to provide intuitive support for mentalism. This is because mentalism explains why our intuitive judgments about these reliabilism are correct:

Deception and envatment: Mentalism implies that all mental duplicates are justificational duplicates. It's independently plausible that I have justification to form beliefs on the basis of perceptual experience. Therefore, mentalism implies that my mental duplicate in the skeptical scenario also has justification to form beliefs on the basis of perceptual experience, despite the fact that his perceptual experience is unreliable.

Clairvoyance and super-blindsight: Mentalism implies that all mental duplicates are justificational duplicates. It's independently plausible that I lack justification to form beliefs on the basis of unconscious information. Therefore, mentalism implies that my mental duplicate in the clairvoyance or super-blindsight scenario also lacks justification to form beliefs on the basis of unconscious information, despite the fact that his unconscious information is reliable.

What these examples illustrate is that varying the reliability of our doxastic dispositions makes no justificational difference when we hold fixed the relevant facts about our mental states. What matters is that we have the same mental states, regardless of whether they are reliably connected to the external world. This suggests that justification is determined not by facts about the reliability of the connections between our mental states and the external world, but rather by facts about our mental states themselves. Hence, these examples not only refute reliabilism, but also provide positive support for mentalism.

The problem with this explanatory argument for mentalism is that my counterparts in these examples are not perfect mental duplicates of mine. At best, they duplicate some of my mental states but not others. After all, my deceived counterpart cannot see everything I can see, since he is merely hallucinating. Meanwhile, my super-blindsighted counterpart can "see" more than I can, since he has unconscious visual information that accurately represents objects outside the conscious field of vision. Intuitively, however, these mental differences make no justificational difference. To suppose otherwise is to succumb to exactly the same counterexamples as reliabilism.

To avoid this problem, we need an answer to the scope question that imposes some restriction on which mental facts are capable of making a justificational difference. Drawing on the conclusions of earlier chapters, I'll argue that only your phenomenally individuated mental states are capable of making a justificational difference. This yields the following phenomenal version of mentalism:

> *Phenomenal Mentalism*: Necessarily, every difference in which propositions you have epistemic justification to believe at any given time is grounded in some difference in your phenomenally individuated mental states at that time.

A *phenomenally individuated mental state* is one that is individuated wholly by its phenomenal character or its phenomenal dispositions. In other words, what it is to be in a phenomenally individuated mental state is to have a certain phenomenal character or a certain phenomenal disposition. If a mental state is phenomenally individuated, then there is some phenomenal character or some phenomenal disposition that is necessary and sufficient for being in that mental state. A *phenomenally individuated fact* is a fact that is wholly about your phenomenally individuated mental states.

Which mental states are phenomenally individuated? In chapter 4, I argued that phenomenally individuated mental states include not only conscious experiences, which are individuated by their phenomenal character, but also consciously accessible beliefs, which are individuated by their phenomenal dispositions. However, these exclude externally individuated mental states, which are individuated by their relations to the environment, and subdoxastic mental representations, which are individuated by their role in unconscious computational processes.

Phenomenal mentalism avoids the intuitive counterexamples to reliabilism and it explains why these intuitive judgments are correct. Anyone who duplicates my phenomenally individuated mental states is also my justificational duplicate. My phenomenal duplicate in the skeptical scenario is not my perfect mental duplicate because we differ in our factive mental states. Nevertheless, we are justificational duplicates because our phenomenally individuated mental states are exactly the same. Similarly, my phenomenal duplicate with a reliable faculty of clairvoyance or super-blindsight is not my perfect mental duplicate because we differ in our subdoxastic mental states and processes. Nevertheless, we are justificational duplicates because our phenomenally individuated mental states are exactly the same. On this view, only a difference in phenomenally individuated mental states can make a justificational difference.

It's worthwhile to consider some restricted versions of mentalism that share the same problems as the unrestricted version. Consider, for example, the version of mentalism defended by Timothy Williamson. He argues that knowledge is a mental state; indeed, it is the most general factive mental state in the sense that all factive mental states are instances of knowledge (2000: ch. 1). He also argues for the E = K thesis, which says that your justifying evidence includes all and only the facts that you know (2000: ch. 9). Hence, Williamson is committed to the following form of mentalism:

Factive Mentalism: Epistemic justification is determined by your factive mental states.

On this view, only factive mental states can make a justificational difference, since any justificational difference holds in virtue of some difference in what you know. Moreover, all factive mental states can make a justificational difference, since any difference in what you know makes a justificational difference.

Williamson's version of factive mentalism faces a version of the new evil demon problem. You and your phenomenal duplicate in the skeptical scenario differ in your factive mental states. After all, you see that you have hands, and thereby know that you have hands, whereas your deceived counterpart merely seems to see that he or she has hands. If Williamson's version of factive mentalism is true, then you and your deceived counterpart are not justificational duplicates because you differ in what you can see to be true. Intuitively, however, this is a mental difference that makes no justificational difference.[7]

Some epistemologists avoid the new evil demon problem by endorsing a nonfactive version of mentalism, which says that only nonfactive mental states can make a justificational difference:

Nonfactive Mentalism: Epistemic justification is determined by your nonfactive mental states.[8]

---

[7] In section 3.4, I argue against Williamson's (forthcoming) response to the new evil demon problem, which appeals to a distinction between justifications and excuses.

[8] Proponents of nonfactive mentalism include Pollock and Cruz (1999), Wedgwood (2002), Conee and Feldman (2004: ch. 3), McCain (2014), and Schoenfield (2015a).

But the restriction to nonfactive mental states is not sufficient to avoid the problems raised by super-blindsight. In this scenario, subjects form beliefs on the basis of unconscious visual information that represents the blind field with a high degree of reliability. These unconscious visual states are nonfactive mental representations: they can misrepresent the blind field. As I argued in section 3.2, however, these visual states cannot justify beliefs about the external world. To explain this, we need to impose some further restriction on which nonfactive mental states can make a justificational difference.

Why not impose the restriction that only phenomenal states—that is, mental states individuated by their phenomenal character—can make a justificational difference? This yields a much stronger version of phenomenal mentalism:

> Strong Phenomenal Mentalism: Epistemic justification is determined by your phenomenal states.[9]

This view avoids both the new evil demon problem and the problems of clairvoyance and super-blindsight. Moreover, it can explain why our intuitive reactions to these examples are correct by appealing to the epistemic role of phenomenal consciousness. The problem is that it cannot accommodate the epistemic role of standing, dispositional beliefs.

In section 4.1, I argued that epistemic justification depends not only on your total experiential state, but also on your total doxastic state. Phenomenal duplicates can differ in which propositions they have epistemic justification to believe owing to differences in background information stored unconsciously in memory. Recall Feldman's (2004: 238–239) example of the expert and novice birdwatchers: they both see a scarlet tanager, and it looks the same way to each of them, but only the expert knows or has any justification to believe that this is how scarlet tanagers look. Even if they are perfect phenomenal duplicates, only the expert has justification to believe the bird is a scarlet tanager. In general, which propositions you have justification to believe on the basis of perceptual experience depends upon vast quantities of background information that is stored unconsciously in the belief system. You cannot bring all of this information into phenomenal consciousness simultaneously in the process of forming justified beliefs, since attention imposes severe limits on the capacity of conscious thought.

Some epistemologists may be tempted to solve this problem by rejecting a synchronic version of strong phenomenal mentalism in favor of a diachronic version:

---

[9] Proponents of strong phenomenal mentalism include Conee and Feldman (2008) and Dougherty and Rysiew (2013).

The Synchronic Version: Epistemic justification is determined by the phenomenal states you have now.

The Diachronic Version: Epistemic justification is determined by phenomenal states you have now or in the past.

The idea is that phenomenal states in the past as well as the present can make a justificational difference right now. For example, the justificational difference between the expert and novice birdwatchers can be explained in terms of differences in their phenomenal history. The problem is that diachronic versions of mentalism are vulnerable to a version of the new evil demon problem. Consider Bertrand Russell's (1921) skeptical hypothesis that you were created five minutes ago by an evil demon who implanted false memories about the past. Intuitively, no such fact about your history can make any difference to which propositions you have epistemic justification to believe right now. In this skeptical scenario, you have epistemic justification to believe the same propositions as any phenomenal duplicate whose memories of the past are entirely accurate.[10]

To avoid the new evil demon problem, we should endorse a *synchronic version* of mentalism: only your current mental states are justificational difference-makers.[11] To accommodate the epistemic role of standing beliefs, we should endorse a *moderate version* of phenomenal mentalism: your justificational difference-makers include mental states that are individuated by their phenomenal character or by their phenomenal dispositions. Combining these claims yields a *synchronic version of moderate phenomenal mentalism*, which says that epistemic justification is determined solely by your current phenomenally individuated mental states.

Andrew Moon (2012) argues that this moderate version of phenomenal mentalism faces its own version of the new evil demon problem. Consider a scenario in which a demon destroys some of your dispositional beliefs but then mimics the dispositions toward judgment normally associated with them. The demon causes you to make judgments, but these judgments manifest the dispositions of the demon, rather than your own dispositional beliefs. According to Moon, your phenomenal duplicate in this scenario is your justificational duplicate: you have epistemic justification to believe exactly the same propositions. If so, then your dispositional beliefs make no justificational difference.

---

[10] Huemer (1999) endorses a diachronic version of strong phenomenal mentalism. See section 12.3 for critical discussion.

[11] Goldman (1999) raises the problem of forgotten evidence as an objection to synchronic versions of mentalism. I agree with Harman (1986) and McGrath (2007) that doxastic conservatism provides the best solution to this problem (section 4.1).

I reject Moon's intuition about this case. We've already seen good reasons to think that phenomenal duplicates can differ in epistemic justification owing to differences in dispositional beliefs that are not manifested in phenomenal consciousness. If your dispositional beliefs can make a justificational difference in these cases, then destroying these beliefs can make a justificational difference too. Hence, we should reject Moon's intuition that your phenomenal duplicate in the demon scenario is your justificational duplicate.

Moon gives two arguments in defense of this intuition. The first argument is that it seems counterintuitive to suppose that you should adopt different beliefs when you're in the demon scenario. In reply, there is a sense in which you should adopt different beliefs, since you should always believe what the evidence supports. But there is another sense in which you shouldn't adopt different beliefs, since you cannot do so in a way that is properly based on your evidence. After all, your belief-forming processes are not at all sensitive to the fact that you are deceived by an evil demon. As a result, it would be unreasonable to expect you to hold beliefs that are properly based on your evidence. The general point is that deontic terms are highly context-sensitive: our intuitions about what we "should" believe don't always reflect what our evidence supports, rather than what we can be reasonably expected to believe given our limited psychological capacities.[12]

Moon's second argument is that you're not in a position to know whether you're in the demon scenario. He writes: "Consider that *you*, at this moment, might be fooled by a demon. . . . You might *think* that you have dispositional beliefs and memories, but you don't" (2012: 349). The claim, presumably, is not that the evil demon scenario actually obtains, or merely that it's metaphysically possible, but that it's epistemically possible: in other words, you're not in a position to know that the scenario doesn't obtain. Moon's conclusion about the case follows from this premise given the further assumption that epistemic justification is "luminous" in the sense that you're always in a position to know which beliefs you have epistemic justification to hold at any given time. Although I accept that epistemic justification is luminous, I deny that it's epistemically possible that you're in the demon scenario. After all, you're in a position to know what you believe, and so you can know by deduction that you're not merely being deceived by an evil demon into forming false higher-order beliefs about

---

[12] We can develop the point further by invoking Lasonen-Aarnio's (2010) distinction between justification and reasonableness. In the demon scenario, your beliefs are not justified by your evidence, but they are reasonable in the sense that they are formed by exercising dispositions that would result in justified beliefs under normal circumstances. Compare my response to Silins's new evil demon problem in section 5.5.2.

what you believe. To suppose otherwise is to make a dangerous concession to skepticism.

The scope question isn't fully settled by the synchronic version of moderate phenomenal mentalism. On this view, the only justificational difference-makers are your current phenomenally individuated mental states. But it's a further question whether all of them, or only some of them, can make a justificational difference. Is there any further restriction on your justificational difference-makers?

Not all phenomenal states justify beliefs about the external world. In chapter 3, I argued that perceptual experience justifies beliefs about the external world only because it represents its contents with presentational force. Not all phenomenal experience represents its contents with presentational force. For example, the experience of visualizing that p gives you no justification to believe that p because it doesn't represent its content with presentational force. Visual imagination doesn't justify believing that its contents are true, but only that they are possible.

In chapter 5, however, I argued for the simple theory of introspection, which says that all phenomenal states give you introspective justification to believe that you're in them. Sometimes you're unable to form introspectively justified beliefs about your phenomenal states—say, because you don't have the requisite concepts, attention, rationality, or powers of discrimination. Even so, you have introspective justification to believe that you're in a phenomenal state just by virtue of the fact that you're in it. Moreover, I extended the simple theory from your phenomenal states to your phenomenally individuated beliefs. On this view, believing that p always gives you introspective justification to believe that p. More generally, any difference in your phenomenally individuated mental states makes a corresponding difference in which propositions you have introspective justification to believe. This completes my answer to the scope question: all and only current phenomenally individuated mental states have the potential to make a justificatory difference.

6.4. The Phenomenal Conception of Evidence

What is the theory of evidence that results from combining evidentialism with phenomenal mentalism? This depends on how the concept of evidence is defined. Evidence can be defined in terms of its epistemic role: your evidence gives you epistemic justification to hold beliefs and other doxastic attitudes by supporting their contents to a fitting degree. Williamson puts the point more succinctly: "evidence is what justifies belief" (2000: 207). As I mentioned in section 6.1, however, there are two distinct ways to understand the justifying role of evidence. Evidence can be defined in terms of its role in *making* a belief justified or its role in *showing* a belief to be justified. Hence, we can define two distinct concepts of evidence corresponding to these two different ways of construing its justifying role.[13]

James Pryor (2005) puts this point in terms of a distinction between what he calls "justification-makers" and "justification-showers." Your evidence in the *justification-making* sense is constituted by the contingent facts that determine which propositions you have justification to believe. In contrast, your evidence in the *justification-showing* sense is constituted by the propositions you have justification to believe, which you are thereby rationally permitted to use as premises in reasoning to further conclusions. In effect, your evidence can be defined either as the facts that make propositions evident to you or as the propositions that are thereby made evident to you. Both conceptions of evidence are perfectly legitimate, but conflating them can lead to serious confusion.

We can spell out the phenomenal conception of evidence by applying this distinction to phenomenal mentalism. Your justification-making evidence is defined by its role in determining which beliefs you have epistemic justification to hold at any given time. Phenomenal mentalism says that this role is played by the phenomenally individuated facts about your mental states. Hence, your justification-making evidence is constituted by the phenomenally individuated facts about your mental states. Your justification-showing evidence, in contrast, is constituted by the propositions that you have justification to believe in virtue of these phenomenally individuated facts about your mental states. To illustrate the distinction, suppose you're hallucinating a dagger. In that case, your justification-showing evidence includes the false proposition that there's a dagger before you, whereas your justification-making evidence includes only the fact—that is, the true proposition—that it visually seems to you as if there's a dagger before you.

Although these two conceptions of evidence are distinct, phenomenal mentalism draws interesting connections between them. On the phenomenal conception, your justification-making evidence is constituted by the phenomenally individuated facts about your current mental states. In chapter 5, I argued that these phenomenally individuated facts about your current mental states are introspectively luminous in the sense that you're always in a position to know whether or not they obtain. As such, you always have justification to believe these justification-making facts and to use them as premises in reasoning. Therefore, all justification-making evidence is justification-showing evidence, although not vice versa.

---

[13] This section draws on my account of perceptual reasons in Smithies (2018b).

Given classical foundationalism, we can add that all justification-showing evidence is either identical with or otherwise grounded in justification-making evidence. Showing your beliefs to be justified by the most demanding standards requires citing the facts that ultimately make them justified. We typically operate with more relaxed standards, but the most demanding standards reveal the ultimate foundational structure of epistemic justification. According to classical foundationalism, introspectively luminous facts about our phenomenally individuated mental states serve as the foundations of this structure. These facts not only determine which propositions you have justification to believe, but also serve as premises in arguments from which these propositions can be justifiably inferred. Hence, your justification-making evidence gives you the foundational premises from which all of justification-showing evidence can be derived. [14]

The same distinction between two concepts of evidence can be applied to other conceptions of evidence, including Williamson's (2000: ch. 9) E = K thesis, which identifies your total evidence with your total knowledge:

The E = K Thesis: One's total evidence is simply one's total knowledge. (2000: 9)

As Williamson notes, this statement of the E = K thesis is ambiguous, since the word 'knowledge' can refer to the factive mental state of knowing that p or to its propositional content that p. Is your evidence identical with the facts you know or with your knowledge of those facts? For example, when you know that p, is your evidence the fact that p or the fact that you know that p? On one reading, your evidence is constituted by what you know: that is, the totality of facts that you know. On the other reading, your evidence is constituted by your knowledge of those facts: that is, the totality of facts about which facts you know. These are two distinct claims about the nature of evidence.

These two readings of the E = K thesis correspond to the distinction we've drawn between two conceptions of evidence and its justifying role. To see the ambiguity, consider the following simple argument for the E = K thesis:

(1) "What justifies belief is evidence."
(2) "Knowledge, and only knowledge, justifies belief." Therefore,
(3) "Knowledge, and only knowledge, constitutes evidence." (2000: 185)

---

[14] Accessibilism is not committed to classical foundationalism: although it is natural to combine these two views, I won't argue for classical foundationalism in this book.

As before, there are two readings of this argument. One reading says that your evidence is what plays the *justification-showing* role: namely, the facts that you know. The other reading says that your evidence is what plays the *justification-making* role: namely, the facts about which facts you know.

Williamson intends the first reading, rather than the second. He says that your evidence is identical with the propositional content of your knowledge, rather than the factive mental state of knowing that propositional content. On this view, the fact that p is included in your evidence if and only if you know that p. This means that he is operating with the justification-showing conception of evidence, rather than the justification-making conception. When you know that p, the fact that p doesn't ensure that you have justification to believe that p. Rather, you have justification to believe that p only because you know that p. Williamson argues that you're rationally permitted to use the proposition that p as a premise in reasoning if and only if you know that p. In the *justification-showing* sense, your evidence is constituted by the facts you know, since these are the facts that you're rationally permitted to use as premises in reasoning. In the *justification-making* sense, in contrast, your evidence is constituted by the facts about which facts you know, since these are the facts that make it the case that you have justification to believe some propositions, rather than others.

Given plausible assumptions, the phenomenal conception of evidence is inconsistent with Williamson's E = K thesis. According to the phenomenal conception of evidence, all phenomenal duplicates have the same evidence. According to the E = K thesis, in contrast, not all phenomenal duplicates have the same evidence, since phenomenal duplicates can differ in what they know. Hence, the phenomenal conception of evidence is incompatible with the E = K thesis. Notice that this argument goes through on both justification-making and justification-showing conceptions of evidence.

Why accept the phenomenal conception of evidence, rather than the E = K thesis? My main argument in this chapter is that the phenomenal conception of evidence explains the intuitive datum that phenomenal duplicates have justification to believe the same propositions, since they have exactly the same evidence. In contrast, the E = K thesis implies that phenomenal duplicates can differ in their evidence when they differ in what they know. This has the counterintuitive consequence that subjects in the bad case don't have the same degree of justification for their beliefs as their phenomenal duplicates in the good case. As we saw in section 3.4, Williamson defends this claim by invoking a distinction between justifications and excuses, but I argued that this defensive strategy fails. Hence, there are compelling intuitive reasons for adopting the phenomenal conception of evidence, rather than the E = K thesis.

In chapter 7, I'll give a further argument for the phenomenal conception of evidence. In brief, the argument is that all evidence is luminous, but only phenomenally individuated facts are luminous, so all evidence is exhausted by phenomenally individuated facts. Williamson's response is to deny that all evidence is luminous; in fact, he denies that anything at all is luminous. His anti-luminosity argument is designed to undercut this argument for the phenomenal conception of evidence by showing that nothing can satisfy the demanding standards of luminosity. I'll reply to this argument in chapter 9.

My aim in this section is not to argue for the phenomenal conception of evidence, but to defend it against Williamson's (2000: 103) arguments for the E = K thesis. After all, the arguments for the phenomenal conception of evidence need to be weighed against the arguments for incompatible alternatives. Here is Williamson's argument in outline:

(1) Only known facts are evidence.
(2) All known facts are evidence.
(3) Therefore, all and only known facts are evidence.

The premises of the argument are contentious, but as Williamson notes, "its aim is simply to divide the contentiousness of the conclusion into manageable portions" (2000: 194). As I'll explain, however, the apparent plausibility of this argument depends on conflating two concepts of evidence. Each premise is plausibly true, given minor revisions, but on different interpretations of the concept of evidence. There is no univocal concept of evidence on which both premises are true.

Let's begin with the justification-making conception of evidence. Your evidence in this sense consists of contingent facts that make it the case that you have justification to believe some propositions, rather than others. Only facts can play this justification-making role. This is because only facts can make it the case that other facts obtain. After all, explanatory contexts are factive in the sense that 'p because q' implies both 'p' and 'q'.

Williamson makes the further claim that only *known* facts are evidence. I reject this claim because facts about your experience can give you justification to believe their contents whether or not you know that they obtain. These facts about your experience are included in your evidence because they play a justification-making role. What enables these facts to play this justification-making role is their phenomenal character, rather than your higher-order knowledge about their phenomenal character (see section 3.2).

Williamson also argues that your evidence must be believed, and hence grasped, in order to play an epistemic role in reasoning. He writes:

One can use an hypothesis to explain why A only if one grasps the proposition that A. Thus only propositions which one grasps can function as evidence in one's inferences to the best explanation. By this standard, only propositions which one grasps count as part of one's evidence. (2000: 195)

I reject this argument for two reasons. First, it overintellectualizes the role of evidence in reasoning. Unreflective creatures, including some human infants and nonhuman animals, can acquire knowledge on the basis of evidence provided by their perceptual experience without having the conceptual abilities required to grasp propositions about their own experience. Second, evidence is defined in terms of its epistemic role as a source of propositional justification, rather than doxastic justification. You can have evidence that gives you propositional justification to form beliefs even if you cannot form doxastically justified beliefs on the basis of your evidence. Your evidence is not constrained in this way by the limits of your doxastic capacities.

I therefore reject Williamson's argument for the E = K thesis as stated. However, this objection leaves a modified version of his argument untouched. The modified version replaces the knowledge constraint on evidence with a knowability constraint:

(1) Only knowable facts are evidence.
(2) All knowable facts are evidence. Therefore,
(3) All and only knowable facts are evidence.

The conclusion of this argument is a weak version of the E = K thesis, according to which your evidence is what you're in a *position* to know, rather than what you *know*. This weak version of the E = K thesis imposes no requirement that your evidence must be believed or even grasped. Even so, it allows that phenomenal duplicates can differ in their evidence, since what you're in a position to know fails to supervene on the phenomenally individuated facts about your current mental states. Hence, even the weak version of the E = K thesis is incompatible with the phenomenal conception of evidence. Nevertheless, the argument for the weak version is not sound: each premise is true on some interpretation of 'evidence', but there is no interpretation on which both premises are true.

On the justification-making conception of evidence, premise (1) is true, but premise (2) is false. On my view, only introspectively luminous facts about my phenomenally individuated mental states are included in my evidence. So I agree that only knowable facts are included in my evidence, but I disagree that all knowable facts are included in my evidence, since not all knowable facts are introspectively luminous. As I've mentioned, Williamson argues that nothing is luminous, but I'll revisit these arguments in chapter 11. My goal here is to reply to his other arguments that the phenomenal conception imposes implausible restrictions on evidence.

One such objection is that we don't usually talk as if evidence is restricted to luminous facts about phenomenally individuated mental states. Thus, Williamson writes:

> If one's evidence were restricted to the contents of one's own mind, it could not play the role that it actually does in science. The evidence for the proposition that the sun is larger than the earth is not just my present experiences or degrees of belief. . . . It is more plausible that the evidence for a scientific theory is the sort of thing which is made public in scientific journals. (2000: 193)

His point is that when scientists argue for the conclusion that the sun is larger than the earth, they don't argue from premises about their own experiences and beliefs. Instead, they argue from facts that are common knowledge in the scientific community. While this observation seems correct, it concerns the justification-showing conception of evidence, which is most pertinent in dialectical contexts in which we're trying to show that our beliefs are justified by arguing for them. However, luminosity is a constraint on the justification-making conception of evidence, which is more germane in theoretical contexts in which we're explaining how epistemic facts are grounded in nonepistemic facts. Hence, Williamson's objection fails to engage its intended target.

Williamson also gives a positive argument that all known, or knowable, facts are evidence. The argument is that if you know that p, or you're in a position to know that p, then it is rationally permissible for you to use the proposition that p as a premise in reasoning. If we define your evidence as what it's rationally permissible for you to use as a premise in reasoning, then it follows that everything you know is included in your evidence. As Williamson writes, "If, when assessing an hypothesis, one knows something e which bears on its truth, should not e be part of one's evidence?" (2000: 203–204).

Again, this argument concerns the justification-showing conception of evidence, rather than the justification-making conception. In the justification-showing sense, premise (2) is true: everything you're in a position to know is included in your evidence, since you're rationally permitted to use anything you're in a position to know as a premise in reasoning. In this sense, however, premise (1) is false: if you have justification to believe a proposition, then you're rationally permitted to use it as a premise in reasoning, even if you're not in a position to know that it's true. In particular, you're rationally permitted to reason from any false premise that you have justification to believe. False propositions can play the justification-showing role of evidence, since they stand in logical and probabilistic relations to other propositions, and thereby serve the evidential functions of confirming, entailing, and ruling out hypotheses.

Peter Unger (1975: ch. 5) gives a semantic argument that you cannot believe or act for the reason that *p* unless it is a fact that *p*. Since evidence is a kind of epistemic reason for belief, it follows that all evidence must be true. Unger notes that sentences like the following sound odd: "Fred's reason for running was that the store was going to close in a few minutes, but in fact it *wasn't* going to close." Moreover, Unger says that such sentences sound odd because they are false. You cannot act for the reason that *p* when it is false that *p*.

Juan Comesaña and Matthew McGrath (2014: 71–76) agree that these sentences sound odd, but they replace Unger's semantic explanation with a pragmatic explanation. Their central claim is that when we say that someone's reason is that *p*, we thereby presuppose that *p* without implying that *p*. They motivate this claim in two ways. First, they note that the presupposition lapses in certain contexts. For instance, in a context in which it's common knowledge that Sally didn't get another offer, but merely thought she did, we can say, "Her reason for turning down the job was that she had another offer." Second, in a context where this is not common knowledge, one can explicitly cancel the presupposition by saying, "Sally's reason for turning down the job was that was that she had another offer; and that made perfect sense; however, her source was lying—she never had the other offer."

One final objection is that the phenomenal conception of evidence threatens to collapse into skepticism. Consider the following skeptical argument:

(1) You have the same evidence as your phenomenal duplicate in the bad case.
(2) If you have the same evidence as your phenomenal duplicate in the bad case, then you know exactly the same facts as your phenomenal duplicate in the bad case.
(3) Your phenomenal duplicate in the bad case doesn't know that he or she has hands.
(4) Therefore, you don't know you have hands.

Williamson blocks this skeptical argument by rejecting premise (1). Given the E = K thesis, you don't have the same evidence as your phenomenal duplicate in the bad case, since you know more facts than your phenomenal duplicate. On my version of phenomenal conception of evidence, in contrast, premise (1) is true. After all, your evidence is restricted to the phenomenally individuated facts about your mental states that you're always in a position to know whether you're in the good case or the bad case. Thus, Williamson writes, "If we presume to know too much about our evidence, we find ourselves knowing too little about the external world" (2000: 15).

In response, however, a better way to block the skeptical argument is to accept premise (1) and reject premise (2) instead. On the phenomenal conception of evidence, you can know more than your phenomenal duplicate even if you have exactly the same evidence. Your evidence is consistent with the hypothesis that you're in the bad case, but the evidential probability that you're in the good case is much higher than the evidential probability that you're in the bad case. Even Williamson (2000: 198) accepts this point. But if your evidence makes it much more probable that you're in the good case than the bad case, then it's not clear why it cannot justify believing that you're in the good case. Moreover, as long as you're in the good case, it is not clear why your evidence cannot serve as a basis for knowledge.[15]

In summary, the argument for the weak version of the E = K thesis depends on an equivocation between two concepts of evidence. In the justification-making sense, premise (1) is true, but premise (2) is false: all evidence is knowable, but not all knowable facts are evidence. In the justification-making sense, premise (2) is true, but premise (1) is false: all knowable facts are evidence, but not all evidence is knowable. There is no consistent interpretation of the argument on which both premises are true.

6.5. The Explanatory Challenge

This chapter argues for *phenomenal mentalism*, the thesis that epistemic justification is determined solely by the phenomenally individuated facts about your current mental states. Phenomenal mentalism can also be combined with *evidentialism*, the thesis that epistemic justification is determined solely by your evidence. This yields the *phenomenal conception of evidence*, which says that your evidence is exhausted by the phenomenally individuated facts about your current mental states.

Phenomenal mentalism is supported by an "argument from below", which appeals to intuitions about cases. Not only does it avoid the intuitive counterexamples to reliabilism, such the new evil demon problem and the problems of clairvoyance and super-blindsight, but it also explains why our intuitive judgments about these examples are correct. This provides strong

---

[15] See Vogel (1990), Pryor (2000), and Wright (2004) for responses to skepticism that are compatible with the phenomenal conception of evidence. Williamson (2011) argues that you have justification to believe that *p* only if the evidential probability that *p* is 1. As Clarke (2013) and Greco (2015) argue, however, the proposition that I have hands may have evidential probability 1 relative to a context in which we ignore possibilities that are too improbable or too outlandish to be worth taking seriously.

intuitive support for phenomenal mentalism. Strictly speaking, however, phenomenal mentalism explains what our counterparts in these scenarios have justification to believe only in combination with plausible background assumptions about what we ourselves have justification to believe: for example, we have justification to form beliefs on the basis of perceptual experience but not on the basis of unconscious perceptual information. Can we provide any further explanation of these background assumptions?

Phenomenal mentalism implies nothing about which propositions we have epistemic justification to believe on the basis of our phenomenally individuated mental states: it just says that every difference in the former is grounded in some difference in the latter. As such, it is compatible with many different views about the nature of epistemic justification, including skepticism. In order to explain which propositions we have epistemic justification to believe, we need to combine the phenomenal conception of evidence with an account of the nature of the evidential support relation, which tells us which propositions are made probable by which phenomenally individuated mental states.

In the first part of this book, I argued for a number of specific principles about the epistemic role of phenomenal consciousness in perception, cognition, and introspection, including the following:

The Content Principle: Necessarily, if you have an experience that represents that p with presentational force, then you thereby have immediate, defeasible justification to believe that p.

Doxastic Conservatism: Necessarily, if you believe that p, then you thereby have immediate, defeasible justification to believe that p.

The Simple Theory of Introspection: Necessarily, if you have an experience e, then you thereby have immediate, indefeasible justification to believe that you have e.

The Extended Version of the Simple Theory: Necessarily, if you believe that p, then you thereby have immediate, indefeasible justification to believe that you believe that p.

These epistemic principles are consistent with phenomenal mentalism, since they only make reference to phenomenally individuated facts about our current experiences and beliefs. At the same time, phenomenal mentalism is not strong enough to explain these epistemic principles without further supplementation. To explain them, we need to combine the phenomenal conception of evidence with more specific claims about the nature of the evidential support relation, such as the following claims about evidential probability:

Necessarily, the fact that it perceptually seems to you that p in the absence of defeaters makes it evidentially probable that p.

Necessarily, the fact that you believe that p in the absence of defeaters makes it evidentially probable that p.

Necessarily, the fact that it perceptually seems to you that p makes it evidentially certain that it perceptually seems to you that p.

Necessarily, the fact that you believe that p makes it evidentially certain that you believe that p.

We can take the intuitive considerations in the first part of this book to support not only the phenomenal conception of evidence, but also these more specific claims about the nature of the evidential support relation.

One of the main goals of the rest of the book is to argue for a further thesis about the nature of the evidential support relation, which can be stated as follows:

> *Accessibilism*: Necessarily, if it is evidentially probable that p to degree n, then it is evidentially certain that it is evidentially probable that p to degree n.

This thesis is not built into the general framework of evidentialism or the phenomenal conception of evidence. It is a further claim about the nature of the evidential support relation that needs independent motivation. In the second part of this book, I'll argue for accessibilism and defend it against objections. Moreover, I'll argue that explaining accessibilism requires commitment to phenomenal mentalism. This means that we can use accessibilism as a premise in an "argument from above" for phenomenal mentalism. If phenomenal mentalism explains accessibilism, and accessibilism is motivated on independent grounds, then phenomenal mentalism is supported by inference to the best explanation.

Why supplement the argument from below with this argument from above? If we could just stop here, that would make for a much shorter book. In my view, however, this would not be a satisfactory stopping point because our intuitions about cases need to be explained, unified, and motivated by appealing to more general theoretical principles concerning the structure of epistemic justification. Let me briefly explain why we need to provide further explanation, unification, and motivation for phenomenal mentalism.

First, there is an *explanatory challenge*. Phenomenal mentalism says that only phenomenally individuated facts about your mental states can make a justificatory difference. But why are these the only facts that can make a justificatory difference? Intuitive judgments about cases might make it plausible that phenomenal mentalism is true, but they don't give us much reflective under-standing of why it is true. To answer this explanatory challenge, we need an argument for phenomenal mentalism that proceeds from general theoretical principles about epistemic justification that can be motivated on independent grounds.

Second, there is a *unification challenge*. Again, phenomenal mentalism says that only phenomenally individuated mental states can make a justificatory dif-ference. But this is a disjunctive answer to the scope question: after all, your mental states can be phenomenally individuated either by their phenomenal character or by their phenomenal dispositions. What do these different kinds of phenomenally individuated mental states have in common that explains why they are both apt to make a justificational difference? We need a theoretical ar-gument for phenomenal mentalism in order to explain what these phenome-nally individuated mental states have in common.

Third, there is a *motivational challenge*. Why should we accept our intui-tive judgments about cases as a basis for building an epistemological theory? Presumably, our intuitive judgments about cases must have some default status, since it is hard to motivate general epistemic principles without relying on some intuitions about cases. But when our intuitions about cases conflict with epistemic principles that are supported by other cases, then their default status can be overridden. A similar point applies when our intuitions are not incon-sistent with our epistemic principles, but when they nevertheless seem arbitrary and unmotivated by those epistemic principles. Ultimately, then, our intuitions about cases cannot simply be taken for granted, but need to be vindicated in light of more general theoretical considerations.

For all these reasons, we need to supplement the argument from below with the argument from above by combining an appeal to intuitions about cases with an appeal to general epistemic principles. My strategy is to argue that phenom-enal mentalism explains accessibilism, and that accessibilism can be motivated and defended on independent grounds, so phenomenal mentalism is supported by inference to the best explanation. This argument from above provides the resources for answering the explanatory challenge, the unification challenge, and the motivational challenge. This sets the agenda for the second part of this book.

PART II
EPISTEMOLOGY

7

Accessibilism

The debate between internalism and externalism about epistemic justification can be defined in many different ways, but it tends to revolve around the following pair of claims:

Mentalism: Epistemic justification is *determined by the mental* in the sense that, necessarily, every difference in which doxastic attitudes you have epistemic justification to hold at any given time is grounded in some corresponding difference in your mental states at that time.

Accessibilism: Epistemic justification is *luminously accessible* in the sense that, necessarily, you're always in a position to know which doxastic attitudes you have epistemic justification to hold at any given time.

What is the relationship between these two claims? There is no immediate logical entailment in either direction between mentalism and accessibilism. For example, Earl Conee and Richard Feldman (2004: ch. 3) argue for mentalism on broadly intuitive grounds, while disclaiming any commitment to accessibilism.[1] Meanwhile, John Gibbons (2006) argues for a view that he calls "access externalism," which combines a version of accessibilism with the wholesale rejection of mentalism.[2]

Nevertheless, I argue in this chapter that mentalism and accessibilism form a coherent and attractive package. More specifically, I argue for a view that I call "phenomenal accessibilism," which combines accessibilism and phenomenal mentalism within a unified theory of epistemic justification. The main goal of this chapter is to argue that phenomenal mentalism is part of the best explanation of accessibilism. In the remaining chapters of this book, I argue for accessibilism and defend it against objections. If phenomenal mentalism is the best explanation of accessibilism, and accessibilism is motivated on

---

[1] Other proponents of nonfactive mentalism who reject accessibilism include Pollock and Cruz (1999), Wedgwood (2002), McCain (2014), and Schoenfield (2015a).

[2] Although Gibbons denies that justification is luminous, he accepts a top-down version of the JJ thesis, which says that if you have justification to believe you have justification to believe that *p*, then you have justification to believe that *p*. Others who combine accessibilism with the rejection of nonfactive mentalism include McDowell (2011), Pritchard (2012), Greco (2014b), and Das and Salow (2018).

independent grounds, then phenomenal mentalism is supported by inference to the best explanation.

The two parts of this book therefore converge on phenomenal mentalism from opposite directions. The first part gives an "argument from below" that proceeds from judgment about particular cases, while the second part gives an "argument from above" that proceeds from general epistemic principles. These arguments are mutually reinforcing, since the judgments about cases provide intuitive support for the general epistemic principles, while the general epistemic principles provide theoretical support for the judgments about cases. The result is an epistemological theory in stable reflective equilibrium.

Here is the plan for this chapter. I begin by defining accessibilism (section 7.1) before arguing that phenomenal mentalism is needed to explain accessibilism (section 7.2). Next, I use accessibilism to defend my intuitions about the cases that motivate phenomenal mentalism—namely, the problems of clairvoyance and super-blindsight (section 7.3) and the new evil demon problem (section 7.4). Finally, I conclude by explaining how accessibilism answers the explanatory challenge for phenomenal mentalism (section 7.5).

7.1. What Is Accessibilism?

What is accessibilism? To a first approximation, accessibilism is the thesis that we always have some privileged kind of epistemic access to the facts about epistemic justification that hold at any given time. This initial statement of accessibilism is vague enough to encompass a wide range of divergent views. To make the thesis more precise, we need to answer the following pair of questions:

Question 1: What are the facts about epistemic justification to which we have privileged epistemic access?

Question 2: What is the nature of our privileged epistemic access to these facts about epistemic justification?

Depending on how we answer these two questions, we end up with very different versions of accessibilism.[3]

On question 1: Any plausible version of accessibilism should be restricted to facts about epistemic justification in the propositional sense, rather than the

---

[3] Accessibilism has a distinguished history, but few contemporary proponents. Descartes is the original standard-bearer, but more recent proponents include Ginet (1975), BonJour (1985), and Chisholm (1989).

doxastic sense. In an evidentialist framework, a belief is propositionally justified whenever your evidence supports its content, whereas a belief is doxastically justified only when it is properly based on evidence that supports its content. The problem is that you don't always have privileged epistemic access to whether your beliefs are properly based on your evidence. Consider Jonathan Schaffer's debasing demon, which "throws her victims into the belief state on an improper basis, while leaving them with the impression *as if* they had proceeded properly" (2010: 231). When you're in this kind of skeptical scenario, you're deceived about whether your beliefs are doxastically justified.

On question 2: We can begin by defining accessibilism as the thesis that the facts about epistemic justification in the propositional sense are "luminous" in the sense that Timothy Williamson (2000: 95) defines. A condition is *positively* luminous just in case you're always in a position to know that it obtains when it does, whereas a condition is *negatively* luminous just in case you're always in a position to know that it fails to obtain when it does. A condition is *strongly* luminous just in case it is both positively and negatively luminous: in other words, you're always in a position to know whether or not it obtains. I'll define accessibilism as the thesis that the facts about epistemic justification in the propositional sense are strongly luminous: in other words, you're always in a position to know whether or not you have epistemic justification to believe any given proposition at any given time.[4]

What does it take to be in a position to know *p*? It doesn't imply knowing *p*, since you don't always succeed in converting your epistemic position into knowledge. Moreover, it doesn't imply having the capacity to know *p*, since nonideally rational agents are not always capable of converting their epistemic position into knowledge. You might have evidence that puts you in a position to know that *p* without having the capacity to know that *p* on the basis of your evidence. To a first approximation, you're in a position to know *p* just when you have evidence that serves as a potential basis for knowing *p* in your current circumstances. Roughly speaking, you would know *p* if you (or some idealized counterpart) were to believe *p* in a way that is properly based on your evidence. This conditional analysis is only a first approximation, since it is vulnerable to counterexamples in "finkish" cases when your evidence changes in the process of forming the belief in question. Even so, it's a good heuristic in nonfinkish cases. A more fundamental account is that you're in a position to know that *p* when you satisfy all the purely epistemic conditions for knowledge, whether or not you're capable of satisfying all the doxastic conditions for knowledge (see section 11.1).

---

[4] Williamson (2000: ch. 4) argues that nothing is luminous, but I will reply in section 11.3.

In summary, accessibilism is the thesis that facts about epistemic justification in the propositional sense are strongly luminous in the sense that you're always in a position to know whether or not they obtain. In other words, these facts are both positively and negatively luminous:

Positive Luminosity: Necessarily, if you have epistemic justification to hold some doxastic attitude D toward the proposition p, then you're in a position to know that you have epistemic justification to hold D toward p.

Negative Luminosity: Necessarily, if you lack epistemic justification to hold some doxastic attitude D toward the proposition that p, then you're in a position to know that you lack epistemic justification to hold D toward p.

Some epistemologists accept positive luminosity, while rejecting negative luminosity. For example, Duncan Pritchard (2012) proposes a version of *epistemological disjunctivism*, which says that you have justification to form perceptual beliefs about the external world in the "good case" of veridical perception, but not in the "bad case" of perceptual illusion or hallucination. On this view, you're in a position to know that you have justification to form perceptual beliefs when you're in the good case, but you're not in a position to know that you lack justification to form perceptual beliefs when you're in the bad case. In other words, justification is positively luminous in the good case, although it is not negatively luminous in the bad case.

Given plausible background assumptions, however, positive luminosity entails negative luminosity. In particular, the entailment holds given the assumption that the following epistemic principles are a priori truths:

Uniqueness: Necessarily, there is exactly one doxastic attitude that you have justification to hold toward any given proposition at any given time.

Closure: Necessarily, if you're in a position to know that p, and you're in a position to know that p implies q, then you're in a position to know that q.

Suppose you lack justification to hold some doxastic attitude D. Given uniqueness, it follows that you have justification to hold some distinct doxastic attitude D*. Given positive luminosity, it follows that you're in a position to know that you have justification to hold D*. Given that uniqueness can be known a priori, it follows by closure that you're in a position to know that you lack justification to hold D. Hence, positive luminosity implies negative luminosity given uniqueness and closure.

Uniqueness principles have recently generated some debate.[5] However, the debate is largely concerned with an evidentialist version of uniqueness, which says that a person's *evidence* at any given time is sufficient to determine some unique doxastic attitude that the person has epistemic justification to hold that at that time. For current purposes, however, we don't need to assume evidentialism. Thomas Kelly (2013) rejects an "interpersonal" version of uniqueness that is restricted to a person's evidence in favor of an "intrapersonal" version that also makes reference to a person's epistemic standards, goals, or reasoning dispositions. To argue from positive luminosity to negative luminosity, the intrapersonal version of uniqueness will serve just as well as the interpersonal version.

Uniqueness is also perfectly compatible with Gilbert Harman's (1986: 12) observations about clutter avoidance. Epistemic rationality doesn't require you to clutter up your mind by believing everything that you have epistemic justification to believe. It requires only that if you have justification to believe a proposition, and you adopt some doxastic attitude toward that proposition, then you should believe it, rather than disbelieving it, or withholding belief altogether. Epistemic rationality doesn't require being fully opinionated in the sense that you adopt some doxastic attitude toward every proposition.

A slightly weaker version of accessibilism says that the justification facts are *lustrous*, rather than *luminous*. A condition is positively lustrous just in case you always have justification to believe that it obtains when it does. A condition is negatively lustrous just in case you always have justification to believe that it doesn't obtain when it doesn't obtain. A condition is strongly lustrous just in case it is both positively and negatively lustrous. Accessibilism says that the justification facts are strongly lustrous in this sense:

Positive Lustrousness: Necessarily, if you have epistemic justification to hold some doxastic attitude D toward the proposition p, then you have epistemic justification to believe that you have epistemic justification to hold D toward p.

Negative Lustrousness: Necessarily, if you lack epistemic justification to hold some doxastic attitude D toward the proposition p, then you have epistemic justification to believe that you lack epistemic justification to hold D toward p.

---

[5] See Kopec and Titelbaum (2016) for an overview of the literature.

As before, positive lustrousness entails negative lustrousness given uniqueness and closure, although in this case we need to formulate the closure principle in terms of epistemic justification, rather than knowledge.

What is the relationship between luminosity and lustrousness? Lustrousness was originally proposed by Selim Berker (2008) as a fallback position in response to Timothy Williamson's (2000) anti-luminosity argument. Williamson argues that nothing is luminous because you're not in a position to know that p when you're close to the margin for error. Suppose that p is true, although there's a close case in which p is false. Williamson argues that you're not in a position to know that p because you're not safe from error: there is a relevantly close case in which you believe falsely that p. Berker replies that you might have justification to believe that p when you're close to the margin for error, since justification doesn't require safety from error. Justification, unlike knowledge, is *nonfactive*: you can have justification to believe that p even if it's false that p. If so, then justification doesn't require safety from error, since the actual case is one of the closest possible cases.

One problem with this fallback response is that justification is *factive* in the special case of strongly lustrous conditions. If C is a strongly lustrous condition, then you have justification to believe that C obtains if and only if C obtains. The right-to-left direction follows from the definition of lustrousness, whereas the left-to-right direction can be shown by the following simple proof: (i) if C doesn't obtain, then you have justification to believe that C doesn't obtain, since C is negatively lustrous; but (ii) you cannot have justification to believe both that C obtains and that C doesn't obtain, since these are contradictory propositions; so (iii) you have justification to believe that C obtains only if C obtains.

With this point in hand, we can argue that all strongly lustrous conditions are strongly luminous conditions (and vice versa). If p is strongly lustrous, then there cannot be a Gettier-style case in which you have justification to believe that p, although you're not in a position to know that p. In a classic Gettier-style case, you're not in a position to know that p because there is a close case in which you have justification to believe falsely that p. Consider Goldman's (1976) fake barn case, in which you see a real barn, but you're surrounded by fake barns that look exactly the same. In that case, you're not in a position to know that there's a real barn ahead, since there is a close case in which the same evidence justifies believing falsely that there's a barn ahead. If p is strongly lustrous, however, then you have justification to believe that p is false in any close case in which p is false. Hence, Gettier-style cases of this kind cannot arise for strongly luminous conditions.

If we define accessibilism as the thesis that justification is strongly lustrous, and we apply this to the special case of belief, then we arrive at the following JJ principle:

The JJ Principle: Necessarily, you have justification to believe that p if and only if you have justification to believe that you have justification to believe that p.

The JJ principle is a biconditional, which comprises a self-intimation thesis and an infallibility thesis. The left-to-right direction says that justification is *self-intimating* in the sense that if you have justification to believe that p, then you have higher-order justification to believe that you have justification to believe that p. Meanwhile, the right-to-left direction says that higher-order justification is *infallible* in the sense that if you have higher-order justification to believe that you have justification to believe that p, then you have justification to believe that p. The self-intimation thesis rules out the possibility of justified agnosticism, while the infallibility thesis rules out the possibility of justified error, about which propositions you have justification to believe. In a slogan, the JJ principle says you can never have justification for agnosticism and error about the justification facts themselves.

Accessibilism can be extended from belief to other doxastic attitudes. The extension from belief to disbelief is quite straightforward, since disbelieving a proposition is just a matter of believing its negation. Meanwhile, the extension from belief and disbelief to withholding follows from the combination of uniqueness and closure. Suppose you have justification to withhold belief that p. Given uniqueness, it follows that you don't have justification to believe or to disbelieve that p. Given negative lustrousness, it follows that you have higher-order justification to believe that you don't have justification to believe or to disbelieve that p. So, given uniqueness and closure, it follows that you have higher-order justification to believe that you have justification to withhold belief that p.

Accessibilism can also be extended from coarse-grained doxastic attitudes of belief, disbelief, and withholding to more fine-grained degrees of confidence. In fact, the extension is hard to resist. Whether you have justification to believe a proposition depends on whether you have justification to be sufficiently confident that it is true. If you can have justification for agnosticism and error about the latter question, then this can sometimes result in justification for agnosticism and error about the former question. Accessibilism should therefore be extended from coarse-grained belief to fine-grained degrees of confidence.

Once we make the extension to degrees of confidence, it is natural to define accessibilism within a probabilistic framework. Probabilistic accessibilism is the thesis that a person's evidential probabilities are "probabilistically luminous" in the following sense:

> Probabilistic Accessibilism: Necessarily, if the evidential probability that p is n, then it's evidentially certain that the evidential probability that p is n.

It is hard to sustain the claim that epistemic justification is luminous within a probabilistic framework unless the evidential probabilities themselves are luminous. I'm not assuming the general thesis that you have justification to believe that p only if it's evidentially certain that p. Suppose instead that you have justification to believe that p so long as the evidential probability that p is high enough to meet some threshold between 0.5 and 1. The problem is that your higher-order evidential probabilities are not always guaranteed to meet this threshold unless they are probabilistically luminous in the sense just defined.

In this section, I've stated various different versions of accessibilism. I've also given some reasons to suppose that these different versions of accessibilism stand or fall together. Even so, much of my discussion of accessibilism in this book will focus on the JJ principle. In this chapter, I use the JJ principle as a premise in defending the intuitions about cases that support phenomenal mentalism. In chapters 8 and 9, I argue for the JJ principle on more general theoretical grounds. In chapters 10 and 11, I'll defend the JJ principle, and other probabilistic versions of accessibilism, against objections. Finally, in chapter 12, I'll conclude by contrasting phenomenal accessibilism with phenomenal conservatism.

7.2. Explaining Accessibilism

If accessibilism is true, then this is a fact that needs explanation. The puzzle is to explain how we're always in a position to know which propositions we have justification to believe. After all, we're *sometimes* in a position to know facts about the external world through perception, memory, or testimony, but we're not *always* in a position to acquire knowledge in these ways. Sometimes our evidence is misleading and sometimes it's inconclusive. But then how can it be that we're always in a position to know which propositions we have justification to believe? This is the puzzle we need to solve.

We can't solve this puzzle by fiat. It's not just a brute fact that we're always in a position to know the justification facts. There must be some explanation of how we're always in a position to know them. Similarly, the justification facts themselves are not brute facts. According to evidentialism, they are grounded in contingent facts about our evidence together with necessary facts about evidential support. This suggests that we need to explain the luminosity of justification facts by appealing to the luminosity of the facts in which they are grounded. In other words, the justification facts are luminous because they are grounded in luminous facts about our evidence together with luminous facts about evidential support.

Given the background framework of evidentialism, the solution to our puzzle must take the following form. The luminosity of epistemic justification is explained by the luminosity of evidence together with the luminosity of evidential support. Necessarily, if my total evidence e justifies believing that p, then I'm thereby in a position to know the following with certainty:

(1) I have evidence e.
(2) If I have evidence e, then I have justification to believe that p. Therefore,
(3) I have justification to believe that p.

This is just to state the form of the solution without stating its content. We still need to explain how facts about my evidence, and facts about the evidential support relation, can be luminous in the sense that I'm always in a position to know with certainty whether or not they obtain. If we can discharge this burden, however, then we'll have thereby explained how justification can be luminous within an evidentialist framework.

We're not begging any important questions by assuming evidentialism, since it has no built-in commitment to either accessibilism or a phenomenal mentalism. On the contrary, evidentialism is compatible with various rival conceptions of the nature of evidence and the evidential support relation. My main goal in this section is to argue that explaining accessibilism within an evidentialist framework requires endorsing a phenomenal conception of evidence. But I'll end this section by showing how evidentialism is an optional component in this explanation. We can explain accessibilism by appealing to phenomenal mentalism without making any commitment to evidentialism.

7.2.1. Evidential Support

According to evidentialism, epistemic justification is grounded in contingent facts about your evidence together with necessary facts about the evidential support relation. When you have epistemic justification to believe a proposition, this is because your evidence supports that proposition to a sufficiently high degree. Whether this condition is satisfied depends not just on facts about what your evidence is, but also on facts about what your evidence supports.

Hence, epistemic justification is not grounded wholly in your evidence, since it is grounded partly in the nature of the evidential support relation. Evidential support facts cannot make a justificational difference, however, because they hold necessarily: if some total body of evidence *e* supports the proposition that *p*, then it is necessary that *e* supports *p*. Hence, while epistemic justification is not *grounded* solely in your evidence, it is *determined* solely by your evidence in the sense that only differences in evidence can make a difference in epistemic justification (see section 6.2).

Evidentialism provides a useful framework for explaining the distinction between a priori and a posteriori justification. On this account, a priori justification is grounded wholly in necessary facts about the evidential support relation, whereas a posteriori justification is grounded partially in contingent facts about your evidence. Any difference in your evidence grounds some corresponding difference in which propositions you have a posteriori justification to believe. In contrast, no such difference in your evidence grounds any corresponding difference in which propositions you have a priori justification to believe, since everyone has a priori justification to believe the same propositions no matter what evidence they have. If we combine this with a phenomenal conception of evidence, which says that your evidence is exhausted by facts about your experience, then we end up with a Kantian conception of the distinction between a priori and a posteriori justification. On this view, a posteriori justification is grounded partially in experience, whereas a priori justification is grounded in a way that is wholly independent of experience.[6]

The key point for current purposes is that there are some propositions that everyone has a priori justification to believe no matter what experiences and beliefs they have. These propositions are supported by your evidence no matter what evidence you happen to have. The nature of the evidential support relation guarantees that these propositions are supported by any possible body of evidence. On a probabilistic conception of evidential support, for example, there are necessary truths that hold at every point in the probability space. On the standard way of interpreting the axioms of the probability calculus, these necessary truths always have probability 1. They are evidentially certain because they are supported by any possible body of evidence to the highest possible degree.

Logical truths are one example. On a standard conception of evidential support, all logical truths are supported by your evidence, no matter what evidence you have, just in virtue of the nature of evidential support. This is because all

---

[6] In chapter 12, I argue against the phenomenal conservatism of Huemer (2001), Chudnoff (2013), and Bengson (2015), according to which a priori justification is grounded in cognitive experiences of intuition. In Smithies (2015a), I argue that experience plays an enabling and disabling role, rather than a justifying role, in the a priori domain.

logical truths are logically entailed by any possible body of evidence. On a probabilistic conception of evidential support, all logical truths have evidential probability 1. Hence, all logical truths are evidentially certain in the sense that they are supported by your evidence to the maximal degree. On this view, ideal rationality requires logical omniscience: it requires that you are certain of all logical truths.

Truths about the evidential support relation are another example. On the version of evidentialism that I've presented, facts about your evidence are contingent, whereas facts about the evidential support relation are necessary. These necessary facts about the evidential support relation are entailed by any possible body of evidence. As such, they are supported by your evidence, no matter what evidence you have, just in virtue of the nature of evidential support. On a probabilistic conception of evidential support, they have probability 1. Hence, they are evidentially certain in the sense that they are supported by your evidence to the maximal degree. On this view, ideal rationality requires omniscience about evidential support: it requires that you are certain of all evidential support facts.

Are all necessary truths evidentially certain in the sense that they have evidential probability 1? The connection between probability and necessity is built into the standard interpretation of the probability calculus, according to which the normalization axiom says that the necessary truths—those that hold at every point in the probability space—have probability 1. Since the probability calculus is just a formal system, however, we need an interpretation to yield the space of possibilities over which probabilities are defined. Different interpretations of this possibility space yield correspondingly different conceptions of necessity. Is it a space of logical possibilities, metaphysical possibilities, epistemic possibilities, or what?

David Chalmers (2011a) proposes an *epistemic interpretation* of probability space, according to which epistemic possibilities are maximally specific propositions about the actual world that cannot be ruled out conclusively on a priori grounds. On this interpretation, the truths that hold throughout the probability space are epistemically necessary in the sense that they are conclusively justified on a priori grounds. Epistemic necessity is broader than logical necessity, but it is narrower than metaphysical necessity. It includes not only logical truths, but also a priori truths about evidential support, although it excludes metaphysically necessary truths that are justified on a posteriori grounds, such as the proposition that water is composed of H_2O molecules. This framework doesn't give us a reduction of a priori justification in more basic terms, but it enables us to draw connections between epistemology, modality, and probability in a theoretically attractive way.[7]

---

[7] Not all propositions that we have a priori justification to believe are epistemically necessary. For example, White (2006) and Cohen (2010) argue that we have a priori justification to believe the

To sum up, I'm suggesting that necessary truths about evidential support have the same epistemic status as necessary truths about logic. They are supported by any possible body of evidence just in virtue of the nature of evidential support. In that sense, they are justified a priori. Moreover, in a probabilistic framework, they are epistemically certain in the sense that they have evidential probability 1. If evidence e makes it probable that p to degree n, then it's certain that e makes it probable that p to degree n. On this view, you're always in a position to know the evidential support facts, since they are conclusively justified on a priori grounds. In short, evidential support facts are luminous by a priori reflection.

This is reminiscent of a central plank of Roderick Chisholm's classic articulation of internalism about epistemic justification:

> The internalist assumes that, merely by reflecting upon his own conscious state, he can formulate a set of epistemic principles that will enable him to find out, with respect to any possible belief he has, whether he is justified in having that belief. (1989: 76)

Chisholm claims, in effect, that epistemic principles are luminous in the sense that we're always in a position to know which of them are true on the basis of a priori reflection alone. Alvin Goldman (1999: 287) criticizes this proposal. He notes that even professionally trained epistemologists struggle to articulate correct epistemic principles; moreover, they disagree among themselves about which epistemic principles are true. Given these sobering facts about the profession, isn't it implausible to suppose that the unwashed masses are in any position to know by a priori reflection which epistemic principles are true? I'll make three points in reply to this objection.

First, there is no commitment to the claim that evidential support facts can be codified into general principles. All we need is the claim that there are evidential support facts that obtain in particular cases, whether or not there are general principles that unify these evidential support facts across particular cases. Just as moral particularism denies that there are any general moral principles, so epistemic particularism denies that there are any general epistemic principles. We needn't take any stand in this debate.[8]

Second, even if particularism is false, it is plausible that our knowledge of general epistemic principles depends upon our knowledge of the evidential support relations that obtain in particular cases, rather than vice versa. After

---

epistemically contingent proposition that our perceptual experience is reliable. This proposition is evidentially probable in virtue of epistemically necessary truths about the evidential support relation.

[8] See Dancy (2004) for an influential defense of moral particularism.

all, we acquire knowledge of general epistemic principles by generalizing from the evidential support relations that we know to obtain in particular cases. Therefore, we don't need to have knowledge of general epistemic principles in order to know which evidential support relations obtain in particular cases. We're in a position to know this a priori given sufficient information about the particular case whether it is real or merely imagined.

Third, it may be difficult for us to know which evidential support relations obtain in particular cases even if we're in a position to know this conclusively on a priori grounds. After all, we are not ideally rational agents. As such, we're not always psychologically capable of converting our epistemic position into knowledge. This point holds for truths about logic as well as truths about evidential support. Just because we're always in a position to know the logical facts, it doesn't follow that it's always easy for us to figure out what they are. Similarly, just because we're always in a position to know the evidential support facts, it doesn't follow that it's always easy for us to figure out what they are.

My goal here is not to argue directly for the thesis that we're always in a position to know the evidential support facts on a priori grounds. Rather, my goal is to argue that we need to assume this thesis in order to explain accessibilism. If accessibilism can be motivated on independent grounds, as I will argue in subsequent chapters, then this will provide indirect support for any thesis that is required to explain it. At the same time, we can make this thesis more plausible by showing how it can be subsumed within a more general theory of a priori justification that applies equally to logic. In chapter 10, I'll pursue this analogy further by arguing that the motivations for regarding logical omniscience as an ideal of epistemic rationality can be extended from logic to the evidential support relation. On this view, ideal rationality requires not only omniscience about logic, but also omniscience about the evidential support relation.

7.2.2. Evidence

In order to explain accessibilism within an evidentialist framework, it's not enough to suppose that necessary truths about evidential support are luminous, since we also need the further claim that contingent truths about your evidence are luminous too. In fact, given how we're understanding accessibilism, we need the claim that contingent truths about your evidence are strongly luminous in the following sense:

Positive Luminosity: Necessarily, if p is included in your evidence, then you're in a position to know with certainty that p is included in your evidence.

Negative Luminosity: Necessarily, if *p* is excluded from your evidence, then you're in a position to know with certainty that *p* is excluded from your evidence.

Again, my goal here is not to argue directly for the thesis that your evidence is luminous, but rather to explain how it could possibly be that your evidence is luminous. Notice that we can't simply extend the same account that we gave for evidential support facts, since facts about evidential support are necessary, whereas facts about your evidence are contingent. Contingent facts about your evidence are not justified a priori in a way that depends solely on necessary truths about the nature of the evidential support relation. If they're justified at all, then they're justified a posteriori in a way that depends on the contingent facts about what evidence you actually have. But how can these contingent facts be luminous?

We can articulate the challenge within a probabilistic framework by appealing to the norm of *regularity*, which says that only necessary truths have evidential probability 1 and only necessary falsehoods have evidential probability 0. Regularity entails that all contingent propositions have an evidential probability that is intermediate between 1 and 0. If so, then contingent truths about your evidence are never probabilistically luminous in the sense that they have evidential probability 1. In that case, there is no guarantee that you're always in a position to know contingent truths about your evidence.[9]

One problem with the norm of regularity is that it conflicts with the norm of *conditionalization*, which constrains how your evidential probabilities change when you receive new evidence. Conditionalization says that if you acquire new evidence *e*, then the new unconditional probability that *h* is equal to the old conditional probability that *e* given *h*. Since the old conditional probability that *e* given *e* is 1, it follows that the new unconditional probability that *e* is 1. Hence, the norm of conditionalization seems to conflict with the norm of regularity. This imposes some theoretical pressure to make an exception to the norm of regularity in the special case of contingent truths about your evidence. On this view, contingent truths about your evidence can have evidential probability 1 after all.[10]

---

[9] Proponents of regularity include Lewis (1980a) and Skyrms (1980), while opponents include Hajek (2012) and Easwaran (2014).

[10] Jeffrey (1965) resolves the tension by proposing a generalization of conditionalization that allows for updating probabilities on uncertain evidence. In contrast, Hajek (2003) defends strict conditionalization by explaining how you can lose evidence that previously had probability 1 and conditionalize on new evidence that previously had probability 0. His key move is to abandon the ratio formula for conditional probability by taking the notion of conditional probability as primitive.

How can contingent truths about your evidence have evidential probability 1? Williamson (2000: ch. 9) argues that your evidence includes everything you know. On this view, the evidential probability of a proposition is its probability conditional on what you know. Everything you know has evidential probability 1, since the probability of what you know conditional on what you know is 1. Hence, your evidence has evidential probability 1.[11]

One objection to Williamson's proposal is that knowledge doesn't require certainty: for instance, you can know that p even if it's not rational for you to accept a bet on p at any odds. If the evidential probability that p is 1, then it's rational to be certain that p, and hence to accept a bet on p at any odds. So not everything you know has evidential probability 1. Williamson (2000: 213) responds to this objection by abandoning the connection between certainty and evidential probability 1. He argues that nothing is certain in a sense that makes it rational to accept bets at any odds. Not even logical truths pass this test: for example, it seems irrational to bet your life against a penny on a complex truth of logic. He therefore recommends interpreting evidential probability in terms of knowledge, rather than certainty.

As Daniel Greco (2013) has argued, one serious cost of this proposal is that it severs an important theoretical connection between probability theory and decision theory. According to standard decision theory, it's always rational to act in ways that maximize expected utility; for instance, by accepting bets that are certain to have a positive payoff. Other things being equal, this connection between probability theory and decision theory is worth preserving. But how can we preserve this connection given the plausibility of Williamson's claim that it's never rational to be certain of anything, including logical truths? I'll make two points in response to this claim.

The first point invokes the distinction between *propositional* and *doxastic* senses of rationality. If p is a logical truth, then it's propositionally rational to be certain that p and hence to accept a bet on p at any odds. However, it doesn't follow that if you're certain that p, and hence prepared to accept such bets, then you're thereby doxastically rational. After all, doxastic rationality requires that your doxastic attitudes are properly based on your evidence. It's not enough that there's a match between what your doxastic attitudes are and what it's rational for them to be, since this could be just a matter of luck. What's required for proper basing is that your doxastic attitudes are held in a way that's reliably sensitive to what your evidence supports. In the case of logical truths, that's just a matter of holding doxastic attitudes in a way that's reliably sensitive to the

---

[11] Williamson's claim that your evidence always has evidential probability 1 doesn't commit him to the further claim that your evidence is luminous, since you can know that p without always being in a position to know that p.

logical truths themselves. The problem is that you cannot be rationally certain that p unless you're perfectly reliable about whether p. Otherwise, it's too risky to accept a bet on p at any odds. Since we're less than perfectly reliable about logic, we cannot be rationally certain of any logical truth.

The second point invokes the distinction between *ideal* and *nonideal* senses of rationality. We are required by ideal rationality to be certain of all logical truths. However, we humans cannot conform to these requirements of ideal rationality because our doxastic dispositions are not perfectly sensitive to the logical truths. Ideal rationality is simply beyond our limited human capacities. So, we can ask, what is the most rational response to the evidence that is possible given our limited human capacities? This is a question about rationality in the nonideal sense. It may be nonideally rational for us to be uncertain of logical truths, even if it's ideally rational for us to be certain of logical truths. The difference is that the requirements of nonideal rationality must be humanly achievable, whereas there is no corresponding constraint on the requirements of ideal rationality.

In summary, it's ideally rational for us to be certain of logical truths, but it doesn't follow that we can be rationally certain of them. Our logical reasoning is simply not reliable enough to satisfy the requirements of ideal rationality. In contrast, the requirements of nonideal rationality are constrained by our limited human capacities. It's sometimes nonideally rational to be uncertain of logical truths and hence to reject bets that are certain to have a positive payoff. Whereas ideal rationality depends solely on evidence, nonideal rationality depends also on our limited human capacities for responding reliably to the evidence.

Assuming that some necessary truths pass the betting test, are there any contingent truths that pass the test? One motivation for the norm of regularity is that it's never rational to bet your life against a penny on contingent truths, since there is always some room for rational doubt about contingent truths, and hence the expected utility of accepting the bet can be negative when the costs of losing are too high. On reflection, however, it is far from clear that contingent truths cannot have evidential probability 1 just as necessary truths can. What about Cartesian propositions, such as the following: I exist, I am conscious, I seem to see red, I am thinking that $2 + 2 = 4$, and so on? Arguably, these contingent truths about your experience are just as well suited to pass the betting test as necessary truths about logic.

In chapter 5, I argued for the simple theory of introspection, which says that some contingent facts about your mental states are luminous in the following sense: if you're in the right kind of mental state M, then you're thereby in a position to know with certainty that you're in M. In an evidentialist framework, the fact that you're in M is evidence that you're in M. On this view, your evidence entails that you're in M and thereby supports the proposition that you're in M to the highest possible degree. On a probabilistic conception of evidential support, it's certain that you're in M, since the evidential probability that you're in M is 1.

The contingent facts that we're in a position to know by introspection have a different epistemic status than the contingent facts that we're in a position to know by other means. I know that I have hands, but I'm not *always* in a position to know whether or not I have hands. Consider a skeptical scenario in which it falsely seems to me that I have hands because I'm deceived by a Cartesian evil demon. In that case, I'm not in a position to know that I have hands, since I'm disembodied; and I'm not in a position to know that I don't have hands, since my evidence is misleading. In contrast, I'm always in a position to know whether or not it *seems* to me that I have hands. Even in the skeptical scenario, I'm in a position to know how things seem. I cannot have misleading evidence about how things seem, since my evidence about how things seem is constituted precisely by how things seem. My evidence includes the fact that it seems that I have hands, whereas it excludes the fact that I have hands. Hence, my evidence entails that it seems that I have hands, whereas it merely makes it probable that I have hands: it's certain that it seems that I have hands, but it's no more than highly probable that I have hands.[12]

It is completely implausible that all of our mental states are introspectively luminous in the sense that we're always in a position to know by introspection whether or not we're in them. The simple theory of introspection therefore needs an answer to the scope question: namely, which facts about your mental states are introspectively luminous? The answer I proposed in section 5.4, is that all and only phenomenally individuated facts about your current mental states are introspectively luminous. If we combine this answer to the scope question with the constraint that your evidence must be introspectively luminous, then we can give the following argument for the phenomenal conception of evidence:

(1) Your evidence is exhausted by introspectively luminous facts about your current mental states.

(2) Only phenomenally individuated facts about your current mental states are introspectively luminous.

(3) Therefore, your evidence is exhausted by phenomenally individuated facts about your current mental states.

---

[12] As Clarke (2013) and Greco (2015) argue, the proposition that I have hands may have evidential probability 1 relative to a context in which we ignore possibilities that are too improbable or too outlandish to be worth taking seriously.

Hence, explaining accessibilism within the framework of evidentialism requires endorsing a phenomenal conception of evidence, according to which your evidence is exhausted by phenomenally individuated facts about your current mental states.

Although evidentialism provides a useful framework for our discussion, it is not an essential component in the explanation of accessibilism. We can remove all mention of evidence from the preceding argument and replace it with reference to facts that make a justificational difference. According to the opponents of evidentialism, these might include nonevidential facts about your epistemic standards, goals, practical interests, and so on. When we remove the commitment to evidentialism, what we are left with is an argument for phenomenal mentalism, defined as the thesis that epistemic justification is determined by the phenomenally individuated facts about your current mental states.

According to this explanation of accessibilism, epistemic justification is luminous only because it is determined by introspectively luminous facts about your phenomenally individuated mental states. Whenever I'm in some phenomenally individuated mental state M that gives me justification to believe that p, I'm thereby in a position to know the following with certainty:

(1) I'm in M [by introspection].
(2) If I'm in M, then I have justification to believe that p [by a priori reasoning].
(3) Therefore, I have justification to believe that p [by deduction from (1) and (2)].

In this way, phenomenal mentalism explains how we're always in a position to know which propositions we have justification to believe on the basis of reflection alone. If phenomenal mentalism is false, and not all the determinants of epistemic justification are introspectively luminous facts about your phenomenally individuated mental states, then there will be counterexamples to accessibilism in which you're not in a position to know which propositions you have justification to believe. Hence, phenomenal mentalism is an indispensable component in the explanation of accessibilism.

In this section, I've argued that phenomenal mentalism is needed to explain accessibilism. In the next two sections, I'll build on this argument by showing how a commitment to accessibilism supports phenomenal mentalism. More specifically, I'll do three things. First, I'll argue that accessibilism can be used as a premise in arguing for the intuitions about cases that motivate phenomenal mentalism—namely, clairvoyance and super-blindsight (section 7.3) and the new evil demon problem (section 7.4). Second, I'll draw out some of the implausible consequences of blocking these arguments by rejecting accessibilism. And third, I'll point to some of the difficulties with versions of access externalism that attempt to explain accessibilism in terms of radically externalist theories of epistemic justification, such as reliabilism.[13]

7.3. Clairvoyance and Super-Blindsight

A simple form of reliabilism says that a belief is justified if and only if it is formed on the basis of a reliable process. As we've seen, however, there are intuitive counterexamples to the thesis that reliability is sufficient for justification. In Laurence BonJour's example, Norman believes that the president is in New York City on the basis of a reliable process of clairvoyance. Similarly, in Ned Block's example, the super-blindsighter—let's call her "Susan"—believes that there is an X in her blind field on the basis of a reliable process of unconscious perception. However, neither Norman nor Susan has evidence that justifies believing that they have any such reliable process at their disposal. Intuitively, these beliefs are unjustified, despite the fact that they are formed on the basis of reliable processes.

Some proponents of reliabilism may be inclined to bite the bullet and maintain that these reliably formed beliefs are justified after all.[14] In response, however, I'll argue that this response cannot be reconciled with accessibilism. In effect, the JJ principle provides the resources for arguing that Susan's super-blindsight beliefs, and Norman's clairvoyant beliefs, are unjustified. Here is the argument in outline:

(1) *The JJ Principle*: Necessarily, you have justification to believe that *p* if and only if you have higher-order justification to believe that you have justification to believe that *p*.

(2) Susan lacks higher-order justification to believe that she has justification to believe that there is an X in her blind field, while Norman lacks higher-order justification to believe that he has justification to believe that the president is in New York City.

(3) Therefore, Susan lacks justification to believe that there is an X in her blind field, and Norman lacks justification to believe that the president is in New York City.

---

[13] The next two sections develop and expand on arguments in Smithies (2016b).

[14] See, for example, Lyons's (2009: ch. 5) verdict on his Nyrmoon case, which is a variation on BonJour's Norman case.

Proponents of reliabilism have two options for responding to this argument. They can either reject the JJ principle or they can maintain that Susan and Norman have higher-order justification for their beliefs after all. I'll argue that both options are implausible.

Option 1 is to reject the JJ principle. Those who take this option can say that Susan has first-order justification to believe that there's an X in her blind field, although she lacks higher-order justification to believe that she has first-order justification to believe this. But then we can ask, which doxastic attitude does she have justification to adopt toward the following metajustificatory proposition: 'I have justification to believe that there's an X in my blind field'? Let's provisionally assume the following existence thesis:

> *The Existence Thesis*: Necessarily, there is always some doxastic attitude that you have epistemic justification to hold toward any given proposition.[15]

Given this assumption, there is some doxastic attitude that Susan has justification to hold toward the metajustificatory proposition. If she doesn't have justification to believe it, then she has justification to disbelieve it or to withhold belief instead. As I'll explain, however, this option has some extremely implausible consequences.

The first implausible consequence is that we can have justification to believe "abominable conjunctions" that are reminiscent of Moore's paradox. Let's assume for the sake of argument that Susan has justification to believe that there is an X in her blind field. And let's assume that she has justification to disbelieve the metajustificatory proposition. In that case, she has justification to believe the following Moorean conjunction:

> There is an X in my blind field, but I don't have justification to believe there is an X in my blind field.

Suppose instead that Susan has justification to *withhold belief* in the metajustificatory proposition: that is, to regard it as an open question whether or not it's true. In that case, she has justification to believe the following Moorean conjunction:

> There is an X in my blind field, but it is an open question whether I have justification to believe there is an X in my blind field.

---

[15] For current purposes, we can even restrict the existence thesis to propositions that you can entertain. The existence thesis is logically weaker than the uniqueness thesis, since it doesn't imply that there is only one doxastic attitude that you have epistemic justification to hold toward any given proposition.

Intuitively, however, you can never have justification to believe these Moorean conjunctions. After all, these beliefs express a kind of epistemic akrasia that is always irrational and hence unjustified. I'll develop this argument in chapter 9.

The second implausible consequence is to sever a plausible connection between justification and critical reflection, according to which a belief is justified only if it can survive a justified process of critical reflection. Critical reflection is the activity of reflecting on which beliefs you have justification to hold and revising your beliefs accordingly. The point of engaging in critical reflection is to bring your first-order beliefs into line with your higher-order reflections about which beliefs you have justification to hold. When critical reflection is performed in a fully justified way, your first-order beliefs are brought into line with your justified higher-order reflections about what you have justification to believe. This means that Susan's belief that there is an X in her blind field cannot survive a fully justified process of critical reflection, since she lacks higher-order justification to believe that she has first-order justification for that belief. It is implausible to suppose that she has justification to believe that there is an X in her blind field, despite the fact that this belief cannot survive a justified process of critical reflection. I'll develop this argument in chapter 8.

Option 2 is to argue that the JJ principle can be reconciled with an externalist theory of justification, such as reliabilism. On this view, Susan not only has justification to believe that there's an X in her blind field, but also has higher-order justification to believe that she has justification to believe this proposition. This is hard to square with our description of the example. We stipulated that Susan has no evidence that justifies believing that she has a reliable faculty of unconscious perception. Her total evidence justifies doubting—that is, disbelieving or withholding belief—that she has any reliable way of forming beliefs about her blind field. But any body of evidence that justifies doubting the reliability of forming beliefs in a certain way also justifies doubting that one has justification to form beliefs in that way. Therefore, Susan lacks higher-order justification to believe that she has justification to form beliefs on the basis of unconscious perception.

What's missing in clairvoyance and super-blindsight? The missing ingredient is perceptual experience. Perceptual experience does a kind of double duty: it not only justifies beliefs about the external world, but also justifies beliefs about perceptual experience. More specifically, perceptual experience justifies introspective beliefs about the phenomenal features in virtue of which it justifies belief about the external world—namely, its phenomenal force and its phenomenal content. For example, when I have a visual experience in which it seems that I have hands, I thereby have justification to believe the following:

(1) I have a visual experience in which it seems that I have hands [by introspection].

(2) If I have a visual experience in which it seems that I have hands, then I have defeasible justification to believe that I have hands [by a priori reasoning].

(3) Therefore, I have defeasible justification to believe that I have hands [by deduction from (1) and (2)].

The key point is that my perceptual experience has introspectible features that seem upon reflection to justify believing that I have hands—namely, its phenomenal force and content. In this way, my perceptual experience provides luminous justification for belief about the external world. In contrast, unconscious perception in super-blindsight doesn't satisfy this constraint because it lacks phenomenal force and phenomenal content. It has no introspectible features that seem upon reflection to justify believing its content. This is why it cannot provide luminous justification for belief about the external world.

Reliability is not luminous in the same way. You're not always in a position to know when you have a reliable way of forming beliefs about the external world. This is exactly what the examples of clairvoyance and super-blindsight are designed to illustrate. In these cases, you have a reliable way of forming beliefs about the external world, although you're not in a position to know that you do. However, some proponents of reliabilism may dispute this. I'll briefly discuss two recent attempts to reconcile a reliabilist theory of knowledge with a version of the KK principle, which says that if you know that p, then you're in a position to know that you know that p. If this can be done, then perhaps we can also reconcile a reliabilist theory of justification with the luminosity of justification, which says that if you have justification to believe that p, then you're in a position to know that you have justification to believe that p.[16]

Daniel Greco (2014b) endorses a broadly reliabilist theory of knowledge, which says that knowledge is a belief state that carries information about the world.[17] According to this theory, you know that p just in case you're in a belief state that carries the information that p. A belief state S carries the information that p just in case normal conditions obtain, and when normal conditions obtain, you're in S only if p. Now, Greco argues that all states carry information about themselves: "If S is in a state that carries the information that p, then *that very state* also carries the information that S is in a state that carries the information that p" (2014b: 184). He uses this point to explain how the KK principle

---

[16] In fact, the extension is not straightforward. The KK principle doesn't entail that justification is luminous unless we assume that you have justification to believe that p only if you know that p. Of course, many proponents of reliabilism reject this assumption.

[17] Dretske (1981) and Stalnaker (1984) defend this informational theory of knowledge, while Stalnaker (2015) also uses it to defend the KK principle.

is true: if knowledge is a state that carries information, and states that carry information thereby carry information about themselves, then knowing that p suffices for knowing that you know that p.

One problem with Greco's argument for the KK principle is that it abstracts away from the belief requirement for knowledge. He relies on the simplifying assumption that any state that carries the information that p thereby causes or constitutes the belief that p. So, for example, if your belief that p carries the information that you believe that p, then you believe that you believe that p. As Greco acknowledges, however, this simplifying assumption is false. The state of being HIV positive carries the information that you're HIV positive, but it doesn't follow that you believe this to be true. After all, people don't always realize when they contract HIV. That's why people take HIV tests.

This makes it much harder to explain how justification can be luminous given a reliabilist theory of justification. What the HIV example shows is that a state that reliably indicates that p doesn't thereby put you in a position to know that p. On many reliabilist theories of justification, a state that reliably indicates that p doesn't thereby justify believing that p unless it grounds a reliable disposition to believe that p. To argue that reliability is luminous, we need to assume that any state that grounds a reliable disposition to believe that p also grounds a reliable higher-order disposition to believe that it grounds such a reliable disposition. But this assumption is false. After all, you can have a reliable disposition to believe that p without having a reliable second-order disposition to believe that you have a reliable disposition to believe that p.

There are two ways this can happen. First, you can have a reliable disposition to believe that p without having any disposition to form second-order beliefs at all. Many human infants and nonhuman animals are in exactly this predicament. Second, you can have a reliable disposition to believe that p while also having a disposition to believe that you have no reliable disposition to believe that p, and hence no justification to believe that p. In that case, you are epistemically akratic, since you believe Moorean conjunctions of the following form: p, but I have no justification to believe that p. Intuitively, this kind of epistemic akrasia is always irrational. The challenge for reliabilist theories of justification is to explain the irrationality of epistemic akrasia given the possibility that you can have reliable first-order dispositions without having correspondingly reliable second-order dispositions.[18]

---

[18] Greco (2014a) explains the irrationality of epistemic akrasia in terms of inconsistency by appealing to a form of expressivism about normative belief. In section 9.1, I suggest that this form of expressivism is implausible insofar as it implies that omissive forms of epistemic akrasia are not only irrational, but also impossible.

Nilanjan Das and Bernhard Salow (2018) propose an alternative reliabilist explanation of the KK principle, which draws upon Alex Byrne's (2005) transparency account of self-knowledge. The key idea is that if you know that p, then you're always in a position to know that you know that p by following the knowledge rule:

The Knowledge Rule: If p, then believe that you know that p!

What it is to follow the knowledge rule is to believe that you know that p on the basis of your knowledge that p. Hence, the knowledge rule is "self-verifying" in the sense that if you succeed in following it, then your resulting belief is guaranteed to be true. Moreover, Das and Salow argue that your belief is guaranteed to be safe from error, since it is true in any close case in which it is formed on the basis of following the knowledge rule. On a broadly reliabilist conception of knowledge, this is all it takes for your belief to be knowledge.[19]

What makes it the case that we have justification to follow the knowledge rule? One answer is that we have justification to follow the knowledge rule because it is self-verifying in the sense that following the rule is guaranteed to yield beliefs that are true and also safe from error. This answer is implausible. Surely we don't have justification to follow all self-verifying rules. Consider the following water rule:

The Water Rule: if x is water, then believe that x is composed of H_2O molecules!

This rule is self-verifying in the sense that beliefs formed by following the rule are guaranteed to be true and safe from error. Even so, we don't have justification to follow the water rule unless we have justification to believe on independent grounds that water is composed of H_2O molecules. Presumably, no one had justification to follow the water rule before the development of modern chemistry. A better answer is that you have justification to follow a self-verifying rule just in case you're disposed to follow the rule. This means that the ancient Greeks had no justification to follow this rule, since they weren't disposed to follow it. However, it does mean that if they had been disposed to this rule, even before the development of modern chemistry, then they would have had justification to do so. And that seems extremely implausible.

---

[19] It's not clear how to extend this account to cases in which you're in a position to know that p, and so you have justification to believe that p, although you don't believe that p. The analogy with self-knowledge has no obvious traction in such cases.

A related problem with this proposal is that it cannot explain the irrationality of epistemic akrasia. Consider an agent who knows that p, but who is not disposed to believe that she knows that p by following the knowledge rule. Instead, she believes that she doesn't know that p because (so she thinks) she doesn't have justification to believe that p. In other words, she believes the conjuncts of a Moorean conjunction of the following form: p and I don't have justification to believe that p. This seems epistemically irrational, but how can we explain why it is irrational? We can't explain it by citing the agent's disposition to follow the knowledge rule, since we've stipulated that she has no such disposition. We might say instead that she is rationally required to follow the knowledge rule, whether she is disposed to follow it or not. But this is to fall back on the implausible claim that you're rationally required to follow all self-verifying rules whether or not you're disposed to follow them.

We can now see a general problem for any reliabilist theory of justification that seeks to explain the luminosity of justification. Any such theory of justification must explain the luminosity of justification by appealing to the reliability of our higher-order doxastic dispositions. But there's no guarantee that agents with reliable first-order dispositions cannot have unreliable second-order dispositions. Such agents are prone toward epistemic akrasia, which seems irrational, but the reliabilist theory of justification cannot explain why epistemic akrasia is irrational in such cases. I'll develop my own explanation of the irrationality of epistemic akrasia in chapters 9 and 10.

7.4. The New Evil Demon Problem

In this section, I'll raise another problem for attempts to reconcile accessibilism with externalist theories of epistemic justification, such as reliabilism. Even if reliabilism can explain how you're always in a position to know what you have justification to believe when you're in the good case, it cannot explain how you're always in a position to know what you have justification to believe when you're in the bad case. This point is best illustrated by considering the new evil demon problem.

My phenomenal duplicate in the skeptical scenario believes that he has hands on the basis of visual experience. In fact, he is merely a disembodied brain in a vat being stimulated to have visual experiences in which it seems as if he has hands. In this skeptical scenario, his visual experiences systematically misrepresent the external world. At the same time, he has no evidence that justifies believing that he is in this skeptical scenario. Intuitively, he has justification to believe that he has hands on the basis of visual experience.

His belief that he has hands is justified, despite the fact that it is held in an unreliable way. Hence, this is a counterexample to the thesis that reliability is necessary for justification.

Some proponents of reliabilism may be inclined to bite the bullet and deny that my envatted duplicate has justification to believe that he has hands. Once again, however, I'll argue that this response is hard to reconcile with accessibilism. The JJ principle provides the resources for arguing in support of the intuitive judgment that my envatted duplicate has justification to believe that he has hands. Here is the argument in outline:

(1) *The JJ Principle*: Necessarily, you have justification to believe that *p* if and only if you have higher-order justification to believe that you have justification to believe that *p*.

(2) My envatted duplicate has higher-order justification to believe that he has justification to believe that he has hands.

(3) Therefore, my envatted duplicate has justification to believe that he has hands.

Proponents of reliabilism have two options for responding to this argument. They can either reject the JJ principle or they can deny that my envatted duplicate has higher-order justification of the relevant kind. I'll argue that both options are implausible.

Option 1 is to reject the JJ principle. On this view, my envatted duplicate has higher-order justification to believe that he has justification to believe that he has hands, although he lacks first-order justification to believe that he has hands. Instead, he has first-order justification to disbelieve or to withhold belief that he has hands. This view is compatible with a plausible explanation of what's bad about the bad case—namely, that when you're in the bad case, you have justification to believe that you're in the good case. As I'll explain, however, it has other implausible consequences.

The first implausible consequence is that my envatted duplicate has justification to believe abominable Moorean conjunctions. After all, he has justification to believe the following metajustificatory proposition: 'I have justification to believe that I have hands'. At the same time, however, he has justification to disbelieve or to withhold belief that he has hands. He thereby has justification to believe one of the following Moorean conjunctions:

(1) I have justification to believe that I have hands, but I don't have hands; or

(2) I have justification to believe that I have hands, but it's an open question whether I have hands.

Intuitively, however, you can never have justification to believe these Moorean conjunctions, since these beliefs express a kind of epistemic akrasia that is always irrational and hence unjustified. I'll develop this argument further in chapter 9.

The second implausible consequence is that my envatted duplicate lacks justification to believe that he has hands, despite the fact that this belief can survive a fully justified process of critical reflection. My envatted duplicate has higher-order justification to believe that he has justification to believe that he has hands. Therefore, his belief that he has hands can survive a justified process of critical reflection. After all, critical reflection is justified when your first-order beliefs are brought into line with your justified higher-order reflections. And yet it is implausible that you lack justification for beliefs that have what it takes to survive a fully justified process of critical reflection. I'll develop this connection between justification and critical reflection in chapter 8.

Option 2 is to argue that the JJ principle can be reconciled with a reliabilist theory of justification. On this view, my envatted duplicate not only lacks justification to believe that he has hands, but also lacks higher-order justification to believe that he has justification to believe that he has hands. This is because he is unreliable not only about whether he has hands, but also about whether he has justification to believe that he has hands. The main problem with this option is that the JJ principle can be extended from belief to other doxastic attitudes, including disbelief and withholding. Here is the extended version of the JJ principle:

The Extended JJ Principle: Necessarily, you have epistemic justification to adopt some doxastic attitude D toward the proposition that p if and only if you have epistemic justification to believe that you have epistemic justification to adopt D toward p.

Assuming the existence thesis, there is some doxastic attitude that my envatted duplicate has justification to adopt toward the proposition that he has hands. If he lacks justification to believe it, then he has justification either to disbelieve it or to withhold belief instead. Given the extended version of the JJ principle, this implies that he has higher-order justification to believe that he has justification either to disbelieve or to withhold belief that he has hands. But this seems absurd. When you're in the bad case, you don't have evidence that justifies believing that you're in the bad case. As Williamson puts the point, "Part of the badness of the bad case is that one cannot know just how bad one's case is" (2000: 165).

I'll now consider two ways of responding to this objection. Option 2.1 says that whenever you're in the bad case, you're in an epistemic position to know that you're in the bad case, although you're incapable of exploiting your epistemic position.[20] On this view, what's bad about the bad case is precisely that you're unable to convert your epistemic position into knowledge. In reply, I'll argue that this diagnosis of what's bad about the bad case has some implausible consequences.

The first implausible consequence is that being in the bad case always involves some failure of rationality in cognition. After all, if you're fully rational, and you're in an epistemic position to know that p, then you're capable of converting your epistemic position into knowledge that p (except in finkish cases). If you're unable to exploit your epistemic position in the bad case, then you must be less than fully rational. As I argued in section 3.4, however, the bad case is more plausibly regarded as a case of perceptual impairment than cognitive impairment. What's bad about the bad case is not that your cognition is any less than fully rational, but rather that your perceptual evidence is limited in ways that guarantee that rational cognition results in ignorance and error about the external world.

The second implausible consequence is that an ideally rational agent is always able to know when she is in the bad case. But the bad case is plausibly much worse than that: not even an ideally rational thinker can know when she is in the bad case. Even a naive realist like Martin (2004) concedes that perfect hallucination is indiscriminable by reflection from veridical perfection in an impersonal sense that abstracts away from the limited cognitive capacities of particular subjects. The indiscriminability of the bad case from the good case holds as much for ideally rational agents as it does for nonideal agents like you and me. Any conception of rationality that denies this is hard to stomach.

Can we avoid this objection by rejecting the existence thesis? This is option 2.2. On this view, there is no doxastic attitude that my envatted duplicate has justification to adopt toward the proposition that he has hands. Moreover, there is no doxastic attitude that he has justification to adopt toward the metajustificatory proposition that he has justification to believe it. These propositions are "epistemically inert" in the sense that there is no doxastic attitude that he has justification to hold toward them. As a result, we cannot apply the JJ thesis in order to derive absurd consequences about the bad case. Even so, I'll argue that this option generates its own implausible consequences.

---

[20] Magidor (2018) argues that some envatted subjects in the bad case are in a position to know that they are envatted so long as they are disposed to form beliefs to that effect in a reliable way. As she notes, however, this strategy cannot be extended to envatted subjects who might easily not have been envatted.

First, there is no good precedent for the claim that propositions about the external world are epistemically inert in the bad case. In general, there is always some doxastic attitude that I have justification to adopt toward any proposition that I can entertain. Consider the proposition that the number of books in my office is even. If I don't have sufficient evidence to justify believing or disbelieving the proposition, then my evidence justifies withholding belief instead. Withholding belief is justified by default whenever my evidence fails to justify believing a proposition or its negation. To deny this in the bad case seems ad hoc and unmotivated.[21]

Second, this option repeats the mistake of diagnosing what's bad about the bad case in terms of cognitive irrationality. But now the situation is even worse because the bad case guarantees cognitive irrationality in a way that does not merely reflect our human limitations. Option 2.1 says that we are condemned to irrationality in the bad case because of our human limitations, although our more ideally rational selves are not. Option 2.2, in contrast, says that no possible agent can form rational doxastic attitudes in the bad case. On this view, the bad case generates a *rational dilemma* in the sense that there is no doxastic attitude that you are rationally permitted to adopt toward the proposition that you have hands. It doesn't matter whether you believe it, disbelieve it, or withhold belief altogether. Whatever doxastic attitude you adopt, it is guaranteed to be irrational. The only way to avoid violating the requirements of epistemic rationality is to adopt no doxastic attitude at all. Insofar as we can make sense of this possibility at all, however, it is very hard to understand why epistemic rationality should ever require us to refrain from adopting doxastic attitudes altogether.[22]

Third, we cannot explain what's bad about the bad case in purely negative terms. When you're in a coma, you don't have justification to adopt any doxastic attitude toward the proposition that you have hands or toward the metajustificatory proposition that you have justification to believe it. These propositions are epistemically inert for you in the sense that there is no doxastic attitude that you have justification to adopt toward them. Intuitively, however, your epistemic predicament when you're in the bad case is quite different from being in a coma. Of course, there are psychological differences between these cases, since you form beliefs when you're in a skeptical scenario, but not when you're in a coma. Even so, the psychological differences between these cases cannot explain the relevant epistemic differences between them.

---

[21] In Smithies (2016b), I explain why de re propositions about objects don't provide a good precedent for rejecting the existence thesis. Even if we restrict the existence thesis to propositions that you can entertain, it can still be applied in skeptical scenarios.

[22] Greco (forthcoming) gives some theoretical reasons to avoid positing rational dilemmas that appeal to various hypotheses about the function of epistemic evaluation.

To illustrate the point, let's contrast your epistemic predicament in the bad case with that of your perceptual zombie twin. Your zombie twin forms beliefs about the external world, just as you do, but these beliefs are formed on the basis of unconscious perceptual information, rather than conscious perceptual experience. Intuitively, there is an epistemic difference between you and your zombie twin, since you are conscious in the bad case even if your perceptual experience misrepresents the external world. However, we cannot explain this epistemic difference in purely negative terms. What's bad about the bad case is not merely that you lack justification to believe that you're in the good case. After all, the same is true of your zombie twin. What's bad about the bad case is that you have positive justification to believe falsely that you're in the good case. If we combine this with the JJ principle, however, it follows that you have justification to believe that you have hands even in the bad case.

7.5. Answering the Explanatory Challenge

In this chapter, I've argued that accessibilism can be explained as a consequence of phenomenal mentalism. Epistemic justification is luminous because it is determined by your phenomenally individuated mental states, which are luminous by introspection, in accordance with epistemic principles about the evidential support relation, which are luminous by a priori reflection. Moreover, it's not clear how to explain accessibilism without commitment to phenomenal mentalism. If epistemic justification is not determined by introspectively luminous facts about your current phenomenally individuated mental states, then there will be counterexamples to accessibilism in which you're not in a position to know which doxastic attitudes you have epistemic justification to hold. I conclude provisionally that phenomenal mentalism is needed to explain accessibilism.

This is one key premise in the "argument from above" for phenomenal mentalism. If phenomenal mentalism is needed to explain accessibilism, and accessibilism is motivated on independent grounds, then phenomenal mentalism is supported by inference to the best explanation. In the remaining chapters of this book, I'll complete this argument by motivating accessibilism and defending it against objections. What I want to do briefly now is to explain how the argument from above provides the resources for answering the three challenges for phenomenal mentalism that I outlined in section 6.5.

First, *the explanatory challenge*: Why are only phenomenally individuated facts about your mental states capable of making a justificational difference? The answer is that only phenomenally individuated facts about your current mental states are introspectively luminous. Given accessibilism, only introspectively luminous facts about your mental states can make a justificational difference. Therefore, only phenomenally individuated facts about your current mental states can make a justificational difference. Hence, accessibilism provides an answer to the explanatory challenge.

Second, *the unification challenge*: What do the phenomenally individuated facts about your mental states have in common in virtue of which they are capable of making a justificational difference? These facts constitute a disjunctive kind: they include not only facts about your conscious experiences, which are individuated by their phenomenal character, but also facts about your consciously accessible beliefs and desires, which are individuated by their phenomenal dispositions. What do your experiences and beliefs have in common in virtue of which they can make a justificational difference? The answer is that these mental states are both introspectively luminous. That is why they are both capable of making a justificational difference. Hence, accessibilism provides an answer to the unification challenge.

Finally, *the motivational challenge*: Why should we accept the intuitions about cases that I used to motivate phenomenal mentalism, including the new evil demon problem and the problems of clairvoyance and super-blindsight? In this chapter, I argued that these intuitions can be supported by arguments that use accessibilism as a premise. They are not just brute deliverances of an untutored faculty of intuition. On the contrary, they are supported by general theoretical principles about the structure of epistemic justification, which can be motivated on independent grounds. Hence, accessibilism provides an answer to the motivational challenge.

The main task for the rest of the book is to argue for accessibilism and to defend it against objections. In chapter 8, I argue that accessibilism is a consequence of a plausible connection between epistemic justification and reflection and I defend this connection against a series of objections raised in recent work by Hilary Kornblith. In chapter 9, I argue that epistemic akrasia always involves some degree of epistemic irrationality, and I use this premise in arguing for accessibilism. In chapter 10, I defend this premise against the objection that epistemic akrasia can be fully rational when we have misleading higher-order evidence about what our first-order evidence supports. My response appeals to a version of accessibilism on which we're always in a position to know with certainty what our evidence is and what it supports. In chapter 11, I defend accessibilism against Ernest Sosa's version of the problem of the speckled hen and Timothy Williamson's anti-luminosity argument. Finally, in chapter 12, I'll conclude by explaining why phenomenal accessibilism is a more plausible version of epistemic internalism than phenomenal conservatism.

8
Reflection

Justification is one among many dimensions of epistemic evaluation. We evaluate beliefs not only for justification and the lack thereof, but also for truth and falsity, reliability and unreliability, knowledge and ignorance, and so on. Justification comes apart from these other dimensions of epistemic evaluation, since justified beliefs fall short of knowledge when they are false or when they are true but unreliable. A theory of justification should explain what justification is and how it differs from these other dimensions of epistemic evaluation.

Knowledge is traditionally analyzed as justified true belief. According to this analysis, justification is the property that turns true belief into knowledge. One of the lessons of Gettier's (1963) counterexamples to the traditional analysis, however, is that there is no unique property that satisfies this description: justification is just one among many properties that are necessary for true beliefs to be knowledge. Given the failure of the traditional analysis, we need an alternative account of what sets justification apart from these other necessary conditions for knowledge.

William Alston (2005) argues that debates about the nature of justification threaten to descend into purely terminological disagreements in which different epistemologists use the term 'justification' to pick out different epistemic properties that are necessary for true beliefs to be knowledge. The danger, Alston writes, is that "controversies over what it takes for a belief to be justified are no more than a vain beating of the air" (2005: 11). His reaction is to urge that epistemology should broaden its focus from traditional questions about the nature of knowledge and justification to include questions about the nature, importance, and interrelations among a much wider range of epistemic desiderata.

Alston's epistemic pluralism is salutary. We should recognize multiple dimensions of epistemic evaluation that matter to us in various different ways. At the same time, we need not follow his recommendation to eliminate use of the term 'justification' in epistemology. Instead, we can avoid the threat of purely terminological disagreement by explicating justification in terms of its distinctive role in epistemic evaluation and then asking what justification must be like to play this role. On this approach, what matters is not so much the terminology that we use to pick out epistemic properties, but rather the role that they play in epistemic evaluation. As David Chalmers writes, "Instead of asking, 'What is X?,' one should focus on the roles one wants X to play, and see what can play that role" (2011: 538).

This is an application of the same methodology that Edward Craig recommends for the theory of knowledge:

> We take some prima facie plausible hypothesis about what the concept of knowledge does for us, what its role in our life might be, and then ask what a concept having that role would be like, what conditions would govern its application. (1990: 2)

The general strategy is to begin by considering the purpose of using a concept in epistemic evaluation and then to use this in constraining an account of the epistemic property to which it refers. An adequacy constraint on a theory of this epistemic property is that it should make sense of the role that our concept of this property plays in epistemic evaluation.[1]

This methodology has several advantages. First, it promises to illuminate the *value* of justification. When we evaluate beliefs as justified or unjustified, these evaluations matter to us. A theory of justification should explain why they matter—that is, why justification is an important dimension of epistemic evaluation. Second, it promises to illuminate the *nature* of justification, since we can ask what justification must be like in order to play its distinctive role in epistemic evaluation. Third, it provides resources for resolving *disagreements* about cases, since we can adjudicate between conflicting intuitions by appealing to theoretical considerations about the role of justification in epistemic evaluation. And fourth, it enables us to avoid *terminological debates* about how to use the word 'justification'. What matters is not which terminology we use to pick out an epistemic property, but rather the nature and importance of its role in epistemic evaluation.

This chapter explores the hypothesis that we use the concept of justification because of its connection with the practice of reflection on the epistemic credentials of our beliefs. According to this hypothesis, justification is the epistemic property that makes our beliefs stable under reflection. Although I draw this hypothesis from the work of William Alston, I'll use it to undermine his theory of justification, which he calls "internalist externalism." Instead, I'll use this hypothesis to argue for a version of the JJ principle, which says that you have justification to believe a proposition just in case you have higher-order justification to believe that you have justification to believe it. Moreover, I'll

---

[1] See also Haslanger's (1999) methodology for building a theory of knowledge that incorporates insights from feminist theory.

defend this proposal against a series of objections raised in recent work by Hilary Kornblith.[2]

Here is the plan. I'll begin by defending the proposal that justification is an epistemic property that makes our beliefs stable under reflection (section 8.1). Next, I'll use this proposal in arguing for the JJ principle (section 8.2). Finally, I'll defend this proposal against Kornblith's objections: the overintellectualization problem (section 8.3), the regress problem (section 8.4), the empirical problem (section 8.5), and the value problem (section 8.6). I'll conclude with some more general reflections on the debate between internalist and externalist theories of epistemic justification (section 8.7).

8.1. Justification and Reflection

The guiding hypothesis of this chapter is that we use the concept of justification in epistemic evaluation because of its connection with the practice of critical reflection. This idea has been clearly articulated by William Alston, who writes:

> Why is it that we have this concept of *being justified in holding a belief* and why is it important to us? I suggest that the concept was developed, and got its hold on us, because of the practice of critical reflection on our beliefs, of challenging their credentials and responding to such challenges—in short, the practice of attempting to *justify* beliefs. (1989: 236)

Critical reflection is the activity that we engage in when we revise our beliefs in light of our higher-order reflections on their justificatory credentials. In critical reflection, we reflect on which beliefs we have justification to hold, and we revise our beliefs accordingly. The aim of this activity is to bring our beliefs into line with our higher-order reflections about which beliefs we have justification to hold.

As Alston construes it, critical reflection is the activity of justifying our beliefs by reflecting on what makes them justified. He is careful to distinguish the activity of *justifying* our beliefs from the property of *being justified*, which is what we reflect upon when we engage in the activity. As I'll explain, having justified beliefs requires neither engaging in the activity of justifying those beliefs through reflection nor even having the psychological capacity to do so. Alston's proposal is not that reflection is what makes one's beliefs justified, but rather

---

[2] This chapter develops my account of the value of justification in Smithies (2015b) and my responses to Kornblith's objections in Smithies (2016c).

that the importance of justification derives from its connection with the activity of reflection.

To add some more detail, the proposal is that the standards for a belief to be justified can be defined by reference to the activity of critical reflection. Alston writes:

> It would, of course, be absurd to suggest that in order to be . . . justified, a belief must have actually been put to such a test and emerged victorious. In suggesting that the concept has developed against the background of such a practice the idea is rather that what it is for a belief to be justified is that the belief and its ground be such that it is in a position to pass such a test; that the subject has what it takes to respond successfully to such a challenge. A justified belief is one that *could* survive a critical reflection. (1989: 225–226)

To a first approximation, the proposal is that a justified belief is *stable under reflection* in the sense that if it were subjected to reflection, then it would survive. Alston denies that a justified belief must actually survive the test of reflective scrutiny, so long as it has the potential to survive the test. Justification on this view is the epistemic property in virtue of which a belief has the potential to survive reflection.[3]

Alston's proposal needs to be qualified in various ways. First, it is vulnerable to the objection that even an unjustified belief could survive reflection if its basis were to change in the process. To avoid this objection, we can say that a justified belief is one that would survive reflection *on its actual basis*. So, for instance, a justified belief held on the basis of perceptual experience could survive reflection on the same basis: of course, the belief is now held reflectively, whereas it was held unreflectively before, but its basis in perceptual experience remains unchanged.

Second, Alston (1989: 226 n. 45) registers doubts about whether the concept of justification can be extended to unreflective creatures, such as animals and children. But we can assuage these doubts by noting that a justified belief has the potential to survive critical reflection in virtue of the basis on which it is held and not in virtue of the subject's reflective capacities. A justified belief is one that would survive on its actual basis if it were subjected to critical reflection by some *idealized counterpart* of the subject with the very same evidence

---

[3] Compare Audi's *process-property integration thesis*, which links the property of justification with the process of justifying: "a belief is justified . . . if and only if it has one or more other (nonnormative) properties such that (i) in virtue of them it is justified, and (ii) citing them, under appropriate conditions, both shows that it is justified and constitutes justifying it" (2001: 24).

together with the capacity for reflection. Animals and children can have justified beliefs in the absence of any capacity to engage in critical reflection, so long as their beliefs could survive reflection in some idealized counterpart who has the relevant capacities.

Third, Alston's proposal is vulnerable to the objection that when reflection is done poorly, justified beliefs can be abandoned and unjustified beliefs can be retained. To avoid this objection, we need to invoke another kind of idealization. We need to idealize not only the subject's capacity to engage in critical reflection, but also the way in which this capacity is exercised. On a revised version of the proposal, a justified belief is one that is stable under reflection that is itself justified. Reflection is justified when you bring your beliefs into line with your justified higher-order beliefs about which beliefs you have justification to hold.[4]

Fourth, Alston's proposal is concerned with doxastic justification, rather than propositional justification: it is a thesis about the conditions for one's beliefs to be justified, rather than the conditions for having justification to hold them. Nevertheless, the proposal can be extended from doxastic justification to propositional justification as follows:

A belief is *doxastically justified* if and only if you hold the belief on some basis on which it would be held after justified reflection.

A belief is *propositionally justified* if and only if you have some basis on which the belief would be held after justified reflection.

The key difference is that doxastic justification, unlike propositional justification, requires proper basing: that is, your belief is justified only if it is held on some basis on which it could survive justified reflection.

I'll now defend this proposal against three objections. The first objection is that the proposal is circular, since it uses the concept of justification in stating the conditions for a belief to be justified. In reply, however, the circularity is not vicious. After all, the proposal is not designed to give a reductive analysis of justification in more basic terms. Moreover, the circularity doesn't trivialize the proposal. Here is the general form of the proposal:

---

[4] Foley (1992) gives a closely related analysis of "egocentric rationality" as invulnerability to self-criticism by one's own deepest epistemic standards. However, Foley's analysis does not allow for idealization in one's epistemic standards, or one's ability to apply them, but only in the conditions in which they are applied. Therefore, Foley's analysis counts some dogmatic and delusional beliefs as rational, where I count them as unjustified because they would not survive appropriate idealization in one's capacity for critical reflection.

A belief is justified if and only if you would hold the belief in ideal conditions C.

If we define ideal conditions as those in which your beliefs are justified, then the proposal becomes trivial. But this is not how we're defining ideal conditions. Instead, ideal conditions are defined as conditions in which your beliefs survive justified reflection. As I've explained, reflection is justified when you bring your beliefs into line with your justified higher-order beliefs about which beliefs you have justification to hold. It is a plausible but nontrivial thesis that beliefs formed in this way are always justified.

The second objection is that the proposal commits the conditional fallacy. After all, the process of engaging in justified reflection may have psychological side effects that change which propositions you have justification to believe. For example, if you were to reflect on whether you have justification to believe that rhubarb is a vegetable, then you would thereby gain justification to believe that you're thinking about rhubarb. As things are, however, you may be thinking about other things, or nothing at all, and so you don't have any justification to believe that you're thinking about rhubarb. To avoid this problem, we need to understand the idealization in a way that brackets these psychological side effects.

Following Michael Smith (1994), we can mitigate this problem to some extent by distinguishing two models of the relationship between one's actual self and one's ideal self, which Smith calls the *example model* and the *advice model*.[5] On the example model, you have justification to believe a proposition if and only if your ideal self would believe it. On the advice model, in contrast, you have justification to believe a proposition if and only if your ideal self would advise that you believe the proposition. The advice model is much more plausible than the example model, since your ideal self would not advise you to follow their example when the idealization changes which propositions you have justification to believe. Hence, which propositions you have justification to believe is determined by the advice, rather than the example, of your ideal self.

I am now inclined to doubt that this provides a fully general response to the conditional fallacy objection.[6] Suppose I have finkish evidence that justifies believing a Moorean conjunction—say, that it's raining and I don't believe it's raining. In that case, my ideal self would neither believe the Moorean

---

[5] Smith (1994: ch. 5) proposes an analysis of normative reasons, according to which you have a reason for action if and only if you would desire that you so act if you were ideally rational. Smith's idealization is rather different from mine, however, since his ideally rational agent is omniscient and infallible about all the facts.
[6] I proposed this response to the conditional fallacy objection in Smithies (2015b), but see the discussion of finkish evidence in Smithies (2016a). See also section 5.3.

conjunction nor advise me to believe it. Neither the example model nor the advice model yields the correct verdict in this case. Ultimately, I think we cannot give a conditional analysis of propositional justification in terms of the hypothetical responses of ideally rational agents. Any such analysis will be vulnerable to counterexamples involving finkish evidence. This doesn't mean we should jettison Alston's proposal altogether, since we can restrict its application to *nonfinkish* cases: that is, cases in which the idealization doesn't affect your justification to believe a given proposition.

Alston's proposal—as I've been refining it—gives an illuminating account of the connection between justification and reflection that holds generally, although not without exception. It fails in finkish cases where engaging in justified reflection changes which propositions you have justification to believe. Nevertheless, it holds in nonfinkish cases when engaging in justified reflection makes no relevant difference. In those cases, you have justification to believe a proposition if and only if you have some basis on which you would believe the proposition after justified reflection.

The third objection challenges the connection between justification and reflection. Why should we define justification in terms of the activity of reflecting on your current evidence, rather than the activity of gathering new evidence? This is largely a terminological issue. Given epistemic pluralism, we can allow that there are some epistemic properties that we care about because of their connection with the activity of gathering new evidence. For instance, one lesson of Gilbert Harman's (1973) assassination case is that knowledge must be stable under the acquisition of new evidence that you could easily possess. Suppose you read in the newspaper that the president has been assassinated, but (unbeknownst to you) the story is retracted in a media conspiracy later that day. In that case, your belief is justified because it is stable under reflection on the evidence that you currently possess. At the same time, your belief is not knowledge because it is not stable under reflection on evidence that is easily available in your social environment. Justification is merely one among many conditions that are necessary for a belief to be knowledge.

Epistemic agents can be idealized along many different dimensions, but many of these are irrelevant for understanding the concept of justification. Justified reflection cannot require being omniscient or infallible about the external world, since this would imply that you have justification to believe all truths and only truths. Justified reflection must be understood in a way that allows for ignorance and error about the external world. Reflection is not a matter of gathering new evidence, but is a matter of reflecting on the evidence that is currently in your possession. Your reflection on your evidence can be fully justified even when your evidence is inaccurate and incomplete. Therefore, justified reflection is compatible with massive ignorance and error about the external world. Even the victim of a skeptical scenario, such as a brain in a vat, can engage in fully justified reflection.

What is the relationship between justification and knowledge? Since Gettier, the usual assumption is that justification is necessary but not sufficient for knowledge, although this is sometimes disputed.[7] This assumption is supported by the thesis that justification is what makes a belief stable under justified reflection. On the one hand, justification is necessary for knowledge, since all knowledge is stable under justified reflection, but only justified beliefs are stable under justified reflection. On the other hand, justification is not sufficient for knowledge, since a belief can be stable under justified reflection even if it is false or true by accident. In such cases, the belief is justified, but it is not a case of knowledge.

8.2. An Argument from Reflection

In this section, I'll use the proposed connection between justification and reflection to argue for a version of accessibilism. More specifically, I argue for the JJ principle:

The JJ Principle: Necessarily, you have justification to believe that *p* if and only if you have higher-order justification to believe that you have justification to believe that *p*.

This is a thesis about propositional justification, rather than doxastic justification: it is not a thesis about which of one's beliefs are justified, but rather about which propositions one has justification to believe. I'll revisit this distinction in section 8.3.

Alston uses the connection between justification and reflection to argue for a rather different version of accessibilism, which he calls "internalist externalism." On the one hand, he argues that a belief is justified, and so has the potential to survive critical reflection, only if its justifying ground or basis—what he calls a "justifier"—is accessible to the subject upon reflection alone. Thus, he writes:

A justified belief is one that *could* survive a critical reflection. But then the justifier must be accessible to the subject. Otherwise the subject would be

---

[7] Foley (1992), Lewis (1996), and Audi (2001) deny that justification is necessary for knowledge, while Sutton (2007) and Williamson (2013) propose that justification is sufficient for knowledge.

in no position to cite it as what provides a sufficient indication that the belief is true. (1989: 226)

On the other hand, Alston claims that your justifiers play their justifying role in virtue of their reliable connections to the external world. On this hybrid view, your justifiers must be accessible to you, but the facts in virtue of which they justify your beliefs—namely, their reliable connections to the external world—need not be so accessible. As a result, you might have access to your justifiers without having access to the facts about which beliefs they justify. Hence, the justificatory status of a belief is not always accessible by reflection: you don't always have access to which beliefs you have justification to hold.

The problem with Alston's internalist externalism is that it conflicts with his own proposal about the connection between justification and reflection. On this view, your beliefs can be justified by their reliable connections to the external world without having what it takes to survive a justified process of reflection. Indeed, Alston seems to acknowledge this point in the following passage:

> To illustrate, let's suppose that experiences can function as justifiers, and that they are accessible to us. I can always tell what sensory experiences I am having at a given moment. Even so, if I am unable to tell what belief about the current physical environment is justified by a given sensory episode, I am thereby unable to regulate my perceptual beliefs according as they possess or lack experiential justification. (1989: 221)

Suppose I form a justified belief on the basis of perceptual experience. And suppose I have access to my perceptual experience, but not the fact that it justifies the belief in question. In that case, my belief is not stable under justified reflection. After all, the aim of reflection is to bring my beliefs into line with my justified higher-order reflections about which beliefs I have justification to hold. My belief cannot survive reflection unless I have justification to believe upon reflection that my perceptual experience justifies holding the belief. Therefore, my justified beliefs are not stable under justified reflection unless what is accessible to me includes not only my justifiers, but also the facts about which beliefs they justify.

My main goal here is not to criticize Alston's internalist externalism, but rather to use his proposal about the connection between justification and reflection in giving an argument for the JJ principle. Here is the argument in outline:

(1) You have justification to believe that p if and only if you have some basis on which you would believe that p after a fully justified process of reflection.

(2) You have some basis on which you would believe that p after a fully justified process of reflection if and only if you have higher-order justification to believe that you have justification to believe that p.

(3) Therefore, you have justification to believe that p if and only if you have
higher-order justification to believe that you have justification to believe
that p.

I defended both premises of this argument in section 8.1. The first premise
restates the proposal that justification is the epistemic property that gives a
belief the potential to survive justified reflection, while the second premise
restates what it is for reflection to be justified. To recap, reflection is justified
when you bring your beliefs into line with your justified higher-order beliefs
about which beliefs you have justification to hold. This is why a belief has the
potential to survive justified reflection just when you have higher-order justification to believe that you have justification for the belief in question. The JJ
principle follows given the further premise that you have justification for a belief just when it has the potential to survive justified reflection.

As I explained in section 8.1, the premises of this argument are vulnerable to
the conditional fallacy objection. My response was to restrict these premises to
nonfinkish cases in which engaging in justified reflection doesn't change your
justification to believe that p. This means that the argument doesn't establish a
fully general version of the JJ principle, but one that is restricted to nonfinkish
cases. Even so, it is reasonable to extend the JJ principle to finkish cases too.
After all, the JJ principle is not vulnerable to the conditional fallacy, since it
is not stated in terms of counterfactual conditionals at all. Indeed, the JJ principle is what grounds the truth of the relevant counterfactual conditionals in
nonfinkish cases. Why is it that if you have justification to believe that p, you
thereby have some basis on which you would believe that p after a justified reflection? The JJ principle supplies the answer: anything that justifies believing
that p also justifies believing that you have justification to believe that p. In
nonfinkish cases, this is enough to guarantee that you have some basis on which
you would believe that p after justified reflection. If you reflect in a way that is
fully justified, then you will form the justified higher-order belief that you have
justification to believe that p, and you'll thereby come to believe that p.

Those who reject the JJ principle must block this argument in a way that
avoids descending into purely terminological disagreement. Replacing the
proposed conditions for justification threatens to change the subject by using
the word 'justification' to pick out a different epistemic property. Given a
reasonable epistemic pluralism, we can recognize many different epistemic
properties that play many different roles in epistemic evaluation. There is no
need to claim that all of these epistemic properties are accessible. The claim

is only that there is *some* epistemic property that is accessible, and this is the property for which we reserve the term 'justification'. To accept that there is such a property, while using the term 'justification' to pick out a different property, is to reject accessibilism on purely terminological grounds. Those who reject accessibilism on substantive grounds must argue that no important epistemic property is accessible in the sense defined.

In the rest of this chapter, I'll defend the proposed connection between justification and reflection against a series of objections raised by Hilary Kornblith. In his book *On Reflection*, Kornblith criticizes what he regards as a chronic tendency in philosophy to overinflate the significance of reflection. More specifically, he argues against theories of knowledge and justification that give a central role to reflection, including those proposed by Laurence BonJour (1985) and Ernest Sosa (1991). In what follows, I'll explain how my theory of justification provides the resources for answering Kornblith's objections. I'll also sketch a more general account of the significance of reflection that withstands Kornblith's criticisms.

8.3. The Overintellectualization Problem

Laurence BonJour (1985: ch. 2) argues for a *doxastic version* of the JJ principle, which says that your belief that p is justified if and only if it is based on a justified higher-order belief that you have justification to believe that p. One of the key premises in his argument against foundationalism is that a belief B is justified if and only if it is held on the basis of a metajustificatory argument of the following form:

(1) B has feature φ.
(2) Beliefs having feature φ are highly likely to be true.
(3) Therefore, B is highly likely to be true.

According to BonJour, "it is necessary, not merely that a justification along the above lines exist in the abstract, but also that [the subject] himself be in cognitive possession of that justification, that is, that he believe the appropriate premises of forms (1) and (2) and that these beliefs be justified *for him*" (1985: 31).

BonJour argues for this metajustificatory requirement by appealing to a connection between justification and epistemic responsibility. The central claim is that a belief is justified only if it is held in a responsible way; moreover, a belief is not held responsibly unless it is based on a metajustificatory argument that the belief is likely to be true. As BonJour writes, "To accept a belief in the absence of such a reason . . . is to neglect the pursuit of truth; such acceptance is, one might say, *epistemically irresponsible*. My contention is that the idea of avoiding such irresponsibility, of being epistemically responsible in one's believings, is the core of the notion of epistemic justification" (1985: 8).

To illustrate the point, BonJour gives the example of Norman the clairvoyant, who believes that the president is in New York on the basis of a reliable clairvoyant power. BonJour argues that Norman's belief is unjustified, and so cannot be knowledge, because it is held in an epistemically irresponsible way. He writes:

> Norman's acceptance of the belief about the President's whereabouts is epistemically irrational and irresponsible, and thereby unjustified, whether or not he believes himself to have clairvoyant power, so long as he has no justification for such a belief. Part of one's epistemic duty is to reflect critically upon one's beliefs, and such critical reflection precludes believing things to which one has, to one's knowledge, no reliable means of epistemic access. (1985: 42)

The claim is that holding beliefs in a responsible way requires fulfilling an epistemic duty to engage in critical reflection on your beliefs. More specifically, you have an epistemic duty to refrain from holding beliefs when you have no justification to believe upon reflection that your evidence makes them likely to be true. Norman has no justification to believe upon reflection that he has any reliable evidence about the location of the president. Therefore, he violates an epistemic duty in believing that the president is in New York.

BonJour's reasoning can be summarized as follows. According to his doxastic version of the JJ principle, a belief is justified only if it is held on the basis of a justified higher-order belief that you have justification to hold the belief. If a belief is not held on the basis of a metajustificatory argument that it is probably true given your evidence, then it is epistemically irresponsible and hence unjustified. Norman's clairvoyant beliefs are unjustified because they fail to satisfy this metajustificatory requirement.

Kornblith argues that BonJour's account of justification faces several problems, including *the overintellectualization problem*. We often form beliefs automatically on the basis of perception, memory, or testimony without first reflecting on whether we have justification to form these beliefs. BonJour's account threatens to have the skeptical implication that these beliefs are unjustified and so cannot be knowledge. As Kornblith writes, "Most of our beliefs are formed without the benefit of critical reflection, and so, on BonJour's view, most of our beliefs are not in fact justified, and we thus have precious little knowledge" (2012: 11).

In response, BonJour might challenge the assumption that reflection is not causally implicated in the formation of our perceptual beliefs. Although we rarely think consciously about the epistemic credentials of these beliefs, we are surely justified in holding the standing belief that perceptual experience is a source of knowledge about the external world. If the justification for this belief is undermined on some occasion—say, when we see mirages in the desert—we tend to refrain from forming beliefs on the basis of perception. In this way, reflection may be poised to inhibit perceptual belief-formation even if our default setting is to form beliefs automatically on the basis of perception.

Whatever the merits of this response, Kornblith's main point is that you don't need any capacity for reflection in order to have perceptual knowledge or justified belief about the external world. Some philosophers argue that the capacity for reflection is required because justified beliefs must be responsive to reasons. In reply, Kornblith argues that responding to reasons doesn't require conceptualizing reasons *as* reasons, and so it doesn't require any capacity for reflection. Moreover, he argues on empirical grounds that many human infants and nonhuman animals have the capacity for cognition with no corresponding capacity for metacognition. In this connection, he cites the broken wing display in piping plovers, termite fishing in chimpanzees, and linguistic abilities in three-year-old children who fail the false belief task. In all of these cases, he argues, information is represented and integrated in ways that manifest the kind of responsiveness to reasons that is required for justified belief.

Although BonJour (2003: 34) denies that human infants and nonhuman animals can have perceptual knowledge of the external world, this is a tough bullet to bite. I'm inclined to agree with Kornblith that unreflective creatures can have perceptual knowledge, so long as their perceptual representations are conscious and their cognitive representations are accessible to consciousness. It doesn't follow that metacognition is required unless we endorse a metacognitive theory of consciousness (which I don't). As far as I'm concerned, the absence of metacognition is no good reason to deny that human infants and nonhuman animals are capable of acquiring perceptual knowledge about the external world.[8]

Sosa (1991) gives a different response to the overintellectualization objection. He agrees with BonJour that justified belief requires the capacity for reflection, while denying that knowledge requires justified belief so construed. He puts the point in terms of a distinction between "animal knowledge" and "reflective knowledge":

---

[8] Presumably, some nonhuman animals are perceptual, cognitive, or affective zombies. In such cases, I'm willing to deny that their representational and motivational states are beliefs and desires, since they don't provide reasons for belief and action (see section 4.4).

For animal knowledge one needs only belief that is apt and derives from an intellectual virtue or faculty. By contrast, reflective knowledge always requires belief that is not only apt but also has a kind of justification, since it must be belief that fits coherently within the epistemic perspective of the believer. (1991: 145)

According to Sosa, animal knowledge is true belief that is "apt" in the sense that it derives from a reliable disposition or "intellectual virtue" of the believer. There is no requirement that animal knowledge must be justified on the basis of reflection. Reflective knowledge, in contrast, requires not only that your true beliefs are formed in a reliable way, but also that they are justified by reflection on the reliability of the way in which they are formed.

My objection is that this proposal collapses the intuitive distinction between perceptual knowledge and clairvoyance or super-blindsight. Sosa makes room for animal knowledge by rejecting the justification condition and replacing it with a reliability condition. On this view, Norman's clairvoyant beliefs satisfy the conditions for animal knowledge, since they are formed in a reliable way.[9] But this is the wrong result: there is no good sense in which Norman's belief is justified and no good sense in which it is knowledge. To avoid this result, we cannot entirely sever the connections between knowledge, justification, and reflection. Instead, we need a more nuanced account of these connections.

My own response to the overintellectualization problem contrasts with both of these. I agree with BonJour, and against Sosa, that a belief is knowledge only if it is justified. While BonJour claims that a justified belief must *actually* withstand reflective scrutiny, I claim (following Alston) that a justified belief is one that has the *potential* to withstand reflective scrutiny. This doesn't mean that the believer must have the reflective capacities needed to realize this potential. A justified belief has the potential to survive reflection in virtue of the basis on which it is held and not in virtue of the believer's reflective capacities. An unreflective subject can have a justified belief so long as it would survive on its actual basis if it were subject to reflective scrutiny by some idealized counterpart of the subject who has the very same evidence but who also has the requisite capacity for reflection.

This provides an alternative to BonJour's diagnosis of why Norman's clairvoyant belief is unjustified and so fails to be knowledge. It doesn't matter whether Norman engages in critical reflection or even whether he has the capacity to do so. What matters is whether his belief is based in such a way

---

[9] Sosa (1991: 240) denies that animal knowledge is available to reflective agents, but we can finesse this point by considering clairvoyants with no capacity for reflection.

that it has the potential to survive a fully justified process of critical reflection. Norman's belief is unjustified because it doesn't satisfy this condition. After all, he has no justification to believe upon reflection that his evidence makes it likely that the president is in New York. Therefore, a reflective and epistemically responsible counterpart of Norman would withhold the belief upon reflection.

The same doesn't apply to perceptual beliefs in animals and children. You don't need reflective capacities in order to satisfy the conditions for perceptual knowledge or justified belief. Animals and children can have justified beliefs in the absence of any capacity for reflection so long as their beliefs are based in a way that gives them the potential to survive an idealized process of critical reflection. Indeed, beliefs formed on the basis of perceptual experience typically satisfy this condition. An idealized counterpart of the subject can reflectively endorse the belief by recognizing that it is justified by the perceptual experience on which it is based.

In conclusion, we can avoid the overintellectualization problem without severing the connections between knowledge, justification, and reflection. Unlike BonJour, we needn't deny that unreflective creatures can have perceptual knowledge, since their perceptual beliefs sometimes have the potential to survive a fully justified process of reflection. Unlike Sosa, we needn't accept that Norman's clairvoyance gives him knowledge, since his clairvoyant beliefs don't have the potential to survive ideal reflection. In this way, we can avoid the problems that arise for both BonJour's and Sosa's theories of justification.

8.4. The Regress Problem

Kornblith's second problem for BonJour is *the regress problem*. On BonJour's account, a first-order belief is justified only if it is based on justified second-order reflection, which is justified only if it is based on justified third-order reflection, and so on ad infinitum. But no finite creature can have an infinite hierarchy of higher-order justified beliefs of infinitely increasing complexity. So BonJour's account generates the skeptical conclusion that no finite creature can have any justified beliefs at all. As Kornblith remarks, "No amount of reflective scrutiny is enough, for, whenever one stops reflecting, there is always some belief playing a would-be justificatory role which has itself gone unreflected upon" (2012: 13).

A similar problem remains if we weaken the conditions for justified belief so that the capacity for justified higher-order reflection must be possessed but need not be exercised. The problem for this account is that the capacity for justified second-order reflection requires a capacity for justified third-order reflection, and so on ad infinitum. And yet no finite creature has unlimited capacity for reflection: there are limits on the length and complexity of the reflective processes that we are capable of undertaking. So this account cannot avoid the skeptical consequence that no finite agent can have justified beliefs.

My proposal avoids these skeptical consequences. A justified belief is stable on reflection in virtue of the basis on which it is held and not in virtue of one's reflective capacities. There are limits on the length and complexity of the reflective processes that we are capable of undertaking, but not on those that our justified beliefs have the potential to withstand. A justified belief has the potential to withstand reflection of any finite length and complexity when conducted by an idealized counterpart of the subject with the very same evidence together with the requisite capacity for reflection. There are no finite limits on the length and complexity of reflective processes that our idealized counterparts can perform.

The point remains that for every finite process of reflection, "there is always some belief playing a would-be justificatory role which has itself gone unreflected upon." But this point is not damning for me in the way it is for BonJour. The problem for BonJour is that one's reflections cannot contribute toward the justification of one's beliefs unless they are justified by reflection themselves. Skepticism follows, since no finite subject can engage in reflection of infinite length and complexity. In contrast with BonJour, however, I don't claim that a belief is justified only if it is based on reflection. A belief can play a justificatory role without being reflected upon, so long as it has the potential to withstand reflection by an appropriately idealized counterpart of the subject.

Unlike BonJour, I formulate the reflective constraints on justification in terms of propositional justification, rather than doxastic justification. The propositional version of the JJ principle generates an infinite regress of propositional justification, but no such regress of doxastic justification. If you have first-order justification to believe that p, then you have second-order justification to believe that you have first-order justification to believe that p, and so on ad infinitum. However, it doesn't follow that your first-order belief is justified only if it is properly based on a justified second-order belief, and so on all the way up the hierarchy. Your first-order belief that p is justified when it is properly based on the evidence that justifies believing that p. It's just that your evidence justifies the first-order belief that p only if it also justifies the second-order belief that your evidence justifies the first-order belief that p, and so on ad infinitum.

The infinite regress for doxastic justification is vicious because it implies the skeptical conclusion that no finite agent can have justified beliefs. In contrast, the infinite regress for propositional justification is benign, since it has no such skeptical implications. It just means that whenever you have justification to believe a proposition, you also have justification to believe an infinite series of metajustificatory propositions. This is no more problematic than the claim that whenever you have justification to believe that p, you also have justification to believe that p or q, and that p or q or r, and so on ad infinitum. In the rest of this section, I'll defend the infinite regress of propositional justification against three objections.

The first objection is that the infinite regress is vicious because it implies that there is a chain of justificatory dependence with no ultimate end point. If so, then none of the beliefs in the chain can be justified, and so the threat of skepticism reappears. In reply, this objection conflates *necessitation* and *dependence*. The JJ principle states necessary and sufficient conditions for justification, but it doesn't attempt to say what justification consists in or depends upon. It implies that first-order justification necessitates higher-order justification, but it doesn't imply that first-order justification depends upon higher-order justification. Whenever my evidence justifies believing that p, it also justifies believing that my evidence justifies believing that p, and so on ad infinitum. But what justifies believing that p is my evidence, rather than my higher-order justification to believe that my evidence justifies believing that p.[10]

The second objection is that the infinite regress implies that we are rationally required to believe infinitely many propositions. This is absurd: finite agents cannot believe infinitely many propositions, but surely we don't violate the requirements of epistemic rationality just by virtue of being finite agents. In reply, this objection assumes an implausible connection between propositional justification and requirements of epistemic rationality. Epistemic rationality requires believing a proposition *only when* you have justification to believe it, but not *whenever* you have justification to believe it. When your evidence justifies believing that p, it also justifies believing that p or q, that p or q or r, and so on ad infinitum. As Gilbert Harman (1986) notes, however, epistemic rationality doesn't require cluttering up your mind with pragmatically irrelevant disjunctions.

The third objection is that the infinite regress of propositional justification implies that you cannot always convert your propositional justification into doxastic justification. Sometimes, you have justification to believe metajustificatory propositions that are so complicated that you're incapable of believing them (or even grasping them) at all. This violates the following doxastic constraint on propositional justification:

The Doxastic Constraint: Necessarily, you have propositional justification to believe that p only if you're capable of believing that p in a way that is doxastically justified.

---

[10] In Smithies (2014a), I make similar points in defending classical foundationalism against the arguments of Sellars (1956), BonJour (1985), and Klein (2005).

In reply, however, I'll argue that there is no compelling basis for accepting the doxastic constraint on propositional justification.

According to evidentialism, your evidence determines which propositions you have justification to believe. In some cases, however, your evidence may justify believing propositions that you cannot believe at all or only in a way that is unjustified. Richard Feldman and Earl Conee make this point in their defense of evidentialism:

> Suppose that there were occasions when forming the attitude that best fits a person's evidence was beyond normal cognitive limits. This would still be the attitude *justified* by the person's evidence. If the person had normal abilities, then he would be in the unfortunate position of being unable to do what is justified. (2004: 87)

We can use this point to generate counterexamples to the doxastic constraint. Suppose Sherlock Holmes and Dr. Watson share evidence about a case that justifies the conclusion that the butler committed the crime. Since the evidence is very complicated, only an expert detective like Holmes can form a justified belief on the basis of the evidence. If Watson forms the same belief, then it is no more justified than beliefs based on blind guesswork, since his beliefs are not sufficiently sensitive to what the evidence supports. Moreover, we can add that Watson is constitutionally incapable of acquiring the same degree of expertise as Holmes. For a more extreme case, consider the patient with Capgras delusion who believes against all the evidence that his spouse has been replaced by an imposter. Because he is delusional, he is incapable of forming justified beliefs about his spouse that are supported by evidence.[11]

Are there any good reasons to accept the doxastic constraint? Some philosophers argue for the doxastic constraint by defining propositional justification in terms of doxastic justification. Here, for example, is a proposal from John Turri:

> Necessarily, for all S, p, and t, if p is propositionally justified for S at t, then p is propositionally justified for S at t because S currently possesses at least one means of coming to believe p such that, were S to believe p in one of those ways, S's belief would thereby be doxastically justified. (2010: 320)

---

[11] See Alston (1989: 95–96), Pryor (2001: 114–115), Feldman and Conee (2004: 88), and Christensen (2004: 161–162) for additional examples of this kind.

According to this proposal, what makes it the case that you have propositional justification to believe that p is that you have some way of forming the doxastically justified belief that p. A consequence of this proposal is that the limits of your doxastic capacities constrain which propositions you have justification to believe.

Turri's proposal is subject to counterexamples involving finkish evidence. Suppose you have meteorological evidence that it's raining, while you also have psychological evidence that you don't believe it's raining. In that case, your total evidence justifies believing the omissive Moorean conjunction: "It's raining, but I don't believe it's raining." But if you come to believe this Moorean conjunction, then your psychological evidence changes, and you no longer have justification to believe it. Since evidence for an omissive Moorean conjunction is always finkish, you cannot satisfy the proper basing relation that converts propositional justification into doxastic justification. However, it doesn't follow—as Turri's proposal implies—that you cannot have evidence that gives you propositional justification to believe an omissive Moorean conjunction in the first place.[12]

An alternative view is that doxastic justification can be defined in terms of propositional justification plus proper basing. Here is a more precise statement:

> Necessarily, for all S, p, and t, S's belief that p is doxastically justified at t if and only if at t, S has evidence e that makes it the case that p is propositionally justified for S, and S believes that p in a way that is properly based on evidence e.

This is not to give a *reductive* definition of doxastic justification in terms of propositional justification. Perhaps there is no way to define proper basing except nonreductively as the relation that converts propositional justification into doxastic justification. Indeed, I suspect that no reductive definition of proper basing is immune from counterexamples of exactly the kind that Turri (2010) proposes. Like many others, however, I regard the project of reductive definition in epistemology as fairly moribund.[13]

The case for the doxastic constraint evaporates on this alternative account of the connection between propositional and doxastic justification. Having the capacity to form a doxastically justified belief that p requires not only having

---

[12] See Smithies (2016a) for a more extended discussion of this point.
[13] In section 11.2, I explicate proper basing in terms of safety from absence of propositional justification, but I doubt that this modal conception of safety can be understood except in terms of doxastic justification. Similarly, Williamson (2000) understands knowledge in terms of safety from error, but he denies that this modal conception of safety can be understood except in terms of knowledge.

evidence that gives you propositional justification to believe that p, but also having the doxastic capacity to believe that p in a way that is properly based on the evidence. But there is no guarantee that meeting the first condition suffices for meeting the second condition. You might have evidence that gives you propositional justification to believe that p without having the doxastic capacity to believe that p in a way that is properly based on the evidence. Indeed, that is exactly what we should say in the examples of Dr. Watson and the patient with Capgras delusion.

We can articulate a much tighter connection between propositional justification and doxastic justification in the case of ideally rational agents. If you're ideally rational, and you adopt some doxastic attitude toward the proposition that p, then you have propositional justification to believe that p if and only if you have a doxastically justified belief that p. But ideal rationality is a standard that we humans are incapable of satisfying. Hence, there is no basis here for accepting the doxastic constraint.

Much of the attraction of the doxastic constraint derives from the reliabilist project of defining propositional justification in terms of doxastic justification, which is then explained in terms of the reliability of our doxastic dispositions.[14] But reliabilism is not the only way to explain how epistemic justification is grounded in nonepistemic facts. In chapter 6, I argued for a version of phenomenal mentalism, according to which epistemic justification is grounded in nonepistemic facts about our phenomenally individuated mental states, rather than by our doxastic dispositions to form beliefs on the basis of those mental states.

A different argument for the doxastic constraint appeals to a deontological conception of justification together with an epistemic 'ought' implies 'can' principle:

(1) *The Deontological Conception of Justification*: Necessarily, if you have propositional justification to believe that p, then you ought to believe that p in a way that is doxastically justified.

(2) *The Epistemic 'Ought' Implies 'Can' Principle*: Necessarily, if you ought to believe that p in a way that is doxastically justified, then you can believe that p in a way that is doxastically justified. Therefore,

(3) *The Doxastic Constraint*: Necessarily, if you have propositional justification to believe that p, then you can believe that p in a way that is doxastically justified.

---

[14] Goldman (1979) is a very clear exponent of this project: he defines ex ante justification in terms of ex post justification, and gives a reliabilist theory of ex post justification.

I'll consider two options for blocking this argument: either (i) reject the deontological conception of justification or (ii) reject the epistemic 'ought' implies 'can' principle. I'll argue that, given the context-sensitivity of 'ought' claims, there is no deep question about which of these options we should prefer.

The first option is to deny premise (1) by rejecting the deontological conception of justification as a source of epistemic obligations. For example, William Alston (1989: ch. 5) argues that we should reject this in favor of an evaluative conception of justification as a source of epistemic values or evaluative ideals. On this view, there is no epistemic obligation to form beliefs rationally on the basis of evidence, but there is nevertheless a distinctive kind of epistemic value in doing so.

The second option is to deny premise (2) by rejecting the epistemic 'ought' implies 'can' principle. Richard Feldman (2004: ch. 7) argues that there are so-called 'role oughts' which apply to anyone who plays a certain role, regardless of how well the person is capable of playing that role—for instance, chefs ought to make delicious food and jugglers ought to keep their balls in the air. Similarly, Feldman argues, there are epistemic 'oughts' that apply to us in virtue of our role as believers: "It is our plight to be believers. We ought to do it right. It doesn't matter that in some cases we are unable to do so" (2004: 175).

Deciding between these options depends on how we understand the relationship between values and obligations. Are we obliged to achieve evaluative ideals or merely to approximate toward them as closely as we can? It seems to me that there is no deep answer to this question. On the one hand, we can recognize a "thin" sense in which we ought to achieve ideals regardless of whether we're capable of doing so. As Feldman and Conee write, "In any case of a standard for conduct . . . it is appropriate to speak of 'requirements' or 'obligations' that the standard imposes" (2004: 87). On the other hand, we can also recognize a "thick" sense in which we can held responsible for fulfilling our obligations in a sense that makes it appropriate to adopt reactive attitudes, such as praise and blame. Our obligations in this thick sense depend on our limited capacities—that is, we're obliged to do only what we're capable of doing. After all, we wouldn't blame someone who violates an ideal, but who nevertheless comes as close as she can.[15]

The argument for the doxastic constraint equivocates between thick and thin senses of 'ought'. Given the context-sensitivity of 'ought' claims, both premises can be given a true reading. However, there is no single reading of the argument on which both premises are true. In the thin sense of 'ought', premise (1) is true,

[15] Pryor (2001: 115 n. 36) draws a similar distinction. My own distinction between ideal and nonideal requirements of epistemic rationality can be regarded as a special case of this more general distinction between thick and thin senses of 'ought'.

but premise (2) is false: we're not always capable of fulfilling our epistemic obligation to form beliefs rationally on the basis of evidence. In the thick sense of 'ought', premise (2) is true, but premise (1) is false: we have no epistemic obligation to form beliefs rationally on the basis of the evidence, but there is nevertheless some distinctive epistemic value in doing so. However we interpret the argument, it fails to establish that rational ideals must be humanly attainable.

In general, there is no good reason to suppose that all evaluative ideals worth caring about must be humanly attainable. We can and do evaluate the performance of human beings along dimensions whose extremes lie beyond human reach. Rational ideals—like ideals of morality, scientific understanding, and chess—may lie beyond our limited human capacities. The ideals themselves need not be humanly achievable so long as we can make sense of better and worse approximation toward those ideals. Christensen (2004: 162) puts the point nicely: "Not all evaluation need be circumscribed by the abilities of the evaluated. In epistemology, as in various other areas, we need not grade on effort."

8.5. The Empirical Problem

The third problem that Kornblith raises is *the empirical problem*. Why suppose that our beliefs are justified only when they have the potential to survive reflection? It is often assumed that reflection makes us more reliable by weeding out logical fallacies, hasty generalizations, baseless prejudice, and wishful thinking. The empirical evidence shows, however, that reflection doesn't always make us more reliable and indeed that it often makes us less reliable. Kornblith concludes, "What commonsense tells us is a way of screening our beliefs in order to make them more accurate turns out, instead, in many cases, to be a route to little more than self-congratulation" (2012: 3).

Here are the key points that Kornblith draws from an extensive review of the empirical literature. There are many cases in which our beliefs are influenced by seemingly irrelevant factors that we are not consciously aware of and whose influence on our beliefs is undetectable by means of introspection. At the same time, we have a tendency to confabulate post hoc rationalizations for these beliefs without recognizing that this is what we're doing. To mention just one classic study, Richard Nisbett and Timothy Wilson (1977) found that subjects showed a strong right-hand-side bias when choosing between qualitatively identical pairs of socks, although subjects were unaware of this bias, and tended to rationalize their choices by citing nonexistent differences in texture, color, and so on. After surveying many other experimental results of this kind, Kornblith concludes: "Asking subjects to introspect more carefully, or think longer and harder about the sources of their beliefs, is entirely useless in many of these cases" (2012: 23).

I'll make three points in response to this empirical problem. The first point is that even if reflection tends to make us less reliable when it is done poorly, it can make us more reliable when it is done well. In Nisbett and Wilson's study, for instance, subjects cannot know by reflection that they're susceptible to right-hand-side bias, so they cannot know the *motivating reasons* for which they act as they do. At the same time, they can know by reflection that there are no good *normative reasons* for choosing the socks on the right, since there is no good reason to believe that they are qualitatively different from the socks on the left. Insofar as these subjects believe they are acting for good reasons in choosing the socks on the right, they are failing to reflect on their reasons in a fully rational way. Of course, what the empirical findings show is that reflection is not always done rationally—we do sometimes engage in confabulation and perhaps much more often than we tend to realize.

The second point, though, is that the empirical evidence about the power of reflection is not universally negative. Reflection can and sometimes does increase our reliability in reasoning about a range of distinct topics. Here are just three examples from a recent review article: (i) *logical reasoning*: Gagne and Smith (1962) found that performance on the Tower of Hanoi problem was improved in subjects who were required to verbalize their reasons for each move; (ii) *moral reasoning*: Small et al. (2007) counteracted the identifiable victim effect by instructing subjects to engage in deliberation about their decisions to donate money to charity; and (iii) *emotion regulation*: Pennebaker and Chung (2007) found that asking subjects to reflect on traumatic personal experiences caused improvements in health that resulted from analyzing the trauma.[16]

The third point is that our account of the reflective stability of justified belief needs to be qualified in light of these empirical facts. When reflection is done poorly, justified beliefs can be abandoned and unjustified beliefs can be retained. So a justified belief cannot be defined as one that is stable under just any empirically realistic process of reflection. Instead, a justified belief should be defined as one that is stable under an *idealized* process of reflection—that is, a process of reflection that is fully rational, reasonable, or justified. Human reflection may never satisfy this ideal, but the crucial point is that it can be evaluated by the degree to which it approximates toward this ideal.

---

[16] See Baumeister et al. (2011). The official topic of the review is the role of consciousness in reasoning, but the authors define consciousness in terms of higher-order reflection, so they also review empirical evidence concerning the role of reflection.

Christine Korsgaard (1996) makes a similar appeal to ideal reflection in her account of the source of normative reasons. She writes:

We need reasons because our impulses must be able to withstand reflective scrutiny. We have reasons if they do. The normative word 'reason' refers to a kind of reflective success. (1996: 93)

Korsgaard argues that normativity has its source in reflection: the correct normative standards are the ones we would endorse upon reflection. This claim is vulnerable to Kornblith's empirical problem. Given the empirical facts about the unreliability of reflection, there is no guarantee that our reflections will converge upon correct normative standards. To solve this problem, Korsgaard invokes an idealization: she appeals to "a person who reasons all the way back, who never gives up until there is a completely undeniable, satisfying, unconditional answer to the question." As Kornblith argues, however, this doesn't solve the empirical problem, since merely idealizing the length of reflection without idealizing its quality does nothing to guarantee that it will converge upon correct normative standards. What Korsgaard needs is an idealization that is understood in more robustly normative terms, but she cannot avail herself of this without compromising her own metaphysical project of explaining the source of normativity.

My response to the empirical problem invokes a normative idealization too: I claim that a justified belief is stable under an idealized process of reflection. Given Korsgaard's project, this kind of normative idealization is illegitimate, since it presupposes normative facts of the very same kind that she seeks to explain. My own project is different from Korsgaard's, however, since I am not trying to give a metaphysical account of the source of normativity. In the context of my project, it is perfectly legitimate to invoke a robustly normative kind of idealization.

Kornblith (2016) challenges this appeal to idealization. If the JJ principle is true, then ideal reflection requires being infallible about which propositions you have justification to believe. Kornblith's objection is that no infallible process of reflection can be regarded as an idealized version of the reflective mechanisms that we actually have. He writes, "the conception of idealized reflective processes which Smithies offers us seems to have lost all connection with the phenomenon of human reflection which it sought to use to illuminate both reflection and knowledge" (2016: 77).

To illustrate the point, Kornblith draws an analogy with vision. Although vision is unreliable under certain kinds of distorting conditions, such as bad light or fog, it is much more reliable under optimal conditions when these distortions are absent. Even so, it's not perfectly reliable, even under these ideal conditions, since it's still vulnerable to certain kinds of visual illusion. Moreover, it's not clear that we can make any sense of an idealization that makes the visual system completely immune from visual illusions. After all, visual illusions result from the proper functioning of the visual system, and not from distortion or outside interference. As Kornblith says, "The human visual system without the visual illusions is not an idealized visual system. It is no visual system at all" (2016: 76).

Kornblith claims that the situation is the same in the case of reflection. Just as vision generates illusions, even in ideal conditions, so does reflection. For example, the subjects in Nisbett and Wilson's experiment took themselves to have direct introspective access to their reasons for action, when in fact they were just confabulating. What the subjects were doing, Kornblith says, is performing an unconscious explanatory inference: "Why did I pick the socks on the right? I must have some good reason for choosing them, so the socks on the right must be somehow preferable." These inferential mechanisms sometimes lead us into error, but they often yield knowledge of our reasons for action. Kornblith's central point is that we cannot make sense of an idealized version of these inferential mechanisms that are entirely immune from error. Kornblith writes, "Talk of idealized reflection which isn't subject to . . . errors postulates a mechanism which is nothing short of a miracle. It is not reflection without interfering factors; it is reflection without reflective processes" (2016: 77).

I'll make two points in response to Kornblith's challenge. The first point is that explanatory inference is required for knowledge of our *motivating* reasons, but not our *normative* reasons: it is required for knowing the reasons for which we believe and act, but it is not required for knowing the reasons we have for believing and acting in the first place. In chapter 7, I argued for a version of accessibilism, which says that you're always in a position to know your normative reasons for belief on the basis of introspection and a priori reflection. Moreover, in chapter 5, I argued that introspection is epistemically privileged over other ways of knowing about the world, including visual perception and explanatory inference. I'm not claiming that the mechanisms of introspection are completely immune from error—they are certainly not—but rather that introspective errors always reflect some failure of epistemic rationality. This epistemic point has no analogue for either visual perception or explanatory inference.

The second point is to make a distinction between two kinds of idealization. Kornblith's idealization considers how a mechanism would function in optimal conditions in which there is no distortion or outside interference. This is a perfectly legitimate kind of idealization, but it is not the same as mine. I'm invoking a more robustly normative kind of idealization on which reflection is ideal when it meets the most demanding normative standards of epistemic rationality. I'm not claiming that all human deviations from ideals of epistemic rationality can be explained in terms of distortion or interference. Epistemic rationality is an ideal that lies beyond our limited human capacities. This doesn't mean it is irrelevant to human concerns. After all, we care about being more or less rational, and the ideal of epistemic rationality is the limiting case that lies at one end of this spectrum. The ideal of epistemic rationality may not be humanly achievable, but that doesn't mean there's no value in getting as close as we can.

8.6. The Value Problem

The fourth and final problem that Kornblith raises is *the value problem*. If justification is the epistemic property that makes a belief stable under reflection, then why should we care about justification? Why should we regard this an important dimension of epistemic value?

One potential answer is that reflection makes us more reliable and hence beliefs that are stable under reflection are objectively more likely to be true. The empirical problem, as we've just seen, is that reflection sometimes makes us less reliable and also less justified. I've argued that we can respond to this problem by invoking an idealization. This doesn't solve the value problem, however, for at least two distinct reasons. First, not even fully rational reflection guarantees reliability, since it's compatible with the kind of massive ignorance and error that obtains in skeptical scenarios. And second, whatever reliability can be achieved through rational reflection can in principle be achieved without it by means of reliable first-order belief-forming processes.

Kornblith's view is that reflection has no distinctive epistemic value. On this view, reflection is just one among many ways of forming beliefs about the world. It is valuable insofar as it makes us more reliable and not otherwise. Here is Kornblith:

> From an epistemological point of view, we should value reflection to the extent that, and only to the extent that, it contributes to our reliability. Epistemologically speaking, there is no reason to value reflectively arrived at belief in general over unreflective belief. (2012: 34)

Here, Kornblith is assuming a form of *epistemic monism*, the thesis that truth is the only intrinsic epistemic value. It follows that the epistemic value of reflection must be explained instrumentally in terms of its reliability or truth-conduciveness. *Epistemic pluralism*, in contrast, says that there are multiple dimensions of epistemic value, not all of which can be explained in terms of reliability. In the present context, it is question-begging to assume that reliability is the only dimension of epistemic value, since many internalist theories deny that the value of epistemic justification can be explained in terms of reliability. Even so, the challenge remains to explain why reflection is valuable given that it is not always guaranteed to increase reliability. Are there any other benefits that reflection provides that cannot be achieved in any other way?

My proposal is that reflection has normative significance because it is the sine qua non for being a *person*—that is, someone who can legitimately be held responsible for her beliefs and actions. On this account, persons are distinguished from other animals by features of their individual psychology—namely, their capacity for reflection. But the significance of this capacity emerges only given its function in the social and interpersonal context of participation in human relationships.

As I use the concept, personhood is a normative kind, rather than a biological kind. Harry Frankfurt puts the point eloquently:

> The criteria for being a person do not serve primarily to distinguish the members of our own species from the members of other species. Rather, they are designed to capture those attributes which are the subject of our most humane concern with ourselves and the source of what we regard as most important and most problematical in our lives. (1971: 6)

Even if *Homo sapiens* is the only species whose members meet the criteria for being persons, there is no reason in principle why members of other species, such as Neanderthals, dolphins, or intelligent aliens, couldn't satisfy these criteria too.

What are the criteria for being a person? Persons are distinguished from other animals by the fact that they can be legitimately held responsible for their beliefs and actions. In this context, responsibility is a matter of *accountability*, rather than *credit*: persons can legitimately be held accountable for believing and acting in accordance with their duties. When people violate their duties, it is legitimate to hold them responsible by subjecting them to what Peter Strawson (1962) calls the "reactive attitudes," such as praise and blame, gratitude and resentment, and so on. We don't normally regard it as appropriate to adopt these reactive attitudes toward other animals. As Kornblith remarks: "When my neighbor's dog runs loose in my garden and destroys the flowers, it is not the dog who is responsible, but my neighbor" (2012: 75).

Responsibility is not the same as rationality: it is a more demanding status. I agree with Kornblith that unreflective creatures can form justified beliefs and perform justified actions that are responsive to good reasons. Even so, we don't regard it as appropriate to hold unreflective creatures responsible for the justification of their beliefs and actions. Why not? It's not enough to be rationally responsive to reasons. What's needed in addition is some capacity for reflection: that is, for considering what you have reason to believe and do and regulating your beliefs and actions in light of these reflections. This motivates the traditional Lockean thesis that persons are distinguished from other animals by their capacity for reflection. According to Locke, a person is "a thinking intelligent being that has reason and reflection" (1689: II xxvii 9).

The argument so far is a kind of inference to the best explanation: the thesis that responsibility requires a capacity for reflection explains why we don't hold rational animals responsible for their actions. We need to say more, however, in order to understand this connection. Why does responsibility require any capacity for reflection? Here it helps to consider the rationale for our social practice of holding each other responsible for our beliefs and actions by adopting reactive attitudes. The point of adopting these reactive attitudes is to make demands on each other to comply with certain normative standards, including standards of morality and practical or epistemic rationality. But a presupposition of the practice is that we all have some understanding of the relevant normative standards and some capacity to bring this understanding to bear in regulating our beliefs and actions. In other words, it presupposes that we all have some capacity for reflection.

This explains why we don't regard it as appropriate to adopt reactive attitudes toward nonhuman animals. When these creatures are responsive to reasons, we can shape their behavior by offering them rewards and punishments. In some cases, these rewards and punishments include expressions of emotion. But this is not to adopt reactive attitudes with their usual social function of making a demand on someone to comply with a certain normative standard. We cannot do this because nonhuman animals cannot understand the normative demands thereby placed on them. They can satisfy normative standards insofar as they are capable of responding to reasons for belief and action. Since they lack the capacity for reflection, however, they cannot understand these normative standards and bring this understanding to bear in regulating their own beliefs and actions. That is why they cannot legitimately be held responsible for their beliefs and actions. Responsibility requires not only responding to reasons, but also appreciating your reasons as reasons, and this in turn requires the capacity for reflection.

This argument gives us an answer to the value problem. Reflection is valuable not just because it tends to make us more reliable, but because it is the sine qua non for being a person. Because we have the capacity for reflection, we are capable of realizing a distinctive kind of rational value—namely, responsibility for the justification of our beliefs and actions. Like other animals, our beliefs and actions can be justified when they are sufficiently responsive to reasons. Unlike other animals, however, we can also be held responsible for the justification of our beliefs and actions. When our beliefs and actions are justified, we can be responsible not only in the sense of accountability, but also in the sense of credit. We gain credit for the justification of our beliefs and actions when this results from the exercise of our reflective capacities. Responsibility is a distinctive kind of rational value that comes only with the capacity for reflection. To explain the value of reflection in terms of reliability alone is to miss the evaluative significance of the distinction between persons and other animals.[17]

8.7. Conclusions

The debate between internalism and externalism in epistemology tends to oscillate between two extremes. Internalist theories tend to overintellectualize the requirements for justified belief by exaggerating the connections between justification and responsibility. According to BonJour, for example, "The idea of avoiding . . . irresponsibility, of being epistemically responsible in one's believings, is the core of the notion of epistemic justification" (1985: 8). On this view, a justified belief is one that is epistemically responsible. As I've just argued, however, an epistemically responsible belief is one that is held on the basis of reflection. The effect of BonJour's proposal, as Kornblith and others have noted, is to rule out the possibility of unreflectively justified belief.

Externalist theories tend to recoil in the opposite direction by severing the connection between justification and responsibility altogether. This dialectical situation is exacerbated by the fact that the connection between justification and responsibility disappears from view when we focus on cases of unreflectively justified belief. After all, as I've argued in this chapter, the significance of the concept of justification emerges only in the context of its role in reflection.

In order to reach a satisfactory resolution of the debate between internalism and externalism in epistemology, we need to allow for the possibility of unreflective justification without losing sight of the significance of justification in the practice of critical reflection. The theory of justification proposed in this chapter is designed to occupy this elusive middle ground. On the one hand, a

---

[17] My account of the value of reflection is strongly influenced by Burge's (1996, 1998) work on critical reflection and its connection with responsible agency.

justified belief must have the potential to withstand an epistemically responsible process of critical reflection. On the other hand, a justified belief need not actually be held on the basis of epistemically responsible reflection. We can therefore preserve the connection between justification and reflection without succumbing to the dangers of overintellectualization.

9

Epistemic Akrasia

This chapter and the next one are about *epistemic akrasia*—that is, the phenomenon of holding beliefs that conflict with your higher-order beliefs about which beliefs you ought to hold. Epistemic akrasia seems irrational—indeed, it is often regarded as a paradigmatic form of irrationality. Recently, however, some philosophers have argued that epistemic akrasia can be a rational response to misleading higher-order evidence about the requirements of epistemic rationality. My response is to turn this argument on its head. This chapter argues that epistemic akrasia is always irrational, while the next chapter argues that you cannot have misleading evidence about the requirements of epistemic rationality.

The main goal of this chapter is to argue from the premise that epistemic akrasia is always irrational to the conclusion that the JJ principle is true. The argument is simple: if the JJ principle is false, then it is sometimes rationally permissible to be epistemically akratic. Since epistemic akrasia is never rationally permissible, however, the JJ principle must be true. I gave a similar argument for the JJ principle in Smithies (2012c), but this chapter goes much further in motivating the premise that epistemic akrasia is never rationally permissible. Meanwhile, the next chapter rebuts the objection that epistemic akrasia is rationally permissible when you have the right kind of misleading higher-order evidence.

Here is the plan for this chapter. I begin by introducing the phenomenon of epistemic akrasia (section 9.1). Next, I present the argument for the JJ principle and I defend the argument against some objections (section 9.2). Finally, I motivate the premise that epistemic akrasia is sometimes rationally permissible by appealing to an epistemic version of Moore's paradox (section 9.3), the thesis that belief aims at knowledge (section 9.4), and the connection between rationality and reflection (section 9.5).

9.1. What Is Epistemic Akrasia?

When Medea betrays her father, King Aeëtes, by helping Jason to win the Golden Fleece, she finds herself torn between duty and romantic love. More specifically, she is torn between believing that she ought to remain loyal to her father and feeling compelled to betray him out of love for Jason. Medea gives expression to this conflict by declaring, "I see the better, and know it is right, but I follow the worse" (Ovid, *Metamorphoses* VII: 20–21).

My own life is characterized by a more mundane conflict between the temptations of gluttony and the need to stay in shape. I believe I ought to go to the gym and work out, but instead I find myself ordering a large slice of cheesecake at a local coffee shop. I believe I shouldn't be doing this, but here I am anyway with the cheesecake in front of me. These are examples—from the sublime to the ridiculous—of akrasia in the practical domain.

We can give similar examples of akrasia in the epistemic domain. Here is an example from T. M. Scanlon:

> I may know, for example, that despite Jones's pretensions to be a loyal friend, he is in fact merely an artful deceiver. Yet when I am with him I may find the appearance of warmth and friendship so affecting that I find myself thinking, although I know better, that he can be relied on after all. (1998: 35)

In Scanlon's example, I cannot shake the belief that Jones is a loyal friend, but I know I shouldn't believe this, since I know from past experience that Jones cannot be trusted.

Akrasia in the practical domain is usually defined as the phenomenon of *acting against your best judgment*—that is, acting in ways that conflict with your considered beliefs about how you ought to act. Similarly, akrasia in the epistemic domain can be defined as the phenomenon of *believing against your best judgment*—that is, holding beliefs that conflict with your considered beliefs about which beliefs you ought to hold. More generally, I'll assume that epistemic akrasia is a matter of holding beliefs that conflict with your considered beliefs about (i) which beliefs it is rationally permissible for you to hold, or (ii) which beliefs you have sufficient epistemic justification to hold, or (iii) which beliefs are supported by your evidence to a high enough degree. These are equivalent in an evidentialist framework that explains epistemic justification and rational permissibility in terms of evidential support.

We can draw a distinction between omissive and commissive forms of akrasia in both practical and epistemic domains:

- *The commissive form*: you ϕ but you believe you ought not to ϕ.
- *The omissive form*: you do not ϕ but you believe you ought to ϕ.

In the practical domain, this is the distinction between doing what you believe you shouldn't do and failing to do what you believe you should do. In the epistemic domain, this is the distinction between believing what you believe you shouldn't believe and failing to believe what you believe you should believe. The first is a sin of commission, whereas the second is a sin of omission.

Broadly construed, epistemic akrasia includes any kind of mismatch between your first-order and higher-order doxastic attitudes. The clearest cases involve a mismatch between your first-order and higher-order beliefs, but a similar kind of interlevel conflict can arise between belief and withholding. So, for example, the following combinations of doxastic attitudes seem irrational in much the same way:

(1) You believe that p, while believing that you ought not to believe that p.
(2) You believe that p, while withholding belief that you ought not to believe that p.
(3) You believe that you ought to believe that p, while believing that not-p.
(4) You believe that you ought to believe that p, while withholding belief that p.

Insofar as you're willing to entertain doubts about whether you ought to believe that p, there is some rational pressure on you to abandon your belief that p and to withhold belief instead. Moreover, if akratic belief is irrational, then the same is plausibly true of more fine-grained degrees of confidence—for instance, it seems irrational to have some degree of confidence that p, while also disbelieving or withholding belief that you ought to have that degree of confidence that p. Epistemic akrasia is not the unique preserve of outright belief.

Philosophical discussion of akrasia tends to revolve around two questions: (i) *the possibility question*: is akrasia possible? And (ii) *the rationality question*: is akrasia rationally permissible? My own view is that akrasia is sometimes possible, but never rationally permissible. I'm primarily concerned with the rationality question, but these questions are related. In particular, if akrasia is impossible, then it follows trivially that rational akrasia is impossible too. The claim that rational akrasia is impossible is much more interesting when it is combined with the view that akrasia is sometimes possible. I'll briefly discuss the possibility question, before turning to the rationality question.

9.1.1. The Possibility Question

There is a long tradition in the history of philosophy of denying that akrasia is a genuine possibility. In Plato's dialogue *Protagoras*, Socrates says:

No one goes willingly towards the bad or what he believes to be bad; neither is it in human nature, so it seems, to want to go toward what one believes to be bad instead of to the good. (358d)

In the twentieth century, this Socratic view was revived as a form of *motivational internalism*, which says that there is a tight conceptual connection between normative judgment and motivation. For instance, R. M. Hare (1952) claims that normative judgment is action-guiding in the sense that any free agent who judges that they ought to act in a certain way is thereby motivated to act in that way. Apparent cases of akratic action are explained away in one of two ways: either the agent is not free but merely acting under compulsion, or the agent is not making a genuine normative judgment but is merely paying lip service to convention and using 'ought' in an "inverted commas" sense.

These attempts to explain away the possibility of akratic action cannot do justice to the phenomenon. When I judge that I should go to the gym, I am thereby giving sincere expression to my belief about what I should do. Moreover, when I go to the coffee shop instead, I am acting freely and without compulsion, though in conflict with my best judgment. Any version of motivational internalism that denies these evident facts is guilty of exaggerating the connections between normative judgment and motivation. However, some versions of motivational internalism weaken this connection in ways that allow for the possibility of akrasia. For instance, Michael Smith (1994) and T. M. Scanlon (1998) propose that if I am fully rational, then my actions are guaranteed to conform with my normative judgments. On such views, the rational function of normative judgment is to motivate action, but there can also be dysfunctional cases in which this connection fails to hold.

Some philosophers claim that there are special reasons for skepticism about the possibility of akrasia in the epistemic domain. For example, Jonathan Adler proposes the following subjective principle of sufficient reason:

The Subjective Principle of Sufficient Reason: "When one attends to any of one's beliefs, one must regard it as believed for sufficient or adequate reasons." (2002: 26)

Adler argues that this excludes the possibility of epistemic akrasia because akratic beliefs are, by definition, those we do not regard as being held for adequate reasons. He concludes, "we cannot in full awareness believe against our best judgment on the evidence" (2002: 67).

Adler's principle only rules out "open eyed" forms of epistemic akrasia in which you believe against your best judgment "in full awareness" of doing so. Perhaps it's impossible to consciously judge that *p* while at the same time consciously judging that one ought not to do so, although I'm very much inclined to doubt it. In any case, this is not built into the definition of epistemic akrasia that I am operating with here. It's sufficient for epistemic akrasia that you believe that p while also believing that you shouldn't believe that p. It's not necessary that you activate both beliefs at the same time in making a single conscious judgment. And it seems hard to deny the possibility of this kind of epistemic akrasia even if the possibility of "open eyed" epistemic akrasia is more questionable.

Compare the phenomenon of inconsistent belief. Donald Davidson (1985) denies that you can believe explicit contradictions of the form: p and not-p. In his view, this would be too flagrant a violation of the rationality constraints that you must satisfy in order to count as a believer at all. But he acknowledges that the human mind can be fragmented in such a way that you can believe contradictory propositions even if you cannot activate both beliefs at the same time in making a single conscious judgment. Thus, he writes: "It is between these cases that I would draw the line: someone can believe p and at the same time believe not-p; he cannot believe (p and not-p)" (1985: 353).

Davidson argues for a negative answer to the possibility question by appealing to a negative answer to the rationality question. More specifically, he argues that certain forms of inconsistency and epistemic akrasia are impossible on the grounds that they violate the rationality constraints on belief. Given what we know about the extent of human irrationality, however, any rationality constraints on belief must be extremely forgiving. An argument of this kind is unlikely to rule out all forms of epistemic akrasia. At best, it rules out those explicit forms of "open eyed" epistemic akrasia that constitute particularly egregious examples of irrationality. Even so, this leaves open the possibility of milder forms of epistemic akrasia that involve some degree of fragmentation, compartmentalization, or division within the mind.

Some theories of belief rule out the possibility of omissive cases of epistemic akrasia, while ruling in the possibility of commissive cases. For example, Daniel Greco (2014a) proposes an expressivist account of normative belief, which says that the belief that you ought to believe that p has the same content as the belief that p, although it has a distinctive etiology or functional role. On this view, omissive cases of epistemic akrasia are impossible because you cannot believe that you ought to believe that p without thereby believing that p. However, commissive cases of epistemic akrasia are possible because you can believe that p while also believing that you ought not to believe that p: this is a case in which you hold inconsistent beliefs. On this view, the irrationality of epistemic akrasia can be explained in terms of inconsistency: no new epistemic norms are required.

This explanation of the irrationality of epistemic akrasia relies on controversial claims about normative belief. On many functionalist theories of belief, the dispositions involved in believing that you ought to believe that p are distinct from those involved in believing that p. For example, these beliefs are associated with different dispositions toward action: if you believe that you ought to believe that p, then you might be disposed to take actions that are calculated to induce belief that p without thereby being disposed to act as if you already believe that p. Moreover, these beliefs are associated with different dispositions toward judgment: you can judge that you ought to believe that p without thereby judging that p, since these judgments have different phenomenal character. Judging that you ought to believe that p is not a way of judging that p any more than deciding that you ought to do something is a way of deciding to do it. Hence, many functionalist theories of belief allow that you can believe that you ought to believe that p without thereby believing that p. This kind of epistemic akrasia seems irrational, but it is not impossible.

Greco's expressivism invites much the same complaint as Hare's motivational internalism: it exaggerates the role of normative judgment in motivation, including its role in motivating belief as well as action. As I noted above, we can maintain that the rational function of normative judgment is to motivate belief and action, while also allowing for dysfunctional cases in which this connection fails. This makes room for the possibility of omissive and commissive cases of akrasia in both practical and epistemic domains.

9.1.2. The Rationality Question

Akrasia—in both practical and epistemic domains—seems irrational. Indeed, it is often regarded as a paradigm case of irrationality. For example, T. M. Scanlon writes:

> Irrationality in the clearest sense occurs when a person's attitudes fail to conform to his or her own judgments: when, for example, a person continues to believe something . . . even though he or she judges there to be good reason for rejecting it, or when a person fails to form and act on an intention to do something even though he or she judges there to be overwhelmingly good reason to do it. (1998: 25)

Of course, it's one thing to note that akrasia is *sometimes* irrational, but it's another thing to claim that akrasia is *always* irrational. In making the universal claim, we need to be sure that we're not guilty of overgeneralizing from paradigm cases.

Nomy Arpaly (2003) argues that there are cases of "inverse akrasia" in which agents act rationally against their own best judgment. For instance, in Mark Twain's novel, Huckleberry Finn helps Jim to escape slavery despite believing that he ought to turn Jim over to the authorities. Arpaly argues that Huck Finn acts rationally in helping Jim because he is responsive to good reasons, despite his belief to the contrary. More generally, she claims that it can be more rational to act against one's normative judgment than to act in accordance with it. However, it doesn't follow that there is nothing irrational or rationally defective about being in an akratic predicament. Arpaly herself is very clear on this point:

> Sometimes, an agent is more rational for acting against her best judgment than she would be if she acted in accordance with her best judgment. I still agree that every agent who acts against her best judgment is, as an agent, less than perfectly rational, as the schism between best judgment and desire indicates a failure of coherence in her mind. (2003: 36)

Our question is not whether akratic beliefs and actions can be rationally based on reasons, but rather whether the overall predicament of an akratic agent can be rational. Huck Finn is no counterexample to the thesis that akrasia always involves some degree of irrationality. After all, his reasons to help Jim are also reasons for him to believe that he should help Jim. His action is rational because it is responsive to those reasons, but his moral judgment is not rationally responsive to those reasons. Arpaly's point is that the rationality of his action is not undermined by any rational defect in his moral judgment or his overall predicament. Nevertheless, the point remains that his overall predicament is less than fully rational.[1]

Some philosophers have recently argued that akrasia can be a fully rational response to misleading evidence about what rationality requires.[2] Suppose, for example, that rationality requires you to φ, while also permitting you to believe that you're rationally required not to φ. In that case, you're rationally permitted to be akratic—that is, to φ, while also believing that you're rationally required not to φ. More generally, the argument runs as follows:

(1) You can have misleading evidence about the requirements of rationality.
(2) If you can have misleading evidence about the requirements of rationality, then akrasia is sometimes rationally permissible.
(3) Therefore, akrasia is sometimes rationally permissible.

---

[1] Audi also gives similar examples: he argues that an incontinent or akratic action can be rational on balance, although "its incontinence counts to *some* degree against its rationality" (1990: 280).
[2] See Weatherson (MS), Coates (2012), and Lasonen-Aarnio (2014, forthcoming a).

In the next chapter, I'll answer this modus ponens with a modus tollens. Since akrasia is always rationally impermissible, you cannot have misleading evidence about the requirements of rationality themselves. To keep things manageable, I'll focus on the epistemic domain, although the same issue arises equally in the practical domain. My main goal in this chapter is to argue that epistemic akrasia is always rationally impermissible and to use this as a premise in arguing for the JJ principle.

Before going further, let me explain what I mean when I say that epistemic akrasia is always irrational. First, I'll argue that epistemic akrasia is always irrational in the *epistemic* sense. Perhaps there is some nonepistemic sense in which it can be rational to be epistemically akratic—say, if someone offers you enough money. I remain skeptical, but this is an issue that lies beyond the scope of the book. Second, I'll argue that epistemic akrasia is always irrational in the *propositional* sense. Since propositional rationality is necessary for doxastic rationality, it follows that epistemic akrasia is always irrational in the doxastic sense too. Third, I'll argue that epistemic akrasia always violates *ideal* standards of rationality. It's a further question whether it ever meets nonideal standards of rationality that take our human limitations into account. I'll revisit this question in section 10.5.

A note on terminology: much of my discussion is couched in terms of justification, rather than rationality. Since I'm concerned with justification by standards of rationality, I'll assume a tight connection between these concepts. More specifically, I'll assume that it's rationally permissible for you to believe that p if and only if you have sufficient justification to believe that p. I'll argue that epistemic akrasia is always rationally impermissible because you can never have sufficient justification to hold epistemically akratic beliefs. Moreover, I'll use this premise in arguing for the JJ principle.

9.2. An Argument from Epistemic Akrasia

In this section, I'll explain how we can use the premise that epistemic akrasia is always irrational in arguing for the following JJ principle:

> *The JJ Principle*: Necessarily, you have justification to believe that p if and only if you have higher-order justification to believe that you have justification to believe that p.

The basic form of argument is simple. If the JJ principle is false, then epistemic akrasia is sometimes rationally permissible. Since epistemic akrasia is never rationally permissible, it follows that the JJ principle is true. In motivating the conditional premise of this argument, I'll also rely on the following pair of assumptions:

> *The Existence Thesis*: Necessarily, there is always some doxastic attitude that you have justification to hold toward any given proposition.

> *The Justification-Rationality Linking Thesis*: Necessarily, if you have justification to hold some doxastic attitude, then it is rationally permissible for you to hold that doxastic attitude.

I'll revisit these assumptions in just a moment, but let me begin by considering each direction of the JJ principle in turn.

Let's start with the left-to-right direction of the JJ principle: if it is false, then there is a possible case in which you have justification to believe that *p*, although you don't have justification to believe that you have justification to believe that *p*. Given the existence thesis, it follows that you have justification either to disbelieve or to withhold belief in this metajustificatory proposition. Therefore, you have justification to be epistemically akratic: that is, to believe that *p* while disbelieving or withholding belief that you have justification to believe that *p*. Given the linking thesis, it follows that epistemic akrasia is rationally permissible in this case. Intuitively, however, epistemic akrasia is never rationally permissible. Therefore, the left-to-right direction of the JJ principle is true.

Now let's consider the right-to-left direction of the JJ principle: if it is false, then there is a possible case in which you have justification to believe that you have justification to believe that *p*, although you don't have justification to believe that *p*. Given the existence thesis, it follows that you have justification either to disbelieve or to withhold belief that *p*. Therefore, you have justification to be epistemically akratic: that is, to believe that you have justification to believe that *p*, while also disbelieving or withholding belief that *p*. Given the linking thesis, it follows that epistemic akrasia is rationally permissible in this case. Intuitively, however, epistemic akrasia is never rationally permissible. Therefore, the right-to-left direction of the JJ principle is true.

I gave a closely related argument for the JJ principle in Smithies (2012c).[3] Similarly, Michael Titelbaum (2015) uses the irrationality of epistemic akrasia as a premise in arguing for the Fixed-Point Thesis, according to which "mistakes *about* the requirements of rationality are mistakes *of* rationality" (2015: 253). Here is Titelbaum's official statement:

---

[3] The main difference is that I'm arguing from premises about the irrationality of epistemic akrasia, rather than the irrationality of believing Moorean conjunctions. I'll explain the connection between these claims in section 9.3.

The Fixed-Point Thesis: "No situation rationally permits an a priori false belief about which overall states are rationally permitted in which situations." (2015: 261)

The JJ principle implies a version of the fixed-point thesis in the epistemic domain: it implies that you can never have justification for false beliefs about which propositions you have justification to believe. Given the rationality-justification linking thesis, it follows that it's never rationally permissible to hold false beliefs about which beliefs are rationally permitted. In fact, the JJ principle rules out not only rational error, but also rational agnosticism, about the requirements of rationality. Moreover, it rules out agnosticism and error about not only the a priori facts about what rationality requires in general, but also the a posteriori facts about what rationality requires in your specific evidential situation. The JJ principle therefore implies a stronger version of the fixed-point thesis than the one that Titelbaum defends.[4]

I'll now defend this argument for the JJ principle against three objections. The first objection is that the existence thesis is false because there are *epistemic dilemmas* in which there is no doxastic attitude that you have justification to hold. This is a very controversial claim and, as such, it needs motivation. Generally speaking, when my evidence is not strong enough to justify either believing or disbelieving a proposition, it justifies withholding belief instead. We need good reasons to suppose there are epistemic dilemmas in which this generalization fails. Some epistemologists argue that misleading higher-order evidence generates epistemic dilemmas, but I'll against this claim in chapter 10. Even if we suppose there are some epistemic dilemmas, however, this no good reason to reject the JJ principle. To generate counterexamples to the JJ principle, we need to assume that some epistemic dilemmas arise at the first-order, but not the higher-order level, or vice versa. Without further motivation, however, this assumption seems ad hoc and implausible.

The second objection is that the justification-rationality linking thesis is false, since we cannot explain the requirements of epistemic rationality solely in terms of what your evidence gives you epistemic justification to believe. Alex Worsnip (2018) argues that there is a sui generis rational prohibition against epistemic akrasia that cannot be explained in evidentialist terms. He argues that when you have misleading higher-order evidence about what your evidence supports, your total evidence justifies holding akratic attitudes that are prohibited by this

---

[4] Titelbaum (2015: 262) allows for rational epistemic akrasia in cases that violate what he calls "situational luminosity," such as Williamson's (2011) unmarked clock case. I reply to Williamson's anti-luminosity arguments in chapter 11.

rational requirement. This gives rise to epistemic dilemmas in which there is an irresoluble conflict between the rational requirement to respect your evidence and the rational requirement to be metacoherent. According to Worsnip, this is one instance of a more general conflict between substantive and structural norms of rationality: that is, between the norm of respecting your evidence and the norm of coherence.

In chapter 10, I'll argue that there can be no conflict between the requirement to respect your evidence and the requirement to be coherent. Instead, I'll argue for a more unified conception of rationality, according to which respecting your evidence guarantees coherence. It is a familiar idea in formal theories of rationality that respecting your evidence guarantees logical or probabilistic coherence. I'll argue on similar grounds that respecting your evidence guarantees metacoherence. On this view, it's impossible to have misleading higher-order evidence about what our first-order evidence supports. This not because of an epistemic coincidence that everyone just happens to have reliable higher-order evidence about what their first-order evidence supports. Rather, it's because there are formal constraints on the evidential support relation, which guarantee that truths about the evidential support relation are always supported by any possible body of evidence.

A third objection is that this argument for the JJ principle relies on a conflation between propositional and doxastic senses of justification. On this view, epistemic akrasia is sometimes justified in the propositional sense, although it is never justified in the doxastic sense. This is because your propositional justification is always *defeated* in the presence of conflicting higher-order attitudes. If so, then we don't need the JJ principle in order to explain the sense in which epistemic akrasia is always irrational. I'll consider two versions of this proposal: the first option says that conflicting higher-order attitudes are doxastic defeaters that make your first-order beliefs doxastically unjustified, while the second option says that they are propositional defeaters that make your beliefs propositionally unjustified.

Michael Bergmann (2005) endorses the first option. He tries to explain away the appeal of higher-level requirements on justification by claiming that higher-order attitudes can serve as defeaters that make your first-order attitudes doxastically unjustified. Bergmann claims that all *believed defeaters* are *actual defeaters*: in other words, if you believe that your belief is unjustified, then it is unjustified. Similarly, he claims, if you merely withhold belief that your belief is justified, then it is unjustified. In other words, if you adopt any doxastic attitude other than belief toward the metajustificatory proposition that your belief is justified, then it is unjustified. Even so, he argues, there is no higher-level requirement on justification, according to which your belief that p is justified only if you have a justified higher-order belief that it is justified.[5]

I'll raise two objections to Bergmann's proposal about doxastic justification. First, it's not true that believing that your beliefs are unjustified is sufficient to make them unjustified. Skepticism about justified belief is not a self-fulfilling prophecy. An undergraduate student can retain justified beliefs about the external world even when she forms unjustified skeptical doubts about their justificatory status. These are epistemic analogues of the phenomenon that Arpaly (2003) calls "inverse akrasia." In these cases, the overall predicament of the akratic agent is irrational, but this irrationality cannot be traced to her first-order beliefs, since they are properly based in a way that is responsive to good reasons or evidence.

Second, Bergmann's proposal cannot explain the irrationality of epistemic akrasia. We agree that it's irrational to believe that p while disbelieving or withholding belief that you have justification to believe that p. In that sense, believing that p rationally commits you to believing that you have justification to believe that p when you consider the question. But now, we can ask, what explains the existence of this rational commitment? As James Pryor explains in the following passage, rational commitments are best explained in terms of more fundamental facts about the structure of propositional justification:

> I think we can understand rational commitments like this. Take a belief the subject happens to have, e.g., his belief in P. Consider what would be the epistemic effects of his *having (decisive) justification* for that belief. . . . If one of the effects is that the subject has decisive justification to believe Q, then his belief in P counts as rationally committing him to the belief in Q—regardless of whether he *really does* have any justification to believe P. (2004: 364)

What explains your rational commitment to form beliefs in accordance with modus ponens? The obvious answer is that if you have justification to believe the premises of a modus ponens argument, then you thereby have justification to believe the conclusion. Similarly, we can ask, what explains your rational commitment to believe that you have justification to believe that p when you believe that p? Again, the obvious answer is that if you have justification to

---

[5] Bergmann doesn't explicitly distinguish between propositional and doxastic versions of the JJ principle. He rejects the doxastic version on the grounds that it entails a vicious infinite regress, but I defended the propositional version against this objection in section 8.4.

believe that p, then you thereby have justification to believe that you have justification to believe that p. I don't see how Bergmann can explain the existence of this rational commitment without assuming that the JJ principle is true.

Clayton Littlejohn (2013) endorses the second option. He argues, in effect, that counterexamples to the JJ principle are "finkish" cases. On the one hand, you can have propositional justification to believe that p, while also having propositional justification to disbelieve or withhold belief that you have justification to believe that p. On the other hand, forming these justified higher-order attitudes thereby defeats your propositional justification to believe that p. As a result, you cannot hold these doxastic attitudes simultaneously in a way that is doxastically justified.

The main challenge for Littlejohn is to explain why forming justified higher-order attitudes should defeat your propositional justification to believe that p. On this proposal, you can have justification to form these higher-order attitudes, while also having justification to believe that p, so long as you don't actually form the higher-order attitudes in question. But then why should forming those higher-order attitudes make any justificatory difference? Littlejohn claims that it makes no sense from your own subjective perspective to maintain beliefs that are inadequately justified by your own lights. I agree, of course, but this is just to reiterate the irrationality of epistemic akrasia without explaining it. What needs to be explained is why forming the relevant higher-order attitudes should affect your propositional justification for the first-order belief in question.[6]

As far as I can see, the best strategy for opponents of the JJ principle is to argue that epistemic akrasia is sometimes justified by your evidence in both propositional and doxastic senses of the term. In the next chapter, I'll rebut an argument for this conclusion, which appeals to the possibility of misleading higher-order evidence. In the rest of this chapter, I'll argue directly for the premise that your evidence never gives you propositional justification for an akratic combination of doxastic attitudes. If so, then epistemic akrasia is never rationally permissible. I'll give three arguments for this claim, which appeal to an epistemic version of Moore's paradox (section 9.3), the thesis that belief aims at knowledge (section 9.4), and the connection between justification and reflection (section 9.5).[7]

---

[6] In more recent work, Littlejohn (2018) suggests that we should explain the irrationality of epistemic akrasia in nonevidentialist terms. This similar to Worsnip's (2018) proposal that the requirements of rationality can conflict with what your evidence supports.

[7] Horowitz (2014) argues that epistemic akrasia is normally irrational, but she makes an exception for cases in which your evidence is not "truth guiding," such as Williamson's (2011) case of the unmarked clock. In contrast, my arguments are designed to establish the more general conclusion that epistemic akrasia is always irrational.

9.3. Moore's Paradox

In its classic form, Moore's paradox is the problem of explaining what's wrong with asserting Moorean conjunctions of the following forms:

(1) p but I don't believe that p.

(2) I believe that p but it's not the case that p.

What exactly is wrong with asserting these Moorean conjunctions? On the one hand, Moorean assertions seem absurd or self-defeating in much the same way as asserting contradictions. On the other hand, these Moorean conjunctions are not contradictions; after all, they can be true. Since I am neither omniscient nor infallible, it can be true that p when I don't believe that p and it can be false that p when I believe that p. Moorean conjunctions can be true, but they cannot be asserted without absurdity. Moore's paradox is the problem of explaining why this is so.[8]

In this section, I'm concerned with a more general form of Moore's paradox. The first point I want to make is that Moore's paradox extends from assertion to belief. Believing Moorean conjunctions seems absurd in much the same way as asserting them. Moreover, it seems absurd to believe Moorean conjunctions whether or not you give linguistic expression to your belief in the speech act of assertion. Since Moore's paradox is not a purely linguistic phenomenon, it cannot be solved just by appealing to linguistic norms, such as Gricean rules of implicature. A more promising strategy is to explain the absurdity of Moorean assertions in terms of the incoherence or irrationality of the Moorean beliefs that they express. As Sydney Shoemaker writes, "An explanation of why one cannot (coherently) assert a Moore-paradoxical sentence will come along for free, via the principle that what can be (coherently) believed constrains what can be (coherently) asserted" (1996: 76).

Second, Moore's paradox can be formulated in terms of knowledge as well as belief. As Moore (1962: 277) observed, it often seems absurd to assert conjunctions of the form

(3) p but I don't know that p.

Since Moore, many epistemologists have claimed that it's always irrational to believe conjunctions of this form.[9] In section 10.4, I'll argue that it's sometimes

---

[8] See Smithies (2016b) for discussion of the classic form of Moore's paradox and Smithies (2012c) on the epistemic form of Moore's paradox.

[9] See, for example, Williamson (2000: ch. 11) and Huemer (2007).

rationally permissible to believe conjunctions of this form based on misleading evidence about the basing relation. However, these complications about the basing relation are not relevant to the more purely epistemic form of Moore's paradox:

(4) p but I'm not in a position to know that p.

In section 9.4, I'll argue that it's always irrational to believe a Moorean conjunction of this form because doing so transparently violates the aim of believing only what you're in a position to know.

Third, the epistemic form of Moore's paradox can be formulated in terms of justification as well as knowledge. Consider conjunctions of the following form:

(5) p but I don't have justification to believe that p.

Believing (5) seems irrational in much the same way as believing (4). Indeed, (4) is entailed by (5), since it's a necessary truth that I'm in a position to know that p only if I have justification to believe that p. Moreover, I have justification to believe this necessary truth on a priori grounds. Given a closure principle for justification, it follows that I have justification to believe (5) only if I also have justification to believe (4). Contraposing, if I cannot have justification to believe (4), then I cannot have justification to believe (5).

Fourth, we can distinguish two forms of Moore's paradox depending on whether the epistemic operator takes wide scope or narrow scope with respect to negation. For instance, we can distinguish the narrow scope form of (5) from the following wide-scope form:

(6) p but I have justification to believe it's not the case that p.

Believing (6) seems irrational in much the same way as believing (5). Notice that there is no wide-scope form of Moore's paradox in the case of knowledge, since knowledge is factive. In contrast, since justification is nonfactive, some instances of this form are true. Even so, believing any instance of this form is irrational. Explaining this irrationality generates another form of Moore's paradox.

Finally, as Shoemaker (1996: 78) notes, certain kinds of agnosticism give rise to Moore's paradox. Agnosticism, or withholding belief that p, is the attitude of regarding it as an open question whether p is true. Now consider the following pair of Moorean conjunctions:

(7) p but it's an open question whether I have justification to believe that p.

(8)   I have justification to believe that p but it's an open question whether p.

The doxastic attitudes expressed by (7) and (8) seem irrational in much the same way as those expressed by (5) and (6). Just as it seems irrational to believe that p while disbelieving that you have justification to believe that p, so it seems irrational to believe that p while withholding belief that you have justification to believe that p. Similarly, just as it seems irrational to believe that you have justification to believe that p while disbelieving that p, so it seems irrational to believe that you have justification to believe that p while withholding belief that p. This generates another form of Moore's paradox.

In this section, I'll use the irrationality of believing Moorean conjunctions to motivate the claim that epistemic akrasia is always irrational. The argument is simple: if epistemic akrasia is ever rationally permissible, then it is sometimes rationally permissible to believe Moorean conjunctions of the form (5)–(8). Intuitively, however, it is never rationally permissible to believe any of these Moorean conjunctions. Therefore, epistemic akrasia is never rationally permissible.

Consider the left-to-right direction of the JJ principle: if it's false, then you can have justification to be epistemically akratic: that is, to believe that p, while also disbelieving or withholding belief that you have justification to believe that p. If you have justification for holding this combination of doxastic attitudes, then it follows by closure that you can have justification to believe one of the following Moorean conjunctions:

(5) p but I don't have justification to believe that p.

(7) p but it's an open question whether I have justification to believe that p.

Now consider the right-to-left direction of the JJ principle: if it's false, then you can have justification to be epistemically akratic in a different way: that is, to believe that you have justification to believe p, while also disbelieving or withholding belief that p. If you have justification for holding this combination of doxastic attitudes, then it follows by closure that you have justification to believe one of the following Moorean conjunctions:

(6)   I have justification to believe that p but it's not the case that p.

(8)   I have justification to believe that p but it's an open question whether p.

Intuitively, however, you cannot have justification to believe these Moorean conjunctions: after all, believing them is always irrational in a distinctively Moorean way.

Someone might resist my argument on the grounds that it relies on the following principle of multipremise closure:

Multipremise Closure: Necessarily, if I have justification to believe that p, and I have justification to believe that q, then I have justification to believe that p and q.

This principle is sometimes rejected on the grounds that the epistemic probability of a conjunction can be less than the epistemic probability of its conjuncts. One standard solution to the preface paradox says that I can have justification to believe each of the claims in my book without having justification to believe the conjunction of all of them; indeed, I can have justification to believe the conjunction is false. This is because the conjunction has much lower epistemic probability than each of its conjuncts.[10]

In reply, we can endorse a probabilistic analogue of multipremise closure, which says that you have justification to believe a conjunction whenever the epistemic probability of its conjuncts is high enough to ensure that the epistemic probability of the conjunction meets a certain threshold. This probabilistic principle is strong enough to generate Moorean paradox whenever the conjuncts of a Moorean conjunction have a high enough epistemic probability. There is no principled motivation for the claim that you can have justification to believe the conjuncts of a Moorean conjunction, although their epistemic probability is never high enough to justify believing the conjunction.

Another objection exploits compartmentalization, rather than probabilities. The objection is that it can be rationally permissible to believe the conjuncts of a conjunction in separate mental compartments even if it cannot be rationally permissible to believe their conjunction within the same mental compartment. For instance, even if it is irrational to believe the explicit contradiction that p and not-p, it can be rationally permissible to believe that p while also believing that not-p, so long as these inconsistent beliefs are stored in separate compartments of the mind.

In reply, there is always some departure from ideal rationality involved in failing to integrate the contents of your beliefs. It's true that believing an explicit contradiction is more egregiously irrational than merely believing each of its conjuncts. We don't always blame people, or call them "irrational," when they have inconsistent beliefs, but they are not thereby immune from rational criticism. Compartmentalization mitigates blame, but it does not absolve us from rational criticism altogether. On the contrary, compartmentalization

---

[10] See Makinson (1965) and Christensen (2004) for this solution to the preface paradox.

is irrational precisely because it reflects a failure of coherence or integration within one's subjective perspective on the world.[11]

The argument from Moore's paradox relies on the assumption that you can never have justification to believe Moorean conjunctions of the relevant forms. The rationale for this assumption is that believing these Moorean conjunctions is absurd, irrational, or in John Koethe's (1978) terms, "Mooronic." To illustrate the point, consider the following exchange between Herman Cain and John Stewart concerning the popular movement to occupy Wall Street in 2011:

> *Herman Cain*: I don't have facts to back this up, but I happen to believe that these demonstrations are planned and orchestrated to distract from the failed policies of the Obama administration.
>
> *John Stewart*: That's all you got? Hey man, if you don't have facts to back it up, why don't you put it more out there? I don't have facts to back this up, but I think the president is a spy from an alternative universe where dinosaurs never went extinct and people are kept as pets.

Why do Cain's remarks merit Stewart's mockery? The problem is not just that Cain believes a theory that is not adequately supported by his evidence. This kind of irrationality is fairly unremarkable. The problem is that he exhibits a distinctively Moorean kind of irrationality in believing a theory that he himself admits is not adequately supported by the evidence—or, as he puts it, is not "backed up by the facts." That is what Stewart is lampooning.[12]

Some philosophers argue that you can have justification to believe Moorean conjunctions when you have misleading higher-order evidence about what you have justification to believe. Suppose I can have justification to believe false epistemological theories on the basis of compelling but fallible reasoning. For example, I might have justification to believe that skepticism about justification is true when in fact it's false. If so, then I can have justification to believe p, while also having justification to believe that I don't have justification to believe that p. By closure, it follows that I have justification to believe a Moorean conjunction of the following form: p and I don't have justification to believe that p.[13]

In the next chapter, I'll answer this modus ponens with a modus tollens. I'll argue that since you cannot have justification to believe Moorean conjunctions,

---

[11] See Stalnaker (1984: 83–84) for the view that compartmentalization constitutes a deviation from ideal rationality.

[12] Thanks to Brian McLean for recommending this example.

[13] Weatherson (MS) explicitly says in response to Feldman (2005: 108–109) that it's sometimes rationally permissible to believe akratic Moorean conjunctions when you have misleading higher-order evidence.

it follows that you cannot have justification to believe false theories of justification. In the rest of this chapter, I'll support this response by arguing that you cannot have justification to believe these Moorean conjunctions. The aim is to draw out some of the theoretical costs, in addition to the intuitive costs, of biting the bullet on this issue.

9.4. Knowledge as the Aim of Belief

It is often said that knowledge is the aim of belief. In this section, I'll argue that epistemic justification for belief is constrained by the aim of believing only what you're in a position to know. Moreover, I'll argue that epistemic akrasia is guaranteed to transparently frustrate this aim. I'll therefore conclude that you cannot have epistemic justification to be epistemically akratic.

The metaphor that belief aims at knowledge commands more agreement than specific attempts to explain what it means.[14] Before we consider rival explanations, however, we can motivate the general slogan by drawing a contrast between belief and high credence. You can have high credence that p, and you can believe that it's highly probable that p, without thereby believing that p. This is an important distinction for our purposes because high credence is not constrained by the aim of knowledge in the same way as belief. Consider the following pair of conjunctions:

(1) p but I'm not in a position to know that p.

(2) It's highly probable that p but I'm not in a position to know that p.

Believing (1) seems irrational in a distinctively Moorean way, whereas believing (2) seems perfectly fine. This is because the rationality of belief, unlike high credence, is constrained by the aim of knowledge. It's irrational to believe that p while believing that you're not in a position to know that p, but it's not irrational to have high credence that p, while believing that you're not in a position to know that p.

This explains why the so-called "Russellian retreat" is an inadequate response to skepticism. Suppose you confront an apparently cogent argument for the skeptical argument that you're never in a position to know anything at all. The Russellian retreat says that you can rationally maintain your beliefs, and regard them as justified by your evidence, without regarding them as justified strongly

---

[14] This slogan is defended in various different ways by Williamson (2000), Adler (2002), Bird (2007), Huemer (2007), Sutton (2007), and Smithies (2012e), among others.

enough to be knowledge. This is to underestimate the threat posed by skeptical arguments. If you concede that you're not in a position to know that p, then you're thereby rationally committed to withholding belief that p. It would be irrational to believe that p while also believing that you're not in a position to know that p.

Objections to the knowledge norm of belief tend to obscure the distinction between outright belief and high credence. Consider a lottery case in which your evidence makes it highly probable that your ticket will lose, although your evidence is not strong enough to put you in a position to *know* that your ticket will lose. In that case, you have justification to give high credence to the proposition that your ticket will lose, but not to believe it outright. After all, you don't have justification to judge, assert, or reason from the premise that your ticket will lose. You don't have justification to inform others that you lost, or to throw your ticket in the trash, until you hear the announcement of the results. Until you hear the results, you don't have justification to believe outright that your ticket did not win.[15]

We've already seen that there is an entailment between the following pair of Moorean conjunctions:

(3) p but I don't have justification to believe that p.
(4) p but I'm not in a position to know that p.

Since (3) entails (4), I cannot have justification to believe (3) unless I also have justification to believe (4). Intuitively, however, I cannot have justification to believe (4). It follows that I cannot have justification to believe (3) either.

We can bolster this argument by noting that these Moorean conjunctions are always unknowable in the sense that I'm never in a position to know them. Every instance of (4) is unknowable because if I'm in a position to know the first conjunct, then the second conjunct is false. Similarly, every instance of (3) is unknowable because if I'm in a position to know the first conjunct, then I have justification to believe it, which makes the second conjunct is false. A similar argument applies to the following Moorean conjunction:

(5) p but I have justification to believe that it's not the case that p.

If I'm in a position to know the first conjunct, then I have justification to believe it, but I cannot have sufficient justification to believe contradictory propositions, so it follows that the second conjunct is false. But I'm in a position to know a

[15] For the claim that you don't have justification to believe that your lottery ticket will lose, but only to have high credence that it will lose, see Nelkin (2000), Williamson (2000: 256), and Smithies (2012e: 281–282).

conjunction only if I'm in a position to know each of its conjuncts. So this conjunction is unknowable too.

How do we get from these premises about knowledge to conclusions about justification? In order to bridge this gap in the argument, we need a further premise linking justification and knowledge. In this section, I'll consider several options for bridging the gap. These provide different ways of explaining the metaphor that knowledge is the aim of belief.

One option is to endorse Williamson's knowledge rule, which says, "one should believe p only if one knows p" (2000: 255–256). If Williamson's knowledge rule is understood to concern the conditions under which you have justification to hold a belief, then it can be restated as follows:

> *The Strong K Principle*: Necessarily, you have justification to believe that p only if you know that p.

We can now use this principle to explain what's wrong with believing Moorean conjunctions. Since you cannot know Moorean conjunctions, it follows that you cannot have justification to believe them.[16]

One problem with the strong K principle is that it collapses the distinction between propositional and doxastic justification for belief. On any plausible theory of justification, you can have evidence that justifies believing that p without thereby believing that p in a way that is properly based on justifying evidence. The strong K principle excludes this possibility because you know that p only if your belief that p is properly based on justifying evidence.

We can avoid this problem by reformulating Williamson's knowledge rule in terms of what you're in a position to know, rather than what you know:

> *The Weak K Principle*: Necessarily, you have justification to believe that p only if you're in a position to know that p.

The weak K principle respects the distinction between propositional and doxastic justification, since you can be in a position to know that p without converting your epistemic position into knowledge. At the same time, the weak version is strong enough to explain what's wrong with believing Moorean

---

[16] Williamson motivates the knowledge rule for belief by appealing to his E = K thesis, which says that your evidence is what you know. In earlier work, Williamson denies that all justified beliefs are knowledge, since false beliefs can be made probable by what you know (2000: 185). In later work, however, he says that a belief is justified only if your evidence entails that it is true (2011: 157). If you should believe only what is entailed by your evidence, and all your evidence is knowledge, then you should believe only what you know (or what is entailed by what you know). This excludes the possibility of justified false beliefs.

conjunctions like (3) and (4). After all, these Moorean conjunctions are un-knowable in the sense that we're never in a position to know them, so it follows that we cannot have justification to believe them.

There are other reasons to reject both strong and weak versions of the K prin-ciple. In deception cases and Gettier cases, you can have justification to believe that p although you're not in a position to know that p because it's false that p or because it's accidentally true that p. In Alvin Goldman's (1976) fake barn case, for example, there's a barn ahead, but you're not in a position to know this, since you're in fake barn country. Even so, you have justification to believe there's a barn ahead, since you're not in a position to know that you're in fake barn country. The K principle gives the wrong results in this case.[17]

Moreover, the K principle fails to explain the intuitive difference between Goldman's original version of the fake barn case and a revised version in which you discover that you're in fake barn country. In the original version, you have justification to believe there's a barn ahead, although you're not in a position to know this. In the revised version, in contrast, your justification is defeated as soon as you discover that you're in fake barn country. In that case, you should withhold belief that there's a barn ahead, since you know you're not in a posi-tion to know whether it is real or fake.

These two versions of the fake barn case provide a clear illustration of Donald Rumsfeld's infamous distinction between "known unknowns" and "unknown unknowns." In both cases, the fact that there is a barn ahead is unknowable to you. The difference is that this fact is unknowably unknowable in the original version, but it is knowably unknowable in the revised version. This makes a jus-tificatory difference, since you have justification to believe there is a barn ahead in the original version, but not in the revised version. The K principle obscures this justificatory difference between these cases, since it implies that you have justification to believe there is barn ahead in neither case.

To explain the justificatory difference between these cases, we might invoke the following principle:

The ~K~K Principle: Necessarily, you have justification to believe that p only if it's not knowably unknowable that p, i.e. you're not in a position to know that you're not in a position to know that p.

Notice that the ~K~K principle is logically weaker than the K principle: it is entailed by the K principle, but not vice versa. Even so, it is strong enough

---

[17] Williamson (forthcoming) claims that your beliefs in such cases are not justified, but merely excusable. I argued against this proposal in section 3.4.

to explain why you cannot have justification to believe akratic Moorean conjunctions of the form (3) and (4). After all, these Moorean conjunctions are not only unknowable, but also knowably unknowable. Moreover, the ~K~K principle avoids the objections to the K principle. It is not falsified by deception cases and Gettier cases in which you have justification to believe that p, although it's unknowable that p. Moreover, it explains the justificatory difference between the original and revised versions of the fake barn case. All this supports the ~K~K principle.

The problem with the ~K~K principle is not that it's false, but that it's not strong enough to explain all the data that needs to be explained. Compare and contrast the following pair of Moorean conjunctions:

(6) p but I don't have justification to believe that p.

(7) p but it's an open question whether I have justification to believe that p.

Intuitively, the doxastic attitudes expressed by (6) and (7) are irrational in much the same way. To be sure, the former seems more egregiously irrational than the latter, but both seem less than fully rational. However, the ~K~K principle cannot explain this. As we've seen, (6) is knowably unknowable: I cannot know that p while knowing that I don't have justification to believe that p. In contrast, the same is not true of (7), since I can know that p while knowing that I regard it as an open question whether I have justification to believe that p. Knowledge is compatible with this kind of higher-order agnosticism. Although there is certainly something rationally problematic in this overall predicament, this is compatible with Arpaly's (2003) core insight that rationality in belief and action is not always undermined by higher-order irrationality.

In order to give a unified explanation of these Moorean phenomena in terms of the idea that belief aims at knowledge, we need to invoke the following stronger thesis:

The JK Principle: Necessarily, you have justification to believe that p only if you have justification to believe that you're in a position to know that p.[18]

The JK principle implies the ~K~K principle, but not vice versa. It is superior because it gives a unified explanation of why you cannot have justification for the doxastic attitudes expressed by (6) and (7). If you have justification to believe that p, then the JK principle entails that you have justification to believe that you're in a position to know that p. Given closure, it follows that you

---

[18] I argue for the JK principle on similar grounds in Smithies (2012e).

have justification to believe that you have justification to believe that p. Given uniqueness, it follows that you don't have justification to disbelieve or to withhold belief that you have justification to believe that p.

The JK principle can be motivated in much the same way as the ~K~K principle. In the revised fake barn case, knowing that I'm in fake barn country defeats my justification to believe that there's a barn before me. In much the same way, knowing that I'm *probably* in fake barn country defeats my justification to believe that there's a barn before me. Indeed, even knowing that there's a *serious chance* that I'm in fake barn country defeats my justification to believe that there's a barn before me. More generally, anything that defeats my justification to believe that I'm in a position to know that p thereby defeats my justification to believe that p. Contraposing, I have justification to believe that p only if I have justification to believe that I'm in a position to know that p.

In summary, the JK principle is motivated in the same way as the ~K~K principle, although it explains a wider range of intuitive data. In particular, it explains the irrationality of agnosticism-based forms of epistemic akrasia as well as error-based forms. Admittedly, the error-based forms of epistemic akrasia are more egregiously irrational than the agnosticism-based forms. But it would be implausible to deny that there's any rational tension exhibited by the agnosticism-based forms of epistemic akrasia.[19]

Let me sum up. It's often said that knowledge is the aim of belief, but what exactly does this mean? I've argued that the K principle is too strong, while the ~K~K principle is too weak, to serve as a plausible interpretation of this slogan. Instead, I've argued that we should accept the JK principle, which captures an important sense in which epistemic justification for belief is constrained by the aim of believing what you're in a position to know. If the JK principle is true, then you cannot have justification for the doxastic attitudes expressed by akratic Moorean conjunctions. Therefore, epistemic akrasia is always irrational.

9.5. Justification and Reflection

In chapter 8, I argued that justification is the epistemic property that makes beliefs and other doxastic attitudes stable under justified reflection. In this section, I'll argue that akratic combinations of doxastic attitudes are not stable under justified reflection. I therefore conclude that you cannot have

---

[19] Williamson (2011, 2014) argues that there are cases of "improbable knowing" that serve as counterexamples to the JK principle, but not the ~K~K principle. I'll discuss these cases, including Williamson's case of the unmarked clock, in section 11.5.

justification for akratic combinations of doxastic attitudes. Here is the argument in outline:

(1) You have justification to hold a doxastic attitude only if you have some basis on which that doxastic attitude can withstand justified reflection.
(2) There is no basis on which akratic attitudes can withstand justified reflection.
(3) Therefore, you cannot have justification to be epistemically akratic.

One virtue of this argument is that it can be extended from beliefs to other doxastic attitudes, including more fine-grained degrees of confidence. Unlike the argument of the previous section, it doesn't assume that knowledge is the aim of belief. If knowledge is the aim of belief, then rationality requires conforming your beliefs to your reflections about what you're in a position to know. If not, rationality still requires conforming your beliefs to your reflections about what you have justification to believe. The argument of this section complements the argument of the previous section, but doesn't presuppose it.

I defended the first premise of the argument in section 8.1. Justification is the epistemic property that gives your beliefs the potential to remain stable under justified reflection. If justified reflection on your evidence would result in your holding a belief, then you have justification to hold the belief on the basis of your evidence. If justified reflection on your evidence would result in withholding belief, then you don't have justification to hold the belief in question. A justified process of reflection cannot result in withholding beliefs that you have justification to hold at that time. After all, justified doxastic processes result in justified doxastic attitudes.[20]

The second premise can be motivated by considering what justified reflection consists in. The point of engaging in critical reflection on the justificatory status of your beliefs is to bring your beliefs into line with your higher-order reflections about which beliefs you have justification to hold. The reflective process has two stages: first, reflecting on which beliefs you have justification to hold; and second, revising your beliefs in light of these reflections. If both stages are fully justified, then your higher-order beliefs are justified and your first-order beliefs are brought into line with your higher-order beliefs. Hence, the result of justified reflection is that you believe that p just in case you have a justified higher-order belief that you have justification to believe that p. Akratic beliefs are not stable under justified reflection because either your higher-order

---

[20] Of course, there are finkish cases in which the process of reflection itself changes which beliefs you have justification to hold, but we can safely set these cases aside. See section 8.1 for some brief discussion.

reflections are unjustified or your beliefs are not rationally responsive to your justified higher-order reflections.

One virtue of this argument is that it explains the irrationality of epistemic akrasia in the full range of cases. Just as it's irrational to believe that p while believing that you don't have justification to believe that p, so it's irrational to believe that p while withholding belief that you have justification to believe that p. Similarly, it's irrational to refrain from believing that p while believing that you have justification to believe that p. In general, rational reflection requires bringing your beliefs into alignment with your justified higher-order reflections about which beliefs you have justification to hold. Moreover, the argument extends from akratic belief to other doxastic attitudes, including more fine-grained degrees of confidence. Just as it's irrational to believe that p while disbelieving or withholding belief that you have justification to believe that p, so it's irrational to have some degree of confidence that p while disbelieving or withholding belief that you have justification for that degree of confidence that p.

How might friends of the rationality of epistemic akrasia respond to this argument? One option is to reject the first premise on the grounds that justified reflection can result in abandoning justified beliefs; or, equivalently, that rational reflection can result in abandoning rational beliefs. Allen Coates endorses this option:

> It is a rational policy to abandon beliefs one judges to be irrational, since this is likely to yield a more rational set of beliefs over the long run. This would allow us to conclude that it is rational of Watson to abandon his belief regardless of whether that belief is rational. But . . . we would then be unable to conclude that Watson's belief is in fact irrational. Instead, we could only conclude that it is rational of Watson to abandon his belief even if that belief is in fact rational. (2012: 121)

It is hard to make sense of this proposal without drawing a distinction between two senses of 'rationality'. How can it be rationally permissible for Watson to hold a belief at a time when he is also rationally required to abandon it? If he is rationally required to abandon the belief at some time, then it is not rationally permissible for him to hold it at that time. So, the proposal generates a contradiction.

A more charitable reading of Coates's proposal avoids contradiction by invoking Maria Lasonen-Aarnio's (2010) distinction between *rationality* and *reasonableness*. Rationality is a matter of proportioning your beliefs to the evidence, whereas reasonableness is a matter of exercising dispositions that generally tend to yield rationally justified beliefs. In these terms, Coates's proposal is that it is sometimes reasonable to exercise dispositions that sacrifice rationality in the short term in order to increase rationality in the long term. To paraphrase: "It is a *reasonable* policy to abandon beliefs one judges to be *irrational*, since this is likely to yield a more rational set of beliefs over the long run." On this view, epistemic akrasia is sometimes reasonable, even if it is never rational. This proposal avoids contradiction, but at the cost of undermining the objection to my argument. In fact, I will argue for an extremely similar view in chapter 10.

Lasonen-Aarnio (forthcoming a) argues for the opposite view, that epistemic akrasia is sometimes rational, although it is never reasonable. Presumably, she would reject the second premise on the grounds that akratic beliefs can withstand reflection in a justified way. The rationale for the second premise is that a belief cannot withstand justified reflection when you have higher-order justification to believe that you don't have justification for the belief in question. But Lasonen-Aarnio maintains that you sometimes have justification to maintain your beliefs even in the face of justified higher-order beliefs that you should abandon them. As she says, "That one should believe that one shouldn't φ doesn't entail that one shouldn't φ" (2014: 343).

The problem with this reply is that it results in an extremely revisionary conception of rational reflection. This connects with a central theme in the work of Tyler Burge: namely, that the unity of one's reflective perspective on the world depends on the existence of immediate rational connections between one's first-order beliefs and one's higher-order reflections on those beliefs. Here is a representative passage:

> If in the course of critical reasoning I reasonably conclude that my belief that a given person is guilty rests entirely on unreasonable premises or bad reasoning, then it normally follows immediately both for the perspective of the review and for the perspective of the reviewed belief that it is reasonable to give up my belief about guilt or look for new grounds for it. . . . This is because the first- and second-order perspectives are the *same* point of view. The reviewing of reasons that is integral to critical reasoning includes the review and reviewed attitudes in a single point of view. (1996: 110)

We can bring this out by contrasting first-person and third-person perspectives on the requirements of epistemic rationality. If I rationally believe that it's irrational for you to believe that p, it doesn't follow that it's irrational for you to believe that p. After all, in the third-person case, I'm subject to what Burge calls "brute errors" in which I form rational but false beliefs about what you're rationally required to believe. In contrast, if I rationally believe that it's irrational for me to believe that p, it does follow that it's irrational for me to believe that p.

After all, rationality requires that I revise my beliefs whenever I rationally believe they're irrational for me to hold. So, in the first-person case, I'm immune from brute errors in which I form rational but false beliefs about what I'm rationally required to believe. According to Burge, this is an essential feature of the unity of my reflective perspective on the world.

Friends of rational epistemic akrasia are committed to denying this. As we'll see in chapter 10, they argue that I'm subject to brute ignorance or error about the requirements of rationality when I have misleading higher-order evidence about what my evidence supports. In such cases, there are no immediate rational connections between my first-order beliefs and my higher-order beliefs. On this view, there is no principled epistemic difference between my first-person perspective on my own beliefs and my third-person perspective on the beliefs of other people.

What is at stake here is the idea that *metacoherence* is a constitutive ideal of rationality. On Burge's view, it is a constitutive ideal of rationality that you have a unified perspective on the world in which your first-order beliefs are coherently integrated with your higher-order beliefs. If we allow for the rationality of epistemic akrasia, then we lose this attractive conception of ideal rationality as requiring coherent integration between first-order beliefs and higher-order reflections within a single unified perspective or point of view. This is not something we should give up too quickly. Abandoning the rational ideal of metacoherence is a serious theoretical cost.

Friends of rational epistemic akrasia tend to argue that this is a theoretical cost that we're forced to accept. After all, rationality always requires respecting your evidence. But respecting your evidence sometimes requires violating metacoherence when you have misleading higher-order evidence about what your evidence supports. Therefore, rationality sometimes requires violating metacoherence. In the next chapter, I'll argue that respecting your evidence guarantees metacoherence, since there are interlevel constraints built into the evidential support relation. In particular, any body of evidence that justifies believing that p thereby justifies believing that your evidence justifies believing that p. On this view, you cannot have misleading higher-order evidence about what your evidence is or what it supports. Hence, your evidence never justifies violating metacoherence.

10
Higher-Order Evidence

This chapter addresses a puzzle about the rationality of epistemic akrasia. What generates the puzzle is the assumption that you can have misleading evidence about anything at all, including facts about what your evidence supports. But if you can have misleading higher-order evidence about what your evidence supports, then it seems to follow that epistemic akrasia is sometimes rationally permissible. Intuitively, however, epistemic akrasia is always rationally impermissible. And yet these plausible assumptions are inconsistent.[1]

In the previous chapter, I argued that epistemic akrasia is always rationally impermissible, and I used this as a premise in arguing for the JJ principle:

> *The JJ Principle*: Necessarily, you have justification to believe that *p* if and only if you have higher-order justification to believe that you have justification to believe that *p*.

In this chapter, I'll address the objection that epistemic akrasia is sometimes rationally permissible when you have misleading higher-order evidence about what your evidence supports. On this view, there are counterexamples to the JJ principle in which your evidence justifies believing that *p*, although your evidence doesn't justify believing that it justifies believing that *p*, or vice versa.

I'll defend the JJ principle against this objection by appealing to the internalist version of accessibilism proposed in chapter 7. On this version of accessibilism, the JJ principle is true because facts about your evidence and facts about the evidential support relation are luminous in the sense that you're always in a position to know with certainty whether or not they obtain. Hence, you cannot have misleading higher-order evidence about what your evidence is or what your evidence supports. I call this view "Upward Push."

The main challenge for this view is to explain away the appearance of counterexamples in which you seem to have misleading higher-order evidence about what your evidence supports. I'll respond to this challenge by drawing on the distinctions drawn in earlier chapters between propositional and doxastic senses of justification and ideal versus nonideal conceptions of rationality. This

---

[1] This puzzle is also discussed in Feldman (2005), Christensen (2010a), Greco (2014a), Horowitz (2014), Titelbaum (2015), Littlejohn (2018), Worsnip (2018), and Lasonen-Aarnio (forthcoming a).

will give me the opportunity to say more about how I'm understanding the role of idealization in the theory of epistemic justification.

What's distinctive about my view is not the distinction between ideal and nonideal conceptions of rationality, but my account of what ideal rationality consists in. My view is that ideal rationality in the epistemic domain requires not only logical coherence and evidential coherence, but also metacoherence: in other words, your beliefs should cohere not only with evidence and logic, but also with your higher-order beliefs. I'll use this metacoherence requirement to argue for an analogy between logic and evidence: just as logical coherence requires logical omniscience, so evidential coherence requires evidential omniscience.

Here is the plan for this chapter. I begin by presenting the puzzle about epistemic akrasia (section 10.1) and a menu of solutions (section 10.2). Next, I defend my own solution against apparent counterexamples (section 10.3). In later sections, I develop this proposal by considering its application to ideally rational agents (section 10.4) and nonideally rational agents (section 10.5). I conclude with some general remarks about the nature of epistemic rationality and the role of idealization in epistemology (section 10.6).

10.1. A Puzzle about Epistemic Akrasia

Our puzzle about the rationality of epistemic akrasia can be stated in the form of an inconsistent triad:

(1) You can have misleading higher-order evidence about what your evidence supports.

(2) If you can have misleading higher-order evidence about what your evidence supports, then epistemic akrasia is sometimes rationally permissible.

(3) Epistemic akrasia is always rationally impermissible.

These three propositions are individually plausible, but they are jointly inconsistent. Which of them should we abandon?

Proposition (1) seems plausible on the grounds that we can have misleading evidence about any subject matter. Consider testimony: when an apparently reliable source tells you that p, you thereby have evidence that p is true. But the testimony of an apparently reliable source can be mistaken. In that case, you have misleading evidence that p is true. Moreover, you can receive mistaken testimony about pretty much anything, including what your evidence supports. So, you can have misleading higher-order evidence about what your evidence supports, just as you can have misleading evidence about anything else.

Proposition (2) seems plausible on the grounds that we are sometimes rationally permitted to form false beliefs on the basis of misleading evidence. In particular, we are sometimes rationally permitted to form false beliefs about what our evidence supports on the basis of misleading higher-order evidence. Suppose your evidence supports p, while at the same time supporting the false proposition that your evidence doesn't support p. In that case, it seems rationally permissible for you to hold akratic beliefs: that is, to believe that p, while believing it is rationally impermissible for you to believe that p.

Proposition (3) seems plausible on the grounds that epistemic akrasia is a kind of incoherence within your own subjective perspective on the world. Fully rational agents are not incoherent in this way. They do not hold beliefs while also believing them to be rationally impermissible. Instead, they hold beliefs only when they believe it is rationally permissible to do so. We humans are not fully rational agents, of course, since we sometimes violate the requirements of epistemic rationality precisely by exhibiting this kind of akratic incoherence within our own subjective perspective on the world.

I'll examine this puzzle as it arises within the framework of *evidentialism*, the thesis that which doxastic attitudes it is rationally permissible for you to hold at any given time depends solely on your evidence at that time. This assumption is inessential, since the same puzzle arises for any view that allows for the rational permissibility of false beliefs about the requirements of rationality. Indeed, these puzzles arise equally in connection with practical and epistemic requirements of rationality. Even so, evidentialism provides a convenient framework for my discussion and one that is presupposed in much of the recent literature on epistemic akrasia. Some authors have recently argued that rejecting evidentialism is the key to solving our puzzle about the rationality of epistemic akrasia, whereas I'll argue that the puzzle can be solved within the framework of evidentialism.[2]

What is higher-order evidence? Thomas Kelly, who originally coined the phrase, defines someone's higher-order evidence as "evidence about her evidence" (2005: 186). The puzzle concerns higher-order evidence about what your evidence *supports*, rather than higher-order evidence about your *response* to the evidence. But Kelly assumes that these two things are connected because evidence about your response to the evidence gives you evidence about what your evidence supports. For example, he argues that peer disagreement gives you higher-order evidence that your evidence doesn't support what you think it does, since your equally reasonable peer holds a different attitude on the basis of the same evidence. As Kelly puts the point, "The fact that a (generally)

---

[2] Christensen (2010a), Littlejohn (2018), and Worsnip (2018) propose solutions to the puzzle that abandon evidentialism.

reasonable individual believes hypothesis H on the basis of evidence E is some evidence that it is reasonable to believe H on the basis of E. The beliefs of a reasonable individual will thus constitute *higher-order* evidence, evidence about the character of her first-order evidence" (2005: 186).

In this chapter, I'll examine cases in which you have misleading higher-order evidence about the rationality of your own response to the evidence. I'll argue against Kelly's assumption that this provides misleading higher-order evidence about what your evidence supports. To focus the discussion, here is a representative example from a recent paper by Sophie Horowitz:

> *Sleepy Detective*: Sam is a police detective, working to identify a jewel thief. He knows he has good evidence—out of many suspects, it will strongly support one of them. Late one night, after hours of cracking codes and scrutinizing photographs and letters, he finally comes to the conclusion that the thief was Lucy. Sam is quite confident that his evidence points to Lucy's guilt, and he is quite confident that Lucy committed the crime. In fact, he has accommodated his evidence correctly, and his beliefs are justified. He calls his partner, Alex. "I've gone through all the evidence," Sam says, "and it all points to one person! I've found the thief!" But Alex is unimpressed. She replies: "I can tell you've been up all night working on this. Nine times out of the last ten, your late-night reasoning has been quite sloppy. You're always very confident that you've found the culprit, but you're almost always wrong about what the evidence supports. So your evidence probably doesn't support Lucy in this case." (2014: 719)

Horowitz describes the abstract structure of the example as follows. Sam has first-order evidence about the case, which justifies believing that Lucy is the thief. In due course, Sam acquires higher-order evidence from Alex, which justifies believing that his first-order evidence doesn't justify believing that Lucy is the thief. Now, the following question arises. What does Sam's total evidence, including both his first-order and his higher-order evidence, give him justification to believe?

Horowitz outlines three contrasting reactions to this example:

> *Level Splitting*: Sam has first-order justification to believe that Lucy is the thief, but he has higher-order justification to believe that he doesn't have first-order justification to believe that Lucy is the thief.

> *Downward Push*: Sam doesn't have first-order justification to believe that Lucy is the thief, since he has higher-order justification to believe that he doesn't have first-order justification to believe that Lucy is the thief.

Upward Push: Sam has first-order justification to believe that Lucy is the thief, so he also has higher-order justification to believe that he has first-order justification to believe that Lucy is the thief.

As she explains, each of these reactions has problems. Upward Push seems to respect the force of Sam's first-order evidence while ignoring his higher-order evidence. Conversely, Downward Push seems to respect the force of Sam's higher-order evidence while ignoring his first-order evidence. Level Splitting has the advantage that it respects both Sam's first-order evidence and his higher-order evidence, but this too comes at a serious cost. On this view, Sam's total evidence justifies epistemic akrasia.

These three reactions to the example correspond to three different strategies for solving the epistemic puzzle:

The first solution—Level Splitting—is to argue by modus ponens from (1) and (2) against (3). On this view, epistemic akrasia is sometimes rationally permissible when you have misleading higher-order evidence about what your evidence supports.

The second solution—Downward Push—is to reconcile (1) and (3) by rejecting (2). On this view, epistemic akrasia is never rationally permissible because misleading higher-order evidence about your first-order evidence always defeats the justification provided by your first-order evidence.

The third solution—Upward Push—is to argue by modus tollens from (2) and (3) against (1). On this view, epistemic akrasia is never rationally permissible because you cannot have misleading higher-order evidence about what your first-order evidence supports.

While the first two solutions have been extensively discussed in the literature, the third has not yet received the same level of critical scrutiny. This is not entirely surprising. After all, Upward Push seems extremely implausible at first glance. Intuitively, it is hard to accept that Sam can rationally remain confident that his beliefs are supported by evidence in the face of higher-order evidence that he is too exhausted to evaluate the evidence properly. This seems like an irrational form of dogmatism. And, theoretically, it is hard to motivate the claim that you cannot have misleading evidence about what your evidence supports, since you can have misleading evidence about almost anything else. Why should facts about evidential support be immune from misleading evidence? My aim in this chapter is to answer these challenges and to argue that Upward Push is the correct solution to the puzzle about epistemic akrasia.

10.2. Solving the Puzzle

In this section, I'll motivate Upward Push by reviewing some of the main problems with Downward Push and Level Splitting. As I'll explain, much of the theoretical motivation for denying the possibility of misleading higher-order evidence emerges from reflection on the problems for these alternative solutions to the epistemic puzzle.

10.2.1. Level Splitting

The first solution to the puzzle of epistemic akrasia—Level Splitting—is to argue by modus ponens from (1) and (2) against (3). On this view, epistemic akrasia is sometimes rationally permissible—namely, when you have misleading higher-order evidence about what your evidence supports. For example, Sam's total evidence justifies believing that Lucy is the thief, while also justifying the higher-order belief that his evidence doesn't justify believing that Lucy is the thief. Therefore, Sam's total evidence justifies epistemic akrasia.[3]

I argued against Level Splitting in the previous chapter, but here is a brief summary of the main points. If epistemic akrasia is sometimes rationally permissible, then it is sometimes rationally permissible to believe Moorean conjunctions, such as the following:

(1)   Lucy is the thief, but I don't have justification to believe that she is the thief.

Intuitively, however, it is never rationally permissible to believe these Moorean conjunctions. Moreover, this intuition can be supported by argument. In general, it's rationally permissible to believe that p only if it's not knowably unknowable that p. Otherwise, believing that p transparently violates the aim of believing only what you're in a position to know. And yet Moorean conjunctions like (1) are knowably unknowable, since being in a position to know the first conjunct makes the second conjunct false. Therefore, it's never rationally permissible to believe them.

Williamson (2014) avoids this objection by endorsing a much stronger version of the knowledge norm for belief, which says that it's rationally permissible

---

[3] Proponents of Level Splitting include Williamson (2011), Coates (2012), Hazlett (2012), Lasonen-Aarnio (forthcoming a), and Weatherson (MS).

to believe that p only if you know (or you're in a position to know) that p. But this version of the knowledge norm is implausible. First, it seems vulnerable to Gettier-style counterexamples, such as Goldman's fake barn case, in which you rationally believe there's a barn ahead, although you're not in a position to know there's a barn ahead because (unbeknown to you) you're surrounded by fake barns. Second, it cannot explain the intuitive distinction between "known unknowns" and "unknown unknowns." For example, if you discover that you're in fake barn country, then it's no longer rationally permissible for you to believe that there's a barn ahead, since you know that you're not in a position to know whether it's real or fake. Third, it cannot explain why it seems irrational to have high confidence in Moorean conjunctions like (1), or to believe probabilistic versions of Moorean conjunctions like (2) and (3):

(2) Lucy is the thief, but I *probably* don't have justification to believe that she is the thief.
(3) Lucy is the thief, but I *almost certainly* don't have justification to believe that she is the thief.

Williamson argues that there are cases of "improbable knowing" in which it's rationally permissible for a person to believe probabilistic Moorean conjunctions like (2) and (3). These are cases in which you're in a position to know that p, although it's evidentially probable that you're not in a position to know that p. However, Williamson's argument for improbable knowing can be blocked by assuming that evidence is luminous, an assumption that I'll defend in chapter 11.

Perhaps the most fundamental problem with Level Splitting is that it yields a revisionary conception of rational reflection. On this view, it's sometimes rationally permissible to believe that p while simultaneously disbelieving or withholding belief that it's rationally permissible to believe that p. This seems irrational because the whole point of reflection is to conform your beliefs to your higher-order reflections about which beliefs it's rationally permissible for you to hold. Given these requirements on rational reflection, it is never rationally permissible for us to believe that p while simultaneously disbelieving or withholding belief that it's rationally permissible to believe that p.

Maria Lasonen-Aarnio (forthcoming a) invokes her distinction between rationality and reasonableness to explain away the intuition that epistemic akrasia is always irrational. To a first approximation, rationality is a matter of respecting your evidence, whereas reasonableness is a matter of exercising more general dispositions that tend to result in respecting your evidence under normal circumstances. She argues that epistemic akrasia is sometimes rational when your total evidence is misleading about itself, although it is never reasonable because it always manifests more general dispositions that tend to result in ignoring evidence in other cases. For example, if Sam continues to believe that Lucy is the thief, while doubting that his belief is justified by the evidence, then he manifests a general disposition to ignore evidence about his own cognitive limitations. As Lasonen-Aarnio writes, "The problem with akratic subjects ... is that they fail to exercise basic epistemic competence" (forthcoming a).

I'll briefly present two objections to Lasonen-Aarnio's proposal. The first objection is that it fails to explain what seems wrong with epistemic akrasia in ideally rational agents. By definition, ideally rational agents are perfectly sensitive to their evidence. As a result, they are epistemically akratic when and only when their total evidence is misleading about what it supports. They can respect their evidence when it requires epistemic akrasia without thereby manifesting general dispositions that lead them to disrespect their evidence in other cases. Intuitively, however, epistemic akrasia seems just as bad for ideally rational agents as it is for nonideally rational agents like us. Lasonen-Aarnio's proposal cannot explain this, since her account implies that their beliefs are not only perfectly rational, but also perfectly reasonable. They are formed on the basis of dispositions that are perfectly sensitive to the evidence.

The second objection is that Lasonen-Aarnio cannot explain what seems right about mild forms of epistemic akrasia in nonideal agents. In section 10.5, I'll argue that epistemic akrasia is sometimes the most reasonable option available to nonideal agents like us, since it manifests general dispositions that enable our first-order beliefs to remain grounded in evidence without requiring us to be dogmatically confident in our higher-order beliefs. It seems too strong to say that epistemic akrasia is always unreasonable, just as it seems too strong to say that violations of probabilistic coherence are always unreasonable. Even if probabilistic coherence is an ideal of rationality, it is sometimes reasonable for nonideal agents to violate this rational ideal. Similarly, even if metacoherence is an ideal of rationality, it is sometimes reasonable for nonideal agents to violate this rational ideal.

In summary, Lasonen-Aarnio's proposal is too weak to explain what seems wrong with extreme forms of epistemic akrasia in ideally rational agents, but it is too strong to explain what seems right about mild forms of epistemic akrasia in nonideally rational agents. To be clear, I have no objection to Lasonen-Aarnio's general distinction between rationality and reasonableness, but only to the way she applies it. In fact, I'll use much the same distinction, but in the opposite way. Lasonen-Aarnio claims that epistemic akrasia is *sometimes rational but never reasonable*, whereas I'll argue that epistemic akrasia is *sometimes reasonable, but never rational*. To put the point in my own favored terminology, epistemic akrasia is sometimes permissible by nonideal standards of rationality, although it's never permissible by ideal standards of rationality.

What is at stake is the idea that metacoherence is a constitutive ideal of rationality. Denying this is a serious theoretical cost. Proponents of Level Splitting argue that this is a cost we must pay, since rationality always requires respecting your evidence, and your total evidence can support epistemic akrasia when you have misleading higher-order evidence about what your evidence supports. It is therefore difficult to explain the irrationality of epistemic akrasia within an evidentialist framework. In response, I'll argue that respecting your evidence guarantees metacoherence, since your evidence cannot be misleading about what it supports. Hence, the rational ideal of metacoherence can be explained as a byproduct of the rational ideal of respecting your evidence.

10.2.2. Downward Push

The second solution to the puzzle of epistemic akrasia—Downward Push—is to reconcile (1) and (3) by rejecting (2). On this view, epistemic akrasia is never rationally permissible, despite the fact that you can sometimes have misleading higher-order evidence about what your evidence supports. This is because misleading higher-order evidence always defeats the evidential support that is provided by your first-order evidence.[4]

Consider Sam, the sleepy detective: he has first-order evidence E that justifies believing that Lucy is the thief, but then he acquires misleading higher-order evidence D that justifies believing that E doesn't justify believing that Lucy is the thief after all. Does his total evidence (that is, E plus D) justify believing that Lucy is the thief? Richard Feldman (2005) says no: this is because Sam's higher-order evidence D defeats the evidential support that is provided by his first-order evidence E. On this view, you can have misleading evidence about what some proper subset of your evidence supports, but your total evidence cannot be misleading about itself. As a result, your total evidence cannot rationally permit epistemic akrasia.

This view is attractive because it promises to explain the irrationality of epistemic akrasia without ruling out the possibility of misleading higher-order evidence. Unfortunately, however, this combination is hard to sustain. I'll argue that Downward Push cannot explain the irrationality of epistemic akrasia without either distorting the facts about evidential support or abandoning evidentialism altogether. It accommodates the force of higher-order evidence at the cost of distorting or neutralizing the force of first-order evidence.

---

[4] Downward Push is the dominant view in the literature on disagreement: its proponents include Feldman (2005), Elga (2007), and Christensen (2007b). Kelly (2010) proposes a qualified version of this view on which the degree of defeat provided by your higher-order evidence depends on its strength compared with your first-order evidence. This is what he calls the "Total Evidence View."

The basic problem, as David Christensen (2010) explains, is that higher-order evidence doesn't function like standard examples of defeat. In the standard examples, I have some evidence e that makes it probable that p, but then I acquire some defeating evidence d, which reduces the probability that p when combined with e. John Pollock and Joseph Cruz distinguish two kinds of defeaters: a *rebutting* defeater provides evidence that a conclusion is false, whereas an *undercutting* defeater "attacks the connection between the reason and the conclusion, rather than attacking the conclusion itself" (1999: 196). Either way, if d defeats the evidential support that e provides for p, then the probability that p given e and d is lower than the probability that p given e alone.

The problem is that higher-order evidence doesn't affect the evidential probability of a conclusion in the way that rebutting and undercutting defeaters do. It doesn't provide evidence against the conclusion, or "attack the connection" between the evidence and the conclusion, but rather leaves this connection intact. This is most clearly apparent in the case of logical truths, which are entailed by any possible body of evidence, and hence which always have evidential probability 1. Even so, the point holds more generally. If the best explanation of Sam's evidence is that Lucy is the thief, then it is evidentially probable that Lucy is the thief, whether or not Sam is capable of appreciating this fact. Suppose Sam acquires misleading evidence that he has taken a reason-distorting drug that impairs his competence in performing abductive inference. It nevertheless remains true that the best explanation of his evidence is that Lucy is the thief, and hence that this hypothesis is probable given his evidence. As Christensen writes, "HOE, unlike ordinary undercutting evidence, may leave intact the connections between the evidence and the conclusion. It's just that the agent in question is placed in a position where she can't trust her own appreciation of those connections" (2010: 198).

I'll consider two potential responses to this objection. The first response is to insist that higher-order evidence does affect the extent to which your first-order evidence supports its conclusion. On this view, higher-order evidence about your deficiencies in logical reasoning can reduce the degree to which logical truths are supported by your evidence. Therefore, degrees of evidential support cannot be understood as probabilities, since logical truths always have evidential probability 1. Abandoning probabilism is already a serious theoretical cost, but this is also a symptom of a more general problem—namely, that we cannot codify any general principles about the nature of evidential support. Consider any general principle of the following form:

If you have evidence e, then the proposition that p is supported to degree n.

The problem is that we can always find counterexamples in which you have evidence e, but the proposition that p is not supported to degree n, since you have misleading higher-order evidence about what your evidence supports.

To avoid this problem, we need to state these principles about evidential support in a way that avoids the possibility of misleading higher-order evidence. But this is to invoke what Christensen (2010: 203–204) calls "the Uber-rule": an overarching rule that specifies the degree of evidential support for every proposition given every possible body of evidence. The idea is that you cannot have misleading evidence about the Uber-rule, since it already takes all of your evidence into account. One problem with this response is that it obscures the distinctive function of higher-order evidence. It is one thing to acquire evidence that makes it less likely that the best explanation of all the evidence is that Lucy is the thief, but it's another thing to acquire evidence that you cannot competently perform inference to the best explanation. The Uber-rule collapses the distinction between these two different kinds of evidence. Another problem is that it's not clear that the Uber-rule can be stated in a finite and nontrivial way, since it is just an infinite list of recommendations for every possible evidential situation. Hence, this response threatens to collapse into a form of epistemic particularism on which there are no general principles about the nature of evidential support that can be finitely and nontrivially stated.[5]

The second response is to abandon evidentialism. As I read him, this is Christensen's view. On this view, rationality sometimes requires you to refrain from believing what your evidence supports—in particular, when you have misleading higher-order evidence about what your evidence supports. The function of higher-order evidence is not to defeat your first-order evidence by undercutting the evidential support that it provides. Rather, it requires you to "bracket" your first-order evidence in the sense that you refrain from using this evidence in forming beliefs. Christensen writes:

> In accounting for the HOE about the drug, I must in some sense, and to at least some extent, put aside or bracket my original reasons for my answer. In a sense, I am barred from giving a certain part of my evidence its due. (2010: 195)

On this view, higher-order evidence is "rationally toxic" in the sense that agents who possess such evidence are thereby required to violate an epistemic ideal— namely, believing what their total evidence supports. Higher-order evidence generates rational dilemmas in which agents are guaranteed to violate one of

---

[5] Christensen (2010a: 203–204) and Lasonen-Aarnio (2014: 330–336) press these objections.

the following epistemic ideals: (i) respecting their first-order evidence, (ii) respecting their higher-order evidence, or (iii) integrating their first-order beliefs with their higher-order beliefs in a metacoherent way.

Alex Worsnip (2018) also defends the view that misleading higher-order evidence generates rational dilemmas. On the one hand, rationality requires respecting your evidence. On the other hand, rationality requires coherence, including metacoherence. These rational requirements—to respect your evidence and to be coherent—come into conflict when your total evidence is misleading about itself. In such cases, respecting your evidence requires epistemic akrasia, whereas coherence requires avoiding epistemic akrasia. According to Worsnip, this is just one instance of a more general conflict between substantive and structural conceptions of rationality: that is, between the rational norm that you should respect your evidence and the rational norm that you should be coherent.

In my view, there are good reasons to resist this bifurcated conception of rationality, according to which norms of coherence can conflict with norms of respecting your evidence. Instead, I'll defend a more unified conception of rationality, according to which respecting your evidence guarantees coherence. Although this is a large issue, I'll make three points that support the unified conception over the bifurcated conception.

The first point concerns theoretical unity. Other things being equal, it is better to explain rational norms of coherence in terms of the rational norm of respecting your evidence, rather than bifurcating these norms of rationality. This is not only for reasons of parsimony, but also because there are plausible connections between these requirements, which we would do well do respect. On the one hand, coherence requires respecting your evidence, since a fully coherent agent is one whose beliefs cohere with all her evidence, and not just with her other beliefs. On the other hand, respecting your evidence requires being coherent, since your total evidence never supports an incoherent set of beliefs. It is a familiar idea that there are formal constraints on the evidential support relation, which ground the rational requirement to be logically or probabilistically coherent. In the same way, I'll argue, there are interlevel constraints on the evidential support relation, which ground the rational requirement to be metacoherent. On this view, respecting your evidence guarantees not only logical or probabilistic coherence, but also metacoherence.[6]

The second point concerns the explanatory costs associated with bifurcating norms of evidence and coherence. How should we weigh these competing

---

[6] See Kolodny (2008) for the view that respecting your evidence guarantees coherence.

norms against each other in cases when they conflict? On the bifurcationist view, there are rational dilemmas in which you're guaranteed to violate either norms of coherence or norms of respecting your evidence. Nevertheless, it's plausible that some ways of weighing these norms are more rational than others. For example, the intuitive motivation for Downward Push is that it's more rational for Sam, the sleepy detective, to bracket his evidence that Lucy is the thief than to be either dogmatic or epistemically akratic. The explanatory problem is that if we bifurcate norms of evidence and coherence, then there are no unified principles of rationality that we can appeal to in weighing these norms against each other. As a result, we cannot explain the intuitive facts about when norms of coherence outweigh norms of respecting the evidence and vice versa. Instead, we seem forced to regard them as brute facts that cannot be further explained.

The same problem doesn't arise on a unified conception of rationality, since there are no fundamental conflicts between norms of coherence and norms of respecting your evidence. Ideally rational agents are never forced to choose between coherence and respecting the evidence. As I'll explain in section 10.5, we nonideal agents are sometimes forced to make this choice, but only because we are less than ideally rational. Since nonideal rationality always involves some deviation from ideal rationality, we sometimes need to make trade-offs between competing dimensions of ideal rationality. Some of these trade-offs are better than others. But there is no theoretical pressure to take these facts about nonideal rationality as primitive and unexplained. On the contrary, we can appeal to principles of ideal rationality in explaining which trade-offs are optimal for nonideally rational agents given their contingent doxastic limitations.

The third point concerns the value of coherence. Does coherence have any genuine epistemic value or is this just a fetish for neat and tidy belief systems? If respecting your evidence guarantees coherence, then we can explain the value of coherence as an essential aspect of the value of respecting your evidence. If these norms come into conflict, however, then the value of coherence is much more difficult to explain. We might try to explain the value of coherence instrumentally in terms of its conduciveness toward respecting the evidence. But it is hard to motivate the claim that coherence has this kind of instrumental value when you can be fully coherent without respecting your evidence. Moreover, it is hard to explain why coherence should have any added value if you can respect your evidence without being coherent. Of course, this skepticism about the value of coherence is grist for the mill of Level Splitting, which says that rationality requires respecting your evidence even when this results in incoherence. But if respecting your evidence guarantees coherence, then the value of coherence cannot be so easily dismissed.

10.2.3. Upward Push

The third solution to the puzzle—Upward Push—is to argue by modus tollens from (3) and (2) against (1). If you can have misleading higher-order evidence about what your evidence supports, then epistemic akrasia is sometimes rationally permissible. However, epistemic akrasia is always rationally impermissible. Therefore, you cannot have misleading higher-order evidence about what your evidence supports.[7]

I'll defend a version of Upward Push that draws on the version of accessibilism proposed in section 7.2. On this view, you cannot have misleading higher-order evidence about what your evidence is or what it supports. This is because facts about your evidence, and facts about what it supports, are luminous with probability 1. If you have evidence e that makes it epistemically probable that p to degree n, then it's certain for you that

(1) I have evidence e.

(2) If I have evidence e, then it is epistemically probable for me that p to degree n.

(3) Therefore, it is epistemically probable for me that p to degree n.

In short, Upward Push explains the rational impermissibility of epistemic akrasia by appealing to the luminosity of evidence and evidential support.

In the next chapter, I'll defend the claim that your *evidence* is luminous against Williamson's (2000: ch. 4) anti-luminosity argument. Here is what's at stake. If your evidence is not luminous, then failures of luminosity generate cases in which it's evidentially probable that p, although it's evidentially improbable that it's evidentially probable that p. These are cases in which your evidence makes it rational to adopt akratic attitudes, such as the following:

(i) Believing that p, while believing that you don't have justification to believe that p; or

(ii) Having high confidence that p, while also having high confidence that you don't have justification for high confidence that p.

In order to rule out the possibility of rational epistemic akrasia, we are committed to the thesis that evidence is luminous.[8]

---

[7] Proponents of Upward Push include Kelly (2005), Smithies (2012c), Van Wietmarschen (2013), Schoenfield (2015b), and Titelbaum (2015). In the literature on the epistemic significance of disagreement, this is sometimes called "the Right Reasons View."

[8] Horowitz (2014) and Titelbaum (2015) allow for rational epistemic akrasia in cases in which your total evidence is misleading about itself, but it is hard to see why epistemic akrasia should be rational in some cases and not others.

My main aim in this chapter is to defend the claim that *evidential support facts* are luminous. The key idea is that truths about the evidential support relation have the same status as truths about logic. Logical truths are entailed by any possible body of evidence. As such, they are supported by any possible body of evidence to the highest possible degree. On a probabilistic conception of evidential support, all logical truths have evidential probability 1. This is why you cannot have misleading evidence about logical truths. After all, the logical truths are evidentially certain given any possible body of evidence.

Similarly, I claim, truths about evidential support, like logical truths, hold necessarily. As such, they are entailed by any possible body of evidence and thereby supported to the maximal degree. On a probabilistic conception of evidential support, all necessary truths about evidential support have evidential probability 1. This is why you cannot have misleading evidence about evidential support facts. After all, the evidential support facts are evidentially certain given any possible body of evidence.

Logical truths and truths about the evidential support relation are examples of what David Chalmers (2011a) calls "epistemic necessities." These are truths that hold throughout the space of epistemic possibilities construed as maximally specific propositions about the actual world that cannot be ruled out conclusively on a priori grounds alone. Another example is the thesis of evidentialism itself: if it is true, then it is epistemically necessary, and so evidentially certain given any possible body of evidence. This means that you cannot have misleading evidence about whether evidentialism is true. After all, evidentialism—like any other epistemic necessity—is evidentially certain given any possible body of evidence.[9]

Why should we accept the view that truths about your evidence, and truths about what your evidence supports, are luminous with probability 1? My answer is that it provides the most attractive overall solution to our puzzle about the rationality of epistemic akrasia. Unlike Level Splitting, it rules out the possibility that epistemic akrasia is rationally permitted by your total body of evidence. Unlike Downward Push, it rules out this possibility without distorting the evidential support relation or abandoning evidentialism altogether. Upward Push has the advantage that it enables us to explain the rational impermissibility of epistemic akrasia within a formally tractable and well-behaved evidentialist framework.

The main problem with Upward Push is that it seems to ignore the force of your higher-order evidence. On this view, you cannot have misleading higher-order evidence about what your evidence is or what it supports. Nevertheless,

---

[9] See Littlejohn (2018) and Lasonen-Aarnio (forthcoming a) for the objection that you can have misleading evidence about the truth of evidentialism.

you can have misleading higher-order evidence about the rationality of your response to the evidence. For example, Sam has higher-order evidence that he is too exhausted to evaluate the evidence properly. Upward Push seems to give Sam a license to ignore this evidence, since he has justification to be certain that his evidence justifies believing that Lucy is the thief. Intuitively, however, it would be irrational and dogmatic for Sam to stick to his guns in the face of higher-order evidence that his belief is irrationally formed. The main goal of the next section is to address this objection.

10.3. The Certainty Argument

David Christensen (2007) argues against Upward Push on the grounds that it licenses an irrational form of dogmatism in response to higher-order evidence. To illustrate the point, let's consider how Sam should respond when Alex tells him that he is too exhausted to evaluate the evidence properly, and hence that the evidence probably doesn't justify his belief that Lucy is the thief. Upward Push says that Sam's evidence not only justifies believing that Lucy is the thief, but also justifies being certain that his evidence justifies believing that Lucy is the thief. Given a plausible closure principle, it follows that Sam has justification to be certain that what Alex says is false, since Alex says his evidence doesn't justify believing that Lucy is the thief. In other words, Sam has justification to dismiss Alex's warning by using the following Certainty Argument:

(1) It is certain that my evidence justifies believing that Lucy is the thief.
(2) If it is certain that my evidence justifies believing that Lucy is the thief, then it is certain that what Alex says is false.
(3) Therefore, it is certain that what Alex says is false.

Intuitively, however, it seems irrationally dogmatic for Sam to dismiss Alex's testimony by using the Certainty Argument. The objection is that Upward Push cannot explain what's wrong with using the Certainty Argument in this way.

If we accept Downward Push or Level Splitting, then it's easy to explain what's wrong with using the Certainty Argument. On either of these views, Sam lacks justification to accept the first premise. Indeed, Sam has justification to reject the first premise, since he has misleading higher-order evidence that justifies doubting that his belief is supported by his evidence. The disagreement between Downward Push and Level Splitting concerns whether these justified higher-order doubts undermine his first-order justification to believe that Lucy is the thief. But there is background agreement that Sam has justification to doubt that his evidence supports believing that Lucy is the thief.

Christensen's objection, in short, is that Upward Push cannot explain what is wrong with using the Certainty Argument. In fact, this objection has two parts. The objection is that Upward Push cannot explain either of the following intuitive data points:

(1) *The Negative Datum*: It's not rationally permissible for Sam to be certain that his evidence supports believing that Lucy is the thief.
(2) *The Positive Datum*: It is rationally permissible for Sam to doubt that his evidence supports believing that Lucy is the thief.

I'll defend Upward Push against this objection by using two distinctions that I've drawn upon elsewhere in this book. I'll explain the negative datum by appealing to the distinction between *propositional* and *doxastic* senses of rational justification. I'll argue that although Sam has propositional justification to be certain that his belief is supported by evidence, he cannot be certain in a way that is doxastically justified. Meanwhile, I'll explain the positive datum by appealing to the distinction between *ideal* and *nonideal* standards of rational justification. I'll argue that Sam is required by ideal standards of rationality to be certain that his belief is supported by evidence, although he is required by nonideal standards of rationality to doubt that his belief is supported by evidence. Here, I'm assuming that Sam is a nonideally rational agent, but I'll explain why these conclusions don't extend to ideally rational agents in the next section.

Let me begin with the negative datum. Upward Push says that Sam has propositional justification to be certain that his belief is supported by evidence. Even so, it doesn't follow that if he is certain that his belief is supported by evidence, then he is doxastically justified. After all, doxastic justification requires not only propositional justification, but also proper basing. I'll argue that nonideally rational agents cannot use the Certainty Argument in a way that is doxastically justified, since their doxastic dispositions are not sufficiently sensitive to the evidence to satisfy the requirement of proper basing. Given that Sam is a nonideally rational agent, he cannot use the Certainty Argument in a way that is doxastically justified.

In a slogan, doxastic justification is propositional justification plus proper basing. That is, a belief is doxastically justified if and only if it is properly based on the facts that make it propositionally justified. In an evidentialist framework, these are facts about what the evidence supports. But what it is for a belief to be properly based on evidence? It is not sufficient that there is a causal relation between the belief and the evidence. The belief must be held in a way that manifests the right kind of counterfactual sensitivity to what the evidence supports. Hence, a belief is doxastically justified only if it is held on the basis of exercising doxastic dispositions that are counterfactually sensitive to the evidence that makes the belief propositionally justified. More specifically, exercising the same doxastic dispositions in similar counterfactual circumstances tends to yield beliefs that are propositionally justified by the evidence. In short, doxastically justified beliefs are safe from the absence of propositional justification.

For illustration, let's consider Ernest Sosa's (2003) version of the problem of the speckled hen (see section 11.2). If my experience represents that the hen has 48 speckles, and I have no defeaters, then I have propositional justification to believe that the hen has 48 speckles. Even so, if I were to believe that the hen has 48 speckles, my belief would be doxastically unjustified. This is because my belief is held on the basis of doxastic dispositions that are not counterfactually sensitive to the evidence in the right kind of way. Exercising the same doxastic dispositions could easily yield beliefs that are not justified by the evidence. For instance, I could easily believe that the hen has 47 or 49 speckles when my experience represents that it has 48 speckles. Similarly, I could easily believe that the hen has 48 speckles when my experience represents that it has 47 or 49 speckles. My doxastic dispositions are too coarse-grained to be counterfactually sensitive to these fine-grained differences in the representational contents of my experience. Given my doxastic limitations, I cannot form the belief in a way that satisfies the proper basing condition for doxastic justification.

Now let's revisit the Certainty Argument. Sam has propositional justification to accept the premises and the conclusion of the Certainty Argument. Even so, he cannot use the Certainty Argument in a way that is doxastically justified. This is because his doxastic dispositions are not counterfactually sensitive to what the evidence supports. By exercising the very same doxastic dispositions, Sam could easily become certain that what Alex says is false when in fact it is true. After all, his doxastic dispositions are not sensitive to the distinction between "good cases" in which Alex's testimony is false and "bad cases" in which it is true. If Sam is disposed to use the Certainty Argument in the good case, then he's disposed to use it in the bad case too. But using the Certainty Argument in the bad case yields beliefs that are not supported by the evidence. So, even in the good case, he cannot use the Certainty Argument without violating the proper basing condition for doxastic justification.

This suffices to explain the negative datum. It is irrational for Sam to use the Certainty Argument in the following sense: if he were to use it, then his beliefs would be doxastically unjustified and irrational. However, it doesn't follow that he lacks propositional justification to use the Certainty Argument in the first place. It just means that his doxastic dispositions are not sensitive enough to the evidence to enable him to convert his propositional justification into doxastic justification. If he uses the Certainty Argument, then he violates the proper basing condition for doxastic justification, since his doxastic attitude is not safe from the absence of propositional justification.

The challenge that remains is to explain not only the negative datum that it's not rational for Sam to be *certain* that his belief is supported by evidence, but also the positive datum that it is rational for him to *doubt* that his belief is supported by evidence. My response here appeals to the distinction between ideal and nonideal standards of rationality. Sam is required by ideal standards of rationality to be certain of the premises of the Certainty Argument. Since he is a nonideally rational agent, however, he is incapable of satisfying these ideal standards of rationality: he cannot be rationally certain of the premises of the Certainty Argument. He is therefore subject to nonideal standards of rationality that take his contingent doxastic limitations into account. Moreover, these nonideal standards of rationality require him to doubt the premises of the Certainty Argument.

The distinction between ideal and nonideal standards of rationality is familiar from discussions of the logical omniscience requirements that are built into many formal theories of rationality.[10] On any probabilistic conception of evidential support, for example, all logical truths have evidential probability 1. Therefore, ideal rationality requires that we are certain of all logical truths. More carefully, it requires that we are certain of any logical truth toward which we adopt any doxastic attitude at all. However, we humans are incapable of satisfying this requirement. Logical omniscience is simply beyond our limited human competence. Hence, we are subject to nonideal standards of rationality that sometimes require us to hold doxastic attitudes that violate logical omniscience. For example, we are sometimes required by nonideal standards of rationality to withhold belief in logical truths when they're too complicated for us to prove, and to disbelieve logical truths when we receive misleading expert testimony that they're false.

I claim that what goes for logical truths goes equally for truths about what your evidence supports. Truths about evidential support always have evidential probability 1. Hence, ideal rationality requires that we are always certain of what our evidence supports. Since we are nonideal agents, however, we are incapable of satisfying these ideal standards of rationality. As such, we are subject to nonideal standards of rationality that take our contingent human limitations into account. These nonideal standards of rationality sometimes require us to entertain doubts about what our evidence supports. Therefore, ideal rationality requires us to use the Certainty Argument, whereas nonideal rationality requires us to refrain from using it.

---

[10] See Christensen (2004: ch. 6) for a helpful discussion of the role of idealization in formal epistemology. In Smithies (2015a), I defend the claim that rationality requires logical omniscience against Christensen's (2007a) objections.

Of course, there are well-known objections to the thesis that rationality requires logical omniscience. Many of the same objections can be leveled against the thesis that rationality requires evidential omniscience. For example, these requirements are much too demanding to serve as standards that we can reasonably use in holding each other to account in our doxastic practices. After all, we are humanly incapable of satisfying them. But then how can they serve as useful standards of rationality for limited agents like us?

This is why we need to draw the distinction between ideal and nonideal standards of rationality in the first place. The requirements of nonideal rationality are constrained by our human limitations—and evidence about our human limitations—in a way that the requirements of ideal rationality are not. Perfect epistemic rationality is an ideal that outstrips our limited human capacities. Even so, our reasoning can be more or less rational insofar as we are capable of approximating toward the ideal. Nonideal rationality is a matter of coming as close to the ideal as can be reasonably expected given our limited human capacities. Of course, the extent of these limitations varies from person to person and for a single person over time. My epistemic limitations change not only as I develop intellectual skills over the course of my lifetime, but as my ability to deploy them waxes and wanes over the course of the day. Nonideal requirements of rationality are sensitive to all this contingent and context-sensitive messiness.

I should add that this distinction between ideal and nonideal standards of rationality is not just an ad hoc maneuver designed to defend the theory against counterexamples. Any theory of rationality needs some version of this distinction to cope with cases in which limited agents are unable to comply with its requirements. We need theories of nonideal rationality to explain what it's "reasonable" for us to do when we know or have misleading evidence that we're unable to satisfy the requirements of ideal rationality. On this view, the value of nonideal rationality is to be explained derivatively as a means toward the end of ideal rationality. The requirements of nonideal rationality have normative force for creatures like us only because complying with them is the best we can do to approximate more closely toward ideal rationality.[11]

In an evidentialist framework, ideal rationality is simply a matter of respecting your evidence. If your evidence supports believing that p, then ideal rationality requires you to believe that p, whether or not you're capable of rationally

---

[11] One promising avenue is to explain ideal rationality in terms of the methods that it would be best for you to follow, while explaining nonideal rationality in terms of the methods that it would be best for you to try to follow: these come apart when you try to follow methods without success. See Lasonen-Aarnio (2010) for this distinction, and Schoenfield (2015b) for arguments that the steadfast response to misleading higher-order evidence is the best method for us to follow, but not the best method for us to try to follow, since trying to follow this method often leads to failure.

believing that p on the basis of your evidence. In contrast, nonideal rationality sometimes requires you to disrespect your evidence. For example, suppose my evidence supports believing that p, although I also have higher-order evidence that I am overestimating the extent to which my evidence supports believing that p. In that case, ideal rationality requires that I believe that p, whereas nonideal rationality requires that I withhold belief that p. Hence, nonideal standards of rationality sometimes require you to disrespect your evidence in response to higher-order evidence about your reliability in responding to the evidence.

As we've seen, Christensen (2010) argues that higher-order evidence about your response to the first-order evidence can sometimes require you to "bracket" the first-order evidence in question. After his conversation with Alex, for example, Sam is rationally prohibited from believing that Lucy is the thief, despite the fact that his evidence supports this conclusion. This proposal can seem puzzling from an evidentialist standpoint. Doesn't ideal rationality require respecting all your evidence? If your total evidence supports p, then ideal rationality requires believing that p, whatever evidence you have about your ability to respond to the evidence. It seems to me that Christensen's proposal is best reconfigured as a proposal about nonideal rationality, rather than ideal rationality. Ideal rationality always requires you to believe what your evidence supports, whereas nonideal rationality sometimes requires that you bracket your evidence when you have higher-order evidence that you're unable to respond to it properly. As a result, nonideal rationality sometimes requires you to believe what is not supported by your evidence.

What is the function of higher-order evidence about your response to the evidence? On this view, it doesn't defeat the support that is provided by your evidence and thereby affect which response is required by ideal standards of rationality. Rather, it affects which response to the evidence is required by nonideal standards of rationality. The requirements of nonideal rationality depend not only on our actual human limitations, but also on our higher-order evidence about those limitations. That is why Sam's conversation with Alex requires him to reduce his confidence that his beliefs are supported by evidence, since it gives him new evidence about his cognitive limitations. Beforehand, nonideal rationality permits him to believe with a high degree of confidence, although not with certainty, that his evidence supports believing that Lucy is the thief. Afterward, however, nonideal rationality requires him to significantly reduce his degree of confidence—for instance, to disbelieve or to withhold belief that his evidence supports believing that Lucy is the thief.[12]

---

[12] In Smithies (2015a) I argued that higher-order evidence defeats doxastic justification by undermining proper basing; see also van Wietmarschen (2013) for a similar proposal about the

To conclude, my aim in this section was to explain what's wrong with using the Certainty Argument. Ideal rationality requires using the Certainty Argument. Nevertheless, nonideally rational agents like Sam cannot satisfy the requirements of ideal rationality in a nonaccidental way because their doxastic dispositions are not sufficiently sensitive to what their evidence supports. Therefore, nonideal rationality requires nonideally rational agents like Sam to refrain from using the Certainty Argument.

10.4. Ideally Rational Agents

In the previous section, I argued that nonideal agents cannot rationally use the Certainty Argument. In this section, I'll argue that this conclusion cannot be extended from nonideally rational agents (NRAs) to ideally rational agents (IRAs). The requirements of ideal rationality, including the requirement to use the Certainty Argument, apply equally to NRAs and IRAs alike. The difference is that IRAs are capable of satisfying these requirements, whereas NRAs are not. This is because IRAs, unlike NRAs, are perfectly sensitive to their evidence.

NRAs cannot rationally use the Certainty Argument because they violate the proper basing condition for doxastic justification. If they use it in the good case in which they have misleading higher-order evidence that their response to the evidence is irrational, then they are disposed to use it also in the bad case in which their higher-order evidence is accurate. This is because their doxastic dispositions are not sufficiently sensitive to the evidential difference between good cases and bad cases. As a result, beliefs formed in the good case by using the Certainty Argument are doxastically unjustified and irrational. In contrast, IRAs can rationally use the Certainty Argument in the good case because their doxastic dispositions are perfectly sensitive to what their evidence supports. As a result, they satisfy the proper basing condition for doxastic justification. I'll now defend this claim against a series of objections.

The first objection is that IRAs cannot rationally use the Certainty Argument because (just like NRAs) they are disposed to use it in bad cases as well as good cases. IRAs are not immune from the effects of sleep deprivation, hypoxia, or reason-distorting drugs. After all, ideal rationality doesn't require having an iron constitution! But the effect of these distorting influences is to make them form beliefs in ways that are insensitive to what their evidence supports.

epistemic significance of disagreement. I now think the function of higher-order evidence is better understood in terms of its effects on nonideal rationality, rather than proper basing, since it may not impact on the reliability of your response to the evidence. Thanks to Sophie Horowitz for helpful discussion here.

Therefore, IRAs are disposed to use the Certainty Argument in the bad case—say, when they are under the influence of reason-distorting drugs.

In reply, we needn't accept the principle "Once an IRA, always an IRA." An IRA can become an NRA by ingesting reason-distorting drugs. Similarly, an IRA can be in danger of becoming an NRA if there are reason-distorting drugs in her environment. But the mere danger of becoming an NRA doesn't make her an NRA any more than the danger of becoming insane makes her insane. After all, her first-order dispositions are perfectly sensitive to what the evidence supports, although she also has a second-order disposition to acquire first-order dispositions that are not perfectly sensitive to what the evidence supports. The effect of ingesting reason-distorting drugs is precisely to change her doxastic dispositions in ways that make them less than ideally rational.

The key point is that an IRA doesn't exercise the same doxastic dispositions in the good case and the bad case alike. In the good case, her doxastic dispositions are perfectly sensitive to the evidence, although she has misleading higher-order evidence to the contrary. In the bad case, in contrast, her doxastic dispositions are not perfectly sensitive to the evidence, since her higher-order evidence to the contrary is accurate. In contrast, NRAs exercise many of the same dispositions in good cases and bad cases alike, since our doxastic dispositions are not perfectly sensitive to what the evidence supports. After all, you don't have to change our doxastic dispositions by giving us reason-distorting drugs in order to induce rational mistakes. We routinely get accurate evidence of our own cognitive imperfection when we are tired and careless. A dogmatic thinker who uses the Certainty Argument is equally disposed to use it whether she is in the good case or the bad case.

The second objection is that an IRA cannot use the Certainty Argument, since otherwise this would allow her to become rationally certain that she is an IRA. This is an implausible result, since an IRA can surely have misleading higher-order evidence that she is less than ideally rational—say, because she has ingested reason-distorting drugs. Moreover, it is not rationally permissible for an IRA to use the Certainty Argument to dismiss this kind of misleading higher-order evidence. As Christensen writes, "Cognitively perfect agents will in general respect misleading evidence scrupulously. And I don't see how the mere fact of our agent's cognitive perfection would make it rational for her simply to disregard the misleading evidence in this case" (2010: 191–192).

In reply, an IRA cannot use the Certainty Argument to become rationally certain that she is an IRA. She can only use it to become rationally certain that a hypothesis is false when it is inconsistent with the facts about what her evidence supports. An IRA can be rationally certain of what her evidence supports, and she can be rationally certain that her beliefs are supported by her evidence, since these facts are luminously accessible. Nevertheless, she cannot be rationally certain that her beliefs are *properly based* on the evidence, since these facts about proper basing are not luminously accessible. Hence, an IRA can never be rationally certain that she is an IRA. At best, she can use the conclusions of the Certainty Argument to increase her confidence that she is an IRA. In some cases, this may be the best explanation of why all of her current beliefs are supported by the evidence. In other cases, this abductive inference may be undermined by much stronger background evidence that she is not an IRA. Either way, she can never be rationally certain about the correct causal explanation of her beliefs.

The third objection is that this reply has Moorean consequences. On this view, an IRA can have evidence that justifies believing that p, while also having misleading higher-order evidence that her belief that p is not properly based on this justifying evidence. If so, then her total evidence justifies believing the following Moorean conjunction:

(1) p and my belief that p is unjustified.

Moreover, since it is an a priori truth that justified belief is necessary for knowledge, she also has justification to infer another Moorean conjunction:

(2) p and I don't know that p.

This might be regarded as a *reductio* of the proposal. When your evidence justifies believing that your belief that p is doxastically unjustified, and hence that you don't know that p, don't you thereby have justification to abandon your belief that p? If so, then your evidence cannot justify believing these Moorean conjunctions. As Christensen remarks, "the rationality of first-order beliefs cannot in general be divorced from the rationality of certain second-order beliefs that bear on the epistemic status of those first-order beliefs" (2007: 18).

I'll argue in reply that your evidence can sometimes justify believing these Moorean conjunctions after all. The key point is that you can have misleading evidence about doxastic justification, although not about propositional justification. In an evidentialist framework, you cannot have misleading higher-order evidence about whether your beliefs are *supported* by the evidence, but you can have misleading higher-order evidence about whether your beliefs are *properly based* on the evidence. Hence, your belief that p can be justified when you have a justified but false higher-order belief that it is unjustified. Similarly, you can know that p when you have a justified but false higher-order belief that you don't know that p.[13]

---

[13] This is the grain of truth in Williamson's (2014) claim that there are cases of improbable knowing in which you know that p, although it's evidentially probable that you *don't* know that p. What I deny is that there are cases in which you know that p, although it's evidentially probable that you're not even in a *position* to know that p.

To see how these Moorean beliefs can be justified, we need to distinguish two sorts of cases. In some cases, you have justification to believe that your beliefs are not supported by your evidence—say, because you are too confident or not confident enough. In those cases, you have justification to revise your beliefs by raising or lowering your degree of confidence. In other cases, you have justification to believe that your beliefs are supported by the evidence but not properly based on the evidence. In those cases, you don't have justification to revise your degree of confidence, but merely to maintain your current degree of confidence in a way that is properly based on the evidence.

To illustrate the point, let's consider Jonathan Schaffer's (2010) debasing demon, whose favorite activity is to ensure that your beliefs are not properly based on the evidence, but without disturbing the coincidence between your beliefs and the evidence. Suppose you know that your beliefs are properly based on evidence, but then you acquire misleading evidence that you're the victim of the debasing demon. What should you do? Nothing at all. There is no rational pressure to revise your beliefs in any way. The rational response is simply to maintain the justified beliefs you already have on the basis on which you already hold them. After all, you know that your beliefs are supported by the evidence, although you don't know that they are properly based on the evidence, since you have misleading evidence to the contrary. In this case, you should just continue to believe that p, while believing—falsely, as it happens—that your belief is improperly based on the evidence.

There is no conflict here with the principle that it's rationally permissible to believe that p only if it's not knowably unknowable that p (see sections 9.4 and 10.2.1). You cannot know Moorean conjunctions of the form (1) or (2) because knowing the first conjunct makes the second conjunct false. Moreover, you can know that you cannot know them on the basis of the proof just given. Even so, it doesn't follow that it's not rationally permissible to believe these Moorean conjunctions. This is because the principle should be understood in terms of what you're in an *epistemic position* to know, rather than what you *can* know. This distinction might seem sophistical at first glance, but it matters crucially in cases where your epistemic position is finkish. These are cases in which you're in an epistemic position to know that p, but you cannot convert your epistemic position into knowledge because your epistemic position changes in the process.

The Moorean conjunctions (1) and (2) are a case in point. Let's suppose you're in a position to know that p, but you don't know that p because your belief is based on wishful thinking. Moreover, you know this fact about your psychology. In that case, you're in a position to know that p, but you're also in a position to know (indeed, you know) that you don't know that p. Hence, you're in a position to know the conjuncts of the Moorean conjunction "p and I don't know that *p.*" Given a plausible closure principle, it follows that you're in a position to know the Moorean conjunction itself. We needn't reject the closure principle in order to explain why you cannot convert your epistemic position into knowledge. You cannot do so because your epistemic position is finkish. If you come to know the first conjunct, then this makes the second conjunct false, and thereby undercuts your epistemic position to know the whole conjunction.[14]

I don't claim that your *evidence* for these Moorean conjunctions is always finkish.[15] When these conjunctions are false, you can form doxastically justified beliefs on the basis of misleading evidence that they are true. Suppose you have misleading higher-order evidence that your belief is improperly based on your first-order evidence. For instance, you might have misleading evidence that you're the victim of a debasing demon. In that case, you're not in a position to know Moorean conjunctions of forms (1) and (2), since they're false. But while these Moorean conjunctions are unknowable, they are not knowably unknowable, since you have misleading evidence that they are true. You therefore have propositional justification to believe them. Moreover, you can be doxastically justified in believing these Moorean conjunctions on the basis of misleading evidence that they are true.[16]

This is exactly the predicament of an IRA who has misleading evidence that she is not an IRA. An IRA can have first-order evidence that justifies believing that *p*, while also having misleading higher-order evidence that her belief that *p* is unjustified because it is not properly based on the evidence. In that case, she has doxastically justified but false beliefs in Moorean conjunctions of forms (1) and (2). There is no inherent rational instability in this predicament. Moorean beliefs are always irrational when they concern propositional justification, but not when they concern doxastic justification.

10.5. Rational Dilemmas

In this chapter, I've argued that epistemic akrasia is never permissible by ideal standards of rationality. Even so, the question remains whether epistemic akrasia is ever permissible by nonideal standards of rationality. Indeed, now

---

[14] Heylen (2016) uses similar Moorean examples to argue that epistemic positions are not closed under conjunction. But his argument relies on the false premise that if you're in a position to know that *p*, then it is in principle possible for you to know that *p*. Although this assumption holds normally, it fails in finkish cases like these.

[15] In section 4.4, I argued that evidence for Moorean conjunctions of the form *p* and I don't believe that *p* is always finkish. See Smithies (2016b) for further discussion.

[16] Note that these are counterexamples to Williamson's (2011) knowledge rule for belief, which says that you have justification to believe that *p* only if you know that *p*.

that we've drawn the distinction between ideal and nonideal standards of rationality, our original puzzle recurs in a slightly revised form. Consider the following inconsistent triad:

(1) Rationality permits uncertainty and error about the requirements of rationality.
(2) If rationality permits uncertainty and error about the requirements of rationality, then epistemic akrasia is sometimes rationally permissible.
(3) Epistemic akrasia is never rationally permissible.

This puzzle arises equally for ideal and nonideal standards of rationality, but my solution cannot be extended in both cases. This is because the requirements of ideal rationality depend solely on your evidence, whereas the requirements of nonideal rationality depend also on facts about your doxastic dispositions to respond to the evidence. Facts about what your evidence supports are luminous in a way that excludes the possibility of rational uncertainty and error, whereas facts about your doxastic dispositions to respond to your evidence are not luminous in this sense. It is therefore much harder the defend the view that epistemic akrasia is never permissible by nonideal standards of rationality.

Moreover, there is considerable intuitive pressure to concede that epistemic akrasia is sometimes rationally permissible by nonideal standards. Consider Richard Feldman's (2005) example of the undergraduate student who is persuaded by apparently cogent arguments for the skeptical conclusion that she never has justification to believe anything on the basis of perception. Assuming that skepticism is false, ideal rationality requires being certain that her beliefs are justified by perceptual evidence. By nonideal standards, however, it would be dogmatic and irrational to remain completely unmoved by apparently cogent skeptical arguments. The student manifests an intellectual virtue of humility in entertaining skeptical doubts about whether she has justification to believe anything on the basis of perception. Even so, it seems much less virtuous for these higher-level doubts to undermine the student's confidence in her ground-level perceptual beliefs. By nonideal standards, it seems reasonable for the student to have much more confidence in her perceptual beliefs themselves than her higher-order beliefs about whether those perceptual beliefs are justified.

As David Hume famously observed, our perceptual beliefs are extremely resilient in the face of skeptical doubts. This is plausible not just as a descriptive claim about human psychology, but also as a normative claim about what makes sense for nonideally rational creatures like us. The functional role of perception is to make a decisive impact on our belief system which has the power to override theoretical doubts. As they say, seeing is believing. Moreover, this is a good way for cognition to be organized in nonideal creatures like us.

Otherwise, there is too much scope for our theoretical constructions to leave us unmoored in reality. As John Campbell notes, "What keeps humans, with their endlessly complex theorizing, anchored in reality is the role played by sensory awareness as an intervention on belief" (2014: 84).

Now, some forms of epistemic akrasia are more egregious than others. It seems much more irrational to hold beliefs you're *certain you shouldn't* hold than to hold beliefs you're *uncertain you should* hold. Perhaps the most extreme forms of epistemic akrasia are always prohibited even by nonideal standards of rationality, but this is consistent with the claim that some moderate forms of epistemic akrasia are sometimes permitted by nonideal standards of rationality. This is perfectly compatible with my central thesis that epistemic akrasia always involves some departure from ideal rationality. Even if it's sometimes the best option available to nonideal agents like us, it is never ideally rational.

One virtue of this proposal is that it explains why our intuitions about rationality are sometimes pulled in different directions. On the one hand, there's some pressure to say that epistemic akrasia is always rationally problematic. On the other hand, there's also some pressure to say that it's sometimes the most reasonable option available for limited agents like us. We can reconcile these apparently conflicting pressures by acknowledging the distinction between ideal and nonideal standards of rationality. Epistemic akrasia is sometimes the most reasonable option that is available to nonideal agents like us, even if it always constitutes some departure from ideal rationality.[17]

David Christensen (2007) argues that higher-order evidence generates rational dilemmas in which you are guaranteed to violate one of the following rational ideals:

(1) Respecting the first-order evidence.
(2) Respecting the higher-order evidence about your response to the first-order evidence.
(3) Integrating your first-order beliefs with your higher-order beliefs about your response to the first-order evidence.

Consider Sam, the sleepy detective. If he opts for a conciliatory response to Alex, then he fails to respect his first-order evidence that Lucy is the thief. If he opts for a steadfast response, then he fails to respect his higher-order evidence that he has responded irrationally to his first-order evidence. If he opts for an akratic response, then he fails to integrate his first-order beliefs with his

---

[17] Compare Harman's (1986) claim that violating logical or probabilistic coherence is sometimes a rational response to paradox. Again, I concede that this is sometimes rationally permissible by nonideal standards, but never by ideal standards.

higher-order beliefs about his response to the evidence. Whatever he does, Sam violates a rational ideal.

On Christensen's view, there are multiple dimensions of ideal rationality that cannot be jointly satisfied when we have misleading higher-order evidence about our response to the evidence. In particular, we cannot respect both our first-order evidence and our higher-order evidence while integrating our first-order beliefs with our higher-order beliefs in a coherent way. In maximizing any one of these dimensions of ideal rationality, we are thereby guaranteed to sacrifice others. As a result, there is no coherent conception of an agent who is ideally rational along all of these dimensions at once. The best we can hope for is an agent who makes optimal trade-offs between these competing dimensions of ideal rationality.

In contrast with Christensen, I've argued that there is no inherent tension between these dimensions of ideal rationality. An ideally rational agent who uses the Certainty Argument is able to respect her evidence, including her higher-order evidence about her response to the evidence, while also integrating her first-order beliefs and her higher-order beliefs in a coherent way. Thus, higher-order evidence doesn't generate rational dilemmas.

There is, however, a grain of truth in what Christensen says. Higher-order evidence is "rationally toxic" in the sense that it puts nonideally rational agents in a predicament where they are forced to trade off some dimensions of ideal rationality against others. As we've seen, nonideally rational agents like Sam cannot rationally use the Certainty Argument. Instead, they must choose between ignoring their first-order evidence, ignoring their higher-order evidence about their response to the evidence, and being epistemically akratic. All of these options involve some departure from ideal rationality. But this is exactly what we should expect. The whole point of nonideal rationality is to rank the options available to nonideal agents when the ideally rational options are beyond their reach. The rational toxicity of higher-order evidence doesn't reflect any inherent tension in the structure of ideal rationality, but merely reflects the limited capacities of nonideal agents.

This proposal has important consequences for the relationship between ideal and nonideal rationality. Should we think about ideal rationality as an extension of nonideal rationality to agents with unlimited capacities? Or should we think of nonideal rationality as an approximation toward ideal rationality in agents with limited capacities? In other words, should we explain ideal rationality in terms of nonideal rationality, or vice versa?

The arguments of this chapter support the conclusion that ideal rationality comes first in the order of explanation. We cannot recover the requirements of ideal rationality by starting with intuitions about nonideal rationality and extending them to agents with unlimited cognitive capacities. Given the conflicting pressures that shape our intuitions about nonideal rationality, extending them to ideal agents risks distorting the structural features of ideal rationality that make it worth caring about in the first place. Instead, we should explain our intuitions about nonideal rationality as tracking various dimensions of approximation toward ideal rationality that take our contingent human limitations into account. On this view, we shouldn't expect our intuitions about nonideal rationality to reflect all the structural principles that govern ideal rationality. Indeed, we shouldn't expect nonideal rationality to be theoretically tractable at all except insofar as it can be understood as a complicated and messy approximation toward ideal rationality.

10.6. Epistemic Idealization

Epistemic rationality is a kind of ideal: it is an epistemic ideal of good reasoning. The main task for a theory of epistemic rationality is to explain what this epistemic ideal consists in. Moreover, a constraint on the adequacy of any such theory is that it should capture an epistemic ideal that has some value for creatures like us and is therefore worth caring about. In this section, I'll conclude by reviewing how this constraint is satisfied by the theory of epistemic rationality proposed in this chapter and throughout this book.

There are many different dimensions of epistemic evaluation. One dimension of epistemic evaluation concerns the degree to which your beliefs are sensitive to the facts. Agents who are ideal along this dimension are "godlike" in the sense that they are omniscient and infallible about everything. Ideal rationality doesn't require being godlike in this sense. You can reason well—indeed, perfectly—by the standards of epistemic rationality without being omniscient or infallible about everything.

Epistemic rationality is a matter of being sensitive to your evidence, rather than the facts themselves. Your beliefs are ideal along this dimension when they are perfectly sensitive to your evidence. And your beliefs can be perfectly sensitive to your evidence without being perfectly sensitive to the facts. This is because your evidence is an imperfect guide to the facts. Your evidence can be misleading and incomplete. This is why ideal rationality doesn't require being godlike. Your response to the evidence can be perfectly rational even if your evidence itself is an imperfect guide to the facts.

Matters are different when we turn from your evidence about the external world to your higher-order evidence about your own evidence. Although you can have misleading evidence about the external world, you cannot have misleading evidence about what your evidence is or what it supports. On this view, ideal rationality requires omniscience and infallibility about what your evidence is, and what your evidence supports, although it doesn't require omniscience or infallibility about the external world. This asymmetry can seem puzzling. Why should ideal rationality require omniscience and infallibility about some facts and not others?

A similar challenge arises for formal theories of ideal rationality that incorporate logical omniscience requirements. According to probabilism, for example, ideal rationality requires that your credences are probabilistically coherent in the sense that they conform to the axioms of the probability calculus. The normalization axiom says that all logical truths have probability 1. Therefore, ideal rationality requires that you are logically omniscient in the sense that you are certain of all logical truths toward which you adopt any doxastic attitude at all. And yet ideal rationality doesn't require that you are empirically omniscient in the sense that you are certain of all empirical truths about the external world. Once again, this asymmetry can seem puzzling. Why should ideal rationality require omniscience about logical truths, but not empirical truths?

A good answer is that violations of logical omniscience have a kind of "trickle down" effect on your logical reasoning. If you violate logical omniscience, and you integrate your reasoning with your beliefs about logic, then your reasoning fails to respect logic. For example, if you doubt that modus ponens is valid, then you might be certain of the premises of a modus ponens argument, but much less confident of its conclusion. Similarly, if you're very confident that affirming the consequent is valid, then you might be confident that its conclusion is true just on the basis of confidence that its premises are true. Reasoning that fails to respect logic in this way seems irrational. The more general point is that uncertainty and error about logic can contaminate your reasoning when you integrate your reasoning with your beliefs about logic. But rationality requires you to reason in ways that respect logic. And rationality also requires you to integrate your reasoning with your beliefs about logic. Therefore, rationality requires logical omniscience.[18]

The thesis that ideal rationality requires evidential omniscience can be motivated in much the same way. After all, violations of evidential omniscience have a similar kind of "trickle down" effect on your reasoning in response to evidence. If you violate evidential omniscience, and you integrate your reasoning with your beliefs about what your evidence supports, then your reasoning fails to respect your evidence. We saw this in the case of Sam, the sleepy detective, who brackets his evidence that Lucy is the thief when he is convinced by misleading higher-order evidence that his belief is not supported by the evidence.

---

[18] Christensen (2004: 153–157), Titelbaum (2015: 254–258), and Smithies (2015a: 2772–2775) propose similar replies to this asymmetry challenge.

More generally, uncertainty and error about what your evidence supports can lead you to disrespect your evidence when you integrate your reasoning with your higher-order beliefs about what your evidence supports. But rationality requires you to respect your evidence. And rationality also requires you to integrate your beliefs with your higher-order beliefs about what your evidence supports. Therefore, rationality requires evidential omniscience: that is, it is requires that you always know with certainty exactly what your evidence is and what it supports.

The upshot is that ideal rationality requires evidential omniscience for much the same reason that it requires logical omniscience. These requirements are connected with independently plausible claims about the nature of ideal rationality. Ideal rationality requires logical omniscience because it requires your beliefs to respect logic in a metacoherent way. Similarly, ideal rationality requires evidential omniscience because it requires your beliefs to respect your evidence in a metacoherent way. Violating these omniscience requirements can contaminate your reasoning in ways that lead you to disrespect logic and evidence. There is rational pressure to disrespect logic and evidence when you integrate your first-order beliefs with false beliefs about logic and evidence in a metacoherent way. Rational agents can respect logic and evidence in a metacoherent way only because they satisfy the rational requirements of logical and evidential omniscience.

In this way, logical and evidential omniscience emerge as natural consequences of an independently plausible account of what ideal rationality consists in. Ideal rationality requires that you are coherent in at least the following three ways:

(1) *Evidential Coherence*: You respect your evidence—that is, your first-order evidence and your higher-order evidence about your own cognitive capacities.

(2) *Logical Coherence*: You respect logic—that is, your beliefs are logically consistent and closed under deduction; or, at a minimum, your credences are probabilistically coherent.

(3) *Metacoherence*: You are metacoherent—that is, you integrate your beliefs with your higher-order beliefs about which beliefs are supported by logic and evidence.

You cannot be coherent in all these ways unless you are logically and evidentially omniscient. The upshot is that ideal rationality requires evidential omniscience for the much the same reason that it requires logical omniscience—that is, because it requires your beliefs to respect logic and evidence in a metacoherent way. This provides an important theoretical rationale for building formal models of rationality that require logical and evidential omniscience. These requirements are not built in solely for reasons of mathematical convenience. On the contrary, they correctly describe the structure of ideal rationality and thereby capture an important dimension of epistemic value.

A commonly held view is that these formal constraints are the result of idealizations of the kind that are ubiquitous in science. We can often safely ignore the false predictions of a scientific theory that is close enough to the truth, especially when these are side effects of mathematical machinery that is otherwise indispensable to the theory. For example, the Lotka-Volterra model in population ecology treats population abundance as continuous when in fact it is discrete. In much the same way, it is often thought that logical and evidential omniscience requirements can be regarded as false predications about epistemic rationality that are side effects of the mathematics of the probability calculus, which can be safely ignored for most concrete applications.

What I've argued in these concluding remarks is that logical and evidential omniscience are idealizations in a more robustly normative sense. These are not false claims about rationality that can be safely ignored for most practical or theoretical purposes. Rather, they are true claims about rationality that can be motivated by appealing to the independently plausible claim that rationality requires respecting evidence in a coherent and metacoherent way. No doubt ideal rationality is too demanding a standard to be fully realized by creatures with our limited human abilities. Even so, it is a valuable epistemic ideal that is worth striving toward. A proper understanding of ideal rationality can inform our plans and policies about how to conduct our limited doxastic lives. As such, it is an epistemic ideal that is worth trying to understand. That is one of the main goals of this book.

11
Luminosity

In this book, I've argued for phenomenal mentalism on the grounds that it is needed to explain the truth of accessibilism, which I have motivated on independent grounds. Here is the argument in outline:

(1) *Accessibilism*: epistemic justification is luminous in the sense that you're always in a position to know which propositions you have epistemic justification to believe.
(2) Epistemic justification is luminous only if it is determined by introspectively luminous facts about your mental states.
(3) *The Phenomenal Individuation Constraint*: all and only phenomenally individuated facts about your current mental states are introspectively luminous. Therefore,
(4) *Phenomenal Mentalism*: epistemic justification is determined by phenomenally individuated facts about your current mental states.

This argument for phenomenal mentalism relies crucially on the premise that phenomenally individuated facts about your current mental states are luminous in the sense that you're always in a position to know whether or not they obtain. Otherwise, phenomenal mentalism cannot explain how epistemic justification is luminous.

The aim of this chapter is to defend this premise against objections. Ernest Sosa (2003) argues that not all phenomenal facts are luminous, while Timothy Williamson (2000) argues for the stronger conclusion that nothing is luminous. My response to both arguments draws on a distinction between *epistemic* and *doxastic* senses of luminosity. I concede that not all phenomenal facts—and perhaps none of them—are doxastically luminous in the sense that we always have the doxastic capacity to know whether or not they obtain. At the same time, I maintain that all phenomenal facts are epistemically luminous in the sense that we're always in an epistemic position to know whether or not they obtain. We don't always have the doxastic capacity to convert our epistemic position into knowledge, but this says more about our own doxastic limitations than it says about the nature of epistemic rationality.[1]

---

[1] This chapter improves upon my response to Sosa and Williamson in Smithies (2012b) and extends the same strategy to defend epistemic iteration principles and to solve the puzzle of the unmarked clock.

Here is the plan for this chapter. I'll begin by drawing a distinction between two senses of luminosity (section 11.1), before applying the distinction to Sosa's version of the problem of the speckled hen (section 11.2), Williamson's anti-luminosity argument (section 11.3), his argument against epistemic iteration principles (section 11.4), and his argument for improbable knowing (section 11.5). Finally, I'll conclude with a more general discussion of what is at stake in these debates (section 11.6).

11.1. Luminosity Defined

Williamson (2000: 95) defines a condition to be *luminous* just in case you're always in a position to know that it obtains when it does. A condition is *strongly* luminous just in case you're always in a position to know whether or not it obtains. In other words, a strongly luminous condition is not only *positively* luminous in the sense that you're always in a position to know that it obtains when it does, but also *negatively* luminous in the sense that you're always in a position to know that it fails to obtain when it does.

What is it to be in a *position* to know that p? You can be in a position to know that p without knowing that p, since you may fail to do what you're in a position to do. You know that p when and only when you exploit your position to know that p. As Williamson says, "If one is in a position to know p, and one has done what one is in a position to do to decide whether p is true, then one does know p" (2000: 95).

This tells us something, but it doesn't tell us what being in a position to know consists in. According to Williamson, the capacity to know that p is neither necessary nor sufficient for being in a position to know that p. It is not necessary because creatures who don't have the concept of pain may still be in a position to know that they feel pain. It is not sufficient because you're capable of knowing many things by gathering new evidence, but you're not in a position to know them until you've acquired the requisite evidence. As Williamson puts the point, "No obstacle must block one's path to knowing. . . . The fact is open to one's view, unhidden, even if one does not yet see it" (2000: 95).

Williamson doesn't attempt to cash out this metaphor more precisely. Instead, reasonably enough, he leaves this task to his opponents. At the same time, he assumes that his anti-luminosity argument succeeds on all acceptable ways of making the notion of luminosity precise. One of the main aims of this chapter is to undermine this assumption by articulating an interpretation of luminosity on which his anti-luminosity argument fails.

The interpretation of luminosity that I propose relies on a distinction between *epistemic* and *doxastic* conditions for knowledge. Of course, there is a broad sense in which all of the conditions for knowledge are epistemic conditions; after all, the Greek word, *episteme*, means *knowledge*. I'll use the term in a more restricted sense, however, to contrast epistemic conditions for knowledge with doxastic conditions, such as belief and proper basing, which concern the subject's doxastic response to her epistemic position.

Knowing that *p* requires satisfying all the epistemic and doxastic conditions for knowledge. We can say that you're in an *epistemic position* to know that *p* just in case you satisfy all the purely epistemic conditions for knowledge. You don't need to satisfy the doxastic conditions for knowledge, or even be capable of satisfying them, to be in an epistemic position to know that *p*. In contrast, you're in a *doxastic position* to know that *p* just in case you satisfy all the epistemic conditions for knowledge, and you *also* have the capacity to satisfy all the doxastic conditions for knowledge. Hence, doxastic positions entail epistemic positions, but not vice versa. You can be in an epistemic position to know that *p* without having the doxastic capacity to convert your epistemic position into knowledge.

What are the epistemic conditions for knowledge? Without attempting to provide an exhaustive list, here are some examples for purposes of illustration:

Truth: Necessarily, you know that *p* only if it is true that *p*.

Propositional Justification: Necessarily, you know that *p* only if you have propositional justification to believe that *p*.

Epistemic Safety: Necessarily, you know that *p* only if it is true that *p* in all close cases in which you have propositional justification to believe that *p*.

These are all epistemic conditions for knowledge because they don't imply anything about the subject's doxastic capacity to know that *p*. Almost everyone agrees that truth is an epistemic condition for knowledge, since knowledge is factive, but the facts are not constrained by your doxastic capacity to know them. If there are no doxastic constraints on propositional justification, as I argued in section 8.4, then propositional justification is an epistemic condition for knowledge. If truth and propositional justification are epistemic conditions for knowledge, then so is the epistemic safety condition: it requires for knowledge that a proposition is not only true and propositionally justified, but also true in all close cases in which it is propositionally justified. In Goldman's (1976) fake barn case, for example, epistemic safety is violated.

We can contrast these purely epistemic conditions for knowledge with the following doxastic conditions for knowledge:

Belief: Necessarily, you know that *p* only if you believe that *p*.

Doxastic Justification: Necessarily, you know that *p* only if you believe that *p* in a way that is doxastically justified.

Doxastic Safety: Necessarily, you know that *p* only if it is true that *p* in all close cases in which you believe that *p* in a relevantly similar way.

These are not purely epistemic conditions for knowledge, since they incorporate doxastic constraints on which beliefs you hold and how you hold them. Epistemic conditions for knowledge concern the quality of your epistemic position, while doxastic conditions concern the quality of your doxastic response to your epistemic position.

There is no commitment here to the project of analyzing knowledge in more basic terms. It may be that some necessary conditions for knowledge cannot be stated without relying explicitly or implicitly on the concept of knowledge. Williamson (2000: 100) suggests, for example, that we cannot understand the doxastic safety condition without using the concept of knowledge in deciding what counts as a relevantly close case. Moreover, there is no commitment here to the project of decomposing knowledge into a conjunction of epistemic and nonepistemic conditions. Some necessary conditions for knowledge may be ineliminably complex in a way that precludes this kind of decomposition. For example, we may be unable to decompose doxastic justification into propositional justification plus proper basing, since there may be way to define proper basing except nonreductively as the condition that converts propositional justification into doxastic justification.

All we need for present purposes is that some of the conditions for knowledge are purely epistemic conditions, while others incorporate doxastic conditions. If so, then the following possibility is left open. You might satisfy the epistemic conditions for knowing that *p* without having the capacity to satisfy the doxastic conditions for knowing that *p*. In that case, you're in an epistemic position to know that *p*, but you're not in a doxastic position to know that *p*, since you lack the doxastic capacity to convert your epistemic position into knowledge. We've already seen many examples of this phenomenon in previous chapters, but as I'll explain, the arguments of Sosa and Williamson generate further examples.

As a rough heuristic, you're in an epistemic position to know that *p* just in case you would know that *p* if your doxastic response to your epistemic position were sufficiently rational. More precisely, you would know that *p* if you were to properly base a doxastically justified belief that *p* on your propositional justification to believe that *p*. This is only a heuristic because there are finkish cases in which you cannot respond rationally to your epistemic position without thereby changing it.[2] In nonfinkish cases, however, it is always possible at least in principle to convert your epistemic position into knowledge by properly basing your beliefs on your evidence in a way that is sufficiently rational. The crucial point for now is that you don't always respond to your evidence in a sufficiently rational way. As a result, there can be discrepancies between what you're in an epistemic position to know and what you're in a doxastic position to know. There is no guarantee that you always have the rational doxastic capacities required to convert your epistemic position into knowledge.

We can now distinguish two senses of luminosity:

A condition is *epistemically luminous* just in case you're always in an *epistemic position* to know that it obtains when it does.

A condition is *doxastically luminous* just in case you're always in a *doxastic position* to know that it obtains when it does.

All doxastically luminous conditions are epistemically luminous, but not vice versa: you don't always have the rational doxastic capacities required to convert your epistemic position into knowledge. In this chapter, I'll use this distinction in replying to Sosa and Williamson. I concede that their arguments show that not all phenomenal facts—and perhaps even none of them—are doxastically luminous. However, these arguments leave intact the claim that all phenomenal facts are epistemically luminous.

Is this a pyrrhic victory? I'll address this objection in the concluding section of this chapter, but the short answer is no. In this book, I've argued for an epistemic version of accessibilism, rather than a doxastic version. Moreover, I've argued that this epistemic version of accessibilism is strong enough to motivate the claims about the epistemic role of consciousness defended in the first part of this book. As a result, there is no theoretical pressure to defend the stronger claim that some conditions are not only epistemically luminous, but also doxastically luminous for limited human agents like us.

11.2. The Problem of the Speckled Hen

Sosa (2003) argues that not all phenomenal experience is luminous: in other words, we're not always in a position to know exactly which phenomenal experiences we're having at any given time. He presents this as a challenge for

---

[2] Moore's paradox is a case in point: see section 5.5 and section 10.4 for further discussion.

classical foundationalism, the thesis that noninferential knowledge of our own phenomenal experience serves as a foundation for all of our inferential knowledge. However, Sosa's challenge arises equally for the version of *phenomenal accessibilism* defended in this book.[3]

Here is Sosa's challenge for phenomenal accessibilism: (i) not all phenomenal facts are luminous, but (ii) there is no way of saying which phenomenal facts are luminous without appealing to externalist facts about the reliability of our doxastic dispositions, so (iii) epistemic justification is not determined solely by phenomenal facts. As Sosa writes: "It is fascinating to find at the heart of givenist, internalist, classical foundationalism a need for the sort of relation so often used by its externalist opponents" (2003: 138).

Sosa's challenge is to explain which beliefs about our own experience are candidates for noninferential knowledge by means of introspection. He writes:

If the classical foundationalist wishes to have a theory and not just a promissory note, he needs to tell us *which* sorts of features of our states of consciousness are the epistemically effective ones, the ones *by corresponding to which specifically* do our basic beliefs acquire epistemically foundational status. Having a visual image with forty-eight speckles seems not to qualify, whereas having a visual image with three speckles may (at least when they are large and separate enough). What is the relevant difference? (2003: 121)

When my visual experience phenomenally represents that the hen has three speckles, I can know this noninferentially on the basis of introspection. When my visual experience phenomenally represents that the hen has 48 speckles, in contrast, I cannot know this in the same way. What accounts for the difference between these two cases? This is Sosa's version of the problem of the speckled hen.[4]

Sosa claims that we cannot solve the problem of the speckled hen without invoking the safety condition for knowledge, which can be stated roughly as follows:

The Safety Condition: Necessarily, you know that p only if you believe that p in a way that is safe from error, i.e. it is true that p in all close cases in which you believe that p in a relevantly similar way.[5]

---

[3] Phenomenal accessibilism is naturally combined with classical foundationalism, but this isn't mandatory: it can also be combined with various forms of moderate foundationalism and impure coherentism.
[4] The problem of the speckled hen was originally raised by Gilbert Ryle as an objection to sense-datum theories of perception. See Ayer (1940: 124–125) and Chisholm (1942) for discussion of Ryle's objection.
[5] To deal with belief in necessary truths, the safety condition is sometimes amended to say that your belief is safe from error just in case there are no close cases in which you falsely believe a relevantly similar proposition in a relevantly similar way.

According to Sosa, the safety condition explains why I'm able to know some facts about my experience but not others. I cannot know that I experience 48 speckles, even if my belief is true, since it is not safe from error: it is formed in a way that could easily yield false belief. For example, I could easily believe that I experience 48 speckles when in fact I experience one more or one less. My introspective belief-forming processes are not sufficiently responsive to these fine-grained differences in the representational contents of perceptual experience. In contrast, I can know that I experience three speckles, since my belief is safe from error: it is formed in a way that could not easily yield false belief. I could not easily believe that I experience three speckles when in fact I experience one more or one less, since my introspective belief-forming processes are generally responsive to this kind of difference in my experience, at least when the speckles are sufficiently clear and distinct.

In response to Sosa, I'll argue that the best solution appeals to a proper basing condition for doxastic justification, rather than a safety condition for knowledge. This gives us all the resources we need to answer Sosa's challenge. On this view, we're always in a position to know all the phenomenal facts, but we're not always capable of exploiting our epistemic position, since we cannot always satisfy the proper basing condition. All the phenomenal facts are epistemically luminous, although not all of them are doxastically luminous. In this section, I'll examine six different proposals for solving the problem of the speckled hen, including Sosa's and my own.

The first proposal appeals to facts about the determinacy of representational content. On this view, the representational content of perceptual experience is much less determinate than Sosa assumes. When I see a hen with three speckles in good viewing conditions, my experience normally represents that it has three speckles. When I see a hen with 48 speckles, in contrast, my experience doesn't normally represent that it has 48 speckles. This is not just because I might fail to see all the speckles. Even if I see all the speckles, and there are exactly 48 of them, it doesn't follow that my experience represents that the hen has exactly 48 speckles. Indeed, there may be no determinate number n such that my experience represents that the hen has n speckles. This is because there is some degree of indeterminacy with respect to the number of speckles represented in the content of my experience.[6]

---

[6] Tye (2009) claims that there is "phenomenal indeterminacy" with respect to the number of speckles represented by your experience. He also claims that you see the speckles collectively, rather than individually, but we don't need this claim here. Even if you see each of 48 speckles individually, it doesn't follow that your experience represents that there are 48 of them, since the contents of experience are not closed under conjunction.

Perhaps we can solve the problem of the speckled hen by exploiting this indeterminacy in the representational contents of experience. On the simple theory of introspection, my experience gives me introspective justification to believe that it represents that *p* if and only if it phenomenally represents that *p*. When I see a hen that has three speckles, my experience phenomenally represents that it has three speckles, so I have introspective justification to believe that my experience has this representational content. When I see a hen that has 48 speckles, in contrast, my experience doesn't phenomenally represent that it has 48 speckles, so I don't have introspective justification to believe that my experience has this representational content. Why isn't this enough to solve the problem?

This response is not sufficient to provide a fully general solution to the problem of the speckled hen. To generate the problem, we just need to find another example in which the contents of perception are more fine-grained than the contents of cognition. Empirical work on the representation of number indicates that our visual representation of "numerosity" is rather coarsegrained: we're not very reliable in making visual discriminations between large numbers of items.[7] Our visual representation of color, in contrast, is relatively fine-grained: it represents not only highly determinable shades, such as red and green, but also much more determinate shades. We don't have words for all the shades we are capable of discriminating on the basis of vision, but we can invent them. Let's use 'red-48' and 'red-49' as names for two of these determinate shades of red. This generates a version of the problem of the speckled hen. I can know noninferentially on the basis of introspection that I experience red, rather than green, when I do. However, I cannot know noninferentially on the basis of introspection that I experience red-48, rather than red-49, when I do. What accounts for the difference between these cases?

To illustrate the problem, consider two color chips: one is red-48 and the other is red-49. I can reliably discriminate the two chips when presented simultaneously but not when presented in sequence. When they are presented simultaneously, I can tell them apart because they look different. My color experience is fine-grained enough to represent the difference between these two different shades. When they are presented in sequence, however, I cannot tell them apart, even though they look different, since I cannot remember exactly what the first one looked like. My experience represents each chip as having a different shade, but these fine-grained differences are not stored in memory long enough for me to use in making reliable judgments about sameness and difference. So, even if my experience represents the chip as having a determinate shade of red-48, I cannot know by introspection that it represents red-48, rather than red-49.

[7] See Deheane (1997: ch. 3) for an accessible survey.

The crucial point is not that I lack words for these specific shades, but rather that I cannot recognize these specific shades from one moment to the next. This is a consequence of what Diana Raffman (1995) calls *the memory constraint*: our capacity for perceptual recognition, unlike our capacity for perceptual discrimination, is constrained by the limits of perceptual memory. Because the informational content of perceptual memory is more impoverished than that of perceptual experience, our capacity for perceptual recognition over time is generally much less reliable than our capacity for perceptual discrimination at a single time. These limits on our perceptual memory generate more realistic versions of the problem of the speckled hen, such as the version just described. Sosa's example may be unrealistic, but having noticed this problem, we can ignore it. It will be harmless to pretend that our experience of numerosity is more determinate than it really is, since our color experience is sufficiently determinate to generate structurally similar problems.[8]

The second proposal appeals to facts about the limited capacity of attention. According to this proposal, we cannot know all the phenomenal facts about our experience because these facts sometimes outstrip the capacity limits of attention. As Sosa writes:

> Much in the intricate character of experience can . . . escape our notice, and can even be mischaracterized, as when one takes oneself to be able to tell at a glance that an image has ten speckles although in fact it has eleven rather than ten. (2003: 121)

I can't know noninferentially on the basis of introspection that I experience 11 speckles, rather than 10, because these numbers fall beyond my limited attentional capacity. I simply can't attend to 10 or 11 things at once. As a result, I don't always notice when my experience represents 11 speckles, rather than 10. In contrast, I can know that I experience three speckles, rather than four, because these numbers fall within the limits of my attentional capacities. I can attend to three or four things at once, but not much more.[9]

Richard Feldman (2004: ch. 8) exploits this point in offering a solution to the problem of the speckled hen. His claim is that the phenomenal properties of your experience are luminous whenever you attend to them. On this view, you sometimes fail to notice the phenomenal properties of your experience, but

---

[8] Adam Pautz notes that the problem for introspection extends more widely than the problem for perception. If you phenomenally represent 48 distinct colors, even if you don't represent that there are exactly 48 distinct colors, this is still a phenomenal fact about your experience that you may well be unable to know by introspection.

[9] The limits on our capacity for attention are explored in much recent empirical work, including Pylyshyn and Storm's (1988) work on multiple-object tracking.

when you attend to them, you are thereby in a position to know noninferentially through introspection that your experience has those phenomenal properties. Thus, Feldman proposes the following principle: "If a person is experientially-aware of property F, and attends to this property, and believes that he is having an experience with property F, and refers to property F in this belief by means of an indexical or phenomenal concept, then the person is foundationally justified in believing that he is having an experience with quality F" (2004: 217).

The problem with this proposal, just like the previous one, is that it doesn't provide a fully general solution to the problem of the speckled hen. When I experience a determinate shade of red-48, I can attend both to the specific shade and to my experience of the shade. The color shade is not so specific that I cannot attend to it at all. Even so, I'm not in a position to know whether my experience represents red-48 or red-49. The problem is not caused by limits on my capacity for attention, but rather by limits on my capacity for memory and recognition. This case is a counterexample to Feldman's principle.

The third proposal appeals to a distinction between demonstrative and recognitional concepts of experience. When I experience a shade of red-48, and then a shade of red-49, perhaps I cannot reliably tell whether my experience is the same or different over time. Nevertheless, I can know noninferentially on the basis of introspection that I am currently having an experience *just like this*. Here, I'm classifying my experience using a phenomenal concept that is demonstrative, rather than recognitional, in kind. Some philosophers argue that introspective beliefs about experience are infallible when they self-ascribe experience under demonstrative phenomenal concepts. The proposed solution is that all phenomenal facts about your experience are luminous in the sense that they can be noninferentially known by introspection under demonstrative phenomenal concepts.

David Chalmers (2003) endorses a version of classical foundationalism that restricts our foundational knowledge to beliefs about experience that are infallible in just this way.[10] He argues that there are "direct phenomenal beliefs" that are guaranteed to be true:

The Incorrigibility Thesis: A direct phenomenal belief cannot be false. (2003: 242)

Moreover, these direct phenomenal beliefs are guaranteed to be justified, at least defeasibly, by your acquaintance with the phenomenal properties of experience that make them true:

---

[10] See also Gertler (2001) and Horgan and Kriegel (2007) for related proposals.

The Justification Thesis: When a subject forms a direct phenomenal belief based on a phenomenal quality, then that belief is prima facie justified by virtue of the subject's acquaintance with that quality. (2003: 249)

A *direct phenomenal concept* is a phenomenal concept whose content is partially constituted by acquaintance with a phenomenal property, which implies that it is available for use in thought only just as long as you are acquainted with that phenomenal property. A *direct phenomenal belief* is a belief that uses a direct phenomenal concept to self-ascribe a phenomenal property on the basis of acquaintance with that phenomenal property. So defined, direct phenomenal beliefs are guaranteed to be true and defeasibly justified because their contents are partially constituted by acquaintance with the phenomenal properties they pick out. In the absence of defeaters, they constitute direct phenomenal knowledge.

The Infallibility Thesis is severely limited in its scope. As Chalmers explains, not all phenomenal beliefs are direct phenomenal beliefs. Some phenomenal beliefs self-ascribe phenomenal properties using standing phenomenal concepts, which can persist in the absence of the phenomenal properties that they pick out. Any capacity to recognize experiences as tokens of the same phenomenal type involves the exercise of standing phenomenal concepts. These standing phenomenal beliefs fall outside the scope of Chalmers's Infallibility Thesis. Moreover, they fall outside the scope of the Justification Thesis, since they cannot be noninferentially justified by acquaintance construed as a relation of partial constitution between a phenomenal property and a direct phenomenal concept. Instead, Chalmers argues that these standing phenomenal beliefs are inferentially justified by their relations to direct phenomenal beliefs. The result is "a sort of limited foundationalism within the phenomenal domain" (2010: 303).

My main reservation about this proposal is that it imposes an implausible restriction on how much we can know about experience noninferentially on the basis of introspection. It implies—quite plausibly—that I cannot know by introspection alone whether I am experiencing red-48. And yet it also implies—much less plausibly—that I cannot know by introspection alone whether I am experiencing red. On this view, introspection only gives me noninferential knowledge that I am having an experience *just like this*. But it's extremely plausible that introspection provides much more noninferential knowledge than that. The proposed solution seems like overkill. If we want an account of introspective knowledge that involves the application of standing or recognitional concepts of experience as well as direct or demonstrative concepts of experience, then the problem of the speckled hen remains.

The fourth proposal retreats from the claim that all experiences are luminous to the claim that all experiences are lustrous. Selim Berker (2008: 20) defines a condition to be *lustrous* just in case you're always in a position to form a justified belief that it obtains when it does. Even if we're not always in a position to *know* all the phenomenal facts that obtain at any given time, perhaps we're always in a position to form *justified beliefs* about them. The key point is that knowledge requires safety from error, whereas justified belief does not require safety from error. After all, justified belief is nonfactive, so you can have a justified belief that is false in the actual world, which is among the closest possible worlds.

This fallback response is unsatisfying because the problem of the speckled hen can be formulated in terms of justified belief as well as knowledge. When my experience represents that the hen has three speckles, I can form a noninferentially justified belief that it does on the basis of introspection. When my experience represents that the hen has 48 speckles, in contrast, I cannot form a noninferentially justified belief that it does on the basis of introspection. Similarly, I can form a noninferentially justified introspective belief that I experience red when I do, whereas I cannot form a noninferentially justified introspective belief that I experience red-48 when I do. What explains the difference between these cases? The problem of the speckled hen remains.

The fifth proposal offers a diagnosis of this point: safety from error is required not only for knowledge, but also for justified belief. This is Sosa's solution to the problem of the speckled hen. He writes:

> How then would one distinguish (1) an *unjustified* "introspective" judgment, say that one's image has 48 speckles, when it is a true judgment, and one issued in full view of the image with that specific character, from (2) a *justified* "introspective" judgment, say that one's image has 3 speckles? The relevant distinction is that the latter judgment is both *safe* and *virtuous*, or so I wish to suggest. It is "safe" because in the circumstances not easily *would* one believe what one now does in fact believe, without being right. It is "virtuous" because one's belief derives from a way of forming beliefs that is an intellectual virtue, one that in our normal situation for forming such beliefs would tend strongly enough to give us beliefs that are safe. (2003: 138–139)

According to Sosa, we cannot solve the problem of the speckled hen without endorsing a version of epistemic externalism that explains epistemic justification in terms of reliable intellectual virtues. As I'll explain, however, Sosa's proposed solution fails to generalize in a plausible way from introspection to perception.

The problem of the speckled hen arises not only for introspective beliefs about experience, but also for perceptual beliefs about the external world. When my visual experience represents that the hen has three speckles in the absence of defeaters, I can thereby form a noninferentially justified belief that the hen has three speckles. But when my perceptual experience represents that the hen has 48 speckles in the absence of defeaters, I cannot thereby form a noninferentially justified belief that the hen has 48 speckles. The same applies to the contrast between cases when my visual experience represents that the hen is red versus red-48. What accounts for the difference between these cases?

Safety from error is a red herring in this context. After all, Sosa's contrast can be drawn whether I am veridically perceiving or merely hallucinating speckled hens. Suppose I hallucinate a red hen, and I believe the hen is not only red, but more specifically red-48. Because I am hallucinating, all my beliefs about the hen are false, and so they are not safe from error. Even so, there is an epistemic contrast to be explained between my justified belief that the hen is red, and my unjustified belief that the hen is red-48. Safety cannot explain this contrast, however, since no false belief is safe from error.

The sixth proposal, finally, is my own. What we need to explain this epistemic contrast is not a *safety* condition for justified belief, but a *proper basing* condition for justified belief. A belief is doxastically justified if and only if it is properly based on the evidence that makes the belief propositionally justified. By definition, proper basing is the relation between belief and evidence that converts propositional justification into doxastic justification. But what is the nature of this relation? Sosa's examples show that a mere causal relation between a belief and some evidence is not sufficient for proper basing unless it manifests the right kind of counterfactual responsiveness to the evidence. A belief is doxastically justified only if it is held on the basis of exercising doxastic dispositions that are counterfactually responsive to the evidence, or the evidential support facts, that make the belief propositionally justified. Exercising the same doxastic dispositions in sufficiently similar counterfactual circumstances should yield beliefs that are supported by the evidence. Hence, doxastic justification requires beliefs to be formed in a way that is safe from the absence of evidential support.

Now let's apply this account to the problem of the speckled hen. My belief that the hen has 48 speckles is doxastically unjustified because it is formed in a way that tends to yield beliefs in the absence of evidential support. For instance, I could easily believe that the hen has 48 speckles when my experience represents that it has one more or one less. My ways of forming beliefs are simply not responsive to these fine-grained differences in the representational content of visual experience. In contrast, my belief that the hen has three speckles is justified because it is formed in a way that tends not to yield beliefs in the absence of evidence. I could not easily believe that the hen has three speckles when my experience represents that it has one more or one less. My ways of forming beliefs are highly responsive to such differences in the representational content of experience. The same applies, mutatis mutandis, to the contrast between my justified belief that the hen is red and my unjustified belief that the hen is red-48.

In summary, justified belief doesn't require safety from error, but safety from absence of evidential support. To a first approximation, the proper basing requirement on justified belief can be stated as follows:

> *The Proper Basing Condition*: Necessarily, your belief that p is doxastically justified on the basis of evidence e only if you believe that p in a way that is safe from the absence of evidential support, i.e. you have evidence e in every close case in which you believe that p in a relevantly similar way.

Suppose you believe that p on the basis of evidence e, but there is a close case in which you don't have e, and yet you believe that p in a relevantly similar way. In that case, your belief is unjustified because it is not properly based on your evidence. For instance, if you believe that the hen has 48 speckles on the basis of an experience that represents 48 speckles, but there is a close case in which you believe the same proposition on the basis of an experience that represents one more or one less, then your belief is unjustified.[11]

Now, in the special case of introspection, there is no distinction between safety from error and safety from absence of evidential support. On the simple theory of introspection, the evidence that justifies your introspective beliefs is constituted by the phenomenal facts about experience that your introspective beliefs are about:

> *Introspective Evidence*: Necessarily, if you have an introspectively justified belief that you have an experience E, then the evidence e that introspectively justifies your belief that you have E is identical with the fact that you have E.

If we combine Introspective Evidence with the Proper Basing Condition, then we can derive the following Restricted Safety Condition:

> *The Restricted Safety Condition*: Necessarily, if you have an introspectively justified belief that you have an experience E, then it's true that you have E in every close case in which you believe that you have E.

---

[11] Williamson (2009: 305–308) defends the safety requirement for knowledge against counterexamples by arguing that if you know that p, then no case in which you falsely believe that p is relevantly close. Similarly, I claim that if your belief that p is properly based on e, then no case in which you believe that p on the basis of different evidence counts as relevantly close. These are nonreductive conditions for knowledge and justified belief, since we need to use the concepts of knowledge and justified belief, respectively, in specifying what counts as a relevantly close case.

In other words, introspectively justified belief requires safety from error because introspective justification has its source in the phenomenal facts that constitute your introspective evidence, and justified belief always requires safety from absence of evidential support.

The problem of the speckled hen is a problem about doxastic justification, rather than propositional justification. Just because I cannot form a doxastically justified belief that I experience 48 speckles, it doesn't follow that I lack propositional justification to believe that I experience 48 speckles. As I argued in section 8.4, propositional justification is not constrained by my doxastic capacities. On the simple theory of introspection, whenever I'm in some phenomenal state, I thereby have introspective justification to believe that I'm in that state. It doesn't follow that I'm able to form an introspectively justified belief that I'm in that mental state. Which propositions I have introspective justification to believe about my experience is determined by the experiential facts themselves, rather than my doxastic capacities for responding to these experiential facts. We can put the point by saying that the experiential facts are epistemically lustrous, even if they are not doxastically lustrous.[12]

For much the same reason, the problem of the speckled hen concerns what I'm in a doxastic position to know, rather than what I'm in an epistemic position to know. I cannot know that I experience 48 speckles, but it doesn't follow that I'm not in an epistemic position to know that I experience 48 speckles. This is because I don't always have the doxastic capacity to convert my epistemic position into knowledge. Suppose I truly believe that I experience 48 speckles (or red-48). My belief is safe from error in epistemically close cases in which I have the same evidence, since the evidence that justifies my belief that I experience 48 speckles is just this fact about my experience. And yet it is not safe from error in doxastically close cases in which I form the same belief in the same way, since I'm equally disposed to believe that I experience 48 speckles when in fact I experience 47 or 49 speckles. Not all doxastically close cases are epistemically close cases, since my doxastic dispositions are not perfectly sensitive to my evidence. As a result, I'm sometimes disposed to give the same doxastic response in cases that nevertheless differ in evidence.

The problem of the speckled hen provides a vivid illustration of the general point that doxastic positions are more demanding than epistemic positions. You can have propositional justification to believe that p without having the

---

[12] Silins (2011) argues that you don't have justification to believe that you experience 48 speckles, but only to spread your credence among a range of competing hypotheses about the content of your experience. While I agree that nonideal rationality permits this kind of credence-spreading, I think this is best explained not as a thesis about what your evidence supports, but rather as a thesis about how nonideal agents can reasonably be expected to respond to evidence that is more fine-grained than their discriminative abilities.

capacity to form a doxastically justified belief that *p*. Similarly, you can be in an epistemic position to know that *p* without having the doxastic capacity to convert your epistemic position into knowledge. As a result, not all epistemically lustrous and luminous conditions are also doxastically lustrous and luminous conditions. As we'll see in the following section, this distinction also spells trouble for Williamson's anti-luminosity argument.

11.3. The Anti-Luminosity Argument

Williamson's (2000: ch. 4) anti-luminosity argument aims to show that there are no luminous conditions except trivial ones. His argument relies crucially on the premise that knowledge requires a margin for error. While Selim Berker (2008) defends luminosity by denying this premise, my own response is rather different. I'll argue that nonideally rational agents need a margin for error to have knowledge, whereas ideally rational agents do not. However, no margin for error is required for being in an epistemic position to know something. This means that when we're close to the margins, we cannot convert our epistemic position into knowledge. This is just a reflection of our nonideal rationality. It doesn't show that there are no epistemically luminous conditions.

The anti-luminosity argument can be presented as follows. Suppose, for *reductio*, that C is a luminous condition. By the definition of luminosity:

(1) *Luminosity*: If C obtains, then you're in a position to know that C obtains.

Let's suppose you're doing everything you're in a position to do with respect to knowing whether or not C obtains. By the definition of being in a position to know:

(2) *Position*: If you're in a position to know that C obtains, then you know that C obtains.

Now we can add Williamson's margin-for-error principle:

(3) *Margins*: If you know that C obtains, then C obtains in every close case.

From these three assumptions, we can infer a tolerance principle:

(4) *Tolerance*: If C obtains, then C obtains in every close case (from (1), (2), and (3)).

But this tolerance principle is falsified by any sorites series of close cases that begins with a case in which C obtains and ends with a case in which C does not obtain.

To illustrate the point, Williamson asks us to imagine a morning in which you feel cold at dawn and then you gradually warm up until you feel warm at noon. The process is so gradual that you cannot notice any change from one moment to the next: any such changes fall below your threshold for discrimination. If feeling cold is a luminous condition, then we can argue as follows:

(1) You feel cold at dawn. (Assumption)
(2) You're in a position to know that you feel cold at dawn. ((1), Luminosity)
(3) You know that you feel cold at dawn. ((2), Position)
(4) You feel cold a moment later. ((3), Margins)

By repeating these moves, we can derive the conclusion that you feel cold at noon. However, this contradicts the initial stipulation that you feel warm at noon. Hence, one of our initial assumptions must be false.

Williamson presents this argument as a *reductio* of the assumption that feeling cold is a luminous condition. Moreover, we can run a similar argument for any other condition that generates a sorites series. If feeling cold is not a luminous condition, then nothing is, since feeling cold is as good a candidate as anything else. Now, one response is to block the argument by denying the premise that knowledge requires a margin for error. But Williamson motivates the margin-for-error principle by appealing to two independently plausible assumptions: first, that knowledge requires safety from error; and second, that there are limits on our powers of discrimination.

To a first approximation, the safety requirement says that you know that p only if there is no close case in which you falsely believe that p in a relevantly similar way. The rationale for this requirement is that if your beliefs are not safe from error, then they are not reliable enough to count as knowledge. In Goldman's (1976) fake barn case, for example, Henry has a justified true belief that there is a barn ahead, but he doesn't have knowledge. Why not? Because there is a close case in which he is looking at a fake barn, rather than a real barn, and so his justified belief is false. The safety requirement explains why we cannot have knowledge in Gettier-style cases of this kind.

There is a gap that needs bridging between the safety requirement and the margin-for-error principle. You can know that p, even if there is a close case in which it is false that p, so long as there is no close case in which you falsely believe that p. As Williamson (2000: 127) notes, you can know that a child is sitting even if she is in danger of falling. Your knowledge is not undermined because you can reliably discriminate between sitting and falling. The extra assumption we need to derive a margin-for-error principle is that your powers of discrimination are limited in such a way that you cannot discriminate between close cases. But what exactly does this mean? It would beg the question to assume that you're not in a position to know the difference between close cases. A more neutral assumption is that your doxastic dispositions are not perfectly sensitive to the differences between close cases. In other words, your degree of confidence that some condition obtains cannot differ too radically between close cases.

Selim Berker (2008) distinguishes two versions of Williamson's argument for the margin-for-error principle: a *coarse-grained* version formulated in terms of outright belief, and a *fine-grained* version formulated in terms of degrees of confidence. According to Berker, neither version of the argument is sound. On the coarse-grained version, the safety requirement is true, but the discrimination principle is false. On the fine-grained version, in contrast, the discrimination principle is true, but the safety requirement is false. He concludes that there is no sound argument for Margins.

Here is the coarse-grained version of the argument for Margins:

(1) *Belief*: If one knows that C obtains, then one believes that C obtains.
(2) *C-Discrimination*: If one believes that C obtains, then in every close case one believes that C obtains.
(3) *C-Safety*: If one knows that C obtains, then C obtains in every close case in which one believes that C obtains. Therefore,
(4) *Margins*: If one knows that C obtains, then C obtains in every close case.

Although some critics have proposed counterexamples to C-Safety, Williamson replies that these counterexamples fail because they rely on a nonepistemic conception of what counts as a relevantly close case.[13] Berker accepts this response and I'm willing to accept it too. Berker's objection in contrast is that C-Discrimination is false because it is falsified by any sorites-style series of cases that begins with a case in which you believe that some condition obtains and ends with a case in which you don't believe that it obtains. This suggests that we need to reformulate the argument in terms of fine-grained degrees of confidence.[14]

---

[13] Neta and Rohrbaugh (2004) and Comesaña (2005a) propose counterexamples to C-safety, but see Williamson (2009: 305–308) for his reply.
[14] See Berker (2008: 7 n. 11) and Srinivasan (2015: 302–305) for discussion of alternative versions of C-Discrimination, which I'll set aside here.

Here is the fine-grained argument for Margins:

(1) *Belief*: If one knows that C obtains, then one believes that C obtains.

(2) *F-Discrimination*: If one believes that C obtains, then in every close case one has a similarly high degree of confidence that C obtains.

(3) *F-Safety*: If one knows that C obtains, then C obtains in every close case in which one has a similarly high degree of confidence that C obtains.
Therefore,

(4) *Margins*: If one knows that C obtains, then C obtains in every close case.

Berker accepts F-Discrimination, but he rejects F-Safety. He argues that F-Safety is false because my reliability is not impugned by the fact that I'm disposed to have high confidence in falsehoods so long as I don't believe them. Why should knowledge require not merely the absence of false belief in close cases but also the absence of false confidence in close cases? This is Berker's challenge.

Anticipating this challenge, Williamson argues that if there is a close case in which you have high confidence in a false proposition, then your belief is not reliable enough for knowledge because it is constituted by "largely misplaced confidence" (2000: 97). The idea is that knowledge requires not merely safety from belief in falsehoods, but also safety from high confidence in falsehoods. To motivate this requirement, Amia Srinivasan gives the following variation on Goldman's fake barn case:

> *Receding Fake Barns*: Mirra is looking at two rows of what look like barns in the distance. The first row is made up of real barns; the second row is fake. In situations like this, Mirra only forms beliefs about the proposition *that is a row of barns*, and she reliably forms only true beliefs about that proposition. The threshold for outright belief is 70% confidence. Of the first row, Mirra believes with 70% confidence that it is a row of barns. Of the second row, Mirra believes with 69% confidence that it is a row of barns. (2015: 314)

In this version of the fake barn case, just like the original version, Mirra fails to know that there are real barns ahead. But in this version, she is in no danger of believing the false proposition that there are real barns ahead. Even so, she doesn't know that there are real barns ahead because she is in danger of having high confidence in the false proposition that there are barns ahead. Hence, F-Safety can be motivated in much the same way as C-Safety.

Berker challenges F-Safety by envisaging a subject whose degree of confidence that she feels cold marches in step with the degree to which she feels cold in such a way that she crosses the threshold for believing that she feels cold just when she crosses the threshold for feeling cold. He takes this to undercut the plausibility of F-Safety:

> What if one's degree of confidence in its being the case that p perfectly tracks the underlying basis for its being the case that p, so that one's degree of confidence that p falls just short of belief at the precise point at which things fall just short of making it the case that p? Why would *that* be a situation in which one's initial belief that p is not reliable enough to constitute knowledge? (2008: 12)

F-Safety implies that the subject is not reliable enough to know that p when the subject is close to the cutoff, since he is disposed to have high confidence that p when it is false that p. Berker thinks this is implausible. He writes: "F-Safety deems as unreliable belief-forming mechanisms that appear to be as reliable as they could possibly be" (2008: 12).

But is it true that Berker's mechanism is perfectly reliable? This depends on how reliability is measured. If we measure reliability in terms of coarse-grained belief, then Berker's claim seems right: the proposed mechanism is perfectly reliable, since it yields belief that p if and only if it's true that p. If we measure reliability in terms of fine-grained degrees of confidence, however, then Berker's claim seems wrong: a perfectly reliable mechanism would yield credence 1 in p when it is true that p and credence 0 in p when it is false that p. A creature with this kind of discontinuous credence profile, who assigns diametrically opposite credences to close cases, satisfies F-Safety by violating F-Discrimination.[15]

Now, it is implausible that humans—or any other physically possible systems—have confidence profiles that are discontinuous in the sense required for being perfectly reliable. As Berker writes:

> Non-idealized physical systems rarely—if ever—exhibit discontinuous phenomena at the macroscopic level, so it seems plausible that, among the degree-of-confidence profiles for which one's belief that one feels cold always counts as being suitably reliable, some of those degree-of-confidence profiles are continuous. (2008: 15)

In effect, Berker suggests that F-Safety is too demanding because it requires the physically impossible: namely, that our confidence profiles are discontinuous.

---

[15] I'm assuming bivalence for simplicity, but even if there are borderline cases in which it's neither true nor false that I feel cold, this wouldn't support Berker's claim that the rational credence distribution is continuous. In a supervaluationist framework, for example, there are some precisifications in which I feel cold, and there are some in which I don't feel cold, but there are none in which it's rational for me to be less than certain about how I feel.

However, there is no need to claim that knowledge requires this kind of perfect reliability. You can know that p on the basis of an imperfectly reliable mechanism so long as you're not too close to the margin for error. But if your belief-forming mechanism is imperfectly reliable, then you cannot know that p when you are too close to the margin, since you're in danger of investing high confidence in false propositions in close cases. In effect, nothing is doxastically luminous for nonideal agents with imperfectly reliable mechanisms. Maybe there are ideal agents with perfectly reliable mechanisms for whom some conditions are doxastically luminous, but since we have imperfectly reliable mechanisms, nothing is doxastically luminous for us.[16]

I conclude that Berker's response to Williamson's anti-luminosity argument fails. Unlike Berker, I accept that F-Safety is a necessary condition for knowledge—and one that applies to ideal and nonideal agents alike. The difference between ideal and nonideal agents is that the former satisfy F-Safety because they violate F-Discrimination, whereas the latter violate F-Safety because they satisfy F-Discrimination. For all we've seen so far, Williamson's argument for Margins fails when it is applied to ideal agents, but succeeds when it is applied to nonideal agents. Since Williamson is primarily concerned with nonideal agents, this is good news for him. The bad news is that another key premise in his argument—namely, Position—holds for ideal agents, but not for nonideal agents, since nonideal agents cannot convert their epistemic position into knowledge when they're close to the margin for error. Hence, Williamson's anti-luminosity argument fails either way.

For simplicity, let's assume that, in the process of gradually warming up from dawn to noon, there is a sharp cutoff between feeling cold and not feeling cold.[17] When ideal agents cross the threshold from feeling cold to not feeling cold, their credence that they feel cold drops sharply from 1 to 0. Ideal agents have discontinuous credence profiles because they are perfectly sensitive to their evidence. As such, they are safe from error even when they are close to the margins. An ideal agent can know that she feels cold, even if there is a close case in which she doesn't feel cold, since she is perfectly sensitive to her evidence, which includes all the facts about how she currently feels. In contrast, we nonideal agents are not perfectly sensitive to our evidence. When we cross the threshold from feeling cold to not feeling cold, our credence that we feel cold changes only incrementally. We cannot know that we feel cold when we are close to the margins because we are not safe from error. If we believe that

---

[16] This is, in effect, Srinivasan's (2015) response to Berker.

[17] Williamson (2000: 103–104) makes this assumption in explaining why the anti-luminosity argument doesn't rely on sorites-style reasoning. As I've noted, however, luminosity is consistent with supervaluationist treatments, as well as epistemicist treatments, of borderline cases.

we feel cold, then there are close cases in which we have high confidence in the false proposition that we feel cold. Therefore, Margins holds for nonideal agents, but it doesn't hold for ideal agents.

In contrast, Position holds for ideal agents, but not for nonideal agents. Williamson's description of the example builds in the assumption that if you're in a position to know that you feel cold, then you know that you feel cold, since you're doing what you're in a position to do throughout the process of warming up between dawn and noon. This assumption is much less innocent than it seems. In effect, it assumes that you're an ideally rational agent. As we've seen, converting your epistemic position into knowledge requires much more than simply considering the question whether you feel cold. After all, knowledge requires safety from error. Ideal agents can satisfy the safety requirement even when they're close to the margin for error, since their doxastic dispositions are perfectly sensitive to the facts that constitute their evidence. In contrast, nonideal agents cannot convert their epistemic position into knowledge when they're close to the margins, since their doxastic dispositions are not sufficiently sensitive to the facts that constitute their evidence. As a result, nonideal agents cannot always convert their epistemic position into knowledge.

In summary, Williamson's anti-luminosity argument fails for both ideal and nonideal agents, but for different reasons in each case. Recall that the argument proceeds by deriving Tolerance from Luminosity given Margins and Position. To accept Luminosity without Tolerance, we need to reject either Margins or Position. In the case of ideal agents, Position is true, but Margins is false: ideal agents don't need a margin for error, since they can convert their epistemic position into knowledge even when they are close to the margin. In the case of nonideal agents, Margins is true, but Position is false: nonideal agents cannot convert their epistemic position into knowledge when they are too close to the margins. Either way, the anti-luminosity argument is unsound.

The key point is that margin-for-error principles don't constrain your epistemic position, but rather your doxastic position. Whenever you feel cold, you're in an epistemic position to know that you feel cold even when there's a close case in which you stop feeling cold. If you're an ideal agent, then you can convert your epistemic position into knowledge even when you're close to the cutoff, since your beliefs about your own experience are safe from error. If you're a nonideal agent, in contrast, then you cannot convert your epistemic position into knowledge when you're close to the cutoff, since your beliefs are not safe from error when you're too close to the margins. Unlike the ideal agent, you're not perfectly sensitive to the evidence provided by your experience, and so you're equally disposed to believe that you feel cold in the close case where you don't feel cold.

Williamson's anti-luminosity argument shows that nothing is doxastically luminous for nonideal agents like us. But it leaves intact the claim that some conditions are epistemically luminous for ideal and nonideal agents alike. It's just that we nonideal agents are not perfectly sensitive to our evidence and so we cannot convert our epistemic position into knowledge when we are too close to the margin for error. Ideal agents are perfectly sensitive to their evidence and so they can always convert their epistemic position into knowledge. All epistemically luminous conditions are doxastically luminous for ideal agents, but not for nonideal agents like us.

11.4. Epistemic Iteration Principles

Williamson (2000: ch. 5) also argues against epistemic iteration principles. His main target is a version of the KK principle, which says that if you know that p, then you're in a position to know that you know that p.[18] As I'll explain, this argument can be extended against the JJ principle, which says that if you have justification to believe that p, then you have justification to believe that you have justification to believe that p. Hence, Williamson's argument against epistemic iteration principles constitutes a direct challenge to the version of accessibilism defended in this book.[19]

In this section, I'll explain how my objections to his anti-luminosity argument can be applied to his argument against epistemic iteration principles. Both arguments rely on margin-for-error principles, although these principles take a slightly different form in each case. My response is that margin-for-error principles constrain your doxastic position, rather than your epistemic position: they are principles about whether you're reliable enough to convert your epistemic position into knowledge. As a result, Williamson's argument leaves intact epistemic iteration principles that are formulated in terms of your epistemic position, rather than your doxastic position.

Williamson constructs a counterexample to the KK principle involving the myopic cartoon character Mr. Magoo:

Looking out of his window, Mr Magoo can see a tree some distance off. He wonders how tall it is. Evidently, he cannot tell to the nearest inch just by looking. His eyesight and ability to judge heights are nothing like that good. . . . Nevertheless, by looking he has gained some knowledge. He knows that the tree is not 60 or 6,000 inches tall. In fact, the tree is

---

[18] Proponents of the KK principle include Hintikka (1962), Stroud (1984), Stalnaker (2009), McHugh (2010), Marusic (2013), Greco (2014b), and Das and Salow (2018).

[19] Smith (2012) and Littlejohn (2013) extend Williamson's argument to the JK principle, which I used in arguing for the irrationality of epistemic akrasia in section 9.4.

666 inches tall, but he does not know that. For all he knows, it is 665 or 667 inches tall. (2000: 114)

Mr. Magoo can't know that the tree is 666 inches tall because his eyesight and his ability to judge heights are not good enough. Even if he truly believes that the tree is 666 inches tall, his belief is not safe from error, since it is formed in a way that could easily yield false belief. His beliefs are not responsive to extremely fine-grained differences in height, so he could easily believe that the tree is 666 inches tall when in fact it is 665 or 667 inches tall.

Williamson uses this example to motivate a margin-for-error principle. Recall that a margin-for-error principle says that you know that p only if there is no close case in which it is false that p. Applying this to Magoo, he knows that the tree is 666 inches tall only if there is no close case in which the tree is 665 or 667 inches tall. Since Magoo cannot make these fine-grained discriminations, these cases count as relevantly close. So if the tree is 666 inches tall, then there is a close case in which the tree is 665 or 667 inches tall. Putting this together, we can conclude that if the tree is 666 inches tall, then Magoo cannot know that it's not 665 or 667 inches tall. More generally, the margin-for-error principle says:

Margins: If the tree is $i + 1$ inches tall, then Mr. Magoo doesn't know that the tree is not i inches tall.

Contraposing, Magoo knows that the tree is not i inches tall only if the tree is not $i + 1$ inches tall. The margin-for-error principle explains why Magoo can't know that the tree is not 665 or 667 inches tall when it is 666 inches tall. He can't know this because knowledge requires a margin for error.

Williamson makes the following assumptions about the case. First, Magoo acquires some knowledge about the height of the tree, even if he cannot know exactly how tall it is. In particular, he knows that the tree is more than 60 inches tall. This is our first stipulation:

Stipulation 1: Mr. Magoo knows that the tree is not 60 inches tall.

Second, the tree is stipulated to be exactly 666 inches tall. Since knowledge is factive:

Stipulation 2: Magoo doesn't know that the tree is not 666 inches tall.

Third, Magoo knows every pertinent proposition that he's in a position to know. In particular, if he is in a position to know that he knows that p, then he knows that he knows that p. Hence, Williamson makes the following assumption for *reductio*:

The KK principle: "For any pertinent proposition p, if Mr Magoo knows p, then he knows that he knows p." (2000: 115)

Fourth, Magoo "reflects on the limitations of his eyesight and his ability to judge heights" and thereby comes to know the margin-for-error principle stated above:

Reflective Margins: "Mr Magoo knows that if the tree is $i + 1$ inches tall, then he does not know that the tree is not i inches tall." (2000: 115)

Fifth, Magoo knows every pertinent proposition that follows deductively from what he knows about the height of the tree and what he knows about what he knows. In other words, Magoo satisfies the following closure principle:

Closure: "If p and all members of the set X are pertinent propositions, p is a logical consequence of X, and Mr Magoo knows each member of X, then he knows p." (2000: 116)

As Williamson argues, these assumptions are inconsistent. The argument runs as follows:

(1) Mr. Magoo knows that the tree is not 60 inches tall. (Stipulation 1)
(2) Mr. Magoo knows that he knows that the tree is not 60 inches tall. ((1), KK)
(3) Mr. Magoo knows that if the tree is 61 inches tall, then he does not know that the tree is not 60 inches tall. (Reflective Margins)
(4) Mr. Magoo knows that the tree is not 61 inches tall. ((2), (3), Closure)

By repeated applications of this argument, we can generate the following absurd conclusion:

(5) Mr. Magoo knows that the tree is not 666 inches tall.

This contradicts Stipulation 2. Since knowledge is factive, it's impossible to know that the tree is not 666 inches tall when it is in fact 666 inches tall.

Williamson presents this argument as a *reductio* of the KK principle. But why not reject Closure or Margins instead? As we've seen, Williamson motivates Margins on independent grounds. Meanwhile, Closure is motivated by the principle that "deduction is a way of extending one's knowledge: that is, knowing $p_1, \ldots, p_n$, competently deducing q, and thereby coming to believe q is in general a way of coming to know q" (2000: 117). Williamson also reworks the argument so that the closure principle applies only to single-premise inferences, thereby blocking probabilistic objections connected with the preface paradox. He concedes that we don't always know the consequences of what we know and that we don't always know the relevant facts about our limited capacities. The point is just that we can stipulate a counterexample to the KK principle in which these principles hold. If so, then we can expect these counterexamples to be pervasive, since "the crucial features of the example are common to virtually all perceptual knowledge" (2000: 119).

Williamson's argument against the KK principle can be extended to the JJ principle by replacing every occurrence of 'knows' with 'has a justified belief'. As before, the following assumptions about Mr. Magoo are inconsistent:

Stipulation 1: Mr. Magoo has a justified belief that the tree is not 60 inches tall.

Stipulation 2: Mr. Magoo doesn't have a justified belief that the tree is not 666 inches tall.

The JJ principle: For any pertinent proposition p, if Mr. Magoo has a justified belief that p, then he has a justified belief that he has a justified belief that p.

Reflective Margins: Mr. Magoo has a justified belief that if the tree is $i + 1$ inches tall, then he does not have a justified belief that the tree is not i inches tall.

Closure: If p and all members of the set X are pertinent propositions, p is a logical consequence of X, and Mr. Magoo has a justified belief in each member of X, then he has a justified belief that p.

Stipulations 1 and 2 are justified by the assumption that Magoo acquires some justified beliefs about the height of the tree, even if they are not very precise. Although justified belief is nonfactive, it remains plausible that Magoo doesn't have a justified false belief that the tree is not 666 inches tall. Reflective Margins remains plausible too, since Magoo knows he is not reliable enough to form justified beliefs about the height of the tree to the nearest inch. Closure is plausible because deduction is a way of extending justified belief as well as knowledge. And we arrive at this version of the JJ principle by assuming that Magoo has a justified belief in every pertinent proposition that he has justification to believe, including metajustificatory propositions about which propositions he has justification to believe. Hence, using the same reasoning as before, we can conclude by *reductio* that the JJ principle is false.

Let me now explain why Williamson's argument fails to threaten epistemic iteration principles that concern epistemic positions, rather than doxastic positions. The argument relies crucially on the assumption that Magoo knows everything he is in a position to know and has a justified belief in everything he has justification to believe. In other words, Magoo always converts his epistemic position into knowledge and justified belief. As before, this assumption is not as innocent as it seems, since it is tantamount to assuming that Magoo is an ideally rational agent. Only ideally rational agents are always capable of converting their epistemic position into knowledge and justified belief. In contrast, nonideally rational agents cannot convert their epistemic position when they are too close to the margin for error. After all, knowledge requires safety from error, while justified belief requires safety from absence of evidential support. Nonideally rational agents violate these conditions when they are close to the margins, since their doxastic dispositions are not sufficiently sensitive to the facts that constitute their evidence. This is one of the morals of my solution to the problem of the speckled hen.

The next point to make is that margin-for-error principles do not constrain our epistemic positions, but rather the doxastic positions of nonideally rational agents. To see this, consider how the following margin-for-error principle is motivated by reflection on the problem of the speckled hen:

Margins: If the hen has $n + 1$ speckles, then you cannot know that the hen doesn't have n speckles.

Suppose you see a hen that has 48 speckles. You cannot know that the hen has 48 speckles, even if you truly believe that it does, since you would believe the same thing even if the hen has one more or one less. Even if your vision is fine-grained enough to represent the difference between 47 and 48 speckles, your doxastic dispositions are sufficiently coarse-grained that you're in danger of believing that the hen has 48 speckles even when your vision accurately represents that the hen has 47 speckles. This is because you are a nonideally rational agent whose beliefs are not perfectly sensitive to your evidence.

These margin-for-error principles do not apply to ideally rational agents whose beliefs are perfectly sensitive to the evidence provided by their experience. For simplicity, let's consider an ideally rational agent with perfectly precise and accurate vision. If the hen has 48 speckles, then our ideal agent can know that it has 48 speckles, and hence that it doesn't have one more or one less. This is a counterexample to Margins. Now, ideal rationality doesn't require having perfectly precise and accurate vision. Ideally rational agents are perfectly sensitive to their evidence, but their evidence can be imperfect. So let's imagine an ideally rational agent with imprecise vision that reliably represents the number of speckles as being within some range: say n speckles plus or minus one. Now consider a case in which the hen has 47 speckles, and the ideal agent's vision accurately represents that the hen has between 47 and 49 speckles. In that case, the ideal agent can know that the hen has between 47 and 49 speckles, and hence that the hen doesn't have 46 speckles. This is another counterexample to Margins.[20]

In summary, the argument fails whether we're considering ideal or nonideal agents. If Magoo is a nonideal agent, then he is not always capable of converting his epistemic position into knowledge or justified belief. If he is an ideal agent, then the margin-for-error principles are false, since he can convert his epistemic position into knowledge or justified belief even when he is close to the margins. Either way, the argument fails to undermine epistemic iteration principles that are formulated in terms of epistemic positions. At best, it undermines epistemic iteration principles that are formulated in terms of doxastic positions. This is a non-trivial conclusion, but it is no objection to the version of accessibilism defended in this book.

11.5. The Puzzle of the Unmarked Clock

Williamson's (2011, 2014) case of the unmarked clock aims to "turn the screw" on his counterexamples to the KK principle. It's not just that there are cases in which it's knowable that p, although it's *unknowable* that it's knowable that p. Worse still, there are cases of "improbable knowing" in which it's knowable that p, but it's *improbable* that it's knowable that p. Similarly, he argues, there are cases of "improbable rationality" in which it's rationally permissible to believe that p, although it's improbable that it's rationally permissible to believe that p. In such cases, Williamson argues, your evidence makes it probable that the following Moorean conjunctions are true:

(i) p but I'm not in a position to know that p.
(ii) p but it's not rationally permissible for me to believe that p.

Of course, these Moorean conjunctions are unknowable, since the second conjunct will be false whenever you're in a position to know the first conjunct. Even so, Williamson argues, the evidential probability of the conjunction can be arbitrarily close to 1. Presumably, however, it is never rationally permissible for anyone to believe these Moorean conjunctions. Hence, these cases of improbable knowing generate a puzzle.[21]

---

[20] Stalnaker (2009) proposes similar counterexamples, but he applies them to nonideal agents, rather than ideal agents.

[21] This puzzle is also discussed by Christensen (2010b), Elga (2013), Horowitz (2014), and Lasonen-Aarnio (2015). I have borrowed from Elga's presentation of the case.

Williamson proposes to solve the puzzle by rejecting the Lockean thesis, which says that it's rationally permissible to believe a proposition just in case its evidential probability is high enough to meet some threshold between 0.5 and 1. Instead, he endorses a knowledge norm for belief, which says that it's rationally permissible to believe that p only if you know that p. Given his E = K thesis, it follows that it's rationally permissible to believe that p only if the evidential probability that p is 1. Since you're never in a position to *know* Moorean conjunctions, it follows that it's never rationally permissible for you to *believe* them. The suggestion is that we can solve the puzzle generated by cases of improbable knowing by endorsing the knowledge norm for belief.

Arguably, however, the puzzle cannot be so easily resolved. Williamson's knowledge norm for belief cannot explain why it's rationally impermissible to be *highly confident* that Moorean conjunctions are true or to believe that they are *probably* true. But this is no less plausible as an intuitive data point to be explained than the claim that it's rationally impermissible to *believe* Moorean conjunctions outright. So even if we accept the knowledge norm for belief, a residual version of the puzzle remains.

Although Williamson claims we are forced to live with the puzzling consequences of improbable rationality, I will suggest otherwise. If we assume that your evidence is luminous, then we can block his argument for improbable rationality. Of course, Williamson argues that nothing is luminous, but I've replied to this argument in section 11.3. My aim in this section is to explain how these arguments stand or fall together.

Suppose you're looking at an unmarked clock whose minute hand moves in discrete jumps from one minute to the next. In fact, the clock reads 12:17. Assuming you know the clock to be reliable, what is it rational for you to believe about the time? On the phenomenal conception of evidence, what it's rational for you to believe about the clock depends not on what it actually reads, but on what it visually appears to read. Absent defeaters, if it visually appears that the clock reads 12:17, then it's rationally permissible to believe that it's 12:17. Presumably, however, your vision is not so precise. At best, it visually appears that the clock reads *approximately* 12:17. For simplicity, let's assume that your vision represents the time as falling within a range of plus or minus one minute:

- When the clock reads 12:17, it visually appears to you that H, i.e. the clock reads 12:18, 12:17, or 12:16.
- When the clock reads 12:18, it visually appears to you that H+, i.e. the clock reads 12:19, 12:18, or 12:17.
- When the clock reads 12:16, it visually appears to you that H−, i.e. the clock reads 12:17, 12:16, or 12:15.

This is where things start to get interesting. Just as you can't know exactly what the clock reads, so you can't know exactly how the clock visually appears to you. You can't know that it visually appears that H because you're not sufficiently reliable about the visual appearances. Let's suppose you're reliable about how the clock appears within a margin of plus or minus one minute. So, for example, when it appears that H, you can know the disjunction that it appears that H, H+ or H−, but you can't know which disjunct is true. Even if you believe that it appears that H, your true belief falls short of knowledge because it is held on the basis of an unreliable disposition. Exercising the same disposition could easily yield false belief in similar counterfactual circumstances. For instance, you might believe that it appears that H when in fact it appears that H+ or H−. This is another application of Williamson's principle that knowledge requires a margin for error.

Now we can generate a case of improbable rationality. Since it visually appears to you that H, in the absence of defeaters, it's rational for you to believe that H. For all you know, however, it visually appears that H+ or H− instead. Assuming that each of these scenarios is about equally probable, it probably doesn't seem to you that H, since it's more probable that it seems that H+ or H−. Moreover, if it seems that H+ or H−, then it's not rational to believe H, since it's rational to believe H+ or H− instead. The upshot is that it's rational to believe H, but it's not rational to believe that it's rational to believe H. In fact, it's rational to believe that it's *probably not rational* to believe that H. In other words, it's rational to be epistemically akratic.

Williamson's own presentation of the argument relies on the assumption that your evidence about the clock is exhausted by what you know about the clock. In contrast, I've assumed here that your evidence about the clock is exhausted by how the clock visually appears to you, which may not correspond to how the clock really is. This is important because it shows how the argument applies even to those (like me) who reject Williamson's knowledge-first conception of evidence and accept the phenomenal conception of evidence instead. Even so, the argument relies crucially on the assumption that what your evidence makes it *rational* for you to believe about the visual appearances depends on what you can *know* about the visual appearances. This is another application of Williamson's claim that your evidence is constrained by what you can know. But suppose we reject this claim and say instead that what it's rational for you to believe about the visual appearances depends just on the visual appearances themselves. On this view, if it seems to you that H, then it's rational for you believe with certainty that it seems to you that H. Now the argument for the rationality of epistemic akrasia is blocked.

My own solution to the puzzle of the unmarked clock is that the evidence provided by visual appearances is *luminous* in the sense that whenever it visually appears to you that *p*, it's rational for you to believe with certainty that it visually appears to you that *p*. If you're looking at an unmarked clock and it visually seems to you that H in the absence of defeaters, then it's rationally permissible for you to believe not only that H, but also the following:

(1) It visually seems to me that H, and I have no defeaters.
(2) If it visually seems to me that H, and I have no defeaters, then it's rationally permissible for me to believe that H.
(3) So it's rationally permissible for me to believe that H.

In conclusion, Williamson's argument for improbable rationality relies on the assumption that evidence is not luminous. If we reject this assumption, then the argument is blocked. Moreover, this undercuts the motivation for allowing some kinds of epistemic akrasia but not others to fall within the limits of rational permissibility.[22]

11.6. What's at Stake?

In this chapter, I've given a partially concessive response to the anti-luminosity arguments of Sosa and Williamson. I concede that no nontrivial conditions are doxastically luminous in the sense that we're always capable of knowing whether or not they obtain. But I maintain that this pessimistic conclusion reflects the limits of our doxastic capacities for responding to our epistemic positions, rather than the limits of our epistemic positions themselves. The anti-luminosity arguments leave intact the claim that some nontrivial conditions are epistemically luminous in the sense that we're always in an epistemic position to know whether or not they obtain. It's just that we nonideal agents cannot always convert our epistemic position into knowledge.

Is this a pyrrhic victory? Once we've abandoned the doxastic version of accessibilism in favor of the epistemic version, it may be said that the resulting view is too attenuated to be worth defending. In this section, I'll consider three versions of this objection which I frequently encounter in conversation: (i) the motivational objection, (ii) the feasibility objection, and (iii) the idealization objection.

---

[22] Elga (2013) presents the puzzle of the unmarked clock as a conflict between two assumptions, which he calls Modesty and Rational Reflection. My solution is to reject Modesty, whereas Elga's solution is to amend Rational Reflection. See Lasonen-Aarnio (2015) for criticism of Elga's solution: one major problem is that it cannot explain the irrationality of a form of epistemic akrasia in which you have credence *n* that *p*, while also being certain that it's rationally impermissible to have credence *n* that *p*.

The motivational objection says that the epistemic version of accessibilism is unmotivated. According to this objection, the main arguments for accessibilism support a doxastic version, rather than an epistemic version, of the thesis. On this view, it's not enough that you're always in an epistemic position to know which propositions you have epistemic justification to believe unless you're also capable of converting your epistemic position into knowledge. If this is right, then the concessive response to the anti-luminosity argument can be dismissed as a pointless compromise, since it doesn't answer to the considerations that motivate accessibilism in the first place.

Accessibilism is often thought to be motivated by what Alvin Goldman (1999) calls "the guidance-deontological conception of justification." On this view, we have an epistemic duty to believe what we have justification to believe. Moreover, we are responsible for fulfilling our epistemic duty: for instance, we can legitimately be blamed for holding unjustified beliefs. As Goldman explains, the guidance-deontological conception of justification is sometimes used to derive an accessibility constraint on justifiers, according to which they must be luminously accessible to the epistemic agent. The basic idea is that you cannot be held responsible for fulfilling your duty unless you're capable of knowing what your duty requires. If this argument is successful, it establishes that justifying conditions are doxastically luminous, and not merely epistemically luminous.[23]

I'll make four points in reply to this objection. First, there are independent reasons to reject the doxastic version of accessibilism. As we saw in chapter 8, it faces an overintellectualization problem, since it implies that you cannot have justified first-order beliefs unless you have the capacity to form justified higher-order beliefs about the conditions that justify them. Moreover, it faces a regress problem, since it implies that you cannot have justified first-order beliefs unless you have the capacity to form an infinite hierarchy of higher-order beliefs of ever-increasing complexity. The epistemic version of accessibilism avoids these objections.

Second, this argument for accessibilism relies on a false premise—namely, a guidance-deontological conception that ties epistemic justification too closely to concepts of duty and blame. In section 8.4, I argued that a Capgras patient who believes that his spouse has been replaced by an imposter is not thereby blameworthy for violating his epistemic duties, despite the fact that his belief is not justified by the evidence. We cannot always be held responsible for failing to believe whatever is justified by the evidence. After all, we're not always

---

[23] Versions of this argument for accessibilism are proposed by Ginet (1975), BonJour (1985), and Steup (1999). This argument has been criticized by many opponents of accessibilism, including Kornblith (1983), Plantinga (1993), Goldman (1999), and Bergmann (2006: ch. 4).

capable of doing so. Blameworthiness is constrained by our doxastic limitations, whereas propositional justification is not.

Third, there is no cogent argument for accessibilism from the premise that the guidance-deontological conception of justification is true. Even if we grant that you must be capable of knowing what your duty requires, it doesn't follow that your duties are determined by facts that are luminously accessible to you. As Goldman points out, your duties may be determined by nonluminous facts about the world that you're nevertheless capable of knowing. The argument is simply fallacious.

Finally, this argument for accessibilism plays no role at all in this book. I've argued for accessibilism on the grounds that it explains intuitions about cases, it explains the irrationality of epistemic akrasia, and it preserves a plausible connection between rationality and reflection. As a result, the motivational objection simply fails to engage with the central arguments of this book.

The feasibility objection says that there are other compelling reasons to hold that propositional justification is constrained by the limits of your doxastic capacities. Perhaps the most compelling version of this objection is that our ordinary epistemic evaluations are in fact sensitive to people's limited doxastic capacities. For instance, we tend to allow that it's reasonable, rational, or justifiable for someone to withhold belief that *p* even when she has strong or even conclusive evidence that *p*, so long as she cannot form a justified belief on the basis of the evidence. This suggests that our ordinary conception of propositional justification is doxastically constrained.

My response is to draw a distinction between ideal and nonideal standards of rationality. Our ordinary epistemic evaluations reflect nonideal standards of rationality that take our limited doxastic capacities into account. These are the standards of rationality for which we can hold each other accountable. But the epistemic value of conforming to these nonideal standards of rationality cannot be explained as an end in itself. Instead, it should be explained derivatively in terms of its conduciveness toward the end of approximating more closely toward ideal standards of rationality. Hence, the epistemic value of nonideal rationality is to be explained in terms of its connection with ideal rationality.

This is not merely an ad hoc maneuver designed to defend accessibilism against objections. Any nontrivial theory of justification needs a version of this distinction to deal with cases in which we're incapable of conforming to its standards. In such cases, we need a distinction between the ideal standards laid down by the theory and the nonideal standards we use when we're incapable of conforming to them. Epistemic ideals need not always be humanly achievable. But when they are not, we need derivative standards to evaluate our strategies for approximating toward the ideal as closely as we can.

The idealization objection says that the epistemic version of accessibilism fails to carve out an important dimension of epistemic value. According to the epistemic version of accessibilism, ideally rational agents are omniscient or infallible about their own evidence, but not about the external world. Why suppose this is an ideal worth caring about? Of course, we can idealize our epistemic capacities along many different dimensions. One kind of ideal epistemic agent is a godlike being who is omniscient and infallible in the sense that she believes that p if and only if it's true that p. And yet it's not plausible that being ideally rational requires being omniscient or infallible in this sense. Rationality is a matter of respecting your evidence, which can be both inaccurate and incomplete. But then why suppose rationality requires omniscience and infallibility in some domains and not others? And why suppose the domain of experience and belief is epistemically privileged in this way?

This objection is structurally parallel to a standard objection to probabilistic theories of rationality. Why suppose that ideal rationality requires logical omniscience, but not empirical omniscience? A standard answer is that violations of logical omniscience have a trickle-down effect. If you violate logical omniscience, and you integrate your reasoning with your beliefs about logic, then your reasoning fails to respect logic. But rationality requires your reasoning to respect logic. And rationality also requires you to integrate your reasoning with your beliefs about logic. Therefore, rationality requires logical omniscience; that is, it prohibits uncertainty and error about logic.

In chapter 10, I argued on similar grounds that rationality requires *evidential omniscience*: that is, it prohibits uncertainty and error about what your evidence is and what it supports. This is because violations of evidential omniscience have a similar kind of trickle-down effect. If you violate evidential omniscience, and you integrate your reasoning with your beliefs about what your evidence supports, then your reasoning fails to respect your evidence. But rationality requires your reasoning to respect your evidence. And rationality also requires you to integrate your reasoning with your beliefs about what your evidence supports. Therefore, rationality requires evidential omniscience: that is, it prohibits uncertainty and error about what your evidence supports.

On this view, your evidence is luminously accessible in the sense that you're always in a position to know with certainty what your evidence is and what it supports. Moreover, I've argued that phenomenally individuated facts about your mental states are the only contingent facts that are luminously accessible in the sense that you're always in a position to know with certainty whether or not they obtain. This is the rationale for embracing a phenomenal conception of evidence, according to which your evidence is exhausted by phenomenally individuated facts about your mental states.

Ideally rational agents are always certain of their own evidence, even if they are not certain of the propositions about the external world that are supported by their evidence. Only facts about experience and belief can play the role of evidence so construed. This is why ideally rational agents are always certain of their own experiences and beliefs, although they are less than certain about the state of the external world.

In conclusion, my concessive response to the anti-luminosity argument is not merely a pointless compromise that preserves the letter of accessibilism while sacrificing its essential spirit. On the contrary, it is strong enough to motivate the phenomenal conception of evidence defended in this book, but it is also weak enough to avoid the implausible psychological commitments that are so often taken to refute accessibilism. Accessibilism stands as an attractive proposal about the structure of epistemic justification and one that is surprisingly resilient against objections.

12

Seemings

What is the epistemic role of phenomenal consciousness? The answer defended in this book—phenomenal accessibilism—combines accessibilism with a phenomenal conception of evidence. Accessibilism says that epistemic justification is luminously accessible in the sense that you're always in a position to know which propositions you have epistemic justification to believe. This principle motivates a phenomenal conception of evidence, according to which your evidence is exhausted by phenomenally individuated facts about your current mental states. On this view, the epistemic role of phenomenal consciousness is to provide epistemic justification in a way that is luminously accessible.

In this final chapter, I'll contrast phenomenal accessibilism with a global version of phenomenal conservatism inspired by the work of Michael Huemer, which grounds all epistemic justification in phenomenal seemings. I'm interested in phenomenal conservatism because of its global ambitions: it seeks to explain all epistemic justification in terms of a single epistemic principle. According to this global principle of phenomenal conservatism, you have epistemic justification to believe whatever seems to you strongly enough on balance to be true.[1]

One of the attractions of phenomenal conservatism is that it offers such a simple and unified framework for explaining the epistemic role of phenomenal consciousness. I will argue, however, that the simplicity of phenomenal conservatism is not a theoretical virtue, but a theoretical vice, since it distorts the epistemological phenomena it is supposed to explain. In effect, phenomenal conservatism seeks to explain all epistemic justification on the same model as perception. But this has the predictable effect of distorting the epistemology of other domains, including introspection, inference, and a priori justification.

This chapter argues against phenomenal conservatism on two distinct fronts. First, it gives an overly restrictive account of the nature of evidence: it says that all evidence consists of phenomenal facts about how things seem. And second, it gives an overly simplified account of the nature of the evidential support

---

[1] See Huemer (2001: ch. 5) for his original defense of phenomenal conservatism. Others who defend similar views include Tucker (2010), Brogaard (2013), Chudnoff (2013), and Bengson (2015), although these authors make no explicit commitment to the fully global version of phenomenal conservatism.

relation: it says that a proposition is supported by your evidence just in case it seems strongly enough on balance to be true. If we relax these restrictions on evidence, or we build more structure into the evidential support relation, then we must abandon the global ambitions of phenomenal conservatism.

Phenomenal accessibilism diverges from phenomenal conservatism on both points. First, it builds more structure into the evidential support relation: accessibilism says that your evidence is always self-evident. And second, it yields a more liberal version of the phenomenal conception of evidence: it says that your evidence includes not just the phenomenal facts about how things seem, but all the phenomenally individuated facts about your current mental states.

There is an important connection between these two points. Accessibilism provides the best theoretical motivation for endorsing the phenomenal conception of evidence in the first place. The main problem with phenomenal conservatism is that both its account of evidence and its account of the evidential support relation are in tension with accessibilism. Phenomenal conservatism is therefore self-defeating in the sense that it undermines its own best motivation. Phenomenal accessibilism provides a more attractive theoretical framework for explaining the epistemic role of consciousness.

12.1. Phenomenal Conservatism

In the course of defending moderate foundationalism about perceptual knowledge, Michael Huemer proposes the following principle of phenomenal conservatism:

> If it seems to S as if p, then S thereby has at least prima facie justification for believing that p. (2001: 99)

This is a principle about foundational—that is, immediate or noninferential—justification. It says that seemings are sufficient to give you noninferential justification: necessarily, if it seems to you that p, then you thereby have at least some degree of defeasible, noninferential justification to believe that p. How much justification you have depends on the strength of your seemings, since the degree of justification provided by a seeming is proportional to its strength. According to Huemer, there are no restrictions on which seemings can play this foundational epistemic role.

Huemer (2001: 99) makes the further claim that the principle of phenomenal conservatism is the only principle of foundational justification. On this view, seemings are necessary as well as sufficient for giving you foundational justification: necessarily, if you have some degree of defeasible, noninferential justification to believe that p, then this is because it seems to you that p. Huemer (2001: 100) draws the corollary that only seemings can defeat the foundational justification provided by other seemings. When your seemings come into conflict, your degree of justification to believe a proposition depends solely on the relative strengths of your conflicting seemings. Hence, all foundational justification has its source in seemings alone.

In more recent work, Huemer (2016) extends phenomenal conservatism from foundational to nonfoundational—that is, from noninferential to inferential—justification. On this view, all inferential justification has its source in inferential seemings. You have epistemic justification to infer a conclusion from some premises just when and because the following conditions hold in the absence of defeaters: (i) the premises seem true, (ii) the conclusion seems to follow either deductively or inductively from the premises, and (iii) the conclusion thereby seems true.[2]

Putting all these claims together, we arrive at the following global principle of phenomenal conservatism:

Necessarily, you have epistemic justification to believe that p just when and because it seems to you strongly enough on balance that p.

The suggestion is that we can explain all epistemic justification in terms of a single unifying principle: you should always believe whatever seems strongly enough on balance to be true. This means that epistemic justification *supervenes* on seemings: there can be no difference in which propositions you have epistemic justification to believe without some difference in which propositions seem true. It also means that all epistemic justification is *grounded* in seemings: every epistemic fact about which propositions you have justification to believe is grounded in some nonepistemic fact about which propositions seem true. All of these claims are concerned with epistemic justification in the propositional sense, rather than the doxastic sense.[3]

The term 'phenomenal conservatism' is used in many different ways, but I'll use it to refer to the view that endorses all three of the following claims:

---

[2] Huemer (2016) focuses on doxastic justification, but it's implausible that inferential seemings are required for doxastic justification unless they are required for propositional justification too. Moreover, denying this would be a significant departure from the global ambitions of phenomenal conservatism. In any case, much of my discussion applies to a nearly global form of phenomenal conservatism that is restricted to foundational sources of propositional justification, although I believe this view has no stable motivation.

[3] Huemer (2006: 151) explicitly endorses the supervenience thesis. I cannot find an explicit statement of the grounding thesis, but it is very much in the spirit of Huemer's view.

(1) *Weak Phenomenal Conservatism*. Seemings are *sufficient* for epistemic justification: necessarily, if it seems to you that p, then you thereby have some degree of defeasible epistemic justification to believe that p.

(2) *Strong Phenomenal Conservatism*. Seemings are *necessary* for epistemic justification: necessarily, if you have some degree of defeasible epistemic justification to believe that p, then this is because it seems to you that p.

(3) *Global Phenomenal Conservatism*. All epistemic justification is *grounded* in seemings: necessarily, you have sufficient epistemic justification to believe that p just when and because it seems to you strongly enough on balance that p.

My own view is partially concessive to phenomenal conservatism: I accept the weak principle, although I reject the strong and global principles. To that extent, I make a much greater concession to phenomenal conservatism than many other critics of the view.[4]

Phenomenal conservatism can be situated within the more general framework of evidentialism. Evidentialism is the thesis that you have epistemic justification to believe whatever is supported strongly enough by your evidence. Any specific version of evidentialism needs two things: (i) an account of the nature of evidence, and (ii) an account of the nature of the evidential support relation.[5]

The evidentialist version of phenomenal conservatism yields an especially strong version of the phenomenal conception of evidence: it says that your evidence includes all and only the phenomenal facts about how things seem to you. Moreover, it combines this account of evidence with a simple account of the evidential support relation: your evidence supports a proposition to the extent that it seems on balance to be true; that is, the more strongly it seems true, the more strongly it is supported by your evidence. This version of evidentialism implies the global principle of phenomenal conservatism, which says that you have epistemic justification to believe whatever seems strongly enough on balance to be true.

Phenomenal conservatism certainly has its attractions. First, as I've noted, it offers a simple and unified epistemological framework that promises to subsume all epistemic justification under a single epistemic principle. Second, it offers an attractive framework for explaining the epistemic significance

---

[4] See Hawthorne and Lasonen-Aarnio (forthcoming) for a more radical critique of phenomenal conservatism that abandons the phenomenal conception of evidence altogether.

[5] See chapter 6 for further discussion of evidentialism. Huemer (2018) criticizes evidentialism, but his critique neglects one of the main points of this chapter, which is that epistemic justification is not wholly grounded in evidence, but partially in facts about the evidential support relation.

of phenomenal consciousness. And, third, it promises to explain so-called "internalist intuitions" about epistemic justification in cases of envatment and demonic deception, clairvoyance and super-blindsight, and so on. Ultimately, however, I'll argue that the global ambitions of phenomenal conservatism cannot succeed.

There are serious problems both with its account of evidence and the evidential support relation. First, its version of the phenomenal conception of evidence is much too restrictive, since it says that only seemings can be evidence. Accessibilism provides no motivation for this restriction, since all phenomenal facts are self-evident, and not just the phenomenal facts about how things seem. Moreover, this restriction generates problems for the epistemology of introspection and memory. There is some pressure to avoid these problems by accepting a diachronic version of phenomenal conservatism, but this conflicts with accessibilism, which provides the best motivation for endorsing the phenomenal conception of evidence in the first place. Hence, phenomenal conservatism threatens to undercut its own best motivation.

Second, the global ambitions of phenomenal conservatism depend on an overly simplified account of the evidential support relation. This account distorts the epistemology of introspection, logic, and inference by subsuming them under the same model as perception. Perception is a bad model for these other domains because there are structural dimensions of epistemic rationality that have no analogue in perception. One instance of this general problem is that phenomenal conservatism cannot solve what Huemer (2011) calls "the puzzle of meta-coherence": in other words, it cannot explain why epistemic rationality requires metacoherence. This is because its account of the evidential support relation is incompatible with accessibilism. Once again, this threatens to undermine the motivations for accepting the phenomenal conception of evidence in the first place.

My own view, phenomenal accessibilism, diverges from phenomenal conservatism both in its account of evidence and its account of the evidential support relation. First, I endorse a more liberal version of the phenomenal conception of evidence. On this view, your evidence includes not just the phenomenal facts about how things seem, but all the phenomenal facts about your experience, and all the phenomenally individuated facts about your beliefs, desires, and other standing attitudes. Second, I endorse a version of accessibilism that builds more structure into its account of the evidential support relation. There are structural constraints on which propositions I can have epistemic justification to believe, which are explained by necessary facts about the evidential support relation, rather than contingent facts about my evidence. Contrary to phenomenal conservatism, it doesn't always make any difference whether a proposition seems true.

My central claim is that the global ambitions of phenomenal conservatism are incompatible with accessibilism. At the same time, accessibilism provides the best theoretical motivation for endorsing the phenomenal conception of evidence in the first place. I therefore conclude that we cannot explain the epistemic significance of phenomenal consciousness within the framework of phenomenal conservatism. We need to adopt the framework of phenomenal accessibilism instead.

Here is the plan for this chapter. Having defined phenomenal conservatism (section 12.1), I'll clarify the central concept of "seemings" (section 12.2). Next, I'll criticize its account of the nature of evidence (section 12.3) and its account of the evidential support relation (section 12.4). Finally, I'll explain how phenomenal accessibilism avoids these problems (section 12.5) and I'll end with some more general conclusions (section 12.6).

12.2. What Are Seemings?

What are seemings? We need to answer this question before we can understand exactly what phenomenal conservatism is saying. In Huemer's (2001) foundationalist account of perceptual knowledge, perceptual experiences are the paradigmatic examples of seemings. At the same time, however, Huemer claims that there are many other kinds of seemings, including introspective seemings, intellectual seemings, and inferential seemings. What do all these different kinds of seemings have in common?

Following Huemer's (2001: 65–79) discussion of perceptual experience, I'll assume that all seemings have three essential features: (i) phenomenal character, (ii) representational content, and (iii) forcefulness. First, seemings have phenomenal character: there is something it is like for you when things seem a certain way. Second, seemings have representational content: when things seem a certain way, you thereby represent the world as being that way; indeed, you sometimes misrepresent the world, when things are not the way they seem. Third, seemings represent their contents with a distinctive kind of force, which Huemer (2001: 77–79) calls "forcefulness." The forcefulness of seemings is what sets them apart from other experiences with representational content, including imaginative experiences of visualization and cognitive experiences of judgment.

What Huemer means by the "forcefulness" of perceptual experience is what I mean, and what others mean, by "presentational force."[6] These are different

---

[6] My own view is presented in chapter 2, but see also Chudnoff (2013) and Bengson (2015) for further discussion of presentational phenomenology.

labels for the distinctive phenomenal character of perceptual experience in virtue of which it plays its distinctive epistemic role. It is only because perceptual experience represents its content with presentational force that it can justify believing its content without standing in need of justification. The presentational force of perceptual experience explains the phenomenal contrast between seeing that p and merely visualizing that p or judging that p. Moreover, it explains why seeing that p plays a distinctive epistemic role that cannot be played by visualizing that p or judging that p. This is because seeing that p involves a perceptual experience in which you represent that p with presentational force. Visualizing that p or judging that p cannot play the same epistemic role because these imaginative and cognitive experiences don't represent their contents with presentational force.

Presentational force—like phenomenal consciousness in general—cannot be defined in more basic terms, but only by example and contrast. It is the kind of phenomenal character that distinguishes the perceptual experience of seeing that p from an imaginative experience of visualizing that p or a cognitive experience of judging that p. Huemer introduces the notion of forcefulness in much the same way. He occasionally lapses into explaining forcefulness in terms of how things seem: for example, "it is the fact that, in the experience, it seems to one that something satisfying the content of the experience actually exists, here and now" (2001: 79). This is problematic because you could imagine or judge this proposition without thereby representing it forcefully. Of course, these experiences are not seemings, but this only goes to show that we cannot define seemings in terms of the representation of distinctive contents. Just as the name suggests, forcefulness is a distinctive kind of representational force, rather than a distinctive kind of representational content.

I've argued in this book that the phenomenal character of perceptual experience can be explained within the more general framework of representationalism.[7] On this view, the phenomenal character of perceptual experience is identical with a way of representing content with presentational force. This representationalist theory of perceptual experience can be combined with the weak principle of phenomenal conservatism, which says that if you have an experience that represents some content with presentational force, then you thereby have defeasible, noninferential justification to believe that content. It follows that perceptual experience justifies believing some content in virtue of its phenomenal character alone. Hence, phenomenal conservatism provides an

---

[7] See chapters 2 and 3 for further discussion of representationalism and its application to the epistemology of perception. The weak principle of phenomenal conservatism corresponds to what I called "the Content Principle" in chapter 3.

attractive framework for explaining the role of phenomenal consciousness in the epistemology of perception.

It's worth noting that Huemer rejects representationalism: he writes, "I view qualia as something over and above representational content" (2001: 67). On this view, the phenomenal and representational properties of perceptual experience are distinct and merely contingently connected with each other. As Huemer notes, however, this threatens to undermine the idea that the phenomenal character of perceptual experience has any essential role to play in explaining our knowledge of the external world:

> If indeed the quale of a perceptual experience is something beyond its representational content, and if the function of perceptual experiences is purely assertive (that is, their function is just to give us information about the world), what, if anything, are qualia good for? Is there any biological reason why we should have experiences with qualia, rather than just having experiences with representational contents and no qualia? (2001: 70)

To rephrase the question: is there any reason why phenomenal consciousness should be needed for acquiring knowledge or epistemically justified belief about the external world? Huemer gives no answer that would explain why unconscious perceptual information in super-blindsight cannot provide knowledge of the external world. In fact, he explicitly mentions super-blindsight and says, "this sort of qualia-lacking awareness plays the same sort of role in our knowledge of the external world as the more typical perceptual experiences" (2001: 67; cf. 89 n. 30).

In order to do justice to the role of phenomenal consciousness in the epistemology of perception, we need to combine weak phenomenal conservatism with representationalism. On this view, the phenomenal character of perceptual experience just is a way of representing contents about the external world with presentational force. Unconscious perceptual states can have representational properties too, but they cannot have exactly the same representational properties as perceptual experience. In particular, they cannot represent contents with the same kind of presentational force as perceptual experience.

Chris Tucker (2010: 530–531) argues that there are weak seemings in blindsight, which explain why subjects make reliable guesses about the blind field. These seemings are explained in terms of feelings of assertiveness, which "make it feel as though the seeming is 'recommending' its propositional content as true or 'assuring' us of the content's truth" (2010: 530). But this characterization fails to distinguish perceptual experiences of seeing from cognitive experiences of judgment. After all, judgment assertively represents its content in the sense that it "recommends" or "assures" that its content is true, but it cannot play the distinctive epistemic role of perception in justifying beliefs without standing in need of justification. Perhaps blindsighted subjects have cognitive experiences—hunches, if you like—that assertively represent propositions about the blind field with a low degree of strength. Nevertheless, these cognitive experiences cannot play the distinctive epistemic role of perceptual experience, since they don't represent their contents with the right kind of presentational force.[8]

The weak principle of phenomenal conservatism provides an attractive framework for explaining the role of phenomenal consciousness in the epistemology of perception. I'll argue that the strong and global principles, in contrast, distort the epistemic role of phenomenal consciousness in other domains, including introspection, inference, and a priori justification. As I've noted, Huemer claims that we have not only perceptual seemings, but also introspective, intellectual, and inferential seemings. Indeed, the plausibility of strong phenomenal conservatism depends on this claim; otherwise, we don't have enough seemings to explain how beliefs are justified in other domains. In this chapter, I'll argue that we have no good reason to believe this claim. In my view, there are no nonperceptual seemings: only perceptual experiences and perceptual memories represent their contents with presentational force.[9]

I'm not denying that we have intellectual, introspective, or inferential experiences that we might report by saying, "It seems to me that p." The problem is that our ordinary use of the term 'seems' is not a good guide to seemings in Huemer's technical sense. For example, when I judge that p, it's perfectly natural to say that it seems to me that p, and yet judgments are not seemings in this sense. This point is crucial for Huemer's purposes, since he denies that judgments can play the same epistemic role as perceptual experience in justifying beliefs without standing in need of justification. This is precisely because the experience of judgment does not represent its content with the right kind of force: it is assertive but not presentational.

I'm not disputing that we have intellectual, introspective, and inferential experiences that assertively represent their contents, but I deny that they have the right kind of forcefulness to justify belief without standing in need of justification. That is not to say that these experiences are reducible to judgments, or inclinations toward judgment, or feelings of confidence, or anything else. I remain agnostic about this. Even if some of these experiences are sui generis,

---

[8] Compare Chudnoff (2013: 30) and Bengson (2015: 719) for the view that there are no seemings in blindsight as characterized in terms of presentational force.

[9] Huemer (2001: 99) claims that we have memory-related seemings in factual memory as well as perceptual memory, whereas I accept only the latter.

and hence irreducible to more familiar categories, it doesn't follow that they have the right kind of phenomenal character to justify belief without standing in need of justification. This further claim is what I am denying.

The question in dispute is whether introspective, intellectual, and inferential experiences have the same kind of phenomenal character as perceptual experiences: the kind that suits an experience to justify beliefs without standing in need of justification. How can we resolve this dispute? As we've seen, ordinary language is too blunt an instrument, since our use of the word 'seems' doesn't track seemings in Huemer's technical sense.[10] Moreover, the dispute cannot be resolved solely by appeal to introspection. Both sides can agree that there are phenomenal similarities and differences between perception and intuition: for example, both are assertive, but only perception is sensory. The question remains whether these experiences are similar enough, and in the right ways, to play the same kind of epistemic role. That is not a question that can be resolved by introspection alone.

Instead, the dispute must be resolved on epistemological grounds. What are the epistemological consequences of assuming that we have introspective, intellectual, and inferential seemings that play the same kind of epistemic role as our perceptual seemings? I'll argue that this assumption, when combined with weak phenomenal conservatism, yields implausible epistemological consequences. Since weak phenomenal conservatism is true, I'll conclude that the assumption is false: we have no introspective, intellectual, or inferential seemings. This is bad news for strong and global versions of phenomenal conservatism. My epistemological argument against phenomenal conservatism has two parts: I criticize its account of evidence in section 12.3 and its account of evidential support in section 12.4.

12.3. Problems about Evidence

What does phenomenal conservatism imply about the nature of evidence when it is combined with the more general framework of evidentialism? The answer is that it yields a strong version of the phenomenal conception of evidence, which says that your evidence includes all and only the phenomenal facts about how things seem. Phenomenal conservatism says these are the only facts that can make a difference to which propositions you have epistemic justification to believe. In other words, your evidence is exhausted by how things seem.

[10] Hawthorne and Lasonen-Aarnio (forthcoming) argue that the semantics of 'seems' locutions provides no empirical support for the existence of seemings in Huemer's technical sense.

As Huemer (2006) argues, one advantage of phenomenal conservatism is that it explains so-called "internalist intuitions" about epistemic justification in cases of envatment and deception, clairvoyance and super-blindsight. Any phenomenal duplicate of yours who is deceived by an evil demon or an evil neuroscientist has epistemic justification to form all the same beliefs on the basis of perceptual experience. This is because things seem exactly the same way to each of you: your perceptual experience represents the same phenomenal contents with the same degree of presentational force. In contrast, subjects with clairvoyance or super-blindsight don't have epistemic justification to form beliefs on the basis of unconscious perceptual information. This is because the information in question is not represented with the distinctive phenomenal character of perceptual experience: there are no seemings in clairvoyance or super-blindsight.[11]

Despite this, I'll argue that we should reject phenomenal conservatism because its phenomenal conception of evidence is much too restrictive. All seemings are evidence, but not all evidence is seemings. Your evidence includes not just phenomenal facts about how things seem, but all the phenomenal facts about your experience. Moreover, your evidence includes all the phenomenally individuated facts about your mental states, including your beliefs, desires, and other standing attitudes. We should endorse a more liberal version of the phenomenal conception of evidence which says that your evidence includes all the phenomenally individuated facts about your current mental states. This view fits better with the motivations for accepting the phenomenal conception of evidence in the first place.[12]

There is no principled motivation for restricting evidence to phenomenal facts about how things seem. We don't need this restriction in order to explain internalist intuitions about cases. All we need is the claim that perceptual seemings are present in your envatted counterparts and absent in your clairvoyant counterparts. The restriction of evidence to seemings is not justified by internalist intuitions alone, but only by the further appeal to theoretical simplicity. As I'll explain, however, the appeal to theoretical simplicity results in epistemological distortion: we cannot explain the epistemology of introspection or memory on the same model as perception.

Moreover, the restriction to seemings is not motivated by accessibilism about epistemic justification. Accessibilism says that epistemic justification is "luminous" in the sense that you're always in a position to know which propositions

---

[11] Huemer (2006) construes clairvoyance as an alien form of perceptual experience, rather than a version of super-blindsight. I agree that this kind of clairvoyance provides defeasible justification, although it may be defeated by evidence of unreliability.

[12] See chapter 6 for this version of the phenomenal conception of evidence and its application to the internalist intuitions. See also chapter 4 for the argument that beliefs and other standing attitudes are individuated by their phenomenal dispositions.

you have epistemic justification to believe. This provides a principled argument for the phenomenal conception of evidence: epistemic justification is luminous only if your evidence is luminous, but your evidence is luminous only if the phenomenal conception of evidence is true. However, this argument supplies no motivation for restricting evidence to seemings. This is because the luminous facts about your mental states include not just the phenomenal facts about how things seem, but all the phenomenal facts about your experience, and all the phenomenally individuated facts about your beliefs, desires, and other standing attitudes. Hence, accessibilism motivates a more liberal version of the phenomenal conception of evidence, which includes all of these facts within your evidence.[13]

Restricting evidence to seemings is not only unmotivated, but also implausible. The benefits of theoretical simplicity are outweighed by the costs of epistemological distortion. This becomes apparent when we shift our focus from perception to introspection. A central insight of phenomenal conservatism is that experience justifies believing its content only if it represents its content with presentational force. This is why perceptual experience justifies believing its content, while imaginative experience does not. Presentational force is necessary for an experience to justify believing its content, but how far does this point extend? Does an experience also need presentational force in order to justify the introspective belief that you have that very experience?

The "simple theory" of introspection says no: whenever you have an experience, you thereby have introspective evidence that puts you in a position to know that you have that very experience. Seemings are not unique in this regard, since all experiences are introspectively luminous in just the same way. This includes not only perceptual experiences of seeing, but also imaginative experiences of visualizing, cognitive experiences of judging, affective experiences of desiring, and so on. All seemings are experiences, but not all experiences are seemings. My introspective evidence includes not just the phenomenal facts about how things seem, but all the phenomenal facts about my experience.[14]

To block this objection, phenomenal conservatism needs to embrace a perceptual model of introspection. On the perceptual model, your introspective evidence is not constituted by facts about your experience, but rather by facts about how your experience introspectively seems to you. These introspective seemings mediate between the experiential facts and introspective beliefs in

---

[13] See chapter 7 for the argument that accessibilism requires commitment to the phenomenal conception of evidence.

[14] See chapter 5 for a defense of the simple theory of introspection and chapter 11 for a reply to Williamson's (2000: ch. 4) anti-luminosity argument.

the same way that perceptual seemings mediate between external facts and perceptual beliefs. Just as your belief that you have hands is justified by the perceptual seeming that you have hands, so your belief that it perceptually seems that you have hands is justified by the introspective seeming that it perceptually seems that you have hands. This is what a global form of phenomenal conservatism needs to say. But do we really have introspective seemings that mediate between our perceptual seemings and our introspective beliefs about them? This claim is hard to defend.

To undermine the perceptual model of introspection, Sydney Shoemaker invites us to conduct a first-person experiment:

> Raise both your hands before you, about a foot apart and a foot in front of your face. Now perform the following two attention shifts. First, shift your attention from one hand to the other. Second, shift your attention from your *visual experience* of the one hand to your *visual experience* of the other. Do you do anything different in the second case than in the first? (1996: 219)

As Shoemaker correctly notes, the only thing that changes in the second case is which aspect of your visual experience you're thinking about. In the first case, we can explain which hand you're thinking about by appealing to the focus of perceptual attention. Shifting perceptual attention from one hand to the other explains why you think about one hand and then other. In the second case, in contrast, we cannot explain which experience you're thinking about by appealing to the focus of introspective attention. This is because shifting introspective attention from one experience to another, where this is something distinct from merely shifting perceptual attention from one hand to the other, is just a matter of thinking about one experience and then the other.

Shoemaker's point reflects a fundamental difference between perception and introspection. Perceptual attention to an object is more primitive than thought about an object and so it can explain which objects you're thinking about. In contrast, introspective attention to your own experience is just a matter of thinking about your own experience and so it cannot explain which experiences you're thinking about. In perception, your ability to think about the external world is mediated by a more primitive form of perceptual representation of the external world. In introspection, in contrast, your ability to think about your own experience is not mediated by a more primitive form of introspective representation of your own experience. Introspective knowledge is not based on introspective awareness of your own experience in the same way that perceptual knowledge is based on perceptual awareness of the external world. To my mind, this is Shoemaker's most powerful criticism of the perceptual model of introspection.

We should reject the perceptual theory of introspection and replace it with the simple theory. Your introspective evidence consists not in facts about how your experience seems to you, but rather in facts about how your experience really is. On the simple theory, there is no motivation for restricting your introspective evidence to phenomenal facts about how things seem. It includes all the phenomenal facts about your experience and all the phenomenally individuated facts about your beliefs, desires, and other standing attitudes. Introspection puts you in a position to know not only what experiences you have, but also what you believe. If you believe that p, for example, then you thereby have introspective evidence that puts you in a position to know that you believe that p. This motivates a more liberal version of the phenomenal conception, according to which your evidence includes all the phenomenally individuated facts about your current mental states.[15]

There is another reason for endorsing a version of the phenomenal conception that is liberal enough to include facts about what you believe within your evidence. Otherwise, it is hard to account for the epistemic role that beliefs play in justifying other beliefs. Any version of evidentialism that restricts your evidence to facts about your experience faces the following barrage of problems:

(1) *The problem of stored beliefs*: What justifies my belief that my name is NN when I'm thinking about other things?

(2) *The problem of forgotten evidence*: What justifies my belief that Washington, DC, is the capital of the United States when I cannot remember how I originally formed my belief?

(3) *The problem of stored defeaters*: What explains why I lack justification to believe your prediction that I can complete the hike to Precarious Peak when I'm temporarily unable to access my knowledge that you've been unreliable in the past?

(4) *The problem of background beliefs*: What explains the difference in epistemic justification between an expert and novice birdwatcher when they both see a spotted flycatcher, and it seems the same way to both of them, but only the expert knows that spotted flycatchers look this way?

---

[15] See chapter 5 for arguments that we need to extend the simple theory of introspection from conscious experience to standing belief.

We can solve these problems by endorsing a principle of *doxastic conservatism*, which says that if you believe that *p*, then you thereby have some degree of defeasible justification to believe that *p*. This contradicts strong phenomenal conservatism, however, according to which phenomenal seemings are the only source of justification.[16]

How can proponents of strong phenomenal conservatism solve these problems? There is some pressure to endorse a diachronic version of phenomenal conservatism, which says that what you have epistemic justification to believe now depends not just on what seems true now, but also on what seemed true in the past. On this view, we can avoid the problems for synchronic versions of phenomenal conservatism by appealing to facts about how things seemed in the past, rather than facts about what you believe in the present.[17]

Huemer (1999) endorses a diachronic version of phenomenal conservatism in response to the problem of forgotten evidence. On this view, beliefs stored in memory can be justified now in virtue of historical facts about how they were formed and maintained in the past. This means that beliefs can transmit the justificatory force of seemings from the past to the present. If on Monday I form a justified belief on the basis of how things seem, and I retain my belief until Friday, then I still have justification to hold the belief on Friday, even if I've forgotten how things seemed to me on Monday. And yet the same doesn't apply to someone who is my phenomenal duplicate on Friday, but whose belief was unjustified when it was formed on Monday. Huemer writes:

> The one person must be counted justified in his present belief (else we have memory skepticism), and the other must be counted unjustified (else we have an unjustified belief converted to a justified belief by the passage of time). It follows that the justificatory status of the belief . . . does not supervene on the current, intrinsic state of the believer. (1999: 352)

Doxastic justification is not determined synchronically, of course, since causal relations of proper basing are often diachronic. Huemer is making the more interesting and controversial claim that propositional justification is not determined synchronically, since intrinsic duplicates can differ in which propositions they have epistemic justification to believe owing to differences in how their beliefs were formed and maintained in the past.

[16] See chapter 4 for further discussion of doxastic conservatism and its role in solving these problems. See also Harman (1986: ch. 3) and McGrath (2007) for more extensive discussion of the problem of forgotten evidence.

[17] This view is hard to reconcile with evidentialism. How can your current evidence include facts about the past that you're no longer in a position to know? And if you no longer have this evidence, then how can it affect what you have epistemic justification to believe?

This diachronic version of phenomenal conservatism conflicts with the natural reading of Huemer's characterization of the internalist intuition about epistemic justification:

There cannot be a pair of cases in which everything seems to a subject to be the same in all epistemically relevant respects, and yet the subject ought, rationally, to take different doxastic attitudes in the two cases—for instance, in one case to affirm a proposition and in the other to withhold. (2006: 151)

On a diachronic version of phenomenal conservatism, epistemic justification doesn't supervene on how things seem now, but merely on the total history of how things seem. In fact, Huemer's position conflicts with this historical version of the supervenience thesis too: he holds that etiological facts about the formation and maintenance of your beliefs can determine whether the justificatory force of past seemings are transmitted to the present, but these etiological facts are not guaranteed to impact how things seem either in the past or in the present.

A more fundamental problem is that the diachronic version of phenomenal conservatism is incompatible with accessibilism. It implies that you're not always in a position to know which propositions you have justification to believe, since you're not always in a position to know how things seemed in the past. Which propositions you have justification to believe now depends on facts about your history that are not luminous to you in the present. According to Huemer, my phenomenal duplicate and I have justification to believe different propositions on Friday owing to differences in how things seemed on Monday. After a busy week, however, neither of us is in a position to recall how things seemed on Monday. As a result, we're not always in a position to know which propositions we have justification to believe at any given time.

One potential reaction is to reject accessibilism, but this has some implausible consequences.[18] Suppose my phenomenal duplicate has justification to believe that p, whereas I have justification to disbelieve that p, owing to some difference in our causal history. Nevertheless, my phenomenal duplicate is not in a position to know that he has justification to believe that p. On the contrary, it seems to him, just as it seems to me, that he has justification to disbelieve that p. So, in the absence of defeaters, he has justification to hold an akratic or meta-incoherent combination of doxastic attitudes: namely, believing that p, while believing that he lacks justification to believe that p, and believing instead that he has justification to disbelieve that p. Intuitively,

---

[18] See chapters 8 and 9 for these arguments for accessibilism.

however, this kind of meta-incoherence is always epistemically irrational. Indeed, Huemer agrees: "If you hold on to your first-order belief while simultaneously denying that it constitutes knowledge, then you are guilty of some sort of irrationality" (2011: 1).

Another implausible consequence is that my phenomenal duplicate has justification to hold a belief that cannot survive a justified process of critical reflection. After all, he has justification to believe that p, but he is not in a position to know that he has justification to believe that p, since it seems to him on reflection that he has justification to disbelieve that p. But it is quite implausible that anyone can have justification to hold a belief that cannot survive justified reflection. Again, Huemer agrees: "A rational person, it seems, ought to be in a position, if he comes to reflect on his doxastic attitudes . . . to approve those attitudes as justified" (2006: 154).

A more general problem is that rejecting accessibilism is self-defeating in the sense that it undercuts the best motivation for phenomenal conservatism. After all, accessibilism provides the best motivation for endorsing the phenomenal conception of evidence in the first place. We cannot fall back on the claim that it's motivated by internalist intuitions about cases. After all, these internalist intuitions need to be supported with principled theoretical arguments if they are to withstand the test of reflective equilibrium. Moreover, the best theoretical arguments for these internalist intuitions appeal to accessibilism.

Can the diachronic version of phenomenal conservatism be reconciled with accessibilism? In section 12.4.3, I'll examine Huemer's (2011) solution to what he calls "the puzzle of meta-coherence." He argues that higher-order justification to believe that you lack justification to believe that p defeats your first-order justification to believe that p. Similarly, he might say, higher-order justification to believe that you have justification to believe that p gives you justification to believe that p. If so, then perhaps my phenomenal duplicate and I have justification to believe the same propositions on Friday, despite the historical differences between us. I'll criticize this solution in due course, but the point to make now is that it cannot succeed in full generality without undermining the diachronic version of phenomenal conservatism. If your past seemings are always trumped by how things presently seem about your past seemings, then they can never make any justificational difference. We are stuck with the synchronic version of phenomenal conservatism and all its associated problems.

In conclusion, we should reject phenomenal conservatism because it imposes implausible restrictions on our evidence. All seemings are evidence, but not all evidence is seemings. To insist otherwise is implausible, since it distorts the epistemology of introspection and memory. Moreover, the resulting view is dialectically unstable, since it threatens to undercut the motivation from accessibilism. In the next section, I'll argue that these problems for phenomenal conservatism are further compounded by its account of the evidential support relation.

12.4. Problems about Evidential Support

Let's turn now from evidence to evidential support. This section argues that the global ambitions of phenomenal conservatism depend on an overly simplified account of the evidential support relation. The global principle says that your evidence supports a proposition to the extent that it seems true: the more strongly it seems true, the more strongly it is supported by your evidence. This view distorts the epistemology of introspection, logic, and inference by subsuming them under the same model as perception. Perception is a bad model to extend because there are structural dimensions of epistemic rationality in these domains that have no analogue in perception.

In an evidentialist framework, epistemic rationality is a matter of proportioning your beliefs to the evidence: an epistemically rational thinker believes whatever her evidence supports.[19] Phenomenal conservatism says that your evidence supports whatever seems true. Hence, an evidentialist version of phenomenal conservatism implies that an epistemically rational thinker believes whatever seems true. The problem is that all sorts of nonsense can seem true, including logical contradictions, Moorean conjunctions, and manifest falsehoods about your own experience. Phenomenal conservatism implies that epistemically rational thinkers can believe all this nonsense. Intuitively, however, this is beyond the pale as far as epistemic rationality is concerned. Therefore, phenomenal conservatism results in a distorted conception of epistemic rationality.

We cannot defend phenomenal conservatism against this objection by invoking constraints on what can seem true to epistemically rational thinkers. Epistemic rationality imposes no constraints on what can seem true, since the requirements of epistemic rationality don't apply to seemings. As Huemer (2001: 97) notes, it makes no sense to say that seemings are rational or irrational: this is a category mistake. There may be contingent constraints on what can seem true to human beings, but there are no necessary constraints on what can seem true to any possible thinker at all. To assume otherwise is to assume

---

[19] Following Huemer (2001: 22), I use 'epistemic justification' and 'epistemic rationality' interchangeably: these are different terms that pick out the same property. Rejecting evidentialism by introducing nonevidential constraints on epistemic rationality would severely compromise the theoretical simplicity and unity of phenomenal conservatism.

that there are brute necessary connections between seemings that cannot be further explained. It is much more plausible to assume a modal principle of recombination on which any seeming can be combined with any other seeming. If there are psychological constraints that apply to all possible thinkers as such, then these must be derived from the nature of epistemic rationality. Since there are no rational constraints on seemings, however, there are no psychological constraints on seemings that apply to all possible thinkers.

This, in a nutshell, is my argument against phenomenal conservatism. In this section, I want to develop this argument by applying it to three kinds of examples: (i) introspective incoherence, (ii) logical incoherence, and (iii) meta-incoherence. I'll argue that phenomenal conservatism cannot explain why these extreme forms of incoherence are incompatible with epistemic rationality. To explain these limits on epistemic rationality, we need to impose structural constraints on the evidential support relation.

12.4.1. Introspection

Phenomenal conservatism says that introspective justification has its source in introspective seemings. On this view, I have introspective justification to believe that it perceptually seems to me that p just when and because it introspectively seems to me that it perceptually seems to me that p. As a general rule, my seemings can be deceptive: things are not always how they seem. Assuming that introspective seemings are no exception to the rule, my first-order seemings and my higher-order seemings can diverge. Suppose it visually seems to me that p, but it introspectively seems that it *doesn't* visually seem that p. Phenomenal conservatism implies that, in the absence of defeaters, I have introspective justification to believe a false proposition about how things visually seem. Indeed, Huemer (2007: 35) explicitly says that false introspective beliefs about your experience can be justified on the basis of false introspective seemings. Are there any limits on how far this can go?

Could there be a case of rational "self-blindness" in which my beliefs about how things seem are fully rational but systematically false? Could I rationally believe, for example, that it seems as if I'm playing basketball with the Los Angeles Lakers, when in fact it seems as if I'm sitting here in my office writing philosophy? Sydney Shoemaker (1996) argues famously against the possibility of rational self-blindness, but his conclusion is much more plausible than his premises. Intuitively, it is just completely irrational to have beliefs about your experience that diverge so wildly from what your experience is really like. And yet phenomenal conservatism cannot explain this.

One potential response is to bite the bullet. It's a familiar Cartesian thought that I can be fully rational when I'm deceived by an evil demon into forming systematically false beliefs about the external world. But then why not say that I can be fully rational when I'm deceived by an evil demon into forming systematically false beliefs about my own experience? This response conflicts with the Cartesian idea that my beliefs about how things seem are epistemically more secure, and less vulnerable to skeptical doubts, than my beliefs about the external world. But what are the implications of rejecting Cartesian orthodoxy?

If I can rationally hold false beliefs about how things seem, then I'll need to revise my beliefs about the external world to cohere with my false beliefs about how things seem. Otherwise, I'm in danger of falling into an incoherent predicament in which I hold beliefs about the world that I believe to be unjustified by how things seem. In the absence of evidence that my seemings are unreliable, it is irrational for me to hold beliefs about the external world that conflict with my beliefs about how things seem. To avoid this kind of incoherence, my experience must be systematically disconnected from my perceptual beliefs about the external world as well as my introspective beliefs about my own experience. And yet this is surely beyond the pale as far as epistemic rationality is concerned.

Let's apply this reasoning to our example. Suppose I can rationally believe that it seems that I'm playing basketball, when it really seems that I'm sitting in my office. What should I believe about where I really am? There is no good answer to this question. One answer is that I should believe I'm teaching philosophy, since that's how things *seem*. Of course, I shouldn't believe that I should believe this, since I shouldn't believe that's how things seem. And yet rationality surely precludes believing something I believe I shouldn't believe. So this answer is no good. Another answer is that I should believe I'm playing basketball, since that's how I should *believe* things seem. And yet surely rationality requires that my beliefs cohere with how things seem and not just with my beliefs about how things seem. So this answer is no good either. And the same point rules out the answer that I should withhold belief about where I am. Either way, phenomenal conservatism generates unacceptable consequences.

The case I am considering is adapted from the "Strange Case of Magic Feldman" that was originally proposed by Richard Feldman:

> Professor Feldman is a rather short philosophy professor with a keen interest in basketball. Magic Johnson (MJ) was an outstanding professional basketball player. While playing a game, we may suppose, MJ had a fully coherent system of beliefs. Magic Feldman (MF) is a possible, though unusual, character, who is a combination of the professor and the basketball

player. MF has a remarkable imagination, so remarkable that while actually teaching a philosophy class, he thinks he is playing basketball. Indeed, he has *exactly* the beliefs MJ has. Because MJ's belief system was coherent, MF's belief system is also coherent. (2003: 68)

He proposes the case as a counterexample to pure coherentism, the thesis that your beliefs are epistemically justified when and only when they cohere with each other. It is a counterexample because Magic Feldman's beliefs are irrational, and so unjustified, despite the fact that they cohere with each other. Intuitively, epistemic rationality requires that your beliefs cohere with your experiences and not just with your other beliefs. Here is what I'm adding to the case: if your introspective beliefs fail to cohere with your experiences, then your perceptual beliefs must fail to cohere with your experiences too. Otherwise, you risk lapsing into meta-incoherence. Therefore, rationality requires that your introspective beliefs must cohere with your experiences. Otherwise, we're forced to accept the counterintuitive result that Magic Feldman can be fully rational.

What we've just seen is an argument that fully rational self-blindness is impossible. If your introspective beliefs are systematically mistaken, then either your perceptual beliefs fail to cohere with your introspective beliefs or they fail to cohere with your perceptual experiences. Either way, you systematically violate the requirements of epistemic rationality. The problem for phenomenal conservatism is that it fails to explain why this kind of rational self-blindness is impossible. If it's sometimes rationally permissible to form false beliefs about how things seem, then why not always? Phenomenal conservatism imposes no principled limits on how far our first-order seemings can diverge from our higher-order seemings. Given that epistemic rationality requires conforming your introspective beliefs to your introspective seemings, it follows that there are no principled limits on how much introspective error is consistent with epistemic rationality.

Perhaps only an alien psychology could produce such a massive divergence between first-order seemings and higher-order seemings. Even so, it is hard to rule out this possibility in principle. After all, delusions like Anton's syndrome provide real-life examples of systematic introspective error in which people who are blind believe they can see. The problem is that phenomenal conservatism cannot explain why such an alien psychology would be irrational. After all, there is nothing irrational about an alien psychology per se.

Another response is to block this objection by endorsing a self-presentational theory of experience, according to which all experiences are "self-presenting" in the sense that they represent themselves with presentational force. On this view, it's a necessary truth that if it seems$_1$ that p, then it thereby seems$_2$ that it seems$_1$

that p. As far as I can see, there are no good reasons to accept this theory aside from its role in rescuing phenomenal conservatism from counterexamples. On the other hand, there are good reasons to reject this theory, since it generates an infinite regress: if it seems$_1$ that p, then it seems$_2$ that it seems$_1$ that p, and it seems$_3$ that it seems$_2$ that it seems$_1$ that p, and so on ad infinitum. Moreover, this infinite regress is vicious, rather than virtuous. It can seem to me that I have hands without thereby seeming to me that any infinitely long and complicated higher-order proposition about my seemings is true. Moreover, these are not just different descriptions of one and the same seeming. After all, my seeming that I have hands has a simpler content and a different subject matter: it is about how things are, rather than how they seem.[20]

A better explanation of the impossibility of rational self-blindness appeals to the simple theory of introspection (see section 12.3). The simple theory says that the phenomenal facts about how things seem are *self-evident* in the sense that they constitute conclusive evidence for themselves:

Self-Evidence of Seemings: Necessarily, if it seems to you that p, then it's evidentially certain that it seems to you that p.

To explain the impossibility of rational self-blindness, we needn't rule out the possibility of alien psychologies in which beliefs about how things seem are systematically divorced from the facts about how things seem. Instead, we should say that this kind of systematic error is epistemically irrational, even if it's psychologically possible, because epistemic rationality requires introspective self-knowledge. Epistemically rational thinkers always know the phenomenal facts about how things seem because these phenomenal facts are self-evident. Epistemically rational thinkers always proportion their beliefs to the evidence: they believe whatever the evidence supports.

12.4.2. Logic and Inference

Phenomenal conservatism says that a priori justification for beliefs about logic has its source in intellectual seemings. On this view, I have a priori justification to believe that p just when and because it intellectually seems to me that p in the absence of defeaters. And yet my intellectual seemings, just like my perceptual seemings, can be deceptive. Suppose it seems to me that affirming the consequent is valid, that modus ponens is invalid, and so on. Phenomenal

---

[20] See Stoljar (2018) for a more detailed presentation of the regress argument.

conservatism implies that, in the absence of defeaters, I have justification to believe all these logical falsehoods. Are there any limits on how far this can go?

Let's revisit the Cartesian thought that I can be fully rational even when I'm deceived by an evil demon into forming systematically false beliefs about the external world. Can we extend this Cartesian thought from contingent truths about my perceptible environment to necessary truths about logic? Intuitively, not: my rationality is compromised by systematic error about logic but not by systematic error about my perceptible environment. Suppose an evil demon ensures that the most basic logical truths seem false and the most basic logical falsehoods seem true. Intuitively, this undermines my rationality, rather than leaving my rationality intact.

As before, one response is to bite the bullet. On this view, epistemic rationality is compatible with systematic error about logic. But we can put pressure on this response by considering the connections between logical belief and logical inference. If you believe that affirming the consequent is a valid form of argument, and you believe that some inference instantiates that form, then you're rationally committed to making the inference: that is, either believing the conclusion or withholding belief in at least one of the premises. Otherwise, you're susceptible to incoherence: you believe the premises of an argument, and you believe the conclusion follows, but you're unwilling to infer the conclusion from the premises. Similarly, if you believe that modus ponens is an invalid form of argument, and you believe that some inference instantiates that form, and no valid form, then you're rationally committed to refrain from making the inference. Otherwise, you're incoherent: you believe the premises of an argument, and you're willing to infer the conclusion from those premises, although you don't believe the conclusion follows from those premises.

To avoid this kind of incoherence, you must be willing to put your logical beliefs into practice by making the corresponding logical inferences. If you believe that affirming the consequent is a valid form of argument, then you must be disposed to make inferences that affirm the consequent. And if you believe that modus ponens is an invalid form of argument, then you must be disposed to refrain from making inferences by modus ponens. And yet these inferential dispositions are beyond the pale as far as epistemic rationality is concerned. Anyone who is systematically disposed to affirm the consequent, but not to infer by modus ponens, is grossly irrational. Epistemically rational thinkers are logical thinkers: they reason in ways that respect logic. Therefore, epistemically rational thinkers, when they are reflective, must form true beliefs about logic. We all make mistakes, of course, but someone whose logical beliefs and logical reasoning systematically fail to respect logic is not an epistemically rational thinker at all.

What we've just seen is an argument that rational blindness about logic is impossible. If your beliefs about logic are systematically mistaken, then either your reasoning fails to cohere with your beliefs about logic or your reasoning fails to respect logic. Either way, you systematically violate the requirements of epistemic rationality. The problem for phenomenal conservatism is that it fails to explain why epistemic rationality prohibits this kind of systematic error about logic. If it's sometimes rationally permissible to form false beliefs about logic, then why not always? Phenomenal conservatism imposes no principled limits on the extent to which our intellectual seemings can be mistaken. Given that epistemic rationality requires conforming our beliefs about logic to our logical seemings, there can be no principled limits on how much logical error is consistent with epistemic rationality.

Similar problems arise for Huemer's (2016) account of inferential justification. On this view, inferential justification has its source in inferential seemings: you have epistemic justification to deduce a conclusion from some premises just when and because the following conditions hold in the absence of defeaters: (i) the premises seem true, (ii) the conclusion seems to follow from the premises, and (iii) the conclusion thereby seems true. As Huemer puts the point, my inferential seeming "represents that a certain conclusion must be correct, in the light of a certain premise that I already accept" (2016: 149).

This account implies that I have epistemic justification to make fallacious inferences whenever the conclusions of such inferences seem true because they seem to follow from premises that seem true. Huemer (2016: 147) defends this claim by giving the case of a skilled but unfortunate mathematician, who makes a subtle fallacy in attempting to prove a theorem. The problem is that Huemer must count as rational not only these subtle and occasional errors in reasoning, but also elementary and chronic errors in reasoning. After all, there is nothing to rule out the possibility that someone might systematically represent all fallacious arguments as valid and all valid arguments as fallacious.

Another problematic consequence is that Huemer is committed to rejecting the following principle of single-premise closure:

Closure: Necessarily, if p entails q, and you have justification to believe that p, then you have justification to believe that q.

Even if the premises of a valid argument seem true, the conclusion may fail to seem true in light of the premises because the argument doesn't seem valid. In light of this point, some proponents of phenomenal conservatism may be tempted to abandon this closure principle and replace it with the following revised version:

Revised Closure: Necessarily, if you have justification to believe that p entails q, and you have justification to believe that p, then you have justification to believe that q.

But Huemer must reject the revised version too. After all, it might seem to you that a conclusion follows from some premises, and it might seem to you that the premises are true, without thereby seeming to you that the conclusion is true. This is what happens to many of us when we consider Vann McGee's (1985) counterexamples to modus ponens. The problem is that phenomenal conservatism imposes no principled limits on how often this can happen. As a result, it allows for epistemically rational thinkers who never infer conclusions that seem to follow from premises that seem true, since those conclusions never seem true. Intuitively, however, such thinkers are grossly irrational.

Can we block these objections by appealing to facts about defeaters? It is not clear that we can, since phenomenal conservatism says that my intellectual seemings can be defeated only by conflicting seemings. Suppose it intellectually seems to me clearly and unequivocally that affirming the consequent is valid, that modus ponens is invalid, and so on. In that case, phenomenal conservatism implies that I have undefeated justification to believe these logical falsehoods, since I have no conflicting seemings.

Can we block the objection by appealing instead to the conditions for possessing logical concepts? The idea is that possessing logical concepts requires some capacity to use them correctly in logical reasoning.[21] On this view, it's incoherent to suppose that someone possesses logical concepts without having any capacity to use them correctly. One problem is that the conditions for possessing logical concepts must be minimal enough to allow for the kinds of logical mistakes that we routinely find in normal and delusional humans. Presumably, you can satisfy these minimal conditions for possessing logical concepts while making enough mistakes about logic to fall below the threshold for epistemic rationality. That is all we need for our argument against phenomenal conservatism to succeed.

A more fundamental problem is that phenomenal conservatism cannot explain why possessing logical concepts should require the ability to use them correctly. This cannot be a general requirement on concept possession. Otherwise, we're forced to deny that the victim of the evil demon can form beliefs about the external world that are systematically false. Why should this requirement apply to logical concepts but not empirical concepts? One good answer appeals to rationality constraints on concept possession together with a more specific connection between epistemic rationality and logical truth. The problem is that phenomenal conservatism makes no such connection between epistemic rationality and logical truth. As a result, it cannot rule out the possibility of

---

[21] See Peacocke (1992: ch. 1) for an account of the possession conditions for logical concepts that requires a disposition to use valid forms of argument.

subjects that use logical concepts in a way that is epistemically rational but nevertheless systematically mistaken.

To explain why systematic logical blindness is epistemically irrational, we need some connection between epistemic rationality and logical truth. Many formal theories of epistemic rationality build such a connection into their account of the evidential support relation. On a probabilistic conception of the evidential support relation, for example, all logical truths are evidentially certain: that is, they always have evidential probability 1. The nature of the evidential support relation guarantees that any possible body of evidence provides conclusive support for any logical truth. On this view, all logical truths are *self-evident* in the following sense:

Self-Evidence of Logical Truths: Necessarily, if it's a logical truth that *p*, then it's evidentially certain that *p*.

If all logical truths are self-evident in this sense, then we can explain why systematic logical blindness is epistemically irrational. This is an egregious violation of the rational requirement that you should proportion your beliefs to the evidence. Epistemically rational thinkers are logically omniscient because they believe whatever their evidence supports and their evidence conclusively supports every logical truth.

12.4.3. Metacoherence

The two problems just considered generate a third problem, which Huemer (2011) calls "the puzzle of meta-coherence." Suppose it seems to me that *p*, although it doesn't seem that I have justification to believe that *p*; in fact, it seems that I *don't* have justification to believe that *p*. This can happen in at least two different ways. First, introspective seemings can be deceptive: it can seem that *p*, although it introspectively seems that it doesn't seem that *p*. Second, intellectual seemings can be deceptive: even if phenomenal conservatism is true, it can intellectually seem to me that it's false, and hence that I don't have justification to believe that things are the way they seem. Either way, it can seem to me that *p*, while it also seems that I don't have justification to believe that *p*.[22]

Here is the problem. Phenomenal conservatism implies that, in the absence of defeaters, I have epistemic justification to be in an incoherent kind of akratic

---

[22] Hasan (2013: 135–136) considers similar examples in exploring the difficulties of reconciling phenomenal conservatism with accessibilism.

predicament: that is, to believe that *p*, while also believing that I lack justification to believe that *p*. If so, then I have epistemic justification to believe a Moorean conjunction of the following form:

p and I don't have justification to believe that *p*.

But this is absurd! Intuitively, I cannot have epistemic justification to believe a Moorean conjunction of this form. Moreover, this intuition can be supported by argument: (i) the Moorean conjunction is knowably unknowable, but (ii) I cannot have epistemic justification to believe that *p* when it is knowably unknowable that *p*, so (iii) I cannot have epistemic justification to believe this Moorean conjunction.[23]

As always, one reaction is to bite the bullet by maintaining that epistemic akrasia is sometimes rational after all. It's noteworthy, however, that Huemer doesn't adopt this response here. Instead, he endorses the following requirement of epistemic rationality:

The Metacoherence Requirement: Categorically believing that *p* commits one, on reflection, to the view that one knows that *p*. (2011: 2)

The idea is that if you believe that *p*, while also believing that you're not in a position to know that *p*, then you're thereby irrational; or, anyway, less than fully rational. On this view, epistemic rationality requires metacoherence.

The problem is that phenomenal conservatism cannot explain why meta-incoherence is always epistemically irrational. This is because it imposes no principled limits on how far our first-order seemings can diverge from our higher-order seemings about justification. As we've seen, it cannot rule out the possibility that it seems to me that *p*, although it seems that I don't have justification to believe that *p*. On this view, epistemic rationality is just a matter of believing what seems strongly enough on balance to be true. But nothing rules out the possibility that Moorean conjunctions might seem on balance to be true. Therefore, phenomenal conservatism cannot explain why epistemic rationality prohibits believing these Moorean conjunctions.

Huemer (2011) proposes to solve the problem of metacoherence by appeal to defeaters. He argues that your justification to believe that *p* is defeated by anything that justifies disbelieving or withholding belief in the metajustificatory proposition that you have justification to believe that *p*. This includes both cases in which it seems that the metajustificatory proposition

---

[23] See chapters 9 and 10 for further discussion of the irrationality of epistemic akrasia and the related phenomenon of believing Moorean conjunctions.

is false and cases in which it doesn't seem that the metajustificatory proposition is true. Either way, your justification to believe that p is defeated. This is how Huemer seeks to explain why you cannot have epistemic justification to believe Moorean conjunctions of the following form: p and I don't have justification to believe that p.

My objection is that Huemer's solution assumes that epistemic rationality requires metacoherence without explaining why it does. His key claim is that anything that justifies disbelieving or withholding belief that you have justification to believe that p thereby defeats your justification to believe that p. Contraposing, you have justification to believe that p only if you lack justification to disbelieve or withhold belief in the metajustificatory proposition. But if you lack justification to disbelieve or withhold belief in the metajustificatory proposition, then you have justification to believe it instead. This is a consequence of the *existence thesis*, which says that you always have justification to adopt some doxastic attitude toward any given proposition. Thus, Huemer's solution assumes the left-to-right direction of the JJ principle:

The JJ Principle: Necessarily, you have justification to believe that p if and only if you have justification to believe that you have justification to believe that p.

Perhaps Huemer will reject the existence thesis unless it is restricted to propositions that you've entertained. Even so, he is still committed to a restricted version of the JJ principle that applies whenever you consider whether the metajustificatory proposition is true.

This structural principle about epistemic justification needs to be explained, but phenomenal conservatism doesn't provide the resources to explain it. Phenomenal conservatism says that you have justification to believe whatever seems strongly enough on balance to be true. But Moorean conjunctions can seem strongly and on balance to be true. So phenomenal conservatism doesn't explain why you cannot have epistemic justification to believe Moorean conjunctions even when they seem true. The upshot is that phenomenal conservatism cannot explain why epistemic rationality requires metacoherence without abandoning its global ambitions to subsume all the requirements of epistemic rationality under a single epistemic principle.[24]

---

[24] More generally, claims about defeat often smuggle in substantive assumptions about the structure of the evidential support relation that are hard to reconcile with the global ambitions of phenomenal conservatism. For example, it's hard to explain why the justification provided by seemings is subject to rebutting and undercutting defeat without appealing to logical and probabilistic constraints on the evidential support relation.

In order to explain why epistemic rationality requires metacoherence, we need to build more structure into our account of the evidential support relation. More specifically, we need the following probabilistic version of accessibilism:

Accessibilism: Necessarily, if the evidential probability that p is n, then it's evidentially certain that the evidential probability that p is n.

This principle explains why epistemic rationality requires metacoherence. Violations of metacoherence are violations of the rational requirement that you should proportion your beliefs to the evidence. Epistemically rational thinkers are always metacoherent because they proportion their beliefs to the evidence and no possible body of evidence supports a meta-incoherent combination of beliefs.

12.4.4. The Overkill Objection

My solution to these problems might seem like overkill. I started with the intuition that epistemic rationality is incompatible with systematic violations of introspective coherence, logical coherence, and metacoherence. I argued that phenomenal conservatism cannot explain these intuitions about the nature of epistemic rationality. Instead, we need to build more structure into the evidential support relation. But this solution implies something much stronger than what we started with: namely, that epistemic rationality is incompatible with even the smallest violation of introspective coherence, logical coherence, and metacoherence. Many philosophers have the reaction that this is simply much too demanding.

My response is that epistemic rationality is an evaluative ideal of good reasoning. Given our contingent human limitations, we are not capable of perfectly realizing this ideal, but we can approximate the ideal to a greater or lesser extent. What our ordinary evaluations of epistemic rationality are tracking, in some rough-and-ready way, are various dimensions of approximation toward the ideal. We count extreme violations of coherence requirements as epistemically irrational because they depart so egregiously from the ideal. We tend to count ourselves as epistemically rational because our own violations are much less egregious: we approximate closely enough to the ideal to meet some contextually determined threshold that takes our human limitations into account. But someone who perfectly realizes the ideal of epistemic rationality never violates these coherence requirements.

I'm not saying that the ideal of epistemic rationality is one that we humans can realize when we're in optimal conditions for the operation of our psychological machinery. We may be constitutionally incapable of realizing the ideal. It seems possible in principle that there could be a perfectly rational agent—perhaps a god or an angel—although its capacities would need to be superhuman and perhaps even infinite. But suppose the possibility of a perfectly rational agent is ruled out by the small print in the laws of metaphysics. It is not at all clear why this should matter. What matters is that we can make sense of degrees of epistemic rationality—whether or not we can model them precisely in a formal framework—and that there is some recognizable epistemic value in having greater, rather than lesser, degrees of epistemic rationality.

Any plausible theory of epistemic rationality needs to account for intuitions about what agents "should" believe and do when they are incapable of complying with its own requirements. Even phenomenal conservatism needs some version of this distinction. After all, we are not always capable of complying with the requirement to conform our beliefs to the way things seem. Sometimes, we cannot form epistemically justified beliefs on the basis of our perceptual evidence, since our belief-forming dispositions are insufficiently sensitive to unattended or fine-grained aspects of our perceptual experience.[25] It makes sense to ask what we "should" believe in light of these psychological limitations: some policies are more reasonable than others as ways of coping with our limitations. This is just another instance of the distinction between ideal and nonideal standards of epistemic rationality. I don't see how any plausible theory of epistemic rationality can do without it.[26]

12.5. Phenomenal Accessibilism

The previous section raised a series of objections to phenomenal conservatism that all have the same basic structure. The starting point is some platitude about the nature of epistemic rationality. For example, all epistemically rational thinkers have the following characteristics:

(1) *Perceptual Coherence*: Necessarily, epistemically rational thinkers hold perceptual beliefs about the external world that cohere with how things perceptually seem.

(2) *Introspective Coherence*: Necessarily, epistemically rational thinkers hold introspective beliefs about how things seem that cohere with how things seem.

---

[25] See chapter 3 for more on conscious perception without attention and chapter 11 on the problem of the speckled hen.
[26] See chapter 10 on ideal versus nonideal requirements of rationality.

(3) *Logical Coherence*: Necessarily, epistemically rational thinkers hold beliefs that cohere logically or probabilistically with their other beliefs.

(4) *Metacoherence*: Necessarily, epistemically rational thinkers hold beliefs that cohere with their higher-order beliefs about which beliefs they should hold.

The objection is that phenomenal conservatism cannot explain all these characteristics of epistemically rational thinkers. According to phenomenal conservatism, epistemic rationality is a matter of believing whatever seems strongly enough on balance to be true. The problem is that things are not always how they seem: if we have introspective, intellectual, and inferential seemings, then these seemings can be systematically deceptive. Therefore, phenomenal conservatism implies that epistemically rational thinkers can be deeply incoherent among all but one of the dimensions listed above. Since this is implausible, we should reject phenomenal conservatism.

Phenomenal conservatism implies that the beliefs of epistemically rational thinkers cohere with their perceptual appearances, although their beliefs need not be introspectively coherent, logically coherent, or metacoherent. In effect, its account of the nature of epistemic rationality preserves some dimensions of coherence at the expense of others. Quite plausibly, however, the beliefs of epistemically rational agents are coherent in all of these ways. There is no principled motivation for privileging just one of these dimensions of coherence over the others. On the contrary, this is merely an artifact of the global ambition to explain all epistemic justification in terms of the perceptual model.

This suggests a diagnosis of why phenomenal conservatism results in such a distorted account of the nature of epistemic rationality. Generalizing the perceptual model of evidential support results in an overly simplistic account of the evidential support relation. Perceptual experience provides defeasible evidential support for its contents by making them seem true: this is why you have justification to believe the contents of perceptual experience. In effect, phenomenal conservatism assumes that this is the only constraint on the evidential support relation. This is the source of the global principle that your evidence supports a proposition just when it seems strongly enough on balance to be true. The problem is that perception is a bad model to generalize to other domains because there are dimensions of epistemic rationality that it fails to explain. Epistemic rationality requires not just perceptual coherence, but also introspective coherence, logical coherence, and metacoherence.

To avoid these problems for phenomenal conservatism, we need an account of the evidential support relation that builds in enough structure to explain all the essential features of epistemically rational thinkers. It is a necessary truth about the nature of epistemic rationality that epistemically rational thinkers are coherent in all these ways. We cannot explain these necessary truths about the nature of epistemic rationality in terms of contingent facts about what seems true to epistemically rational thinkers. After all, epistemic rationality doesn't impose any constraints on how things seem. Instead, we need to explain the nature of epistemic rationality in terms of necessary truths about the evidential support relation that hold for all thinkers regardless of the contingent facts about what evidence they happen to have. That is the overarching point that I want to insist upon.

Let's start with perceptual coherence: why do epistemically rational thinkers hold perceptual beliefs about the external world that cohere with how things perceptually seem? We can explain this in terms of a probabilistic constraint on the evidential support relation:

Explaining Perceptual Coherence: Necessarily, if it seems to you that p in the absence of defeaters, then it is evidentially probable that p.

According to this principle, it's an a priori necessary truth about the evidential support relation that things are probably the way they seem in the absence of defeaters. This explains why epistemically rational thinkers form beliefs about the world that cohere with their perceptual appearances. Epistemically rational thinkers proportion their beliefs to their evidence: they believe what is sufficiently probable given their evidence.[27]

Here is a related question: why do epistemically rational thinkers tend to rely on the contents of their beliefs as premises in reasoning? Again, we can explain this in terms of a formal constraint on the evidential support relation:

Explaining Doxastic Coherence: Necessarily, if you believe that p in the absence of defeaters, then it is evidentially probable that p.

According to this principle, it's an a priori necessary truth about the evidential support relation that things are probably the way you believe them to be in the absence of defeaters. This is why epistemically rational thinkers tend to use the contents of their beliefs as premises in reasoning. After all, epistemically rational thinkers proportion their beliefs to the evidence: they believe what is sufficiently probable given their evidence. Beliefs don't raise the probability of their contents as much as perceptual seemings. After all, when conflicts arise, epistemically rational thinkers tend to revise their beliefs in light of their

[27] There are probabilistic constraints on what counts as a defeater: if d defeats the support that e provides for p, then the evidential probability that p given the conjunction of e and d is lower than the evidential probability that p given e alone.

perceptual seemings, rather than regarding their perceptual seemings as unreliable. Even so, this default can be overridden by strong enough evidence that your perceptual seemings are unreliable.

What about introspective coherence, logical coherence, and metacoherence? In section 12.4, I argued that we can explain these essential features of epistemically rational thinkers by building the following structural constraints into the evidential support relation:

> *Self-Evidence of Seemings*: Necessarily, if it seems to you that p, then it's evidentially certain that it seems to you that p.

> *Self-Evidence of Logical Truths*: Necessarily, if it's a logical truth that p, then it's evidentially certain that p.

> *Accessibilism*: Necessarily, if the evidential probability that p is n, then it's evidentially certain that the evidential probability that p is n.

These structural constraints on the evidential support relation explain why epistemically rational agents are not only perceptually coherent, but also introspectively coherent, logically coherent, and metacoherent. Epistemically rational agents are always coherent in these ways because they always proportion their beliefs to the evidence and their evidence always supports a coherent set of beliefs.

Now we face a unification challenge. Is there anything that unifies this laundry list of constraints on the evidential support relation? If not, then the lingering suspicion will remain that we should prefer phenomenal conservatism on grounds of theoretical unity and simplicity. My answer to the challenge is that the principles in this list can be unified within the framework of accessibilism. I'll make three points in this connection.

The first point is that we can derive the conclusion that all seemings are self-evident from the premise that all seemings are evidence together with the further premise that all evidence is self-evident:

> *Self-Evidence of Evidence*: Necessarily, if your evidence includes the fact that p, then it's evidentially certain that p.

In section 12.3, I argued that all seemings are evidence, though not all evidence is seemings. But why suppose that all evidence is self-evident? The evidential probability that p is equal to the probability that p conditional upon your evidence: if your evidence includes the fact that p, then your evidence entails that p, and hence the evidential probability that p is 1. This means that epistemically rational thinkers always know what their evidence is, including the phenomenal facts about how things seem.

The second point is that the self-evidence of logical truths can be derived from the more general principle that all epistemically necessary truths are self-evident, including truths about the evidential support relation as well as truths about logic. On this view, evidential support facts are self-evident in just the same way as logical facts:

Self-Evidence of Evidential Support: Necessarily, if evidence e makes it evidentially probable that p to degree n, then it's evidentially certain that evidence e makes it evidentially probable that p to degree n.

Epistemically necessary truths are truths that are conclusively justified on a priori grounds. On David Chalmers's (2011a) epistemic interpretation of the probability calculus, they are true everywhere in the probability space, and so they have evidential probability 1. I've given no general formula for deciding which truths are epistemically necessary in this sense, but there are good reasons to include truths about logic and evidential support.

The third point is that accessibilism is true just because facts about your evidence, and facts about the evidential support relation, are self-evident in the sense just defined. Necessarily, if your evidence e makes it evidentially probable that p to degree n, then it is evidentially certain that (i) you have evidence e, and (ii) if you have evidence e, then it is evidentially probable that p to degree n, so (iii) it is evidentially probable that p to degree n. Hence, accessibilism is not an extra constraint on the evidential support relation: it stands or falls with the other constraints just mentioned, rather than dangling loosely on its own.

What motivates all these constraints on the evidential support relation is that epistemic rationality requires metacoherence. It is hard to explain this unless we suppose that facts about your evidence, and facts about what it supports, are self-evident. If you can have misleading higher-order evidence about what your evidence supports, then it is sometimes rationally permissible to be meta-incoherent. Since it is never rationally permissible to be meta-incoherent, it follows that you can never have misleading higher-order evidence about what your evidence supports. This is precisely because facts about your evidence, and facts about the evidential support relation, are self-evident in the sense we've defined. On this view, epistemically rational agents are not only logically omniscient, but also evidentially omniscient in the sense that they are always certain of what their evidence is and what it supports. This explains why epistemically rational agents are always metacoherent.[28]

---

[28] This argument is developed at length in chapter 10.

This answer to the unification challenge illuminates the unity of the epistemic virtues. Epistemic rationality requires being coherent along multiple dimensions: perceptual coherence, introspective coherence, logical coherence, and metacoherence. What do all these dimensions of coherence have in common? We can now see what unifies these virtues of epistemic rationality. Epistemically rational thinkers are coherent because they believe what their evidence supports and their evidence is guaranteed to support coherent beliefs. These coherence constraints are built into the nature of the evidential support relation in a principled and unified way. The resulting theory is admittedly more complex than phenomenal conservatism, but it is also much simpler and more unified than it might initially seem. Moreover, the additional complexity of the theory is justified by its explanatory power, since we need this extra structure in our account of the evidential support relation in order to explain the nature of epistemic rationality.

In summary, phenomenal conservatism cannot explain why epistemic rationality requires coherence. This is because it operates with an overly simplified account of the evidential support relation, according to which your evidence supports a proposition to the extent that it seems true. In order to explain why epistemic rationality requires coherence, we need to build more formal structure into our account of the evidential support relation. In particular, we need to endorse accessibilism: the thesis that facts about your evidence, and facts about the evidential support relation, are self-evident.

Why can't proponents of phenomenal conservatism simply abandon the project of explaining the evidential support relation and settle for an account of evidence instead? There is nothing wrong with combining a phenomenal conception of evidence with accessibilism about the evidential support relation: indeed, that is exactly my view. But this is to abandon all but the weakest of our three principles of phenomenal conservatism. Here's why. Even if your evidence is exhausted by how things seem, your evidence can support p, and thereby give you epistemic justification to believe that p, even when it doesn't seem that p. This is because the nature of the evidential support relation guarantees that you have epistemic justification to believe certain propositions even when they don't seem true.

Logical truths provide the simplest illustration of this point. On a probabilistic conception of evidential support, every logical truth is entailed by your evidence, and thereby conclusively supported by your evidence, whether or not it seems true. This generates counterexamples to the strong principle of phenomenal conservatism, since you have epistemic justification to believe logical truths even when they don't seem true. The same point holds more generally in the following examples:

(1) If it seems that p, then you have justification to believe that it seems that p, even when it doesn't seem that it seems that p. More generally, if you have evidence e, then you have justification to believe that you have evidence e, even when it doesn't seem that you have evidence e.

(2) If your evidence e supports p, then you have justification to believe that evidence e supports p, even when it doesn't seem that e supports p. More generally, you have justification to believe any epistemically necessary truth that p, even when it doesn't seem to you that p.

(3) If you have justification to believe that p, then you have justification to believe that you have justification to believe that p, even when it doesn't seem to you that you have justification to believe that p.

(4) If you have justification to believe that p, and p entails q, then you thereby have justification to believe that q, even if it doesn't seem to you that q is true in light of p.

The general point is that, even if your evidence is exhausted by seemings, it can support a proposition that doesn't seem true. This is because some propositions are supported by your evidence in virtue of structural facts about the evidential support relation that hold necessarily whatever evidence you contingently happen to have. Epistemic justification is not grounded solely in how things seem, since it is grounded partially in facts about the nature of the evidential support relation. This is another reason why the global ambitions of phenomenal conservatism are doomed to fail. Its account of the evidential support relation, as well as its account of evidence, is much too simple.

A corollary of this argument against phenomenal conservatism is that we have no good reason to believe that we have introspective, intellectual, or inferential seemings. This is not to deny that we have experiences associated with introspection, intuition, or inference, which assertively represent their contents to be true. The claim is, rather, that these experiences do not have the right kind of phenomenal character to play the same epistemic role as perceptual experience. The argument for this claim depends on epistemological considerations, rather than introspection or semantics. As we've seen, the global ambitions of phenomenal conservatism are doomed to fail because these experiences cannot play the same kind of epistemic role as perception.

To contrast my own view with phenomenal conservatism, I propose to call it "phenomenal accessibilism." The main point of agreement between these views is that we need a phenomenal conception of evidence. One point of disagreement concerns whether your evidence is restricted to phenomenal facts about how things seem. In section 12.3, I argued for a more liberal version of the phenomenal conception of evidence, which includes all the phenomenally individuated facts about your experiences and standing attitudes. Another point of disagreement concerns the evidential support relation. Phenomenal conservatism says that your evidence supports a proposition to the extent that it seems true. In contrast, phenomenal accessibilism says that your evidence supports a proposition to the extent that it is probable given your evidence, where evidential probability is constrained by a probabilistic version of accessibilism. This disagreement is more fundamental. Even if we assume that your evidence is constituted by facts about how things seem, a proposition can be probable given your evidence when it doesn't seem true. Phenomenal conservatism and phenomenal accessibilism deliver different verdicts in such cases.

The contrast between phenomenal conservatism and phenomenal accessibilism becomes crucial when we consider the motivations for endorsing the phenomenal conception of evidence in the first place. The best argument appeals to accessibilism: epistemic justification is luminous only if your evidence is luminous, but your evidence is luminous only if the phenomenal conception of evidence is true. I've argued that phenomenal conservatism conflicts with accessibilism both in its account of evidence and in its account of the evidential support relation. Hence, phenomenal conservatism undermines its own best motivation. To defend the phenomenal conception of evidence in a principled way, we need to endorse phenomenal accessibilism instead.

12.6. Conclusions

Here is a summary of the main conclusions of this chapter.

Conclusion 1: Weak phenomenal conservatism is true. This explains why perceptual experiences justify believing their contents. After all, perceptual experiences are seemings: they are experiences that forcefully represent their contents. Moreover, it is because they forcefully represent their contents that they can justify believing their contents without standing in need of justification themselves. Weak phenomenal conservatism, in combination with representationalism, implies that perceptual experience justifies belief about the external world in virtue of its phenomenal character alone. Hence, weak phenomenal conservatism provides an attractive framework for explaining the essential role of phenomenal consciousness in the epistemology of perception.

Conclusion 2: Global phenomenal conservatism is false. We cannot explain all epistemic justification on the perceptual model, since this results in a distorted account of the nature of epistemic rationality. On this view, your evidence supports a proposition whenever it seems true. Since epistemic rationality requires believing whatever your evidence supports, it follows that epistemically rational thinkers believe whatever seems true. This fails to explain why epistemically rational thinkers are not only perceptually coherent, but also introspectively coherent, logically coherent, and metacoherent. To explain these essential features of epistemically rational thinkers, we need to build more structure into our account of the evidential support relation.

Conclusion 3: Strong phenomenal conservatism is false. Building more structure into our account of the evidential support relation generates counterexamples in which you have epistemic justification to believe propositions that don't seem true. This is because your evidence can support propositions in virtue of structural features of the evidential support relation, which hold necessarily whatever evidence you contingently happen to have. On this version of evidentialism, epistemic justification is not grounded wholly in contingent facts about your evidence, but partially in necessary facts about the evidential support relation.

Conclusion 4: There are no seemings besides perceptual seemings: only perceptual experience and perceptual memory represent their contents with presentational force. We have intellectual experiences of intuition, inference, and introspection, but these experiences do not have the right kind of phenomenal character to play the same epistemic role as perceptual experience. This conclusion is not based on introspection, or ordinary language, but on epistemological considerations. The arguments against strong and global phenomenal conservatism show that cognitive experience cannot play the same epistemic role as perceptual experience.

Conclusion 5: To explain the essential features of epistemically rational thinkers, we need to abandon phenomenal conservatism in favor of phenomenal accessibilism. On this view, there are structural constraints built into the evidential support relation, which guarantee that your evidence always supports a coherent set of beliefs. More precisely, facts about your evidence, and facts about the evidential support relation, are self-evident in the sense that they are made certain by your evidence. Epistemically rational thinkers are not only perceptually coherent, but also introspectively coherent, logically coherent, and metacoherent, because they always believe what their evidence supports.

Conclusion 6: Phenomenal accessibilism fits better than phenomenal conservatism with the theoretical motivations for endorsing the phenomenal conception of evidence. The strongest argument for the phenomenal conception appeals to accessibilism: epistemic justification is luminous only if your evidence is luminous, but your evidence is luminous only if the phenomenal conception of evidence is true. Phenomenal conservatism cannot explain this structural constraint on the evidential support relation without abandoning its own global ambitions. Hence, phenomenal conservatism is self-defeating in the sense that it undercuts its own best motivation.

Conclusion 7: There is no principled motivation for a version of the phenomenal conception that restricts your evidence to phenomenal facts about how things seem. This restriction is not motivated by accessibilism, which provides the best argument for the phenomenal conception in the first place. Moreover, this restriction results in an implausible account of the epistemology of introspection and memory. There is some pressure to avoid these problems by endorsing a diachronic version of the phenomenal conception of evidence, but this is inconsistent with accessibilism. Once again, the restricted version of the phenomenal conception of evidence undercuts its own best motivation.

Conclusion 8: We should endorse a more liberal version of the phenomenal conception of evidence, which includes not only phenomenal facts about how things seem, but all phenomenal facts about your experience, and all phenomenally individuated facts about your standing propositional attitudes, including your beliefs, desires, and intentions. On this view, your evidence includes all and only the phenomenally individuated facts about your current mental states. This results in a more plausible account of the epistemology of introspection and memory. Moreover, it fits better with the motivations for endorsing the phenomenal conception of evidence in the first place.[29]

---

[29] A version of this chapter, "On the Global Ambitions of Phenomenal Conservatism," is forthcoming in *Analytic Philosophy*.

References

Adler, Jonathan E. 2002. *Belief's Own Ethics*. MIT Press.

Alston, William. 1989. *Epistemic Justification*. Cornell University Press.

Alston, William. 2005. *Beyond Justification: Dimensions of Epistemic Evaluation*. Cornell University Press.

Armstrong, David. 1968. *A Materialist Theory of the Mind*. Routledge.

Armstrong, David. 1973. *Belief, Truth and Knowledge*. Cambridge University Press.

Arpaly, Nomy. 2003. *Unprincipled Virtue: An Inquiry into Moral Agency*. Oxford University Press.

Audi, Robert. 1990. "Weakness of Will and Rational Action." *Australasian Journal of Philosophy* 68 (3): 270–281.

Audi, Robert. 1994. "Dispositional Beliefs and Dispositions to Believe." *Noûs* 28 (4): 419–434.

Audi, Robert. 2001. "An Internalist Theory of Normative Grounds." *Philosophical Topics* 29 (1–2): 19–46.

Ayer, Alfred Jules. 1940. *The Foundations of Empirical Knowledge*. Macmillan.

Ayer, Alfred Jules. 1963. *The Concept of a Person: And Other Essays*. Macmillan.

Ayers, Michael. 1991. *Locke: Epistemology and Ontology*. Volume 1. Routledge.

Baumeister, Roy, E. J. Masicampo, and Kathleen Vohs. 2011. "Do Conscious Thoughts Cause Behavior?" *Annual Review of Psychology* 62: 331–361.

Bayne, Tim. 2009. "Perception and the Reach of Phenomenal Content." *Philosophical Quarterly* 59: 385–404.

Bayne, Tim, and Maja Spener. 2010. "Introspective Humility." *Philosophical Issues* 20: 1–22.

Bengson, John. 2015. "The Intellectual Given." *Mind* 124: 707–760.

Bennett, Karen, and Brian McLaughlin. 2005. "Supervenience." *Stanford Encyclopedia of Philosophy*.

Bergmann, Michael. 2005. "Defeaters and Higher-Level Requirements." *Philosophical Quarterly* 55: 419–436.

Bergmann, Michael. 2006. *Justification without Awareness: A Defense of Epistemic Externalism*. Oxford University Press.

Berker, Selim. 2008. "Luminosity Regained." *Philosophers' Imprint* 8: 1–22.

Bird, Alexander. 2007. "Justified Judging." *Philosophy and Phenomenological Research* 74 (1): 81–110.

Block, Ned. 1978. "Troubles with Functionalism." *Minnesota Studies in the Philosophy of Science* 9: 261–325.

Block, Ned. 1986. "Advertisement for a Semantics for Psychology." *Midwest Studies in Philosophy* 10 (1): 615–678.

Block, Ned. 1990. "Can the Mind Change the World?" In *Meaning and Method: Essays in Honor of Hilary Putnam*, edited by George S. Boolos, 137–170. Cambridge University Press.

Block, Ned. 1995. "On a Confusion about a Function of Consciousness." *Behavioral and Brain Sciences* 18 (2): 227–247. Reprinted in Block, Flanagan, and Güzeldere 1997: 375–415.

Block, Ned. 1996. "Mental Paint and Mental Latex." *Philosophical Issues* 7: 19–49.

Block, Ned. 2002. "The Harder Problem of Consciousness." *Journal of Philosophy* 99 (8): 391–425.

Block, Ned. 2007. "Consciousness, Accessibility, and the Mesh Between Psychology and Neuroscience." *Behavioral and Brain Sciences* 30 (5): 481–548.

Block, Ned. 2016. "The Anna Karenina Principle and Skepticism about Unconscious Perception." *Philosophy and Phenomenological Research* 93 (2): 452–459.

Block, Ned, Owen Flanagan, and Güven Güzeldere. 1997. *Nature of Consciousness: Philosophical Debates*. MIT Press.

Boghossian, Paul. 1989a. "Content and Self-Knowledge." *Philosophical Topics* 17 (1): 5–26.

Boghossian, Paul. 1989b. "The Rule-Following Considerations." *Mind* 98: 507–549.

Boghossian, Paul, and David Velleman. 1989. "Color as a Secondary Quality." *Mind* 98: 81–103.

BonJour, Laurence. 1985. *The Structure of Empirical Knowledge*. Harvard University Press.

BonJour, Laurence, and Ernest Sosa. 2003. *Epistemic Justification: Internalism vs. Externalism, Foundations vs. Virtues*. Blackwell.

Bortolotti, Lisa. 2010. *Delusions and Other Irrational Beliefs*. Oxford University Press.

Bourget, David. 2010. "Consciousness Is Underived Intentionality." *Noûs* 44 (1): 32–58.

Brewer, Bill. 1999. *Perception and Reason*. Oxford University Press.

Brewer, Bill. 2006. "Perception and Content." *European Journal of Philosophy* 14 (2): 165–181.

Brogaard, Berit. 2018. *Seeing and Saying: The Language of Perception and the Representational View of Experience*. Oxford University Press.

Burge, Tyler. 1982. "Other Bodies." In *Thought and Object: Essays on Intentionality*, edited by Andrew Woodfield, 97–121. Oxford University Press.

Burge, Tyler. 1986. "Individualism and Psychology." *Philosophical Review* 95: 3–45.

Burge, Tyler. 1988. "Individualism and Self-Knowledge." *Journal of Philosophy* 85: 649–663.

Burge, Tyler. 1996. "Our Entitlement to Self-Knowledge." *Proceedings of the Aristotelian Society* 96 (1): 91–116.

Burge, Tyler. 1997. "Two Kinds of Consciousness." In *The Nature of Consciousness: Philosophical Debates*, edited by Ned Block, Owen Flanagan, and Güven Güzeldere, 427–433. MIT Press.

Burge, Tyler. 1998. "Reason and the First Person." In *On Knowing Our Own Minds*, edited by Crispin Wright, Barry Smith, and Cynthia Macdonald, 243–270. Oxford University Press.

Burge, Tyler. 2003. "Perceptual Entitlement." *Philosophy and Phenomenological Research* 67 (3): 503–548.

Burge, Tyler. 2010. *Origins of Objectivity*. Oxford University Press.

Byrne, Alex. 2001. "Intentionalism Defended." *Philosophical Review* 110 (2): 199–240.

Byrne, Alex. 2005. "Introspection." *Philosophical Topics* 33 (1): 79–104.

Byrne, Alex. 2009. "Experience and Content." *Philosophical Quarterly* 59: 429–451.

Campbell, John. 2002. *Reference and Consciousness*. Oxford University Press.

Campbell, John, and Quassim Cassam. 2014. *Berkeley's Puzzle: What Does Experience Teach Us?* Oxford University Press.

Campion, J., R. Latto, and Y. Smith. 1983. "Is Blindsight an Effect of Scattered Light, Spared Cortex, and Near-Threshold Vision?" *Behavioral and Brain Sciences* 6 (3): 423–486.

Carruthers, Peter. 2000. *Phenomenal Consciousness: A Naturalistic Theory*. Cambridge University Press.

Carruthers, Peter. 2011. *The Opacity of Mind: An Integrative Theory of Self-Knowledge*. Oxford University Press.

Cassam, Quassim. 2014. *Self-Knowledge for Humans*. Oxford University Press.

Chalmers, David. 1996. *The Conscious Mind: In Search of a Fundamental Theory*. Oxford University Press.

Chalmers, David. 2002a. "Does Conceivability Entail Possibility?" In *Conceivability and Possibility*, edited by Tamar Szabo Gendler and John Hawthorne, 145–200. Clarendon Press; Oxford University Press.

Chalmers, David. 2002b. "The Components of Content." In *Philosophy of Mind: Classical and Contemporary Readings*, edited by David Chalmers, 608–633. Oxford University Press.

Chalmers, David. 2003. "The Content and Epistemology of Phenomenal Belief." In *Consciousness: New Philosophical Perspectives*, edited by Quentin Smith and Aleksandar Jokic, 220–272. Oxford University Press.

Chalmers, David. 2004. "The Representational Character of Experience." In *The Future for Philosophy*, edited by Brian Leiter, 153–181. Oxford University Press.

Chalmers, David. 2011a. "The Nature of Epistemic Space." In *Epistemic Modality*, edited by Andy Egan and Brian Weatherson, 60–107. Oxford University Press.

Chalmers, David. 2011b. "Verbal Disputes." *Philosophical Review* 120 (4): 515–566.

Chisholm, Roderick. 1942. "The Problem of the Speckled Hen." *Mind* 51: 368–373.

Chisholm, Roderick. 1989. *Theory of Knowledge*. Prentice Hall.

Chomsky, Noam. 1965. *Aspects of the Theory of Syntax*. MIT Press.

Chomsky, Noam. 1976. *Reflections On Language*. Temple Smith.

Chomsky, Noam. 1980. "Rules and Representations." *Behavioral and Brain Sciences* 3 (1): 1–61.

Christensen, David. 2004. *Putting Logic in Its Place: Formal Constraints on Rational Belief*. Oxford University Press.

Christensen, David. 2007a. "Does Murphy's Law Apply in Epistemology? Self-Doubt and Rational Ideals." *Oxford Studies in Epistemology* 2: 3–31.

Christensen, David. 2007b. "Epistemology of Disagreement: The Good News." *Philosophical Review* 116 (2): 187–217.

Christensen, David. 2010a. "Higher-Order Evidence." *Philosophy and Phenomenological Research* 81 (1): 185–215.

Christensen, David. 2010b. "Rational Reflection." *Philosophical Perspectives* 24: 121–140.

Chudnoff, Elijah. 2013. *Intuition*. Oxford University Press.

Churchland, Paul. 1981. "Eliminative Materialism and the Propositional Attitudes." *Journal of Philosophy* 78: 67–90.

Clark, Andy, and David Chalmers. 1998. "The Extended Mind." *Analysis* 58 (1): 7–19.

Clarke, Roger. 2013. "Belief Is Credence One (in Context)." *Philosophers' Imprint* 13: 1–18.

Coates, Allen. 2012. "Rational Epistemic Akrasia." *American Philosophical Quarterly* 49 (2): 113–124.

Cohen, Stewart. 1984. "Justification and Truth." *Philosophical Studies* 46 (3): 279–295.

Cohen, Stewart. 2010. "Bootstrapping, Defeasible Reasoning, and A Priori Justification." *Philosophical Perspectives* 24: 141–159.

Comesaña, Juan. 2005a. "Unsafe Knowledge." *Synthese* 146 (3): 395–404.

Comesaña, Juan. 2005b. "We Are (Almost) All Externalists Now." *Philosophical Perspectives* 19: 59–76.

Comesaña, Juan, and Matthew McGrath. 2014. "Having False Reasons." In *Epistemic Norms*, edited by Clayton Littlejohn and John Turri, 59–80. Oxford University Press.

Conee, Earl, and Richard Feldman. 2004. *Evidentialism: Essays in Epistemology*. Oxford University Press.

Conee, Earl, and Richard Feldman. 2008. "Evidence." In *Epistemology: New Essays*, edited by Quentin Smith, 83–104. Oxford University Press.

Craig, Edward. 1990. *Knowledge and the State of Nature: An Essay in Conceptual Synthesis*. Oxford University Press.

Crane, Tim. 2003. "The Intentional Structure of Consciousness." In *Consciousness: New Philosophical Perspectives*, edited by Quentin Smith and Aleksandar Jokic, 33–56. Oxford University Press.

Crane, Tim. 2013. "Unconscious Belief and Conscious Thought." In *Phenomenal Intentionality*, edited by Uriah Kriegel, 156–173. Oxford University Press.

Dancy, Jonathan. 2004. *Ethics without Principles*. Oxford University Press.

Das, Nilanjan, and Bernhard Salow. 2018. "Transparency and the KK Principle." *Noûs* 52 (1): 3–23.

Davidson, Donald. 1985. "Incoherence and Irrationality." *Dialectica* 39 (4): 345–354.

Davidson, Donald. 1986. "A Coherence Theory of Truth and Knowledge." In *Truth and Interpretation: Perspectives on the Philosophy of Donald Davidson*, edited by Ernest LePore, 307–319. Blackwell.

Davies, Martin. 1987. "Tacit Knowledge and Semantic Theory: Can a Five Percent Difference Matter?" *Mind* 96: 441–462.

Davies, Martin. 1989. "Tacit Knowledge and Subdoxastic States." In *Reflections on Chomsky*, edited by Alexander George, 131–152. Blackwell.

Davies, Martin. 1995. "Consciousness and the Varieties of Aboutness." In *Philosophy of Psychology: Debates on Psychological Explanation*, edited by Cynthia Macdonald, 356–392. Oxford University Press.

Davies, Martin. 1997. "Externalism and Experience." In *The Nature of Consciousness: Philosophical Debates*, edited by Ned Block, Owen Flanagan, and Güven Güzeldere, 244–250. MIT Press.

Dennett, Daniel. 1971. "Intentional Systems." *Journal of Philosophy* 68: 87–106.

Dennett, Daniel. 1991. "Real Patterns." *Journal of Philosophy* 88 (1): 27–51.

Dickie, Imogen. 2015. *Fixing Reference*. Oxford University Press.

Dougherty, Trent, and Patrick Rysiew. 2013. "Experience First." In *Contemporary Debates in Epistemology*, 2nd edition, edited by Matthias Steup, John Turri, and Ernest Sosa, 10–16. Blackwell.

Dretske, Fred. 1981. *Knowledge and the Flow of Information*. MIT Press.

Dretske, Fred. 1995. *Naturalizing the Mind*. MIT Press.

Dretske, Fred. 1997. "What Good Is Consciousness?" *Canadian Journal of Philosophy* 27 (1): 1–15.

Dretske, Fred. 2003. "How Do You Know You Are Not a Zombie?" In *Privileged Access: Philosophical Accounts of Self-Knowledge*, edited by Brie Gertler, 1–14. Ashgate.

Dretske, Fred. 2006. "Perception without Awareness." *Perceptual Experience*, 147–180.

Dummett, Michael. 1978. *Truth and Other Enigmas*. Harvard University Press.

Easwaran, Kenny. 2014. "Regularity and Hyperreal Credences." *Philosophical Review* 123 (1): 1–41.

Egan, Frances. 1995. "Computation and Content." *Philosophical Review* 104 (2): 181–203.

Elga, Adam. 2007. "Reflection and Disagreement." *Noûs* 41 (3): 478–502.

Elga, Adam. 2013. "The Puzzle of the Unmarked Clock and the New Rational Reflection Principle." *Philosophical Studies* 164 (1): 127–139.

Evans, Gareth. 1981. "Semantic Theory and Tacit Knowledge." In *Wittgenstein: To Follow a Rule*, edited by Steven Holtzman and Christopher Leich, 116–137. Routledge.

Evans, Gareth. 1982. *The Varieties of Reference*. Oxford University Press.

Farkas, Katalin. 2008a. "Phenomenal Intentionality without Compromise." *The Monist* 91 (2): 273–293.

Farkas, Katalin. 2008b. *The Subject's Point of View*. Oxford University Press.

Farkas, Katalin. 2013. "Constructing a World for the Senses." In *Phenomenal Intentionality*, edited by Uriah Kriegel, 99–115. Oxford University Press.

Feldman, Richard. 2003. *Epistemology*. Prentice Hall.

Feldman, Richard. 2005. "Respecting the Evidence." *Philosophical Perspectives* 19: 95–119.

Fernández, Jordi. 2013. *Transparent Minds: A Study of Self-Knowledge*. Oxford University Press.

Fine, Kit. 2001. "The Question of Realism." *Philosophers' Imprint* 1: 1–30.

Firth, Roderick. 1978. "Are Epistemic Concepts Reducible to Ethical Concepts?" In *Values and Morals: Essays in Honor of William Frankena, Charles Stevenson, and Richard Brandt*, edited by Alvin Goldman and Jaegwon Kim, 215–229. Kluwer.

Fodor, Jerry. 1975. *The Language of Thought*. Harvard University Press.

Fodor, Jerry. 1980. "Methodological Solipsism Considered as a Research Strategy in Cognitive Psychology." *Behavioral and Brain Sciences* 3 (1): 63–73.

Fodor, Jerry. 1983. *The Modularity of Mind*. MIT Press.

Fodor, Jerry. 1985. "Fodor's Guide to Mental Representation: The Intelligent Auntie's Vade-Mecum." *Mind* 94: 76–100.

Fodor, Jerry. 1987. *Psychosemantics: The Problem of Meaning in the Philosophy of Mind.* MIT Press.

Foley, Richard. 1992. *Working without a Net: A Study of Egocentric Epistemology.* Oxford University Press.

Frankfurt, Harry. 1971. "Freedom of the Will and the Concept of a Person." *Journal of Philosophy* 68 (1): 5–20.

Frege, Gottlob. 1956. "The Thought: A Logical Inquiry." *Mind* 65: 289–311.

Fumerton, Richard. 1995. *Metaepistemology and Skepticism.* Rowman and Littlefield.

Gagné, Robert, and Ernest Smith. 1962. "A Study of the Effects of Verbalization on Problem Solving." *Journal of Experimental Psychology* 63 (1): 12–18.

Gendler, Tamar Szabó. 2008a. "Alief and Belief." *Journal of Philosophy* 105 (10): 634–663.

Gendler, Tamar Szabó. 2008b. "Alief in Action (and Reaction)." *Mind and Language* 23 (5): 552–585.

Gertler, Brie. 2001. "Introspecting Phenomenal States." *Philosophy and Phenomenological Research* 63 (2): 305–328.

Gertler, Brie. 2007. "Overextending the Mind." In *Arguing about the Mind*, edited by Brie Gertler and Lawrence Shapiro, 192–206. Routledge.

Gertler, Brie. 2011. *Self-Knowledge.* Routledge.

Gettier, Edmund. 1963. "Is Justified True Belief Knowledge?" *Analysis* 23 (6): 121–123.

Gibbons, John. 2006. "Access Externalism." *Mind* 115: 19–39.

Ginet, Carl. 1975. *Knowledge, Perception and Memory.* Springer.

Goldman, Alvin. 1976. "Discrimination and Perceptual Knowledge." *Journal of Philosophy* 73: 771–791.

Goldman, Alvin. 1979. "What Is Justified Belief?" In *Justification and Knowledge*, edited by George Pappas, 1–25. Reidel.

Goldman, Alvin. 1986. *Epistemology and Cognition.* Harvard University Press.

Goldman, Alvin. 1993. "The Psychology of Folk Psychology." *Behavioral and Brain Sciences* 16 (1): 15–28.

Goldman, Alvin. 1999. "Internalism Exposed." *Journal of Philosophy* 96 (6): 271–293.

Goldman, Alvin. 2006. *Simulating Minds: The Philosophy, Psychology, and Neuroscience of Mindreading.* Oxford University Press.

Gopnik, Alison. 1993. "How We Know Our Minds: The Illusion of First-Person Knowledge of Intentionality." *Behavioral and Brain Sciences* 16 (1): 1–14.

Greco, Daniel. 2013. "Probability and Prodigality." *Oxford Studies in Epistemology* 4: 82–107.

Greco, Daniel. 2014a. "A Puzzle about Epistemic Akrasia." *Philosophical Studies* 167 (2): 201–219.

Greco, Daniel. 2014b. "Could KK Be OK?" *Journal of Philosophy* 111 (4): 169–197.

Greco, Daniel. 2015. "How I Learned to Stop Worrying and Love Probability 1." *Philosophical Perspectives* 29: 179–201.

Greco, Daniel. Forthcoming. "On the Very Idea of an Epistemic Dilemma." In *Epistemic Dilemmas*, edited by Nick Hughes. Oxford University Press.

Grice, Paul. 1957. "Meaning." *Philosophical Review* 66 (3): 377–388.

Hájek, Alan. 2003. "What Conditional Probability Could Not Be." *Synthese* 137 (3): 273–323.

Hájek, Alan. 2012. "Is Strict Coherence Coherent?" *Dialectica* 66 (3): 411–424.

Hare, Richard. 1952. *The Language of Morals.* Oxford University Press.

Harman, Gilbert. 1973. *Thought.* Princeton University Press.

Harman, Gilbert. 1986. *Change in View.* MIT Press.

Harman, Gilbert. 1987. "(Nonsolipsistic) Conceptual Role Semantics." In *New Directions in Semantics*, edited by Ernest LePore, 55–81. Academic Press.

Harman, Gilbert. 1990. "The Intrinsic Quality of Experience." *Philosophical Perspectives* 4: 31–52.

Hasan, Ali. 2013. "Phenomenal Conservatism, Classical Foundationalism, and Internalist Justification." *Philosophical Studies* 162 (2): 119–141.

Haslanger, Sally. 1999. "What Knowledge Is and What It Ought to Be: Feminist Values and Normative Epistemology." *Philosophical Perspectives* 13: 459–480.

Hatfield, Gary. 2002. "Perception as Unconscious Inference." In *Perception and the Physical World: Psychological and Philosophical Issues in Perception*, edited by Dieter Heyer and Rainer Mausfeld, 113–143. Blackwell.

Hawthorne, John, and Maria Lasonen-Aarnio. Forthcoming. "Not So Phenomenal!"

Hazlett, Allan. 2012. "Higher-Order Epistemic Attitudes and Intellectual Humility." *Episteme* 9 (3): 205–223.

Heavey, Christopher, and Russell Hurlbut. 2008. "The Phenomena of Inner Experience." *Consciousness and Cognition* 17 (3): 798–810.

Heck, Richard. 2000. "Nonconceptual Content and the 'Space of Reasons.'" *Philosophical Review* 109 (4): 483–523.

Heylen, Jan. 2016. "Being in a Position to Know and Closure." *Thought* 5 (1): 63–67.

Hintikka, Jaakko. 1962. *Knowledge and Belief.* Cornell University Press.

Horgan, Terry, and George Graham. 2012. "Phenomenal Intentionality and Content Determinacy." In *Prospects for Meaning*, edited by Richard Schantz, 321–344. De Gruyter.

Horgan, Terry, and Uriah Kriegel. 2007. "Phenomenal Epistemology: What Is Consciousness That We May Know It So Well?" *Philosophical Issues* 17: 123–144.

Horgan, Terry, and John Tienson. 2002. "The Intentionality of Phenomenology and the Phenomenology of Intentionality." In *Philosophy of Mind: Classical and Contemporary Readings*, edited by David Chalmers, 520–533. Oxford University Press.

Horowitz, Sophie. 2014. "Epistemic Akrasia." *Noûs* 48 (4): 718–744.

Huemer, Michael. 1999. "The Problem of Memory Knowledge." *Pacific Philosophical Quarterly* 80 (4): 346–357.

Huemer, Michael. 2001. *Skepticism and the Veil of Perception.* Rowman and Littlefield.

Huemer, Michael. 2006. "Phenomenal Conservatism and the Internalist Intuition." *American Philosophical Quarterly* 43 (2): 147–158.

Huemer, Michael. 2007. "Moore's Paradox and the Norm of Belief." In *Themes from G. E. Moore: New Essays in Epistemology and Ethics*, edited by Susana Nuccetelli and Gary Seay, 142–157. Oxford University Press.

Huemer, Michael. 2011. "The Puzzle of Metacoherence." *Philosophy and Phenomenological Research* 82 (1): 1–21.

Huemer, Michael. 2013. "Epistemological Asymmetries between Belief and Experience." *Philosophical Studies* 162 (3): 741–748.

Huemer, Michael. 2016. "Inferential Appearances." In *Intellectual Assurance: Essays on Traditional Epistemic Internalism*, edited by Brett Coppenger and Michael Bergmann, 144–160. Oxford University Press.

Huemer, Michael. 2018. "A Probabilistic Critique of Evidentialism." In *Believing in Accordance with the Evidence: New Essays on Evidentialism*, edited by Kevin McCain, 199–222. Springer.

Hurlburt, Russell T. 1990. *Sampling Normal and Schizophrenic Inner Experience*. Springer.

Hurlburt, Russell T., and Sarah Akhter. 2008. "Unsymbolized Thinking." *Consciousness and Cognition* 17 (4): 1364–1374.

Jackson, Frank. 2003. "Narrow Content and Representation—or Twin Earth Revisited." *Proceedings and Addresses of the American Philosophical Association* 77 (2): 55–70.

James, William. [1890] 1981. *The Principles of Psychology*. Volume 1. Dover.

Jeffrey, Richard. 1965. *The Logic of Decision*. University of Chicago Press.

Johnston, Mark. 1992. "How to Speak of the Colors." *Philosophical Studies* 68 (3): 221–263.

Kelly, Thomas. 2005. "The Epistemic Significance of Disagreement." *Oxford Studies in Epistemology* 1: 167–196.

Kelly, Thomas. 2010. "Peer Disagreement and Higher Order Evidence." In *Disagreement*, edited by Richard Feldman and Ted Warfield, 111–174. Oxford University Press.

Kelly, Thomas. 2013. "Evidence Can Be Permissive." In *Contemporary Debates in Epistemology*, 2nd edition, edited by Matthias Steup, John Turri, and Ernest Sosa, 298–312. Blackwell.

Kim, Jaegwon. 1984. "Concepts of Supervenience." *Philosophy and Phenomenological Research* 45: 153–176.

Kim, Jaegwon. 2005. *Physicalism, or Something Near Enough*. Princeton University Press.

Klein, Peter. 2005. "Infinitism Is the Solution to the Epistemic Regress Problem." In *Contemporary Debates in Epistemology*, edited by Matthias Steup and Ernest Sosa, 131–140. Blackwell.

Koch, Christof, and Francis Crick. 2001. "The Zombie Within." *Nature* 411: 893.

Koethe, John. 1978. "A Note on Moore's Paradox." *Philosophical Studies* 34 (3): 303–310.

Koksvik, Ole. 2017. "The Phenomenology of Intuition." *Philosophy Compass* 12 (1): 1–11.

Kolodny, Niko. 2008. "Why Be Disposed to Be Coherent?" *Ethics* 118 (3): 437–463.

Kopec, Matthew, and Michael Titelbaum. 2016. "The Uniqueness Thesis." *Philosophy Compass* 11 (4): 189–200.

Kornblith, Hilary. 1983. "Justified Belief and Epistemically Responsible Action." *Philosophical Review* 92 (1): 33–48.

Kornblith, Hilary. 2012. *On Reflection*. Oxford University Press.

Kornblith, Hilary. 2016. "Replies to Boghossian and Smithies." *Analysis* 76 (1): 69–80.

Korsgaard, Christine. 1996. *The Sources of Normativity*. Cambridge University Press.

Kriegel, Uriah. 2009. *Subjective Consciousness: A Self-Representational Theory*. Oxford University Press.

Kriegel, Uriah. 2011. *The Sources of Intentionality*. Oxford University Press.

Kriegel, Uriah. 2013. "The Phenomenal Intentionality Research Program." In *Phenomenal Intentionality*, edited by Uriah Kriegel, 1–26. Oxford University Press.

Kriegel, Uriah, and Kenneth Williford. 2006. *Self-Representational Approaches to Consciousness*. MIT Press.

Kripke, Saul. 1979. "A Puzzle about Belief." In *Meaning and Use*, edited by Avishai Margalit, 239–283. Reidel.

Kripke, Saul. 1982. *Wittgenstein on Rules and Private Language*. Harvard University Press.

Lasonen-Aarnio, Maria. 2010. "Unreasonable Knowledge." *Philosophical Perspectives* 24: 1–21.

Lasonen-Aarnio, Maria. 2014. "Higher-Order Evidence and the Limits of Defeat." *Philosophy and Phenomenological Research* 88 (2): 314–345.

Lasonen-Aarnio, Maria. 2015. "New Rational Reflection and Internalism about Rationality." *Oxford Studies in Epistemology* 5: 145–179.

Lasonen-Aarnio, Maria. Forthcoming a. "Enkrasia or Evidentialism? Learning to Love Mismatch." *Philosophical Studies*.

Lasonen-Aarnio, Maria. Forthcoming b. "Virtuous Failure and Victims of Deceit." In *The New Evil Demon Problem*, edited by Julien Dutant. Oxford University Press.

Lau, Hakwan, and Richard Passingham. 2006. "Relative Blindsight in Normal Observers and the Neural Correlate of Visual Consciousness." *Proceedings of the National Academy of Sciences* 103: 18763–18768.

Lee, Geoffrey. 2013. "Materialism and the Epistemic Significance of Consciousness." In *Current Controversies in Philosophy of Mind*, edited by Uriah Kriegel, 222–245. Routledge.

Lee, Geoffrey. 2019. "Alien Subjectivity and the Importance of Consciousness." In *Themes from Block*, edited by Adam Pautz and Daniel Stoljar, 215–242. Oxford University Press.

Lehrer, Keith. 1990. *Theory of Knowledge*. Routledge.

Levine, Joseph. 1983. "Materialism and Qualia: The Explanatory Gap." *Pacific Philosophical Quarterly* 64 (4): 354–361.

Levine, Joseph. 2011. "On the Phenomenology of Thought." In *Cognitive Phenomenology*, edited by Tim Bayne and Michelle Montague, 103–120. Oxford University Press.

Lewis, David. 1972. "Psychophysical and Theoretical Identifications." *Australasian Journal of Philosophy* 50 (3): 249–258.

Lewis, David. 1974. "Radical Interpretation." *Synthese* 27 (3–4): 331–344.

Lewis, David. 1980a. "A Subjectivist's Guide to Objective Chance." In *Studies in Inductive Logic and Probability*, volume 2, edited by Richard C. Jeffrey, 83–132. University of California Press.

Lewis, David. 1980b. "Mad Pain and Martian Pain." In *Readings in the Philosophy of Psychology*, volume 1, edited by Ned Block, 216–222. MIT Press.

Lewis, David. 1996. "Elusive Knowledge." *Australasian Journal of Philosophy* 74 (4): 549–567.

Littlejohn, Clayton. 2009. "The Externalist's Demon." *Canadian Journal of Philosophy* 39 (3): 399–434.

Littlejohn, Clayton. 2013. "A Note Concerning Justification and Access." *Episteme* 10 (4): 369–386.

Littlejohn, Clayton. 2018. "Stop Making Sense? On a Puzzle about Rationality." *Philosophy and Phenomenological Research*, 257–272.

Loewer, Barry. 1997. "A Guide to Naturalizing Semantics." In *A Companion to the Philosophy of Language*, edited by Crispin Wright and Bob Hale, 108–126. Blackwell.

Lormand, Eric. 1996. "Nonphenomenal Consciousness." *Noûs* 30 (2): 242–261.

Lycan, William. 1995. "Consciousness as Internal Monitoring." *Philosophical Perspectives* 9: 1–14.

Lycan, William. 1996. *Consciousness and Experience*. MIT Press.

Lyons, Jack. 2009. *Perception and Basic Beliefs: Zombies, Modules, and the Problem of the External World*. Oxford University Press.

Magidor, Ofra. 2018. "How Both You and the Brain In a Vat Can Know Whether or Not You Are Envatted." *Aristotelian Society Supplementary* Volume 92: 151–181.

Makinson, David. 1965. "The Paradox of the Preface." *Analysis* 25 (6): 205–207.

Mandelbaum, Eric. 2013. "Against Alief." *Philosophical Studies* 165 (1): 197–211.

Markie, Peter J. 2005. "The Mystery of Direct Perceptual Justification." *Philosophical Studies* 126 (3): 347–373.

Marr, David. 1982. *Vison*. Freeman.

Martin, Charles. 1994. "Dispositions and Conditionals." *Philosophical Quarterly* 44: 1–8.

Martin, Michael. 2004. "The Limits of Self-Awareness." *Philosophical Studies* 120 (1–3): 37–89.

Marušic, Berislav. 2013. "The Self-Knowledge Gambit." *Synthese* 190 (12): 1977–1999.

McCain, Kevin. 2014. *Evidentialism and Epistemic Justification*. Routledge.

McDowell, John. 1994. *Mind and World*. Harvard University Press.

McDowell, John. 1995. "Knowledge and the Internal." *Philosophy and Phenomenological Research* 55 (4): 877–893.

McDowell, John. 2011. *Perception as a Capacity for Knowledge*. Marquette University Press.

McGee, Vann. 1985. "A Counterexample to Modus Ponens." *Journal of Philosophy* 82 (9): 462–471.

McGinn, Colin. 1989. "Consciousness and Content." In *Proceedings of the British Academy*, volume 74: *1988*, 225–245.

McGrath, Matthew. 2007. "Memory and Epistemic Conservatism." *Synthese* 157 (1): 1–24.

McGrath, Matthew. 2013. "Phenomenal Conservatism and Cognitive Penetration: The 'Bad Basis' Counterexamples." In *Seemings and Justification: New Essays on Dogmatism and Phenomenal Conservatism*, edited by Chris Tucker, 225–247. Oxford University Press.

McHugh, Conor. 2010. "Self-Knowledge and the KK Principle." *Synthese* 173 (3): 231–257.

Mendelovici, Angela. 2018. *The Phenomenal Basis of Intentionality*. Oxford University Press.

Millikan, Ruth. 1984. *Language, Thought and Other Biological Categories*. MIT Press.

Milne, Peter. 1991. "A Dilemma for Subjective Bayesians—and How to Resolve It." *Philosophical Studies* 62 (3): 307–314.

Milner, David, and Melvyn Goodale. 1995. *The Visual Brain in Action*. Oxford University Press.

Milner, David, and Melvyn Goodale. 2006. *The Visual Brain in Action*. 2nd edition. Oxford University Press.

Moon, Andrew. 2012. "Three Forms of Internalism and the New Evil Demon Problem." *Episteme* 9 (4): 345–360.

Moore, G. E. 1962. *Commonplace Book, 1919–1953*. Macmillan.

Moran, Richard. 2001. *Authority and Estrangement: An Essay on Self-Knowledge*. Princeton University Press.

Morrison, John. 2016. "Perceptual Confidence." *Analytic Philosophy* 57 (1): 15–48.

Munton, Jessie. 2016. "Visual Confidences and Direct Perceptual Justification." *Philosophical Topics* 44 (2): 301–326.

Nagel, Jennifer. 2016. "Knowledge and Reliability." In *Alvin Goldman and His Critics*, edited by Hilary Kornblith and Brian McLaughlin, 237–256. Blackwell.

Nagel, Thomas. 1974. "What Is It Like to Be a Bat?" *Philosophical Review* 83: 435–450.

Nelkin, Dana. 2000. "The Lottery Paradox, Knowledge, and Rationality." *Philosophical Review* 109 (3): 373–409.

Neta, Ram. 2011. "The Nature and Reach of Privileged Access." In *Self-Knowledge*, edited by Anthony E. Hatzimoysis, 9–32. Oxford University Press.

Neta, Ram, and Guy Rohrbaugh. 2004. "Luminosity and the Safety of Knowledge." *Pacific Philosophical Quarterly* 85 (4): 396–406.

Nichols, Shaun, and Stephen Stich. 2003. *Mindreading: An Integrated Account of Pretence, Self-Awareness, and Understanding Other Minds*. Oxford University Press.

Nisbett, Richard, and Timothy Wilson. 1977. "Telling More Than We Can Know: Verbal Reports on Mental Processes." *Psychological Review* 84 (3): 231–259.

Nozick, Robert. 1981. *Philosophical Explanations*. Harvard University Press.

O'Callaghan, Casey. 2010. "Experiencing Speech." *Philosophical Issues* 20: 305–332.

Orlandi, Nico. 2014. *The Innocent Eye: Why Vision Is Not a Cognitive Process*. Oxford University Press.

Overgaard, Morten, Katrin Fehl, Kim Mouridsen, Bo Bergholt, and Axel Cleeremans. 2008. "Seeing without Seeing? Degraded Conscious Vision in a Blindsight Patient." *PLOS ONE* 3 (8): e3028.

Pautz, Adam. 2010. "Why Explain Visual Experience in Terms of Content?" In *Perceiving the World*, edited by Bence Nanay, 254–309. Oxford University Press.

Pautz, Adam. 2013. "Does Phenomenology Ground Mental Content?" In *Phenomenal Intentionality*, edited by Uriah Kriegel, 194–234. Oxford University Press.

Pautz, Adam. Forthcoming. "The Arationality of Perception: Comments on Susanna Siegel." *Philosophy and Phenomenological Research*.

Peacocke, Christopher. 1992. *A Study of Concepts*. MIT Press.

Peacocke, Christopher. 1993. "Externalist Explanation." *Proceedings of the Aristotelian Society* 67: 203–230.

Peacocke, Christopher. 1994. "Content, Computation and Externalism." *Mind and Language* 9 (3): 303–335.

Peacocke, Christopher. 1998. "Conscious Attitudes, Attention, and Self-Knowledge." In *Knowing Our Own Minds*, edited by Crispin Wright, Bob Smith, and Cynthia Macdonald, 63–98. Oxford University Press.

Peacocke, Christopher. 1999. "Computation as Involving Content: A Response to Egan." *Mind & Language* 14 (2): 195–202.

Peacocke, Christopher. 2007. "Mental Action and Self-Awareness (I)." In *Contemporary Debates in the Philosophy of Mind*, edited by Jonathan D. Cohen and Brian P. McLaughlin, 358–376. Blackwell.

Pennebaker, James, and Cindy Chung. 2007. "Expressive Writing, Emotional Upheavals, and Health." In *Foundations of Health Psychology*, edited by H. S. Friedman and R. C. Silver, 263–284. Oxford University Press.

Phillips, Ian. 2016. "Consciousness and Criterion: On Block's Case for Unconscious Seeing." *Philosophy and Phenomenological Research* 93 (2): 419–451.

Pitt, David. 2004. "The Phenomenology of Cognition, or, What Is It Like to Think That P?" *Philosophy and Phenomenological Research* 69 (1): 1–36.

Pitt, David. 2013. "Indexical Thought." In *Phenomenal Intentionality*, edited by Uriah Kriegel, 49–70. Oxford University Press.

Plantinga, Alvin. 1993. *Warrant: The Current Debate*. Oxford University Press.

Pollock, John, and Cruz, Joseph. 1999. *Contemporary Theories of Knowledge*. 2nd edition. Rowman and Littlefield.

Prinz, Jesse. 2007. "All Consciousness Is Perceptual." In *Contemporary Debates in Philosophy of Mind*, edited by Brian McLaughlin and Jonathan Cohen, 335–357. Blackwell.

Prinz, Jesse. 2015. "Unconscious Perception." In *The Oxford Handbook of Philosophy of Perception*, edited by Mohan Matthen, 371–389. Oxford University Press.

Pritchard, Duncan. 2012. *Epistemological Disjunctivism*. Oxford University Press.

Pryor, James. 2000. "The Skeptic and the Dogmatist." *Noûs* 34 (4): 517–549.

Pryor, James. 2001. "Highlights of Recent Epistemology." *British Journal for the Philosophy of Science* 52 (1): 95–124.

Pryor, James. 2004. "What's Wrong with Moore's Argument?" *Philosophical Issues* 14: 349–378.

Pryor, James. 2005. "There Is Immediate Justification." In *Contemporary Debates in Epistemology*, edited by Matthias Steup and Ernest Sosa, 181–202. Blackwell.

Putnam, Hilary. 1975. "The Meaning of 'Meaning.'" *Minnesota Studies in the Philosophy of Science* 7: 131–193.

Pylyshyn, Zenon, and Ron Storm. 1988. "Tracking Multiple Independent Targets: Evidence for a Parallel Tracking Mechanism." *Spatial Vision* 3 (3): 179–197.

Quine, Willard Van Orman. 1960. *Word and Object*. MIT Press.

Quine, Willard Van Orman. 1970. "Methodological Reflections on Current Linguistic Theory." *Synthese* 21 (3–4): 386–398.

Raffman, Diana. 1995. "On the Persistence of Phenomenology." In *Conscious Experience*, edited by Thomas Metzinger, 293–308. Schoningh.

Ramm, Brentyn. 2016. "Dimensions of Reliability in Phenomenal Judgment." *Journal of Consciousness Studies* 23 (3–4): 101–127.

Rescorla, Michael. 2012. "Are Computational Transitions Sensitive to Semantics?" *Australasian Journal of Philosophy* 90 (4): 703–721.

Rescorla, Michael. 2015. Review of Nico Orlandi, *The Innocent Eye: Why Vision Is Not a Cognitive Process*. *Notre Dame Philosophical Reviews*.

Rescorla, Michael. 2017. "From Ockham to Turing—and Back Again." In *Turing 100: Philosophical Explorations of the Legacy of Alan Turing*, edited by Juliet Floyd and Alisa Bokulich, 279–304. Springer.

Robinson, William. 2005. "Thoughts without Distinctive Non-imagistic Phenomenology." *Philosophy and Phenomenological Research* 70 (3): 534–561.

Roessler, Johannes. 2009. "Perceptual Experience and Perceptual Knowledge." *Mind* 118: 1013–1041.

Rosen, Gideon. 2010. "Metaphysical Dependence: Grounding and Reduction." In *Modality: Metaphysics, Logic, and Epistemology*, edited by Bob Hale and Aviv Hoffmann, 109–136. Oxford University Press.

Rosenthal, David. 1997. "A Theory of Consciousness." In *The Nature of Consciousness*, edited by Ned Block, Owen Flanagan, and Guven Güzeldere, 729–753. MIT Press.

Russell, Bertrand. 1912. *The Problems of Philosophy*. Home University Library.

Russell, Bertrand. 1921. *The Analysis of Mind*. Macmillan.

Ryle, Gilbert. 1949. *The Concept of Mind*. Hutchinson.

Scanlon, Thomas. 1998. *What We Owe to Each Other*. Harvard University Press.

Schaffer, Jonathan. 2009. "On What Grounds What." In *Metametaphysics: New Essays on the Foundations of Ontology*, edited by David Manley, David Chalmers, and Ryan Wasserman, 347–383. Oxford University Press.

Schaffer, Jonathan. 2010. "The Debasing Demon." *Analysis* 70 (2): 228–237.

Schellenberg, Susanna. 2011. "Perceptual Content Defended." *Noûs* 45 (4): 714–750.

Schellenberg, Susanna. 2013. "Experience and Evidence." *Mind* 122: 699–747.

Schoenfield, Miriam. 2015a. "Bridging Rationality and Accuracy." *Journal of Philosophy* 112 (12): 633–657.

Schoenfield, Miriam. 2015b. "Internalism without Luminosity." *Philosophical Issues* 25: 252–272.

Schroeder, Mark. 2011. "What Does It Take to 'Have' a Reason?" In *Reasons for Belief*, edited by Andrew Reisner and Asbjørn Steglich-Petersen, 201–222. Cambridge University Press.

Schwitzgebel, Eric. 2010. "Acting Contrary to Our Professed Beliefs or the Gulf between Occurrent Judgment and Dispositional Belief." *Pacific Philosophical Quarterly* 91 (4): 531–553.

Schwitzgebel, Eric. 2011. *Perplexities of Consciousness*. MIT Press.

Schwitzgebel, Eric. 2013. "Reply to Kriegel, Smithies, and Spener." *Philosophical Studies* 165 (3): 1195–1206.

Schwitzgebel, Eric. Forthcoming. "The Pragmatic Metaphysics of Belief."

Searle, John. 1983. *Intentionality*. Oxford University Press.

Searle, John. 1990. "Consciousness, Explanatory Inversion, and Cognitive Science." *Behavioral and Brain Sciences* 13 (4): 585–596.

Searle, John. 1992. *The Rediscovery of the Mind*. MIT Press.

Sellars, Wilfrid. 1956. "Empiricism and the Philosophy of Mind." *Minnesota Studies in the Philosophy of Science* 1: 253–329.

Shoemaker, Sydney. 1996. *The First-Person Perspective and Other Essays*. Cambridge University Press.

Shoemaker, Sydney. 2009. "Self-Intimation and Second Order Belief." *Erkenntnis* 71 (1): 35–51.

Siegel, Susanna. 2004. "Indiscriminability and the Phenomenal." *Philosophical Studies* 120 (1–3): 91–112.

Siegel, Susanna. 2010. *The Contents of Visual Experience.* Oxford University Press.

Siegel, Susanna. 2012. "Cognitive Penetrability and Perceptual Justification." *Noûs* 46 (2): 201–222.

Siegel, Susanna. 2017. *The Rationality of Perception.* Oxford University Press.

Siegel, Susanna, and Nicholas Silins. 2015. "The Epistemology of Perception." In *The Oxford Handbook of Philosophy of Perception,* edited by Mohan Matthen, 781–811. Oxford University Press.

Siewert, Charles. 1998. *The Significance of Consciousness.* Princeton University Press.

Silins, Nicholas. 2008. "Basic Justification and the Moorean Response to the Skeptic." *Oxford Studies in Epistemology* 2: 108–140.

Silins, Nicholas. 2011. "Seeing through the 'Veil of Perception.'" *Mind* 120: 329–367.

Silins, Nicholas. 2012. "Judgment as a Guide to Belief." In *Introspection and Consciousness,* edited by Declan Smithies and Daniel Stoljar, 295–327. Oxford University Press.

Silins, Nicholas. 2013. "Introspection and Inference." *Philosophical Studies* 163 (2): 291–315.

Silins, Nicholas. Forthcoming. "The Evil Demon Inside." *Philosophy and Phenomenological Research.*

Skyrms, Brian. 1980. *Causal Necessity: A Pragmatic Investigation of the Necessity of Laws.* Yale University Press.

Small, Deborah, George Loewenstein, and Paul Slovic. 2007. "Sympathy and Callousness: The Impact of Deliberative Thought on Donations to Identifiable and Statistical Victims." *Organizational Behavior and Human Decision Processes* 102 (2): 143–153.

Smith, Martin. 2012. "Some Thoughts on the JK-Rule." *Noûs* 46 (4): 791–802.

Smith, Michael. 1994. *The Moral Problem.* Blackwell.

Smithies, Declan. 2011a. "Attention Is Rational-Access Consciousness." In *Attention: Philosophical and Psychological Essays,* edited by Christopher Mole, Declan Smithies, and Wayne Wu, 247–273. Oxford University Press.

Smithies, Declan. 2011b. "What Is the Role of Consciousness in Demonstrative Thought?" *Journal of Philosophy* 108 (1): 5–34.

Smithies, Declan. 2012a. "A Simple Theory of Introspection." In *Introspection and Consciousness,* edited by Declan Smithies and Daniel Stoljar, 259–293. Oxford University Press.

Smithies, Declan. 2012b. "Mentalism and Epistemic Transparency." *Australasian Journal of Philosophy* 90 (4): 723–741.

Smithies, Declan. 2012c. "Moore's Paradox and the Accessibility of Justification." *Philosophy and Phenomenological Research* 85 (2): 273–300.

Smithies, Declan. 2012d. "The Mental Lives of Zombies." *Philosophical Perspectives* 26: 343–372.

Smithies, Declan. 2012e. "The Normative Role of Knowledge." *Noûs* 46 (2): 265–288.

Smithies, Declan. 2013a. "On the Unreliability of Introspection." *Philosophical Studies* 165 (3): 1177–1186.

Smithies, Declan. 2013b. "The Nature of Cognitive Phenomenology." *Philosophy Compass* 8 (8): 744–754.

Smithies, Declan. 2013c. "The Significance of Cognitive Phenomenology." *Philosophy Compass* 8 (8): 731–743.

Smithies, Declan. 2014a. "Can Foundationalism Solve the Regress Problem?" In *Current Controversies in Epistemology*, edited by Ram Neta, 73–94. Routledge.

Smithies, Declan. 2014b. "The Phenomenal Basis of Epistemic Justification." In *New Waves in Philosophy of Mind*, edited by Jesper Kallestrup and Mark Sprevak, 98–124. Palgrave Macmillan.

Smithies, Declan. 2015a. "Ideal Rationality and Logical Omniscience." *Synthese* 192 (9): 2769–2793.

Smithies, Declan. 2015b. "Why Justification Matters." In *Epistemic Evaluation: Point and Purpose in Epistemology*, edited by David Henderson and John Greco, 224–244. Oxford University Press.

Smithies, Declan. 2016a. "Belief and Self-Knowledge: Lessons from Moore's Paradox." *Philosophical Issues* 26: 393–421.

Smithies, Declan. 2016b. "Perception and the External World." *Philosophical Studies* 173 (4): 1119–1145.

Smithies, Declan. 2016c. "Reflection On: *On Reflection*." *Analysis* 76 (1): 55–69.

Smithies, Declan. 2018a. "Access Internalism and the Extended Mind." In *Extended Epistemology*, edited by Adam Carter, Andy Clark, Jesper Kallestrup, Orestis Palermos, and Duncan Pritchard, 17–41. Oxford University Press.

Smithies, Declan. 2018b. "Reasons and Perception." In *The Oxford Handbook of Reasons and Normativity*, edited by Daniel Star, 631–661. Oxford University Press.

Smithies, Declan. Forthcoming. "On the Global Ambitions of Phenomenal Conservatism." *Analytic Philosophy*.

Smithies, Declan, and Jeremy Weiss. 2019. "Affective Experience, Desire, and Reasons for Action." *Analytic Philosophy*.

Sobel, Jordan Howard. 1987. "Self-Doubts and Dutch Strategies." *Australasian Journal of Philosophy* 65 (1): 56–81.

Sosa, Ernest. 1991. *Knowledge in Perspective*. Cambridge University Press.

Sosa, Ernest. 2003. "Privileged Access." In *Consciousness: New Philosophical Perspectives*, edited by Quentin Smith and Aleksandar Jokic, 238–251. Oxford University Press.

Speaks, Jeff. 2009. "Transparency, Intentionalism, and the Nature of Perceptual Content." *Philosophy and Phenomenological Research* 79 (3): 539–573.

Speaks, Jeff. 2010. "Attention and Intentionalism." *Philosophical Quarterly* 60: 325–342.

Spener, Maja. 2015. "Calibrating Introspection." *Philosophical Issues* 25: 300–321.

Srinivasan, Amia. 2015. "Are We Luminous?" *Philosophy and Phenomenological Research* 90 (2): 294–319.

Stalnaker, Robert. 1984. *Inquiry*. Cambridge University Press.

Stalnaker, Robert. 2009. "On Hawthorne and Magidor on Assertion, Context, and Epistemic Accessibility." *Mind* 118: 399–409.

Stalnaker, Robert. 2015. "Luminosity and the KK Thesis." In *Externalism, Self-Knowledge, and Skepticism: New Essays*, edited by Sanford Goldberg, 19–40. Cambridge University Press.

Steup, Matthias. 1999. "A Defense of Internalism." In *The Theory of Knowledge: Classical and Contemporary Readings*, 2nd edition, edited by Louis Pojman, 373–384. Wadsworth Publishing.

Stich, Stephen. 1978. "Beliefs and Subdoxastic States." *Philosophy of Science* 45: 499–518.

Stich, Stephen. 1983. *From Folk Psychology to Cognitive Science: The Case against Belief.* MIT Press.

Stich, Stephen. 1992. "What Is a Theory of Mental Representation?" *Mind* 101: 243–261.

Stich, Stephen, and Ted Warfield. 1994. *Mental Representation.* Blackwell.

Stoljar, Daniel. 2004. "The Argument from Diaphanousness." *Canadian Journal of Philosophy* 30: 341–390.

Stoljar, Daniel. 2012a. "Introspective Knowledge of Negative Facts." *Philosophical Perspectives* 26: 389–410.

Stoljar, Daniel. 2012b. "Knowledge of Perception." In *Introspection and Consciousness*, edited by Declan Smithies and Daniel Stoljar, 65–89. Oxford University Press.

Stoljar, Daniel. 2018. "The Regress Objection to Phenomenal Reflexive Theories of Consciousness." *Analytic Philosophy* 59, no. 3: 293–308.

Strawson, Galen. 1994. *Mental Reality.* MIT Press.

Strawson, Galen. 2008. "Real Intentionality 3: Why Intentionality Entails Consciousness." In *Real Materialism and Other Essays*, edited by Galen Strawson, 279–297. Oxford University Press.

Strawson, Peter. 1959. *Individuals: An Essay in Descriptive Metaphysics.* Methuen.

Strawson, Peter. 1962. "Freedom and Resentment." *Proceedings of the British Academy* 48: 1–25.

Stroud, Barry. 1984. *The Significance of Philosophical Scepticism.* Oxford University Press.

Sutton, Jonathan. 2007. *Without Justification.* MIT Press.

Teng, Lu. 2018. "Is Phenomenal Force Sufficient for Immediate Perceptual Justification?" *Synthese* 195 (2): 637–656.

Titelbaum, Michael. 2015. "Rationality's Fixed Point (or: In Defense of Right Reason)." *Oxford Studies in Epistemology* 5: 253–294.

Travis, Charles. 2004. "The Silence of the Senses." *Mind* 113: 57–94.

Tucker, Chris. 2010. "Why Open-Minded People Should Endorse Dogmatism." *Philosophical Perspectives* 24 (1): 529–545.

Turri, John. 2010. "On the Relationship between Propositional and Doxastic Justification." *Philosophy and Phenomenological Research* 80 (2): 312–326.

Tye, Michael. 1995. *Ten Problems of Consciousness: A Representational Theory of the Phenomenal Mind.* MIT Press.

Tye, Michael. 2009. "A New Look at the Speckled Hen." *Analysis* 69 (2): 258–263.

Unger, Peter. 1975. *Ignorance: A Case for Scepticism.* Oxford University Press.

Van Wietmarschen, Han. 2013. "Peer Disagreement, Evidence, and Well-Groundedness." *Philosophical Review* 122 (3): 395–425.

Vogel, Jonathan. 1990. "Cartesian Skepticism and Inference to the Best Explanation." *Journal of Philosophy* 87 (11): 658–666.

Watzl, Sebastian, and Wayne Wu. 2012. "Perplexities of Consciousness, by Eric Schwitzgebel." *Mind* 121: 524–529.

Weatherson, Brian. MS. "Do Judgments Screen Evidence?" Unpublished manuscript.

Wedgwood, Ralph. 2002. "Internalism Explained." *Philosophy and Phenomenological Research* 65 (2): 349–369.

Wedgwood, Ralph. 2013. "A Priori Bootstrapping." In *The A Priori in Philosophy*, edited by Albert Casullo and Joshua Thurow, 226–246. Oxford University Press.

Weiskrantz, Lawrence. 1997. *Consciousness Lost and Found.* Oxford University Press.

White, Roger. 2006. "Problems for Dogmatism." *Philosophical Studies* 131 (3): 525–557.

Williamson, Timothy. 2000. *Knowledge and Its Limits.* Oxford University Press.

Williamson, Timothy. 2007. "On Being Justified in One's Head." In *Rationality and the Good: Critical Essays on the Ethics and Epistemology of Robert Audi*, edited by Mark Timmons, John Greco, and Alfred Mele, 106–122. Oxford University Press.

Williamson, Timothy. 2009. "Replies to Critics." In *Williamson on Knowledge*, edited by Duncan Pritchard and Patrick Greenough, 279–384. Oxford University Press.

Williamson, Timothy. 2011. "Improbable Knowing." In *Evidentialism and Its Discontents*, edited by Trent Dougherty, 147–164. Oxford University Press.

Williamson, Timothy. 2014. "Very Improbable Knowing." *Erkenntnis* 79 (5): 971–999.

Williamson, Timothy. Forthcoming. "Justifications, Excuses, and Sceptical Scenarios." In *The New Evil Demon Problem*, edited by Julien Dutant. Oxford University Press.

Wilson, Robert. 2003. "Intentionality and Phenomenology." *Pacific Philosophical Quarterly* 84 (4): 413–431.

Worsnip, Alex. 2018. "The Conflict of Evidence and Coherence." *Philosophy and Phenomenological Research* 96 (1): 3–44.

Wright, Crispin. 2004. "Warrant for Nothing (and Foundations for Free)?" *Aristotelian Society Supplementary Volume* 78 (1): 167–212.

Yablo, Stephen. 1992. "Mental Causation." *Philosophical Review* 101 (2): 245–280.

Zangwill, Nick. 2005. "The Normativity of the Mental." *Philosophical Explorations* 8 (1): 1–19.

Zimmerman, Aaron. 2004. "Basic Self-Knowledge: Answering Peacocke's Criticisms of Constitutivism." *Philosophical Studies* 128 (2): 337–379.

Zimmerman, Aaron. 2007. "The Nature of Belief." *Journal of Consciousness Studies* 14 (11): 61–82.

Index